THE AMERICAN
JOURNA
2010

This page: Jack Tackle on Tangled Up in Blue, the first route on the north face of Thunder Mountain, Alaska Range. *Jay Smith*

Cover: Luka Lindic approaching the second bivouac on Bhagirathi II (6,512m), with Bhagirathi III (6,454m) in the background. *Marko Prezelj*

Jon Walsh following the crux pitch on a new line on the
South Tower of Mt. Asgard, Baffin Island. *Chris Brazeau*

CONTENTS

16 **Reincarnation, by Denis Urubko**
A bold new route on the southeast face of Cho Oyu in Nepal.

25 **Rejuvenation, by Marko Prezelj**
An invigorating trio of new routes in India's Bhagirathi group.

34 **Discovering What Lies Within, by Kyle Dempster**
A lost mentor shows the way on the north face of Xuelian West, China.

42 **A Bit of Luck, by Andy Houseman**
The alpine-style first ascent of Chang Himal's north face in Nepal.

48 **Alone on Annapurna South, by Dodo Kopold**
Some time to kill in base camp produces a bold new route.

52 **Jobo Rinjang, by Joe Puryear**
The alpine-style first ascent of a little-known Nepalese peak.

58 **Thriller, by Jens Holsten**
Four major routes in two weeks on Alaska's Stikine Ice Cap.

64 **Catharsis, by Jack Tackle**
After 28 Alaskan expeditions: the trip of a lifetime.

70 **Project Victory, by Gleb Sokolov**
A bold new route on the north face of Pobeda in Kyrgyzstan.

78 **Free Mountaineering, by Yan Dongdong**
An inside look at modern Chinese alpinism.

87 **The Golden Peak, by Kim Hyung-il**
A new route on Pakistan's Spantik raises the bar for Korean alpinism.

CLIMBS AND EXPEDITIONS

90 Contiguous United States
110 Alaska
136 Canada
150 Greenland
164 Mexico
165 Colombia, Venezuela, Guyana, Brazil
170 Peru, Bolivia
176 Argentina, Chile
193 Antarctica
201 Middle East (Oman, Yemen)
207 Africa (Morocco, Mali, Namibia, Malawi)
218 Norway
231 CIS: Russia, Tajikistan, Kyrgyzstan
253 Afghanistan
258 Pakistan
280 India
299 Nepal
326 China
351 Tibet
357 Malaysia
360 AAC Grants

362 Book Reviews, edited by David Stevenson
New books by Daniel Arnold, Jerry Auld, Dean Fidelman and John Long, Steve House, Bree Loewen, Robert Marshall, Royal Robbins, David Roberts, and Ed Viesturs.

373 In Memoriam, edited by Cameron M. Burns
Remembering Stimson Bullitt, Riccardo Cassin, Jonathan Copp, Micah Dash, Charles Snead Houston, Tomaž Humar, Craig Luebben, Clifton H.W. Maloney, Robert Model Jr., and Sean Patrick.

386 Club Activities, edited by Frederick O. Johnson

391 Index

400 International Grade Comparison Chart

Submission guidelines, expanded reports, additional photos, topos, and comments are available at aaj.AmericanAlpineClub.org

Jiri Splichal and Martin Klonfar on a new variant to the original winter route on Rulten during the International Winter Meet in Lofoten, Norway. *Marko Prezelj*

Industry Friends

of the

AMERICAN ALPINE
JOURNAL

*We thank the following for their generous
financial support:*

SUMMIT PARTNER

patagonia®

BENEFACTOR

PATRONS

ARC'TERYX

Black Diamond™

DESTINATION
HOTELS & RESORTS

GUARANTEED
TO KEEP YOU DRY
GORE-TEX
PRODUCTS
GORE

MOUNTAIN GEAR

Kate Rutherford leading out on the first ascent of 10 Pounds of Tequila (V, 5.12c, R), on the east face of Acopan Tepui, Venezuela. *Mikey Schaefer*

Friends

of the

AMERICAN ALPINE JOURNAL

We thank the following for their generous financial support:

BENEFACTORS
Yvon Chouinard
H. Adams Carter American Alpine Journal Fund

PATRONS
Gordon A. Benner, M.D.
Ann Carter
Richard E. Hoffman, M.D.
John G. McCall, M.D.*
In memory of John Fischer, Charlie Fowler and Randall Grandstaff
Joseph E. Murphy
Edith Overly
Glenn E. Porzak
Verne and Marion Read
Mark A. Richey

SUPPORTERS
William A. Burd
Jim Edwards
Z. Wayne Griffin, Jr.
John R. Kascenska, II
William R. Kilpatrick, M.D.
Michael J. Lewis, Jr.

SPECIAL THANKS
David Harrah
Steve Schwartz
Samuel C. Silverstein, M.D.

Approaching the summit of Mt. Sarmiento, in Chile's Tierra del Fuego. *Ralf Gantzhorn*

The American Alpine Journal, 710 Tenth St. Suite 100, Golden, Colorado 80401
Telephone: (303) 384-0110 Fax: (303) 384-0111 E-mail: aaj@AmericanAlpineClub.org
www.AmericanAlpineClub.org

ISSN: 0065-6925   ISBN: 978-1-933056-23-4   ISBN: (e-book) 978-1-933056-24-1

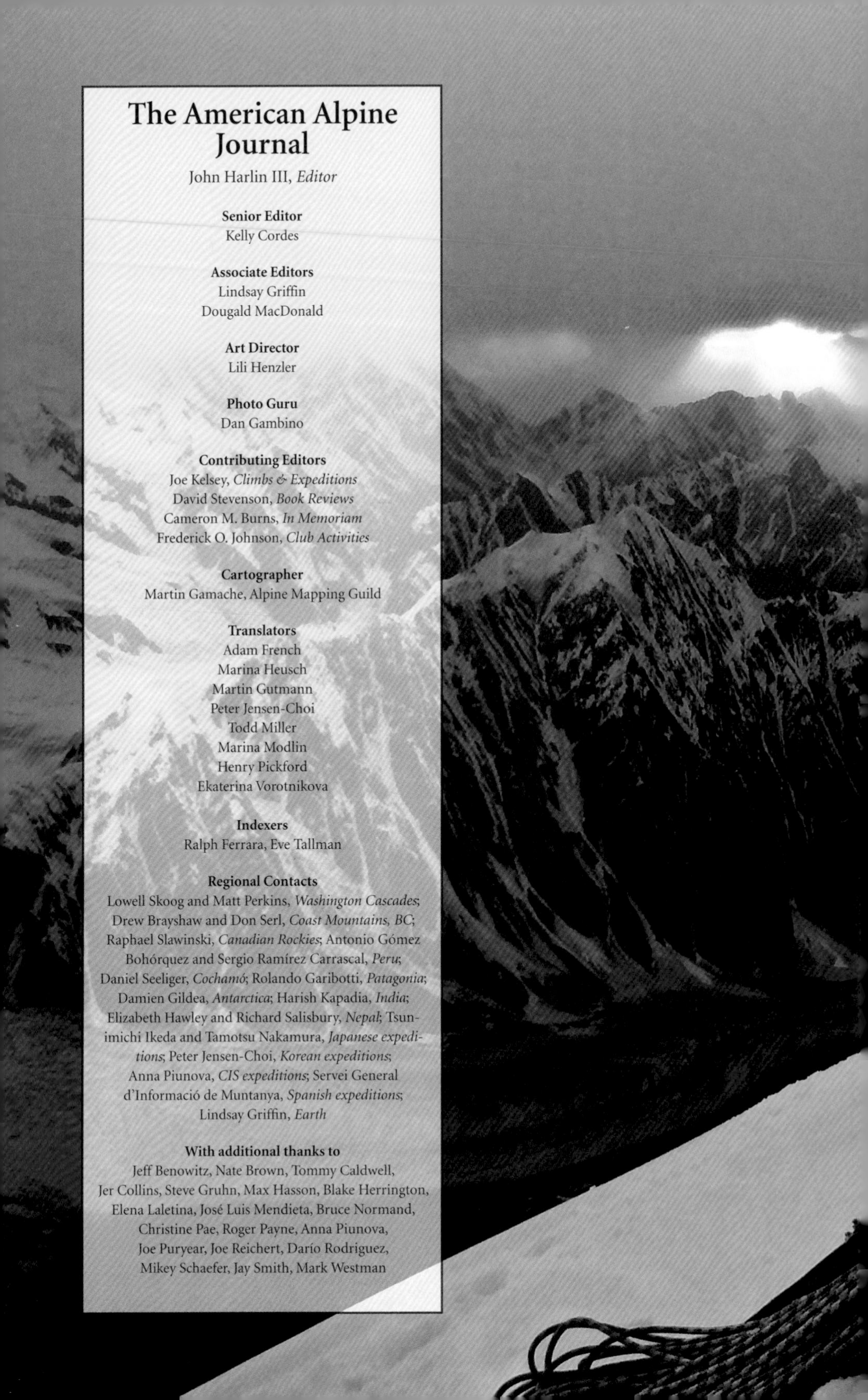

The American Alpine Journal

John Harlin III, *Editor*

Senior Editor
Kelly Cordes

Associate Editors
Lindsay Griffin
Dougald MacDonald

Art Director
Lili Henzler

Photo Guru
Dan Gambino

Contributing Editors
Joe Kelsey, *Climbs & Expeditions*
David Stevenson, *Book Reviews*
Cameron M. Burns, *In Memoriam*
Frederick O. Johnson, *Club Activities*

Cartographer
Martin Gamache, Alpine Mapping Guild

Translators
Adam French
Marina Heusch
Martin Gutmann
Peter Jensen-Choi
Todd Miller
Marina Modlin
Henry Pickford
Ekaterina Vorotnikova

Indexers
Ralph Ferrara, Eve Tallman

Regional Contacts
Lowell Skoog and Matt Perkins, *Washington Cascades*;
Drew Brayshaw and Don Serl, *Coast Mountains, BC*;
Raphael Slawinski, *Canadian Rockies*; Antonio Gómez
Bohórquez and Sergio Ramírez Carrascal, *Peru*;
Daniel Seeliger, *Cochamó*; Rolando Garibotti, *Patagonia*;
Damien Gildea, *Antarctica*; Harish Kapadia, *India*;
Elizabeth Hawley and Richard Salisbury, *Nepal*; Tsun-
imichi Ikeda and Tamotsu Nakamura, *Japanese expedi-
tions*; Peter Jensen-Choi, *Korean expeditions*;
Anna Piunova, *CIS expeditions*; Servei General
d'Informació de Muntanya, *Spanish expeditions*;
Lindsay Griffin, *Earth*

With additional thanks to
Jeff Benowitz, Nate Brown, Tommy Caldwell,
Jer Collins, Steve Gruhn, Max Hasson, Blake Herrington,
Elena Laletina, José Luis Mendieta, Bruce Normand,
Christine Pae, Roger Payne, Anna Piunova,
Joe Puryear, Joe Reichert, Darío Rodríguez,
Mikey Schaefer, Jay Smith, Mark Westman

THE AMERICAN ALPINE CLUB

OFFICIALS FOR THE YEAR 2010
*Directors ex-officio

EXECUTIVE COMMITTEE

HONORARY PRESIDENT William Lowell Putnam	**PRESIDENT** Steven J. Swenson*	**VICE PRESIDENT** Charles B. Franks*
HONORARY TREASURER Theodore (Sam) Streibert	**SECRETARY** George Lowe III*	**TREASURER** Jack Tackle*

DIRECTORS

TERMS ENDING 2011	**TERMS ENDING 2012**	**TERMS ENDING 2013**
Charlotte Fox	Ellen Lapham	Cody J Smith
Aimee Barnes	John R. Kascenska	A. Travis Spitzer
Doug Walker	Eric Simonson	Pete Takeda
Dave Riggs	Doug Colwell	Mark Kroese
	Roanne Miller	Paul Gagner
	Rob BonDurant	

SECTION CHAIRS

Alaska Harry Hunt & James Brady	**Great Lakes** Bill Thompson	**Southern Appalachian** David Thoenen
Blue Ridge Simon Carr	**Heartland** Jeremy Collins	**Southwest** James Pinter-Lucke
Cascade Eddie Espinosa & Roger Strong	**New England** Nancy Savickas	**Tetons** Brenton Reagan
Deep South Chadwick Hagan	**New York** Philip Erard	**Western Slope** Jim Donini
Front Range Chris Pruchnic	**Northern Rockies** Brian Cabe	**Wyoming** Don Foote
	Sierra Nevada Tom Burch	

EDITORS

THE AMERICAN ALPINE JOURNAL John Harlin III	**ACCIDENTS IN NORTH AMERICAN MOUNTAINEERING** John E. (Jed) Williamson

STAFF

Executive Director – Phil Powers	**Communications & Content Manager** – Emily Kreis
Director of Operations – Penn Burris	**Bookkeeper** – Carol Kotchek
Marketing Director – David Maren	**Events Coordinator** – Brittany Griffith
Development & Conservation Director – Deanne Buck	**Library & Museum Director** – Sarah Wood
Technology Manager – Craig Hoffman	**Assistant Director & Preservation Librarian** – Beth Heller
Outreach Manager – Dana Richardson	**Special Collections Manager** – Gary Landeck
Executive Assistant & Grants Manager – Janet Miller	**Ranch Manager** – John Clegg
Membership Coordinator – Lauren Shockey	

Sunset from near the final camp on the new Korean route on Spantik, Pakistan. *Kim Hyung-il Collection*

PREFACE

*An Open Letter to Managers of Peak Fees and
Permits in the Greater Ranges.*

Your high peaks are beautiful, as are the people who live in their valleys. They attract visitors from all over the world, which is a source of pride for those who live in mountain communities. However, many of the rules that apply to visitors are relics of a bygone era and are now stumbling blocks to climbing in the Greater Ranges. If you simplify your regulations, you'll more easily and effectively protect the environment, support rural communities, and help mountaineers.

Our biggest concern involves the requirement to choose in advance a peak and even a route up that peak. This may be less of an issue for a big group going to a well-known summit, such as a commercial expedition. But for modern climbers—especially the exploratory and new-route climbers represented in the *American Alpine Journal*—there is a great need for flexibility in the field. We may have seen a photo of a beautiful peak that inspired us to fly halfway around the world to try to climb it. But on arrival we might discover that snow conditions are bad, access routes are dangerous, or the route is unsuited to our skills. Also, the fee structure should not discourage a modern expedition of two climbers operating in very lightweight style. A small group of friends climbing together is the future of climbing, even on the most difficult and remote mountains.

There is only so much that can be planned back home in Paris, Denver, or Tokyo. Rigid rules, high fees, inflexibility regarding changes of plans, all discourage visits by responsible climbers, and they can be counter-productive by encouraging rule breaking.

All parties would benefit, especially the rural communities that provide goods and services, if the permit process was modernized. Many good ideas have been floated, and they all point toward simplicity and flexibility. Here are key points for your consideration:

- A blanket fee and permit could apply to a valley or region, instead of to a specific peak (i.e. give climbers the same freedom as trekkers).
- Liaison officers, who generally have little to do on small expeditions, could be replaced by a system of "rangers," who would follow good-practice environmental guidelines for protected-area management.
- Approved tour companies could fulfill most of the roles currently undertaken by liaison officers, and they could deal with permits on the spot or with minimum wait.

Over 100 years ago, the pioneers of Himalayan mountaineering were climbing in small teams. In the 1930's Eric Shipton wrote of his longing to "...wander with a small, self-contained party through the labyrinth of unexplored valleys, forming plans to suit circumstances, climbing peaks when the opportunity occurred, following topographical clues and crossing passes into unknown country."

Those heady days of exploration, when so much was open to enterprising travelers, may be over. But today, if you simplify your regulations, you will not only help mountaineers, you'll also find that climbers will be easier to manage, the environment can be better protected, and happier visitors will bring more business to support rural communities.

John Harlin III
Editor

Biyong Village, Tibet, with the east face of an unnamed and unclimbed 6,030m peak behind. *Tamotsu Nakamura*

If you like the AAJ, you'll love the AAJ Online. There you'll find extra panoramic photos, topos, longer reports, and more. Space in the printed AAJ is very tight, so we can't include everything. When you find a report about a place you're interested in, be sure to check out aaj.AmericanAlpineClub.org; you might find a lot more good info. You can also leave comments and see corrections.

THE AMERICAN ALPINE CLUB
From the 2009 Annual Report.

In the face of a tough economy, our club was able to achieve its overall goals. With substantial effort, we met our fund-raising targets and exceeded our membership goals. We also moved forward on many fronts.

This year's Craggin' Classic was held in Utah's Wasatch Range. After two years of operating the Craggin' Classic, it is clear that smaller, more frequent events, operated in cooperation with our sections and local climbing organizations, will be the model for the future.

Our rekindled involvement in the international climbing community continued with another International Climbers' Meet in Indian Creek. The brainchild of past president Jim Donini, the ICM will make its way to Yosemite Valley this fall. The international theme continued when Greg Mortenson, author of *Three Cups of Tea*, spoke at our Annual Benefit and Awards Dinner. The AAC helped Greg during his early days of trying to build schools in Pakistan, and he received our David Brower Conservation Award in 1998. In turn, he drew a wonderful crowd to the dinner, and, from a fund-raising perspective, it was our most successful ever—grossing over $75,000, plus an additional $15,000 raised for conservation.

Last spring, John Clegg came on as the new manager of the Grand Teton Climbers' Ranch. With help from Ranch Committee chairman Bill Fetterhoff, this was a great year for the Ranch. Fund-raising was up in general, and then was multiplied by a grant from the Community Foundation of Jackson Hole.

Our trail building and conservation work in Patagonia continued for a second year under the dedicated leadership of Rolando Garibotti. His efforts have inspired a way for the AAC to support conservation work at local climbing areas in the United States. Modeling our effort after the Civilian Conservation Corps of the 1930s, we plan to put the muscles of climbers to work restoring and improving trails, staging areas, and signage. If you have needs at your local crag, work with your section chair to bring the new CCC—the Climber Conservation Corps—to your area.

We continued to focus our advocacy efforts on issues of national prominence or ones that bode to set a national precedent. Last year, we worked successfully on preventing fee increases for climbers in Denali National Park—an issue that I fear we will have to address again. Moving into 2010, our attention has been focused on the Merced River Plan in Yosemite and the Minnewaska State Park management plan in New York.

While my forecast that 2009 would be a challenging year held true, it also was a successful one. The budgeted net operating loss for the club was slightly less than expected. Kudos are due to the marketing team for membership growth that exceeded our plan. I am proud of the marketing and messaging coming out of the club these days; we are telling our story better than ever. Underneath that

Warming up at the AAC's 2009 International Climbers' Meet. *Andrew Burr*

success, however, are indications that substantial changes for the club's programs and operations are in order. Ultimately, the best measure of success for the AAC is the degree to which committed climbers vote for our relevance with their dues dollars. If there are 500,000 committed climbers in the U.S., or even only 250,000, our membership of 8,000-plus is a tiny share. Our programs must be improved to fully deliver on our mission to "provide knowledge and inspiration, conservation and advocacy, and logistical support for the climbing community."

AAC member Rolo Garibotti repairing trails during a four-year AAC/Patagonia Inc. project. *Doerte Pietron*

We are well positioned to make substantial changes. Our board has been reformed into a more nimble committee structure, our financial position is sound, and we are led by a president, Steve Swenson, who cares deeply that change is made in a process that's thoughtful and appropriate.

This effort began in an ad hoc fashion in 2009 when the board launched three, independent processes:

- With the IT Project, the board established funding for a substantial overhaul of our electronic delivery systems for information.
- A research project on how to improve our Grants Program is under way.
- Our Knowledge Committee is building a plan to restructure our publications in 2011 and beyond.

Steve Swenson has asked that we use our three ad hoc planning processes as input into a five-year plan due to the board in draft form in October. Initial meetings with the board indicate that this process will, for the first time in many years, call for significant changes to the AAC's core programs. Current programs like our rescue benefit and the AAJ must be evaluated and improved. Programs and membership benefits that are no longer as relevant will be reduced or eliminated. New programs will be added. The board populated a task force of active climbers chaired by board member Paul Gagner to help with this work. Once the draft strategic plan is delivered to the board of directors in October, there will be a comment period followed by revisions before a final plan is presented to the board in February 2011. Your input is essential.

This year bodes to be at least as challenging as last year was, but I am grateful that the club leadership recognizes that these times also present opportunities for real change. I hope you take a serious look at how our club can evolve into a community that includes all climbers. Suggestions of any kind can be sent to the Planning Task Force at: planning@americanalpineclub.org

Lastly, please vote with your dollars for a better, stronger American Alpine Club. As climbers and club members, we know the importance of partnership—of watching out for one another and banding together to do something great. If we can pool contributions, and go in on this together, then the kind of substantial change our club is seeking is within reach.

Phil Powers
Executive Director

REINCARNATION

A bold new route on the southeast face of Cho Oyu in Nepal.

DENIS URUBKO

Denis Urubko leading the steep rock wall at ca 6,000m on the southeast face of Cho Oyu. Switching between boots and rock shoes, Urubko found moves up to 6b (5.10). *Boris Dedeshko*

Cho Oyu is generally considered simple among the 8,000ers. For serious alpinists it has often been used as a place to get high-elevation experience. But in 2001 I happened to catch a glimpse of Cho Oyu's southeast wall, with a logical line from the foot to the summit. It was terrifying and beautiful. For years I was obsessed with this route.

One day my old friend Denis Gichev, with whom I served in the army—and thanks to whom I ended up in the Central Sports Club of the Army of Kazakhstan—spoke to me about his planned trek to the foot of Mt. Everest.

"Take a look into the Gokyo Valley," I told him. "That will be a real journey, not for couch potatoes."

"And what's there?"

"There's the wall of Cho Oyu, Den! I want you to photograph it for me."

Denis set off on his trip, convinced I was nuts, but he brought back the photos. They were fantastic views, showing in detail the relief, the traps, the dangers. I spent hours examining them on my computer—zooming in for details, backing off to understand the scale.

In the spring of 2009 Boris Dedeshko and I finally examined the wall with our own eyes; it was more complicated that even our wildest presuppositions had hinted. Our base camp was tucked behind old moraines of the Ngojumba Glacier, by the fifth lake of the Gokyo gorge, and in order to catch sight of Cho Oyu we had to hike beyond a bend to the sixth lake. There we sat under the bright sun by huge rocks and studied the wall through binoculars.

"What do you think, Den?"

"Errr…my head is swimming. We'll climb those lower faces by, uh, I don't know how we'll climb."

"A direct assault?" Boris spread his hands, gesturing helplessness. "And what about acclimatization?"

My turn to shrug. I poked my finger farther to the east, in the direction of Gyachungkang, just shy of 8,000 meters. "We'll acclimatize on those slopes, or somewhere in the vicinity," I said. To touch our route on Cho Oyu would have been unsporting. We wanted to climb it alpine style, in a dash from foot to summit.

I shook hands with Chokra and Mingma, our cooks. "If we don't return after eight days, go to the wall and take a look," I said.

"And if we're not back in 10 days, you can take down base camp and go home," Boris cheerfully added.

During our reconnaissance of the approach, we had built small cairns to show the way, and thus we arrived in just two hours at the base of Cho Oyu, at 5,300 meters, where we had left a tent. The silent surrounding mountains intensified our emotions. One wanted to race away to freedom, away from these somber, claustrophobic walls.

We began the ascent in the depths of night on May 7. We carried only the inner half of the tent and two of its four poles. We had food for five or six days and two large gas canisters. We carried eight ice screws, half a dozen nuts, a set of cams, and 12 pitons, some of which we had sawed off to save weight. Our plan was to descend from the summit via the Austrian route (Furtner-Koblmüller, 1978) on the east side of the face.

Our climb began at 5,600 meters. We belayed with two 9mm ropes as we moved up the lower slabs. It was necessary to choose the line carefully, for above were several icefalls. During this day and the night that followed, several times avalanches and rocks flew by, two or three meters away. Sometimes we could climb in rock shoes, but often we had to wear crampons. We belayed six pitches, up to 6b, with a fair amount of 6a on the slabs. At day's end we were at 6,100 meters, still below the overhanging bastion. After spending the night half sitting up,

Denis Urubko and Boris Dedeshko needed most of two days to climb the rock "bastion" on Cho Oyu, following a line above and to the right of the climber. They had to sit up in their tent throughout the first night on the wall. *Boris Dedeshko*

we continued the ascent in fog and mist.

The rock overhang extended for about 80 meters, and we climbed most of it with aid. The weather was bleak. The world narrowed to the dimensions of a dull glass box 10 meters on a side. I couldn't see Boris; now and then we communicated with short phrases: "take in," "hold fast," "slack on the blue rope." We spent most of the day climbing two and a half pitches. Beyond a bend of the rocky bastion appeared a series of icy slabs and chutes, and we followed these as snow began to fall until we attained an altitude of 6,600 meters. Here, under the cover of a serac at the beginning of a crescent icefield, we set up our tent.

"We've climbed the most difficult part," Boris said. Sipping thin soup, I nodded. We were full of optimism.

"And do we have enough provisions and gas?" Boris furrowed his brow.

"Six servings of Bystrov kasha [porridge], four of Chinese noodles, sugar, tea...oh...here's a lot of sausage! So we have to think we have enough provisions," I concluded.

"It will be necessary to 'have to think.'" Boris laughed.

A beautiful morning was our reward for the previous day's hardships. Mountains extended to the edge of the world, and I felt like a speck of dust in this chaos. Like a palisade, the peaks circled the horizon, eliciting the sensation that we were alone on the planet. And like a gigantic guard to the east, Everest rose quite close. My lord! So much had happened in just a few months: the desperate ascent of Makalu with Simone Moro in February, and now, in May, here I was again, hanging between heaven and earth on an unclimbed wall of an 8000er.

Along a series of icy ridges we confidently reached 6,900 meters, and then a powerful storm bore down. As a whole, I should note, the weather in the spring of 2009 was different from the norm in the Himalaya. Instead of daily afternoon snowfalls with rare storms lasting two or three days, the weather had more contrast: bright periods extending four or five days, after which a storm would follow for several days.

As the storm continued, we managed to get to 7,100 meters. It's better not to recall how I fearfully traversed those unstable pillows of snow. But it worked out. We squeezed our tent into an icy niche at a small bergschrund, widening it with our ice axes. At night several powerful avalanches flew by, causing the ice to rumble and shake under our sleeping mats. It was terrible.

Morning did not bring improvement in the weather, but, sheltered by the bergschrund, we continued obliquely upward, finding secure anchors in small rock ridges. Along these we ascended to 7,300 meters, where we traversed to the left under a zone of seracs. We were lucky, because the new snow had not stuck to these steep walls, and avalanches had tamped down the snow underfoot, so we progressed relatively easily. At one point, though, a half-meter avalanche slid from under me, knocking Boris off his feet at the belay. As we turned up through icy overhangs, we had to work desperately hard. In one section the snow was up to our waists, but the proximity of the icy walls allowed us to set up a belay. As darkness approached we reached 7,600 meters and again hid our tent under a small bergschrund.

With the snow conditions that had developed, our planned descent of the Austrian route did not seem feasible. Moreover, the completely independent route we'd hoped to follow to the top of the face led to the left into a dangerous couloir. Thus we decided to climb up onto the southeast rib, where we would join the Polish route (Berbebka-Heinrich-Kukuczka-Paw-likowski, February 1985) and follow it to the top. We would have to descend by the route of our ascent.

△

During the night the storm quieted a bit. Nonetheless, it was terribly cold when we woke at 2 a.m. on May 11. Just before sunrise, at around 4 a.m., we left our tent and began a diagonal traverse up to the right, belaying on rocks and icy outcrops. We carried a few slings, a complete set of nuts and cams, and six ice screws. Again we were lucky because the fresh snow had sloughed off, and the layer underneath was harder. Still, sometimes, when crossing couloirs, we were waist-deep in snow. In midmorning, via two simple rock walls, we reached the southeast ridge at about 7,950 meters. Here I left my pack in the snow as a landmark.

We made our way relatively slowly, belaying off ice axes or sometimes an ice screw. We were dead tired and did not always belay sufficiently, but we made headway. The weather was repugnant: light wind, tedious snow, and dense fog. We oriented ourselves by a rock tower to the left of our route. Or rather, that was our best guess. At times we could see the rock bands and seracs lining the summit plateau. A steep final chute presented dangerous avalanche conditions, and we sat down and thought about turning around. We rested in the snow a long time, trying to get used to the idea that again a large risk awaited. Moreover, darkness had descended.

Urubko spent most of the second day aid-climbing an overhanging 80-meter headwall. *Boris Dedeshko*

Do you know what this feels like? When, using up the last shreds of strength and nerve, step after step you strive to move forward, summoning your will into a fist. But then hope reaches its limit, and you cannot muster the resolve to take the next step. Around us was dark, grey emptiness. Boris and I sat, afraid to stir.

"How does the saying go, Boris?" I joked darkly. "If you go one way, you'll lose your horse. Go the other, and you'll lay down your life. But in those old stories, the hero finds a way."

Borya nodded toward the summit. "Shall we risk it?" His muscles twitched under his sunken, unshaven cheeks.

"Let's risk it.

With that decision we buried ourselves. By all conceivable laws, we were not destined to return. The sad experiences of Boukreev, Khrishchaty, Terzyul, and other alpinists who did not find in themselves the strength to halt in time, to retreat, say that one has to *run* away in such situations. Ghosts of those buried in the snows circled around me. They walked along our path; from the darkness their eyes attentively followed us, hoping and believing that we would overcome this insanity.

Falling snow, carried by a west wind, had piled up on the eastern slopes. It was necessary to plow ahead at full steam. Tramping down a track in the snow, hardly daring to breathe, praying to the saints, I leaned carefully into each step so that it would not collapse, unleashing an avalanche. Because if the slope took off, we would too. Atheism or faith—what difference does it make? Just so we remain alive.

Finally, along the ridge, just 200 meters from the summit, the snow was only knee-deep. I began to breathe easier. And at 8:10 p.m. we reached the summit plateau of Cho Oyu. The ridge widened, the slope diminished, and we could make out the far side, descending into Tibet. I crumpled onto my side, devoid of strength.

I felt nothing. I was empty and transparent, like glass. I just lay there and tried to calm my breathing. In the murky darkness the wind and snowflakes rushed through me, the mountain lay below me like a beast grown quiet. I watched dully as a light indicated Boris approaching. He dropped next to me in the snow.

"That's it?" he exhaled.

"We've arrived, Boris." I was scarcely able to answer. "And now for a photo."

"What photo?" He waved his hand in the darkness.

"Just of ourselves." I shrugged.

Many have experienced similar impassivity, when a longed-for goal is finally attained but one doesn't have the strength to understand it. When one is empty of emotion despite a great success. But I remember one thing clearly: anger at myself for proceeding, under the prodding of my own stubbornness multiplied by ambition. The ascent was a trap, into which we fell. Now, sitting on the summit, I believed we had no chance of descending alive.

△

After taking a few photos, we set off.

It was easy to follow our deep path in the snow. Moreover, my pack was lying at the turn at 7,950 meters, showing us the way. As we lost altitude our strength began to return, as if the mountain were giving back what it had taken. Boris' lamp was almost dead, but mine continued to work, and the light gave us hope. We descended past the cliffs without problem and at 12:30 a.m. reached our tent at 7,600 meters. Here was a stove, imagined warmth, and safety. We drank a few swallows of water and collapsed into sleep.

That night it began snowing hard again. Very early in the morning, we tried to start down but set off a couple of avalanches that raced down the mountain with an unbelievable roar. We decided to wait. Soon, though, avalanches from above began to cover the tent, despite the shelter of the overhanging bergschrund. A few times the tent was buried completely, and, clenching our teeth, we supported it with our bodies until the snow stopped moving. We went outside to dig it out each time. Everything inside was covered in frost crystals.

Dedeshko arrives on Cho Oyu's summit in deep snow, darkness, and storm. *Denis Urubko*

"It's impossible to go to the bathroom!" Boris hollered above the wind. "My pants are full of snow."

"And the tent, the tent!" I giggled nervously, idiotically. "It's like a sieve. Look, there's snow all over my sleeping bag!"

Imagine our joy, then, when around 8 a.m. a hole suddenly appeared in the clouds to the east, revealing Everest and Lhotse. Despite the obvious idiocy of descending in such dangerous conditions, Boris and I decided to try to force our way lower, although bad weather was again pressing in; it was better than sitting and waiting for death. We successfully rushed across the most dangerous place below the zone of seracs, but as we rappelled Boris knocked loose a piece of ice or rock that smacked me in the head.

I moaned, blood seeping through the hood of my jacket and flowing between my fingers. Stunned, I couldn't recall who and where I was.

"Den, forgive me," Boris said, repeatedly, seeing snow turning scarlet with blood. "Den, forgive me."

"Nothing serious," I finally managed to wheeze, coming to my senses a bit. "I'm the one responsible, for leaving my helmet below."

Boris brightened. "You just can't be killed!"

We spent that night in an ice cave below another bergschrund. The snowfall continued. Avalanches cascaded around us, at times flying across the bergschrund, covering the tent in dust. Our remaining provisions included nothing more than tea and 100 grams of dried horsemeat.

Next morning, same story. At 8 a.m. the sun shone for several minutes, and we decided to risk continuing downward. We rappelled 25 meters at a time on a doubled rope, having left the other rope at our second bivy site. Two avalanches hit Boris, who was descending first. He dangled from the rope like a hooked fish in a swift current, but the screws were in reliable ice, and they bore the weight. Around 5 p.m., as we reached 6,600 meters, the weather suddenly cleared and it became terribly cold.

In the morning, after drinking some water, we continued our descent. For the first time in five days it became warm; soon the sun was burning. As we descended the rock bastion, we had to swing in on the rope to touch the wall. Near dark we reached the glacier and stayed there for the night. That evening the gas ran out.

The next day, collapsing into snow-covered pits on the moraines, dodging pools of water but without the strength to drink our fill, we descended for six hours to base camp. Fortunately, the cooks were still there despite our instructions to leave after 10 days.

In the village of Gokyo the Nepalese arranged a party for us. This was a celebration we could enjoy only with great effort. We were so exhausted. Boris and I had each lost about 10 kilograms. For the second time in my life I could encompass one of my thighs with my fingers.

Back home in Kazakhstan, I awoke one morning in a state of confusion. Popping up from the mattress on the floor, I looked at the empty walls. Through the window curtains I perceived the gray sunrise as if through a shroud. What? Where? It felt as if I were back on the summit of Cho Oyu, on *that* night. I felt empty and unconscious, like the specters that had circled in the storm. I had just seen their eyes in my dreams.

Then, suddenly, I understood that I had died on Cho Oyu. It was so simple and clear that I wasn't surprised. It was as though the pieces of the puzzle that had tormented me since the beginning of the winter had taken preordained places. First the storm on Makalu, like a razor tearing nerves and flaying skin. Then the sand and warmth of Goa, where I pulled myself

The Kazakh route on 8,188m Cho Oyu. The foot of the wall is at ca 5,600m. *Denis Urubko*

Urubko braces the tent against avalanches during the pair's stormy descent. *Boris Dedeshko*

together and turned to the future. And then the otherwordly storm on Cho Oyu, without a hope of survival…and I had died.

All that remained on this earth was merely a shadow. I (or it) had become an empty little cloud, without nerves or strength. But now the time had come to fill that void, piece by piece, selecting only what was necessary and correct. To arise out of the ashes of burned-out feelings, broken personality, and tortured body. It was as if Fate, having laughed its fill at absurdity, now offered a second chance, the gift of another opportunity to test my endurance. I was alive again; life was only beginning. I strode across the room and flung open the curtain. The crimson sunrise met my eyes. Extending my arms, I stretched wide at the open window.

SUMMARY:

Area: Mahalangur Himal, Nepal

Ascent: Alpine-style new route on the southeast face of Cho Oyu (8,188m), Boris Dedeshko and Denis Urubko, May 7–14, 2009 (five days up from advanced base camp and three days down, via the ascent route). The 2,600m route went at 6b A2/3 M6, with steep snow and ice.

A NOTE ABOUT THE AUTHOR:

Born in 1973, Denis Urubko lives in Almaty, Kazakhstan. With this ascent of Cho Oyu, he completed the list of the world's 14 8,000-meter peaks. Urubko's first winter ascent of Makalu, with Simone Moro, was featured in the 2009 AAJ.

Translated from the Russian by Henry Pickford, with assistance from Elena Laletina and Anna Piunova.

Urubko in sunnier times on Cho Oyu. *Boris Dedeshko*

REJUVENATION

An invigorating trio of new routes in India's Bhagirathi group.

MARKO PREZELJ

Rok Blagus and Luka Lindic make their way toward the eastern summit of Bhagirathi III (6,454m), the second of three peaks climbed by the Slovenian expedition in 2009. In the background: Satopanth (7,075m), on the left, and Bhagirathi I (6,856m). *Marko Prezelj*

After my expedition to Makalu in the fall of 2008, a big project that demanded lots of time and energy—and ultimately was frustrated by poor conditions—I felt the need to recharge my motivation. That winter I went to the Lofoten Islands of Norway, where we climbed lots of interesting ground in good company. In late spring I went to Alaska, where I met many motivated climbers. In the summer I guided in Europe and began to build a new house for my family. My life was intense from many perspectives, and I began to feel a fresh enthusiasm for climbing.

In the fall I joined forces with Rok Blagus and Luka Lindic, who belong to the young generation of Slovenian alpinists—the generation that is upgrading "old school" alpinism with a sport approach. Luka is just 22, a student, and Rok is 28, finishing a doctoral degree in statistics. I was 44, and last autumn I was surprised (again) by the fact that I could still push my limits. Once again I found that alpinism has the power to stop time and refresh one's perspective.

Our original goal for the fall expedition was Rimo III, which borders the Siachen area in the eastern Karakoram. However, at the last minute, one month before our departure, the Indi-

Base camp and Shivling in moonlight. After this photo was taken, it rained and snowed for a week. The tent in the photograph, which served as our eating quarters, collapsed in the middle of the night under the weight of the wet snow. We made emergency repairs, but two days later the tent gave way completely. Here, Luka looks through the new "window" in our dining tent. *Marko Prezelj*

an army refused to give us permission to climb there—*after* we had made all the logistical arrangements and bought our plane tickets. We quickly shifted plans to visit the Bhagirathi group. We knew only a little about the Bhagirathis or what routes had been done. With this "onsight trip," we didn't have any specific expectations besides having fun climbing big mountains. The seeds of spontaneity were sown.

When we left home our idea was to attempt to free climb the Catalan route on Bhagirathi III's west pillar. But after we set up base camp it snowed and rained for a week. We knew we'd have to be very patient and lucky to do any rock climbing. As a result, we looked for lines that were less technical and would be useful for acclimatization; for that reason, and not because of any greedy ambitions for an unclimbed summit, we chose the route on Bhagirathi IV. During the approach to that climb, we spotted a logical line on Bhagirathi II, but we knew we'd need very good acclimatization for that serious route. So, for our second climb, we chose Bhagirathi III, which we hoped would be climbable even though the rock was still snowy; we followed mixed ground at the beginning and just looked for the most logical line up wet rock in the middle. In general we just followed our intuition: "Look, that is a logical and interesting line. Let's try to free climb it."

The most intense part of this experience was juggling all the options. It's a great feeling when you see that you've made the right decisions and you are able to realize your ideas despite a lot of uncertainty. On this expedition my motivation for climbing was fully reinvigorated, and I proved to myself that I'm not yet ready for retirement, even in the company of young, strong climbers. I felt the same joy as I had when I was much younger and more naïve.

With the steepest faces inaccessible because of new snow, we decide to attempt the easiest and lowest of the three summits, Bhagirathi IV (center). *Marko Prezelj*

Luka leads an ice pitch on the upper third of Bhagirathi IV. Our route follows the most logical line up the peak from the west. The week of snowfall had covered the hard ice and loose rock, and there was just enough fresh ice where water might run normally. In warmer conditions this route might be risky due to rockfall. We had to break trail through deep snow near the top, and it took us a long time to cross the ridge from the saddle to the summit. We were lucky with the weather: In the morning it was clear; at noon it started to snow (good for preventing rockfall); and in the evening it cleared again as we were descending. In short, it was perfect. *Marko Prezelj*

On the southwest face of Bhagirathi III, Luka made a decisive start on a strip of snow and ice, but he soon realized that this way wasn't safe. After descending to the foot, he started again on this variation from the right. Behind, Bhagirathi III and IV. *Marko Prezelj*

Here I'm climbing the second pitch on the rocky part of the face. After another pitch in the dark we found a short, narrow ledge where we spent the night. The rock above us was very icy, and in the morning we decided to make a diagonal rappel to another ledge, from which we were able to continue climbing. *Rok Blagus*

We weren't sure which of Bhagirathi III's summits was the highest, so we climbed them both; now we think the western peak is slightly higher. Here Rok and Luka are starting the descent. All the exultation of the summit was swiftly smothered by anxiety. After five long rappels we found a suitable place for a bivouac, and the next day we continued down the southeast ridge and northeast face. *Marko Prezelj*

Luka breaks trail through crusty snow toward the dry Vasuki Valley, along which we trekked back to base camp. We used some of the same track while descending from Bhagirathi II about a week later, and that time we made it from the summit to base camp in just three and a half hours. *Marko Prezelj*

Luka on the crux move of the second ropelength of Bhagirathi II's south-southwest face. We were aiming for the ice line on the upper left of the picture. The climbing took more time than we expected, and the sun reached the ice before we did, which resulted in challenging conditions. *Marko Prezelj*

A line of waterfall ice had attracted us from our first view of the face. Before leaving for the climb, we drew lots with pieces of dry spaghetti to decide who would start leading the next morning and who would continue on the next block. When Luka, the youngest, drew the longest piece and so led the first four pitches, I was rather envious, since leading is more interesting than going second. But my envy soon evaporated. My pitches began with demanding climbing over ice-covered rock and continued with vertical and overhanging ice, where, after a time, I was truly pumped. *Luka Lindic*

Rok and Luka like two ravens at the first bivy. This was our third climb and the first bivy spot where we could find a "comfortable" place for only two of us. Rok rushed to settle in at the ledge before we even started cooking, and I had to jokingly remind him that we were a party of three. While they were building their nest, I cooked and sorted the gear. After dinner I climbed 10 meters higher to a sloping ledge where I fought with gravity all night. In the morning I rappelled down and found a young couple waiting for breakfast. *Marko Prezelj*

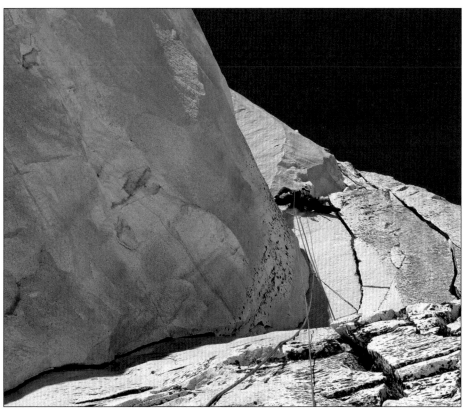

Luka reaching high for a hold on the upper wall. We were lucky to find very good rock on our line, and we managed to free climb all but a five-meter tension traverse 50 meters below this point. *Marko Prezelj*

In the afternoon we climbed along the upper southwest ridge (Ravaschietto-Sarchi, 1984), which surprised us with its exposure. Luka, climbing last, was bent double under the weight of the haul bag. After three pitches we found a good place for a bivouac. The next morning we threw the bag with the equipment we didn't need over the face. The jubilation over this move was accompanied by anxiety over the climb to the summit and descent down the far side of the mountain. After returning to base camp, we collected the haul bag from below the face. Only one ice screw was missing. *Marko Prezelj*

On top of Bhagirathi II: Marko Prezelj, Rok Blagus, and Luka Lindic (from left). We had similar smiles, but my missing hair reveals the difference in years. For me it was a privilege to observe the honest, joyful enthusiasm of two young friends on this expedition. In their eyes I could clearly see why I like alpinism. *Marko Prezelj*

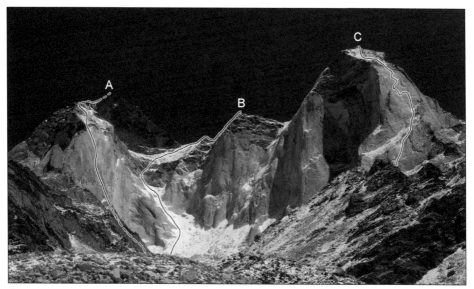

The new Slovenian routes on the southwest flanks of (A) Bhagirathi II, 6,512m; (B) Bhagirathi IV, 6,193m; and (C) Bhagirathi III, 6,454m. *Marko Prezelj*

AREA: GARHWAL HIMALAYA, INDIA

Ascents: Southwest couloir and north ridge of Bhagirathi IV (1,000m, D+), September 15, 2009, possibly the first ascent of the peak. The climbers descended the same route with four rappels and downclimbing. New route on the southwest face of Bhagirathi III (1,300m, ED 6b M5 WI5, two rappels), September 21–22, 2009. The route lies between the 1982 Scottish Route and the 1993 Czech Route, and it shares a few pitches with the former. The climbers descended by the southeast ridge and northeast face, with another bivouac en route. New route on the south-southwest face of Bhagirathi II (1,300m, ED+/ABO- 6b+ WI6+ M8, one tension traverse), September 29–October 1, 2009. The climbers descended by the east face. All ascents by Slovenian climbers Rok Blagus, Luka Lindic, and Marko Prezelj. See Climbs and Expeditions for more details and a route photo from Bhagirathi II.

A NOTE ABOUT THE AUTHOR:

Born in 1965, Marko Prezelj lives in Kamnik, Slovenia. His first ascent of the northwest pillar of Chomolhari, with Boris Lorencic, was featured in the 2007 American Alpine Journal.

DISCOVERING WHAT LIES WITHIN

A lost mentor shows the way on the north face of Xuelian West, China.

KYLE DEMPSTER

The 2009 expedition was only the second to approach the Chinese Tien Shan from the north. In the background: Khanjaylak II (5,380m; left, in clouds; climbed in 2008), and Khanjaylak III and IV (twin 4,900m peaks, both unclimbed). *Bruce Normand*

We were lost. It was late in the afternoon of our second day on Xuelian West's north face, and storm clouds were building, descending, and darkening. Everywhere was steep, chalky marble, malleable with a firm swing of an ice axe and extremely difficult to protect. My anxiety about the terrain and weather had brought up a brief discussion about bailing, but quitting seemed premature, so we faced the terrain above. With no accord on which direction was best, or even passable, I opted for Bruce's suggestion, took a deep breath, and cast off into the unknown.

Every time it happens, the process is similar. A picture or story yields curiosity, curiosity evolves to captivation, and captivation leads to intimidation. With time and preparation we eventually commit, and from commitment we always grow.

Kelly Cordes had e-mailed me in January about joining an expedition to the Chinese Tien Shan with Jed Brown and Bruce Normand. Just six weeks earlier I'd had one third of my ring finger amputated due to frostbite sustained while soul-searching on a big wall in Pakistan. I'd regained some of the 40 pounds I lost when the soul-searching became a lesson in survival, and I was beginning to feel well enough to think about future trips.

The unclimbed walls and massive peaks in the photos Kelly sent were breathtaking. They made me feel inexperienced and unqualified, at least compared with Kelly's lengthy list of accomplishments, but I found comfort knowing that I'd be climbing with and learning from him. One picture in particular, the steep north face of Xuelian West, intimidated the hell out of me. I couldn't comprehend the level of commitment necessary to climb something of that size and exposure.

"We are going climbing because it's fun and I need a belay," was Drew's sales pitch. He was my older cousin; we were 15 and 13. Throughout our childhood I followed his lead, whether it was drinking whiskey or going climbing. Climbing quickly became both of our passions, though at first in different ways. I loved pushing my physical limits safely in bouldering and sport climbing, while Drew found satisfaction in the mentally demanding adventures of trad and big-wall climbing.

I remember sitting at the dinner table one Christmas when I was about 17, our big family fixated on Drew's harrowing desert climbing adventures. He was a good storyteller, and I sensed he was exaggerating a bit to impress his audience, and it worked—they shook their heads in awe. But as my cousin grew more animated, eyes widening and smile broadening, I also saw the genuine passion the adventure had ignited within him. Again, I was sold. After high school I moved to California to explore bigger stone and new aspects of climbing.

In early February I committed to the Tien Shan expedition and began the most rigorous training program I had ever pursued. Before the surgeon gave me clearance, I returned to the gym and began learning how to climb with 9.66 fingers. Absolutely dedicated to climbing and training, I sold most of my possessions, slept in my parents' basement, and navigated between the climbing gym, weight room, yoga studio, and the local hills by bicycle.

Because of generous contributions from the Shipton-Tilman and Lyman Spitzer grants, I had a bit more money than expected and in early May decided on a last-minute trip to Alaska. I wanted to see how well I was recovering and check the progress of my training. It was my first time returning to big mountains since my injury, and as a testament to how much I worried about my finger I packed six pairs of gloves. Nate Opp and I managed the Bibler-Klewin route on Hunter's north buttress, topping out just above the Bibler Come Again exit and returning to base camp in 37 hours. Considering we had never climbed together and that neither of us had been on an alpine face that big, there was not much reason for complaint. However, deep down I was concerned about my fatigue at our high point. I flew home to Salt Lake City six days after I'd left and immediately increased my training load.

Drew bellowed his mighty laugh as he cruised tenuous aid pitches on a frigid wall on Baffin Island. He mocked the difficulties in a pirate voice or cheesy English accent. I'd chuckle faintly and then ask, "So...is that piece good? 'Cause falling there might suck." Drew could make a beginning climber believe he could send 5.14 in his first week. His lighthearted enthusiasm for serious climbs often got him into situations over his head, yet these were the experiences that made him grow beyond his years. A searcher, he was always on the move, looking for the next lesson that life has to offer.

After we topped out on our 750-meter first ascent, during the second day of our descent, my cousin Drew Wilson rappelled off the end of a rope and began the journey into his next life.

The 2,600m north face of Xuelian West. After four days on the face, Jed Brown, Kyle Dempster, and Bruce Normand topped out in midmorning and descended to the west (right) to return to the foot of the wall. *Kyle Dempster*

As I held his lifeless body in my arms and tears streamed down my face, rain began falling from the sky and the powerful energy of death and life buzzed in and around me.

It was 2005, and I spent the next year in a depressed haze. I climbed a little but was fixated on one thing: returning to Baffin. I hoped a solo return to the Arctic would restore some clarity to my mind. I felt a strong pull to the otherwise insignificant snow ledge where Drew had come to rest after his fatal fall. I wanted to say goodbye to it all: to the Arctic, to Drew, and to that part of my life. A year to the day after I'd held my dead cousin, I sat in the same place, and that same energy of life and death pulsed through my head and my heart. "Drew, is that you? I miss you."

I had hoped to reach some conclusions, so I could move on with my life, but instead I found continuation, the desire to keep questioning and searching. Drew's pursuit of happiness, discovery, and challenge had sparked my passion for climbing, and now I began exploring aspects of the sport that push the mind much deeper.

One month before our Tien Shan expedition, news of Jonny Copp's death reached Kelly at University Hospital in Colorado. Kelly had spent the past several weeks living by his fiancé's hospital bedside while doctors desperately tried to figure out what was happening to her. As if the news of his close friend's death wasn't difficult enough, the health and survival of his love was in question. I had a good idea of the emotional instability that Kelly was experiencing, and deep down I knew we wouldn't be climbing together in China.

Another friend from Colorado, Jared Vilhauer, soon joined the expedition. He and I had climbed once together, in 2007, on the frozen waterfalls outside of Canmore, Alberta. He is a dedicated climber and motivated adventurer, and for the last eight years had been searching for the right partner for climbing in Asia. I was happy at the chance to climb with Jared, but I sensed a role reversal taking place; with Kelly off the team, I would have to step up as the more experienced partner on the biggest climbs I'd ever attempted.

Drew was far beyond the most influential climbing mentor I've ever had. He encouraged me to go beyond my comfort level, to push myself both as a climber and as an individual, and to reflect on these experiences afterward. Our climbing partnership was both competitive and highly supportive—forged from 22 years of knowing each other, from growing up in diapers through the delin-

Dempster (left) and Normand follow a pitch of low-angle ice during the second day of climbing. *Jed Brown*

quent years of getting into trouble, and culminating on an Arctic big wall. Since his death, finding a similar influence in my life has been impossible. But because of his death, I have had the opportunity to climb with many new partners. All of these partners, most of whom have become friends, test me in different ways than Drew did.

In late July we boarded a bus at Urumqi and rode across the immense agricultural plains of Xinjiang Province. Countless acres of sparkling wheat fields and blinding yellow safflower provided a golden pedestal for a little-explored backdrop, the northern peaks of the Chinese Tien Shan.

Our two-day journey to the end of the road at the little Sino-Kazakh village of Xiate gave ample time for our small team to get to know each other. We were four: Bruce Normand, Jed Brown, Jared, and I, plus Mr. Xu, our liaison officer, and David, our Chinese cook.

I knew Jed only by the impressive climbs that he has written about in past *AAJ*s. He was raised in the Alaskan bush and now lives in Switzerland, finishing his Ph.D. in something I can barely pronounce. Also a Ph.D., Bruce works as a research physicist at whatever university will hire him for long enough to pay for the next climbing expedition. Fifteen years older than me, he's done about as many expeditions as years I've been alive. Bruce's 2008 reconnaissance had inspired this expedition, and as we rode the bus toward Xiate we pored over his photos of the Xuelian massif [*AAJ* 2009, "Untapped Potential"]. Our group would be only the second expedition to approach the Xinjiang Tien Shan from the north.

At the end of the road, at midnight, rain beat down on a canvas yurt. The deafening noise seemed to amplify the intensity of negotiations going on inside by flickering candlelight. We needed to hire the teenage Kazakh horsemen whose 15 horses foraged outside, hobbled and drenched after their long journey down from a summertime pasture. In the early morning light, negotiations concluded with an agreement, they loaded our 1,200 kilograms of gear onto their horses, and we began the 22-kilometer approach to base camp.

Green fields stretched for kilometer after kilometer, decorated with purple forget-me-nots, yellow milkwort, and other aromatic flowers. Towering pines lined the trail, as our caravan of climbers, horses, and equipment wound uphill. Kazakh shepherd families emerged from their summertime yurts to greet us and offer naan, chai, and a bitter, pungent cheese. I envied their traditional way of living, self-sustained and deeply connected with their animals. They smelled of fire and

Dempster leads a thin mixed pitch. During a 2008 reconnaissance of Xuelian West, Normand concluded from a distance that the golden rock must be granite. Instead, the team found soft, difficult-to-protect marble. *Bruce Normand*

horse, a brute leathery smell that once was common on the American frontier and that I imagine when I turn the pages of Cormac McCarthy novels.

On day two of the approach we crested Muzart Pass and descended slightly to base camp, at 3,580 meters on the edge of the impressive Muzart Gorge. Camp had all the attributes of an alpine climber's Elysium: fresh drinking water and a nearby waterfall for brisk showers, grassy alpine slopes patched with flowers, and red, sun-baked boulders. And directly across the gorge and dominating the view from base camp: the 2,600-meter north face of Xuelian West. After months of preparation, countless hours of training, and days of travel, a place that had existed only as pictures had finally become reality. As we ate dinner and watched the orange glow of day's end bleed from Xuelian West, the soothing colors gave the face a welcoming feel. I could feel my intimidation fading. However, committing to the face would take time.

At the beginning of August, as planned, we split into two teams: Bruce and Jed, and Jared and I. We wished each other luck and set off to pursue different goals. After a week of acclimatization and a reconnaissance of various objectives, Jared and I started up a 1,700-meter route on Xuelian's 6,400-meter eastern sub-summit. The initial 900 meters on the north face consisted of 60°–70° ice, with snow-covered rock pitches up to M5 and plenty of waist-deep snow. We

rested for a day at 5,500 meters and the following morning crested onto the east ridge. To our
surprise the amazing view included two climbers kicking steps up the ridge. Jed and Bruce had
departed early that morning for a push to the
summit of Xuelian East; we hadn't seen them for
10 days and now ran into them at this unlikely
intersection. As a team of four we climbed the
remaining 800 meters to the summit in rapidly
deteriorating weather.

Jed and Bruce had already climbed one
big new route on Xuelian North (6,472m). After
they headed back to base camp, Jared and I
managed another first ascent on the north face
of Yanamax II (6,180m). The 1,600-meter route,
Yanamaniacs, took us three days and climbed
difficulties up to M4. After the climb Jared and I
trekked the 15 kilometers back to base camp and
began stuffing our faces with delicious Chinese
food. We then focused our attention on the most
intimidating mountain we'd ever seen.

Dempster leads the delicate crux traverse late on the
second day, with spindrift compounding the difficulties. *Jed Brown*

Jared and I spent an entire day in base
camp resting and discussing Xuelian West. With a frostbitten toe, he eventually decided to
forgo an attempt at the massive peak and instead explore smaller peaks along our approach
route. Late the next day Bruce and Jed returned from an attempt on Xuelian's northeast satellite. By now we were well-acclimatized and had a good feel for the daily weather patterns.
While drinking coffee on the grassy slopes of base camp, I asked Jed about his climbs so far. As
if reading my mind, he said, "I'm ready for something harder." With six days left on our permit
and our liaison officer getting antsy, Bruce, Jed, and I began packing for Xuelian West.

A blunt prow of complex rock divides the north-northeast and true north faces of Xuelian West. Both faces are capped with huge seracs, and the prow offers the only passage that
is relatively free of objective dangers. The route up the top third of the face appeared fairly
straightforward, but as we looked through binoculars we couldn't agree on the best route
through the bottom two-thirds. By committing, we began the process of finding a solution. On
the afternoon of August 24 Bruce, Jed, and I walked over to an advanced camp directly below
the face. Before dawn the next day we began kicking steps up a 400-meter snow cone.

Jed led the first block, angling left from the snow. The first four pitches were moderate
and allowed us to climb together until Jed ran out of gear; he would then bring Bruce and me
up and rerack. Pitch five entered a narrow 80° gully on very thin ice; protection was difficult
and our pace slowed. I took over the lead, delicately exiting the gully and climbing another
four pitches on immaculate 70° ice. This put us on a wide-open icefield, where we spent two
hours chopping a bivy ledge wide enough for five butt cheeks. The weather during the night
remained stable, and I fell asleep very curious about the terrain above.

Jed began leading the following morning in the dark. Two pitches of slab covered with
rotten ice gave way to four pitches of amazing ice, rivaling in steepness and quality some of

the best frozen waterfalls I have ever climbed. These brought us to another open ice slope with a view of the entire left side of the prow. Here I took the lead. As we simul-climbed for 120 meters up a snow and ice field, dark clouds descended and dimmed the light, as if setting the stage for something tremendous. Snow began to fall as I led two more mixed pitches of classic and unique M5 climbing. Then, right on the prow, I reached a dead end. Ten meters above the semi-hanging belay were roofs and blank-looking terrain. I brought up Bruce and Jed, hoping they would see a path. For 45 minutes we looked around and discussed the options. Eventually Bruce said, "I think you should lead out that thin ramp to the left."

The angle of the wall began to ease during the third day, but the climbing remained thin and poorly protected. *Jed Brown*

We were somewhere near 5,000 meters, and a steep seam arced to the left 40 meters and then wrapped around a near-vertical corner, in the direction of anyone's best guess. It looked too steep, too blank. "This is for someone else," I thought. As I tiptoed farther from my last gear and into absolute self-accountability, I tried to breathe deeply and calm my mind. Spindrift ripped down the face, and I squeezed my tools, hoping that whatever they were connected to wouldn't break. A comfortable lightness began building within me.

As the snow pummeled against my hood, I began to laugh. With a strange accent I cursed at the cascade of snow, as if to mock the danger and absurdity of the situation, just as I'd heard Drew do many times. Waves of heat flowed through my body, and my forearms pulsed with each thump of my heart. With the picks of my tools slotted in a flared seam and pricked in a pancake of thin ice, I pushed deeper and felt a familiar energy buzzing inside me. "Drew is with me." Way beyond commitment, I delicately continued upward to the end of the pitch.

Jed took over the lead and climbed a horribly rotten pitch that tested him equally. Day two continued well into the night, as we searched for a place to bivy. Eventually we cut snow blocks from a 60-centimeter-deep snowfield and stacked them to create a makeshift ledge. We sat with our backs to the wall, as spindrift piled against the tent and threatened to push us into the void. A problem with the stove gave us symptoms of hypoxia and forced us to abandon our efforts to rehydrate. Fortunately, in the morning we were able to get the stove working and melt enough water for the day.

After a slow start I led six long, poorly protected pitches of snow-covered 5.7 rock, as the angle of the wall began to ease. Late in the afternoon we began to realize that success was likely, and Jed and I shared a fatigued smile at a belay. An intense electrical storm rumbled over us that night, and again spindrift built up between the tent and the wall. Selflessly, Bruce spent an hour outside shoveling away the snow.

In the morning the climbing continued to ease, with snowfields separated by bits of 5.7 rock. Strong winds prevailed for most of the day, and we decided to camp just shy of the corniced ridgeline leading to the summit. On day five, in only an hour, we climbed the final 200 meters to the top. Engulfed in fast-moving clouds, we exchanged hugs and congratulations.

Time has slowly and inevitably corroded my memories of Drew; his face and the sound of his voice are fading. But there are moments in my life, as on Xuelian West, when I know he's still present. On top, I took some of his ashes from my pocket and rubbed them onto my face, a final act of physical connection. From my sleep-deprived eyes streamed the best tears imaginable. Letting Drew go into the wind, I turned and continued the search.

Summary:

Area: Tien Shan, Xinjiang Province, China

Ascents: First ascent of the 6,427m northern satellite of Xuelian Feng via the west ridge, August 8–9, 2009 (Jed Brown and Bruce Normand). First ascent of Xuelian's east satellite (6,380m) via the north face (1,700m, AI3 M5, Kyle Dempster and Jared Vilhauer), August 11–14, and via the east ridge (Brown-Normand), August 13–14. Both parties descended the east ridge. First ascent of Yanamax II (6,180m) via its northwest buttress (Yanamaniacs, 1,600m, AI3 M4, Dempster-Vilhauer), August 18–20. First ascent of Xuelian's western satellite (6,422m) via the north face (The Great White Jade Heist, 2,600m, AI5 M6 5.7R, Brown-Dempster-Normand), August 25–29. All ascents were completed alpine style; see more details and route photos in Climbs and Expeditions.

A Note About the Author:

Kyle Dempster was born in 1983 and lives in Salt Lake City, Utah. He is co-owner of a coffee shop and experiences the joys of small-business ownership, heavy taxation, and working too much. In the future he hopes to spend time exploring wherever his heart guides him.

The expedition acknowledges the generous contributions of the American Alpine Club's Lyman Spitzer Cutting-Edge Award, W.L. Gore's Shipton-Tilman Grant, and the support of the British Mountaineering Council and the Mount Everest Foundation. Thank you!

Dempster checks out the ruins of advanced base camp before climbing Xuelian West. *Jed Brown*

A BIT OF LUCK

The alpine-style first ascent of Chang Himal's north face in Nepal.

ANDY HOUSEMAN

What do you need for a good trip? A partner, a mountain, and a bit of luck?
The first was easy. My climbing partnership with Nick Bullock had been forged over the last few years, strengthened through friendship, mutual respect, and trust in each other in the mountains. We shared a flat in Chamonix in the winter of 2006-'07, me the keen and inexperienced youth, Nick the wise old man. Conditions were favorable that winter and our route tally kept growing, the only problem being that neither of us had much enthusiasm for leaving a bivy early.

The second factor, the mountain, we owe to Lindsay Griffin and his contribution to the *Alpinist* article "Unclimbed" (*Alpinist 4*). One of Lindsay's picks was the stunning 1,800-meter north face of Chang Himal (6,802m, also known as Ramtang Chang or Wedge Peak). Situated in the remote northeast corner of Nepal, this is one of many impressive mountains that form the Kangchenjunga Himal. We'd thought about going there in the autumn of 2008, but my attempt at full-time work back in U.K. limited my time away. After a two-day jeep ride and 10-day trek to reach base camp, we would barely have had time to acclimatize, let alone attempt that face on Chang Himal.

Luck, well that's a tricky one. We didn't have it that autumn, when, without time to get to Chang Himal, we opted for the quickly accessed Hinku Valley. While resting at a teahouse down the valley from our base camp, everything there was robbed, apart from the garbage bag, before we'd even tied into a rope.

One year later, though, karma seemed to be on our side. With no daily forecast being sent to us at base camp below Chang Himal, we had no way of knowing if the good weather we experienced upon arriving would hold, but day after day it did. And we were lucky with conditions, too. In 2007 a Slovenian attempt (the only proper attempt on the face prior to ours) had failed at less than half height due to bad snow. We didn't have bomber, squeaky névé up the entire face, but we weren't complaining.

We also had a fourth lucky charm: Buddy, our cook. Without a doubt, he made the trip. Day after day he produced pizza and chips, lasagne, fresh bread, apple pies, burgers—you name it and he'd cook it.

We arrived at base camp, situated at 5,050 meters, above the Kangchenjunga Glacier, in mid-October. The 10-day trek with three friends had been mellow and sociable; we could almost forget what we were there for. After our good-byes at base camp, the trip suddenly took on a serious note, a kick up the backside, so to speak. The daunting north face of Chang Himal was not even a mile away over the jumbled chaos of the glacier. "Umm…bitten off more than you can chew here," I thought. From the time we woke to the end of each day of acclimatizing on the 6,000-meter mounds of scree behind base camp, Chang Himal was omnipresent—there was no escaping it.

For 10 days, we watched the face and our bodies slowly adapted to the altitude, Buddy producing tasty food day after day. With a route cairned across the glacier, the rack and food debate finished, and our kit stashed below the face, only an hour and half away, we were out of excuses. We spent a couple of days just eating, resting, and watching for any telltale signs of a change in the weather. None came and so, after a leisurely lunch, we followed our cairned path across the glacier and settled down for the night in a small cave below the face.

Sleep came surprisingly easy. After an early alarm and a quick breakfast, we entered the rocky gully that leads onto low-angled snow slopes at the bottom of the face at 2:30 a.m. Climbing onto the snow cone, we felt silent relief as we stood on a crust of firm snow instead of sinking to our waist in bottomless powder as we'd feared. We zigzagged up the slope, avoiding front-pointing till the last possible moment, saving our calves for what was to come. But instead of running up the firm snow, I moved as slowly as if I were wading through powder; I could barely keep pace with Nick as he kicked steps in front. I'd come out to Nepal not as fit as I'd have liked, but I'd felt better than this while acclimatizing. Bent over my axes, I threw up in the snow—"Not now!" I silently screamed. We'd both managed to keep well on the trip. What if I blew our only weather window?

Standing in the dark silence, I shouted up to Nick, dreading his reply. Without a moment's hesitation or the slightest anger in his voice, he replied, "No worries, youth, we can go down and give it a few days."

The Bullock-Houseman line on the 1,800m north face of Chang Himal. The two men bivied twice at their high camp, for a total of four nights on the face—none on a ledge big enough for their small two-man tent. *Nick Bullock*

Houseman begins the difficulties on Day 2. "I'll head up this way, I think. Looks straightforward." *Nick Bullock*

There it was: a chance to bail, to run away. Was this what I'd been looking for? Was it all psychological? This was the biggest face I'd been on, and of course I felt nervous—anyone who says he doesn't is bullshitting. Nick's laidback response almost made it too easy. But the drive was still there. "I want to continue!" I shouted up. If Nick could kick the steps, I'd try to keep up.

We slowly soloed up the steepening snow slope, moving as quickly as my weak body would allow through the "Narrows," the most threatened part of the route. With the arrival of dawn we had started up the broad gully that eventually would lead us back left onto the spur proper. The odd steep step or a few moves on unconsolidated, bottomless snow limited my daydreaming. The vomiting had stopped, but my body felt empty. Nick thought giardia. I wasn't sure, but the excitement of the unknown climbing above had taken over, keeping me going.

Nearly halfway up the face we stopped just to the right of the spur, chopping a small ledge for a rest and refuel. Feeling wasted but no longer ill, I asked Nick if he'd mind taking the first technical pitch of the route while I tried to down as much food and liquid as possible. I was feeling stronger with each bite. Above, Nick battled with steep snow and rotten ice, interspersed with time-consuming searches for gear in the shattered and blocky granite. This would be the norm for the rest of the route.

Feeling I should at least kick a few steps, I took the lead for the first time and ran out the ropes another 150 meters over steep snow to reach the crest of the spur, just over 1,000 meters up the face. It was early, but we'd covered a lot of ground and we both were tired. We set about chopping a ledge, knowing that a bivy here would catch a welcome few minutes of warming sun at dawn.

Sleep and more food helped revive me through the night, and after savoring the brief rays of morning sun I grabbed the rack for the first pitch. An obvious corner with a steep exit led straight up from the bivy.

"I'll head up this, I think. Looks straightforward."

Nick smiled knowingly, but all he said was, "Okay."

Some minutes later, breathing hard, I looked a long way down at my last bit of decent gear as I searched for an axe placement at the top of the corner. Nick's sly grin filled my memory. After finding a good cam, I swung left and felt the reassuring thunk of a pick in good névé. Legs bridged wide to take the weight of the pack off my arms, I pulled a few moves over the bulge and the cam disappeared far below as I reached easier ground and started the hunt for a belay.

Pulling over the steep step, Nick glanced up with an I-told-you-so look and said, "Umm, bet that was stimulating." My payback was to hand Nick the rack for what turned out to be the crux pitch of the route: a long, steep corner with a capping overhang of rotten ice. "Watch me, youth!" That was daunting: I'd never heard Nick shout that in the mountains before. But the rope slowly ran through my belay plate, the jerk of a fall thankfully never coming. Dismantling the meager belay, I started following as Nick moved up easier terrain, trying to find a belay. I pulled through the bulge on what usable thin ice was left, arms screaming and lungs bursting. An impressive lead.

The next four pitches were less steep but just as slow going, as we tried to unearth protection and belays in the shattered rock. Leaving Nick's belay and a possible bivy, I started a long traverse to the right under a huge roof that had been obvious from base camp, a feature that we hoped marked the end of the steepest section of the face. The ropes came tight, and while I waited a few minutes for Nick to start moving I got out my headlamp. Moving again, I passed the end of the roof, but the beam from my headtorch showed no sign of a belay stance. I kept going toward a

Bullock leads the route's crux pitch (M6). *Andy Houseman*

The third bivy: biggest bivy ledge of the route. *Nick Bullock*

slight rib I could just make out in the gloom, hoping to find snow deep enough to carve a ledge for a bivy. But the rib proved useless, and after placing two screws into the bulletproof ice just a few inches below the snow, I slumped onto the anchor and brought Nick across.

Through the darkness we could just make out a snow arête above the roof we'd passed. Nick quickly led upward, hoping for a comfy ledge. But in the end we settled for a foot-wide stance just off to one side of the spur. A fitful night's sleep was ensured, though hope that the hardest climbing was behind us made it slightly more bearable. We had climbed only 200 vertical meters that day.

Packing away one rope, we began the next morning moving together up a broad, right-trending snow ramp. Good névé and easy-to-find gear were nice changes, and soon we'd covered as much ground as we had the entire previous day. After traversing across a couple of flutings, only one unconsolidated, rotten snow arête remained to get 'round before we'd reach a deep gully that we knew would lead up to the easy-angled west ridge below the summit. Two attempts of levitating around the arête proved useless—a longer Peruvian apprenticeship needed for me.

Plan B was a short, rotten mixed step to reach one of the flutings directly above—more direct but, unlike the deep gully, with an unknown end. The rock step led into unconsolidated snow and a grovel over a few bulges before horrendous rope drag stopped me about 20 meters below the fluting's vertical headwall. Nick quickly took us up to the top of the fluting, where we dug the biggest bivy ledge of the route. (But still not big enough for the single-wall tent we carried and never used.) Brewing up that evening, just 300 meters below the summit, we feared we might have climbed ourselves into a dead end, and the thought of rappelling back down and trying to find another way into the deep gully to our right wasn't too appealing.

We woke to a very cold morning, and Nick went for an exploratory "poke your head around the corner" look to the left. He returned to the bivy ledge 10 minutes later with a grin that said it all. Another fluting appeared to lead straight to the west ridge. Stashing the bivy gear, Nick left the ledge again, moving quickly with no pack. Following, I removed a screw from the last bit of ice we would find on the route and reached Nick, belayed to his axes and a not-so-inspiring bollard. As I took over the lead, I forgot the joy of being close to the summit and instead started contemplating downclimbing this Peruvian-style fluting during our descent, as it appeared that any chance of finding ice for rappel anchors would be fruitless.

Moving together, the rope between us pointless but for some reason still there, we pulled onto the ridge and into the full force of the wind that had been blowing long plumes off the high summits of Kangchenjunga during the past two weeks. For the first time in four days we

Houseman searches for the exit from the face toward the end of Day 3. *Nick Bullock*

could see the summit, barely 150 meters away. I followed Nick's boot pack up the 45° slope and quickly joined him on the knife-edge top.

What a feeling as we embraced and took in the full panorama: the gigantic north face of Kangchenjunga towering behind us, Jannu's impressive north face poking up in the distance, base camp a tiny dot below. After only 30 minutes on the summit, the cold and our anxiety about the descent forced us to leave. Easy downclimbing brought us to the point where we'd exited onto the ridge. Hoping to avoid downclimbing the insecure snow flutings, we started digging as fast as the thin air allowed. After 20 minutes, though, we'd found only rotten snow. Accepting defeat, I started down after Nick, a few meters below me, plunging each tool as far as possible into the snow, holding my breath each time I weighted a foothold, expecting it to collapse. Finally we reached ice and quickly drilled a V-thread. A single 60-meter rap brought us back to the bivy ledge. It was late in the afternoon, and neither of us had the energy to chop another ledge lower down the face, so we spent a while enlarging the previous night's ledge and settled in for one last night on the face.

After 14 hours of rappelling the next day, we crashed out in the cave at the base of the face, our rack gone but at last the true feelings of success sinking in. It was almost like standing on the summit again—but this time there were no niggling thoughts of unknowns still to overcome, just pure satisfaction.

SUMMARY:

Area: Kangchenjunga Himal, Nepal

Ascent: Alpine-style first ascent of the central spur (1,800m, ED+ M6) on the north face of 6,802m Chang Himal (a.k.a. Wedge Peak or Ramtang Chang), October 29–November 2, 2009, by Nick Bullock and Andy Houseman. The two bivouacked at the base of the wall before and after the climb, for a total of six nights away from base camp.

A NOTE ABOUT THE AUTHOR:

Born in 1981, Andy Houseman is from North Yorkshire, England, but lives in Chamonix, France, where he is training to become a UIAGM guide.

Bullock (left) and Houseman relax at the foot of the face, after 14 hours of rappelling. *Nick Bullock*

ALONE ON
ANNAPURNA SOUTH

Some time to kill in base camp produces a bold new route in Nepal.

DODO KOPOLD

Annapurna South from Annapurna Lodge. (1) Dodo Kopold's route on the 1,700m east face topped out near the north summit (ca 7,100m). (2) Kopold traversed the ridgeline southwest to reach the main summit of Annapurna South (7,219m). (3) Approximate site of crevasse fall during Kopold's nighttime descent. *Courtesy of Dodo Kopold*

People say that Annapurna is dangerous from the north, dangerous and difficult from the northwest, and steep, dangerous, and difficult from the south. My first experience with Annapurna was in the autumn of 2008, when I tried to climb the northwest face in alpine style. After five days of climbing, Petr Masek, Martin Minarik, and I reached 7,500 meters. Strong wind, freezing cold, and heavy snowfall during our summit push drove us down. Nobody wanted to try again.

But one day....

In the spring of 2009 I returned to Annapurna, this time to the south face, with Martin Minarik from the Czech Republic and Elisabeth Revol from France. We reached base camp on March 19 and soon started acclimatizing. The weather was predictable: In the morning it was clear and warm, and in the afternoon there were thunderstorms with snow. Every day the same, plus huge avalanches. The conditions this season were not the best.

Our dream was to climb the Bonington Route in alpine style, but really we just wanted to find any safe route to the summit of Annapurna. After a few weeks in the Annapurna Sanctuary, we decided that, indeed, the Bonington Route would be the best choice. The route has more than 3,000 meters of climbing, with demanding rock and ice passages. Our idea was to climb the face in seven days, and then we had two options: traverse the Annapurnas eastward to Manang village, or rappel the route we had climbed. We chose the second.

We took two superlight tents, light sleeping bags, 200 meters of 6mm rope, two snow anchors, pitons, ice screws, a few carabiners, and personal gear. We started April 4. The weather was unchanged: sunny mornings, afternoon snow.

During our first two days we reached 6,100 meters. Conditions were not good: deep snow and warm. But we were fast and full of power. On the third day we woke early and the sky was filled with long clouds. As we started to climb, heavy fog lay everywhere, and soon it started to snow. Martin checked the forecast in late morning: strong winds and heavy snowfall during the next few days.

Kopold on Annapurna Main's south face, after a bivouac at 6,000m. Storms soon forced a retreat. *Dodo Kopold*

The decision to retreat was not easy, but we knew it was the only way to survive. In deep fog, we retreated to our campsite at 6,100 meters and then to base camp the next morning. We were sad because I would not have time for another attempt. It snowed during the next few days, and our thoughts were simple: go home, go sailing. But suddenly we got a new forecast—the weather would improve for several days. Our tent was quiet; the chessmen stopped moving. Martin's goal was clear: He wanted to try Annapurna again with Eli, this time by the Joos-Loretan Route on the east ridge.

It was Tuesday, April 7, and Martin and Eli planned to start on Friday, when the weather was expected to improve. And me? I still had several free days before my flight home, but I didn't have time to attempt Annapurna. I wondered how I would kill time in base camp. Then, after a night of reflection, I decided to try Annapurna South.

△

Before this, Annapurna South had only been one of the peaks visible from base camp—we could clearly see its 1,700-meter east-southeast face, split by a shallow prow that leads directly to the northern summit at ca 7,100 meters. Now I wondered why nobody had climbed it from this side. I knew only the peak's altitude and that there was a route from the south (Bashkirov-Cherny-Lobankov-Minibaev-Shataev, 1994). Nothing about the descent, nothing about the history of the peak. Maybe that was why I decided to climb it.

Friday, April 10. It reminded me of the day in 2005 when Gabo Cmarik and I stood beneath Great Trango Tower, selecting the gear for a huge wall. Only the most important things. But today I had to do it alone. My idea was to climb the virgin face in a single push. I wanted to be light and fast, enjoying the climbing, feeling the air, and not carrying heavy loads. I had soloed difficult walls in winter and had a lot of experience with high altitude; I was well-acclimatized from our attempt on the Bonington Route. I felt good, and I wanted to use everything in my power, not only to summit but also to make a technically difficult, nonstop ascent.

I packed only a 40-meter 6mm rope, eight pitons, eight ice screws, ten quickdraws, three energy bars, some dried meat, a stove, and a down parka. I didn't take a sleeping bag, tent, mattress, food for cooking, spare clothes, or bivy sack.

I left base camp with Martin, Eli, and two Sherpas on Friday afternoon. After crossing the glacier to Annapurna Lodge, we stopped and I looked into Martin's eyes. He was happy. Eli was also full of power and optimism, as usual. Only I seemed worried about their

Oblique view of Annapurna South's east face from base camp. *Dodo Kopold*

climb—they planned to spend an unbelievably long time up there (about 12 days), and they carried heavy loads. But I believed they could climb the east ridge.

I ordered soup and pizza and a cup of tea. I smoked two cigarettes. Then, at 7 p.m., I left the safety of the friendly lodge.

⬡

The sky was clear and Annapurna South rose in front of me. I crossed the glacier and found the entryway to the face: vertical and overhanging water ice, the only way to reach the snow ridge in the middle of the face.

I had climbed 150 meters and it was already midnight when I reached a mixed section where I thought I might have to retreat. These were the hardest moves of my life—like drytooling on a sport route. The ice was good, but climbing it in the dark with only the small light of my headlamp was more than serious.

After a whole night of climbing, I finally reached the snow ridge and continued up to the steep first rock band. Now I felt safe. The sun was up, and the steep ice and avalanche terrain were behind me. I thought the route would be easier, but it was not. I struggled to find a way through the rock band. Ice fell everywhere. Then came the second rock band, steeper, with many tricky sections. I established a belay from two rock pitons and used my 6mm rope to protect myself. I had to make many moves without gloves. Unreal exposure! I could see the sunny valley, holy Machapuchare, Annapurna III, Ganggapurna, and somewhere down there the Annapurna Lodge. Beer, pizza, people. I was a big attraction for the tourists that day. Again, I believed I'd soon be on good terrain, but I was wrong again.

The conditions were getting worse. The ice and snow were melting, and it was much harder to find good belays. I climbed strange snowy ribs with no protection. After that came a wet rock wall with icy sections. The wall was steep, with thin, wet cracks, but I had no choice. I had to climb it.

Higher up I had to use more protection, and that made me slower. But finally, at 3:20 p.m., I reached the ridgetop, at about 7,100 meters. From here I thought the only possible descent would be to traverse southwest toward the main summit (7,219m) and continue down the east ridge toward Hiun Chuli; I had seen a snow gully that seemed to lead to the glacier from this ridge. It was late afternoon, and the way along the ridge was very long and in places dangerous and difficult, with ice towers and crevasses. But the snow conditions were perfect, and the weather was very good. When I reached the ridge down to Hiun Chuli, it looked too sharp and dangerous, but I could see the top of Annapurna South was not far, so I kept going. After another 40 minutes on easy ridge, I reached the summit at 6:18 p.m.

I decided to return to the saddle and descend directly to the east. There were huge seracs, deep snow, and hidden crevasses everywhere around me. Where to go? What was the safest way? Suddenly I fell five meters into a hidden crevasse; only a snow bridge stopped me from falling deeper. It was dark except for a bit of light from the hole I'd left above. I anchored myself to my tools and an ice screw, and fished for my headlamp in my pack. Then I climbed quickly toward one end of the crevasse, clawing through the soft snow near the exit.

Outside it was dark. I wondered if I should bivy and continue down the next morning. I don't know why, but I chose to continue. Exhausted, I finally reached Annapurna Lodge a little after 3 a.m. The lodge was closed, so I continued toward base camp, two hours away. As I started walking, an enormous avalanche fell from the serac atop the east face, crashing across the route I had just descended. I started to cry. I was happy that my decision to descend that night had been correct.

Forty hours after leaving, I returned to base camp. Our cook Temba helped me walk the last few meters and prepared tea and soup. My ascent had given me everything I wanted: I felt the thin air, climbed high into the unknown, and used all my experience from climbs I'd done before. It is hard to say how difficult the line I climbed really was, but that's not important. The mountain just gave me one chance to climb a perfect line in a fair style.

The next day I ran down to Pokhara and started toward home. When I finally got home to Slovakia, I fell ill with a fever; I still had a strong cough as I traveled to Chamonix to join the Piolets d'Or jury. During my time there, I got a sad message. Martin Minarik was missing on Annapurna. *[Editor's note: Elisabeth Revol, forced to descend alone when Minarik could no longer move, made it down safely.]* I couldn't believe it. Only a few days earlier Martin and I had played chess in base camp, and now he was gone. And with him his smile and dreams.

SUMMARY:

Area: Annapurna Himal, Nepal

Ascent: Solo, single-push first ascent of the central line on the east face of Annapurna South, also known as Annapurna Dakshin or Modi Peak (1,700m, ABO V+ WI6), Dodo Kopold, April 10–12, 2009. From the ridge crest at ca 7,100m, Kopold traversed southwest to reach the main summit at 7,219m, then returned to a saddle and descended to the east. The central prow on the east face had two known previous attempts, by a Japanese party that disappeared while trying the route in the mid-1980s and by a British team in the spring of 1989.

A NOTE ABOUT THE AUTHOR:

Born in 1980, Jozef "Dodo" Kopold began climbing in 1997. He lives in Bratislava, Slovakia, with his wife and two children. Kopold wrote about a new route on Great Trango Tower in the 2006 American Alpine Journal *and about ice climbs in Trango Valley in 2007.*

JOBO RINJANG

The alpine-style first ascent of a little-known Nepalese peak.

JOE PURYEAR

The south and east flanks of the Lunag massif, as seen from Kyajo Ri. Proposed names: (1) Little Lunag, 6,492m; (2) Lunag I, 6,895m; (3) Lunag II, 6,891m; (4) Jobo Rinjang, 6,778m; (5) Lunag III, 6,795m; (6) Lunag IV, 6,781m; (7) Lunag V, 6,550m. *Joe Puryear*

It was cold and clear on the summit, without a breath of wind. Unlikely conditions, considering where we were. Laid out before us were the iconic peaks of the Nepal Himalaya. Mountains you dream about while growing up. Mountains I had already seen from the valley bottoms. But now, through the lean air above 6,700 meters, I gained a whole new appreciation. Lost were the lush green jungles, the sprawling juniper and rhododendron forests, and the tiny Sherpa

villages sprawled across the hill-
sides. From up here it was all raw
mountains of ice and rock, and we
were the first people to view them
from this perch.

It was October 2008, and
David Gottlieb and I stood atop
Kang Nachugo (6,735m). It was
the first time we'd summited
an unclimbed peak together in
Nepal, and we were beginning to
recognize the vast potential that
remained, even among these well-
explored mountains. In the distance to the north, rugged peaks
framed the seemingly endless
Tibetan Plateau. Gaurishankar,

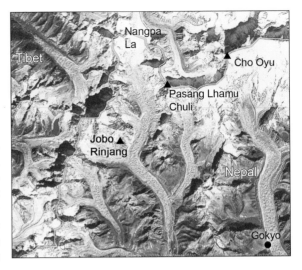

Menlungste, Cho Oyu, Gyachungkang, Pasang Lhamu Chuli—many peaks we could easily
identify. But one monstrous massif stood out, and we had no idea what it was. It was shorter
than the surrounding giants, but its bulk and steep vertical relief on all sides were impressive.
On its western edge a series of pointy summits jutted along the Nepal-Tibet border. And spur-
ring to the east was a solitary pyramid, connected to the main massif by a knife-edge ridge over
two kilometers long.

"What the hell is that?" David exclaimed. I was asking myself the same question. Our
desire to identify and explore this peak was now second only to getting off Kang Nachugo
safely. Four months later, we'd be back in Nepal.

⟁

In Nepal there are around 60 unclimbed peaks for which permits can be obtained. Lists of
these peaks are widely available. The tricky part is sifting through this information to find worthy
independent summits. Many of the "peaks" are small sub-summits or BORs (bumps on a ridge).
And, unsurprisingly, many are labeled with the wrong elevations, coordinates, and even names.

We found several different names for the pyramidal mountain we'd seen from Kang
Nachugo. After much research, including talking to locals, we concluded that Jobo Rinjang,
elevation 6,778 meters, was as close as we were likely to come to a definitive name. More
important to us: Although Jobo Rinjang had been attempted at least once (by a Swiss team in
October 2008), it was still unclimbed.

In early March we spent three weeks in Nepal acclimatizing for an alpine-style attempt.
First we completed a grand trekking loop through the Khumbu region, crossing Renjo La and
Cho La, and hitting five points over 5,400 meters. Next we climbed the southwest ridge of
Kyajo Ri (6,186m) in a one-week roundtrip from Namche Bazaar. From our high camp on
Kyajo Ri, we got a splendid view of Jobo Rinjang, about 18 kilometers to the northwest.

A week later we commenced the two-day trek north from Thame to the remote outpost of
Lunag. Old, dilapidated stone huts hinted of perhaps better times. Lunag is the first place where
Tibetan traders coming over Nangpa La can find meager shelter and graze their yaks. But we

David Gottlieb and Joe Puryear climbed the 1,700m south face of Jobo Rinjang with one bivouac, high on the face. After two nights on the summit, they descended by approximately the same route. The south ridge (right foreground) and southwest pillar (far left) were attempted by Swiss-Nepali teams in 2008 and 2009, respectively; see Climbs and Expeditions. *Joe Puryear*

found it empty and desolate, as the border between Tibet and Nepal had been temporarily closed.

We spent the next several days exploring this magnificent area. Just to the west of Jobo Rinjang is a string of peaks lining the border with Tibet. Given that the nearby village and the glacier below the south side of the massif are named Lunag, we have proposed that this chain be called the Lunag Massif. The highest peak (6,895m) is on the south end of the chain; this we've dubbed Lunag I. We've called the prominent points farther north Lunag II, III, IV, and V. Jobo Rinjang, attached to Lunag I by a two-kilometer ridge, rises above the 1.5-kilometer-wide confluence of the Lunag and Nangpa La glaciers.

Nearly all of the Lunag Massif, including Jobo Rinjang, was a chaotic mess of steep, disintegrating rock and precariously perched ice. Only one line seemed the least bit sane: a beautiful swath of ice on the south face of Jobo Rinjang, gaining nearly 1,700 meters.

On April 20 we left the relative comfort of Lunag and headed across the confluence of glaciers—an endless maze of huge, shifting boulders teetering on steep ice walls—toward the foot of Jobo Rinjang. From the moraine, the glacier looked like a war zone, as dust from falling blocks hung in the air like smoke, and explosions boomed across the valley. With our heavy packs, the four-kilometer trek was arduous, but by late afternoon we'd settled onto a small patch of sand in a nook between boulders for a few hours of rest.

Gazing up at Jobo Rinjang, we studied the looming ice cliffs bracketing our proposed line. At one point the behemoth on the right let loose a spectacular show. Cool, it completely missed our route! We guessed the left cliff would drain left. As for the multiple rock bands streaking across the upper route, we assumed—mistakenly—that because they were well above 6,000 meters they would remain frozen and stable.

We could not see any safe bivy site in the middle of the face. Although we felt that we could mitigate the rockfall dangers while moving, we didn't want to risk pitching a tent without shelter. Nor did either of us have the inclination to chop blue ice for several hours for a cramped bivy. Banking on our four weeks of acclimatization, we decided to aim for the top of a hanging glacier high on the face in a single push; we assumed a bench and bergschrund there would provide a safe and comfortable night's rest. But nearly 1,400 meters of calf-burning blue ice stood in our way.

⚐

A true alpine start was in order, and so, after only a few hours of anxious sleep, we awoke before midnight. I was first out of camp and began stumbling through huge boul-

ders in the dark. Looking down, I would catch
glimpses of David's faint headlamp meander-
ing along the moraine's edge. The moraine
gave way to steep, fine scree and then slabby
rock, which we cautiously soloed. Eventually
we reached a little ledge at the base of the first
ice swath, where we donned crampons and
watched the sun rise.

It had been a particularly dry winter
and spring, and abnormal amounts of ice
showed on the high peaks. On Kyajo Ri we
had expected the southwest ridge to be an easy
snow trek but instead were treated to 12 pitches
of alpine ice. Under different conditions, our
icy route on Jobo Rinjang might be easier than
we found it; on the other hand, we enjoyed the
security of good ice screws for protection and
belay anchors.

Gottlieb arrives at the bivy (6,500m) at 11 p.m., 21
hours after starting. *Joe Puryear*

For the first few hours, the climbing was monotonous. Starting at around 45 degrees, the
ice quickly ramped up to 55 degrees. I led the first simul-climbing "pitch" of 400 meters, and,
after a short break, David swung into the lead. We crested a small roll, and the angle backed off
a little as we headed into the gut of the mountain between the two ice cliffs. Suddenly a rock
the size of a beer cooler sped past us, sounding like a helicopter as it skimmed over the surface
of the ice.

"Holy shit, did you see that?" I yelled.

David's reply was unemotional, a simple "yeah." My mind raced. But quickly I realized
he had already understood our situation. Keep going up. We'd get out of danger quicker if we
continued up. David turned back to the ice and continued kicking away.

I leaned back from the anchor and studied the route above. All I could see were bands
of stacked boulders and blocks. As I followed the rest of David's leading block, I kept my head
up, scanning for projectiles so he could concentrate on the climbing. We hugged the steeper ice
on the far left of a wide gully, hoping to avoid debris. Several other blocks flew by at a distance,
and smaller samples whizzed by our heads. By the time David's block was up, my neck was as
tired as my calves.

It was now early evening, and we were level with the base of the hanging glacier. The ice
was turning to sn'ice, and protection was becoming harder to find. At times we climbed with
no pro between us. Darkness fell as we entered runnels leading through the ice cliffs. I crossed
one runnel and used the slot left behind in the snow as my only protection. A fast-moving
storm had enveloped the mountain, and soon it started to snow. In a daze I just kept plodding, looking for anyplace we could dig in. I hadn't seen David in over an hour—the darkness,
storm, and terrain hid the glow of his headlamp. I had to assume he was still on the other end
of the ropes that trailed behind me.

Finally I reached a bergschrund and followed its outer lip until it widened enough that
we could excavate a flat bivy site. I hauled in the ropes as David wearily plodded toward me. It
was around 11 p.m. We had succeeded in our push.

Cold, soaked, and completely spent, we dug a small platform and settled in for a long night of melting water. "I'd register that as definitely one of the harder days of my existence," David murmured through steamy breath. It was still snowing heavily. Toward morning, however, the snow tapered off, and we awoke to clear skies. Our position was exposed, but we were safe now from falling rocks. We slept in and waited until the sun swung around and warmed us. We knew this would be a shorter day—we were only about 300 meters from the top.

In late morning on April 22, David led out from our high perch, moving right and down around the bergschrund. On 45-degree firm snow, we made quick progress until we reached another bergschrund below a fluted headwall. Since no anchor was possible, David launched right up the steeper ground, and we continued to simul-climb with no pro, crossing sugary flutings. Soon, though, the terrain rolled over and David was reeling me onto the summit. As on Kang Nachugo, our partnership and strategies had proved successful. Even better, we had spent 100 of the past 200 days together and were still best friends. We stood on top and took in the surroundings—once again an entirely new vista unfolded.

◬

We reveled in our success, but we were not happy with the idea of descending the dangerous route we'd climbed, and we were keen to explore more of the massif. Our plan now was to descend the west ridge of Jobo Rinjang toward the Lunags, try to link other peaks, and hopefully find a different descent route. We had carried a week's worth of food and were only on day three away from the Lunag settlement. We pitched our tent right on the summit, the safest and flattest spot we had encountered in a few days.

After a night on top of Jobo Rinjang, Gottlieb and Puryear attempted to traverse the two-kilometer ridge west toward the main Lunag massif, but warm temperatures and fragile cornices turned them back. *Joe Puryear*

The clear weather was holding, but it was cold and windy. Our ultra-light tent was battered all night. The next day we packed and descended toward the Lunags. The ridge was racked with huge cornices, and snow conditions were awful in the warming air. When the way along the ridgeline was no longer feasible, we debated rappelling to the north in hopes of finding a way around.

"Are you sure you want to go down there and pull the ropes?" David asked cautiously.

"Let's just not rap off anything we don't want to lead back up," I replied.

And that's what happened: After three rappels, we reached another dead end. Before long we were back at the ridge. After half a day of trying to pick our way across the ridge, we had to accept that it was too dangerous in these conditions, and so we returned to the summit of Jobo Rinjang, where we camped for another night on the summit.

Now we had to descend the way we'd come up, which would expose us to rockfall for most of a day. In the morning we downclimbed to the southwest, putting us in line with the gully we had ascended between the two ice cliffs. After several ropelengths we reached a patch of blue ice, where we sank the first of many V-thread rappel anchors. With each V-thread, we pulled the climbing rope through the hole instead of tying tat through it, thus leaving no trace of our descent or ascent.

After 20 rappels we started downclimbing again. The ice was turning to slush, and water ran down the surface. At one point rocks smashed into the terrain around David, nearly wiping him off the face, but he escaped unscathed. Finally down on the moraine, we wearily made our way back to our tiny bivy on the glacier, and the next day commenced the arduous journey back to Lunag. Our desire to explore the world's unclimbed mountains had strengthened, and our next expedition was already developing in our imaginations.

Summary:

Area: Rolwaling Himal, Nepal

Ascent: Alpine-style first ascent of Jobo Rinjang (6,778m) via the south face (1,700m, 75°), David Gottlieb and Joe Puryear, April 21–24, 2009. The team descended by approximately the line of ascent.

A Note About the Author:

After 15 years of climbing as often as he could in Alaska, Joe Puryear has turned his focus to unclimbed peaks of the greater Asian ranges. Born in 1973, Puryear lives with his wife in Leavenworth, Washington, where he works in writing, photography, and graphic design. He writes: "I thank the American Alpine Club for giving us the Lyman Spitzer Cutting Edge Award for our climb of Jobo Rinjang. It truly made the difference in helping us follow our dreams of exploration."

David Gottlieb (left) and Joe Puryear on top. *Joe Puryear*

THRILLER

Four major routes in two weeks on Alaska's Stikine Ice Cap.

JENS HOLSTEN

Burkett Needle (left) and Mt. Burkett, from Silly Wizard Peak to the east. Max Hasson and Jens Holsten did the first free ascent of Burkett Needle's South Pillar, generally following the left skyline. Their route National Public Ridge (5,700', 5.10R AI3) takes the longest line on the south face of Mt. Burkett. Previous ascents (Cauthorn-Collum, 1994; Hoyt, 2005) followed straightforward glaciers on either side of the ridge to approximately the elevation of the Hasson-Holsten bivouac site (marked) before climbing the upper southeast face. Hasson and Holsten descended their route to the bivy site, then rappelled to the glacier to the east and followed this down to the top of the steep rockband below their line; they descended these rocks and a snow couloir to reach the glacier. *Max Hasson*

Millions of stars stabbed through the darkness; a dusty ledge was our bed, stones our pillows. Inadequate bivy gear and general gumbiness were turning my first Yosemite climb with Max Hasson into an epic. Up with the dawn, Max threw himself at the Kor Roof, the crux lead on Washington Column's South Face. I floundered with my jumars as I tried to clean the overhang, and soon I lowered in a sweaty haze of itchy pain. (A few days before, I'd wiped my ass with poison oak.) As we rappeled toward the Valley floor I wondered, "Will Max ever climb with me again?"

He let my shortcomings slide, and soon we were back on the rock. My fevered motivation seemed to complement Max's analytical style. It was the summer of 2002, and as our skills grew we climbed a stack of walls, including our first El Cap route, a 24-hour sufferfest on the Zodiac. Hanging at a belay with a sea of granite all around and a sickle moon overhead, I sensed greater adventures ahead.

For the next several years, Max and I traveled the American West, our program built around solos in Joshua Tree, splitters in Utah, and the iconic walls of Yosemite. Inspired by California's Stonemasters, we traced a learning curve that emphasized a simple climbing style dependent upon movement skills and mental strength rather than equipment. When we started to put the pieces together high in the mountains, we realized a passion. The combination of adventure and athleticism in the world's wildest places seemed to us like the perfect game.

Long before that first trip to Yosemite, I'd seen a photo of a freshly rimed spike of granite in southeast Alaska called Burkett Needle. The image had burned in my mind for years, an ember of inspiration that still held heat when Max and I finally felt ready for Alaska in 2007. Then life threw me some curveballs, stalling our trip for two years. When we finally touched down on the "Burkett Glacier"— the south arm of the Baird Glacier—on June 9, we were like two monkeys let out of a cage. It had been a long time coming.

The splitter weather at base camp did not give us time to sit nervously under misty peaks, endless cups of tea clutched between sweaty palms. Immediately we began preparing for a free effort on the magnificent South Pillar of Burkett Needle. Established in 1995 by Dan Cauthorn, Greg Collum, and Greg Foweraker, this classic ridge featured moderate yet steep climbing, with a single overhanging pitch of modern A3. Our plan was to approach the climb like we would any other: a lead line, a tag line, a small rack of cams and nuts, and some shoulder-length slings with biners. We would try to use only our hands and feet for upward movement.

A hurried ascent through a disintegrating ice cliff was the first order of business. The moderate terrain passed quickly below my boots; Max swung up behind me. Past all the difficulties, I began to mantel onto the glacier but never finished the move, a portable blade of névé sending me for a 50-foot tumble. Sixty feet to my right, a gripped Max shouted, "What's keeping us on?"

"One screw," I responded in disbelief.

"Well, are you OK?"

Upside down, my tools' umbilicals wrapped around me, I took inventory. My side was badly bruised, and at first I felt sure I had a concussion, but as the adrenaline wore off my thoughts were coherent and my motivation strong. Ten minutes later, on top of the ice cliff, I unbuckled my helmet and discovered it had split like a melon.

It took a few hours to put the fall behind us, but we regained our flow as we started up the rock pitches. I quickly sensed this would be one of the best climbs I had ever done. Max bypassed the route's single question mark, the pitch of A3, with a surprisingly moderate 5.10+ variation. Another 5.10 pitch and a sweeping arc over a golden slab put us back on the original route. The climb had exceeded years of building expectations: 2,000 feet of moderate climbing on flawless, gold-plated granite, with reasonable protection and magnificent views.

Holsten follows the third of three new pitches that bypass the A3 overhang on the original line of Burkett's South Pillar. *Max Hasson*

Clicking into cruise control, we raced up the summit tower, each lost in amazement, the never-ending alpenglow of Alaska twilight seeming like a big slice of heaven.

After our free ascent of the Needle we needed a rest day. The skies remained splitter and our spirits high. Climbing without guidebooks, it was exhilarating to imagine lines up castles of rock and ice that we knew nothing about.

At the head of the glacier, to the southeast of Mt. Burkett, a 3,000-foot face of complex ridges and gullies rose to several minor summits. We wanted nothing to do with such faces in mid-June, as tears of boulders and melting ice mourned the exit of spring. But on the right side of the wall a southwest-facing arête of gendarmes and snow patches shot upward. Choosing the safety of the ridge, we crossed the glacier, found an unlikely path through the icefall to the right of the peak, and carefully negotiated a rubbly 5.7X pitch onto the arête.

Steep slabs, fourth-class ground, and 50° snow slopes stretched for a couple of thousand feet; we ditched the ropes and hardware where a ledge would allow us to retrieve them from the glacier during our descent, and we made quick progress up the easy ground above. Alaska always dishes out a little extra, however, and from a false summit we could see that the next 800 feet would be no exception. The terrain was classic: a traverse in the sky at around 5.7, with delicate foot matches in mountain boots and the knife-edge ridge top in our hands. Calling on all of our free-solo experience, we enjoyed a sense of untethered freedom.

At the saddle beyond the summit, we tried to dial in a forecast on our radio. Mt. Burkett and the Needle hovered powerfully in the warm air. Between bites of summer sausage and cheese, we sat back and enjoyed our position, the music of Scotland's Silly Wizard band slipping among the towers and ice slopes around us. Heel-plunging down the backside, we decided on a name: Silly Wizard Peak. Later, we'd name our route the Thriller Arête, a tribute to its airy excitement and to Michael Jackson, who died while we were in the mountains.

The next morning, through the filtered light of a cloudy day, yet another peak begged for my attention: an obvious 3,000-foot fin of granite, directly across the glacier from Burkett, its northwest ridge slicing between steep snow slopes and somber rock walls.

Max emerged from the tent, rubbing puffy eyes. I booted up the stove, and within minutes he was sipping hot, oily coffee. "That peak across from us has a sweet ridge. I can't believe it didn't stand out to me before," I said. Max rummaged for his tobacco amid a heap of drying gear. He twisted up a cigarette before looking at the mountain. Exhaling smoke, he offered,

"Looks cool," and opened a rat-ravaged book he had found in the talus.

"Maybe one more rest day," I thought.

The Thriller Arête follows the right skyline about 3,000 vertical feet to Silly Wizard Peak, one of a cluster of summits east of Mt. Burkett. *Max Hasson*

A day later, our psyche was so high that we set out despite deteriorating weather. Gone were the Yosemite skies, but the temperatures were reasonable and we thought we'd just continue upward as long as we could. The approach passed quickly, and after a quick brew we started up snow and mixed climbing that would lead to the spine of granite above. Although the climbing was not difficult, it was subject to significant objective hazards. Both of us clung to a protrusion of polished granite as a bouncing block the size of a TV sent snow sliding evilly around us. When the snow stopped moving, we literally sprinted for safer ground.

Once on the ridge we found solid rock and parallel cracks. The climbing was no harder than 5.8, but tiptoeing in crampons through falling snow and fog kept things interesting. Finally, we could climb no further, even the impenetrable mist unable to disguise our location on the summit. Then, magically, the weather turned and bold beams of sunlight pushed back the angry clouds; rimed towers poked their heads into the pink light of evening. To the southwest, steep ice and rock fell 6,000 feet to the Devil's Cauldron, while across the Burkett Glacier we saw a huge, snaking granite arête splitting the snow climbs on Mt. Burkett's south face. A chord rang within me—the immensity and obvious difficulty of that feature demanded my attention. But for now I forced my eyes toward our descent route via the crevassed western slopes.

A faded green handkerchief on top suggested our route reached a previously climbed summit. However, the mountain was still unnamed (a fact we confirmed after discussing the climb back in Petersburg with Dieter Klose, the Stikine's most inspired and accomplished explorer). When Max suggested we call the peak Mt. Suzanne, I readily agreed. Two years earlier, as we had laid our initial plans to climb in Alaska, I was forced to stay home and scale a different kind of mountain, as my mother, Suzanne, died from ovarian cancer. Although she has left this Earth, I saw her beauty and spirit in that high sunset on Mt. Suzanne, and her guiding hand showing us the way toward a safe descent. Having struggled with my decision to dedicate my life to climbing, I felt at that moment as if she had blessed my choice. Now I was ready to see what Max and I were really capable of. I began to wonder about that huge ridge on Mt. Burkett's south face.

Two days later I was run-out on 5.10, the slammed-shut seams of Mt. Burkett forcing me to believe in my ability rather than my pro. Our single rack of cams seemed inadequate for the steep, steel-gray rock above. Just when I began to wonder about our chance of success, Max found an escape route through a band of loose diorite. Immediately, the angle eased and the terrain allowed us to blast another 1,000 feet up the ridge that evening.

By the time we had eaten, high, thin clouds were lazily swimming up valley. I knew the weather had plans and, sure enough, the next morning those high clouds had transformed into a smothering blanket of moisture. Max was experiencing shooting back pains, and so down we went, Max wincing at the pain, and me at the double loads I carried. Many tense moments later, we snowshoed toward camp, feeling the weight of defeat more acutely than the sodden ropes we pulled through the snow. Despite all the great climbs we'd already done, this now seemed like the line we had come for.

Two days later, Max was feeling better than ever and the weather had improved. "Should we get up on the ridge again?" he asked. Within seconds I was shoving gear into my pack. Judging by the weather pattern of the last few days, the partly cloudy skies might give way to rain and snow within hours. We needed to use the window of good weather to reclimb the run-out 5.10 of the initial buttress. Above that, our plan was to climb upward regardless of weather.

Aided by the knowledge gleaned from our previous attempt, we passed our highpoint within a few hours, climbing into increasingly poor weather. A sidewalk of spongy moss and alpine flowers led around an enormous tower and onto a snow patch. Max was barely visible in the gloom. Snow, talus, and then blocky steps evolved into a monstrous knife-edge. We crawled carefully across this 800-foot ridge, the consequences of falling equally grotesque for leader and follower. Finally, the precarious shimmy ended against the mountain's upper bowels, tentacle-like couloirs squiggling everywhere. Using nuts and cams, we pinned our tent into an airy position, with steep cliffs on both sides.

We stared at the tent ceiling for two nights, as National Public Radio out of Petersburg kept us entertained. The storm shrieked, the mountain wearing its anger in a coat of rime ice and sugar snow. Closing my eyes that second evening, I accepted the notion of bailing. The food was nearly gone, and fresh snow pressed down on the tent. I slept soundly.

Cold air stung my face as I looked outside well before dawn. "*You won't believe it, man!*" Max sat up and cracked the door to see the stars for himself, rubbed his eyes, and zipped the door again. We readied ourselves to leave our cocoon. I rejoiced in the good fortune of unexpected clear skies, but also knew the suffering they would bring. The air was cold enough to consider frostbite, and the slopes were loaded with fresh snow. We moved humbly and quickly across mixed terrain, steep snow arcing like a bow, and up a couloir glistening with alpine ice.

Summits on the south side of the "Burkett Glacier," opposite Mt. Burkett. (1) Unnamed peak, ca 7,240'. (2) Mt. Suzanne, ca. 7,190'. The Hasson-Holsten route began with the steep glacier to the right of the peak (arrow) and then followed the rocky northwest ridge to the top. *Max Hasson*

Crystalline rime daggers shattered on the rocks as sun touched the upper face. I dragged our heavy rope as quickly as my burning calves would allow.

Topping the couloir brought a sobering view of the massive upper basin. We slipped under crushing ice cliffs, their stability waning in the warming air, and then blasted up never-ending 70° snow slopes toward the summit. Six hundred feet from the top, I dropped my head onto my axe. Saliva fell from a corner of my cracked lips. With no calories to fire up my empty muscles, I tried to scrape together what mental strength I had left. As Max approached I thought of all the friends and family pulling for us. "It's about time I kicked a few steps," he said. I gladly gave up the lead and watched as Max pushed ahead. When the rope came tight, I started moving again, following quickly in his steps. Near the summit, clouds began to spin around us. Through the fog I could barely see Max as he negotiated a tricky mixed step with no pro. I dug my tools deeply in the snow and prayed for my friend above.

"You're on!" Through the swirling clouds I could see Max had made the pointy, whipped-cream summit. I punched my way toward the top and joined him. Icy wind swept up Mt. Burkett's giant north face, but the sun-warmed slopes we had to descend were melting into a dangerous mush. For a few hundred feet, solid bollards facilitated quick retreat, but soon no ice could be found anywhere. More than a few times I gingerly tested an anchor only to have Max yell, "*Stop! That won't work!*" Like a knife through warm butter, our rope cut at every anchor we tried to build. In desperation I began to downclimb toward a vertical ice cliff, resigned to a solo mindset. Then I noticed a ramp that allowed us to slip down and around the cliff, leading us to easier ground.

We had a long, tedious descent ahead, but it was nothing compared to the danger of that last stretch. Racing down the final bowling alley of a couloir and onto the flats of the glacier was sweet release. Fear and anxiety crumbled away, leaving only tired awe.

SUMMARY:

Area: Stikine Ice Cap, Alaska Coast Mountains

Ascents: First free ascent of the 2,500' South Pillar of Burkett Needle (ca 8,500') by a three-pitch 5.10+ variation, June 10, 2009; likely the fourth ascent of the peak. First ascent of Silly Wizard Peak (ca 7,350') via the Thriller Arête (southwest arête, 3,000', 5.7X 50°), June 13, 2009. First ascent of the northwest ridge (3,000', 5.8 M4 60°) of Mt. Suzanne (ca 7,190'), June 16-17, 2009. First ascent of National Public Ridge (direct south ridge, 5,700', 5.10R AI3) on Mt. Burkett (9,730'), June 22-24, 2009. All climbs by Max Hasson and Jens Holsten.

A NOTE ABOUT THE AUTHOR:

Born in 1982, Jens Holsten has been enjoying the mountains for nearly 20 years, thanks to a father who took his kids on long climbs and hikes in the Cascades rather than to Hawaii or Disneyland. He works at a small, family-owned winery in central Washington when he's not climbing locally or abroad.

CATHARSIS

After 28 Alaskan expeditions: the trip of a lifetime.

JACK TACKLE

A) Kahiltna Queen (12,380'). (B) Top of the "Scottish Wall." (C) The 10,300' south peak of Mt. Huntington, with the line of Prizefight (Smith-Tackle, 2009). (D) Mt. Huntington (12,240'). (E) Denali (20,320'). (F) "My Private Idaho," the hanging cirque where pilot Paul Roderick landed for the first time ever to drop off Jay Smith and Jack Tackle. The Rooster Comb is out of view to the right. *Jack Tackle*

There is a rare feeling of completeness and calm that can only come after concerted effort and toil, sacrifice and vision. As the Beaver lifted off from the Kahiltna, and Jay and I headed for Talkeetna and home, I felt more at peace than I can ever remember feeling. The previous 18 days in the Alaska Range had cleansed some lingering doubts and demons; now all I had to do was breathe.

This trip culminated an odyssey of recovery from two significant health challenges, the first in 2001 and another the following year. Contracting and surviving a rare auto-immune disorder called Guillain-Barré syndrome was by far the most serious medical event of my life. Everything else has been a mosquito bite. I could write a book about it, and many people tell me I should, but I can barely do my taxes on time. Recovering from near-complete paralysis, learning to walk again, and retraining my muscle memory were only parts of the process. Suffice it to say that many, many friends and family members, along with my loving wife, Pat, helped me through this, and to them I am forever indebted.

Eighteen months after I came down with Guillain-Barré, an attempt to get back on the horse went bad. I started up an unclimbed face on Mt. Augusta with Charlie Sassara, and 2,000 feet up I was hit by a falling rock that broke my neck and back. The parajumpers and my friends rallied to pull my sorry ass off the wall—

Jay Smith leads the crux ice pitch of the Black Pearl. *Jack Tackle*

again, chapters in a book yet unwritten. But I survived it all, and now, finally, I was back home in the Alaska Range with Jay Smith—who could ask for more?

On May 7, Jay and I flew into a small cirque below the south peak of Mt. Huntington, thanks to Paul Roderick's skills and his awesome Otter ski plane. No one had ever landed in this cirque, a hanging arm above the upper Tokositna Glacier which I called "My Private Idaho." Our objective was a new route on Huntington's main peak, but after a day of reconnoitering the line, we knew it was not going to happen: too much wall climbing, too slow. Dejected, we wondered what to do next. Jay suggested the Rooster Comb: "Hey, we're here, let's at least climb something."

On May 9 we left a tent below the east side of Huntington, climbed to the col between Huntington and the Rooster Comb, and continued up what's likely the 1978 route from the West Fork of the Ruth. We summited in 7½ hours—possibly the fifth ascent of the peak—and were back at the tent nine hours later. The next day, as we labored back to base camp, Jay gazed around our Private Idaho. Jay has more new routes to his credit than anyone I know, and now he pointed out potential routes everywhere. From past experience, we both knew the alpine granite on Huntington is as good as any in the Alaska Range. The lines looked worthy, and the weather was splitter.

We spent the next week doing three new routes right above our base camp. The first was Prizefight on the south side of Huntington's 10,300-foot south peak. On May 13 we started

The Scottish Wall, south of Mt. Huntington's south peak: (1) Lagavulin (5 pitches) and (2) the Black Pearl (8 pitches). *Jack Tackle*

up an obvious left-leaning ramp across the rock wall that comprises the lower half of the route. We led with packs in three-pitch blocks over immensely enjoyable moderate terrain, with short challenging cruxes of mixed climbing. Jay pulled out his rock shoes (the only pair we'd brought) for the key pure-rock section (5.9R), two pitches leading directly up from the end of the ramp, the first of which was like plated City of Rocks granite. Above this was mostly snow, with the occasional rock step or short section of mixed terrain. Nineteen hours after we left the tent, in darkness, I manufactured a snow hole for a brief bivy without sleeping bags. After three hours of "sleep," we emerged from our cocoon to forge upward through poor snow to just below the summit of the south peak; the last 20 meters were too rotten to climb safely. We made 17 or 18 rappels down a different line from that we'd climbed, and 39 hours after leaving we were back at the tent.

It snowed the next day—the only snowy day of the trip—but that didn't matter. We were toasted, and we just slept, made margaritas, and rested some more—perfect timing, for once.

Sometimes things just line up, though most of the time they don't. My success ratio sucks generally, and especially in Alaska. But as the soreness left our bodies, we again gazed around our solitary alpine arena and saw more routes we had to climb. South of Prizefight was a wall with unique parallel chimneys formed by intrusive diorite dikes. We called it the Scottish Wall; it was maybe 20 minutes from the tent. (This made up for my 75-mile approach to Mt. Kennedy in the Yukon in 1978.)

Lagavulin, our first climb on the Scottish Wall, started with a splitter 5.10 crack that I dry-tooled up, and the rest of the five-pitch route followed an obvious weakness, with thin but protectable WI4+/5 pitches. Just to the right was a longer, harder line we dubbed the Black Pearl. (Clearly, Jay had watched *Pirates of the Caribbean* with his stepson Grady more than once.) The Black Pearl started with M5 mixed climbing; it had one of the best alpine WI5+ pitches I have seen, which Jay fired in one 70-meter lead; and the sting in the tail was a poorly protected M6 pitch that I struggled up while looking for gear the whole way. We were 14 hours up and down the eight-pitch line.

I was back at home in the Alaska Range, and I'd done four climbs (three of them new routes) in less than two weeks, with an old friend—who could ask for more? Well, we did.

When Paul flew us out from My Private Idaho, he stopped at Kahiltna base to pick

Jack Tackle leads the start to Lagavulin on the Scottish Wall. *Jay Smith*

up more climbers, and I casually asked him to fly by the north face of Thunder Mountain (10,920') on the way out to Talkeetna. I had spied a potential route on Thunder in 1996, when Doug Chabot and I did a new route on the south face of Hunter's south peak (The Sound of Freedom), directly across from Thunder. It had been on the list ever since. I knew of a couple attempts by very good climbers, but poor ice and snow had likely prevented success. It's all about timing. Now, 13 years later, Jay and I clicked away with our cameras as we flew by. It was in! Before we'd landed in Talkeetna, we had decided to return. We could have gone home content, but how many times do things line up so well?

After three days of rest, reracking, getting new ropes, and drinking draft beer, we were ready to go back. We landed on an arm of the Kahiltna underneath the face. It was, to the day, the 10th anniversary of my friends Jim Donini and Malcolm Daly's epic on the south side of Thunder. The imposing 4,000-foot north face had an obvious line. Also obvious were the hanging glaciers and massive seracs just left of it. Careful study and two weeks in the range made us confident we could climb fast and safely to a point where the objective danger was no longer an issue. After a few hours of scrutiny with the binoculars and strategy discussions, we packed two-pound sleeping bags, a canister of fuel, and one and a half days of food. We'd seen a small crevasse more than halfway up that might offer a bivy site.

Our packs weighed 17 pounds when we crossed the 'schrund at 5 a.m. and simul-climbed the first 900 feet. Jay took the first block of three pitches, and the climbing was deceptively steep. In fact, he had to leave his pack to haul with the tag line while I jumared, because the climb-

The line of Tangled Up in Blue (4,000', VI- AI6 M7) on the north face of Thunder Mountain. *Jack Tackle*

ing was, as Jay described it, "as hard as any pitches I've ever led in the mountains." That's saying something. Protection was hard to find; there were slightly overhanging sections where you swore there wouldn't be; and it was mostly compact snow over thin ice, not just stick and go. Each 70-meter pitch took Jay one to two hours to lead.

Above this the angle eased somewhat, but the concrete ice was relentless. We did five more 70-meter pitches in order to reach the bivy crevasse at 1 a.m., about 20 hours after we started. Happy we had scouted this bivy site from below, we rearranged some snow for comfort, brewed and ate, and fell asleep as it began to snow. Seven hours later it was still snowing lightly enough that we talked ourselves into brewing and eating some more, before launching once again.

At midday I left the comfort of the crevasse and headed toward the upper face. Until this point, it hadn't been clear if the line would connect easily at the top, because of the ominous seracs on either side. But, again, the route proved safe, with beautiful ice and mixed ground. Jay got another great mixed lead around pitch 13, but this one had good gear and better rock (generally the rock improved the higher we got). Near the top of the day's nine pitches, we could sense a weakness through the final barriers. The last pitch eased onto flat terrain and we left the vertical world in which we had lived for the past two days.

Near the summit I found another crevasse, and we crawled inside to escape the wind. Jay slept for two hours, but I only dozed, believing I needed to eat and rehydrate more than I needed to sleep. Initially we had planned to rappel a parallel line down-glacier from our route, but by now doubt and concern over dropping into the unknown abyss had filled our minds. We also thought it might be possible to downclimb unknown terrain off the west side and thus reach the Kahiltna. After some deliberation, we decided to go for the longer but less technical way down. In hindsight, I could have said to myself, as I am fond of saying to others, "How does it feel to be wrong?"

During our trip back to base we experienced some of the most heinous, deep, soft isothermal snow either of us had ever seen. We ended up all the way down on the main Kahiltna and had to wallow back uphill for miles to reach our tent. (The descent totaled eight miles.) At times we would sink waist-deep in the soft snow, only held up by our packs. We were out of food, fuel, and water, so there was no real benefit to stopping, and so we just kept struggling. At one point, for the first time in my life, I was not confident that I could just keep going for the barn. It was that bad. Only the bottle of tequila in the tent kept us moving. That and the fact that stopping wasn't going to solve the problem. Sixty-seven hours after we left the tent, we returned—wasted, parched, hungry, almost delirious. I had never felt better.

Jay and I agreed that if we'd just gotten out of the plane on May 7 and attempted Thunder, things probably wouldn't have gone as well, or at all. This climb was not only the highlight of the trip, but also, in many ways, the culmination of 75 years of alpine climbing between us. Sometimes it takes a while to get warmed up. I recently read Malcolm Gladwell's book *Outliers*, and one of the major premises is that no matter who you are, or how much opportunity and natural talent you have, it takes 10,000 hours of doing what you are passionate about to be the best—or at least, as Garrison Keillor says, "above average." All of our collective experience in the mountains had paid off.

Partnerships are talked about so much they have become something of a cliché in climbing stories. But, for me, one of the lasting values of this kind of climbing is sharing a unique experience with another person whom you trust implicitly—and he you—and never letting the other person down. Commitment, Vision, and Trust has always been my mantra in alpine climbing. And the beauty is, when everything lines up and a climb goes perfectly, nothing can ever take that away from you. And therein lies the essence of life: perfection in an imperfect world.

SUMMARY:

Area: Alaska Range

Ascents: Ascent of the Rooster Comb via the Huntington–Rooster Comb col and west ridge (May 9, 2009). First ascent of Prizefight (2,000', 5.9R M6 AI5) on the 10,300' south peak of Mt. Huntington, May 13-14. First ascent of Lagavulin (800', 5.10 WI4+/5, May 17) and the Black Pearl (1,500', WI5+/6 M6, May 18), both on the "Scottish Wall," an east-facing cliff south of Huntington's south peak. First ascent of the north face of Thunder Mountain via Tangled up in Blue (4,000', VI- AI6 M7, May 23–25; 67 hours round-trip, with one bivouac and a brief rest en route). All ascents by Jay Smith and Jack Tackle.

A NOTE ABOUT THE AUTHOR:

Jack Tackle, treasurer of the American Alpine Club, lives in Victor, Idaho, with his wife, Pat. He first climbed in Alaska in 1976.

Jay Smith (left) and Jack Tackle on the summit of Thunder. *Jay Smith*

PROJECT VICTORY

A bold new route on the north face of Pik Pobeda in Kyrgyzstan.

GLEB SOKOLOV

(1) Pik Pobeda (7,439m) from the north. (2) Pobeda West (6,918m), with the Medzmariashvilli Route (1961) on the buttress in the foreground. The Camel Buttress line is marked in the center of the face. After eight days on the 2,000m face, Vitaly Gorelik and Gleb Sokolov headed toward the summit but were driven back over Pobeda West and down the Medzmariashvili Route by a fierce storm. *Roger Payne*

A bove my head there's a loud bang, as though a gigantic door is slamming shut. The snowy whirlwind condenses into foamy syrup. "The most important thing is not to breathe…don't breathe!" I clutch my ice axe and press my head against the ice. A mass of snow rumbles and hisses past, tugging at my legs softly but persistently. Seconds later, more snow. I shake off the powder, and my thoughts gallop: If I had stood a meter lower, it would be over…Vitalya could not have held me…the rock protected me…there is no place for the tent… this is bad, but where is it better?"

It's nearly dark, though there must be at least an hour still before sunset. In the gloom and blowing snow, I can barely see my partner standing under a rock wall 20 meters to my left.

From above, to the left, to the right, comes the roar of large avalanches. As the next flies over me, I press into the ice again. I have to get back to Vitalya. There's no good tent site where he's standing, but at least the crazy snow trains are not running past him. The avalanches seem to be falling every three to four minutes. Immediately after the next slide I leap from behind the protection of the rock, race across the snowy couloir, and arrive at the belay as thunder announces the arrival of the next train.

"Did you look to the right? How are things there?"

"Total shit. A river of avalanches."

"So, we have to dig in right here."

A glacier hangs overhead; who knows what might break off in this horrid weather. We had planned to spend the night much higher and farther to the right, in a relatively safe place, but the conditions and weather have decided otherwise. The blizzard does not let up. We chop at brutally hard ice for three hours by headlamp, trying to carve a tent platform. The slope is very steep, and the work progresses slowly. Finally we hit rock and have to take seats on a narrow shelf, half of our tiny tent hanging in the air. We anchor the tent to the rock and fix a sleeping pad above it to deflect the snow.

The snowfall is not quite as scary now, and at 10:30 p.m. we crawl into the tent. We anchor everything: backpacks, boots, gloves. We drink and eat as much as we can; we are still only at 5,400 meters, and our appetites are strong. Around 1 a.m. we go to sleep, facing each other on a single pad. We each have a down jacket, and half sleeping bags cover our legs. We are not cold yet. The mountain rumbles all night, but gradually calms. By morning the avalanches have stopped shaking our squalid dwelling.

My obsession with this line on Pik Pobeda began four years ago, but really it dates to long-ago 1976. That's when, in a second-hand bookstore, I accidentally bought *The Spring Behind Nine Ranges,* a simple black-and-white picture book that changed the course of my life. "The elderly colonel cried in the tent. Cried, because he summited Pobeda, and because he returned from Pobeda...." Those photos of

Vitaly Gorelik studies the north wall of Pobeda two days before starting the climb. *Gleb Sokolov*

Gorelik leads bulletproof ice during the second day on the Camel Buttress. *Gleb Sokolov*

Pik Pobeda—the name mean "victory"—grabbed hold of me and never let go. As soon as summertime comes, like an old regimental horse reacting to the sound of a trumpet, I am eager to go only one place: the South Inylchek Glacier, below Pobeda.

Since 2006 Vitaly Gorelik and I had focused our thoughts on the north face of "our" mountain. Our goal was a new line between the Dollar Route (Smirnov, 1986) to Pobeda's 7,439-meter main summit and the classic route to 6,918-meter Pobeda West (Medzmariash-villi, 1961). Standing on Dikiy Pass, at the foot of the Medzmariashvilli Route, one can see a vague buttress on the north face that leads directly to the Camel, a minor peak on Pobeda's west ridge. It's called the Camel because huge cornices give the skyline a distinctive humped shape; it's an apt name, but like most camels this one is vicious and treacherous. The southern slopes are prone to avalanches that can be a serious hazard to summiting Pobeda via its west ridge. To the north, where our route lies, the Camel is also prone to avalanche. We hoped to reach it by climbing bands of brown, black, and dirty-yellow rocks below. The overhanging walls of glacial ice to either side of these rocks reminded us of the bushy brows of certain for-mer leaders of our country. Together with the snow that accumulates on the face during foul weather, they presented a serious danger.

Vitaly is 42 years old and lives in wonderful Akademgorodok, next door to me. Togeth-er with various friends, we celebrate holidays, drink, ski, and climb mountains. We climbed together on the west wall of K2 in 2007. Vitaly is an all-rounder, reliable on both rock and ice. He was undoubtedly the leader on Pobeda.

The mountain had easily defeated our first two attempts, in 2006 and 2008. Each time, a crazy snowfall started the night before we were to begin climbing. We woke to a cacophony of uninterrupted avalanches and ran down the glacier, while Pobeda rumbled and sighed, as if to say, "Next time, guys, I am not now in the mood." But as we boarded the helicopter to leave base camp, Pobeda would give us a sunny smile. "See you next summer, boys!"

In 2009, adapting ourselves to the mountain, we postponed our arrival for a week and a half, so we wouldn't begin climbing the face until the end of August. To summit Pobeda you need very good acclimatization, and usually I go to the Himalaya to climb an easy 8,000er, or I climb Khan Tengri two or three times, before attempting Pobeda. I had already climbed Manaslu in 2009, and Vitaly acclimatizes quickly, so we planned only one ascent of Khan Tengri.

By the middle of August we had been to Khan Tengri's summit, at around 7,000 meters, taken a rest, and prepared to meet our "one and only." The weather began to deteriorate, with a little snowfall every afternoon. This rang the alarm—we needed to hurry. The north face does not get much sun, and one huge storm can close the mountain for the season.

⌂

On August 18 we catch a ride up the glacier by helicopter and walk for several hours to advanced base camp on the glacier under Dikiy Pass. The day is bright but not very warm; it already feels like fall on the glacier. We walk over for a look at the approach. The bergschrund appears to be mostly covered with snow—difficult, but possible. There are few fresh traces of avalanches or falling ice, raising our hopes. In the evening we drink a beer, eat a little, talk for a while, and go to sleep. In the night it starts snowing.

Is this again the end? Should we return to base camp for sympathetic words that never give consolation? We are smothered in fury and disappointment. We drink tea and decide to sit in the tent for a day. From time to time the tent flutters in the wind from nearby avalanches. We wait for a miracle. If we turn back, there will not be time for a new attempt.

And the miracle happens! After midday the snowfall stops, the fog disappears, and the wall eventually becomes quiet. Stars gleam in the dark-blue evening sky. It is absolutely silent.

Early on the morning of August 20 we hurry for two kilometers along the base of the wall, exposed to the dangers from above. "Hurry" is an exaggeration. Knee-deep snow slows us, but we move as fast as we can to the bergschrund. Under its protection we catch our breath, take a gulp from the thermos, and quickly begin moving again. For now the wall is silent. The bergschrund is not bridged, as it had seemed from below. It takes an hour and a half to overcome an overhanging five-meter wall, using aid. At midday there is a huge ice avalanche to our left, and two hours later a big powder avalanche from the right crosses our tracks below. The mountain is letting her dogs out.

Above the second bergschrund, we are absolutely unprotected on a snow slope, so we head up toward the shelter of some rocks. We had hoped to climb much farther today, at least to the level of the serac that now hangs overhead. As soon as we arrive at the rocks, snow starts falling again. (It has already been snowing for some time in the vicinity of Pobeda West, nearly two kilometers overhead.) Pobeda has awoken and begun to grumble. It's time to look for shelter.

Above my head something bangs, as though a gigantic door is slamming shut. The snowy whirlwind condenses into foamy syrup....

⌂

We are exhausted from the previous day's adventures and do not want to get up. There is no wind, and the sun is shining, but we are cold in the shade. When we light the stove, the ice covering our tent evaporates. After breakfast we crawl out into the chilly air. That glacier still hangs above our heads. We should get out of here.

We work our way up to the right. The ice is amazingly hard, like steel plate, though it had looked like névé from below. Slowly we climb out of danger from the left glacier, only to find ourselves in danger under the right one. We squeeze ourselves alongside rocks that create an illusion of safety. Dusk catches us on a steep, hard ice slope. Nothing can be done about it, but at least it is relatively safe. We chop the ice endlessly to dig out a platform. At midnight we try to make ourselves comfortable in our cramped house, melting ice for water and cooking supper. The night skies are clear, and this is nice, but it is too cold.

The third day is much like the second. Again we climb steep, nearly impenetrable ice. We work slowly, but gradually climb out from under the most dangerous avalanche terrain and icefalls. We spend the night under a belt of yellow rock, the spot we had hoped to reach on our first day. As always, we work late and only crawl into the tent near midnight. The platform supports just half of the tent. We will only be able to lie down side by side for two nights out of the seven on this route. Our fingertips are splitting from all the work we do with half-frozen hands, and it's desperately hard to manipulate the lighter to ignite our stove. Only after we warm up inside the sleeping bags can we work the lighter and turn on the gas.

Now we finally begin climbing the upper rock wall, if you can call it rock. We can carve handholds in the rotten yellow stone with ice tools; the smell of sulfur fills our nostrils. The belay anchors are scary. Holds break under our hands and feet. And now the weather deteriorates again. The wind blows, and spindrift pours down the wall. We finish the yellow rock band in the dark. Again, there is no place for the tent. At around 6,000 meters, by the light of headlamps, we find a rock big enough for two people to sit. We erect the tent over us but repeatedly fall off the rock ledge during the night.

Thanks to God, the weather is totally calm and sunny on the morning of our fifth day on the face. Even though we are still in the shade, it's nice. We can even take pictures. I have a simple point-and-shoot camera (we call it "soap dish"); a good camera is too heavy and inconvenient on a two-person climb. With a soap dish you can sometimes take good pictures with one hand. We climb semi-rotten rocks all day. It's definitely not easy, but it's a pleasure compared to the previous day. At the end of the day, we find a wonderful tent platform on a névé slope. We drink and eat to make up for the previous days.

The following day the weather is again cold but clear, and all day we climb snow-covered rock. It is steep, but the rock is better, and cams and pitons provide good protection. (We will pass five different rock types during this ascent.) We often belay using ice screws in the frozen runnels between picturesque rocks—they resemble whimsical gargoyles. We chop the crest off a névé ridge at 6,500 meters for a tent platform and enjoy our second consecutive good night.

In the morning, however, the weather is worse. It is our seventh day on the wall—we had hoped to climb it in five—and the ridge top is not far above, but the next rock band is steep and covered with a thin layer of ice. The climbing is extremely difficult. We have to pendulum a couple of times. Now and then Vitaly has to rappel after finishing a lead and jumar back up with his pack. Thank God, the rock is solid. Small powder avalanches never give us the opportunity to relax. That night there is no place for the tent, and we are back to the old routine, piling snow on a rock slab, trying to level out a platform. Inside the tent is wet from our breath,

Day 4: very difficult mixed climbing on the rotten yellow band at ca 6,000m. *Gleb Sokolov*

Gorelik heads into difficult mixed ground high on the face. *Gleb Sokolov*

and we struggle to light the stove. We can't light the matches, and our fingers hurt too much to work the lighter. We nearly give up and just lie shivering in our sleeping bags. But in another hour, after warming the lighters, we manage to light the stove, melt snow, and prepare food. Immediately the world becomes not so awful. Life is good.

Above, we can see the snowy ridge leading to the Camel. But soon we are dealing with the infamous Tien Shan snow—and with hard ice underneath. When you step on such snow, it does not consolidate but instead flows like a river onto the belayer. We have to work with maximal caution so we don't clumsily peel off the whole slope. Slowly, slowly, we crawl upward. Our limbs are like robotic arms under the guidance of a half-dead processor. The trench we carve could be seen by telescope from base camp, many kilometers away, but by late afternoon it is snowing hard and the trench is obliterated.

It seems we must be close to the cornices of the Camel, but we can see nothing. We navigate by feel. The wind blows the warmth out of us. It's okay when we stomp our feet into the snow and climb, but as soon as we stop to belay we feel doomed. At some point during the nightmare of the blizzard, for a fraction of a second the Camel is lit by the evening sun, a grayish-pink giant. It takes another two or three hours to reach the crest. There is no place for the tent, so without discussion we continue along the ridge, circling below the south side of the Camel. Only primitive thoughts occupy our minds: "Careful…hope we don't fall…God, help us…." At 11 p.m., after traversing along vertical walls, we find ourselves back on the ridge top.

During the seventh day, the climbers found better rock, but the weather deteriorated. *Vitaly Gorelik*

We anchor the tent with ice screws, so it won't blow away in the hurricane winds. We squirm into the sleeping bags with our boots on; if the tent is destroyed, we want to be ready.

In the morning, August 28, the hurricane is still blowing. We do not even discuss going to Pobeda's main summit, though it would only be an hour and a half away in good conditions. We just want to escape, to survive. At 8 a.m. there is zero visibility. At 10 a.m., no visibility. At 12 p.m., no visibility. We lie in the tent with our clothes on, so we can make a break for it as soon as it clears. Finally, at 2 p.m., we gain some visibility. We immediately gather our stuff and start moving back along the ridge toward Pobeda West, toward home.

The clouds rush toward us; the ridge seems endless. We often have to stop to wait for small openings in the clouds, so we won't stray off the ridge. Our energy and power have vanished. At last we turn down off Pobeda West and quickly lose altitude. We spend one more night out, at 6,400 meters, among big boulders. Our gas is gone, and our batteries are dead. The wind rips at our tent like a dog tearing a rug.

Late at night on our 10th day we reach camp and friends and warmth and tea and vodka. When we wake the next day, we are astonished to find that neither of us has frostbite. We each have lost 12 to 14 kilograms. The weather deteriorates completely, and we have to wait four days for a helicopter to carry us toward home. Only then do we see the mountain again. It is absolutely white.

SUMMARY:

Area: Tengri Tag, Kyrgyzstan

Ascent: Alpine-style first ascent of the "Camel Buttress" (ca 2,000m, 6B) on the north face of Pik Pobeda, Vitaly Gorelik and Gleb Sokolov, August 20–29, 2009. The two men spent eight days climbing the face and finished on the west ridge at ca 6,950m. They descended via the Medzmariashvili Route over the 6,918m summit of Pobeda West (Vazha Pshavela Peak).

A NOTE ABOUT THE AUTHOR:

Gleb Sokolov, 55 at the time of this ascent, lives in Novosibirsk, Russia, and works as a photographer. He has completed more than 50 ascents of 7,000-meter peaks, including a speed ascent of 7,439m Pik Pobeda (20 hours) and an eight-day solo traverse of the massif. In 2003, he led a new route on the north face of 7,100m Pik Armenia, continuing over the summit of Pobeda.

Translated from the Russian by Ekaterina Vorotnikova.

Vitaly Gorelik (left) and Gleb Sokolov. The climbers each lost 12 to 14 kilograms during the 10-day route. *Gleb Sokolov*

FREE MOUNTAINEERING

An inside look at modern Chinese alpinism.

YAN DONGDONG

China likely holds more unclimbed 5,000m and higher peaks than any other country on Earth. But Chinese alpinists face serious difficulties tackling these objectives without government or commercial sponsorship and supervision. Here, unclimbed 6,000m peaks above Lake Jambo Tso and the Maraipo Glacier, Nyaiqentanglha East, Tibet. *Tamotsu Nakamura*

When the words "Chinese" and "mountaineering" are used together, you probably think of siege-style expeditions on big-mountain routes established 50 or 60 years ago, involving large teams, huge amounts of time, money, and gear, and the "reach-the-summit-by-whatever-means-for-national-glory" ethos.

That was an accurate description until pretty recently, and there are still examples today, such as the 2008 Everest expedition that took the Olympic torch to the summit. However, such climbs do not monopolize the scene as they once did, nor do the commercial expeditions that arose in the past decade and have since grown into a large industry.

Let me define the term "free mountaineering" as used in this article. It covers climbs on which there are neither government officials and subordinates nor guides and clients, but only climbers who go to the mountains because they really want to climb them, and who stand as equals on the team, each taking his or her own share of responsibilities. I had considered using the term "alpine-style mountaineering," but this article is not about climbing style; it's about the climber's spirit. A free mountaineer is someone who doesn't climb for national glory or another lofty goal, nor for profit; it's someone who is ready to match his abilities against the pressures and dangers of mountaineering, and prepared to face the consequences (thereby excluding the commercial client from the definition). I think it is a China-specific term because no other mountaineering community in the world needs such a clarification.

The reason I'm stressing this is because there are many "official climbers" getting paid by the Chinese Mountaineering Association (CMA, a governmental organization) and local mountaineering associations, and still more commercial guides and clients, but relatively few free mountaineers in China—perhaps no more than 100, and only a handful of these attempt first ascents. I believe the differences between free mountaineers and the other types of climbers are much greater than the differences between free mountaineers who choose alpine style and those who go in large teams and fix ropes. I also believe China is only going to have a robust, healthy mountaineering community when there are enough free mountaineers.

ORIGINS OF FREE MOUNTAINEERING

In 1989 the first Chinese student mountaineering club was started at Peking University in Beijing. This was a time when recreational outdoor activities were supposed to take place in well-developed scenic areas with paved trails, and only soldiers, surveyors, and nomadic minorities slept in tents. There were no training programs, no translated textbooks, no gear stores, and the Internet was a distant concept. The student climbers had to learn basic techniques (mostly Russian-oriented) from sympathetic CMA officials, and they borrowed gear wherever possible. In the earlier days, when kernmantle ropes were not available, they tied military bedroll strings together and used waist belays to protect rock climbs in nearby hills.

All of this sounds very crude today, but it marked the beginning of modern free mountaineering in China. In August 1990, Peking University student climbers summited Mt. Yuzhu (6,178m, Kunlun Mountains, Qinghai), which was likely the first time a Chinese team climbed a high-altitude mountain just because the climbers themselves wanted to. They climbed the easy southern slopes, reaching the summit in three separate groups. CMA instructor Xiong Jiping went with the team and escorted the summit groups.

After this, the Peking University students' team continued to climb a mountain each summer vacation, mostly without outside help, and similar student clubs soon emerged at other universities and colleges in Beijing, most notably at Tsinghua University and Beijing Institute of Technology. (I began climbing during my freshman year at Tsinghua in 2002.) Many of the student team members dropped climbing after graduation, but some carried on.

In 1994 a team of 10, consisting partly of ex–student climbers, attempted 6,268m Anemaqen II in Qinghai. Team leader Wang Xiaozheng was severely injured in an avalanche after

Mt. Yuzhu (6,178m) in the Kunlun Mountains was climbed by Peking University students in 1990, "likely the first time a Chinese team climbed a high-altitude mountain just because the climbers themselves wanted to." *Luo Biao*

the summit assault and died after two days of exposure. Of the two others in the rope team, Wang Junbiao headed back toward base camp alone to seek help and was not seen again, while Sun Ping staggered back into camp after eight days on the mountain. This was the first time a free-mountaineering accident in China had resulted in deaths. Sun later wrote an article titled "Eight Days and Nights on Anemaqen," which became the Chinese version of *Touching the Void*.

The normal Chinese bureaucratic response to something like the Anemaqen deaths would have been a ban on free mountaineering, but fortunately, because of the lack of a government agency directly responsible for it, no officials got pressured enough to issue such a ban. However, several newspapers and magazines reported the incident, causing the word "mountaineering," if not the actual concepts behind it, to be more familiar to Chinese people.

So student clubs continued to exist and climb, more often independently than not, and other people began to learn of and get into mountaineering. The tiny community of free mountaineers in China grew at a slow but steady rate.

OFFICIAL COMMERCIAL MOUNTAINEERING

With the growth of the mountaineering community came the first commercial expeditions on high mountains, but at first such expeditions were few in number and poorly organized. (Some say the aforementioned Anemaqen expedition had a commercial element, as the deceased team leader, Wang Xiaozheng, went partly for profit.) In 1999 the CMA organized its first commercial expedition, to Yuzhu. The climb was successful, and the same clients went the next spring on a second commercial expedition, also organized by the CMA, to Changtse, the 7,543-meter peak just north of Everest.

Just after the Changtse expedition, the Qinghai Mountaineering Association (QMA) hosted the first Yuzhu mountaineering festival, a gathering of several commercial expeditions. Due to a sudden snowstorm, two of these expeditions went badly wrong, and five clients were killed over two days. The leaders of the two expeditions bore the blame; the QMA did not. CMA officials and guides from Changtse were called on to help with the body searches, and several of the clients also went to Yuzhu to help. One of these clients, Liu Fuyong ("Big Liu"), wrote a narrative on the search titled *Yuzhu in Tears*.

Several months later, in October 2000, the CMA held its own Yuzhu festival, and 50 clients reached the summit in six groups and came back safely. Large festivals then became one of the chief ways in which provincial mountaineering associations organized commercial events. Tibet held its first mountaineering festival on Jiangsang Lamo (6,325m) in 2001, and Xinjiang on Muztagh Ata (7,546m) in 2002.

Such festivals might seem to have little to do with free mountaineering, but with the growth of "official" commercial mountaineering in China, more people came to understand mountaineering, and more joined the related online discussions (including armchair climbers), making for a bigger and noisier scene. In addition, the success of such commercial expeditions prompted the CMA to offer training courses on modern technique, which had a direct positive influence on the Chinese free-mountaineering community. On the downside, the rise of commercial mountaineering also resulted in more rigid regulations, which were created with commercial expeditions in mind but also applied to free mountaineers, and which have now become one of the greatest obstacles to the development of free mountaineering in China.

TIBET MOUNTAINEERING GUIDE SCHOOL

With the rise of commercial expeditions, the need for qualified, competent mountain guides was pressing. The Tibet Mountaineering Guide School, established in 1999, soon got support from the CMA, the China Tibet Mountaineering Association, and Ozark Equipment (China's leading outdoor brand at that time). The school began a lasting cooperation with the École Nationale de Ski et d'Alpinisme (ENSA), the French guides' and ski instructors' school.

The Tibet Mountaineering Guide School recruited students exclusively from Tibetan families, and with the help of CMA and ENSA it quickly turned these sturdy Tibetan boys into good Himalayan guides. The best students in each class (the school took in a new batch every two to three years), along with a select few climbers from the CMA, got the chance to climb for a few weeks in Chamonix with ENSA professionals each year. When the first batch of students graduated, a company called Himalayan Expedition was set up to provide them with jobs.

For the first time, China had a number of trained, certified modern commercial guides, ready to be dispatched anywhere when they were not on duty with Himalayan Expedition, and their numbers grew every few years. This stimulated the growth of official commercial mountaineering, but also indirectly caused the demise of student clubs as free mountaineering organizations, as we shall see.

CMA TRAINING COURSES

With several successful commercial expeditions and rock and ice climbing courses under its belt, the CMA began to contemplate more advanced training courses for the rapidly growing numbers of mountaineering enthusiasts. In October 2003 the first CMA Guide Course was held, on a mountain in Sichuan, which was then named Guide Peak (5,800m). This course was not as successful as hoped, because none of the students was skillful or experienced enough to begin training as a professional guide. After this, the CMA changed the course's name to the CMA Mountaineering Skills Course and held it every one or two years.

Under the leadership of Ma Xinxiang (director of the CMA's training department) and Sun Bin (once a member of the Peking University students' team, and later sent to Chamonix by the CMA for guide training), these training courses were the first in China to explicitly advocate the "light and fast" style of climbing. Students were eager to try out this new attitude on real rock, ice, and mountain routes.

In 2007 the CMA and Ozark launched the first Chinese Mountaineering Development Institute [CMDI] program, a guide-training course that was open only to candidates from provincial mountaineering associations. The program was taught by ENSA instructor Olivier Balma and Chinese instructor Kang Hua. Since the first batch of eight trainees graduated in 2009, additional sessions have begun.

A Chinese Mountaineering Development Institute guide-training class at Moon Hill in Yangshuo, Guangxi Province. *Luo Biao*

REGULATIONS AGAINST FREE MOUNTAINEERING

In 2002 the summit group of the Peking University students' team was hit by an avalanche on Shishapangma West (7,292m, Tibet). All five climbers were killed. Before this, there had been a set of Regulations on Domestic Mountaineering, issued by the Chinese National Sports Bureau in 1997, but the rules were neither comprehensive nor strictly followed. After the Shishapangma incident, the National Sports Bureau urged the CMA to make a new set of rules, and to carry them out more ardently.

The immediate result was that student teams were required to hire at least three certified professional guides for their expeditions, and the guides would be in complete control of the climbing. Until the guides' schools were created, such a requirement would have been difficult or impossible to meet, but by 2003 the first batch of Tibet Mountaineering Guide School students had graduated. This regulation was the beginning of the end of Chinese student clubs as free-mountaineering organizations.

In addition, provincial mountaineering associations were urged to follow the previously neglected 1997 regulations to the letter. These required all mountaineering expeditions to be "organized by an entity with corporate capacity," in other words, by a registered company or agency. Free mountaineers could not register unless they could find a corporation willing to back them up.

In 2004 a new version of Regulations on Domestic Mountaineering was issued, which further required all expedition members to "have graduated from at least one climbing skill-training course held by the CMA or one of the provincial mountaineering associations," and all expeditions to "hire at least one certified professional guide for every four members." Free mountaineers could not register a team for an expedition unless they could (1) find a corporation willing to back them, (2) find the time and money for a training course, and (3) pay the wages of one or more guides. This was true even if the climbers were totally competent and willing to assume full responsibility for their own safety.

Moreover, there might have been enough Tibet Mountaineering Guide School graduates to meet the guiding requirements for student clubs' summer-vacation climbs, but their numbers were definitely inadequate for free-mountaineering expeditions throughout China. And after its unsuccessful guides' course in 2003, the CMA never certified any guides other than the few CMDI graduates.

In the province of Sichuan, especially after 2005, these regulations have not been carried out as rigorously as elsewhere, so some free-mountaineering teams have managed to register to climb. In the province of Yunnan, where there are mountains but not a fully functional mountaineering association, the regulations don't mean much. But in Xinjiang and Qinghai, and particularly Tibet, the registration of a free-mountaineering expedition is either impossible or prohibitively expensive, costing up to tens of thousands of RMB (1,000 RMB equaled $146 in May 2010.)

The first ascent of the west face of Xuebaoding (5,588m, Sichuan) in 2004 was a milestone in Chinese alpine-style climbing—and poaching. *Zhou Peng*

UNOFFICIAL COMMERCIAL MOUNTAINEERING

In the spring of 2003 the Arête Alpine Instruction Center (AAIC) was founded in Sichuan by Chinese climber Ma Yihua and American Jon Otto, who had studied at Peking University and had been involved with the students' team there. It was one of the earliest companies of its kind in China, and certainly the most famous. Ma, Otto, and their people not only led commercial expeditions, but also explored new mountain areas and routes whenever possible. *[Editor's note: Jon Otto's reports have frequently appeared in the* AAJ, *including this edition.]*

Ma left China after his colleague Liu Xinan, one of the most accomplished Chinese alpine climbers, got killed in a rappelling accident in 2007, and Liu's family demanded large compensation, which Ma couldn't pay. The AAIC stopped operating last November.

Although the AAIC was a commercial company, it strongly promoted the spirit of free mountaineering. The same could be said of a couple of other unofficial mountaineering companies, including the Shu Shan (literally "Sichuan Mountains") and the Ultimate Mountaineer, which went out of business after its founder and director, Li Hongxue, was killed on Celestial Peak last June. However, most such companies (especially those outside of Sichuan) are not really interested in anything other than profit, and whether more companies like the AAIC will emerge remains to be seen.

Another form of unofficial commercial mountaineering has been on the rise in some mountainous areas, particularly the Qionglai Range in Sichuan. Because the CMA and local mountaineering associations have long provided their own high-altitude porters, liaison officers, and other technical services for foreign expeditions, local yak and camel herders living in mountain areas never learned modern mountaineering techniques from foreigners, as Nepalese Sherpas did. But now some local people have become part-time guides, escorting tourists up easier mountain routes. Some of these local guides have learned to be good technical climbers, while others barely know how to handle ropes. The Sichuan Mountaineering Association (SMA) has been providing training courses and certification for such guides, but the licenses are valid only within the province. Some local guides are talking about banding together to form their own companies, so their expeditions can be insured against accidents. This is a very good start, but they still have a long way to go.

An ascent of Bogda Feng (5,445m, Xinjiang) in 2000 by Cao Jun, Chen Junchi, Xu Xiaoming, and Yang Chunfeng may have been the first alpine-style climb of a technical route by Chinese climbers. *Luo Biao*

MOUNTAIN POACHING

For Chinese free mountaineers, the only way to climb most mountains without joining a guided or officially sanctioned expedition is to do it illegally— in other words, to "poach" their summits. Many of the notable Chinese free-mountaineering events after 2002, including the alpine-style first ascent of Xuebaoding's west face (5,588m, Sichuan, 2004), the solo first ascent of Jianshanzi (5,472m, Sichuan, 2005), and the recent first ascent of Zalaqueni (the 5,476m main peak of White Horse Mountain, Yunnan), were done illegally.

Some provincial mountaineering associations, especially Sichuan Province's, tend to turn a blind eye; others, most notably Tibet's, have done what they could to stop these poachers and to fine them when possible.

One of the major problems with an illegal expedition is that, if you get killed or injured, an insurance company is not going to pay up. In the winter of 2005-'06 a team of three and another team of two were lost on Lamo-She (6,070m) in Sichuan. Neither had registered. I'm not sure who paid the bill for the body search, but certainly no insurance company was involved.

Mountain poaching is still widely practiced among both free mountaineers and unofficial commercial guides. Unless the regulations are changed, or the practice of free mountaineering (and unofficial commercial mountaineering, for that matter) comes to an end, I don't see how this problem can be solved.

ALPINE STYLE

As far as alpine-style climbing goes, the 2000 ascent of Bogda Feng (5,445m, Xinjiang), by Cao Jun, Chen Junchi, Xu Xiaoming, and Yang Chunfeng, was among the earliest alpine-style successes on a technical route by Chinese climbers, if not the first. Among other early alpine-style endeavors by Chinese free mountaineers were attempts on the west face of Xueba-

Steep ground on The Free Spirits, a new route on the south face of Siguniang (6,250m) climbed by Yan Dongdong and Zhou Peng in November 2009. Zhou is employed by the Chinese Mountaineering Association, but the pair registered for the ascent as individual climbers and completed the difficult ascent alpine-style after two previous attempts. *Yan Dongdong*

oding in 2000 and a 2001 expedition to Yulong (5,596m, Lijiang, Yunnan). Before that, there had been some small-party, single-push ascents of 5,000ers and 6,000ers, but not on truly technical routes.

In the years since, alpine-style climbs have become more common, though many of these are difficult to trace because the climbers poached their summits and wouldn't want to talk openly about them. By 2004, when Xuebaoding's west face route was finally accomplished, the term "alpine-style" was commonly known, though perhaps not commonly understood. (There are always more armchair climbers on the Internet than there are real mountaineers.) Most of these climbs have been in Sichuan, Yunnan, and the parts of Qinghai more neglected by the QMA.

China has perhaps the greatest number of unclimbed peaks above 5,000 meters in the world, and huge potential for new routes. Naturally many alpine-style attempts have been aimed at new summits or new routes, but the success rate of such attempts has not been high. Of all the new routes established by Chinese parties in the past five years, fewer than 30 have been alpine-style ascents (as far as I know—no one currently keeps a record of these things).

THE FUTURE

At the National Mountaineering/Rescue Conference in January 2010, CMA officials stated frankly that if the Regulations on Domestic Mountaineering were to be changed, it would only be toward the stricter side. In Tibet, with the CTMA/Himalayan Expedition monopoly on commercial expeditions, free mountaineering is regarded as both troublesome and unprofitable, and they have been rather successful at suppressing it, especially since Tibet is so far from the rest of China that few free mountaineers go there anyway. In Xinjiang and Qinghai, the provincial mountaineering associations also frown upon free mountaineering, but poaching is easier and more frequently done. In Yunnan, the main obstacle is not the mountaineering association; it's local governments and tourism offices that neither understand nor desire mountaineers coming on their own instead of paying thousands to join commercial festivals.

The most hopeful case is Sichuan, where any Chinese team can register for less than 200 RMB [ca $29 in May 2010] to climb any mountain below 7,000 meters, whether it's unclimbed or not, as long as the climbers can provide a photocopy of a company's business license and a photocopy of an SMA-certified guide's license. (The company does not actually have to organize the expedition, and the guide himself need not come on the team; this is understood though never stated.) This is why most Chinese free-mountaineering expeditions in the past few years—and certainly every free-mountaineering expedition that's been properly registered—have taken place in Sichuan.

Perhaps in the next 10 or 20 years, the number of free mountaineers in China will become so great that the CMA and other officials will be forced to recognize our presence and hear our voices. But in China, things are usually done the hard way. Perhaps Tibet will not be officially open to free mountaineers until climbers have poached every unclimbed summit, leaving the mountaineering associations no first ascents for which to charge big fees to foreign expeditions. Meanwhile, free mountaineers will have to be content to climb legally in Sichuan and to poach summits elsewhere—and be very careful not to be caught.

A NOTE ABOUT THE AUTHOR:

Born in 1984, Yan Dongdong lives in Beijing and works as a freelance translator. He summited Mt. Everest in May 2008 as part of the Olympic torch expedition, and since then has focused on free mountaineering, including a new route on Siguniang (6,250m) in 2009 and the first ascent of Wuse Shan (5,430m) in early 2010, both in Sichuan Province. Both of these ascents are reported in the Climbs and Expeditions section of this Journal.

Yan Dongdong (left) and Zhou Peng at a bivouac during an attempt on Siguniang in February 2009. *Zhou Peng*

THE GOLDEN PEAK

A new route on Pakistan's Spantik raises the bar for Korean alpinism.

KIM HYUNG-IL

The Korean Route on the northwest face of Spantik (7,027m). The Korean climbers spent two nights at their second bivouac and two nights at their high camp, for a total of seven days on the mountain. (A) The Golden Pillar, first climbed in 1987 by Mick Fowler and Victor Saunders. (B) The "Descent Route" followed by Fowler and Saunders, as well as various teams since. This line was first ascended in 2004 by a Japanese expedition. *Kim Hyung-il Collection*

I can't remember when I first saw a picture of Spantik, the Golden Peak, in Pakistan, but it's easy to recall the strong impression I felt. I couldn't imagine how one would climb that lofty pillar on the northwest face, and I was humbled by the achievement of Mick Fowler and Victor Saunders, who did it first in 1987. Over the years I've experienced much joy and discouragement on my climbing journey, and always I dreamed of that golden summit in the photo. Finally, in 2008, I visited beautiful Spantik and spotted the line for a new route. As for tactics, there was no doubt: alpine style.

Korean climbers have a strong history of ascents on Himalayan big walls. The Korean Baintha Brakk expedition of 1983 was probably the first of these, and it led to other important high-altitude ascents, such as the Shining Wall (northwest face) of Gasherbrum IV, Thalay Sagar's north face, Trango Tower, the southwest face of Everest, the north face of Annapurna, and Shishapangma's south face. These days, perhaps one third of the expeditions that depart from Korea attempt to climb high-altitude walls.

However, I would guess that 90 percent of the significant Himalayan climbing done by Koreans is with the help of high-altitude porters and fixed lines. Most is not lightweight alpine-style climbing. I believe we Korean climbers should re-examine ourselves and how expedition style has come to prevail among us. For one thing, the large majority of big-name expedition leaders in Korea employ these methods. Because of their influence, other expedition leaders have followed suit. Also, because these tactics have proven successful and are judged to be safe, this has remained the popular way to climb high-altitude walls. Moreover, the Korean mentality, from early in our climbing history, has fixated on the summit as the sole objective of mountaineering. These are the root causes of our ongoing focus on heavy, siege-style tactics.

But there always has been a small number of climbers who believe differently. For about 10 years, this small community of climbers has done a fair share of alpine-style climbing, putting up new routes in this style in the Himalaya and Karakoram. A few of us eventually decided to try a new route on Spantik in pure alpine style, despite the uncertainty of such an attempt. We wanted to do our best to leave a strong impression on young Korean climbers, showing that we could climb without harming the environment or leaving any trace of our passage.

In 2009 I returned to Pakistan with two other climbers, Kim Pal-bong and Min Jun-young, plus a cameraman, Rim Il-jin, and a friend, Seo Jung-hwan, for support. Due to the threat of terrorism in the Swat area, we gave up on taking a bus along the Karakoram Highway and flew to Skardu instead.

After arriving at base camp in early June, we acclimatized on several unnamed 6,000-meter peaks and planned our tactics for Spantik. We decided to simul-solo the lower parts of the mountain, and then in the middle we would lead in blocks. On the highest, most difficult section, the Black Tower, the lead climber would fix the ropes once he had finished a pitch, and the two others could climb the fixed line, jugging where necessary for speed.

We planned to spend six days on the route—five on the wall and one on the upper snowfields to reach the summit. Beginning on June 15 it snowed for several days, and we had to wait. We read and worried, trapped in our tents. After a long, anxious wait, we finally started climbing on June 28.

Toward the end of our third day, we reached the bottom of the Black Tower. There we were caught in a fierce snowstorm. We couldn't decide whether to continue or head down. We returned to the previous bivy site, and the next day, July 1, descended to base camp.

After a week of rest, we started up again on July 8. For the first 1,000 meters above the glacier, we soloed steep snow, up to 60°. By 11 the next morning, we had reached our previous high point near the base of the Black Tower. For another 200 meters, we continued to solo and then began belaying on difficult mixed ground. We climbed five pitches on snow-covered rock, with sections of very thin ice. Good anchors were difficult to find. At 7 p.m. we found a ridge of snow where we were able to chop a ledge and set up the tent.

That night it snowed hard, and we didn't get much sleep. On July 10 the snowfall eased but then got heavier again, off and on all day. We spent an uneasy day in the tent, wondering if we would go up or down. The snow stopped early in the morning of July 11, and we began climbing loose, vertical rock covered with snow. Ice runnels only 10 centimeters wide led through some of the rock, and on these we might as well have been soloing because we could not get any good gear. This day brought the steepest climbing of the route, and also the coldest. The sun didn't reach the face until after 11 a.m., and I struggled with the pain of frostbite injuries I'd suffered a decade earlier. After three pitches, Kim Pal-bong took over and faced a new problem. As the sun hit the face, his anchors quickly melted out of the ice, leaving us vulnerable to the slightest slip. We had no choice but to stay calm and take extreme care with each move.

We chopped a bivy ledge out of another snow ridge and got into the tent around 9 p.m. The next morning two pitches up rocky gullies brought us to the final snow wall. The serac on top of the mountain was so close that it looked like we could grab it with our hands. But the snow was up to chest-deep, and soon snow began to fall again. The storm seemed never-ending, and the longer we waited for it to stop the more desperate we felt. At last, by the grace of God, the snow stopped, and after 30 minutes of climbing we reached the gentle slopes above the northwest face. As we set up our final bivy, I contacted base camp and shouted, "We've made it!" In a flush of emotions, we all burst into tears.

On July 13, at 4 a.m., after sipping a cup of tea, we started toward the summit; however, we soon had to return to the tent because it was too dark to deal with an ice wall and several hidden crevasses. We waited two hours for the sun to rise before heading out again. We climbed up and up, and our nerves tightened in the faint light of dawn, but finally, at around 10:45, we were on top. After a moment of joy, we all felt exhausted. Our energy had been burned down by whiteout and snowstorm.

We decided to spend one more night on the ridge before descending. Kim Pal-bong and I were showing symptoms of snow blindness, and with the pain in our eyes we weren't able to sleep at all that night. Moreover, an overnight storm brought wind and snow. But at 2 p.m. the next day, the wind suddenly stopped, and we immediately packed up and began the descent. Hours later, after many rappels in the dark, we downclimbed the steep snow at the base of the wall and arrived on the glacier around midnight. Our friends Jin Rim-il and Seo Jung-hwan stood in the darkness to welcome us. How can we forget the bright light of their headlamps and the cold water we sipped!

SUMMARY:

Area: Rakaposhi Range, Karakoram, Pakistan

Ascent: Alpine-style new route on the northwest face of Spantik (7,027m), by Kim Hyung-il, Kim Pal-bong, and Min Jun-young, July 8–14, 2009. The Koreans called the 2,300m route Dream 2009 and graded it VI WI4 M8. They descended by the snow and ice buttress to the right (west) of their ascent route.

A NOTE ABOUT THE AUTHOR:

Born in 1967, Kim Hyung-il has led or joined expeditions to Nepal, India, and Pakistan, including teams that climbed a new route on Trango Tower (2005) and attempted the south face of Lhotse in winter (2006).

Translated from the Korean by Peter Jensen-Choi.

Min Jun-young, Kim Pal-bong, and Kim Hyung-il (left to right) on Spantik's summit. *Kim Hyung-il Collection*

CLIMBS AND EXPEDITIONS

2010

Accounts from the various climbs and expeditions of the world are listed geographically. We generally bias from north to south and from west to east within the noted countries, but the priority is on a logical flow from one mountain range to the next. We begin our coverage with the Contiguous United States and move to Alaska in order for the climbs in Alaska's Wrangell Mountains to segue into the St. Elias climbs in Canada.

We encourage all climbers to submit accounts of notable activity, especially long new routes (generally defined as U.S. commitment Grade IV—full-day climbs—or longer). Please submit reports as early as possible (see Submissions Guidelines at aaj.AmericanAlpineClub.org).

For conversions of meters to feet, multiply by 3.28; for feet to meters, multiply by 0.30.

Unless otherwise noted, all reports are from the 2009 calendar year.
Longer versions, extra photos, and additional information for many of these
reports can be found at aaj.AmericanAlpineClub.org

NORTH AMERICA
CONTIGUOUS UNITED STATES

Washington

Summary of activity. [This summary supplements individual reports, mostly of bigger routes, below—Ed.] What may have been the first new Cascade alpine route of the 2009 summer season came on June 26, with Wayne Wallace and Steph Abegg climbing Twin Needles in the Southern Pickets (Thread of Ice, III AI3). On July 22 Kurt Hicks and Forest McBrian did a new route on Formidable, climbing the direct/complete Northeast Buttress (III+ 5.9) in a 15-hour roundtrip.

The Northeast Buttress, on Mt. Formidable. *Kurt Hicks*

Mario Moreno, Sandy Weil, Keith Luther, and Seth Pollack climbed a new route on Middle Challenger, the South Ridge (1,100', 5.7), on August 5. The next day, Luther and Pollack established Birthday Route (east ridge, six pitches, 5.9) on West Challenger.

A great deal of Washington crag climbing goes unreported, and the *AAJ* does not contain a complete record, even of significant climbs, but one of the longer crag routes of the year was established on Squire Creek Wall, near Darrington, by Chris Greyell (the Holy Grail, III 5.10c).

December 2009 was unusually good for ice climbing, and climbers flocked to waterfalls around the state. Many had not been previously explored, and many hadn't seen ascents in years. On February 21, 2010, Wayne Wallace and Rolf Larson climbed a new route on the northeast face of Pyramid Peak, with eight pitches to the summit (III WI5, plus a point of A0). On March 7, 2010, Daniel Jeffrey and Tom Sjolseth made the first ascent of the long-sought Assassin Spire, a satellite of Lincoln Peak in the Black Buttes area, via the Shooting Gallery (2,000', IV WI4+), on the northwest face.

MATT PERKINS, *Northwest Mountaineering Journal, AAC*

Dome Peak, Gran Torino and East Ridge. On July 12 Wayne Wallace and I cruised the waters of Lake Chelan on the buxom yet buoyant Lady of the Lake, on our way to check out the unclimbed southeast face of Dome Peak's southwest summit. I saw the 1,800' granite face on a reconnaissance flight with John Scurlock back in 2005 and filed it in my pain-in-the-ass list of obscure climbs that would probably suck and take forever to get to—although the face was probably one of the, if not the, largest unclimbed faces in the Cascades. Dome Peak already had a reputation for taking days to reach, but this side of the mountain was even more remote. The big problem with logistics was that I had flown in from Salt Lake to climb with Wayne somewhere different. But when bad weather dashed our original plans, I preyed on Wayne's vulnerability and convinced him with lies and promises. For Wayne to agree, we had to fit eight days worth of crap into 40-liter backpacks, while keeping our pack weights under 30 lbs. So after three days of bushwhacking, crossing glaciers, sketchy low-5th scrambling, and drinking 120-

Gran Torino, on the southeast face of Dome Peak. *Layton-Wallace photo*

Dome Peak from the southeast, showing Gran Torino.
John Roper

proof alcohol that had reacted with its plastic container, we arrived at a high camp below the base of the face.

We began our approach from the remote, boat-accessed town of Stehekin, hiking up the Agnes Creek Trail and bushwhacking to the Spruce-Icy Col. From the col we made a multi-glacier traverse over subpeaks and ridges, careful routefinding eventually bringing us to the base of the route. The next morning we climbed the glacier and crossed the moat onto the lower slabs, where we did a few clean, moderate pitches, before the headwall reared up. We encountered well-protected pitch after pitch of clean, polished granite splitters and chickenheads. The climbing on Gran Torino, as we named the route, was so good and so straightforward that we managed to do the route in four-and-a-half hours. The 15 pitches were mostly 5.7–5.9, with a few sporty moves of 5.10. We downclimbed the unclimbed East Ridge (5.6) and traversed back to camp, which took about as long as the ascent. The approach to the climb takes you by the fabled Gunsight Range, so on the way out Wayne and I repeated the Gunrunner Traverse (IV 5.9+) to complete an excellent Cascade adventure.

MICHAEL LAYTON

Sloan Peak, Fire on the Mountain. Rad Roberts and I established a new route on the southwest face of Sloan Peak that, compared to new routes established in the 'Rado or California, would be a grade IV. But going by the AAC's use of the IV definition being a "full day of technical climbing," we think it's more fairly a grade III+. The whole grade thing is messed up and pretty vague, though, so here's what we did:

We did 1,200' of steep climbing, and then 500' of class 3-type stuff to the summit. Pitches were probably: 5.11- (1), 5.10 something (6), and a couple around 5.8. We started climbing at maybe 9 a.m., and it took around 11 hours to the summit.

BLAKE HERRINGTON, *AAC*

Squire Creek Wall, Slab Daddy. In September 2008 Dan Dingle, Bill Enger, and I completed Slab Daddy (V 5.10+ A0) on Squire Creek Wall near Darrington. The 22-pitch route, which took four years to complete, goes free except for a 10' section on pitch 20. There is a good bit of the bolt-protected slap-and-pray climbing that Darrington is known for, but there are also enough flakes, cracks, and features to require a light rack, with at least one piece of five or six inches. The bottom half of the route consists of slabs punctuated by large ledges. Several earlier pitches are 5.10, but most are 5.8 or 5.9. The increasingly steep upper half of the route features more-difficult climbing and reaches 5.10+ in several places.

Squire Creek Wall is 80 miles northeast of Seattle, on the western slope of the Cascades. Just minutes from the rustic logging town of Darrington are several valleys blessed with large granite formations. The 2,000' Squire Creek Wall first made it into print in 1976, with Fred

Beckey's original Darrington & Index guide, but rumors of blank rock and nasty approaches kept most away. Surprisingly, the near end of Squire Creek Wall has a fairly civilized approach. The massif is reached after a 1½-mile walk along a decommissioned logging road. From the road a quick descent to the creek leads to a crossing immediately beneath the route itself. Slab Daddy takes the obvious full-height stroke of rock on the northern end of the wall and tops out on the fin-like ridge at nearly 4,400'.

Several excellent bivouac ledges exist, the most usable being the Reservoir Bivy at the top of the 6th pitch and the Balcony Bivy at the top of the 11th, where we spent many nights. The Reservoir Bivy features a large pocket that holds water through much of the season.

Slab Daddy, on Squire Creek Wall. *David Whitelaw*

The 2009 season marked a 40-year history of rock-climbing on the Darrington crags. Until recently almost all of that history had taken place in the adjacent Clear Creek drainage, and indeed features like Exfoliation Dome, Three O'Clock Rock, and the Green Giant Buttress, though far from climbed out, could be said to be approaching mature status. Now the feature once thought least accessible turns out to be among the more easily reached. After 40 years, this and Chris Greyell's new routes on the Illusion Wall and Salish Peak point to an exciting future for climbing in the backcountry of Darrington's domelands.

DAVID WHITELAW

Mt. Stuart, Gorillas in the Mist. Mt. Stuart is a Cascades icon, featuring 3,000' climbs on excellent stone or dependable ice. I'd assumed its major faces and ridges had been completed, until I saw photos of an unclimbed 1,000' buttress towering over the glacier, between Stuart Pass and Goat Pass. While winter trip planning, Sol Wertkin and I dubbed this the "West Face Wall."

Gorillas in the Mist. *Steve Smith*

We dreamed of sunny rock and exchanged e-mails from two parties who'd attempted the climb. Phrases like "giant roof," "full pitch of thin nailing," and "all day…at least" brought cautious inspiration. Jens Holsten, who had attempted the wall in 2006, joined us at the last minute. We set off as a trio at 5 a.m. on July 8.

Above treeline we entered a swirling fog that made locating the climb an adventure in itself. Jens had predicted sunny skies, and Sol's wedding anniversary was the next day, so our gear consisted of wind shirts, climbing equipment, and two daypacks. We started up a splitter crack, just right of looming orange overhangs. Two pitches of corners and arêtes led to a bolted anchor stamped "1993." We'd later hear from the 1993 climbers, who climbed three-fourths of the wall in big-wall style.

Jens unlocked the key route-finding puzzle on pitch 3, leading the rightward "Monkey Traverse" while pausing, mid-crux, to trundle. We followed flakes and corners for six more foggy pitches until joining the West Ridge route amid decreasing temperature and visibility. While negotiating icy towers, Sol and I got separated from Jens, who'd soloed while we'd simuled. Hours of nervous shouting through howling winds resulted in three sore throats but eventual reunion. Under darkening gloom we settled for a bivy and hardcore cuddling. The coldest night of our lives (but best spooning) ended at 4 a.m. We reached a sunrise summit under clearing conditions, fingers still too numb to manipulate iced-up cams. Gorillas in the Mist (IV+ 5.11).

The Sherpa Glacier downclimb and hike out went quickly, as we knew friends would be worried. Bouncing down the dirt road, we encountered an all-star rescue squad, hastily assembled by Sol's nervous wife. She was happy to have her husband back and treated Jens and me to the best homemade sandwiches of our lives. Their marital bliss preserved, we avoided the potential for jealousy and never mentioned the spooning.

BLAKE HERRINGTON, *AAC*

Colchuck Balanced Rock, The Scoop. After an early June ascent to check out and clean the more difficult pitches, Matt Clifton, Evan Cabodi, and I returned to Colchuck Balanced Rock (CBR) on August 9 and completed a free ascent of our new line. The Scoop (III+ 5.11c), named for the crux pitch, which looks like it was carved by a giant ice cream scoop, follows a line of beautiful cracks, linked with excellent belay ledges, to the right of the West Face and the Tempest.

The first three pitches provided climbing up to 5.10a, to reach "Launch Ledge" and the base of the Scoop pitch. On our exploratory ascent we found it clogged with black lichen; the overhanging upper half of the 60m pitch looked to be a difficult seam requiring much cleaning before a free ascent might be possible. Loaded with aid paraphernalia, I set out on the Scoop's namesake pitch. With each step I found easy cam placements in the crack, and I knew with a little work this would be a stellar, sustained free pitch. Over the next two days we climbed the last two difficult pitches through a series of fun roofs and cleaned the lichen-filled cracks.

The West Face, Tempest, and Scoop routes (L to R) on Colchuck Balanced Rock. *Matthew Clifton*

Returning in August, we had only slightly better weather, but the approach was easier without aid gear. Our goals were to complete the route to the top of the peak and free the previously aided pitches. We nearly accomplished our goals by the second day, with Evan almost sending the Scoop pitch, and Matt and I freeing the upper roof pitches at 5.10b and 5.10a, respectively. We finished with a simul-climb of the last four pitches to the summit of CBR. Freeing the Scoop took several attempts over the next couple of days, but on our last day Evan successfully led the pitch clean, and I followed it, completing one of the best 5.11 hand-and-finger cracks any of us has done in the Pacific Northwest. We left no bolts or fixed gear for the climbing, only leaving natural anchors for the descent. The route can be rappelled with two 60m ropes, to avoid the loose descent.

STEWART MATTHIESEN, *AAC*

California

YOSEMITE VALLEY

Middle Cathedral Rock, Border Country. On a rainy day in early spring 2005, I walked below Lower Cathedral Rock and Middle Cathedral Rock. As I came to the base of the Gunsight, the gully that splits Lower and Middle, I gazed at the sweeping north-northwest face of Middle. A hasty check of the guidebook revealed that this part of the wall was almost untouched. I was instantly enticed, though other projects kept me from returning to it for four years.

Finally I enlisted Jeremy Collins, of Kansas City, and Dana "Mad Dog" Drummond, of New Hampshire. In early May we started up, moving slowly due to wet rock and the difficult ground-up climbing. After a week we reached the North Face Traverse, a ledge system cutting across the wall at midheight. Using both bolts and traditional gear, we had to here established a fine line that was going free at 5.10+. Jeremy had obligations back home, leaving Dana and me to finish the upper half.

While the lower half had low-angle incipient cracks and small flakes connecting larger features; the upper half was going to be different. The angle steepened to near-vertical, and the

Border Country, on Middle Cathedral Rock. *Jeremy Collins*

features diminished. We would be connecting golden knobs and flat edges, devoid of cracks for natural protection, forcing us to use the drill more. Four steep, beautiful, hard pitches led us to the northwest shoulder, where our route ended, but one could continue on class 3 terrain to the summit. Mid-June had come, and my season in the Valley was over. We left with the route completed but without a free ascent.

In mid-September, under cooler temps, I returned. Before we could go for the redpoint, though, we wanted to get the route into perfect shape. On our initial foray we had placed ¼" bolts and needed to replace them with ¹/₄". After doing that tedious work, Dana and I cruised the initial first half, enjoying climbing without hammer and drill. Above, the crux 5.12- and 5.12 pitches slowed us, but we redpointed both first try. With aching feet we continued up the sting-in-the-tail 5.11+ pitches above. Dana got the final hard lead and dispatched it as usual, with me just eking-out the pitch on toprope. Thankfully, the final, run-out 60m was only 5.9, as the sun had dipped well below the horizon. Quickly we started headlamp-less rappels down the face.

Within the next two months the route had seen over five attempts but no one has yet grabbed the second free ascent.

MIKEY SCHAEFER, *AAC*

SIERRA NEVADA

Watchtower, new routes. While planning a trip to remote Tower Peak (11,755'), on the northern border of Yosemite National Park, my interest shifted to an unnamed subpeak ¾-mile north, locally called the Watchtower or Watchtower Peak (10,820'). My research found no record of climbing, beyond the 2nd-class route from the saddle between Watchtower and Tower Peak.

In August Alyse Bertenthal, Jay Kumar, Bob Steed, Paul Tieslau, and I hiked 15 miles from Leavitt Meadows on the Sonora Pass highway, up the West Walker River to the base of the north face, which rises 1,500' above an avalanche meadow. Over 10 days our group established four

Watchtower: (1) Northeast Face. (2) North Face. (3) Where There Is a Will There Is a Way. (4) Where There Is a Wall There Is a Way. (5) Over the Hill. *Dan Merrick*

routes. While we were there, a second party, whose research had also unearthed no climbing history, arrived and established one route. All five routes lead to the north summit.

We found no evidence of previous climbers on the routes or the summit. This is not the highest of the peak's three summits, but it is the hardest to reach and to descend from. (We left rappel anchors.) At an obvious ledge on the Beacon we found a 30+-year-old pilot's distress beacon that we think was accidentally dropped, since it was still in its pouch. We also found an old military-type piton near the summit, but it was not where it would be useful as a belay or rappel point. We assume the summit was reached by helicopter, perhaps in connection with the nearby Marine Corps Mountain Warfare Training Center. The beacon could have been dropped from the summit and ended up where we found it. We have contacted the Navy and other agencies to see if they know anything.

Routes:

(1) Northeast Face (the Beacon; Merrick-Steed, 9+ pitches, III 5.7). Approach the left side of the north face and begin at a ladder of small horizontal dikes. Ascend directly up and enter the gully to the left of the large arête.

(2) North Face (Bertenthal-Kumar-Steed, 10 pitches, III 5.7+), begin 300' right of the Beacon. The first pitch ascends the right of an obvious pair of parallel, vertical cracks. Continue up and right of a large arête.

(3) Where There Is a Will There Is a Way (David Blattel-Bill Leventhol-Will Oxx, 8 pitches, III 5.8), starts at a black water streak 200' right of the North Face.

(4) Where There Is a Wall There Is a Way (Steed-Tieslau, 5 pitches, II 5.8), starts at a double crack system 150' right of Will…, after five pitches joining Will. Continuing to summit via Will is nine pitches (III).

(5) Over the Hill (Steed-Tieslau, 9 pitches, III 5.8), begins right of Wall…, at the right side of the north face.

Descent: Rappel from bolts in a large block facing the south summit, pass around the south summit on the left via 3rd/4th-class ledges, and go west to the saddle above Tower Lake. Hike down past Tower Lake to the trail.

DAN MERRICK

Mt. Walt, Northwest Ridge. While cragging on the west side of Little Slide Canyon, one naturally admires the Incredible Hulk, across the drainage. Less obvious is Mt. Walt, lurking above and behind the Hulk. A low-angle but sharp ridge descends from the summit area before fading into the face below. This face, which is immediately left of the Hulk, has an obvious left-facing corner system that leads to the sharp ridge. Micha Miller and I had climbed the corner for five pitches a few years earlier but got chased off by a thunderstorm. We returned in August 2008 and worked our way up, finding fun, exposed climbing on the narrow ridge and challenging cracks and corners above. We unroped after 10 pitches (5.10a) and scrambled to the exposed summit pinnacle. An easy descent to the northeast leads into the Blacksmith Creek drainage and eventually the car. Fun day.

DAVID HARDEN, *AAC*

Mt. Ritter, West Arête. The west escarpment of Mt. Ritter (13,157') stretches over the headwaters of the San Joaquin River. This impressive wall is steep and the rock suspect, but an arête leading from Ritter Lakes basin to the summit too hard to resist, especially since there weren't any climbing routes on this side of the peak. I mobilized the smarter-with-age squad of Mort Testerman and Jim Keating. As we planned the trip, the days of living our lives out of our cars seemed a hundred years ago, but divvying up the gear at the trailhead we stepped back into a like-yesterday routine. Who gets the rack, who gets the rope, did you bring matches? No, but I brought film for the Brownie. We camped at the west end of Thousand Island Lake, ahead of the Labor Day backpacker invasion. The next morning we hiked past Lake Catherine and over to Ritter Lakes. Hiking time: two ibuprofen.

The obvious arête looked great from the lakes. From the inlet of the middle Ritter Lake we gained a couple of hundred feet to the toe of the arête. We stayed either on the arête or on the north side to the summit. Two thousand vertical feet of class five, up to 5.7, with some easier scrambling, brought us to the summit.

We made it back to camp by 6 p.m., twelve non-stop hours after we'd started. It was great to dust off the hardware of the rack and the software of our minds.

CLAUDE FIDDLER, *AAC*

Ken Minaret, Broken Rib. The northeast face of Ken Minaret features a sharp ridge that leads directly to the summit. In August 2008 Kevin Hartigan and I climbed nine pitches (Broken Rib, 5.9) along this prominent rib in a long day from Devil's Postpile. We enjoyed great views and I was happy to tag my final Minaret summit. R.J. Secor lists 19 named Minarets in his guidebook, and though some folks have cruised most of them in a day, I am pleased to have spread it out over 37 years since my first attempt on Clyde in 1971.

DAVID HARDEN, *AAC*

Disappearing Dome, Do It Don't Spew It. On September 9 my daughter Lynnea, my wife Sigrid, and I completed a new route on 1,100' Disappearing Dome, in the San Joaquin River gorge. Although this is a steep, prominent formation, it has only one other reported route, done over 30 years ago and more than a half mile away (Memphis Blues, IV 5.11c, Lawrence-McCabe-Stoddard, 1978).

A foreshortened photo of the upper part of pitch one and the initial six pitches of Do It Don't Spew It, on Disappearing Dome. *Jerry Anderson*

The easiest way to find the dome on a map is to follow Minarets Road from North Fork, near Bass Lake, past Mammoth Pool Reservoir and look for Squaw Dome (Paiyu Dome on more recent and p.c. maps). Disappearing Dome is the next formation to the southeast, about one-half mile from Squaw/Paiyu Dome and across the gorge from Balloon Dome. On Google Earth it is at 37° 28' 17.60"N, 119° 15' 27.96"W. Lots of luck with the maze of old logging roads! We eventually found a 4x4 road that came within a few hundred meters of the dome—not that it helped with the final approach.

This long, difficult approach starts on the south side of the dome and follows steep, brushy slopes and loose gullies below the east side to an obvious gully on the northeast side. Scramble up the gully for 100' over class 3/4 chockstones to the second left-facing open book. A bolt protecting the moves into the book marks the start of the route.

Figuring that two of the nine pitches would require bolts, we wanted to make sure that the line would actually go, rather than blindly climbing and drilling, so we rappelled our line first. We then completed the route over several sessions. Some may criticize previewing a route, but when drilling is going to be involved we feel a responsibility to the rock to not just bash away and hope for the best.

The climb is on perfect granite and starts up a corner system, with fun laybacking and jamming to the crux 5.11b moves out of the corner to a flake system. Two pitches up the flakes (5.10a and 5.9) lead to a vertical dike. Where the 5.11a dike ends, a 30' traverse leads to another crack system. This crack goes for a pitch at 5.7; then a beautiful featured 5.8 face leads to an easier 5.7 face and crack climbing for three pitches to the top. The route's name celebrates a mantra of on-line climbing forums: Do It Don't Spew It (IV 5.11b).

Jerry Anderson, *AAC*

Ruby Peak, East Corner. Out of Mosquito Flats, and past Ruby Lake, on September 26 Miguel Carmona and I established the East Corner (IV 5.9) on the steep Ruby Wall (east wall) of Ruby Peak. The route climbs eight pitches to a summit where the East Arête and Left East Arête also most likely finish.

Miguel and I had made our first trip to the Ruby Wall two weeks earlier. We started on the left side, climbed five pitches in a big corner, but retreated in intermittent snow and hail. We returned and reclimbed to our prior belays, added another long pitch, and finished with easier climbing to the summit.

The route starts on the left side of the main wall between the East Arête (Rowell-Wilson) and Central Route (Rowell-White). An elevated platform marks the start, and lower-angled pitches (5.7 and 5.4) lead to the corner. The third pitch moves right, then back left through steeper flakes to arrive at the 400' right-facing corner that defines the route. Steep, sustained pitches end on excellent ledges. The final section eased slightly and finished to the left, on a big platform, and our first warm sun for most of the route. We then finished the pitches to the top. The long descent involves going south along the ridge, dropping into notches, re-attaining the summit plateau, and dropping down a very loose slope to the Mono Pass Trail.

JOE LEMAY, *AAC*

Ruby Wall of Ruby Peak: (1) East Corner (LeMay-Carmona, 2009). (2) East Arête (Rowell-Wilson, 1984). (3) Central Route (Rowell-White, 1982). (4) Daphne (Parker-Houston-Selters, 2000). *Joe LeMay*

Mt. Langley, Horizontal Thought Movement. I'd been eyeballing this line on the 1,500' north face of Mt. Langley for a year, since I noticed that Rest and Be Thankful, the north arête route put up by Alois Smrz and Miguel Carmona 10 years ago, was the only route on the face.

It felt like summer was slipping away. My friends Shay Har-Noy and Luke Stefurak had been up to the face the previous weekend, trying to scoop "my" line, but luckily (for me) they failed, climbing a detached tower that led nowhere and which they called the Unstoppable Tango Tower. With some idea of where not to

Approaching the north face of Mt. Langley, with the arrow indicating the start of Horizontal Thought Movement, with the first four pitches to the skyline visible. *Nate Ricklin*

go, I found a willing partner. Ben Cohen had never been in the High Sierra, never climbed an alpine route, never been to 14,000', and never simul-climbed, but I knew he'd be solid.

Our route starts at the base of the sweeping arête that curves down from the summit, to the right of Rest and be Thankful. Four vertical pitches, including a wide crack, zig-zagging through blocky towers, and a hand crack through a small roof, lead to the arête's most prominent feature, a huge horizontal jog. Easy climbing along the arête soon leads to a huge open book, which we climbed directly, with a tricky face exit to the left. A few more pitches of easy fifth lead to the summit. We topped out on September 6 and descended the northeast couloir straight to our base camp.

We named the route Horizontal Thought Movement (5.8), a mash-up between a Franklin Merrell-Wolff book chapter and the big horizontal jog on the route.

NATE RICKLIN, *Pullharder Alpine Club*

Utah

Fisher Towers, various ascents. Spaniards David Palmada and Esther Ollé established a route to which they gave the unprecedented rating of A6+ (the standard aid scale tops out at A5+). Their route, Look Out! Danger, took 13 days and climbs the northwest face of the Titan in 11 pitches. They drilled on one blank section, but did not bolt any belays.

On the south face of King Fisher, Jeremy Aslaksen and Paul Gagner put-up Weird Science (V 5.7 A4 R), which begins 50' left of Death of American Democracy. The route took four days and, according to Aslaksen, ascends "a very thin series of seams/corners and blankety-blank."

Over the course of a few trips that included a 50' ledge fall and a broken foot, Jason Haas and Rob Pizem freed each pitch of West Side Story (9 pitches, 5.12c R), for the first free ascent of Cottontail. Haas later returned (foot healed), and freed every pitch on lead.

ZION NATIONAL PARK

Mt. Kinesava, Tatooine. In February Joe French, Zach Lee, and Caleb Padgett found, equipped, and freed a fantastic crack system on the south face of Kinesava. The route is the farthest left of the established routes (left of Arrakis), and a few bolts in a slightly overhanging di-himney mark the start. It is characterized by one continuous crack that rarely opens up to anything larger than hand-size. There is a comfortable bivy for four atop pitch five. The upper buttress is reminiscent of Moonlight. Wherever the crack pinches off, face holds appear. The route is well equipped for speedy ascents and is sure to be a classic desert free-climb. Tatooine (15 pitches, IV 5.11).

NATHAN BROWN

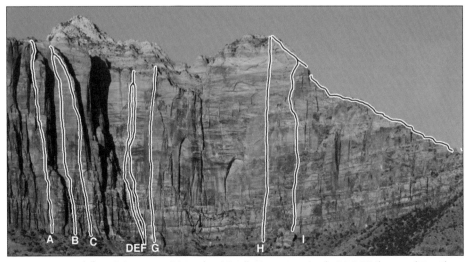

Mt. Kinesava, south face: (A) Tatooine. (B) Arrakis. (C) Jolly Green Jam Crack. (D) & (E) Lhasa and Free Lhasa (unclear where they split). (F) Shake That Bear. (G) King's Corner. (H) Plumb Line. (I) The Millennium Falcon. (J) Cowboy Ridge. *Bryan Bird*

Mt. Majestic, Cracking the Emerald. In November Ryan Frost and I climbed Cracking the Emerald (IV/V 5.10 C1), a steep new six-pitch route on the southwest face of Mt. Majestic, in the Emerald Pools area. We ascended a striking corner near the center of the face, with dark rock on the right, lighter rock on the left. Part way up the corner is a roof, split by a one-inch crack. The climbing was mostly hand-and-finger cracks, with clean aid climbing and ledges at every belay.

Shortly after our ascent, Ben Williams free-climbed the route, leading every pitch. Three pitches were 5.11, and the fifth was 5.12-. We were surprised this route hadn't been done before, because of the quality of the climbing and the close proximity to the pools. The setting is spectacular.

BRIAN SMOOT

The southwest face of Mt. Majestic: (1) Cracking the Emerald (Frost-Smoot, 2009). (2) Leaving Llamaland (Tarr, solo, 1998). *Brian Smoot*

Sentinel, Red Chamonix Ridge. This incredibly bad idea originated years ago on spring break, when some friends and I got in way over our heads on Rodeo Queen. While freezing our butts off, we noticed this amazing gendarmed ridge on the Sentinel, with Birdbeak Spire being the ridge's most prominent tower.

It took a few years for memories of choss to fade, but on April 5, 2008, Joe French, Zack Lee, and I cast off with two packs, a big rack of birdbeaks, down coats, and not enough water. We left the car at 5 a.m., and Joe led the first block. Around pitch five or six Zack and I heard the dreaded rumble of *big* rockfall. Down the fall line came a 5'x5'x5' boulder, but no yelling. And the rope kept going up. WTF? We got to Joe, who nonchalantly explained that he'd man-tled onto the thing and had to jump off when it started to go.

We moved along at a good clip for 15 pitches, snaking through broken towers, where the climbing stayed around 5.9, with some big runouts, loads of choss, and vertical talus.

The Sentinel: (1) Mountaineers' Route. (2) Bird-beak Spire (climbs to a detached spire along ridge) (Middendorf-Oxx, 1993). (3) Belly of the Buddha (Draper-Littman, 1998). (4) Red Chamonix Ridge (Brown-French-Lee, 2008). Rumors exist of a 1966 route on the Sentinel, but we were unable to uncover details. *Nathan Brown*

After pitch 17 we plopped onto a comfortable ledge on the south side of Birdbeak Spire and screeched to a near halt: 70' of beaks, followed by a 10-hole ladder, followed by another 60' of beaks. We then scampered around to the gully, skipping the last 60' to the top of Birdbeak. Another three loose pitches brought us near the summit cap of the Sentinel. Totally dark.

Zack rope-gunned 200' of white sandcakes, and we untied for the final 400' of 4th-class, which included step-kicking up a snowfield. Joe brought a summit register, which we signed at 11 p.m. And then the real danger began: a sleep-deprived descent of the Mountaineer's Route, where we endured a forced bivouac. Red Chamonix Ridge (V 5.9 A4).

NATHAN BROWN

Streaked Wall, Lord Helmet. According to www.alpinist.com and confirmed by Brian McCray, he and Chad Umbel established Lord Helmet (9 pitches, VI 5.9 A4) over 11 days in May, spread over two trips. They drilled about 60 holes (including belay anchors), mostly on the final two pitches.

Streaked Wall, Wet Stone Wall. This high-adventure route climbs through the site of the seasonal flash waterfall on the right side of the wall. Ryan Frost, Joe French, and I stole a few precious days (October 9–13) from our busy schedules to race up the wall. The climbing was generally hard (1,700', VI 5.10 A4), with lots of difficult nailing, technical hooking, run-out free climbing, and serious vertical bushwhacking. The bivy ledge atop the arch is one of the finest I have laid bags on. We placed 45 bolts, 30 for anchors. Future parties should bring a bolt kit, as we left about 20 or so holes unfilled, for hooking. Most of the holes are on the ladder pitch. The route is equipped for rappel descent.

NATHAN BROWN

The Streaked Wall: (1) Rodeo Queen. (2) Tale of the Scorpion. (3) Latitudes. (4) Lord Helmet. (5) Wet Stone Wall. (6) Farmer Brown. *Nathan Brown*

Sub Peak or Confluence Peak, Satan's Waitin'. On October 26 Zach Lee and I did a new route on the west face of the peak north of, and connected to, Bridge Mountain, The peak is officially unnamed but known locally as Sub Peak or Confluence Peak. We dubbed our effort Satan's Waitin', after a Bugs Bunny-Yosemite Sam cartoon where, to escape his fate of remaining in hell, Yosemite tries to replace himself with Bugs. The route follows a natural line

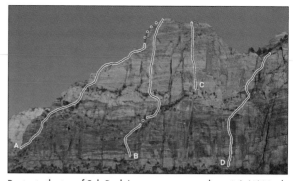

Routes to the top of Sub Peak (many crag routes also exist): (A) North Ridge. (B) Satan's Waitin'. (C) Golden Gate (original start unknown). (D) Take Back The Rainbow. *Bryan Bird*

up the left side of the main wall, directly below the summit. I had previously attempted the route with Eric Draper and Brody Greer in 2006 or 2007. We climbed about half the route, stopped at the base of a large roof, drilled a single bolt, and bailed. At the time the off-width bulge seemed too much for us, and proved to be the crux when Zach and I finally sent it. The lone half-inch bolt below the crux remains the route's only fixed gear.

The route begins in the center of the peak, in a high recessed area that sports several fine cragging routes. One long pitch off of the ground accesses an area that allows for some soloing through the vegetated ramps in the middle of the face. We roped up for seven pitches, onsighting the entire route (IV 5.11). It's an enjoyable adventure, albeit a bit on the sandy side, and it accepted cams and stoppers its entire length. To descend, we hiked south to the saddle between Confluence Peak and Bridge Mountain, toward the Bridge Mountain Arch, and rappelled a route called Take Back The Rainbow. It is possible to descend TBTR with one 60m rope, though two 60m ropes allow for smoother sailing.

BRYAN BIRD

Wyoming

Teton Range, Death Canyon, Alien Wall. I remember the night in 1987 when Jim Donini and Jack Tackle established Predator. My worried mother and other friends dispatched my dad and me to collect Jim and Jack after they had failed to return home at what she deemed a "reasonable time." It seemed that even those two consummate climbers could not escape the watchful eye and worried mind of my mom. We met them safe and sound on the trail around midnight, and I was enthralled and horrified by their story of a mini-tornado whipping through the canyon, fouling their ropes up. Since then, every time I've climbed the Snaz or Caveat, I've gazed at the virgin rock across the canyon and promised myself to do something about it. But summer moves into fall and my intentions slip away.

Death Canyon is a special place for me, because I learned to climb there as a kid. Donini taught me the basics of wide cracks as he hauled me up The Snaz. Alex Lowe conned me into wandering around the Omega Buttresses looking for interesting new lines. Tim Toula would leave notes on ledges and in cracks; unfolding them would reveal beta: "PULL DOWN HERE!"

or "THIS SLOT PROBABLY HAS SNAKES!" The most special times have been spent with my dad. We climbed Apocalypse Couloir in June, and in July he fired the Snazette variation on the Snaz. At 69 he is a total inspiration and a reminder of what is possible with kindness, patience, and a good attitude.

With all this in mind, Joel Kauffman and I set out on September 2 to explore the south wall. After crossing the creek and 'shwacking through the alders, we reached the face. The first 150m were easy 5th-class, with a few moderate roped pitches of run-out face climbing. We eventually gained the bench where the real climbing starts. After an initial pitch of 5.6, we veered from Predator onto the steep face to the left. As Joel bravely traversed out, the sun hit the wall, the angle eased, and the climbing got even better. We kept going and climbed the route in seven 55m pitches. The Alien Wall (400m, IV 5.10-) follows a fairly direct line left of Predator, with wild and varied climbing for the grade—steep face-climbing, stem-box corners, thin flakes, and cracks, from cranking fingerlocks to a small offwidth section. Pitch 4 would be a face-climbing classic anywhere, with some of the wildest rock I've seen in the Tetons: dense, dark, and solid, with knobs and chickenheads twisted into psychedelic forms. Pitches 5–7 were also stellar. Nine long rappels from trees, plus some downclimbing get you to the base of the wall and back to terra firma. My thanks to Joel for making the climb so special.

MARK GIVENS (1971–2009), *AAC*

WIND RIVER MOUNTAINS

Twenty-Hour Tower, You Gotta Want It and Alexander's Band; Flat Top Mountain, Trundler. Laramie boys Oliver Deshler and I made two trips into the Clear Creek valley in the northern Winds this summer. As a warm-up, on June 23 we climbed the previously unclimbed north-facing wall of Flat Top Mountain, via the northeast arête: Trundler, 9 pitches, III 5.5–5.8. Descend via the gully behind the wall, hooking west and then north back down to the valley. Moving at 4:30 the next morning, we started up the giant buttress/pinnacle [later revealed as Twenty-Hour Tower, as named by Paul Horton and Sean O'Malley, who'd climbed it on June 7, 1997] on the north side of the valley, west of Mt. Osborn's Forlorn Pinnacle. The granite was of extraordinary quality and we climbed directly up the center of the formation, with Deshler leading the crux 5.11 layback finger crack. After 15 pitches of mostly 5.8 to 5.10, we summited at dusk, then rapped in the dark, at one point using a ridiculously dangerous bush as an anchor. About halfway

Twenty-Hour Tower, from left: Alexander's Band (Deshler-Jenkins, 2009), You Gotta Want It (Deshler-Jenkins, 2009), Horton-O'Malley (1997). *Mark Jenkins*

down the face, exhausted, I took off my pack (with $1,000 worth of climbing gear) and managed to forget it. Too beat to climb back up, we got back to camp at 3 a.m. We walked out the next day, naming the route You Gotta Want It (IV 5.11). Three months later, Deshler and I returned on a recovery mission. On September 13 we climbed a route (8 pitches, 5.10R) to the left of YGWI. It ties into YGWI at its 10th pitch, and we retrieved the pack. It was spitting sleet and snow the whole day, then began to rain; then a double rainbow came out just at dusk, prompting us to name the route Alexander's Band.

MARK JENKINS, *AAC*

East Fork Valley, various routes. The north-south ridge between Ambush and Raid contains a lot of rock. A long, attractive east-facing slab two buttresses north of M Buttress, two buttresses south of Raid, lured us in. On August 28 Felix Hörmann and I started at the lowest toe of the slab, near two vertical brown dots on the granite, and 4th-classed up and right to a two-bolt ledge. (We bolted belays while rapping the route, with other bolts drilled on lead.) Son of Raid (1,150', III 5.10) climbs interesting features more or less straight up for seven pitches. Two 60m ropes allow a quick rappel descent. We placed two

The East Fork Valley, with Son of Raid (marked) and the obvious M Buttress of the left. *James Garrett*

cairns up top, at the ridgeline, to facilitate finding the raps for climbers descending from Raid, which is otherwise long and involved.

In the same valley, back on July 23, 2006, Franziska Garrett and I climbed 10 pitches (1,300', III 5.9) on the east face of Ambush, starting at the lowest part of the face and ending directly below the huge roof, where difficulties drastically change. We called it Ambush Plaisir; *plaisir* is a Swiss word meaning pleasurable and casual at the same time. With belay/rappel stations installed, this makes for a low-commitment Winds outing. A week later we established Triple Shot (9 pitches, 1,500', IV 5.7+), which traverses three gendarmes to the top of Ambush. A huge dike forms the letter M at the lower part of an east-facing wall/arête that's really its own mountain, north of the north summit of Ambush. We started climbing at the far left lower side of the M and followed the beautiful left-facing dihedral, and then the arête, to the top of the first tower, which is part of a huge ridge leading to the top of the mountain.

JAMES GARRETT, *AAC*

Watchtower, Hay Fever. In mid-July 2008 Dave Stewart and I climbed what we believe to be a new route on the east face of Watchtower. We started from camp in the Cirque and approached up the broad scree directly below the formation. Our route takes nondescript rock left of the

East Gully route, near the toe of the face. After three pitches of run-out 5.10, we traversed hard right to the huge left-facing dihedral that is the most prominent feature on the face. We followed the dihedral for two pitches, at 5.11 A0, until it ends at a large roof where we found an old pin [Joe Kelsey, author of *Climbing and Hiking in the Wind River Mountains,* adds that a fixed pin or stopper high on a route seems to be an essential ingredient of new routes in the Winds, where many routes and significant attempts have gone unrecorded—Ed.] From here we downclimbed, traversed right, and then back up to a large grassy ledge 30' above the roof. One pitch of low-end 5.10 and another 400' of simul-climbing got us to the summit. We pulled on gear on two pitches to get around vegetation in the big dihedral, but these should go free at 5.11. People have climbed on this face before, but we found no record of previous ascents near where we climbed. Hay Fever (5.11 A0, with 5.10R).

BEN ROSENBERG, *AAC*

The east face of the Watchtower, showing the probable new route Hay Fever. Other routes known on the formation: South Buttress (Raymond-Robbins, 1964; farther left, not clearly visible; FFA Copp-Merriam, 1997) and East Gully (the nasty gully right of H.F., first descended after climbing a route on the gully's right edge, by Bollinger-Orear-Yodh, 1953). *Ben Rosenberg*

Temple Peak, Last Go Round. On September 12 Ty Mack, Mike Anderson, and I made the first ascent of Last Go Round, on the northwest buttress of Temple Peak. The route takes a pronounced splitter crack on the far left side of the buttress. I had attempted the route in the fall of 2006 with Todd Skinner, but we were turned back by a very hard last pitch. This time I stacked the odds in my favor by taking two of the best climbers I know. The day was cloudy and windy, and the warmest we were all day was on the glacier approach.

The climb was a team-free ascent, with Mike and Ty climbing well on hard terrain. The crack varies little in width: mostly thin hands and hands for the first four pitches. We climbed most of the route in down jackets. By the time we got to the last pitch, none of us was ready to pull hard. The pitch, a left-leaning seam feature, looked to need bolts and considerable scrubbing, so we opted for a 5.10 face traverse left to an alcove. Ty then led a steep dihedral to the top of the buttress.

We rappelled the route from the buttress crest, judging that continuing to the summit would be superfluous—an ascent of a 4th-class rubble gully that would only taint the quality of the climbing we'd done. Plus, we were freezing. We named our route in memory of our friend Todd; our 2006 attempt was his last sojourn into the mountains of his youth. With pitches of 5.10, 5.11, 5.12, 5.12 and 5.11, it ranks as one of the Wind Rivers' hardest climbs.

STEVE BECHTEL

Colorado

Black Canyon of the Gunnison, Suffer Pony at the Disco. Early morning on September 20, Joe Forrester and I descended the SOB Gully to climb the Porcelain Arête (IV 5.10). When we arrived at the base of the PA buttress, though, we were disheartened by a lack of significant crack or corner systems. Undeterred, we roped up and began climbing. We later discovered that we had followed the first pitch of the PA before we headed right. Several mostly 5.7 and low-angle 70m pitches wandered through the occasional bush and onto the arête proper, where Joe led through a steep, sharp roof crack at 5.9. The next pitch remained directly on the arête, via tricky 5.10 face moves, before we followed a 5.9 crack around the right side of the buttress. More committing face moves (5.10R) led straight up, back to the arête. After traversing around a giant pegmatite tower, we climbed two easier pitches to the rim. In staying much closer to the arête (the Porcelain Arête climbs left of the arête), we shared only the first pitch and probably the final pitch

Suffer Pony at the Disco (right) and the Porcelain Arête. The Painted Wall rises to the left. *Joe Forrester*

with the PA. Our route, Suffer Pony at the Disco (IV 5.10R) is by no means a Black Canyon classic, but offers a moderately graded adventure with spectacular views. A topo is available at the North Rim Ranger Station.

JEREMY ROOP, *AAC*

The North Shore, with dots marking belays, on the NW face of The Big Island. Kor's Echo Canyon route follows the wide right-facing corner visible at the left edge of the formation, and Wild Bill's Wall is around the corner on the NE face. *Vera Schulte-Pelkum/Alpinecreative.com*

Black Canyon of the Gunnison, Big Island, North Shore. In June, Jared Ogden and I completed the North Shore (5.11+), a new route on the northwest face of the Big Island. The Big Island is a huge flat-topped formation off Cross Fissures Overlook. The climb follows an invisible line on excellent rock with sustained difficulty, similar in character to Eldorado Canyon. Be looking for a pile of white rocks amid the black, marking the start of the North Shore. The route begins in thin cracks up improbable-looking rock, with good but challenging protection. Ten pitches to the summit, a 60m rappel into a notch, and two easy pitches to Cross Fissures Overlook finish the adventure. Take triple sets of thin cams. Ours was probably the third ascent of the Big Island, after Layton Kor's mysterious Echo Canyon route and Wild Bill's Wall. The unpopular nature of the Big Island is no surprise; finding this quality line around the dirty slabs, bushy corners, and discontinuous cracks took several seasons. A topo can be found at the North Rim Visitor Center.

TOPHER DONAHUE

Alaska

BROOKS RANGE

Sukakpak Mountain, Arctic Haze. Sukakpak (typically pronounced *suka-pak,* 4,459') is a prominent landmark to Euro motorcycle tourists, RVers, and long-haul truckers who ply the Dalton Highway north of Coldfoot. To a climber, Sukakpak's west face is even more conspicuous. Its 2,000' high and two-mile-wide wall of "Marble of Devonian Age Skajit Limestone" (from some book I once saw) beckons, and climbers have established several water-ice lines. Most likely, bygone Fairbanks hardmen (or placer miners on a drunken dare) have clambered over the rock faces too, though we know of no complete ascent, and there were no signs of previous ascent on the face.

In one sense, Sukakpak is remote, six hours north of Fairbanks and north of the Arctic Circle, at 67°37'. From an Alaskan perspective however, it could not be more accessible. Looking for an adventure and inspired by a post on the Black Diamond website about a "chossaineering" trip in Utah, Andy Sterns and I traveled north in his battle-scarred F-150 on July 25. Smoke hung heavy from forest fires across the state when we pulled off the trans-Alaska pipeline road below Sukakpak. We gawked at the massive face, stunned, before tenting on the banks of the Middle Fork of the Koyukuk River.

Saturday morning we drank coffee, glassed potential lines, racked, and starting walking up tussock and talus slopes until finally standing under what appeared to be a promising and fairly solid-looking start. Between the recon, approach, and back-and-forth about suitable lines, much of the day had passed. We agreed to stash water and rack at the base and return for an early start the next morning, anticipating a long, long day on the route.

We returned early, and the climbing began well. Two consecutive rope-stretchers danced between lousy rock, fun corners, exposed face moves, and run-out slab. After this initial progress, things deteriorated. We angled farther right than intended. It was only 5.5, but steep, gravelly mud was curiously bonded to the face. We were tethered to the face in theory only, with nearly worthless anchors and pro, belay ledges collapsing below our feet. We finally rounded a massive

Arctic Haze on Sukakpak, with the untouched head-wall awaiting the masses. *Matt Klick*

yellow block and delicately traversed onto an expansive belay meadow, six pitches—but only 600' vertical—from the start of the climbing. We looked at the massive face looming above, capped by huge overhanging blocks of dubious rock, and looked at our skimpy rack. A direct line was not in the cards. We untied and traversed back left along the ledge, sucking water from seeps through straws snagged at the last truck stop, and then scrambled to the distinguishable ridge. We continued by scrambling and hiking the ridge to the summit, topping out in a beautiful, smoky, Arctic midnight-blue haze, with a view over the Brooks Range. After a long half-circumnavigation of the massif, we finished by tussock-hopping back to Andy's truck, 20 hours after we left.

The Voice of America boomed from Andy's shortwave radio while we snacked, brewed, and discussed the projecting necessary for a big-wall route on Sukakpak's face, happy to be off safely. We called our unfinished (because we wanted to go direct) route Arctic Haze (5.9+ A0) and clambered out of the smoky air and swarming mosquitoes, into our tents, before the bumpy ride back home.

MATT KLICK, *AAC*

KIGLUAIK MOUNTAINS

Suluun, new routes. Last July Andy Sterns of Fairbanks and I made several ascents on a remote and spectacular chunk of granitic gneiss at the Glacial Lake headwaters. We flew in from Nome with Ben Rowe in a Bering Air helicopter to a base camp in the spectacular western cirque of Suluun. First came a 17-hour epic climbing its West Ridge (IV 5.7) to the west summit, lots of ups and downs across several tors, followed by a hideous gully descent. Two days later we returned to bag the true, east summit of the mountain, the Sulu Tor (II 5.8, from the notch at the base), a soaring pinnacle I had faced alone on earlier attempts. Lastly, we climbed an eight-pitch line, the Steely Focus Buttress (III/IV 5.9), up a patch of tolerable rock in the western cirque of the mountain. The normally scree-laden approaches were ameliorated by huge amounts of residual snow.

IAN MCRAE

Suluun's west and main summits, and the Steely Focus Buttress. The West Ridge route takes the left skyline. *Ian McRae*

Mosquito Pass Wall (Peak 2,911'), Hidden Couloir. On a cold day in February, Jeff Collins and I snow-machined in to Mosquito Pass and climbed a narrow, 1,700' sinuous couloir (with some WI2 and M3) on the wall of gneiss to the west of Mosquito Pass.

IAN McRAE

Note: Reports of several previously unreported new routes in the Kigluaik are posted at aaj.american alpineclub.org

ALASKA RANGE

Geographical note: While the well-known peaks in Denali National Park are often called "The Alaska Range," these peaks form just one part of the immense Alaska Range, which contains many significant subranges, including the Hayes and Delta ranges, and the Revelation, Kichatna, and Tordrillo mountains.

HAYES RANGE

Mt. Balchen, Alchemy Ridge. When my 2009 expedition plans fell through due to partner injury, I scrambled to salvage the season and found a partner in fellow Fairbanks climber Matt Klick. At home in Fairbanks we waited two days to fly in to a gravel strip at the base of the northwest ridge of Mt. Hayes in Rob Wing's Super Cub. From the base of Hayes, we walked seven miles to our base camp in the Hayes basin at 6,500'. After arriving at base camp, we did some recon and made plans to attempt the north ridge of Mt. Balchen as our first objective. Due to bad weather it would be the only route we attempted, and we received only five hours of clear weather while on route. Of our 15 days from June 10–24, 12 had bad weather.

Alchemy Ridge on Mt. Balchen. Johnson and Klick started from the opposite (Hayes Glacier) side of this photo, climbed to the col and ascended the sky-line ridge. *Jeff apple Benowitz*

As we left base camp we could see a dense haze approaching from the north and told ourselves we'd bail if the weather got too nasty. Over about 36 hours to and from base camp, we battled marginal weather to complete the first ascent of Balchen's Alchemy (north) Ridge in 14 long pitches. We climbed a beautiful line true to the ridge (V AI4 M7 in the conditions we found, could be IV when dry). To descend we made six raps onto the east face, then downclimbed to the 'schrund and ran under a serac to return to our skis. The route would be a classic in a more traveled range, as would the other routes on Balchen. In dry or even just non-stormy conditions, it would be a pleasurable outing, with many options through the two steeper rock bands, and could be completed in one day from our base camp below the Hayes basin. That was the plan, but due to the weather we endured a sitting bivy on a ledge chopped into a 70° rime slope, with just bivy sacks and belay jackets. It was a very cold night.

SAMUEL JOHNSON, *AAC*

DENALI NATIONAL PARK

Denali National Park and Preserve, summary. The 2009 climbing season once again featured great tri-umphs and moving tragedies. Four deaths occurred on Mt. McKinley, and 47 climbers were stricken

Sam Johnson on cruxy mixed ground on Alchemy Ridge. *Matt Klick*

with injuries or illnesses that required medical intervention by the National Park ranger staff and volunteers.

Two Colorado women, Sarah Fritz and Irena Overeem, received the Denali Pro Award for initiating and leading an independent technical rescue of an injured climber on the Moose's Tooth. Starting in 2010, the award will be renamed the Mislow-Swanson/PMI Denali Pro Award to honor former recipients John Mislow and Andrew Swanson, who died on a 2009 climb of the West Rib.

Quick Statistics—Mt. McKinley and Mt. Foraker:

- *Mt. McKinley: Average trip length: 16.4 days. Busiest summit day: June 7, with 77 summits. Average age: 38. Women constituted 12.4% of all climbers.*
- *The five most represented nations on Mt. McKinley were: U.S. (698 climbers), Poland (47) Canada (44), Japan (38), and U.K. (38).*
- *McKinley was attempted by 1,161 climbers, with 59% reaching the summit; 1,078 attempted the West Buttress, with 60% summiting. Fifteen climbers attempted Mt. Foraker, with eight summiting.*
- *The complete Mountaineering Summary can be found at www.nps.gov/dena/planyourvisit/ summaryreports.htm*

Summarized from the DENALI NATIONAL PARK & PRESERVE ANNUAL MOUNTAINEERING SUMMARY

Other notable activity. On April 12 Norwegians Nils Nielsen and Eiliv Ruud climbed a like-ly new six-pitch variation (AI4/5) of the modern classic Shaken Not Stirred, on the Moose's Tooth. They took a rarely forming ice smear to the left of the Narrows section (marked "pos-sible new variation" on the topo in Joe Puryear's *Alaska Climbing*) for three pitches and contin-ued up snow and ice, rejoining Shaken Not Stirred one pitch below the col. They climbed the route in a 15-hour round-trip from camp in the Ruth Gorge.

After an impressive effort on Mt. Huntington's Harvard Route (27 hours round-trip, with retreat just below the summit), on May 21 Chris Thomas and Rick Vance returned and climbed a difficult new variation. The Community College Couloir (1,000', M7+ WI5) starts on the West Face Couloir and angles to the Harvard Route, joining it at the Nose pitch, before

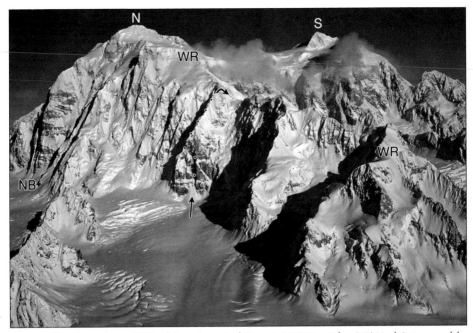

Mt. Hunter from the northwest: (N) North Summit, (S) South Summit, (WR) West Ridge, (NB) North Buttress, and the arrow showing the new Swiss route. *Mike Gauthier*

the climbers descended. It's the highest of the many slashing systems below the West Face Couloir. The Puryear-Westman (2000) variation, below and to its right, is the only other of these systems known to have been climbed.

The famed North Buttress of Mt. Hunter continued to be a showcase for speed and technical proficiency, seeming like an Alaskan El Capitan. In May, Bjørn-Eivind Årtun (Norway) and Colin Haley made the fourth and fastest ascent of the difficult French Route (Grison-Tedeschi, 1984), in less than 40 hours roundtrip from base camp, including a descent of the long and complex West Ridge. They had first attempted the Bibler-Klewin route (Moonflower, as named by Mugs Stump after climbing high on the buttress in his attempt with Paul Aubrey in 1981, though true first ascent credit belongs to Todd Bibler and Doug Klewin, 1983). Årtun and Haley climbed from 'schrund to Cornice Bivy in 16 hours, eventually retreating 100m below the summit, eschewing any rationalization of a "modern ascent" (i.e. stopping wherever you feel like stopping).

A small group of Swiss climbers flew in to Kahiltna base camp at the beginning of May, and made several impressive ascents over 24 days in the range. One such ascent was Simon and Samuel Anthamatten's fastest ascent, by far, of Mt. Hunter's Bibler-Klewin/Moonflower. They topped-out the buttress in 15 hours of climbing, bivied at the Cornice Bivy, continued to the summit, and descended the same route, making the roundtrip from base camp in 36 hours. Also on Mt. Hunter, the Anthamatten brothers and Andreas Steindl climbed a likely new route on a prominent face west of the Rattle and Hum Buttress. Their line (2,500', M4+ WI4+ AI5) weaves up mixed terrain, with seracs on either side, and continues along a heavily corniced and mushroomed "Himalayan-like" ridge until joining the West Ridge route, from where they

Samuel Anthamatten leading the lower gully on the team's new route on Hunter. *Simon Anthamatten*

descended (Simon and Samuel had already summited Hunter). Toward the end of their trip, one of their friends received a birthday delivery of pizza, booze, and cake. Samuel wrote (www.anthamattens.ch), "I would have paid $100 extra for some fresh apples."

Canadians Dave Edgar and J Mills made a rapid repeat of Deprivation (Backes-Twight, 1994), with a significant variation between the second and third ice bands, where the original route does a big zig-zag. Edgar and Mills essentially climbed straight up from the left side of the second ice band—yet still right of The Knowledge (Cartwright-Parnell, 2000)—adding five pitches of WI5 before joining the Moon-flower for the Bibler Come Again Exit. Photo at www.cdnalpine.blogspot.com. They made the massive roundtrip from basecamp to summit and back in 45 hours.

In mid-May Japanese climbers Genki Narumi and Katsutaka Yokoyama made a

Looking up Wasabi Gully. *Kei Taniguchi*

free and extremely rapid attempt (with variations) on perhaps the hardest line on the North Buttress, the Wall of Shadows (Child-Kennedy, 1994). Carrying only fanny packs, they started with the logical, albeit easier, Gilmore-Mahoney (2001) variation, and made variations to the Enigma pitch, the Somewhere Else Wall, and also a thin ribbon pitch above. They rated their climbing 5.10- M6R WI5+, reached the Cornice Bivy in 29 hours (including a six-hour brew stop), and retreated from there.

On May 25 Iku Mitoma, Hiroki Suzuki, and Kei Taniguchi (Japan) climbed a beautiful, albeit threatened, mixed line on the north-facing wall between the Mini-Mini Moonflower (or Micro Moonflower) and Kahiltna Queen, about two hours east of Kahiltna Base Camp. Wasabi Gully (M4x WI4+) climbs eight pitches and ends at the serac band.

In early July, Ryan Bougie and Marcus Waring made the first ski descent of Mt. Foraker's Archangel Ridge. Making a giant loop from the Kahiltna Glacier, the pair climbed Sultana Ridge, skied Archangel down to the wild, remote north side of the peak, then climbed back out via Mt. Crosson's northwest ridge and skied Crosson's southeast ridge back to base camp.

Wedge Peak, west ridge attempt. Rob Wing and I established a camp near the northwest face of Wedge Peak (10,239') on July 3, after hiking in via Glacier Creek and the Muldrow moraine. We attempted the unclimbed west ridge of Wedge but were turned around by the gravity of our situation after passing three of about a dozen rock towers. The granitic rock itself left something to be desired.

JEFF APPLE BENOWITZ

Thunder Mountain, Tangled Up in Blue; and other new routes. Alaska veterans Jay Smith and Jack Tackle climbed four new routes in May, culminating in the prized first ascent of the 4,000' north face of Thunder Mountain, climbed in lightweight alpine style by a route they named

Wedge Peak: (1) North Ridge (FA unknown; descent route for (2)). (2) Northwest Face (Benowitz-McRae,1996). The 2009 Wedge attempt was the ridge left of (3). Ragged Peak: (3) East Ridge (Benowitz-McRae,1995). The top of the North Ridge (Bayer-Benson-Colby-Collins, 1988) of Ragged is barely visible on the right skyline. *Jeff apple Benowitz*

Tangled Up in Blue (VI- M7 AI6), in 67 hours roundtrip from camp. Their trip started on a small fork of the Tokositna Glacier, south of Mt. Huntington, where no one is thought to have previously climbed. They warmed-up with a rapid ascent of the Rooster Comb, with a possible new start, and then established Prizefight (2,000', 5.9R M6 AI5) on the 10,300' south peak of Huntington, and Lagavulin (800', 5.10 WI4+/5) and the Black Pearl (1,500', M6 WI5+/6) on a formation they called the Scottish Wall. Tackle, who has established many major new routes in Alaska since his first trip in 1976, called it "maybe my best trip ever to Alaska." See his feature article earlier in this *Journal*.

Peak 11,300', Night of the Raging Goose; Mt. Church, Amazing Grace. After climbing the fantastic ice line of Shaken Not Stirred (2,200', V AI5) on the south face of the Moose's Tooth, James Clapham and I returned to the unclimbed 5,000' east face of Peak 11,300', which we'd tried upon our early April arrival. This time we rationalized away the objective dangers of the central couloir, *the* line on the face. Although it looked technically easier than the line we'd tried, much of the couloir was threatened by a large, partially detached serac.

Night of the Raging Goose, on Peak 11,300'. The South Ridge descent approximately follows the left skyline. *Gavin Pike*

Reasoning that what we couldn't see wouldn't hurt us, we climbed most of the couloir at night, emerging past a couple of pitches of steep ice and onto the upper section of the face, out of the firing line, as dawn broke. But the top of the face proved to be a maze of crazy hanging snow formations, some the size

Dawn on the upper face, Night of the Raging Goose, Peak 11,300'. *Gavin Pike*

of buses, a danger that hadn't been visible from the glacier below. Clambering happily onto the cornice at the top of the face, we eyed the summit slopes a mere stone's throw away, at the junction with the South Ridge descent. But the next few pitches were some of the most involved of the route, with vertical serac ice, sketchy rappels from snow mushrooms, and a final overhanging cornice exit. The South Ridge's endless downclimbing and rappels through hip-deep sugar seemed to take an age, but we knew we were safe. We named the route Night of the Raging Goose (5,000', V WI5).

Returning to the Ruth Gorge, we looked to the aesthetic north face of Mt. Church. Despite its prominence from the entrance of the Gorge, this face had only seen one ascent. We

High on the east ridge of Mt. Church, completing Amazing Grace. *Gavin Pike*

chose a new line to the left of the original Japanese route (Memorial Gate, Ichimura-Sato-Yamada, 2007). Four hours of simul-climbing past several short sections of steep ice saw us high on the upper face. Progress then ground to a halt, as we hit the steep, unconsolidated snow flutings that seem to be a feature on Church. The next 100m took many hours, as we excavated to the top of the face.

As we were learning, ridges in Alaska are not to be sniffed at, and a sizeable section of the unclimbed east ridge lay between us and the summit. The ridge sported extremely delicate cornice formations, proven by James's ride down the north face when a bus-sized section broke away. Certain death was fortuitously averted by my position on the other side of the ridge, and James, although beaten-up by his tumble, was otherwise uninjured.

The north face of Mt. Church: (1) For Whom the Bell Tolls (Bracey-Helliker, 2009). (2) Amazing Grace (Clapham-Pike, 2009). (3) Memorial Gate, (Ichimura-Sato-Yamada, 2007). *Jon Bracey*

Progress from here was slow, and though we weren't enamored with the prospect of spending the night on an Alaskan summit, with only a survival bag between us and the abyss, the situation necessitated an unplanned bivouac. But the temperatures were balmy by Alaskan standards, and the night proved eminently bearable.

After negotiating the summit the next morning and completing the first ascent of Amazing Grace (4,000', V AI4), we made a slow, water-deprived descent of the north ridge, followed by a long, interminable ski back up the glacier to the safety of our base camp. Our time in the Ruth Gorge had certainly been memorable.

GAVIN PIKE, *U.K.*

Mt. Grosvenor, Meltdown; Mt. Church, For Whom the Bell Tolls. Matt Helliker and I landed in the Ruth Gorge on May 6 to unseasonably warm weather and spotted a good unclimbed line on Mt. Grosvenor. Superb thin ice and mixed climbing in the center of the north face, between the Walsh-Westman routes Warrior's Way and Once Were Warriors, gave us a great day's climbing (Meltdown, 1,300m, ED3 VI AI/M6+). We downclimbed the southeast face to the Church-Grosvenor col and continued down the steep glacier back to our skis.

After a rest, on May 15 we climbed the Japanese Couloir to the summit of Mt. Barrill in bad weather, in search of missing climbers. Thankfully, after a grim night out near the summit, they returned safe and well.

We waited a day for good snow before heading off on May 17 to try a new route on the north face of Mt. Church, up a large fault system

Mt. Grosvenor: (1) South Face (Walsh-Westman, 2005), upper part hidden behind ridge. (2) Warrior's Way (Walsh-Westman, 2006). (3) Meltdown (Bracey-Helliker, 2009). (4) Once Were Warriors (Walsh-Westman, 2005). (5) North Ridge (Bocarde-Head-Lee-Thomas, 1979). *Jon Bracey*

east of the summit. This 1,150m face gave superb climbing (For Whom the Bell Tolls, 1,150m, ED2 V AI/M6), and there are plenty more unclimbed lines on this face. We downclimbed to the Church-Grosvenor col and back to our skis.

Matt Helliker on Meltdown, Mt. Grosvenor. *Jon Bracey*

Jon Bracey leads the crux pitch on Meltdown, Mt. Grosvenor. *Matt Helliker*

The next day the weather forecast was for a week of prolonged storms, so we quickly packed and got a flight out to Talkeetna. We later learned that planes were grounded by weather for the next five days, so we were lucky to get out.

JON BRACEY, *U.K.*

Sugar Tooth, South Ridge; Missing Toof, first ascent; Tooth Traverse, attempt; Mt. Barrill, Cobra Pillar, speed ascent. In alpine climbing you do your best to anticipate the potential crux of a trip. You physically and mentally prepare for bad weather, loose rock, huge days, anything you can imagine. This time getting on the airplane and deciding to go was the hardest part of our trip. The day before Renan Ozturk and I left for Alaska we attended Jonny Copp's memorial service. The day before that we said farewell to our friend Micah Dash. We could have never prepared enough for this.

But in late June, after postponing our trip for two weeks after our friends had gone missing in China, we arrived in Talkeetna. It had been an unusually warm June, so our pilot denied our flight request, saying it was too risky to land in the Kichatnas and that we "should have been here last week." So we went to the Ruth and within a couple of days after leaving home were beneath Mt. Barrill, racking up for a single push attempt of the famous Cobra Pillar (Donini-Tackle, 1991). It was happening too quickly. We wanted a week of snow, a mental rest to try to absorb the loss of our friends. Before we knew what was happening we were halfway up the route, feeling great. The weather was stable, the climbing engaging, and 12 hours after starting we topped out, possibly the fastest ascent to date. We descended the Japanese Couloir in the coldest hours of the day and reached our tiny tent at the base in a 20-hour roundtrip.

Renan Ozturk on the initial section of the new route on Sugar Tooth. *Zack Smith*

Ozturk nearing the highpoint of the Tooth Traverse attempt—the obvious spire in the center of the photo ("Missing Toof"). The background summits are the Bear Tooth (right) and Moose's Tooth (left). *Zack Smith*

After several days of rest at our deluxe base camp in the Don Sheldon Amphitheater, we began to motivate for another route. Back home we had talked about the possibility of enchaining the major summits of the Tooth group. Starting with the Sugar Tooth, up and over the Eye Tooth, onto the Bear Tooth, dropping down and then tagging the two summits of the Moose's Tooth. The link-up would be enormous, technically challenging, committing, and aesthetic.

On the morning of July 4 we started up Espresso Gap, which gains the unclimbed south ridge of the Sugar Tooth. After a few hours of simul-climbing and soloing we established a new route to the top of the Sugar Tooth, for its third known ascent (2,000', 5.10, two rappels). We did a 70m rappel into the notch between the Eye Tooth and the Sugar Tooth and climbed onto the Talkeetna Standard (Hollenbaugh-House, 2003). On the summit of the Eye Tooth we rested and collected running water. For the next eight hours we climbed along the insanely exposed snow ridge between the Eye Tooth and the Bear Tooth. The climbing proved to be much more time-consuming and taxing than we anticipated. Because of warm temperatures we became soaked and were getting increasingly committed to an unknown descent down exposed snowfields. We stopped at a spiky summit between the Eye and the Bear that we suspect was unclimbed and unnamed, so we'd like to call it the Missing Toof. [An ice and mixed route, Unforgiven (James-Ramirez, 2004), is on the west face of this spire but ends at seracs well below the summit—Ed.] The climbing ahead looked more difficult and exposed, and after a cold night wrapped in our tarp without sleeping bags, we painfully retraced our steps along the ridge. When we arrived back at the summit of the Eye Tooth we rappelled the 3,000' Dream in the Spirit of Mugs (Bonapace-Haas-Orgler, 1994) and returned to our skis. We climbed about 5,000' of rock, ice, and horizontal snow, but were less than halfway across the Tooth Traverse.

I feel so fortunate to have received the McNeill-Nott Award for this trip. The grant is set up for amateur climbers like me who would not otherwise be able to afford these kinds of adventures. Thank you so much to the AAC for their time and support.

ZACK SMITH, *AAC*

Route lines on Mocha and Coffee spires. Inset: Mocha. *Jay Rowe*

Mocha Spire, first ascent; Broken Tooth, attempt with new variation. On May 2 Paul Roderick of Talkeetna Air Taxi landed Cody Arnold, Peter Haeussler, and I, all from Anchorage, at 5,600' on the northwest fork of the Coffee Glacier. Over the next four days we made an attempt on the west ridge of Broken Tooth. Starting left of the 1987 Lewis-Bauman west ridge start, we climbed a new five-pitch variation (WI4+ M5) to the ridge crest via the left of two ice couloirs. One more pitch up the ridge led to an exposed but safe bivouac spot. We spent the next two days tent-bound, while 24" of snow fell. After the storm the route was out of condition and hazardous avalanche conditions prompted a quick descent.

We then turned our attention to a 1,000' unclimbed rock spire that lies on the divide between the Coffee and Ruth glacier drainages, a short distance from camp. Cody and I had climbed its taller neighbor to the north, Coffee Spire, the year before. On May 9 we enjoyed a sunny and moderate six-pitch free climb to the summit. We chose the name "Mocha Spire" because of the chocolate color of the rock. Our line went more or less straight to the summit, starting just right of center at the bottom of the east face and ending just left of center at the top. The first pitch started in the left of two parallel cracks. This pitch is the steepest of the route, but was well protected at easy 5.10 on solid rock. The second pitch moves up and around blocks and slabs at 5.8, until reaching a large ledge. We followed this ledge system up left for a pitch at 5.6 and traversed under the large dihedral above. We then ascended the left side of the summit tower for three more pitches, at 5.7. We descended via a snow couloir south of the summit, with downclimbing and two rappels. This is a fine, moderate day climb.

JAY ROWE, *AAC*

REVELATION MOUNTAINS

Ice Pyramid, Southwest Ridge. In April, Clint Helander and I flew onto the Big River Glacier in the remote Revelation Mountains. The previous year we had attempted an unclimbed 9,250' peak we called the Ice Pyramid (*AAJ 2009*) but were turned back by deteriorating weather after 18 pitches. In 2009, with the help of a Mugs Stump Award, Clint and I planned to finish our route on the southwest ridge.

We left base camp on May 2, with three days of food, and climbed 15 long pitches of unrelenting mixed terrain to a small alcove. Our second day dawned clear, and the crux came early and hard on stiff fingers and brittle ropes. The hours slid by in 12 pitches of mixed rock and snow, with a final 80° snow mantle to the summit. After topping out we made one rappel down the mountain's southern flank to scope future objectives in the Swift Valley. On a

Ice Pyramid's first ascent route, with the arrow showing the rappel to the south on the descent. *Clint Helander*

seemingly non-glaciated sub-summit we unroped and Clint punched into an 80' deep crevasse up to his chest. After extracting him and carefully stepping across the hole, we re-climbed our ropes and made several rappels down the ridge. An airy rock outcropping served as a cramped bivy, with half of our tent hung hammock-style over space.

The third morning dawned cold and gray, and we rappelled into a deep gash on the south side into the Swift Valley, rather than descend the extremely technical and unknown 2,500' west face. Streaks from rockfall and avalanches painted the gash's huge walls. Racing to get out of danger, we rapidly downclimbed unroped 2,000' of steep snow and ice. We found ourselves safe from the mountain, but one valley south of our skis and base camp. We needed to climb over the mountain's lower southwest ridge and ski the final 2,500' to base camp. A critical pass on the ridge, which we believed to have been used by Dave Roberts as part of his Butterfly Traverse in 1967 (*AAJ 1968*), proved more technical and dangerous than it had appeared.

Seth Holden nearing the summit ridge on the first ascent of Ice Pyramid. *Clint Helander*

Nasty avalanche conditions and zero visibility hindered us. Hungry and exhausted but relatively safe, we camped on the flat glacier. The next day, on wooden legs and fueled with the last of our hard candy, we tediously climbed over the pass, where only steep snow and a 70° cliff separated us from our skis. Four rappels (three on single-picket anchors) brought us to the Big River Glacier in a whiteout. We stumbled to find our skis, but in our base camp an hour later we enjoyed the best Cinco de Mayo fiesta ever. Southwest Ridge of Ice Pyramid, AK Grade IV+, 2,800'.

After several days rest, we further explored around the three main forks of the Big River Glacier and climbed a gigantic couloir on the west face of the Ice Pyramid. We climbed snow and ice up to 70° to the top of the couloir, which we called Cataclysmic Couloir, at about 9,000'. A gendarme-like ice feature blocked easy access to the upper ridge and without adequate ice protection we bailed.

Two days later we hiked 22 miles down the Big River to Rob Jones' lodge and flew out from there.

SETH HOLDEN

Snowcap Mountain, first ascent and clarification. A prominent rock peak with an unusual summit icecap, located between the upper forks of the Stony River, southeast of the nearby Revelation Mountains, is identified incorrectly on current topographic maps. The true Snowcap Mountain (ca 8,350') is unquestionably about three miles southwest of the summit, which has no permanent summit snow or ice, so named on these maps.

In 1928 geologist and topographer Stephen R. Capps completed the difficult wilderness trek from Cook Inlet across Merrill Pass to the Stony River. His precise report of this unexplored region clearly indicates the mountain's correct position, verified by my two expeditions to the region. The true Snowcap Mountain, its name and position marked on his map about 20 miles north-northeast of Two Lakes, is clearly visible from Capps' route along the river, while the summit named on the newer maps is not in sight.

May 21, 2008, dawned a glorious morning. Pilot Rob Jones had already landed Zach Shlosar, Richard Baranow, and me on a narrow, tumbling glacier to the east of true Snowcap. I

An aerial view of the true Snowcap Mountain, from the northeast. The route ascends the glacier tongue starting in the lower-right corner, and continuing near the peak's right skyline to the summit. *Fred Beckey*

had suffered a mysterious leg cramp and was resigned to remaining in camp, but my partners headed upslope, skiing near the right flank of the glacier until it was necessary to make a steep boot pack. Zach then led a section of vertical ice above a gaping bergschrund. The last portion of the glacier route involved cramponing a steep section, with the exposure of blue ice walls underneath. They navigated around two more 'schrunds, then completed the route to the virgin summit. The route climbs a strange corkscrew-shaped glacier that, from the summit, flows briefly northwest, then curves north, then broadens to the northeast down to our camp. After absorbing the spellbinding views of this remote portion of the range, one that included numerous difficult-appearing unclimbed peaks, they skied back to camp, sometimes roped while jumping impasses. Richard punched though a crevasse and somersaulted onto a steep slope, to highlight the descent.

FRED BECKEY, *AAC*

NEACOLA MOUNTAINS

First ascents and descents. In late April 2006 Dustin Schaad and I were dropped by ski plane near Glacier Fork [a.k.a. The Pitchfork Glacier, which drains to the Glacier Fork of the Tlikakila River]. Our pilot, Doug Brewer, knew of no one being flown into this spot before. Over two weeks in late April and early May, we explored ridges and couloirs surrounding our base camp. Although we weren't there to peak-bag, we topped out some impressive couloirs, ticking off a handful of 3,000–4,000' first ascents (climbed with crampons and axes) and descents (on skis). [Maps and photos at aaj.americanalpineclub.org]

DARON HUCK

First ascents and exploration. On April 21 Gerard van den Berg and I installed camp at the top of the Pitchfork glacial cirque [They initially reported being on the North Fork Glacier, but their maps and coordinates show the Pitchfork, which drains to the Glacier Fork of the Tlikakila River. The North Fork is a few miles southwest of the Pitchfork—Ed.], near Neacola Mountain (2,873m). The next day

Pacific Warrior, on Aguja Ulysses. *Curro González*

we prepared to explore the endless spectacular climbing and skiing, but a storm dropped two meters of snow, trapping us for six days. When the sun timidly emerged, the mountains were heavily loaded, so we headed toward summits that we felt were safer and had five good days. Peak and route names are ours, as we believe our ascents were all firsts:

Day 1. We climbed Pacific Warrior (360m, 6b [French] A2 M6 WI4) on the southwest face of Aguja Ulysses (2,150m, section 22 on Lake Clark (D1) map, N60°51'042/W153°20'846). From the Hill of Geese (so called for the constant migration of these birds, even in bad weath-

Puntas Rik (left) and Jimmy Boy. *Curro González*

Little Horses, on La M. *Curro González*

Curro González on Pacific Warrior. *Gerard van den Berg*

er), we approached via a ramp, up to 50°, for 150m to the foot of a narrow gully. In five pitches (210m), we climbed a mixed chimney/gully of ice, snow, and rock to the summit. We made a long rappel down the other side and downclimbed to our skis.

Days 2-3. Unstable conditions, so we descended the glacier for 15 miles to new targets. We established camp atop a side glacier, after ascending 600m on 30° slopes while pulling 80kg sleds.

Day 4. Day of fun: climbed several things, so we could ski virgin terrain. We also went up 600m (40° max) to a 2,250m col between two needles, which we climbed via their east faces. We called the left needle Punta Rik (60°, with a step of 4+ rock) and the right one Punta Jimmy Boy (60°, 3+ rock) (map section 35, N60°54'634/W153°7'575). Then we climbed the 800m southeast face of the cirque's highest mountain, with snow to 60° and three or more needles near the summit: Pico Jeanet (2,300m, map section 35, N60°54'880/W153°07'771). We descended on skis (EBA ski difficulty, similar to S3), with some downclimbing.

Day 5. Constant avalanches.

Day 6. With bad weather forecast and the Redoubt Volcano on the verge of erupting again, we decided to leave. But first we had to climb, full speed ahead. We climbed the south-southwest face of La M (2,100m, map section 31, N60°55'031/W153°05'136), calling our route Little Horses (300m, 5+ A2 WI3). A 250m snow-ice ramp (70° max), led to El Collado del Silencio. From there we first climbed the more difficult left needle, a 40m pitch at 5+ A2, and rappelled to the col. We then climbed the 50m right needle, about 6a A0. [Maps at aaj.americanalpineclub.org]

CURRO GONZÁLEZ, *Spain*

CHUGACH MOUNTAINS

Mt. Yukla, West Ridge. Rod Hancock and Stuart Parks climbed the Complete West Ridge of Yukla in 2004 for the first ascent, after quite a few local attempts (including a near miss by Charlie Sassara and Marty Schmidt during the winter of 1983-84). They completed the route, which gains 2,050m in elevation, in 11½ hours. I completed the second ascent and first solo (without really any beta) this August, in 11 hours. The route is huge but probably goes at IV 5.7.

SAMUEL JOHNSON, *AAC*

Toilsome Peak, first ascent; Worrisome Peak, northwest ridge. Ross Noffsinger, David Stchyrba, and I helicoptered with Pollux Aviation to a 5,500' saddle on the ridge northwest of Troublesome Glacier, in the western Chugach, on June 26. We scrambled a mile northeast to Peak 6,325' and found no summit cairn, though it's been previously ascended (southwest ridge and south face) by Jim Sayler and possibly others. We retraced our route and descended to 4,000' on Troublesome Glacier. From here we made the first ascent of Toilsome Peak (5,250'), via the chossy southern slopes, and the second ascent of Worrisome Peak (5,690'), via a new route (50° snow) up its northwest ridge. We descended Richard Baranow and Sam Pepper's 2005 southern route. We climbed back up to our landing site and moved camp to Blissful Lake (3,300') at the base of notorious Baleful Peak (7,990'). However, a summer storm had deposited several inches of snow and ice on the 5,000' 4th-class northeast ridge, turning us back at 6,300'. We hiked out to Eklutna Lake over the next two days.

DAVE HART, *AAC and Mountaineering Club of Alaska*

"Pass Out Peak," first ascent; "Far Out Peak," northwest slopes. On September 5 the two of us set out to attempt two western Chugach peaks we thought might be unclimbed. From Richard's home, we hiked up the North Fork of Eagle River and Twin Falls Creek before setting Camp 1 at Blue-Eyed Lake. The next day we crossed Thunder Creek, ascended to Blackout Pass, and crossed the Whiteout Glacier to establish Camp 2 at Whiteout Pass. On September 7 we traveled down the Whiteout Glacier and up a tributary glacier to the south to access Peak 5,940' (61.13652° N, 148.80742° W), some three miles east of Whiteout Peak. Finding no evidence of a previous ascent, Richard assigned the name "Pass Out Peak" in reference to his partner's state of fatigue. The ascent of the north ridge involved two pitches of ice and one pitch of exposed low-fifth-class rock. Due to our desire to avoid the substantial crevasse fields in the dark, on the descent we bivied 1,100' below the summit. The following morning we set out for Peak 5,750' (61.13894° N, 148.77698° W). We descended the glacier to the northwest of our objective to about 4,500', rounded a rock buttress, ascended the glacier to 5,600', and kicked steps in firm snow for the final 150'. We found a cairn on the summit. We don't know when the peak was

Far Out Peak (left) and Pass Out Peak, with the bivy site (X). *Richard Baranow*

first climbed or who first climbed it, but, for easy reference, rather than yet another Peak 5,750',
Richard suggested the name "Far Out Peak," because it was far out from his front door. We
returned to Camp 2 at Whiteout Pass late that evening and reached the trailhead two days later.
Not counting zigzagging through the numerous crevasse fields, we had traveled ca 52 miles
with ca 18,000' of elevation gain. The glaciers have receded tremendously from their positions
depicted on USGS maps. Additionally, the glaciers have thinned significantly, so that many
previously covered rock features are now evident at locations where the maps indicate only ice.

RICHARD BARANOW *and* STEVE GRUHN, *Mountaineering Club of Alaska*

ALASKA ST. ELIAS MOUNTAINS

Peak 9,365', first ascent and ski descent, and exploration. In April,
Tory Dugan, Jason Kwiatkowski, and I began a month-long kite-assisted ski expedition with a goal
of traveling from the Hubbard Glacier to the Miles Glacier, a distance
of nearly 200 miles. We skied many couloirs and features along our
route, the most notable on April 30, when we made what we believe to
be the first ascent and ski descent of

The northeast face of Peak 9,365'. The route of first ascent/descent
takes the sun/shade glacier line left of the rock ribs. *Ryan Hokanson*

Peak 9,365', approximately 12 miles west of Mt. Saint Elias. From the Bagley Icefield we climbed and skied the northeast face, with 2,000' of relief, numerous large crevasses, and névé snow to 60°. I cut a finger tendon with a pocketknife and had to be evacuated, but Jason and Tory completed the route to the Miles.

RYAN HOKANSON, *AAC*

Eastern Barnard and upper Tittmann Glacier, climbs and exploration. On May 3 Paul Claus flew us from the Ultima Thule Lodge to a 10,500' base camp at the head of the eastern branch of the Barnard Glacier, five miles south of Mt. Bear. We were Brad Gessner, Hans Neidig, Stuart Parks, Wayne Todd, Jeannie Wall, Carrie Wang, and I. Over the next seven days, our group summited several peaks:

Peak 12,382' ("Wetterhorn"), east ridge, new route (2nd peak ascent, entire party), AK grade 2.

Point 11,500', southwest slopes (entire party) and Peak 11,570', northeast slopes, first ascent (Hart-Wall; repeated by Gessner-Neidig-Parks-Todd-Wang), AK grade 1.

Peak 12,850', southwest ramp, new route (Gessner-Parks-Todd-Wang; repeated by Hart-Neidig-Wall), AK grade 1.

Peak 12,007', southwest slopes, first ascent (entire party, AK grade 2).

Peak 12,850', traverse via west ridge over Point 12,410' (5th ascent, Hart-Wall, new route, 13 pitches, 50° snow/ice).

Paul Claus, Ruedi Homberger, Christine Kopp, Peter Stadler, and Stefan Wyss had previously spent time in this area, making first ascents of Peak 12,382' in 1996 (Ruedi and Paul have clarified that this is the "13,000' border peak just south of Mt. Bear," as referenced on p.

Some of the first ascents and new routes on the eastern Barnard Glacier. *Dave Hart*

Pk 11,570'

Pk 11,500'

10,500'
base camp

More first ascents on the eastern Barnard Glacier. *Dave Hart*

185 of the 1997 *AAJ;* they called it "Wetterhorn.") and Peak 12,850' in 1994 (Claus solo).

On May 12 Jeannie, Wayne, Carrie, and I flew to a new base camp three miles south at 8,500' on the upper Tittmann Glacier, a spot where Paul Claus had not previously landed. We reached 11,000' on the southwest ridge of unclimbed Peak 11,610', before weather turned us back. Storms continued until Paul returned for us on May 17. Several more unclimbed peaks in this area beckon, including the challenging Peaks 11,610' and 11,050', the striking Peak 10,455', and walkup Peak 10,385'.

DAVE HART, *AAC and Mountaineering Club of Alaska*

Good Neighbor Peak, Southwest Spur, first alpine-style ascent. In the spring, Simon Yates and I did what we thought was the first ascent of the massive Southwest Spur of the South Summit of Mt. Vancouver (Good Neighbor Peak, 15,700') on the Alaska-Yukon border. The line is clearly visible in a Bradford Washburn photo published in the 1994 *AAJ,* p. 88—the prominent ridge left of the South Spur climbed by Diedrich and Pilling in 1993. We flew in from Haines and were dropped

Good Neighbor Peak, with the Southwest Spur on the skyline, and the South Spur (Diedrich-Pilling, 1993) the next spur to the right, in the center of the photo. *Paul Schweizer*

in a high glacial cirque on the Alaskan side, directly below the start of the route. We began climbing at dawn on April 29, soloing the 1,000' headwall at the back of the cirque to reach a col and get established on the ridge. Then we followed the line of least resistance—generally left of the ridge crest. We had perfect weather, and it took five days to reach the summit, with hidden ice runnels and surreal gargoyles near the top. The perfect weather broke during the descent, and we were stormbound on a high col, nearly out of food, on day 6. Day 7 dawned clear, and we continued down the east ridge to a side spur, which entailed a series of unpleasant rappels and a lengthy detour. We finally arrived back in base camp at 10:30 p.m. on day 7.

A subsequently unearthed Japanese article revealed that our route was the ridge climbed by a large Japanese expedition in 1968, starting from the Canadian side. They climbed the ridge expedition-style with a 10-member team, using fixed ropes and camps. Three of their team died in the process, and only two reached the summit, after 13 days on the mountain. So we actually did the second ascent, but first alpine-style, with a new start from the Alaskan side.

It's an excellent route, very long and committing. Done alpine-style, we reckon it warrants an alpine grade of ED, with climbing up to Scottish grade V ice and VI mixed, and an 8,000' vertical height gain.

PAUL SCHWEIZER, *Alpine Club*

FAIRWEATHER RANGE

Mt. Bertha, Northwest Ridge; Fifty Years of Alaskan Statehood, South Face. The Johns Hopkins Glacier is one of the major glaciers of the west arm of Glacier Bay, southeast Alaska, and is surrounded by major summits of the Fairweather Range, from Mt. Quincy Adams in the north to Mt. Crillon in the south. Thanks to the local knowledge and enthusiasm of our ski-plane pilot, Paul Swanstrom, in April Guy McKinnon and I became the first climbing party to access this glacier. The price was an inconvenient 2,000' descent, from the landing site on the west shoulder of Mt. Abbe to the 2,000' contour on the south arm of the glacier. A number of earlier parties had been thwarted by the broken tidewater area and, from the south

The first ascent line on Peak 8,599' ("Fifty Years of Alaskan Statehood"). *Paul Knott*

and east, by crevasse-strewn cols. The only previous climbs even overlooking the Hopkins Glacier appear to be those in the Mt. Abbe group by the 1977 Wickwire party. (The 1991 Gove-Pilling ascent of Mt. Abbe was on the north side, accessed from the inlet via a side glacier and overlooking Hopkins Inlet.)

Our aerial reconnaissance showed problems with icefalls and seracs on the approach and descent from our original objective, the long-coveted north ridge of Mt. Crillon. Instead, we took advantage of the stable forecast to tackle the unclimbed northwest ridge of Mt. Bertha (10,200'). Bradford Washburn's 1940 party was the first to climb Mt. Bertha, and the mountain had since received three more ascents, all from the Brady Glacier to the east. Four

The remote Mt. Abbe massif, with Peak 7,260' (presumably unclimbed) the obvious spire on the left, as seen from the Northwest Ridge of Mt. Bertha. *Paul Knott*

The Northwest Ridge of Mt. Bertha, from the Johns Hopkins Glacier. *Paul Knott*

miles long and rising 7,100' from the glacier, the undulating northwest ridge turned into a trial of stamina as we successively encountered unconsolidated winter powder, breakable melt-freeze crust, and compressible wind deposits. Long sections of ridge also featured typically exposed southeast Alaskan cornices. We reached the summit on our fourth climbing day, April 26, enjoying panoramic views from the expansive Brady Ice Cap to the mixed alpine faces of the Mt. Fairweather group. Our descent was rapid, down the same ridge.

After two days refueling our bodies at base camp, with continued good weather we tackled the striking unclimbed 8,599' peak that lies north of Mt. Crillon and east of Mt. Orville. Somewhat tongue-in-cheek, we propose the unofficial name "Fifty Years of Alaskan Statehood" for this peak, following an old Russian naming tradition. Taking the only amenable line we could see, we waded up isothermic snow on the shallow east rib. We stopped early at our second camp, at 7,560' in the bowl below the upper south face, and spent the day watching avalanches let loose on the face. Early on May 2 we crossed the bergschrund above the bowl and continued up the south face via a couloir and snowed-up rock rib to reach the summit in pre-dawn light. We left a three-foot trench as we descended the lower east rib through wet snow that was close to sliding.

With the sea-level pressure falling rapidly, we flew out on May 5, before bad weather set in. The next day, Juneau reverted from record high temperatures to cold, wet, and windy.

PAUL KNOTT, *New Zealand*

Knott has written a brief report on the history of attempts to access the John Hopkins Glacier, based on his extensive research for this trip. The report can be found at aaj.americanalpineclub.org

COAST MOUNTAINS

Mendenhall Towers; Main Tower, Iron Curtain; Tower 4, Resisting A Rest, and Resignation Arête.
Alaska has been called the Great White North and the Last Frontier, a land where tough, cold peaks are scaled by gruff, bold climbers. So why was I a thousand feet up a new route sweating through my T-shirt? Sun-burned eyes squinted through the white glare that reflected off glaciers, granite, and my shirtless partner. A thousand feet up a new route in the Mendenhall Towers, we couldn't believe it. Welcome to southeast Alaska!

In mid-July Jason Nelson, from Ouray, CO, joined me on a two-week trip to the Mendenhall and Taku Towers, 30km north of Juneau. We opted for the helicopter approach to the south side of the Mendenhalls on July 9 and began climbing on the 10th. In record-breaking heat we crossed the edge of the glacier, jumped the rapidly melting moat, and headed up the previously climbed Southeast Buttress of the Main Mendenhall Tower (IV 5.10), finding a

Iron Curtain (left) on the Main Mendenhall Tower, and Resisting A Rest (middle) and Resignation Arête on Tower 4. One previously existing route is thought visible in this photo: the Southeast Buttress of the Main Tower, starting left of the gully left of Iron Curtain. *Herrington/Nelson*

potentially new 5.10+ splitter headwall pitch to the north of the buttress crest. If this route were located anywhere accessible, it would have frequent traffic.

The morning of the 11th we began climbing "the Curtain," a previously untouched wall that spans the gap between the Main Tower and Tower 4, to the east. The Curtain is the longest, steepest section along the south face of the towers. After eight pitches of clean white granite on the left side of the Curtain, we topped out the wall and turned left. From here we followed vertical cracks and steps for five more pitches to the summit, establishing the Iron Curtain (IV+ 5.12a).

Jason Nelson leading a thin-hands splitter up the headwall on the Southeast Buttress of the Main Mendenhall Tower. *Blake Herrington*

Jason's crux lead pulled a thin-hands roof—something straight out of Indian Creek.

After and day of recon, we used consecutive periods of 20-hour daylight to establish two more routes. Resisting A Rest (IV 5.10+) follows a long corner system farther right on the Curtain, crosses a vertical chasm between two towers (one rappel), and finishes with three pitches on the west ridge of Tower 4. We dubbed our final climb the Resignation Arête in honor of Ms. Palin's sudden departure from the governor's mansion. It follows the distinct south arête of Tower 4 for 12 pitches, with a 5.11+ crux on the peak's headwall.

Two days of walking, skiing, rappelling, crevasse jumping, bushwhacking, and hitchhiking brought us back to the stormy Alaskan capital, where we accepted the generous hospitality of our friend Ryan Johnson. This trip would not have been possible without help from the AAC's Mountain Fellowship Grant.

BLAKE HERRINGTON, *AAC*

Burkett Needle: (1) South Pillar (Cauthorn-Collum-Foweraker, 1995), with (v) the 2009 Hasson-Holsten free variation. Not shown, on the steep face to the right, is the Heaton-Reichert 1995 attempt (see topo, *AAJ 1996*, p. 182) which ends high on what soon became the South Pillar; and Le Voyage des Clochards Celestes (Daudet-Foissac, 1999), which traverses into the face from the col on the right (the pillar rising east from the col is a sub-spire of Mt. Burkett). (2) Smash and Grab (Burdick-Frieh, 2009). *John Scurlock*

Stikine Ice Cap, new routes and first ascents. Climbing from the Baird Glacier's unnamed south arm ("Burkett Glacier" to climbers) in June, Max Hasson and Jens Holsten made several impressive ascents. They made a free ascent of Burkett Needle (ca 8,500') via a new variation (5.10+) to the 2,500' South Pillar (V 5.10 A3+, Cauthorn-Collum-Foweraker, 1995); did the first ascent of Silly Wizard Peak (ca 7,350') via the Thriller Arête (southwest arête, 3,000', 5.7X 50°); first ascent of the northwest ridge (3,000', 5.8 M4) of Mt. Suzanne (ca 7,190'); and a huge new route, National Public Ridge direct south ridge; 5,700', 5.10R AI3) on Mt. Burkett (9,730'). See Holsten's feature article earlier in this *Journal*.

Burkett Needle, Smash and Grab; Pipsqueak Peak, East Ridge. Three years ago Fred Beckey pulled out his little black book (actually a tattered FedEx envelope) and showed me a blown-out photocopy of the unclimbed west side of Burkett Needle. Of course, no tactical information could be gained from scrutinizing the fuzzy blobs and lines on the page, but it showed that half of an amazing peak on the Stikine Ice Cap remained overlooked. That summer Fred, Micah Lambeth, and I flew to Petersburg and then helicoptered in to the Burkett Boulder. During that trip Micah and I attempted the west ridge of the Needle and, on July 4, 2006, climbed the East Ridge (5.7) of a 6,700' pyramidal-shaped rock peak. This peak, which we dubbed Pipsqueak Peak, is situated on the left (west) side of the major col west of the Needle.

It took several summers for everything to align, but on July 3 John Frieh and I caught a helicopter flight with Wally from Temsco Air in to the Burkett Boulder. The weather was set to be absolutely gorgeous for at least the next two days. We quickly packed in the afternoon sun and hiked east a quarter-mile to the base of a ridge that allows access to the upper glacier under the Needle. We followed the scrambly ridge (3rd and 4th class) for 1,800' to a small, flat campsite on a knife-edge ridge. On the morning of the 4th we left camp and climbed the glacier to the base of the South Pillar (Cauthorn-Collum-Foweraker, 1995). From here we traversed on steep snow into a couloir that led to the col at the base of the unclimbed west ridge. One long mixed pitch (M4) got us onto the rock. From here we simul-climbed perfect granite along the crest for many enjoyable pitches (up to 5.8). Higher, we climbed two tricky mixed pitches (M4) to the top of the false summit, then made a short rappel to a col below the imposing summit pinnacle. A short knife-edge traverse with great exposure led to two more fantastic rock pitches, following cracks up and right toward the summit (5.6). A final pitch up an icy fist crack and the last dollop of snow led us to the summit. We rappelled the beautiful South Pillar route, touching down in the hot-pink glow of the setting sun.

We named our route Smash and Grab (IV 5.8 M4), after Dieter Klose's expression for climbers who smash into town and grab a summit before the Stikine's clouds realize what's happened.

DAVE BURDICK, *AAC*

Canada

ST. ELIAS RANGE

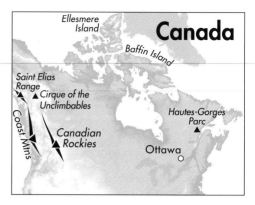

Stairway Glacier, probable first ascents. Jenny Foister, Pete McCombie, Glenn Wilks, and I spent three weeks on the Stairway Glacier in Kluane National Park, climbing nine probably unvisited peaks that varied from straightforward snow plods to technical ridges. [The area is shown in the upper right quadrant of the map on p. 220, *AAJ 2004.*]

May 20 dawned staggeringly bright, as we set off for a beautiful day's snow plodding that took us over three summits (N 60.31.14, W 139.04.58, 3,250m; N 60.32.24, W 139.04.48, 3,345m; and N 60.32.14, W 139.03.53, 3,330m). We crossed lynx tracks on the descent. Two days later we climbed two more peaks (N 60.31.14, W 139.05.29, 3,280m, and N 60.30.47, W 139.05.01, 3,385m), one with a fine slender summit ridge with spindrift pouring over its knife-edge crest.

We set off in clouds for our sixth peak, on our sixth day. It turned out well; the cloud lifted, and we had our first steep and sustained ice face and ridge. We popped out onto a satisfyingly small summit (N 60.30.03N, W 139.04.40, 3,482m), with a great-looking ridge stretching away across further peaks.

We then moved on to an impressive peak to the east, but twice retreated from the upper portions in terrible snow and absent protection.

We climbed three more excellent peaks, one (N 60.32.52, W 138.58.58, 3,250m) via great Scottish grade 2 mixed through tottering pinnacles and up gullies of melting snow. The hour's magnificent climb along the ridge to the top was worth the whole trip. Another (N 60.34.18, W 139.02.30, 3,410m) took us from the bottom up a sustained snow slope directly to the summit ridge. A thousand meters of steep snow and ice; airy and exposed, requiring a steady head on the way down. Our last climb took us to a great summit (N 60.34.08, W 138.57.06, 3,248m), but only after we dealt with bottomless snow on the glacier and during the ascent.

The weather was mostly good, with some days of snow and wind but no major storms. The avalanche danger became extreme toward the end. All of the routes we climbed and most visible faces slid during the heat of the last day, and we climbed at night.

MARK WEEDING, *U.K.*

LOGAN MOUNTAINS

Middle Huey Spire, Power of Silence; East Huey Spire, Riders on the Storm, first free ascent. After a long journey in mid-July, Lisi Steurer (Austria) and I arrived in one of the most beautiful and wildest rock-climbing areas in the world, the Cirque of the Unclimbables, in Nahanni National Park. It was real Canadian wilderness—hard to believe for Euros like us. The first days

The south face of Middle Huey Spire, with the Power of Silence (left) and the 1977 route. *Chris Atkinson*

we worked on the first free (redpoint) ascent of Riders on the Storm, on East Huey Spire, a 400m climb supposedly of Yosemite quality. The first pitch, a 5.9 offwidth, showed us how hard trad climbing can be. Later we enjoyed dihedrals and finger cracks, figuring out how finger- and hand-jamming is supposed to work. On our fourth day of effort, we redpointed the full route and yelled from the tiny summit.

Back at camp we visited neighbors from the U.S., who'd recently climbed Lotus Flower Tower. With them were two girls—their ground staff—cooking for their heroes. Food was well prepared. We thought about finding a boys ground staff for us, and suggested it to our friends Chris Atkinson and Marc Piche, who had invited us to the Cirque and were work-ing on photographs for a new book. They just laughed—absolutely not, stupid idea!

At 5 a.m. the next day we started climbing the classic Southeast Buttress of the Lotus Flower Tower by headlamp. The first 5.10 pitch took me a while, because of wet rock and fatigue. I was completely fucked and could not think about 17 more pitches, up to 5.10c, that day. But it got better. The day was sunny, not a cloud, and we felt so lucky and privileged. Climbing the headwall gave me a big, big smile. Perfect cracks and chickenheads, long pitches and fast climbing. Just before the top I dropped a climbing shoe and climbed the last pitch barefoot, but we reached the top at 2:30 p.m., nobody there, just me and Lisi and the immense scenery of the Mackenzie Mountains.

The next day we saw a beautiful crack system in a huge dihedral with huge roofs on the south face of Middle Huey Spire. The 400m face had just one route (5.9 A3), done by an Austrian team in 1977 (Kosy-Lackner-Weilguny), but the left side of the face—the most solid part, also the steepest—was untouched. After a thunderstorm, we started up again in sunny weather, followed by thousands of mosquitos. We began with the first two pitches of the Austrian line (one was an awkward, wet offwidth), before heading into our dihedral. The rock got steeper and solider. Excellent finger- and hand-cracks led to a face pitch. We were installing bolt anchors, but I had tried hard to avoid setting protection bolts. After I took an eight-meter whipper onto a small pecker, though, screaming and stopping next to Lisi, and after another try, I was ready to set a few bolts. In three days of work we finished our route, with some aid. We placed four protection bolts, enough for freeing the route. After a rest day we returned, and I redpointed every pitch. Power of Silence (11 pitches, 5.12+/5.13-).

Our fantastic three weeks were over, and we loaded our heavy packs. Chris had been kayaking the Nahanni River, and when we reached the lake he was waiting for us, with great tasting beers and chips and blueberries.

INES PAPERT, *Germany*

Coast Mountains

Southern Coast Mountains and Canadian Cascades. It's been a slow few years in the mountains of southwestern British Columbia. There is energy and talent concentrated in the Vancouver-Squamish-Whistler-Pemberton corridor, but the focus remains at Squamish. When these talented climbers focus on the alpine, it seems they go to established areas like the Waddington Range, the Bugaboos, the Adamants, and Patagonia, rather than hunting for new climbs closer to home.

First, a couple of older things that have recently come to light. In November 2008, on the left side of the north face of Dalton Dome, one of the summits of the Garibaldi massif, Damien Kelly and Trevor Hunt climbed a nice snow/frozen rock/gully line, avoiding trouble-some seracs and finishing near the summit. The line is 350m long and AI3. In August 2007 Kelly, with Derek Flett and Justin Cassels, climbed a difficult new route on the right edge of the north pillar of Mt. Joffre. The left edge of the pillar was climbed in 1995 by Rich Prohaska and Bruce Kay, at 5.10c, but the right side is steeper for longer. The 2007 climb began with a few easy pitches, soloed, then six roped pitches, up to 5.11c (400m, TD).

The 2009 season saw more failed attempts on the East Face route on Mt. Slesse. Put up in 1997 by Sean Easton and Dave Edgar, at ED2 VI 5.9 A3+, this climb remains unrepeated. In the mid-2000s Craig McGee, with various partners, worked on free-climbing it, redpointing the first seven pitches, at 5.12c, but failed to make further progress. Last summer Squamish hotshots Will Stanhope and Andrew Boyd retreated after a few pitches, spooked by poor rock, run-out climbing, tricky route finding. Next, Washington hardmen Colin Haley and Dylan Johnson tried, bailing after about seven pitches. Haley blogged that he thought it was the

The approximate line of the Easton-Edgar (1997; first two pitches hidden). See *AAJ 2003*, p. 258, for other routes on this side of the Slesse massif. *Drew Brayshaw*

hardest route in the Cascades.

Across the Nesakwatch Creek drainage from Mt. Slesse lies the Mt. Rexford massif, well-loved by local climbers for its solid granite. In late June, Jesse Mason, Marc-Andre Leclerc, and I took advantage of reopened logging roads on the east side of the massif to climb a new route on the subsidiary Nesakwatch Spires, following the buttress just right of the Priest-Coupe Couloir to the summit of the South Nesakwatch Spire. The line went at D-, III 5.9, with 10 pitches, mostly in the 5.7 range but with a couple of short, probably avoidable cruxes.

Finally, Mt. Robie Reid has a massive northeast wall rising 1,700m vertically to the summit ridge. The true face has one route, the awesome Pacemaker (ED1/2, VI 5.10a A1), established over eight days, on the third attempt, by John Black, Reinhard Fabische, and Chris Rowe in August 1998. Last September, Chris Geisler and Tony Richardson finally made the second ascent and first free ascent of Pacemaker. They walked in from the logging road in five hours and bivied near the base, then climbed

Pacemaker, on Robie Reid. *Scott Pick*

20-some pitches, with much simul-climbing and long runouts to mid-5.10, past bolt anchors destroyed or damaged by a 2007 rockfall, to the Ice Block Ledge bivy, near the edge of the rockfall scar. Geisler estimated it at 50' wide, 60' high, and 30' deep, creating a massive new roof to circumvent. The next morning they climbed another eight long or simul-climbing pitches to the top of the face (28 pitches total, vs. nearly 40 on the first ascent), descended the standard route, and were back at their car before dark, with the route going at ED1/2, VI 5.10R.

DREW BRAYSHAW, *Canada, AAC*

Mt. Desire, East Ridge. On July 17, with the support of the American Alpine Club and the McNeill-Nott Award, Brianna Hartzell, Eric Dalzell, Mike Pond, and I made our way to the Bella Coola Valley. Our objective was the unclimbed east ridge of Mt. Desire, 15 miles southeast. The brief glimpse we got of the route as the helicopter landed was our only beta. With a stellar forecast, the following morning we descended the crevassed glacier, downclimbed a 50° snow slope to a small band of rock, and climbed a ramp to the ridge proper. We began simul-climbing along the crest, occasionally pitching-out short sections of 5.7. We skirted an imposing gendarme to its north, returned to the ridge, and followed a beautiful knife-edge snow arête with amazing exposure.

Our first glimpse of the headwall gave us a collective sense of "Holy Shit!" As Mike and I studied the rock, we saw weaknesses and became enthusiastic. Brianna and Eric were less optimistic and descended, while Mike and I continued.

The East Ridge of Desire. *Matt Van Biene*

Mike and I descended into a notch in three rappels, bringing us to a rock bridge and the base of the headwall. We mostly simul-climbed, up 5.8. The climbing stayed engaging, the rock quality improved, and our position kept improving. The final section gradually steepened to just shy of vertical, with a final snow mushroom mantle. This was our introduction to first ascents (1,200', III+ 5.8), making for a special moment. We found a cairn on top, which we presumed was from John Clarke, who arrived in 1993 from the west and south [*CAJ 1994*, p. 78]. Our descent to the west began by a scramble down to a small col, then rappels down a steep snowfield and bergschrund, which put us within a hundred yards of our camp.

Mike and I climbed another two new routes, on unnamed peaks along the south ridge of Desire. Menergy Ridge ascends the west ridge of Gayle Needle (III 5.8, optional 5.9+ variation on summit block). The Wanderlust Traverse bags Wanderlust Peak (south of Gayle) via a three-pitch rock and snow climb (5.10) that gains the north ridge, climbs to the summit, then continues along the east ridge over two smaller peaks.

MATT VAN BIENE, *AAC*

Defiance, on the southeast face of Mt. Combatant. The initial prominent tower is the Incisor, home to two other routes: Belligerence (Child-Collum-Mascioli, 1994), to the left of Defiance, and Smoke Show (Furneaux-Maddaloni, 2004), to the right. Perseverance (Cusick-Kearney, 2000) climbs the next buttress to the left on Combatant, mostly out of view. All continue to Combatant's summit. The thin rib right of the Incisor, across the glaciated couloir, is Southwest Bartizans (Condon-Edwards, 2002) on Mt. Tiedemann. *Joshua Lavigne*

Mt. Combatant, Defiance. After warming up on über-classic Skywalk Buttress (600m, ED1 5.9) with my girlfriend Carlyle Norman and our friend Scott Everett, Craig McGee and I turned our attention to a line on the southeast face of Mt. Combatant, with hopes of establishing a free climb up the Incisor and continuing along the ridge to the summit.

On August 26 Craig and I climbed the lower portion of the Incisor, encountering steep technical climbing with multiple loose, run-out 5.11 pitches. The crux pitch had intricate thin crack climbing that required cleaning and two pins (the only gear we left). After the crux pitch we discovered several pins, probably from the route Belligerence. (We think we shared three or four pitches with it). After seven pitches of intricate, sustained climbing, we rappelled, fixing our two lines and leaving gear at the base.

Two days later we returned and quickly reached the crux pitch. After a couple of attempts and additional cleaning, Craig sent the pitch. However, the wall then steepened, with thin, bottoming cracks forcing us to resort to aid for 20m. After 15 sustained pitches, we found a comfortable bivy directly below the summit of the Incisor and fell asleep under a clear sky, with warm temperatures.

The next morning we continued along the Jawbone, a knife-edge ridge that connects the Incisor to the upper ridges of Mt. Combatant in eight chossy pitches. We exited this section after lunch and continued to the base of the Toothless Tower, where we stashed gear and simul-climbed a mostly independent line to the summit. (We descended the gully to the northwest of the Toothless Tower in eight rappels.) The rock on the Toothless Tower, in contrast to the Jawbone, was some of the most spectacular rock either Craig or I had ever touched; we padded our way up scooped dishes of bulletproof granite to the summit. After 20 hours of climbing, we sat on the summit enjoying the fruits of our labor: a warm breeze, a jaw-dropping view of Mt. Waddington, and a route to remember. Defiance (4,500', ED2 5.12 A3). Thanks to Mountain Equipment Co-op for making this trip possible.

JOSHUA LAVIGNE, *Canada*

Mt. Bute, School of Rock. In mid-August, Jimmy Martinello, Jay Sinnes, and I flew northwest out of Squamish for the head of Bute Inlet. Once there we transferred for a quick bump to the head of Galleon Creek, below the 6,000' west buttress of Mt Bute. The next morning saw us simuling and rope-stretching up a few spooky pitches of slab, aiming for a single corner system

Mt. Bute, with (1) the 50-pitch School of Rock (Kay-Martinello-Sinnes, 2009), and (2) West Face (Foweraker-Serl, 1986). The Northwest Buttress (Down-Fletcher, 1991) roughly takes the left skyline. Soon after the Foweraker-Serl ascent, starting just left and joining it at the first big ledge (where (2) traverses right), is the Beckey-Lewis-Nelson 1986 variation. *Jimmy Martinello*

breaching the lower wall. Numerous pitches put us at our first bivy with glorious views of the Waddington Range and down the Inlet.

Next morning Jay solved our lower crux with some tricky routefinding and mixed free and aid, putting us at a snow patch for rehydration and R&R. We really should have brought a few beers.

Then it was up and over Point Steffannie to bivy 2, below the upper buttress, which had largely been solved by Mike Down and Greg Foweraker on a previous attempt. The following day gave further spectacular granite ridge-climbing, until we tagged the summit in the evening light. We were finally caught by darkness on the descent, at Rat Terrace, where we spent the night in remarkable comfort though occasionally tormented by an enormous, prehistoric pack rat.

Next day we rapped the ridge and bailed down the huge slope below the West Face route (Foweraker-Serl, 1986). The west face is certainly one of the finest pure rock features in the Coast Range; it deserves a free ascent. Next day after consuming all consumables, we hammered our way out Galleon Creek, taking a vague but highly recommended trail located on the north side and traversing high above the creek. If you find it, stay on it at all costs!

A brief but tranquil evening, enjoying Chuck and Sharon's hospitality at Homathko Camp, was followed by a return flight to Squamish. It all happened so fast it seemed like a dream.

School of Rock (Complete West Buttress, 50 pitches, VI 5.11 A2), with much appreciation to the Mugs Stump Award and Mountain Equipment Co-op.

BRUCE KAY, *Canada*

Sendero Norte and Labyrinth, on the east face of Snowpatch Spire. Dots are belays (fixed on SN). *Jon Walsh*

BUGABOOS

Bugaboos, various ascents. On the next tower right of Fingerberry Tower (and bordering the Pigeon Feather access gully), in an August snowstorm Christophe Dumarest and Ben Rosenberg made the probable first ascent of the steep west face, via the Tiffen Route (6 pitches, 5.10 A2). They propose naming the formation in honor of recently departed friends: Lost Friends Pinnacle.

Desnivel.com reported that Martin and Florian Riegler established the Flying Penguin (300m, 5.12b A3), in the middle of the south face of a tower in the Pigeon Feathers. The tower, between Fingerberry Tower and Lost Feather Pinnacle, was dubbed Snaffle Puss Pillar by Nick Martino and Renan Ozturk after their likely first ascent in 2003, via Ride the Snafflehound (6 pitches, 5.10a), which takes the left side of the tower.

Jason Kruk, Matt Segal, and Will Stanhope made the FFA of the west face of Central Howser Tower, via the North Vancouver/Miami variation to Chocolate Fudge Brownie (Isaac-Webster, 1999), at V 5.12+. With Hazel Findlay, they also made a strong attempt at the coveted FFA of Sendero Norte, on Snowpatch Spire, established and nearly freed in 2006–08 by Chris Brazeau and Jon Walsh. The FFA eventually fell to Stanhope at V 5.12+.

Snowpatch Spire, Labyrinth. Jon Simms and I spent three-and-a-half days, over two weekends in August, establishing a 14-pitch route on the 600m east face of Snowpatch Spire. Tricky routefinding (hence the name Labyrinth) and crack-gardening kept us busy on the lower half the first weekend. The following weekend, on day one we reclimbed the first seven pitches, with our previous cleaning efforts making the pitches sendable and more enjoyable. On pitch seven, we hand-drilled three bolts and fixed three knifeblades, to protect the bouldery moves through the roof. We then sent the pitch and made two rappels to a good bivy ledge. The next day we joined the 1977 Brayshaw-Parker route for the last five pitches. We climbed the face in 14 pitches, plus a couple of 4th-class ropelengths along the summit ridge to the north summit. Two pitches clock in at 5.12-, four at 5.11, and the rest are 5.10, making Labyrinth a good moderate by east face standards.

JON WALSH, *Canada*

CANADIAN ROCKIES

Canadian Rockies, summary. The most notable ascent of the otherwise quiet Canadian Rockies summer, despite a noteworthy succession of cloudless days, came in early August, when J Mills and Dana Ruddy slogged over Woolley Shoulder and sent the Lowe-Glidden on the north face of Mt. Alberta. The route has lost little of its reputation since its 1972 first ascent, and has likely been climbed fewer than ten times. Mills and Ruddy confidently set out from the hut below the east face, made the first one-day ascent of the route, and returned to the hut after a 30-hour roundtrip. They also nearly nabbed the first free ascent, with only a few hangs on the crux A2/3 pitch (5.10 A0).

Last winter (2009-10) a small crew of dedicated locals made essentially all the bigger sends of the season. Tool-swinging got off to a good start in late October with the first ascent of Facile Monster (420m, M5 WI5) by Mills, Steve Holeczi, and Eamonn Walsh. The route is tucked away in a remote drainage behind Mt. Murchison, and its ascent owes much to Mills' encyclopedic knowledge of the mountains around the Saskatchewan River Crossing.

Mills and Walsh continued the charge, in January 2010 making the second ascent and first

Tangle Ridge's new routes (all are independent), from left: Undertow, Can't Touch This, and Boobquake. *Raphael Slawinski* free ascent of rarely formed Suntori (1,500m elevation gain from road, discontinuous climbing and approach steps, M7 WI6), a striking ice line on the massive south face of Mt. Wilson. In February, Walsh and I climbed the parallel line Living in Paradise (1,500m elevation gain from road, WI6+), continuing from the end of the water-ice pitches up snow and mixed ground to the summit ridge, making likely the first integral ascent of the route. Among Walsh's many other winter alpine ventures, in January he and Rob Smith made possibly the first winter ascent of Mt. Fryatt, via the Southwest Face.

Around the corner from the classic Curtain Call, climbers were lured by big unclimbed ice lines on the northeast side of Tangle Ridge. It was not until April, though, that Holeczi, Mills, and Mike Verway found the right combination of gumption and conditions and plucked the plum of the cliff, Undertow (600m, WI6). The route, with a long approach and endless succession of largely moderate but excellent pitches, received several repeats that confirmed it as one of the finest ice routes in the range. Walsh and I were then drawn to a less-obvious line to the right, resulting in Boobquake (600m, WI4+ M5). We returned the following weekend, finding Can't Touch This (600m, WI5+ M6) between Undertow and Boobquake. Who would have thought there would still be big unclimbed ice easily seen from the road? Those are the Canadian Rockies for you, a big range with still plenty of potential.

RAPHAEL SLAWINSKI, *Canada, AAC*

BAFFIN ISLAND

Broad Peak, North Face; Beluga Spire, attempt. Baffin is a landscape of frozen fjords, exotic wildlife, massive big walls, and sea ice as far as the eye can see. I went to the island in early April and did not leave until the second week in June, having the experience of a lifetime along the way.

I took the full arsenal of toys—big-wall and alpine climbing gear, ski-touring equipment, and enough food and fuel for a few months. My outfitter dropped me in the Walker Arm of the Sam Ford area, in a climber's and skier's paradise. I set up base camp in a central location, at the foot of the impressive Polar Sun Spire. I climbed or skied almost every day, despite -30° temperatures. The skiing was great, with an abundance of couloirs and chutes that had a deep layer of powder. I also made forays into other fjords, sometimes traveling 35 miles at a time. On

The unclimbed north face of Beluga Spire, with Turner's attempt. *Dave Turner*

windy days I would kite-ski across sea ice, being pulled at 40mph!

Once the temps rose in early May, I started climbing. The biggest unclimbed wall in the area is the north face of Beluga Spire, situated between Polar Sun Spire and the Walker Citadel. The 1,400m monster had been BASE jumped, but never climbed. I slimmed my gear to a minimum, leaving portaledge, bolts, static rope, and partner (obviously). After three days of climbing, I retreated from halfway, due to cold affecting my toes, which I'd frostbitten a few weeks earlier while ski-mountaineering.

I tried Beluga again a few days later, going even lighter—no second rope, haulbag, or anything extra—but got shut down again by my toes.

The new route on the north face of Broad Peak. *Dave Turner*

I switched objectives to a new route on the north face of Broad Peak, a 1,400m rock and mixed giant. I knew I could do it if I brought all the big-wall gear, but I wanted to continue my light-and-fast strategy and try a continuous ascent. I took one 70m rope, my one-man tent, and food and fuel for 48 hours. I spent 39 non-stop hours on the ascent, taking advantage of the 24-hour Arctic sunshine to keep going without a bivy. The line was beautiful—a few pitches of mixed to get onto a spur, then a difficult knife-edge arête that led to an easier hanging snow-field, the 400m crux headwall (5.10 A3), and a super-rad ice arête to the summit. It was one of my biggest climbs, set in the most beautiful area I have seen.

By the beginning of June it was time to go home, and my Inuit friend came to get me. But not before I got to see polar bears, seals, caribou, foxes, crazy big walls, super couloirs, virgin peaks, and so much more than words can describe.

DAVE TURNER, *AAC*

Mt. Asgard, South Tower, South Face; North Tower, East Face; and other activity. Chris Brazeau and I spent four weeks in Auyittuq National Park, climbing the granite walls and ridges of the Weasel Valley. We left home with inspiring photos, vague beta, and a lot of excitement. In the fishing village of Pangnirtung in early July, we met Belgian friends and hired a boat to take us to the trailhead at the end of the fjord. Our main goal was to climb beautiful Mt. Asgard, which requires a 42km

The South Face route on Asgard's South Tower. *Jon Walsh*

approach. As the Weasel Valley is stacked with amazing mountains, the objectives along the way were plentiful and the views always mind-blowing.

Of our 28 days in the park, we spent seven climbing, 11 schlepping loads, and 10 resting. We did our routes in light, clean style, trying to find challenging, aesthetic lines. Our two most significant climbing achievements were:

Asgard's South Tower, South Face (600m, 5.12-). We thought we were on a new route until we found a bolt at the crux, on the second-to-last pitch. Not sure, but we probably climbed 50% new terrain and 50% the Italian Route. After 300m of 4th-classing, we continued with nine amazing 60m pitches of mostly 5.10, except for the 5.12- crux pitch. It was probably the first free ascent of the South Tower, taking 16 hours roundtrip from a camp alongside the Caribou Glacier.

Chris Brazeau on a repeat of Stories in Stone, Mt. Walle, Baffin Island. *Jon Walsh*

Asgard's North Tower, Northeast Face (800m, 5.11+ C1). Hard to say whether the first half had been climbed, but we climbed about 10 nice pitches, up to 5.11-, to the headwall. We then followed an obvious crack system, to the right of Line of Credit, that provided the highlight of the trip. Eight 60m pitches, six of which were 5.11 and often involved run-out, delicate face climbing that linked cracks, on some of the best quality stone we've ever touched. Wet rock forced us right near the top, and one body-length didn't go free due to wetness. Probably 5.12- free, but we onsighted the rest of the headwall. The Favresse brothers repeated the first two-thirds of the headwall, and drier conditions permitted a more direct finish. Camp-to-camp took us 22½ hours, with at least two hours of approaching.

We also repeated the Scott Route (5.11-) on Asgard's North Tower and the South Ridge (5.8) of Mt. Thor, both classics; the 600m South Ridge of Mt. Menhir (Salvaterra's route; perfect rock, of similar character to the Northeast Ridge of Bugaboo Spire), with 5.10 variations; and Stories in Stone (600m, 5.12- A0) on Mt. Walle, a sustained 16 pitches with bolted belays, one of the best routes either of us has climbed. It's a physical route, with chimneys and offwidths on an amazing red pillar; it required our biggest effort, taking 25 hours camp-to-camp.

On Mt. Tirokwa's west face we attempted a new route to the left of Chocolate Boomerang [see below], climbing about 400m out of 700m, before run-out face climbing shut us down. This could be a great route, but a couple of bolts seem necessary to pass an obvious white rock scar.

The expedition unfolded smoothly, we had a great time, and the weather was great. We climbed more than we anticipated, and the adventure was everything that we hoped it would be. Thanks to Arc'teryx for helping make this trip possible.

JON WALSH, *Canada*

Chocolate Boomerang, on Mt. Tirokwa. *Nicolas Favresse*

Mt. Tirokwa, Chocolate Boomerang; Mt. Odin, Le Bic Rouge de Odin; Mt. Asgard, South Tower, the Belgarian; North Tower, Whisky Gonzales. Over 45 days from early July through mid-August, Sean Villanueva, Stephane Hanssens, Olivier Favresse, and I had an awesome trip to Baffin Island. We hiked ca 600km, ferrying loads for only two weeks of climbing; it seems ridiculous, but the climbing and the place is so unique and amazing, and the potential for free-climbing and first ascents seems endless. All along the way to Mt. Asgard we found innumerable boulders, with perfect soft tundra landings, to keep us in shape.

Expert aid-climbing soloist Silvia Vidal, from Catalonia, traveled with us. She originally planned to solo a wall and then trek, but when she arrived at the base of her objective she didn't feel motivated, so we invited her to join us. We figured we free-climbers could learn from her aid skills. Plus, she had a portaledge, which was nice since we'd taken just one portaledge and two hammocks to be lighter. Now only one of us would have to sleep in a hammock.

As we hiked up the Weasel Valley, many walls appeared. After a few days of hard hiking, we had to climb something. We split into two teams and went for it. Sean and Steph most likely made the first ascent of the northwest buttress of Tirokwa, to its main summit, by putting up Chocolate Boomerang (700m, 5.11) in a 24-hour push camp-to-camp. The line was previously attempted by Australians; the rock is excellent, with thin climbing and run-out sections. Meanwhile, my brother Olivier and I went for a virgin tower detached from Mt. Odin. We climbed the most obvious feature, up the prow, in an onsight push, likely making the first ascent of the spire, via Le Bic Rouge de Odin (800m, 20 pitches, 5.10).

Le Bic Rouge de Odin.
Nicolas Favresse

With a bit of climbing in, we felt better ferrying loads to the base of our main target, Mt. Asgard. After a reconnaissance of two established aid routes, Inukshuk on the North Tower and the Bavarian Route on the west face of the South Tower, we attempted to free-climb the latter.

The climbing was excellent and sustained, with a bunch of pitches in the 5.12–5.13 range. After 11 days on the wall, dividing the hard leads among us, we almost succeeded in freeing a line. But ice has melted since the first ascent, in 1996, leaving the route's original start 15m above the ground, and now the route has a new first pitch, on blank rock. After a failed attempt to free-climb it ground-up, we sent Silvia up with her babies (copperheads, hooks, and other funky tools) to solve what turned out to be "a really nice A4+," in her words. For the rest of us, the groundfall potential of hanging on a #1 copperhead seemed nasty. We had to headpoint that pitch, and it went free at 5.12X or E8. Most of the harder pitches had to be redpointed and a few headpointed, to avoid adding bolts. The rock and the climbing were outstanding.

The west face of Asgard's South Tower, with the original Bavarian Route (stroked line) and the Belgarian variations. *Nicolas Favresse*

Most of the pitches were splitter cracks, combined with hard face-climbing joining one crack to another. On pitch 7 I couldn't link a one-meter section. I did all the moves, so the route should go free, probably at a minimum of 5.13+. It was just a bit too hard for us, especially after all the hiking, so we had to use a move of aid. We should also mention that we redpointed some other pitches after we reached the summit.

In order to free-climb, we made many variations, and almost half of the route is new. We called our variation the Belgarian (850m, 5.13 A1) to recognize the joint effort of Bavarians and Belgians. We must say, though, that the original ascent wasn't done in best style, with many bat-hook holes, rivet ladders, and a few bolts next to perfect cracks.

Asgard's North Tower, stroked line showing Northeast Face (Brazeau-Walsh, 2009), black line Whisky Gonzales (Favresse-Favresse, 2009). *Nicolas Favresse*

After a few days of recovery and jamming with accordion, mandolin, tin whistle, harmonica, and drums, we set off for the North Tower, to climb it in alpine style. Sean and Stephane repeated the Porter Route (5.12 A4) in 24 hours. They onsighted all but three pitches, which they say would go free with a bit of work.

Olivier and I created a new line, we believe, on the northeast face of the North Tower. Our line, Whisky Gonzales, follows classic Yosemite-like splitters, and the quality is amazing. Both of us freed it onsight, in about 24 hours. The upper middle part shares pitches with the Brazeau-Walsh line. The climb is very sustained in the 5.10–5.11 range, and the climbing is sometimes delicate, with runouts on faces between cracks.

We had an awesome time climbing on Baffin. The weather was great, with comfortable temperatures and almost no precipitation. In summer there are no nights on Baffin, so it's great for long alpine pushes—we never used headlamps. We definitely have to go back. The future of big-wall free-climbing is there.

NICOLAS FAVRESSE, *Belgium, AAC*

NEWFOUNDLAND AND LABRADOR

Chaleur Bay, new routes and exploration. Janet Bergman, Kirsten Kremer, and I loaded my 1991 Toyota van with two-and-a-half weeks of food and climbing gear and drove for 15 hours from New Hampshire to the tip of Nova Scotia, making the overnight ferry to Newfoundland with less than 30 minutes to spare. The boat had eight floors and accommodated over a hundred vehicles, even tractor trailers. Lucky for us, there was also a bar.

Another ferry got us to François, population 113, a remote fishing village that dates to the 1700s. The next morning George Durnford and George Fudge, captain of the intrepid *Royal Oak*, took us on a boat tour of the cliffs. The Georges dropped us on a small beach in Chaleur Bay, the only fjord in the region that had not yet been explored by climbers. Two miles of unclimbed granite cliffs stretched before us.

For the next two weeks of September, we paddled around the fjord in a little plastic rowboat, crawled up 50° slopes of fern and moss, climbed gorgeous, virgin cracks and crumbly, flaky horror-shows, and ate tons and tons of wild blueberries. We established three new routes—Billfish Dihedral (800', 5.10+), on Chaleur Blow Me Down; an unnamed 400' 5.10+ on St. Ilian's (St. Elias), in Rencontre Bay; and Squid Cracks (400', 5.10+), on an unnamed wall in Chaleur Bay. We left one unfinished line, a 500' 5.11 left of Billfish Dihedral. The rock was unbelievably climbable; we sent our routes onsight and free. And the famous Newfoundland weather? Well, a storm did come, the last day. The ferry bucked and swayed in the surf as we pulled out of François into the open Atlantic.

SARAH GARLICK, *AAC*

Looking west from base camp in the English Mountains. The tallest visible cliffs rise ~1,300' vertical. *Michael Lederer*

English Mountains, M & M Ridge. In early spring fellow New York Section-AAC member Mike Barker and I explored this low subarctic range that comprises the easternmost and highest part of the Mealy Mountains, protected as part of the Mealy Mountains National Park Reserve. They reach elevations of approximately 4,000', with bare alpine summits, and are flanked by cliffs of clean anorthosite and granite. The English Mountains have no record of technical climbing.

M & M Ridge. *Mike Barker*

On March 27 we traveled by turbine single-Otter ski plane from Goose Bay to a dramatic cirque at N53.626° W58.506°, where we established a base camp for a week. Several harsh, extended arctic windstorms hampered our climbing. However, we had a sufficient break in the weather to climb the snow and rock ridge (M & M Ridge: the ice melts in your mouth *and* in your hands) that rose north-northwest from our base camp. It took three days to figure out, due to complex routefinding, but on day three we climbed a 1,300' vertical route that bypassed four cliff bands, with scrambling over moderate rock and variable snow, and put us onto exposed snow slopes up to 60°, before the long, flat walk to the summit.

The English Mountains have lots of untapped climbing and winter sports potential. There were abundant continuous, fully formed water-ice falls and steep, narrow, firm snow chutes, some in excess of 2,000' vertical, on stable, featured rock, much of it clean granite. We saw almost no evidence of rockfall or avalanches. There were also lots of possibilities for skiing. Scenically, this truly wild area struck me as a cross between a lower-elevation Baffin and an inland Norwegian fjord, with some granite faces reminiscent of the southern Columbia Mountains of British Columbia. All of this in an area about the same air distance from midtown Manhattan as Miami Beach.

We thank the AAC-New York Section for giving us the honor of carrying its expedition flag. We are also grateful to Big Agnes for their support, and to AAC-NY Section member Martin Torresquintero, our communications coordinator, duct tape consultant, and weatherman.

Michael Lederer, *AAC*

Greenland

WEST COAST

Uumannaaq Fjord, several routes. In summer 2009 Giovanni Cristofori and Cristina Rapisardi decided to spend time on the west coast of Greenland. They own an ocean-going yacht, *Billy Budd,* and Christina likes to climb. In 2006 we put up new routes on the northeast coast of Baffin Island, operating from the yacht. The plan was for Christina and Giovanni to sail up the Greenland coast to Aasiaat, where fellow guide Daniele Bernasconi and I would join them in mid-July for two weeks of exploration around the fjord of Uumannaaq, farther north.

The weather was on our side; there was no fog or cold. We could sail without heavy clothing, see icebergs, and climb in T-shirts.

On Adgap Island Christina, Daniele, and I opened an 11-pitch, 520m rock route using only traditional protection. Three pitches were 6a and the rest 5b-5c. We named the route Pavlova, in honor of excellent

White Seagulls and descent route, on Qingussaq Island. *Michele Maggioni*

cake eaten the previous night, and walked down the opposite side of the island to be collected by boat. At the top of the route our GPS gave a reading N 70°52.122', W 51°40.104'.

On Qingussaq Island we opened another rock route, this one of 10 pitches (400m), up to 5c. Again, we used only traditional protection, naming the route White Seagulls. (The face was full of them.) At the top the GPS read N 71°23.569', W 53°04.219'. We descended the east flank of the island, using a ledge system that required difficult route-finding. We needed a rope to downclimb the last section to the shore.

Finally, on Qioqe Peninsula Daniele and I climbed Peak 1,831m

Pavlova, on Adgap Island. *Michele Maggioni*

West side of Peak 1,831m, on Qioqe Peninsula.
Michele Maggioni

(N 71°11.726', W 52°27.317') from the south coast. We believe this is the peak climbed by Kurt Diemberger's seven-member expedition in 1971, but from the opposite side. We followed moraine, ice, and finally a rock ridge, using ice axe and crampons but no rope. From the summit we could see many fine unclimbed objectives on the Alfred Wegener Peninsula and the island of Upernavik O.

MICHELE MAGGIONI, *Italy*

Akuliarusinguaq Peninsula, various ascents; Sortehul Fjord, Old Man's Benefit; Northumberland Island, traverse and various ascents. I've now made five Tilman-type expeditions to Greenland. The latest, in summer 2009, involved sailing my Westerly 10m Discus from Scotland across the Atlantic and up the west coast of Greenland, calling at various locations to make first ascents from the boat. Our first venue was the Akuliarusinguaq Peninsula (N 71°50', W 52°50'), where we enjoyed spectacular successes and failures. I had explored this region on several previous expeditions, but a number of difficult-to-access 2,000m peaks remained unclimbed. These provided our initial objectives.

We failed. On the first, north of the anchorage at Puartdlarsivik, we were beaten by distance. With just three climbers available at any one time, the logistics of getting gear up a huge icefall and a long crevassed glacier proved impracticable. On the second, approached from Nugatsiaaq Tunua in the south, we climbed boulder fields and a long glacier to a bivouac.

Agparssuit (540m) guards southern entrance to Sortehul Fjord, on southeastern side of large Qaesopssuaq Island. Close to here is Iterdlagssuaq and the route Old Man's Benefit. At west end of Qaesopssuaq lies Sanderson's Hope (1,042m), a famous headland with two big wall routes 800m high (see photo *AAJ 2001*). *Bob Shepton*

Tom Howard (left) and Bob Shepton during failed attempt to reach a 2,000m summit on Akuliarusinguaq Peninsula. Immediately behind (right) is Peak 2,060m, climbed in 1998 by Shepton and Danuska Rycerz. Karat Fjord lies beyond, with the island of Upernavik O, Wegener Peninsula, and Qioqe Fjord behind first line of mountains. Shepton was awarded his second Tilman Medal for this 2009 sailing expedition. *Thomas Gough - Bob Shepton Collection.*

The next day we pushed on up a long snow shoulder to Solo Snow Dome, a peak I had climbed in 2004 (solo, because my partner would not come up for a second attempt). Our peaks lay well beyond this, and weariness, lack of stove and food, and the distance over a thin connecting ridge defeated us. However, we established that Solo Snow Dome was 2,090m and not 2,060m, as I had previously recorded. Before returning, we climbed a small subsidiary peak of 2,060m on a shoulder to the west of Solo Snow Dome.

Chastened, we retired to the southwestern end of the peninsula, which we had not previously explored. We found a cirque of peaks around a glacier flowing north. Mike Bowley and Tom Howard climbed all six main summits, the highest the pleasing Snow Dome SW (1,598m, N 71°43.416', W 53°06.636'). I climbed four peaks on the ridge running southwest from the head of the cirque and two minor gendarmes. The highest was 1,311m. We climbed 10 virgin peaks (and two minor points), so honor was satisfied.

We sailed north to Sortehul Fjord, close to Upernavik (N 72°40', W 55°59'). Most rock climbs in this area are big walls and serious under-

Unclimbed rock walls on east side of Upernavik O. *Bob Shepton*

takings. However, at Iterdlagssuaq, at the southern end of the fjord, a "day" cliff gives routes of 200m on good rock and in sunshine. It is accessed from a beach, rather than requiring one to climb directly onto the rock from a dinghy. There was only one previous route, climbed in 2006 by Italians Gianni Predan and Cristina Rapisardi. Tom and I added Old Man's Benefit (British HVS 5a, 200m, eight pitches), which took the central of three corner grooves on the main face, finishing up with a chimney-groove (the crux). Guess who the old man was? I'm glad to say there is still scope here for the under-70s.

The main goal of the expedition was exploration and ascents on Northumberland Island, at N 77°25', W 72°00'. Tom Howard and Andy Prosser completed a two-day, technically difficult ski-mountaineering traverse across most of the spine, making first ascents of six peaks. The journey involved steep descents, an uncomfortable bivouac, and big crevasses.

As Tom reported, "We landed by dinghy and were soon on glacier. Our first summit was Peak 1,030m, which gave a steep run on excellent snow down the far side. Skins were replaced for a straightforward ascent of Peak 827m. We avoided a third summit and bivouacked in a boulder field, unable to erect the tent. Next day, August 21, we returned to make a quick ascent of the third summit (930m) and then faced a horrendous crossing of gravel and boulder fields, carrying our skis. From the top of our fourth summit, Peak 1,000m, we rapidly reached our fifth (950m) and sixth (also 950m). We continued to the top of Sermiarssugssuaq Glacier, which gave a crevasse-jumping descent, finishing with Cairngorm skiing over ice, mud, and mogul fields. After a never-ending slog on a terminal moraine, we pitched camp on the shore, only to be disturbed at 3 a.m. when Andy realized we were about to drown in the rising tide. Next morning the boat made its way through ice floes to collect us."

In the meantime Mike and I made the first ascent of Peak 900m, situated on Josephine Headland; Peary's winter camp, where his wife Josephine joined him, was visible on the mainland opposite. Later Mike made the first ascent of Peak 930m on the southern side of the island. Andy and Tom repeated this ascent on skis. Finally Mike, Thomas Gough, and I climbed Peak 1,010m, which had been unreachable from the ski traverse. This completed ascents of most peaks on the island, including the highest.

Before returning we continued a little farther north to set up an automatic weather station on Littleton Island in Smith Sound/Nares Strait. The Scottish Association of Marine Science and the Danish Space Agency are now using it as part of their research into arctic weather and the flow of ice down the Strait from the Arctic Ocean. We sailed back along the west coast as far as Aasiaat, where I left the boat for the winter.

BOB SHEPTON, *Alpine Club*

EAST GREENLAND

LIVERPOOL LAND

Lillefjord, Peak 710m, The Last Inuit; Peak 715m, King of His Lost Empire-Nanoq. In April, Anna Boldinger and I planned first ascents in the Sylfjeldene region of Liverpool Land, 35km north of Ittoqqortoormiit. In general the rock throughout Liverpool Land is rotten and loose, the best possibility for steep climbing is on mixed terrain, and to find good conditions requires visiting the area in April and May, when it is really cold (-20°C). In July and August there is no ice on the steep walls, only rotten rock, with the risk of stonefall. Our idea was to reach the region using

Peak 710m from southwest. The Last Inuit climbs rock pillar immediately left of central couloir. *Ed Birnbacker.*

dog sledges and a local hunter, and ski back on our own to Ittoqqortoormiit pulling pulks.

When we arrived at Ittoqqortoomiit, the weather had been bad for a week, and there was a meter of fresh snow. We had to wait a week for fine weather, but the forecast only guaranteed a good spell for five or six days. Because of the deep snow and lack of time, we opted for the nearer region of Lillefjord, south of Heywood Berge, only 20km to the north. We climbed two peaks, which we think may have been previously untrodden. Daytime temperatures were -15°C, and we found tricky conditions, with some danger of avalanche.

Peak 715m and (right) Peak 770m from north. King of His Lost Empire-Nanoq climbs rocky ridge immediately left of broad central couloir to east ridge, then follows crest on rock and snow up right to summit. *Ed Birnbacker*

Our first route was on Peak 710m, which lies northwest of Peak 770m on the east side of the southern part of Lillefjord. Peak 770m is marked on the 1:250,000 map, and in reality Peak 710m is simply a subsidiary summit. We climbed it by the pillar on the west face left of the central couloir. The 500m-high route, which we named the Last Inuit, had 60-75° ice/snow, pitches of M6, and few pure rock sections of UIAA V+. From the summit we rappeled and down-climbed the route, leaving only a few pitons.

Our second route was the north pillar and east ridge of Peak 715m, directly east of another Peak 770m (also marked on the map) on the west side of the southern part of Lillefjord. We named the line King of His Lost Empire-Nanoq. It was

Ed Birnbacker on King of His Lost Empire-Nanoq, Peak 715m. *Anna Boldinger*

600m high, 400m of which were on the pillar. The difficulties were M4/M5 UIAA V 55-70° snow/ice. We rappeled and down-climbed the east ridge.

EDUARD BIRNBACKER, *Germany*

REN LAND

Southeast Ren Land, Cenotaph, McDonnell Peak, Small Lion. Inspired by pictures from an expedition in 2007 led by Dick Griffiths and reported in *AAJ 2008*, four of us from the Netherlands, supported by the Dutch Alpine Club, visited Southeast Ren Land from August 8-30, operating from a base camp at the head of Skillebugt Inlet.

Niek de Jonge and Jelle Staleman planned to make alpine-style first ascents, their main goal being a 900m-high loose standing pillar named the Cenotaph, a photo of which had appeared in the *AAJ* report. Gerke Hoekstra and I hoped to make the first ascent, in big-wall style, of the main Shark's Tooth [The Shark's Teeth lie above the Shark's Teeth Glacier, which flows north into the Edward Bailey. This glacier was visited and the Teeth photographed by a British team in 2008: see *AAJ 2009*].

The Cenotaph from the east showing (1) de Jonge-Staleman attempt (UIAA VII, 600m), (2) Controversy (UIAA VII, 900m), and (3) First Ascent Route (UIAA VII, 900m). *Niek de Jonge.*

The Cenotaph is a 16km walk from base camp up the Apusinikajik Glacier, and on August 12 de Jonge and Staleman made their first attempt on this formation, trying to climb a direct line up the east face. The initial 250m consisted of bad-quality gneiss, and above an obvious spire, a blank section proved to be impassible without considerable drilling. They were not prepared for this and retreated after climbing 600m. up to UIAA VII. Descent proved particularly dangerous on the lower, loose section of the face.

Meanwhile Hoekstra and I found our approach cut by impassible rivers, and the Shark's Tooth inaccessible from Skillebugt. Deciding that the poor rock on the Cenotaph was not conducive to a big wall ascent, we tried a free ascent in alpine style. We climbed the first five pitches of the de Jonge-Staleman attempt and fixed rappel anchors for a safe return, then on the 17th all four of us set out to attempt two different lines. After re-climbing those five pitches, Hoekstra and I branched right and climbed to the summit by the line of least resistance. First Ascent Route (UIAA VII, 900m). De Jonge and Staleman took a more direct option and finished on the last few pitches of our climb, arriving at the summit an hour later. They named their route Controversy (UIAA VII, 900m).

Niek de Jonge on the First Ascent Route, The Cenotaph. Below is the Apusinikajik Glacier. *Martin Fickweiler.*

McDonnell Peak, showing the line of the first ascent. The final pitch was the crux. *Martin Fickweiler*

On the 25th de Jonge and Staleman climbed a 2,000m peak on the east side of the Apusinikajik. Expecting an easy ascent, they to took the bare minimum: one pair of crampons, one ice axe, one rope, and a few cams and wires. The first 1,300m proved straightforward: a debris slope with big boulders, followed by scrambling to a shoulder. From there they climbed névé and mixed ground, up to 50°, to the final 200m, which was of surprisingly good quality, with difficulties up to VII-, and the final, crux, pitch (VII+ with minimal protection). They named the summit McDonnell Peak after Gerard McDonnell, who died on K2 in 2008. They believe that a person who risks his own life trying to save others is a true hero.

On the 28th Hoekstra and I made the first ascent of a 1,000m peak close to and north-northeast of base camp. We simul-climbed up and down (UIAA IV, 450m) and in thick cloud made a big cairn on what we felt to be the top. A few days later, when the weather cleared, we confirmed through binoculars that we had reached the true summit, which we have named the Small Lion.

MARTIN FICKWEILER. *The Netherlands*

Northwest Ren Land, various ascents. Chris Larvin, Jonny Phillips, Rob Porter, and I, from Imperial College London, arrived at Constable Pynt in early August, only to find that much of our equipment and food, which we had freighted by sea, had not arrived. In fact, after investigation, we found it had not left Copenhagen. The carrier was at fault and agreed to fly it out. However, due to the infrequency of air flights to Constable Pynt, we were forced to wait a week.

After a few nights in an airport hangar, we relocated to the town of Scoresbysund (Ittoqqortoormiut) by boat. Here we were lucky to be given a week's food by two girls from Oslo University, who happened to be leaving. This enabled us to spend a few days hiking in Liverpool Land. After renting two tents from Nanu Travel, we headed

Pk. 1,636m from the east, showing the line of the first ascent. *Dominic Southgate*

across the peninsula to Lillefjord and made an ascent of Trefoden (1,110m). This not only allowed us to adjust to the local terrain but also gave us our first sightings of musk oxen and arctic hares.

On return to Scoresbysund we found our freight had arrived, so the following day we headed up-fjord on a 250km boat journey to a previously unvisited area in Northwest Ren Land. The journey took around six hours, after which we spent a day ferrying loads across a glacier to establish base camp 30 minutes walk from the coast. The next day we explored the two main glaciers of the area, looking for attractive objectives.

Chris Larvin at ca 1,500m on route to the subsidiary summit of ca 1,700m. *Rob Porter*

On August 16th, for their first outing, Chris and Rob chose a mixed route up the nearest ridge east of base camp. Ascending scree, rock, snow, and ice (AD with one pitch of Scottish 4) to ca 1,700m, they reached a subsidiary summit. They were unable to continue to the main summit, which lay much farther back on the icecap. Jonny and I attempted an obvious zigzag line up Pk. 1,636m, opposite camp on the west side of the larger of the two glaciers. On our first try we failed to find a route off the far side of the glacier, due to crevasses and a 30-40m drop. Our second attempt involved a rappel and a river crossing, but we finally reached the base of the mountain and climbed it over the next two days, the 17th-18th, up scree slopes and friction slabs (British V Diff).

Chris and Rob then made a two-day exploratory trip up the length of the larger glacier and onto the ice cap, reaching a high point of ca 2,100m. In the meantime Jonny and I headed back across this glacier and up a western side valley to attempt a snow peak via a series of subsidiary glaciers. After a camp at 850m, we made our ascent on the 23rd, reaching a 1,950m summit after 1,100m of snow and ice at PD. Chris and Rob's third outing took them to the same valley, where they climbed a similar route (snow and ice at PD) for 1,000m to reach a 1,816m summit on the ridge opposite our peak.

Jonny, Rob, and I made the final outing of the trip, attempting a route on the ridge east of the smaller of the two main glaciers. After camping at 600m, we climbed 1,000m the next day. We had to stop at ca 1,600m, short of the ridge crest and summit tower, due to snowfall making for difficult conditions on steep slabs above. Returning, we were picked up promptly by our chartered boat.

After a night's stopover in Southeast Ren Land, where we picked up a group of Dutch climbers, we returned to Constable Pynt. Here, our final highlight was seeing a polar bear while camping at the airport, albeit through binoculars at a safe distance.

Throughout our stay the weather was mostly fine, with snow level at 1,700m, dropping to 1,200m after bad spells. Although base camp was vegetated, we had to deal with much scree elsewhere. In addition to our climbs (first ascents as far as we are aware), we took many photographs to provide information for future expeditions, and noted some good objectives. One member analyzed the geology of the region, and we studied the flora, taking specimens back to the U.K. for expert examination.

DOMINIC SOUTHGATE, *U.K.*

The unclimbed rock summit east of base camp attempted to 1,600m by Phillips, Porter, and Southgate. *Dominic Southgate*

SCHWEIZERLAND

Tupilak, south face of east ridge, Cake Walk; Duck Walk Wall, Via Nossnoj; Ravtanna; Whiskey Pillar, Unknown Expectations. During four weeks in the summer of 2006, Anna Backlund and I climbed on gneiss walls in the Tupilak area, Schweizerland. We left Sweden in the first week of June and flew to Kulusuk via Iceland. Our food, climbing equipment, skis, and camping gear weighed 105kg, and the flight would have been very expensive if I'd not managed to negotiate a deal with the airline for free baggage. From Kulusuk we flew to a base camp on the September 16 Glacier, southeast of the summit of Tupilak. We'd expected to melt snow but found a stream, which saved much fuel and time.

During our first days we reconnoitered and climbed a small peak east of camp called Schartenspitze (1,720m). It was an easy alpine climb, which someone had been on before, as we found a piton and sling though no other signs of traffic elsewhere on the mountain. [Schartenspitze (1,720m) has been climbed by various lines, including difficult Italian and Austro-British rock routes on its south face.] We descended snow slopes easily to our skis, and then had several days of snowfall.

South face of east ridge of Tupilak, Cake Walk marked. On reaching crest climbers descended ridge to (D), then down face. The two main Tupilak summits (east and west) lie well off-picture to left. *Krister Jonsson*

Our next goal was Tupilak. We wanted to climb the north face, but there was too much snow, so we opted for a line on the south face. There was 24-hour daylight, so when the weather cleared at midday, we set off immediately, ascended the heavily crevassed glacier to the base of the wall, filled our water bottles and started to climb. From farther away we'd spotted a promising line but now found we were unable to reach the start, so we opted for a crack system toward the center of the face. Fine pitches took us to an area of compact wet rock, but after a few ropelengths of poor quality climbing, we once again laid hands on steep, mostly solid gneiss. Just before midnight, and after 17 long pitches, up to UIAA VII-, we reached the snow ridge. We descended the crest east before rappelling and downclimbing to the glacier, reaching camp by 7:30 the following morning. We called our route Cake Walk. [Cake Walk lies above the glacier bay east of the one leading to the true south face of Tupilak and established German,

Duck Walk Wall, showing line of Via Nossnoj. From far end of the ridge first ascensionists rappeled into snow gully immediately right. *Krister Jonsson*

Ravtanna, showing line of first ascent. From summit climbers rappeled far side into steep couloir descending left. *Krister Jonsson*

British, and Austrian routes. Cake Walk finishes at a point on the east ridge of a secondary summit east of Tupilak's east summit, and is the first known route on the wall above this bay.]

Our main goal fulfilled, we turned to a smaller wall on the south side of the September 16th Glacier, opposite base camp. The wall, which faces southwest, we named Duck Walk Wall and climbed it in nine pitches, to UIAA VII+, on excellent gneiss. We saw no sign of previous visits to the summit of this formation, which we traversed to the southeast, before rappelling into a snow gully right of the face. We named our line Via Nossnoj. [Duck Walk Wall is a subsidiary buttress on the west ridge of a complex massif, the main summit of which was called Sonnblick (ca 1,800m) in 2000 by Austrians Julian Neumeyer and Jorg Susnik, who were probably the first to climb it (northeast face to east ridge)].

The next objective was a fine spire northeast of Tupilak called Ravtanna (Fox Teeth), which is more or less at the foot of the southwest ridge of the previously climbed Red Wall (2,070m). We climbed the spire by its south-southwest ridge in seven pitches, up to UIAA VII, and rappeled into a snow gully on the far side. Our route could be the first part of a much longer climb to the higher peak. With time left for one more route, we focused on a large detached tower that lies close to the base of the south ridge of Rodebjerg (2,140m). We dubbed it

Whiskey Pillar and climbed a line up the center of the southeast face in a 21-hour push. The climbing was amazing, with everything from superb hand and finger cracks, to runout climbing on compact gneiss with small roofs. We used three points of aid and called our 19-pitch line Unknown Expectations (UIAA VIII+ A1).

After a few days relaxing at base camp, we packed sledges and began our seven-day ski trip back to the coast, the Tasilaq Mountain Hut, and Kungmiut, where we were picked up by chartered boat and returned to Kulusuk. This proved a fine ending to an already great trip.

KRISTER JONSSON, *Sweden*

Unknown Expectations on Whiskey Pillar. Buttress behind and to right is part of south ridge of Rodebjerg. *Krister Jonsson*

Part of Fox Jaw Cirque. (A) Molar. (B) Incisor. (C) Cavity Ridge. (D) Left Rabbit Ear. (E) Right Rabbit Ear. Approximate lines of (1) El Cavajo dell'angel, (2) Ingirumimusnocte, (3) Emozione Polare, and (4) Il Gemello Diverso. See AAJ 2008, p.209, for older lines. *Richard Felderer*

Fox Jaw Cirque, various ascents. During July, Matteo Della Bordella, Richard Felderer, Lorenzo "Pala" Lanfranchi, and Simone Pedeferri from the Ragni di Lecco climbed four new routes in the Fox Jaw Cirque.

The team climbed five routes in 20 days and enjoyed an experience that an unusually loquacious Pedeferri described as "aesthetically very beautiful." If this climber-artist feels this way, then it must be true. He added, "Tasiilaq Fjord, where we established base camp, is one of the most beautiful and wildest I've ever seen. The granite walls in the cirque are fantastic, with truly superb rock." He concluded with a statement all alpinists dream of hearing: "You're so isolated, and there are still so many walls to be climbed, it seems as if you're in Patagonia 30 years ago."

Pedeferri describes the area as so wild that "it is nature that dictates the rules—nature as unbeatable as the absurd number of mosquitoes that infested our base camp." However, there

Opening Ingirumimusnocte on Molar. *Richard Felderer*

were "no mosquitoes on the rock faces, and you could climb for 20 hours non-stop, with constant daylight. What you usually achieve in three days, you manage in just one."

Emozione Polare, put up by all four climbers, ascends the Incisor in the same area of rock as Beers in Paradise (V 5.10+ A0, 600m, American-Canadian team, 2007). Pedeferri described it as "perfect, on extraordinary rock, one of the most beautiful routes I know." The four ascended the 15-pitch line during July 15 and 16, in a 26-hour push from base camp to summit and back, with difficulties up to UIAA VIII. They placed one protection bolt and equipped some belays for rappels.

Using minimal gear was a fundamental aspect of the style they wished to achieve. "We wanted to climb clean—British style—on-sight and without leaving a trace," explained Pedeferri, who with Lanfranconi had already put up two routes. On July 8 they produced Il Gemello Diverso (7b, 630m of climbing, 20 hours camp-to-camp, no bolts), a 13 pitch line on Left Rabbit Ear in the same vicinity as Naeterqaabin-Jebbananee (IV 5.10, 550m, 13 pitches, American-Canadian team, 2007). On the 12th they climbed El Cavajo dell'angel (7b, 420m, 16 hours camp-to-camp) on the Molar, again with no bolts. "We didn't think we'd be able to climb El Cavajo dell'angel without bolts, but in the end we managed, thanks to our combined experience" stated Pedeferri. The route appears to be near to the line attempted in 2007 by Becknar, Furman, and Panagoulis.

Also on the Molar, Della Bordella and Felderer spent two days making the first ascent of Ingirumimusnocte, a beautiful 420m line with difficulties up to 7b+, 6c+ obl. Although they placed 28 bolts, including belays, this is a truly psychological outing, with long runouts. (Della Bordella is well-known for his scary climbs at Wendenstock, the European temple of bold routes.) Later, Della Bordella and Felderer repeated Doublemint Direct (III 5.8, Lundin-Warten, 2007) on Baby Molar, which they graded UIAA VI.

Pedeferri complimented the other climbers, in particular Della Bordella who, despite being on his first expedition (or perhaps because of it) proved unstoppable. "Matteo has attributes I've rarely seen in other climbers. He really is talented and incredibly at ease when on-sighting a big rock face. He has a pure, insatiable passion for climbing." And then the climber-artist concluded, "Yes, I'm really happy. In Greenland I really felt free to climb!" As everyone knows, there is nothing better for a climber.

FABIO PALMA, *ITALY*, AND LINDSAY GRIFFIN, *Mountain INFO*

More Fox Jaw history. Some history of climbing in the Fox Jaw Cirque was reported in *AAJ 2008*, pp. 207-211. In addition, in 2000 Christoph Mauerhofer and friends from Switzerland climbed two routes. The first was seven pitches to the summit of Baby Molar (Milk Tooth Spire), where they found a cairn. Their route appears to lie between routes (1) and (2) on the photo in AAJ 2008. The difficulties were reported to be moderate, and the team noted several other lines on this face that would offer enjoyable first ascents. They equipped the descent with 8mm bolts. The second route led to the summit referred to as Cavity Ridge, climbing the obvious right-hand pillar below (F) on the photo in 16 pitches. The Swiss completed the route alpine-style in a long day at 6a, spending three hours waiting on a ledge during darkness. All belays were equipped with hand-drilled 8mm bolts.

In 2006 Gemma Woldendorp and Natasha Sebire spent two weeks in the area but experienced only two days without rain. They climbed a line on Baby Molar up the face left of (3). After four pitches up to 6a A2, they retreated just short of an easy scramble leading to the summit. Prior to this they climbed in an area called the Col de Phantome. At the back of the cirque they climbed five pitches (up to 6a A2+) on a peak shaped like a vertical shield, but were stopped just short of the summit due to loose rock.

FROM INFORMATION PROVIDED BY GEMMA WOLDENDORP, *Australia*

SOUTH GREENLAND

CAPE FAREWELL REGION

Tasermiut Fjord, Nalumasortoq (2,045m), Life is Beautiful, first free ascent. On June 28, Oskar Alexandersson and I made the first free ascent of Life Is Beautiful (VI 5.9 A2+, 600m, Suzuki-Yamaoka, 2000) at 5.13- or F7c+. Both of us led and followed free in a 19-hour push. I had tried to free climb the route the previous summer with Martin Jakobsson, and knew it was possible. That year the weather wasn't on our side, so we had to leave without getting a shot at a free ascent. This year we climbed the route ground up on our second attempt. We climbed the route ledge to ledge, therefore not always using the belays from the first ascent. On the crux pitch I fell, lowered, stripped the gear and handed over the lead to Oskar. He sent the pitch and

Nalumasortoq with the line of Life is Beautiful on the Left Hand Pillar. For the whereabouts of other lines on this face see AAJ 2004, p. 263. *Erik Massih*

we climbed the remainder of the route, which for me was unknown ground, via mainly 5.11 cracks, topping out at midnight in beautiful moonlight.

The first four pitches of the route give fun and varied climbing on rock that while generally safe, features many loose or crumbling flakes. We dubbed this section the "Knäcke (Wasa) Pitches" after Sweden's national hard bread. Above the ledge at the top of pitch 5 the rock quality improves and the climbing is pure pleasure – well, save for the last two pitches, but they were also pretty fun.

Later, Oskar and I climbed War and Poetry, the Bechtel-Bechtel-Lilygren-Mallamo-Model-Piana-Skinner free version (5.12c) of the Geneva Diedre (6b and A4, 1,000m, Dalphin-Piola-Probost-Wiestlibach, 1983) on the West Face of Ulamertorssuaq (1,830m). We climbed the route on-sight, ground up, and then rappelled, all in a 30-hour push. Each climber led or followed free, the only flaws being three hangs by the second climber on pitches 12, 15, and 26. On each occasion he lowered to the stance (on pitch 15 to a marginal stance) and re-climbed the pitch. We fixed no ropes nor made any stashes, though we did receive hugs and a few mouthfuls of tea from a group of girls in a portaledge just below the Black Heart.

Norwegian-Swedish parties repeated the Original British Route on the Left Hand Pillar (British E4 and A2, ca. 600m, Anderson-Dring-Dring-Tatersall, 1995) of Nalumasortoq. Magnus Eriksson with Peter Lothegius (Sweden), and Hilde Björgaas (Norwegian) with Hanna Melin

Erik Massih on the sixth pitch (5,13-) of Life is Beautiful, Nalumasortoq. *Oskar Alexandersson*

(Sweden) climbed without jumars but with some aid here and there, mainly on the top pitches. Nathan Martin and Timmy O'Neil climbed the 18-pitch route free in 2003 on the third overall ascent at 5.12+.

ERIK MASSIH, *Sweden*

Mexico

Mexico

Nuevo León, Tatewari, Nayeri. La Huasteca still has many walls to explore, and this 500m south-facing wall of limestone, just 15 minutes from Monterrey, had two routes and an unfinished project. David Tirado (Mexico), my wife Marisol Monterrubio (Mexico), and I started with the first pitch and the three first bolts of the second pitch of Carlos Garcia's route Cola de Venado. We then went a little right, then mostly straight to the summit. Nayeri (11 pitches, V 5.12 [obligatory 5.11]) is named after our one-year-old daughter, is sustained, and is set among wild scenery. The route is fully bolted, with gear optional for some easy runouts. Descend by rappel.

We took a week in late December to create the route, sleeping on the valley floor and usually waking late before jumaring back up. On the last day we slept on the summit, which is a vegetated ridge with rocks and thorny plants, but we cleaned it and made a perfect bivy for four or five climbers.

Directions: From Monterrey enter La Huasteca National Park. Follow the paved road for 5km to a gravel turn-off on the right. Tatewari is visible on the right, past the other beautiful wall of Pico Erin. Just in front is the Don Simon ranch, with the entrance to Guitarritas Canyon on the other side. The approach takes 30 minutes.

ORIOL ANGLADA, *Catalonia, Spain*

Nuevo León, Tatewari, Fiducia al Sentiero. In December 2009 and early January 2010, Alessandro Baù and I opened Fiducia al Sentiero (500m, 10 pitches, 7b+ [5.12c; 7a obligatory]) on Tatewari's south wall. The route is a mix of bolts and trad: six pitches trad, with

the rest having bolts where you cannot place anything else. There are two bolts at each rappel station, though. We took three days in late December to open the route, climbing and fixing the first four pitches on day one, then returning and opening three more pitches to a good bivy spot, where we spent the night before finishing the route the third day. We returned on January 2, 2010, for the redpoint, alternating leads.

MATTEO DELLA BORDELLA, *Club Alpino Accademico Italiano and Ragni di Lecco,* AAC

Tatewari: (1) Via Suiza (5.10). (2) Cola d Venado (5.12c). (3) Nayeri (5.12b/c). (4) Tu Quieres Tu Puedes (5.11c). (5) Project. (6) Fiducia al Sentiero (5.12c). *Oriol Anglada*

Colombia

Ritacuba Blanco, Tierra de Condores. In February 2010, on the east face of Ritacuba Blanco (5,350m) in Colombia's Cordillera del Cocuy, Fernando Gonzalez Rubio (Colombia), Ivan Calderon (Venezuela), Simon Kehrer (Italy), and I (Italy) established Tierra de Condores (800m, 7a+) in seven days of excellent weather, with six bivouacs on the wall. We used bolts at the belays and traditional protection for climbing. The first 14 pitches are very overhanging, on good alpine rock; the last 300m are

Helmut Gargitter on Tierra de Condores. *Simon Kehrer*

not so steep but are loose. With melting ice, the top part is dangerous. We rappelled the route and freed the pitches we hadn't yet freed. The rock is hard sandstone that looks like granite. There are two more routes on this wall, both established more than 10 years ago: one on the extreme right, climbed by Fernando Gonzalez Rubio and friends, and one on the extreme left, a then-mixed route (since melted), soloed by Swiss climber Daniel Anker.

HELMUT GARGITTER, *Italy*

Ritacuba Blanco, east face: (1) El Llano en Llamas (Anker [solo], 1996). (2) Viviendo Entre Tinieblas (González Rubio-Mazzieri-Wilke, 2001). (3) Buscando la de Anker (Caceres-González Rubio, 2008). (4) Tierra de Condores (Calderon-Gargitter-González Rubio-Kehrer, 2010). *2010 expedition photo*

The first four (of six) peaks of the Laguna Grande de la Sierra traverse. From Left: Pre-Concavo, Concavo, Concavito, and Portales. *Camilo Lopez*

Laguna Grande de la Sierra, traverse. Over five days in late November, Anna Pfaff and I traversed the six peaks of the Laguna Grande de la Sierra, on the west side of the Cocuy mountains. Starting from a base camp at the edge of Laguna Grande, eight miles from the last farm on the road called Hacienda La Esperanza, we quickly climbed to the summit of Pre-Concavo (5,100m). After a couple of rappels, we continued along the steep snow ridge to the second summit, Concavo (5,215m). From its summit mushroom we downclimbed, traversed under a small cornice, and then back onto the ridge and up 45° névé to Concavito (5,115m). We then retraced our steps and camped on the glacier below. Next we crossed a crevasse-filled glacier to the fourth summit, Portales (4,920m), which had 200m of 5.7–5.8. We rappelled back to the base and established our second high camp. The fifth summit, El Toti (5,125m), had a long approach over exposed ledges that led to a 50° snowfield and 120m of moderate mixed to the talus summit. We downclimbed and rappelled to the base and made our third high camp. We climbed summit six, Pan de Azucar (5,235m), through a large north-facing headwall leading to the steep glacier below the summit. We combined 800m of 5.8–5.9 rock with a 70° snow ramp below El Pulpito del Diablo. From the base of El Pulpito del Diablo, we crossed the glacier and gained the steep ridge to the overhanging mushroom summit of Pan de Azucar (5,235m). After rappelling to the base of Pan de Azucar, we made our fourth and final high camp. The following day we hiked back to Hacienda La Esperanza.

CAMILO LOPEZ

Venezuela

Acopan Tepui, various routes. Several routes went up on Acopan Tepui, not all of which are reported here. In December, Polish climbers Boryslaw Szybinski, Maciej Dziedzic, and Michal Szeliga teamed with Venezuelan Cheo García to establish Lapa, Yuca y Kachiri (300m, 7 pitches, 7c+). From January 21 to February 2, 2010, on the left side of the Gran Torre, between the routes Uñate Arête and Pizza, Chocolate y Cerveza, the Polish-Venezuelan team of Marcin Tomaszewski, Marcin Szczotka, Jaret Wacko, and Cheo García established Misterios (630m, 18 pitches, 7c [7b obligatory]). Later, as reported on www.desnivel.com, over 11 days Adolfo

Madinabeitia and André Vacampenhoud climbed a new route, Mundo Perdido (650m, 16 pitches, 7a A3), which takes a line between Pizza, Chocolate y Cerveza and the new route Misterios.

Exact locations of routes on the massive, monolithic Tupuis can be difficult to describe but, as Mikey Schaefer said after his visit and new route (below): "The locals know exactly where each route starts. They can point them out from town...and they will certainly be the ones leading the way."

Additional routes are reported below, and www.ClimTepuyes.com has information on many climbs in the region.

Lapa, Yuca y Kachiri, on Acopan Tepui. *Cheo García*

Acopan Tepui, El Sendero De Los Indigenas. Ján Smoleň (Slovakia) and Ondra Beneš, Jiří Lautner, and Tomáš Sobotka (Czech Republic) established El Sendero De Los Indigenas (7c/UIAA 9), on the east face of Acopan Tepui from Jan 7–11. The 425m route has 11 pitches: 3, 7a, 7c, 7c, 7b, 6b, 6a, 6c+, 6b, 6b+, 5. They climbed ground-up with fixed ropes, no chipping, and freed all the pitches in redpoint style.

10 Pounds of Tequila (left) and El Sendero De Los Indigenas, two of the new routes on the east face of Acopan Tepui. *Mikey Schaefer*

Brittany Griffith headed for happy hour on the 5.12a sixth pitch of 10 Pounds of Tequila. *Mikey Schaefer*

They placed 19 protection bolts and 11 at belays, and left five fixed pitons. El Sendero De Los Indigenas has a sport-alpine character and requires Friends, nuts and long slings.

VLADO LINEK, *JAMESÁK, Slovakia*

Acopan Tepui, 10 Pounds of Tequila. On February 9 Kate Rutherford, Brittany Griffith, Jonathan Thesenga, and I arrived in the small village of Yunek, below Acopan (Akopan) Tepui. The local Pemon people were happy to see us and eager to porter a few loads, and soon we were on our way to the Boulder Camp. Two locals helped us reach the base of the wall the next day, and after a couple of false starts we found an appealing line on the east face. Over the next five days we slowly made our way up the wall, fixing pitches, then returning to base camp at night. We climbed mostly free but couldn't free a few short sections on our initial attempt (but freed on the next attempt). The climbing involved difficult route-finding on fairly solid rock, with the occasional 5.10+ runout.

After fixing 170m, we committed to a camp on the wall, with J.T. and I hauling and shooting photos, while Brittany and Kate climbed from the ground, freeing the initial seven pitches at 5.12-. Over the next three days, we established eight more pitches on the overhanging headwall. Most of the climbing was in the 5.10+ range with one pitch of 5.12c R. The last few pitches to the top turned into a vertical jungle. After a short, thirsty trip to the summit, we reversed our ascent route, cleaning our ropes and camp, rapping off of horns, blocks, pins, stoppers, and five bolts. We then hiked to base camp, where our celebratory prize of 10 pounds of tequila waited. 10 Pounds of Tequila (V 5.12c R).

MIKEY SCHAEFER, *AAC*

Guyana

Monte Roraima, Guerra de Luz e Trevas. After 12 days on Monte Roraima, Márcio Bruno, Fernando Leal, and I achieved the first ascent of a new route from the Guyana side: Guerra de Luz e Trevas (War Between Light and Darkness; 650m VI 5.11a A3 J4).

We reached the wall by a 50-minute helicopter flight, starting from the Santa Elena Uiarén in Venezuela. The partial landing/hover was on a 4x5m block, just below the highest waterfall on the mountain (on a low water day), and we quickly jumped out. It is believed that this is one of the few possible landing points in the area; other expeditions have used a heli point 3km away. The first part of the route is full of jungle climbing and loose blocks, but after 50m the rock improved. The stone is quartzite and offers many cracks for protection. There are many possible bivy ledges, but many are wet, and spiders and scorpions are found even in

X marks the landing spot on Monte Roraima's Guyana side; Guerra de Luz e Trevas (inset) begins just to the right. *Eliseu Frechou*

vertical places. A storm interrupted our climb on the fifth day and forced us to spend four days on a four-square-meter ledge.

The first ascent of this mountain from Guyana was made 1973 by legendary British climbers Joe Brown, Don Whillans, Mo Anthoine, and Hamish MacInnes. U.S. expeditions opened routes nearby in 2003 and 2006: the Scorpion Wall and Cutting the Line.

ELISEU FRECHOU, *Brazil*

Brazil

Pedra Riscada, Place of Happiness. In July on Pedra Riscada, near São José do Divino in the state of Minas Gerais, Horacio Gratton (Argentina), Stefan Glowacz, Holger Heuber, and Klaus Fengler (Germany), and I opened Place of Happiness (850m, 5.12d). It is a magic line in an amazing place.

EDEMILSON PADILHA, *Brazil*

Pedra Riscada, showing the new route, Place of Happiness (stroked line), and Onde o Vento Faz a Curva. The normal route is farther left; no other routes are visible in this image. *Edemilson Padilha*

Peru

CORDILLERA BLANCA

Urus Central, El Vuelo del Inca. After hiking to an advanced camp (4,900m) in the Ishinca Valley on October 16, Beto Pinto and Eric Albino began climbing the south face of Urus Central (5,495m). The initial 360m had loose snow and mixed climbing, to 80°, along with falling blocks of ice. They passed this section in two hours and continued on hard 70° snow for another six 60m pitches, reaching the summit at 12:30 p.m. They descended a ridge, with three rappels, and returned to camp by 6 p.m. El Vuelo del Inca (360m, MD+ 6a M5 70–90°).

SERGIO RAMÍREZ CARRASCAL, *Peru*

Nevado Ranrapalca, La Paliza del Ranrapalca. The south face of Ranrapalca (6,162m) ca 6km wide, with rock, ice, and snow rising for 750–850m. Peruvian mountaineers and guides (AGMP-UIAGM) Eloy Salazar Obregón, Octavio Salazar Obregón, and Eric Albino (aspirant guide) started in the Cojup Valley on August 26, proceeding until a fork of the valley brought them to a spot below the face, where they camped at 4,800m. The next day, in bad weather, they scouted a possible route. The glacier leading to the base was in horrible condition, with fragile ice, huge crevasses, and delicate ice bridges. After feeling confident about their route, they returned to camp. Surprisingly, the weather improved, so they ate a light meal, tried to sleep, and at 11 p.m. began their attempt. Early on August 28 they crossed a bergschrund and, a few meters higher, another, at ca 5,150m. The first 240m had loose 50–60° snow, which they simul-climbed. They then belayed 40m of mixed climbing and resumed simul-climbing on hard snow for 240m, reaching hard ice near the top of the face. After an overhanging final passage, they entered an 80° couloir that in 120m led directly to the ridge. On the ridge they hiked to the summit, which they reached at 6:30 p.m. They descended the 55° east face and returned to camp, completing the ascent in 20 hours and the descent in nine hours. La Paliza del Ranrapalca (850m, ED 50°–90°/95°).

SERGIO RAMÍREZ CARRASCAL, *Peru*

Urus Central's south face, with El Vuelo del Inca. *Americo Serrano*

La Paliza del Ranrapalca, on the south face of Ranrapalca. *Eric Albino*

Nevado Rurec, traverse. From June 8 to 10 two Spaniards, Eloi Callado and Joan Sole, and I traversed the twin summits of Nevado Rurec (5,696m) from the east. We originally wanted to climb the south side of Huantsan from a base camp beneath the southeast face, which we approached from Chavin in two days with burros. Our climb went up the east face of Huantsan's south ridge to its crest at ca 5,600m, where we bivied. Then, however, rather than continuing up Huantsan, we headed west over the summits of Rurec and descended north into the Quebrada Rajucol-

The line to the crest of Huantsan's south ridge, from where Buhler, Callado, and Sole headed west over the twin summits of Nevado Rurec. *Carlos Buhler*

ta, then went on to Huaraz. Our cook brought our gear, with *arrieros*, from our base camp back to Chavin and then Huaraz. I don't think anyone had traversed Nevado Rurec from east to west before. It wasn't so much a spectacular route, but more of an extended alpine traverse.

CARLOS BUHLER, *AAC*

Pucaraju, Juego de los Reyes to summit ridge. In July, Nate Farr and I with the support of the AAC's McNeill-Nott climbing grant attempted a new line on Caraz II, but were stopped by loose, overhanging rock down low. We returned to Huaraz, disheartened and without a mission.

Adam French came to town and renewed our spirits with pictures of the southwest face of Pucaraju (5,320m), in the Yana-

The southwest face of Pucaraju, from left: Mururoa, Adam et Eve, Choose Life, Hotline, Princesa au Petit Pois, and the new route, Juego de los Reyes, with the arrows showing the descent. *Marcus Donaldson*

mara subrange. Nate and I hopped a ride to Lake Queracocha and in half a day's hike were bivied in a cave 2,000' below the face. As we hiked up on July 26, much of the face appeared covered in unconsolidated snow from a wet winter. However, a thin white line seemed to snake nearly unbroken all the way up the sunnier right side of the face. Game on!

The first pitch was 60m of sustained thin ice and mixed climbing on a three-foot-wide ice ribbon. The friable rock offered uncertain protection, so we took belays whenever we could on the succeeding pitches of névé, ice, and rock. Steeper and more delicate mixed climbing, up to M6, in the upper couloir culminated in a narrow chute filled with classic Andean sugar snow.

Upon reaching the ridge, we downclimbed and rapped the south ridge and a snow couloir to the climber's right of our line. Juego de los Reyes (300m, 5.8 WI4 M6) ascends the first corner system right of a major slab bisecting the southwest face.

MARCUS DONALDSON, *Portland, OR, AAC*

CORDILLERA HUAYHUASH

Puscanturpa, Barne Sua. From June 27 to 29, Spanish (Basque) climbers Mikel Bonilla and Aitor Abendaño climbed the north face of Puscanturpa via a variation to the 2000 French route, Macanacota (*AAJ* 2001, p. 284). They began up a diagonal crack with a succession of unstable blocks. (A carabiner is visible 10m from the base.) The next pitches ascend grooved rock and cracks to a big ledge. Pitches 5–10 increase in difficulty, through dihedrals, overhangs, and chimneys, before a 10m traverse joins the route to Macanacota, which it takes to the summit. The team left bolts and pitons on their variation. They descended Macanacota by rappel. Barne Sua (750m, 7a+).

SERGIO RAMÍREZ CARRASCAL, *Peru*

CORDILLERA CENTRAL

Nevado Vicuñita, Last Inca. In late January, Peruvians Beto Pinto, Steven Fuentes, Roger Lliuya, and Darío Yucra, students of CEAM (the official mountain guiding school of Peru), made camp at Lake Paccha (4,600m), below the southwest face of Nevado Vicu-ñita (5,550m). They began at 3 a.m. on the 27th and at 6 a.m. reached 120m of unstable mixed ground below a hanging glacier. Above, a 100m, 60°–90° ice couloir took two hours and was the most difficult part of the wall. A 50°, 120m wall with loose snow then led to the north ridge. Following the north ridge they reached the main summit

Last Inca, on Nevado Vicuñita. *Beto Pinto*

at midday. The next day they descended to the village of San Mateo and named the route Last Inca (400m, MD+ 6a 65–90°).

SERGIO RAMÍREZ CARRASCAL, *Peru*

CORDILLERA YAUYOS

Nevado Ticlla, southwest and southeast face. Ticlla (5,897m) is highest *nevado* of the Cordillera de Yauyos (east of Lima), located in the Reserva Paisajistica Nor Yauyos Cocha and accessed from the town of Miraflores (3,600m), whose residents call the peak "Cotoni." French climbers Jean Francois Fillot, Sylvain Mellet, and Nicolas Whirsching trekked to a pass at 4,750m and continued to Lake Huascacohca (4,200m). They went north toward Ticlla and made base camp at 4,600m, close to a little unnamed lake. To reach the bottom of the southwest face, they climbed the very left side of rock bands and, at 4,900m, traversed just under the seracs to the right. They reached the glacier, passed the bergschrund on the right, and climbed directly toward the rock bands close to the summit. At 5,550m they climbed over a cornice onto the southeast face, 100m below the summit. Most of the route was 45°–50° and was done unroped. The southeast face is continuous 50°–55° snow from 5,400m to 5,850m and then

Nevado Ticlla, with the route of ascent (left) and descent. Sylvain Mellet

becomes easier. The climbers, who made the climb on May 8, perceived the overall difficulty as 900m D.

Nicolas and Sylvain then skied the southeast face (500m, 50°–55° continuous), while Jean Francois downclimbed it to 5,750m, but became ill and could not continue. His teammates and the Miraflores people worked together to rescue him.

Also, all three climbed and descended on skis the north face of Ranrapalca, in the Cordillera Blanca.

SERGIO RAMÍREZ CARRASCAL, *Peru*

Bolivia

Cordillera Apolobamba, first ascents. From the village of Pelechuco, we (Daria Mamica-Galka, Jakub Galka, Wojciech Chaladaj, and Marcin Kruczyk) hired five mules and trekked to the Huancasayani Valley. To the best of our knowledge the valley had been the target of two previous expeditions—German in 1998 and New Zeland/American in 2008. Thanks to materials and information obtained from James Dempster, a member of the latter expedition, and a copy of Paul Hudson's map, presented by Royal Geographical Society, we identified summits and made rough plans. A three-day trek took us over three passes above 4,500m. About two km before Puina we turned west into the Huancasayani Valley and continued for several more hours, reaching a perfect base camp (4,600m) on the edge of a side valley falling from Coquenzi, 2–3 hours from Lusuni Pass.

After two days of acclimatization, we attacked our first target—the probably unclimbed, unnamed four-summit ridge, which we called Trata Tata, falling to the north from Pacasqua Mukuku (ca 5,050m). On July 19 three of us (Jakub, Wojciech, Marcin) climbed the second highest summit in the Trata Tata massif, following the northwest ridge from the lowest pass, which is easily accessible from both sides (rock difficulty II, with several pitches up to V; very loose rock). We returned to camp via the east face, with two rappels and a three-hour walk. Two days later we reached the unclimbed west peak of Coquenzi (5,150m; its main summit was climbed by both previous expeditions) via the southwest ridge and descended via the German route, after a rappel from the summit. The most serious problem with this AD climb (glacier to 70°, rock/mixed to M4) was extremely fragile rock. Our third aim was the possibly unclimbed Nevado Losoccocha on the western ridge of Kura Huari, on the Peruvian side (5,100m). Two of us (Wojciech and Marcin) climbed and descended it on July 23, following the shepherds' and smugglers' path to Lusuni Pass, then crossing a glacier and scrambling the east ridge. The whole climb is easy (F+, 20–40° glacier, rock I-II) but unpleasant due to poor rock. After a rest day, we focused on the 5,000m unclimbed, unnamed summit on the main ridge extending south from Kura Huari. We ascended it on July 25, via the east face, encountering difficulties of AD. We christened it La Indigna, due to its inconspicuous figure. An easy rock face led to a chimney (M3), then a glaciated couloir (70° max) to a pass (which separates La Indigna from FAE 5 [climbed and named by the Germans]), from which we summited with a single, easy (M2) pitch. Due to a strong wind, snowfall, and difficult climbing, we did not climb

Trata Tata, from base camp. *Marcin Kruczyk*

Coquenzi West, as seen from Trata Tata. Solid line is ascent, dashed the descent. *Marcin Kruczyk*

Looking northwest from Trata Tata. (KH) The Kura Huari massif, on which several spires have been climbed by the two previous parties in the area (close-up photo on p. 190, *AAJ 2009*). (I) La Indigna. (3) & (5) FAE 3 & 5 (1997 German expedition). (CW) Coquenzi West. *Wojciech Chaladaj*

the 7m rock monolith crowning the summit. On the last day of our stay, three of us (Jakub, Wojciech, and Marcin) repeated the German route to the summit identified in their report as FAE 3, finding easy terrain. On July 29 we returned to Pelechuco, and a few days later, back at El Carretero hostel in La Paz with a bottle of wine, we considered our expedition a success. [A map and other photos are posted at aaj.americanalpineclub.org]

MARCIN KRUCZYK AND WOJCIECH CHALADAJ, *Poland*

Cordillera Real, Peak Austria, Caporales Celtica. Paddy Englishman, Paddy Scotsman, and Paddy Irishman (Jim Osborne, Rob MacCallum, and I) arrived in La Paz in one piece but subsequently fell apart when we reached base camp in the Condoriri Valley. A heady cocktail of AMS, gastroenteritis, mild HAPE, and chronic trots got us off to a flying start. As we recovered, in July we made several attempts and ascents, including what we believe to be new route on Peak Austria (5,320m). It has a beautiful buttress—La Fortaleza Buttress (Fortress Buttress)—that offered a welcome change from snow-plodding, and MacCallum and I put up a superb rock route on its eastern arête. The line had lots of character, 350m long, V Diff, alpine grade AD, climbing ribs, towers, and a ridge crest, all on quality sedimentary rock, with a dramatic backdrop of the Cabeza and surrounding peaks. Naming the route was the hardest part. We settled on Caporales Celtica—*caporales* being a traditional Bolivian dance performed by African slaves in the court of the Spanish Conquistadors. Celtica being our version.

Caporales Celtica, on the eastern arête of La Fortaleza Buttress, Peak Austria. *Gerry Galligan*

GERRY GALLIGAN, *Ireland*

Cordillera Real, Illimani, Pacha Brava. Lionel Terray, French idol of the 50s, wrote about Illimani's huge south face: "The human being who succeeds in climbing this frightening and steep wall isn't born yet." Decades later the French Alain Mesili and the Japanese Giri-Giri Boys ascended several serious routes on the southeast wall. The south face is a challenge, it's dangerous, it's a great game, it's the longest face in Bolivia's Andes. It's 12km wide, up to 1,400m high, and very complex. [This face is around the corner, to the left, of the "southeast face" shown on p. 237, *AAJ* 2007 (called "south face" in the 2007 report).] Even villagers living in Pinaya, below Illimani's west side, don't know about the remote south side, other than that it exists. So I made an orientation trip: three days of perfect loneliness.

Shortly after my exploration I returned with Porfirio Chura. He is a young Aymara born below Illimani, and one of a few Bolivian extreme climbers living in La Paz. At 3 a.m. one day in mid-August, we started to climb. At sunrise we were high up the face, mostly simul-climbing 60–75° ice, with mixed passages connecting the icefields, on a wall with no end. Every step was is clear and simple, life in its purest form. A steep but short icefield above a crevasse was the crux: 8m of overhanging ice (115°). At midday thick fog enveloped us, but, almost blind, we continued up. As soon as we left the south wall and traversed west we left the fog and our doubts behind.

"This wall is a bitch," said Porfirio.

"It *was* a bitch," I answered with a smile.

The long traverse to Illimani's south summit and the descent, westward near the Bonatti Route, stole the whole afternoon. At nightfall we passed Puente Rotto (base camp for the normal route to the south summit). Forty minutes later we reached Pinaya. Here we spent the night with Porfirio's sister and her family, in the tiny adobe hut where he was born.

Pacha Brava, "couraged grass," is a tough pioneer plant that grows where no other plant could survive: between rocks and in the poorest traces of soil. We search for happiness in simplicity, and *Pacha Brava* makes a good symbol of that.

ROBERT RAUCH, *Germany and Bolivia*

Argentina and Chile

NORTHERN ANDES, ARGENTINA

New routes. In April we established several new routes in northern Argentina. The most difficult was a mixed line on the south face of Chañi Chico (5,570m): Marcados por el Chañi (600m, M5 85°) climbs 13 pitches to the summit, and took 12 hours of climbing, with a 16-hour round trip. The other routes: Pachamama (1,000m, 5+/6a), a rock route on the south face of Morro Von Ronsen (5,450m); Vitoria-Gasteiz (550m, 80°), an ice route on the south face of Aguja Negra (5,350m); and Gure Etxea (850m, 60°), on the north face of Punta Ibañez (5,800m), with a traverse to General Belgrano (Chañi's main summit, 5,896m).

JABI BARAIAZARRA, AND ENEKO *and* IKER POU, *Basque Country, Spain, AAC*

Volcán Salín, northeast face. This 6,029m volcano, in Salta, Argentina, was first ascended by pre-Columbian Indians. Hans-Martin Schmitt from Germany and Adrian Germishuizen from South Africa climbed it on May 20, opening a new route on the northeast face for the fifth modern ascent.

MARCELO SCANU, *Buenos Aires, Argentina*

Marcados por el Chañi, on the south face of Chañi Chico. *Jabi Baraiazarra*

Pachamama, on the south face of Morro Von Ronsen. *Jabi Baraiazarra*

Pissis, West Glacier. The West Glacier of Pissis, Argentina, is 40km square, the biggest in the region. It can only be reached after a difficult 200km off-road ride. The only attempt on the route was by Mexicans in 1994. In March a team led by Guillermo Almaraz, with Eduardo Namur, Nicolás Pantaleón, and Daniel Pontín, erected base camp at 5,000m (S 27 43 04.5, W 68 54 00.8) in the valley that accesses the West Glacier. They made Camp 1 at 5,600m beside the glacier (S 27 44 03.1, W 68 51 40.8), and the next day traversed the 7km glacier, camping at 5,950m near the ridge used by the Polish on the 1937 first ascent (S 27 44 48.3, W 68 48 45.5). The final summit bid was made by Almaraz, Namur, and Pantaleón, ascending the snowy face and reaching the ridge that is the final part of the original route. They continued to a minor summit (Gendarmería Nacional, 6,675m), then to a col between it and the main summit, which they reached shortly after midday on March 14. The group believes the last unofficial measurement, 6,795m (official is 6,882m), to be accurate.

MARCELO SCANU, *Buenos Aires, Argentina*

CENTRAL ANDES

Cerro Presidente Perón, first ascent; Cerro Bifurcación, south face and ridge. In February 2010 Pablo González and I accessed the Quebrada San Lorenzo at 4,200m, in the Cordillera de Olivares, Agua Negra zone, in Argentina's San Juan province, near the border with Chile. The next day, February 8, we followed a destroyed mining trail to camp at 4,625m. On February 9 González climbed a new route on the south face and south ridge of Cerro Bifurcación (5,223m), first ascended by friends and me in 1991 (*AAJ 1992*, p. 161). On the 11th we climbed the west face of a fine 5,774m virgin summit, finding terrain similar to the Normal Route on Aconcagua and naming the peak Cerro Presidente Perón, because the three-time Argentine president was a climber and supported expeditions in Argentina and abroad.

MARCELO SCANU, *Buenos Aires, Argentina*

La Ramada Range, Rio Colorado Valley, ascents. La Ramada is a remote, little-visited range in Argentina, 200km northwest of Mendoza, without a precise map. With Argentine climbers, I've climbed in this area, specifically the Rio Colorado Valley, three times. Access involves a four-hour drive from Mendoza to the nice village of Barreal and then the *gendarmerie* post of Santa Anna, the beginning of the walk. Then a two-day, 30km, trek with 1,400m elevation gain, to base camp (3,600m). In 2005, with an Argentine climber, we repeated two existing routes: the South Face of Pico Negro and the East Face (Serac Route; French D) of Pico Polaco, considered the most beautiful mountain in the area. Then, in January 2008, Anibal Maturano (Argentina) and I climbed a 5,700m peak that had no known previous ascents; Anibal called it Pico Franco-Argentina. Our route, St. Jean de Passy, begins at 4,100m, above the upper valley, and climbs the east-northeast face. It was nice, but not technical (French PD). We made two camps above base camp (4,300m and 4,900m; a porter came with us to our highest camps on these trips), explored the glacier, and climbed two parallel couloirs (45°) en route to the summit.

It was a pleasure to return in December 2009 for 10 days, with Gabriel Fava (Argentina) to the valley's fantastic landscapes, home of the agile guanacos, and our calm base camp dominated by the impressive south face of Mercedario and the pyramid of Pico Polaco. Above base

(1) Veronica y Seis Hijos, on La Mesa (dots for hidden portions). (2) St. Jean de Passy, on Peak 5,700m (Pico Franco-Argentina). (3) The Serac Route on Pico Polaco. The first two were new routes, and (3) a repeat. *Anibal Maturano*

camp we established two camps on the Italian Glacier to reach the base of La Mesa, distinguished by its long summit ridge. We climbed a direct route to its central summit (6,130m) on December 15, gaining 1,130m on the northeast face near a ridge, difficulty D-/D. It was 45°/50° max, with a final 10m of 60° to reach the ridge. In the absence of previous known ascents, we named the route Veronica y Seis Hijos, dedicated to my wife and six children. The best time to climb this mountain is usually November and December; November could be colder, and in January the Italian Glacier can be impassable and the faces icier.

HENRY BIZOT, *France, AAC*

Aconcagua (6,962m), 2009–10 overview. This season had fewer climbers and more trekkers than last season, with 3,712 attempting the summit, compared to 4,048 last year. Foreign climbers rose to 89%. The first two weeks of January 2010 were the busiest for climbing. There were fewer evacuations and only one death. The historic summit cross was stolen. On past occasions the wind had taken, but it was found. This time anonymous thieves made off with it. Now there is a new one.

In addition to Chad Kellogg's solo (below), the massive south face saw other ascents. Young Argentine climber Mariano Galván soloed the Messner variation of the French Route, beginning February 11, 2010, and taking 34 hours. He went without a tent, in very low temperatures. Also in February, Argentines Gabriel Fava and Anibal Maturano ascended the original 1954 French Route.

MARCELO SCANU, *Buenos Aires, Argentina*

Aconcagua, Medicine Buddha to summit ridge. After acclimatizing on the Normal Route, on the summer solstice I scoped the 3,000m south face with intent to attempt a new route on the left side of the face, between the original French Route and the Romanian variation to the Slovenian Route. The bergschrund looked crossable, but the initial vertical ice pitch gushed with water. I walked away, and minutes later a huge avalanche swept the route and cone where I had stood. I tried to steel my nerves against the possibility that I could be swept into the debris at the base from any point on the route. I told myself that this was my route, and in eight hours I would be on it.

Back at Plaza Francia I was confident that I could climb the south face via a new route in a day, so I did not take a sleeping bag or tent, just 30m of 8.1mm rope,

Medicine Buddha, on the south face of Aconcagua, with the spot of Kellogg's shiverfest bivy also indicated. *Chad Kellogg*

some climbing hardwear, a stove, food, and extra clothes. I rested for a few hours before rising at 1:30 a.m. I centered myself with a meditation session before preparing for my departure.

I left camp at 4 a.m. I crossed two large crevasses before reaching the bergshrund, and headed up until I hit a dead-end. Finally, after 3½ hours I was in the couloir proper. Suddenly a massive avalanche rushed past, putting me on constant alert. I kept climbing and at mid-route reached a large ice step near an island of rock. Then I heard and felt a huge serac release and looked up to see ice shooting off the top of the rock island, followed by a billowing avalanche cloud. I ran, looking for somewhere to hide—nothing. I flopped on my face, with my arm cocked for an air pocket and prepared to be buried. Fine snow and 40–60 mph winds blasted me. When I continued, a solid pitch of WI4 led past the rock island and into a large, scoured basin, directly below the upper seracs. I crossed the basin to its left and looked back just as another serac released down the ice pitch. Timing is everything.

An hour later, at nearly 20,000', I climbed a 25' section of gently overhanging ice to surmount a bulge, and, above, I moved away from the seracs and onto the upper glacier. I had completed the first 2,000m in 12½ hours [to approximately where he joined the Messner Route—Ed.], but soon I encountered horrible unconsolidated sugar snow that dissolved underfoot. My progress slowed to less than 200' per hour. I had nearly 3,000' to go. At 11 p.m., after 19 hours of climbing, I knew I would not reach the summit in a day, and thought of how to counter hypothermia and frostbite. I descended to a block of ice on the hanging glacier and sought protection from the wind, as the temperature dipped below 10°F. I shivered away the night until the sun's greeting licked away the cold.

Tenuous sections of vertical ice led to the open face of the upper Argentine Route. I was within 1,200 vertical feet of the summit ridge, but half a day away in the deep sugar snow. At 2 p.m. I was above 21,500', but stuck in poor snow, daggering with both axes for upward purchase. I had been out of water since mid-morning and had used my last fuel canister. I desperately needed to reach the summit ridge by nightfall, and all of my life force clawed slowly upward. Then the sun went behind the ridge and the temperature dropped. I strained to keep up with the sun, because I knew that darkness was close behind. There were six corpses on the south face, and I did not want to join them. Eventually I traversed left for 1,500', directly below the ridge, working steadily. At 8 p.m., with a frostbitten thumb, I radioed my position to Gonzalo with the Guardaparques office. He encouraged me to push on and told me that rangers would be waiting at Camp Nido de Condores when I descended. I reached the ridge between the south and north summits at 10 p.m, welcomed by 50 mph wind. I walked like a drunken sailor. Around midnight I reached the Canaleta and descended familiar terrain. I had spent 42 hours on the south face, 35 of those climbing. I named the route Medicine Buddha (6,500' new, VI WI4 M4), after my favorite meditation *sadhana*. The *sadhana* is about the healing qualities of the Ocean King. Speaking the mantra is supposed to protect someone from an untimely death.

At 1:30 a.m. I made it to the ranger station at Nido. Oscar, Gonzalo, and Juan greeted me and offered hot drinks and a place to sleep. I related the story until 4 a.m. Then I crawled into my sleeping bag and slept soundly.

CHAD KELLOGG, *AAC*

Cerro El Cuerno, Direct South Face. On Cerro El Cuerno (5,462m), near Aconcagua, in February 2010 Argentines Jorge Ackermann and Tomás Aguiló opened a direct route (500m, 90° WI5) on the south face.

MARCELO SCANU, *Buenos Aires, Argentina*

Various climbs, Cordón de la Jaula. A group has been active in this area of Argentina, west of the Cordón del Plata, near Aconcagua but much more isolated. Access has been by the El Plata-Vallecitos col and Quebrada del Peine, after the Quebrada de la Jaula. On October 17 Pablo González, Gabriel Barral, and Alcides Massa left a 4,000m moraine camp and ascended the west face of a virgin 5,147m peak, which they christened Pico El Fede, in honor of Federico Campanini, who died on Aconcagua. They then traversed west and ascended two other peaks, making the second ascents of 5,168m Pico San Esteban and 5,165m Pico Rosa . All three climbs were on 40° snow. A few days earlier Gabriel Moretta, Matías Cruz, and Pablo Ruiz made the first ascent of a 5,245m peak near El Fede, calling it Pico Campanini, by coincidence also in honor of Federico Campanini. (The two groups were unaware of each other.) Their route climbs the south face via a 700m couloir, with 40–70° ice, and a crux 20m serac with ice to 90°. Above the couloir they continued, with climbing to 70°, up a ridge and to the summit.

MARCELO SCANU, *Buenos Aires, Argentina*

Cerro Freile, Inanición. On January 10, 2010, Waldo Farias and I did a new route, Inanición ("Starving"), on Cerro Freile (4,598m), Marmolejo Valley, Chile, 100km west of Santiago. The mountain is an island of granite between the typical bad rock of the Central Cordillera, and we thought it could offer good climbing. The route ascends the prominent east ridge. The first 300m are 5.5, but

Inanición, on Cerro Freile. *Waldo Farias*

with bad rock. Then the climbing steepens, 75°–80°, through loose granite blocks, 5.8 with poor protection, before traversing right (north) along a terrace through more bad rock, exposed, with minimal protection but easy, until emerging on the east face. Above, we found more vertical climbing, no harder than 5.8, with better rock. After 450 meters of climbing, we reached the upper ridge, very exposed and with more bad rock. Another 600m of climbing/scrambling along the ridge

Fernando Fainberg climbing Inanición, on Cerro Freile. *Waldo Farias*

brought us to the summit. The descent, via the 1942 first-ascent route, required care, between the terrible rock (not granite), exposure, and a 40° snow slope. We did the route in one day, taking 17 hours camp-to-camp; the vertical gain is 1,000m.

FERNANDO FAINBERG, *Chile*

Torres del Brujo, new routes. In late November 2008 Bernd Rathmayer and I traveled to Chile's Torres del Brujo, north of Patagonia, to find virgin rock. After several days of travel with horses and mules, we installed base camp at the foot of these great granite walls for three weeks. Because of the excellent rock and consistent good weather, we opened four new routes, all in alpine style and, with one exception, without bolts [see topos at aaj.americanalpineclub.org]:

In a sea of granite on a new route in the Torres del Brujo. *Aaron Richiger*

-Linea de los Suenos Sueltos (470m, 13 pitches, 6b A3), Torre Grande. A beautiful line, but with loose rock in the first seven pitches, it climbs the obvious first large, straight crack system right of the Gandalf route, with a dangerous start due to serac exposure. Descend by 60m rappels.

-Un Mantra para Machos (400m, 6 pitches + scrambling, 5.12b), on Torre 3. A beautiful line, on often perfect granite, and with an awesome fist crack in the middle. Upper pitches sometimes blocky, but good rock on the crux pitch. It's the first good line right of the huge dihedral. Some serac danger on the glacier approach. Rappel descent, max 63m but 60m ropes will work.

-Deceleracion (430m [250m climbing], 7 pitches plus scrambling, 6c+), on Torre Universidad. Superb route, excellent rock, good intro to the area. Begins in rounded dihedrals just right of Un Rato Para Maltrato. Descend by scrambling north to below a col, then continue easily to 65m above the snowfield and rappel (60m) from jammed blocks.

-Ahab (320m [200m climbing], 6 pitches plus scrambling, 7b), on Torre Universidad. Begins 50m above Deceleration. Same descent as Deceleration.

AARON RICHIGER, *Switzerland*

Cajon de Arenales, El Cohete, Gracias por el Aguante. El Cohete, known for its splitter cracks and the longest routes in Arenales, has a frequently climbed east face, but the other faces are practically unexplored. Its north face had no known routes until, after four days of vertical gardening and rock-tumbling in November, Ignacio Elorza, María-José Moisés, and I completed Gracias por el Aguante (600m, 7a+ (5.12-) [6b obligatory]). The route meanders up crack systems in the middle of the north face, beginning with a few ropelengths of easy climbing. Then one chooses between a 5.10 dihedral (recommended) and a slightly easier fist crack just to the left. A few more ropelengths of moderate climbing traverse leftward, to the base of a prominent dihedral that splits the face into two. We climbed the dihedral for 20m, then followed a thin crack that splits right and turns the corner for another 20m (5.10). A lot of weed pulling exposed a great 5.10+ finger crack that dies

Gracias por el Aguante, likely the first route on the north face of El Cohete. *Ignacio Elorza and María-José Moisés*

after 30m; the pitch ends with memorable slab moves out right to another system. Next comes the crux, a finger crack out a small roof, with a pocket of crystals that offer a salvation hold after the most difficult moves. Majo and Nacho dubbed the pitch El Techo de las Faldas (The Roof of Skirts), when, on the onsight attempt, I yelled out that I was wearing my skirt. Above are four more quality pitches, including El Paseo de los Cristales, where the wall has a sea of crystals embedded in the cracks. The last pitch is a strenuous, slightly overhanging fist crack in a red dihedral. As we were finishing the route with the last light, it started snowing—time to get our butts down. We drilled nine two-bolt anchors for 60m rappels (starting just right of the route and heading straight down; some of the rap anchors correspond with belays). Juan Tarrditti and I returned to add a really sweet three-pitch variation, El Cicatriz (The Scar), that branches left at a bolt on a ledge after the sixth pitch. It's a slightly overhanging dihedral to a flaring roof, then splitter hands in a corner before regaining Gracias por el Aguante.

CRYSTAL DAVIS-ROBBINS, *AAC*

CENTRAL PATAGONIA

Cerro Condor, first ascent, and other climbs and exploration. In mid-September, near the end of calendar winter, a group of 17 students and Jose Luis Troncoso, Pedro Binfa, and I, instructors from Patagonia Alpine Guides, mounted an expedition to several Chilean valleys, glaciers, and peaks that had had few, if any, visits and about which there was little information.

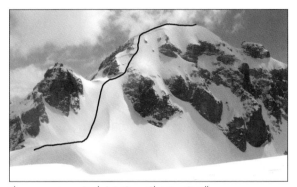

The new route on Peak 2,143m. *Christian Steidle*

Spring took an extra month to arrive, with furious winter conditions persisting. Temperatures fluctuated between -15°C and 12°C, snow was generally dry, and snowshoes made for efficient travel. Approaching from the south side of Monreal Lake, we spent a month covering terrain, going past Aislado Peak, and popping into the far end of the Orqueta Valley. We started with 10 days of food and at Orqueta got a 10-day resupply, before going onto Peñon Glacier, east of Cerro Castillo. On our way to this impressive, narrow

The route of first ascent on Cerro Condor. *Christian Steidle*

glacier tongue, we were distracted by a gorgeous 1,753m peak far to the northwest. We decided to try it and went with four days of food, caching the rest, intending to return and continue with the original plan.

On September 27 Jose Luis, Pedro, and I climbed Peak 1,753m, starting from the west, gaining the shoulder, climbing the south ridge, and gradually moving onto the southwest face and following it to the summit. The climb gained 3,300' of elevation, and, climbing unroped, we took three hours round-trip from camp. The last 1,000' had consistently 60° snow, with a small section of ice, taking us to the end of the ridge and a perfect summit platform. We named Peak 1,753m "Cerro Condor," an admittedly popular name given to several other Patagonian peaks. On September 28, another perfect day, all the students and we instructors repeated the climb. This time we protected the terrain and simul-climbed throughout.

The following day we returned to our cache and continued on our original way. On October 4 we reached the New Zealand Camp, where porters brought us 10-days food and fuel. Here, instead of going through Cerro Palo Pass and looping north and down-valley, we camped for 10 days and got familiar with the area. On October 6 seven students and we three instructors climbed Peak 2,050m from the north (not likely a first ascent). On October 11, 10 of us climbed the southeast aspect of Peak 2,143m (probably the second ascent), another pretty mountain, with 900' of consistent 70° snow on the face we climbed. We broke through an 80–85° corniced ridge, gaining a beautiful knife-edge ridge, and arrived on the rocky summit. We did most of the ascent and descent under strong winds and cold snow, making the fire back at camp even more enjoyable.

On October 15 nine of us attempted Peak 2,237m, in front of Cerro Palo, retreating from 2,150m after seven pitches of 65–75° hard snow, with a 20m section of 60° ice. The final portions of the summit ridge, a mix of snow and loose rock, remained. On October 17 we left the mountains, thankful for a good trip and with dreams of future projects.

CHRISTIAN STEIDLE, *Chile*

NORTHERN PATAGONIA

Cochamó, Pared de los Placeres, Hay Que Disfrutar and Erotica. In early February, Zoroastro Eduardo and I established two new routes in Cochamó, on Pared de los Placeres: Erotica and Hay Que Disfrutar, each 500m, 8 pitches, 5.10b. We placed no bolts, and the descents are walk-offs.

THIAGO C. PORTO, *Brazil*

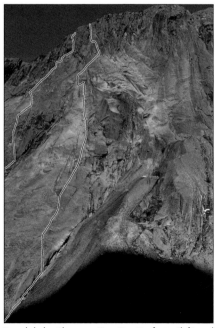

Cochamó, Señor Cara de Papa, La Cara de Decepción. Mid-January, 2010, after two weeks of consistent rain, Matt Othmer and I established the first route on the last formation before the pass to El Monstruo, across the valley from Trinidad Sur. We called it Señor Cara de Papa (Mr. Potato Head), and our line, La Cara de Decepción (5.11+ A2+), climbed the beautiful north face on what looked to be perfect splitter granite cracks. Cochamo's face of deception was quite ugly. The splitter cracks turned out to be moss-covered and flared as hell, the moss creating an illusion of deep splitters. We placed four bolts on

Pared de los Plazeres: Hay Que Desfrutar (left) and Erotica. *Thiago C. Porto* lead and Matt used his nut tool as a bird beak, but we got to the top of the face in six pitches, from where a fourth-class scramble would take you to the summit. We started rapping, and established a rappel line down the face. I do not recommend this route without either serious aid intentions or cleaning equipment. The best line on the formation will be if the waterfall dries up on the left side of the east face.

ASA FIRESTONE, *AAC*

Cochamó, Cerro Trinidad, La Orca. Juan Tarditti and I arrived in Cochamo, Chile, mid-February 2010 after a long rainy season. The trails that approach the Refugio Cochamó in La Junta had become rivers; people and horses were engulfed in knee-deep mud. We arrived to stories of rain, rain, rain, yet blue overwhelmed the skies. First we climbed the classic Bienvenidos a Mi Insomnio, a 20-pitch route that meanders up the east face of Trinidad. We were so charmed by the endless white granite and technical climbing on Trinidad that we decided to give Trinidad another attempt, this time on the 500m south face.

La Cara de Decepción. *Matt Othmer*

La Orca starts with moderate climbing through a series of flakes and continues up a crack system with discontinuous dihedrals. A long horizontal ledge then traverses right for 30m (3rd class), to the giant dihedral. Sev-

Cerro Trinidad, La Orca. *Crystal Davis-Robbins*

eral pitches head up the dihedral, ranging from fingers to offwidth. We freed everything on lead (up to 5.11) until the final 30m of the dihedral, which was a jungle. It's a drainage pipe from the summit and had grown an inch-thick layer of black moss and a diversity of plants. We cleaned it, but the vegetation will probably return. At this point you reach a huge ledge, and 20m left the route finishes with a fun moderate dihedral that leads to 150m of 3rd class and the summit. Descend the standard way, with two rappels to a col and then walking.

CRYSTAL DAVIS-ROBBINS, *AAC*

Central Patagonia

Cerro Kristine, first ascent. For ten years Yvon Chouinard and Doug Tompkins had been eyeing what they called "Cerro Geezer"—an unnamed, unclimbed ca 7,500' mountain a few kilometers west of Cerro Jeinimeni. The peak is the highest in a small range on the northern margin of Chilean Patagonia's Chacabuco Valley, a crucial habitat area that Kristine Tompkins' (Doug's wife's) Conservacion Patagonica purchased as the centerpiece of the future Patagonia National Park.

Yvon and Doug decided to give it a go the year before, but they were immediately thwarted by technical difficulties. Ten steps into the long approach Yvon's 30-year-old mountain boots shattered. Maybe this year, Yvon said, Cerro Geezer will finally give way to a geriatric ascent. I was honored by their invitation to tag along. Yvon was 69 and Doug 65. I realized this could be their last first together.

It took a day to get to high camp. We drove from Maillin Grande, on the north side of the Jeinemeni Reserve, up the Rio Furioso road to the abandoned mine, entered Conservacion Patagonica land near the top of the road, unlocked the gate, and continued into the reserve. We then walked east across the tops of a small range of low peaks. Our planned route rose in the distance, up the west ridge and trending north as it twisted toward the summit. On a wide, slightly sloping ridge next to a glacier at 3,000', tucked under a windbreak we made from rocks, we traded stories over dinner. I asked Yvon what he wanted to call the route if we got up it.

"Nothing," he said, "Just climb it…and walk away."

The next morning we arrived at the upper reaches of the glacier just as the sun glanced around the northern flanks. The last section had near-vertical ice, above the glacier, and brought us to the base of some technical rock. I had brought a rope and a small rack, and asked Yvon if we should rope up.

"Every man for himself!" he said with a hearty laugh and took off up the rock.

Doug was already up there, free-soloing an exposed slab that led to the upper ridgeline. I followed.

Early afternoon we reached the shoulder that led to the summit. Just below the summit blocks Doug stopped and stepped aside. In his typical gentlemanly fashion, he gestured for me to pass.

Cerro Kristine, near Chilean Patagonia's wild Chacabuco Valley. *Jeff Johnson*

"Here you go," he said, knowing that I'd never made a first ascent. "It's all yours."

I stopped, Yvon standing behind me.

"Go ahead," said Yvon. "Go for it."

I looked up at the virgin peak, the clear blue sky, and the vast wilderness of mountains and glaciers and rivers that surrounded it. We were three insignificant souls on the precipice of wonder.

Doug and Yvon have been friends for over 40 years. They had eyed this mountain for ten years, and they had already failed once. There was no way I was going to do this. With due respect I said, "It's yours Doug. You go."

The three of us stood on the summit in the afternoon of March 7, 2008. It was dead quiet while we took in the panorama. Wondering if they were serious about "Cerro Geezer," I turned to Doug and asked what he wanted to name it.

Doug looked out over the world and trailed off a bit in thought. Then he said quietly, "Cerro Kristine. Cerro Kristine. I think she would like that."

A few days later the three of us sat near Rio Chacabuco, sipping *mate* beneath the shade of poplar trees.

"How do you two do it?" I asked Doug and Yvon. "Most people when they get older tend to get more conservative in their political ideals, as if all that radical stuff was just a phase they went through as young adults. And most people your age aren't climbing mountains."

There was a long pause, as with all questions I had asked them. Then Doug said, "Don't hang out with old people."

The two of them began to laugh. Then Yvon, slapping his knee chimed in, "Always make sure you are the oldest person in the room."

Far in the distance, below a mass of cotton-ball clouds stood Cerro Kristine, resplendent in the setting sun.

JEFF JOHNSON

SOUTHERN PATAGONIA

Chalten massif, summary. The biggest news in Patagonia this season was not related to an ascent but to an attempt. David Lama's attempt to free the Compressor Route was well-publicized, but in spite of his spending close to three months in El Chalten, nothing came of it. Nothing except the further damage that Lama's film team did to the mountain. They fixed—and subsequently abandoned—ropes from the glacier to the bolt traverse, more than 700m, and added more than 60 bolts. These bolts were placed where not even Maestri had bolted back in 1970, on his infamous siege, when he dragged up a 400-pound air compressor. While Argentine guides removed the fixed ropes months later, the bolts remain, and many of the fixed ropes were abandoned in a haul bag above the bergschrund. One has to wonder what climbers in the Alps would say if the same was done to one of their most iconic peaks by a team of foreigners. In 1985 Fulvio Mariani made one of the best climbing movies of all time with *Cumbre*, documenting Marco Pedrini's solo ascent of Cerro Torre. They fixed three ropes, nothing more. Unfortunately, Lama and his entourage displayed a big regression.

Weatherwise this season was almost identical to the previous one, with much good weather at the start and end, in early December and late February. However, snow and ice conditions

Poincenot, east face: (1) Whillans-Cochrane (1962). (2) Fühl Dich Stark aber Nicht Unsterblich (Gietl-Schäli, 2009). (3) Patagonicos Desesperados (Piola-Anker, 1989). (4) Whisky Time (Pitelka-Eggler, 1994). (5) Potter-Davis (2001). *Rolando Garibotti*

remained mostly bad during the clear spells, with much snow and ice on the peaks. This prevented any ascents of Cerro Torre and focused activity on the Fitz Roy massif.

The weather forecasts continue to define a new climbing era, where Fitz Roy is regularly climbed with running shoes instead of boots, where hard-shells have vanished from climbers' packs, and where gradually the search for difficulty has taken the stage. Less constrained by weather, this is a natural evolution. The main beneficiaries of weather forecasting have been locals, who have stormed "their" mountains recently. Fourteen people stood atop Fitz Roy one day in late February, 12 of them Argentine—the *andinismo* is alive and kicking.

Apart from reports below of individual climbs, there were several ascents worth noting:

Luciano Fiorenza and Federico Arletti climbed a new route on the north face of Guillaumet, right of the Fonrouge-Comesaña, which they called Guillotina (300m, 5.11).

Also on Guillaumet, a route on the west face was reported two years ago, which was then thought to be new (Lost Men [*AAJ 2008*]). It turns out that Lost Men was a repeat of Padrijo, put up by Erich and Stefan Gatt in 1993, as confirmed by the Gatts; confusion seemed to exist about Padrijo's location. In the *AAJ 2009* photo, p. 208, line #3 is actually Padrijo, though perhaps with a variant finish. Line #4 does not exist (yet) as a route.

Argentine Milena Gomez and German Doerte Pietron completed the fifth ascent of the Afanasieff route on Fitz Roy, making the second all-female ascent of Fitz.

On the east face of Aguja Poincenot, Simon Gietl (Italy) and Roger Schäli (Switzerland) established a difficult new route. Over four days, which included fixing a few ropes along the Whillans ramp to reach the left side of the steep east face, they put up Fühl Dich Stark aber Nicht Unsterblich (Feel Strong, but not Immortal; 6c A3+ M5).

Also on Poincenot, Austrians Erich and Stefan Gatt climbed an interesting new route on one of the pillars attached to the west face. The 14-pitch Tango Viejo (400m, 5.10 A3) reaches a small summit that they christened Punta Mercedes Sosa. Also on Poincenot, Argentines Esteban De Gregori and Nicolas Benedetti climbed a seven-pitch variation to the Fonrouge-Rosasco route on the south face.

On the opposite side of the massif, in the Piergiorgio Valley, Americans Joel and Neil Kaufmann and Jim Toman climbed a new route on the north face of Aguja Tito Carrasco (300m, 5.10). Theirs was the second ascent of the tower.

ROLANDO GARIBOTTI, *AAC*

Cerro Fitz Roy, Historia Sin Fin and new pitches. At the end of February 2010 Luciano Fiorenza, Tomy Aguilo, and I—all Argentines—completed a new route on the west pillar of Fitz Roy,

on the face right of Supercanaleta and just right of Ensueño. On the first day we hiked from Chalten and climbed six pitches to a big ledge, where we fixed two pitches above and then bivied. The next day we climbed 10 pitches up steep, well-featured rock, placing natural protection, except for one belay bolt. After those 10 pitches we joined No Brain No Pain and bivied again. The following morning we climbed on, joining Tonta Suerte and eventually the Supercanaleta, reaching the summit in late day. We climbed close to 40 pitches, of which 18 were new, with difficulties to 5.10. The rock proved better than expected, and the climbing on the ridge (on Tonta Suerte and Supercanaleta) required weaving around gendarmes and other alpine trickery. We name our new line Historia Sin Fin.

The following week, with another good weather forecast, Luciano, Matias Villavicencio, and I made another foray on Fitz Roy, this time on the north face. On the first day we climbed to the Grand Hotel, a big ledge halfway up, following a line to the far left of Tehu-elche, just right of the French Route, for 15 pitches (some shared with the French Route). At the Grand Hotel we took a rest day and waited out some weather. On day three we started to the right of Hoser Chimney, with much offwidth climbing leading to a roof and a long traverse to the right, followed by a chimney that we avoided by climbing the face to the side. In the evening we reached the north ridge, 350m below

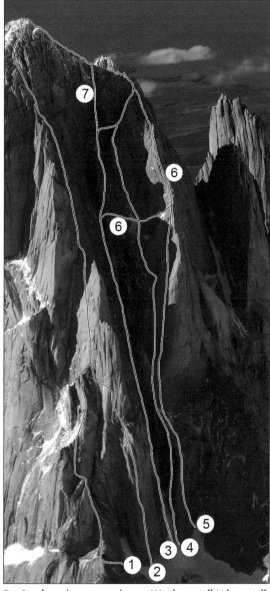

Fitz Roy from the west-northwest: (1) Afanassieff (Afanassieff-Afanassieff, 1979). (2) Chercheurs d'Absolu variation (Clouet-Dumarest, 2008). (3) Supercanaleta (Comesaña-Fonrouge, 1965). (4) Ensueño (Girardi-Nadali-Sarchi, 1995). (5) Historia Sin Fin (Ackermann-Aguilo-Fiorenza, 2010). (6) No Brain No Pain (Inselvini-Lerjen, 2007). (7) Supercanaleta Diretta (Demarchi-Mercolli, 1987). *Rodrigo Diaz*

The andinistas send: Historia Sin Fin, on Fitz Roy. *Milena Gomez*

the summit, and descended to the Grand Hotel via Hoser Chimney. We climbed 28 pitches, up to 5.11, dubbing our effort "Clinica de Aventura."

JORGE ACKERMANN, *Bariloche, Argentina*

TORRES DEL PAINE

Torre Central/Norte, Waiting for Godot to col. As reported on www.planetmountain.com and elsewhere, in January Austrians Hansjörg Auer and Much Mayr climbed a new line near the east-facing cleft between Torre Central and Torre Norte. Waiting for Godot (750m, 7b M6) ends at the col between the two towers. They fixed ropes partway up, using some aid on the initial ascent. While rappelling to their portaledge after their successful push, they stopped, and Mayr redpointed the crux, which they had not yet freed. The next day, in a storm that turned their line into a waterfall, they completed their descent.

Los Gemelos, The Slash. Graham Zimmerman and I left camp at 10:45 a.m. on January 25, 2010, just after it stopped raining and snowing. At 2:30 p.m. we stood at the base of the previously unclimbed east face of Cerro Los Gemelos, or the Twins. The first pitch was a 5.9R face, with laybacking up verglassed flakes. Then a 5.8 rising traverse, with a little aid and some 5.10, got us onto the ridge. A few pitches of easier 5.10 brought us to the notch that divides the much higher

Los Gemelos: (1) Audios Ayer (Matthews-Turner, 2009). (2) The Slash (Nicholson-Zimmerman, 2010). *Ian Nicholson*

north peak from the lower south peak. The next two pitches were more complicated than we'd expected, and around 11 p.m. we hit a steep, blank slab, just as it got dark and started snowing hard. Graham tried repeatedly to climb the unprotected slab, to no avail. Then we saw a small seam out to our right, and Graham set off into the darkness. It went! One more pitch, and we topped out at 12:40 a.m. in an increasing storm, becoming the third party to summit the higher of the Gemelos. We descended in a full-on storm, with near 100mph winds that blew us off our stances and pinned us down. At one point 100' of the rope escaped and went horizontal, slithering like a snake into the sky. We finished the last rappel at 4:30 a.m. and trudged down the glacier and out the ultra-shitty moraine, returning to camp after 22 hours on the move. The Slash (1,200', 10 pitches, IV+ 5.10b A2).

IAN NICHOLSON, *AAC*

TIERRA DEL FUEGO

Monte Sarmiento, west summit, La Odisea de Magallanes. At the western end of the Darwin Range in Chile's Tierra del Fuego rises one of the most beautiful mountains in the world, the ca 2,200m Monte Sarmiento. The mountain is 150km from the nearest human settlement and is only accessible by boat. Bad weather and overhanging ice mushrooms present major obstacles. The only successful climb of the main peak (east summit) was in March 1956 (Carlo Mauri

Monte Sarmiento, west summit: (1) Italian Route (1986). (2) La Odisea de Magallanes (2010). The main (east) summit is the peak to the left. *Ralf Gantzhorn*

and Clemente Maffei, no photos, strange description). The western peak was climbed by Italians in 1986 (again, no published photos and contradictory descriptions) and, well-established, in 1995 by Stephen Venables, John Roskelley, and Tim Macartney-Snape.

In 2010 Robert Jasper, Jörn Heller and I climbed the western peak in a 39-hour single push, with a short bivouac. [Unbeknown to the 2010 party at the time, their route was a variation to the 1986 Italian route, traversing into the face via the north ridge, while the Italians climbed the face directly—Ed.]

We sailed from Ushuaia on the *Tari II* (Skipper Micki Fischer) for 11 days to the east side of Sarmiento, at Caleta Escandallo, 20km from the peak. After three unsuccessful attempts, we started again at 10 a.m. on April 1. We crossed the rainforest and climbed a slippery ramp to the glacier at 600m, then crossed a heavily crevassed icefield to Collado Este (ca 1,000m), a pass at the beginning of Sarmiento's east ridge. Because of a snowstorm, we bivied in a snow cave. At 2 a.m. we left, going by the rule: "If you see a single star, move out." From Collado Este we crossed to Collado Norte, where the north ridge starts. We moved quite fast, despite short vertical passages, and before sunrise we were about 80m below the western summit. Huge ice mushrooms stopped us, and we had to downclimb 150m onto the ca 70° north face. We traversed 300m east to where we could cross the bergschrund and climb the face (some vertical-to-overhanging passages) [joining the 1986 Italian route]. After four ropelengths we reached the ridge between the east and the west summits. The ridge to the east summit was full of ice mushrooms, so we headed for the west summit. After a ropelength, again, though, same problem: huge, vertical mushrooms. Weaving around, we found a passage, reaching the summit around midday (La Odisea de Magallanes, WI4+). After half an hour on the western summit, we downclimbed the entire route—rappelling was impossible given the bad ice. At 1 a.m. on April 3 we reached Caleta Escandallo and *Tari II*.

RALF GANTZHORN, *Germany*

Antarctica

Antarctica

All ascents reported took place in the 2009-2010 season, unless otherwise stated.

ELLSWORTH MOUNTAINS

Vincent Massif summary. Around 120 people summited Mt. Vinson (4,892m), somewhat fewer than in recent years. Antarctic Logistics & Expeditions (ALE) guide David Hamilton and friend Patrick Bird made the second ascent of Mt. Rutford (4,477m), probably the ninth highest mountain in Antarctica. The pair finished their trip with another ascent of Vinson the following day, this time using the right-hand variation on the summit pyramid, climbing from west to east. This route was popular more than a decade ago, but now nearly all climbers follow the eastern ridge of the summit pyramid and descend the same way.

In the southern section of the Ellsworth Mountains several parties did numerous small climbs. Several people from ALE climbed minor peaks around the Union Glacier, in the vicinity of Connell Canyon and Henderson Valley. British climber Dominic Spicer and ALE guide Robin Jarvis also climbed in this area and farther south, toward Patriot Hills. The duo made two ascents above the Henderson Glacier—one a subpeak of Hoinkes Peak, overlooking Connell Canyon, and another overlooking the Union Glacier. They also climbed farther south in the range, making the second ascent of Gliozzi Peak (1,477m), via the northwest ridge. This summit lies in the Douglas Peaks, a small massif on the eastern side of Horseshoe Valley. Across the valley, in the Independence Hills (behind the Patriot Hills), they made an ascent of the west summit of Simmons, climbed a minor 1,356m summit south of Geissel Peak, and made the first ascent of Beitzel Peak, just south of the impressive marble pyramid of Minaret Peak.

DAMIEN GILDEA, *Australia*

ANTARCTIC PENINSULA

Mt. Foster, Mt. Parry, Savoia, False Cape Renard, Wandel Peak, Mt. Statham, Lars Christensen Peak. The highlight of the Antarctic season was undoubtedly the string of big climbs done by the French team of Mathieu Cortial, Lionel Daudet, and Patrick Wagnon, traveling aboard Isabelle Autissier's

Vol du Sérac on west spur of Mt. Foster, Smith Island. *Lionel Daudet*

Lionel Daudat on difficult, precarious rime, Le Vol du Sérac, Mt. Foster. *Patrick Wagnon*

Mt. Parry, Brabant Island, from the west. Nouvelle Vague ascends northwest ridge, which slants down left 2,500m from summit to ocean. *Lucas Trihey*

West face of Savoia from Jabet Peak, showing Bon Anniversaire Tristan. French descended south ridge to point marked D, then directly down to glacier. *Damien Gildea www.antarcticmountains.com*

Ada II. This was Daudet's third voyage to the mountains of the far south, having climbed new routes on Kerguelen in 2006 and traversed South Georgia—with a new variant on Mt. Paget—in 2007. This third installment of his southern trilogy was arguably the most significant and successful climbing expedition to the Antarctic Peninsula in modern times.

On their journey south the team first came to the massive Smith Island, highest of the South Shetland Islands, near the northern section of the Peninsula. The highest peak, Mt. Foster (2,105m), was climbed for the first time in 1996 after years of effort by various teams. It had become famous for its huge vertical relief and terrible weather. The French decided to try a new route on what they refer to as the western spur of the northeast summit. The first 1,000m were uneventful, but the terrain got harder as they climbed higher, and both Cortial and Daudet took roped falls, the latter while climbing an overhanging serac that plunged 1,000m toward the sea. After tunneling through steep rime mushrooms, they reached the summit at 2 a.m. on January 12, after 15 hours climbing. They then began a 15-hour descent. They named their 1,600m route Le Vol du Sérac (Flight of the Serac).

Their next stop south provided the jewel in the crown for the French expedition— the northwest ridge of Mt. Parry (2,520m) on Brabant Island. Only days after their adventure on Smith Island, the three made the coveted first ascent of the enormous northwest ridge, which rises over 2,500m directly from the sea. Though often looked at and talked about, the ridge had never been attempted and had become likely the biggest and best-known unclimbed objective on the Antarctic Peninsula. This season it was also the target of a primarily New Zealand team aboard the yacht *Australis;* on hearing that the French were there first, the New Zealanders climbed elsewhere.

Parry had been climbed three times before, always from the east: British in 1984, Chileans in 1993, and French in early January 2010. On that third ascent, Ludovic Challeat led Alwin Arnold, Arnauld De Fouchier, Thierry Garnier, Ulrich Goerlach, Vincent Logerot, and Philippe Poncin from the south and east, on skis. After making one camp on the route, they had a spectacularly clear but very cold and windy summit day, January 13. This team then moved across to the Arctowski Peninsula, making the probable first ascent of Scheimpflug Nunatak (1,150m), on the southern side of Laussedat Heights, and climbing to 650m on higher Pulfrich Peak in the northern half of the Peninsula.

Ada II delivered Cortial, Daudet, and Wagnon to Brabant Island eight days later, most of that time having been spent moored safely at the Melchior Islands. Dropped near the base of the northwest ridge, the three climbed over 1,000m up soft snow, before bivouacking in poor weather. They set off again 39 hours later, enjoying another 1,000m of climbing up an elegant arête, hampered only by several crevasses. The last 500m of this route are decidedly steeper; here the climbers encountered the hardest climbing, on soft, wet snow. Wagnon and then Daudet needed four hours to climb the last 100m, but all three arrived on

Zerua Peak, False Cape Renard. Spot the line. From exit of couloir, 42 Balais et Toujours pas Calmé finishes up crest of ridge to summit. Azken Paradizua (7a 90° M6, ca 600m, Baraiazarra-Pou-Pou, December 2007) climbs left ridge in its entirety. *Patrick Wagnon*

East face of Wandel Peak, Booth Island, showing La Mystique des Corniches...ons. 2006 Spanish route came across glacier plateau on right, below skyline ridge. *Damien Gildea www.antarcticmountains.com*

High on summit ridge of Wandel Peak, looking north.
Patrick Wagnon

Perplex Ridge, Pourquoi-pas Island. Bohemios y Locos to Mt. Statham marked. Arrow indicates attempted direct finish up partially overhanging chute. *Patrick Wagnon*

top at 6 p.m. on the 23rd. It took 19 hours to descend, and rough seas delayed their pickup. This did not seem an immediate problem, as they had brought sufficient food and equipment to counter such a delay. But a giant wave hit their site and washed away most of the food and gear. They shivered through the night, before the yacht could retrieve them the next day. Over the years there have been several incidents of large waves hitting climbers and camps close to shore, sometimes causing injury and loss of equipment. Prospective Antarctic climbers would do well to take this into account when operating in these areas. The French named their route Nouvelle Vague (New Wave).

The expedition continued south, arriving at increasingly popular Wiencke Island. The highest summit there is Savoia Peak (often incorrectly called Luigi de Savoia, or variants), the first real mountain climbed on the Peninsula, by Charcot's men in 1905. It has now been climbed several times. When seen from the west, its most obvious feature is a narrow ribbon of ice on the left side of the face. Climbers had talked of this but been deterred by avalanches down the face. The three French approached Savoia on skis, pulling sleds. On the 28th they were turned back by poor weather, but two days later tried again. The route gave 800m of steep ice climbing in the gully, followed by another 300m up the ridge to the summit, reached after 13 hours. They named their route Bon Anniversaire Tristan and graded it ED+. They descended the south ridge, thus traversing the peak, and rappeled the gully separating Savoia from the first peak on a serrated ridge running south. This ridge has seven summits, known colloquially as the Seven Sisters of Fief; several have been climbed. The first sister, closest to Savoia, was climbed this season by the New Zealand team aboard *Australis*.

Leaving the relative civilization of Wiencke Island and the tourists at Port Lockroy, the French headed south, but could not resist stopping at a small but enticing piece of False Cape Renard: the triple-summited feature at the northern end of the Lemaire Channel, just south of the more famous Cape Renard Tower (Una's Tits). Only one of the peaks on False Cape Renard has been climbed; the Pou brothers in 2007 created the technical route Azken Paradizua up the northwest buttress of the western summit, which they named Zerua Peak. Just right of that line is an unusually straight, narrow ice chute that had attracted the eye of passing climbers but had not been touched. Cortial, Daudet, and Wagnon climbed 550m up the couloir and ridge above, naming their line 42 Balais et Toujours pas Calmé, as a tribute to the fact that it was

Daudet's 42nd birthday and that he has not lost the burning energy to climb such adventurous routes.

The insatiable French then aimed for Wandel Peak (980m), the high point of steep, narrow Booth Island, which forms the western side of beautiful Lemaire Channel, one of the most photographed places in Antarctica. Wandel has been attempted many times over the years, usually from the north. On the east face, rising directly from the Lemaire Channel, is an obvious couloir, a straight shot to the

On narrow crest of Statham Peak, Perplex Ridge. *Patrick Wagnon*

summit. It is steep and somewhat threatened by seracs and overhanging cornices. The French climbed the couloir, reaching the summit ridge just north of the highest point, and proceeded toward it, negotiating the sinuous crest and wild cornices. Looking 900m straight down to the Lemaire Channel, they could see cruise ships passing by. Near the summit was a large crevasse, which Cortial fell into on the descent. The trio found that the top of Wandel Peak consists of two summits separated by a short, narrow ridge. They visited both, noting the smaller, steeper southerly summit to be a few meters higher. In February 2006 a Spanish team claimed the first ascent of Wandel, having climbed the north ridge, but it later transpired that they stopped 15m from the highest point. The French named their direct route La Mystique des Corniches...ons, a play on French slang, *Cornichons*—Mystical Idiots.

The team's last success was the probable first ascent of Mt. Statham, at the southern end of Perplex Ridge on Pourquoi-pas Island. This involved hard climbing up the west-northwest face. Perplex Ridge, which runs northeast to southwest in the northwestern section of Pourquoi-pas Island, has two named high points: Statham Peak and Matthews Peak. The latter is named after BAS geologist David Matthews, who in 1965 made the first ascent of Mt. Verne, one of the most notable peaks on the island. Approaching Statham Peak on February 18, the French climbed a couloir to reach a chute of extremely steep and overhanging ice high on the face, probably the steepest ice ever climbed in Antarctica. Part way up Wagnon backed off, so the team traversed right to easier ground and reached the summit after 12 hours climbing. They named the route Bohemios y Locos, originally referring to their summit as Peak Ada 2, not realizing they were on Mt. Statham.

Pourquoi-pas Island has a rich history of French activity. It was discovered by Charcot during his second expedition of 1908-1910 and was the scene of one of the earliest private yacht-based climbing adventures in Antarctica. In 1983 two separate French teams converged on the island, climbing and skiing on Mt. Verne and Mt. Arronax and flying ultralight aircraft.

One reason the expedition aboard *Ada II* devoted so much time to the Antarctic Peninsula—most teams charter a yacht for only 30 days—was so they could get to the big unclimbed peaks on Alexander Island, where no private expedition has climbed. However, poor weather and severe sea ice stopped them close to their goal, so they moved on to their final objective. Peter 1 Island (sometimes seen as Peter I øy) is one of the most isolated and windswept pieces of mountain on earth. The highest point is Lars Christensen Peak (1,640m), which is guarded by steep cliffs of rock and ice and rough seas with much pack ice. The seemingly unstoppable French managed to get onto the eastern side of the mountain on March 5, only to be stopped after 500m of climbing, by bad weather and large crevasses. They escaped to *Ada II* and were in Ushuaia two weeks later, finishing an expedition of 75 days. A stunning collection of photos from the expedition can be seen at http://nomansland.project.free.fr.

DAMIEN GILDEA, *Australia*

SOUTH GEORGIA

Punta Billy Budd and other ascents. In January 2009 Italians Giovanni Cristofori and Maria Cristina Rapisardi, a globetrotting couple from Milan who spend most of their free time sailing their sloop *Billy Budd* in Arctic or Antarctic seas, visited South Georgia with guides Luca Argentero and Matteo Pellin. The plan was a leisurely counterclockwise circumnavigation of the island, making touch-and-go ascents from the boat, thus avoiding the need for overnight stay permits. An adventurous and light approach was to be used—no contact between ship and climbers, no on-call weather forecasts.

Mt. Ashley, looking south from Bay of Isles. *Crag Jones*

While the sailing went well, difficult landing conditions and typically unstable weather limited climbing time. Nevertheless, in addition to several repeat ascents, Luca and Matteo climbed four peaks in the Nordenskjold area thought to be previously virgin.

The most interesting was Punta Billy Budd (ca 1,800m), where the long access from the coast was made more interesting by enormous crevasses that required ingenuity to cross. Steeper slopes and crevassed areas led to the base of the main ridge. An avalanche cone, a snow gully, and a 50° snow slope led to three technical mixed pitches, which Pellin found reminiscent of climbs on the Tour Ronde (Mt. Blanc Massif). The overall grade was TD+.

The other three peaks—Punta Luca, Punta Caterina, and an unnamed mountain near Nordenskjold—provided less technical but eminently enjoyable ski mountaineering. Pellin, who has a reputation for exploratory climbing on the south side of Mt. Blanc, feels that South Georgia is a treasure chest of unexplored technical lines.

LUCA SIGNORELLI, *Italy*

Mt. Ashley (1,145m, 1,136m GPS). Our main target had been Nordenskjold (2,355m), but we were beaten back below the summit ridge by a typically ferocious South Georgia storm. Sailing back along the north coast of the island in clear weather, we made an impetuous decision as majestic Mt. Ashley came into view. Skip Novak and I decided to make a one-day attempt during what would be our last day on the island. While with a group of Swiss and Italians in 2006, Skip had bookmarked Ashley as a nice unclimbed summit, easily accessible from above Salisbury Plain. We camped ashore on the night of October 29, behind Start Point on the edge of the Plain. It was a filthy night for weather. We got up at 2 a.m. and by 4:00 were skiing up the Grace Glacier. We reached its headwall at 5:30, stashed skis, and climbed to the col. The back end of the range is a broad, undulating glacial slope, overlooking the outer part of King Haakon Bay. After many waits for visibility, we identified what we thought was the highest point, the second of four summits in a chain stretching more than 1.5 km to the southeast. We proceeded up easy slopes to a col between the first and second summits, from where 100m up a steep icy dome led to the second summit. We belayed the last pitch from ice screws.

I waited for a clearing to confirm that we were higher than the distant third or fourth summits, but Skip noted that the ridge behind us, leading to the first summit, rose worryingly for more than 100m until it disappeared in cloud. We descended to the col and climbed the ridge to the first and highest summit. Though spectacular, with vast drops to the north, the broad ridge gave straightforward climbing, and we moved together through hoar-frosted towers to a flat summit, where we took a GPS reading of S 54° 06.963', W 37°21.650', 1,136m. It was 1 p.m. [Ed. note: The southern side of the Mt. Ashley falls gradually down to King Haakon Bay, the starting point for the legendary traverse in May 1916 by Tom Crean, Ernest Shackleton, and Frank Worsley.]

CRAG JONES, *Alpine Club*

QUEEN MAUD LAND

Orvin Fjella, various ascents. The first Austrian expedition to Queen Maud Land comprised Karl Pichler, Paul Koller, and me. Our goal was to ski east from the well-known Ulvetanna Group in the Fenriskjeften to the Holtedahlfjella, Kurzefjella, and Conradfjella. In November we flew from Cape Town to Novo Airbase and from there were lifted by Twin Otter to our starting point near Holtanna base camp. Our route, traversing some of the most spectacular rock and ice scenery in the world, was challenging. On the way we climbed 15 summits, of which 11 were first ascents.

Part of Holtendahlfjella, showing peaks climbed and named by Austrian expedition. (3) Roteck. (4) Austrian Peak. (5) Tiroler Spitze. (6) Styria. (7) Alexey Turchin. (8) Kamelbuckel. (9) Galileo Nunatak. (10) Steinskar Nunatak. (11) Galileo. (12) Peak of Silent Solitude. *Christoph Höbenreich*

We repeated Tungespissen (2,277 m), Mundlauga (2,455 m), and Sandneshatten (2,208 m). The first two, relatively close to Ulvetanna, were first climbed in January 1994 by Norwegians (*AAJ 1996*), the last in 2006, again by Norwegians (*AAJ 2007*). Sandneshatten in the

Rappeling from Tiroler Spitze. Snowy humped peak behind is Kamel-buckel, while rock peaks to left belong to Vinten-Johannsenegga Massif. *Christoph Höbenreich*

Two peaks in Skorvestallen Massif, first climbed by Austrians in 2009: Peak of Silent Solitude (left) and Mount Galileo. *Christoph Höbenreich*

Peak Alexey Turchin was ascended via snow slope from left to right. Big wall awaits future parties. *Christoph Höbenreic*

Conradfjella involved friction climbing on granite at UIAA II and III, though the final few meters to the summit were exposed and UIAA V. We used the rope for both ascent and descent.

Our most prominent first ascents and new named peaks were Tiroler Spitze (2,201m, S 71°52'15.8", E 8°55'00.6"); Austrian Peak (2,177m, S 71°52'27.9", E 8°54'50.6"); Peak Alexey Turchin (2,232m, S 71°51'19.8", E 9°00'12.7"); Kamelbuckel (Camel's Hump, 2,184m, S 71°50'28.1", E 9°00'01.5"); Mt. Galileo (2,528m, S 71°55'23.6", E 9°01'38.8"), and Peak of Silent Solitude (2,550m, S 71°54'59.2", E 9°03'28.1"). Tiroler Spitze involved real rock climbing up to UIAA IV; we had to remove our warm expedition outers and climb in inner thermal boots. Other summits were not difficult; some involved rock scrambles. We completed all ascents during November.

We had outstanding weather for our three weeks in the area, with brilliant blue skies and only one day when we were hit by a severe katabatic storm that produced winds in excess of 100km/hour. Daytime temperatures were between -15° and -20°C; the lowest we recorded at night was -36°C. However, the air is dry, and while skiing during daylight hours in strong sunshine we could be sweating at -15°C. This was my 11th polar expedition, many as a IFMGA qualified guide, and with new ideas I am inspired to return in the near future. If you are interested in taking part in an exploratory ski trip, please contact me at christoph.hoebenreich@aon.at

CHRISTOPH HÖBENREICH, *Austria*

Oman

WESTERN HAJAR

Jabal Nakhus, east face, F-Sharp; Jabal Dhawi, west ridge. Ian Gough organized a trip to Oman in January 2009, after learning about its limestone peaks from Paul Knott, another local of Christchurch, New Zealand. During 2004 Ian and I climbed together in New Zealand's Southern Alps. Five years later he produced an ultimatum: either buy and ship gear to him from the U.S., or join him on a Middle Eastern adventure. After some exploratory cragging on Wadi an Nakhur's 1,000m canyon walls and an attempt on Jabal Misht, we discovered two major desert limestone new-route possibilities by accident, while touring the Western Hajar. A rental sport-utility vehicle and the guidebook Oman Off-Road, proved invaluable in getting around the country.

On January 8, driving to the start of the hike up the Chains in Wadi ad Dil, we were greeted at the entrance to this narrow slot canyon by a virgin face. After a short hike up the can-

Joe Sambataro leading the 5.10 off-width on pitch two of F-Sharp. *Ian Gough*

The west ridge of Jabal Dhawi. Gough and Sambataro parked their car at the pass, and then traversed down and around to the foot. *Joe Sambataro*

yon, we returned for a closer look, spotting a direct crack system up the steepest part of the face and the general location of a possible descent. After lunch at the car, we racked up and made our way to the base. Three pitches of corner, off-width, and roof climbing led to easier ground, which we simul-climbed to the top. Unfortunately, the desert limestone was a sharp contrast to the polished sea walls of Thailand, where I'd spent the week before; our ascent left deeper gashes in our skin and a gnarled rope from rockfall. We reached the summit at dark and descended in moonlight, downclimbing and rappelling an unclimbed buttress to the north.

Ian's parents had joined us for half the trip. (Peter Gough was well known in the 1970s for establishing groundbreaking routes in the New Zealand Alps.) Unbeknown to us, Ian's father had been calling off local villag-ers' rescue efforts, climbers being an uncommon sight in this part

Joe Sambataro on the west ridge of Jabal Dhawi. *Ian Gough*

of Oman. Next morning a local herder informed us that the peak was called Jabal Nakhus, and we named our route F-Sharp (III 5.10, 500m).

On the road to Yasab we caught an intriguing view of Jabal Dhawi and drove across the As Sahtan bowl on the 12th to reach a mountain pass only a few hundred meters below the peak's summit. We traversed down and west across the lower slopes to reach the toe of its west ridge, which gains ca 350m of elevation. We roped up for a long pitch that led to an upper plateau and then, to keep it interesting, followed the crest of the ridge to the summit. This gave a rewarding 1,000m of fun 4th- to mid-5th-class climbing. We continued down the east ridge, before reaching a notch, from which we stretched the rope on a 35m rappel.

We met no other climbers during the trip and went weeks without seeing another tourist. Everywhere we traveled, Omanis extended their generosity and friendliness. They also showed us how to celebrate the first-ever Omani football victory in the Gulf Cup of Nations.

JOE SAMBATARO, *AAC*

Jabal Asala, Lulu. During our two-week stay in Oman, Marc Kuhn and I climbed one possible new route on the north side of Jabal Asala. Initially we wanted to repeat Petit Journée (D+ F5/5+, Frédéric and Magali Salle), but we had no proper route description and only a photo of the face. We found ourselves too far right of the route. (We now think it is on a different face.) The first 100m were a system of easy ledges (3) followed by a compact black slab. We roped up above the slab and left a sling through a thread at the first belay. The next four (50m)

North face of Jabal Asala with approximate lines of a selection of routes: (1) Omanic (UIAA VI+, Brachmayer-Precht, 2002). (2) Route 1 (British VS 4b/c, Davison, solo, 2002), (3) Route 2 (British HS 4b, Davison, solo, 2002), (4) Ramadan for Bolts (UIAA VI+, Brachmayer-Eisendle, 2002), (5) Rock Fascination, and (6) Lulu. *Pascal Trividic*

pitches, over slabs with cracks, were F5+ and led to a series of overhangs, below which we traversed left (60m, 6a/b, the crux). We left slings in place on this pitch. We then followed the easiest line, which slanted left to reach a large ledge. We followed this ledge rightward to the crest of the pillar and then climbed straight up for 200m (3/4) to the top, exiting 100m left of the summit. We climbed this route, Lulu, on January 14, 2010. Although it is 550m long

Marc Kuhn climbing excellent rough limestone on fifth pitch of Lulu. *Pascal Trividic*

and TD, only the first 250m are difficult. The main five pitches have excellent rough rock with lovely *gouttes d'eau* [pockets common in limestone].

PASCAL TRIVIDIC, *France*

Editor's note: Lulu appears to follow similar ground to (though perhaps left of) Sigi Brach-meyer and Albert Precht's 2001 North Pillar (TD), before moving left, crossing Rock Fascina-tion (TD, UIAA VII-, Brachmayer-Precht, 2001), and eventually slanting right to finish on the top section of North Pillar.

Jabal Kawr, M'Seeb Rappers, Anhydrous Living; Jabal Misht, Vultures' Keep; Amqah Tower; Jabal Nakhus, Hand Grater. During late December 2009 and early January 2010, Graham Rowbotham and I completed five new routes on the exotic limestone of the Western Hajar. Starting on the southwest face of Jabal Kawr near M'Seeb hamlet, we climbed an old watercourse on the shallow buttress immediately left of the Kawr Tower. Some sources record this as the line of the 1984 route National Day Climb (500m, D-), but I had concluded after a visit in 2007 that that route likely took an easier line much farther left (*AAJ 2008*, p.283). Nevertheless we found several rusty pitons on the opening pitches, and immediately below a capping overhang a hawser-laid cord around a tree and another peg with an old Joe Brown carabiner. An awkward, cam-protected traverse on friable rock allowed us to continue, and we found no further signs of passage. We named the route The M'Seeb Rappers (463m of climbing, TD- VI-).

Farther northwest on the same face lies the Kawr Pillar and its slightly more laid-back twin, which we named Mabos Pillar, after one of the nearby villages. We approached the Mabos Pillar by scrambling up a dry water-slide gully to bivouac in the hanging valley above. The crucial passage on the climb was an orange buttress at half-height. With careful

Right-hand end of southwest face of Jabal Kawr, showing (1) M'Seeb Rappers, and (2) Queen of Sheba (British E1 5a, Hornby-Ramsden, 1999). Wadi Girls (TD, Barlow-Nonis, 1999) takes front face of tower marked (3). *Paul Knott*

Southwest face of Jabal Kawr showing (1) The Full Qaboos (Chaudry-Hornby, 1999, solid line; Eastwood-Ramsden, 1999, dotted line) on Kawr Pillar, and (2) Anhydrous Living on Mabos Pillar. *Paul Knott*

Left end of Jabal Misht's south face. (1) West ridge (Eastwood-Ramsden, 2000). (2) Mishts of Time (V, Hornby-Knott, 2004). (3) West col (AD+, Davies-King-Searle, 1982). (4) Vultures' Keep. (5) Rock Vulture (VI, Knott-Simpson, 2008). (6) Madam Butterfly (VI, Chaudry-Hornby, 2000). *Paul Knott*

500m east face of Jabal Nakhus. (1) F-Sharp (5.10, Gough-Sambataro, 2009). (2) Hand Grater. (3) Descent route. *Joe Sambataro*

Graham Rowbotham on orange buttress of pitch 11 of Anhydrous Living. Kawr Pillar visible behind. *Paul Knott*

route finding, we avoided other steeper walls. As we returned by torchlight to the bivouac site, we passed a remote hamlet, far from any apparent water source. The inhabitants greeted us enthusiastically and plied us with dates and coffee. This encounter and our own water-constrained days led to the route name Anhydrous Living (924m of climbing, TD- V).

Also on the southwest side of Jabal Kawr, the newly completed but already blocked road to Nadan helped us access the main western arête of the Nadan Pillar. We completed 315m of climbing up to V+ on variable rock. At a prominent steep step on the arête, we could see no way to continue and retreated by rappel. We felt fortunate that the ropes pulled cleanly, as the stiff breeze threatened to snag them on endless spikes and flakes.

We were keen to include a route on Jabal Misht, so on January 3 we walked in moonlight to the far left end of the south face. Starting 100m left of Rock Vulture, we found superlative climbing, finishing near the main arête on the left side of the first tower. We named the route Vultures' Keep (456m of climbing, D+ V+) in honor of the residents of the tower. After this we drove north to seek out Jabal Murri, a mysterious rocky massif visible from high on Jabal Misht. We ascended Amqah Tower, the westernmost of Jabal Murri's distinctive set of towers, taking the best orange rock but finding only one pitch of IV in reaching this excellent viewpoint.

Finally, we took the main highway via Wadi Hawasinah to investigate the alluring east face of Jabal Nakhus, first climbed in January 2009 by Ian Gough and Joe Sambataro. Wary of the numerous off-width corners, we took a narrower crack line up the center of the main face. This provided solid, well-protected climbing, but the sharp rock bloodied our hands mercilessly. We continued to the ridge to complete Hand Grater (338m of climbing, VI or British HVS 5a+) and descended by rappel close to the Gough-Sambataro descent. Although the local villagers seemed concerned about our antics, the inaccessible summit ridge featured a pair of large, expertly constructed cairns.

After this, we took a much-needed soak in the Nakhl hot springs before returning to Muscat. In contrast to my previous visits, the weather on this trip was persistently cool with frequent afternoon clouds. Otherwise nothing had changed: the people remain as hospitable as ever, and we saw no other visitors except at well-known attractions.

PAUL KNOTT, *New Zealand*

Yemen

Socotra Island, Mashanig Towers. Several years ago I explored the eastern islands off the coast of Papua New Guinea, looking for steep rock formations that had yet to see humans on their summits. I found amazing spires. There I met an ornithologist who was also following his passion. I gave him my contact and asked that if he ever saw big, steep walls or towers on his travels, could he please send details. A year later he sent me information about Socotra Island off the coast of Yemen, saying there were big rocks in the mountains. That was enough for me; I had to go. There was little information about these mountains; this was perfect. I first planned

Twin towers of Mashanig, Yemen, looking from southwest: Daddy and Daughter. Rock bridge is visible in notch.
Mike Libecki

to go solo, but the political situation became intense, especially for Americans. I invited Josh Helling, one of my best friends and the best climber and partner I know. Political mayhem pointed to not going, but after he digested all the information, Josh decided to join me.

Mike Libecki on first ascent of Mashanig Daughter. *Josh Helling*

Our trip lasted from November 17 to December 17. We flew Utah-Germany-Ethiopia-Sana'a (the capital of Yemen). We didn't leave the Sana'a airport, as it was safer to fly straight to Socotra. The island is remote and little known, and it is likely we were the first climbers to visit. We arrived in the rainy season, but it was manageable. Locals were most helpful. We toured the island and hiked many miles to reconnoiter climbing potential. We had set our eyes on the highest part of the island and the two most prominent rock towers: Mashanig and its neighbor. I called them the Daddy and Daughter. We shuttled loads to a perfect base camp, with a nearby stream, and climbed routes on both towers.

At the base of the Daughter a spire, as big as a whale, had fallen between the towers to make a magnificent bridge, like a plank off a pirates' ship. We walked this plank and started our route right off the bridge, wonderful and exotic. Encased in clouds and rain, we spent one day climbing the north face on the time-bomb-slippery, lichen-painted rock, before reaching the summit in a white-out. From the pirates' plank bridge to the was just over 600' and 5.10.

Weather on the towers was unique. In the notch between the two there was wind, clouds, and rain 24 hours a day, and for our entire time on the Daughter we endured moisture mayhem. On the Daddy we started on the east face, and the tower became our shield. As we climbed, wind and clouds raced by, leaving us in a sanctuary from this torment. We reached a ledge just below the summit and bivouacked there, having enjoyed beautiful free-climbing in lichen-and moss-caked cracks. Next day we stood on the summit, above the clouds and rain. It was powerful and magical, to say the least, and we naturally put on our Year of the Ox masks and celebrated. The 800' route was also 5.10. We drilled no holes on either route and left only slings for rappel anchors.

We are going back to this island, because there is another mystery. Someone had been to the spires before, as on top of the Daddy, and also on a ledge beneath the summit, we found stacked rocks similar to those that locals would pile at gravesites. They were caked with lichen that formed a shell around the structure and had obviously formed after the rocks were stacked. A Yemeni botanist thinks these rocks were stacked at least 80-100 years ago and that a local may have found a way to the top of the spires for religious or magical reasons, or maybe to pass on to his next life. We hope to know more after our next trip. There may have been an easier route to the summit than the one we took, but we had a good look around. On any route up the tower an unroped fall would be fatal.

MIKE LIBECKI, *AAC*

Africa

MOROCCO

TAGHIA

Jbel Tadline, west face, Fugitivos del Paraiso. Arnaud and I hadn't climbed together in Taghia for four years, but as an amateur or guide, I have returned each year since. In 2005, with Thomas Berges, Michel Bourdet, and Joel Tost, I spent three days in the depths of the Akka n'Tazarte canyon, opening two routes on Jbel Tadline. There was still another line on the west face, more difficult, certainly, than the preceding ones. But without doubt exceptional. I had this project on my mind during the spring of 2008, and Arnaud told me he had similar plans.

With Martin Elias, we arrived in Taghia to find 80 climbers had just left and the guesthouse owned by the Messaoudis, returning it to a state of relative calm.

At Zaouia, I asked Moa to join the other mule-drivers and accompany us to the base of Akkas. Moa is one of those people I like to use again and again. Mohamed, Said's brother, played a useful part in the journey: he knows the way well, and sometimes storms change the normally dry riverbed and the path becomes difficult for donkeys. In that case we have to shift rocks and make walkways to aid the progress of our precious quadrupeds.

We arrived at the cave opposite the face by early afternoon. Binoculars changed hands

The west face of Jbel Tadline and the line of Fugitivos del Paraiso. *Christian Ravier*

The west face of Jbel Tadline and the line of Deux Anes et un plus fin. *Christian Ravier*

Jbel Timghazine with the line of Oeil de Lynx. Only pitches four to seven are visible. The obvious line to the right is the Diedre Pikort. *Christian Ravier*

Falaise de Machkour with the line of Alambic Sortie Sud. It is the pitch above the large roofs that still requires two points of aid. *Christian Ravier*

Arnaud Guillaume following a hard crack on Oeil de Lynx, Jbel Timghazine. *Christian Ravier*

and a line emerged on the great red wall. I won the draw and got the first pitch. I was anxious to leave the ground, a situation that suits me perfectly but would also please my companions. After the first few meters the message was clear: we would have to fight. An obvious line led up to a roof, then two bolts protected a rising traverse left to a belay. Above, the wall had no real weakness, but it was Martin's turn.

"Bon, bon, on va y aller" (alright, alright, let's go), he said in a French he has learnt with disconcerting ease. I know few people who can infiltrate slang into our most refined language with such elegance.

Martin climbed the difficult wall and succeeded in placing a bolt. However, it was directly above the belay, and if he were to fall, it would hurt. He trembled and then managed to place a hook, from where he drilled another bolt. Seconding this section, Arnaud and I fully appreciated the skill of our friend from La Rioja in northern Spain. It proved to be the crux of the route. At the belay we fixed our haul line, and then descended to the cave, a woodfire, and food and drink.

We continued with some anxiety due to the performance of our drill on the first day: we were only able to place six bolts before our first battery ran out. After Martin equipped the fifth belay, logic suggested that we only have enough power left in our second battery for one more bolt. Several tens of meters above, the wall gave way to less steep and more broken terrain, but before that a roof system and, on the right, a vague spur blocked our view. To the west we heard the rumbling of a storm and were immediately faced with moments of doubt. Martin found a few more good words, and Arnaud decided to see what lay to the right. He climbed under the roofs and then traversed right on beautifully sculptured rock. The last bolts were placed: he bypassed the spur, and knew that we would now get up. The rain arrived and then intensified. I climbed a long easy pitch and Martin led through to the top, soaked.

It was a magnificent eight-pitch climb, and is one of the best in Taghia. We quickened our pace in order to find the descent back into the canyon before nightfall.

Jbel Tadline, west face: Fugitivos del Paraiso (ABO- 7b+ 7a+ obl, 350m, Martin Elias-Arnaud Guillaume-Christian Ravier, June 6-7, 2008). The start is 50m left of Amazigh. Deux Anes et un plus fin (TD+ 6c, 250m, Elias-Guillaume-Ravier, June 9, 2008)

Jbel Timghazine, Akka n'Tafrawt: Oeil de Lynx (ED 7a+ 6c obl, 250m, Guillaume-Ravier, June 10, 2008). Situated to the left of Diedre Pikort.

Falaise de Machkour: Alambic Sortie Sud (7a+ and two points of aid on the third pitch, which has yet to be freed, 6b+ obl, 130m, Elias-Guillaume-Ravier, June 12, 2008). The start is a little to the right of Le Peau de l'Ours.

All routes require a full rack of natural gear.

CHRISTIAN RAVIER, *France (translated by Marina Heusch)*

Jebel Tadrarate, southwest face, Raum der Wünsche. During our successful trip to Taghia in 2008 (*AAJ 2009),* we discovered an untouched wall in the Tadrarate Canyon. Situated between the classics La Rouge Berbère (560m of climbing, 14 pitches, 7b, Guillaume-Ravier-Thivel, 2002) and Sul filo della Notte (570m of climbing, 12 pitches, 7c+, 7b obl, Larcher-Oviglia-Paissan, 2003) on the southwest face of 2,803m Jebel Tadrarate, the wall looked simply perfect, yet large and demanding. It was obvious we had to return in 2009.

The Tadrarate Canyon. Part of the southwest face of Jebel Tadrarate, showing the line of Raum der Wünsche. La Rouge Berbère takes a corner system in shadow to the right. *Rüdiger Helling*

Rüdiger Helling makes a balancy move on the initial section of Raum de Wünsche . *Tino Kohbach*

We had left some of our equipment, including bolts, at Mohammed's gîte (village guest house) in Zaouiad-Ahansal, so this time we had no problem with excess baggage on the flight. However, reaching Taghia gave unforeseen problems, due to the long, cold winter. Even by April the main pass to Zaouiad-Ahansal was still closed by deep snow, and the river crossings on the trek were difficult. We found much snow in the deep canyons and experienced a cold start to our climbing.

On our previous visit there had been two sheltered bivouac caves in the canyon, only 20 minutes from the start of our proposed route, but we discovered that one had been destroyed by rockfall during the winter. The other was good, but had room for only three people. Tino Kohbach, Michael Petters, and I stepped inside and slept there for nearly two weeks.

We worked on the route ground-up, finding the first third of the wall to be perfect gray, vertical limestone with excellent features. But due to the cold, our progress was slow, and at best we added only two new pitches each day. Once we got higher, the sun hit the wall earlier and stayed longer, motivating us to push hard. In the middle section of the face we followed a thin crack, which gave outstanding climbing at 7a+ and proved to be one of the best pitches on the route. Above, we discovered a good bivouac ledge below the overhanging headwall. Route-finding skills now became important as the rock was loose in places, unclimbable in others. But we found a weakness, traversing the lip of the big roof right, with great exposure. Two more airy pitches through the orange headwall led to easier ground and a system of corners. After 14 pitches, many 60m in length, we reached the top, having climbed nearly 700m with difficulties up to 7c.

After a couple of days' rest in Taghia village, we returned for the redpoint, adding a few more bolts in crucial areas and establishing a direct rappel line through the headwall to make descent more convenient. Our route name, Raum der Wünsche (Room of Requirements), was inspired by the Harry Potter stories. During our days on the wall and resting in the village all of us found what we were looking for: peace and quiet; friendly people; a great landscape, deep emotions, and an outstanding climbing experience. We hope the next party on our route has the same pleasures. For more information on climbing in Taghia, we recommend visiting the excellent Spanish website www.onaclimb.com.

RÜDIGER HELLING, *Germany*

Tagoujimt N'Tsouiant, northeast face, Cosmic Roof. At the end of April, Luka Krajnc, Alenka Lukic, Miha and Milena Praprotnik, and my wife Tanja and I, accompanied by Moroccan climber Jonathan, traveled to Taghia village, situated in an incredible canyon landscape of the High Atlas. Snowy peaks, green river valleys, traditional local life, vast houses of stone and mud, and transportation provided by mules and donkeys made us feel we were in the Himalaya, not Africa.

The first afternoon saw us running to the nearest wall, and in the next 20 days we climbed meter after meter, route after route. Formations above the village rise to an altitude of more than 3,000m, and the region has more than 10 walls over 800m high. There are more than 100 routes of all difficulties. We climbed a number of excellent routes, both easy and hard.

Luka and I also made a spectacular first ascent, Cosmic Roof (a.k.a. Separate African Reality, 7b, 750m) on the northeast face of Tagoujimt N'Tsouiant. We followed the obvious crack/corner system to the left edge of a huge 20m roof in the middle of the wall, climbed

Vast northeast face of Tagoujimt N'Tsouiant with Cosmic Roof marked. *Andrej Grmovsek*

over it, and exited via the ramps of Via del Sostre (UIIAA V+ and A3). In the lower part we crossed the bolted route Fantasia (7c) and in the chimneys above found two old bolts. Above, we climbed virgin rock, occasionally quite loose and dirty. On the super-steep crux roof I battled gravity for more than half an hour, negotiating gravel-covered loose rock and wide cracks, with poor protection. (We took only one 4 Camalot). We climbed the route in 13 hours, and in contrast to other ascents on these walls, used only traditional removable protection. We recommend future parties take two sets of Friends up to #4.

We repeated many difficult and beautiful routes, including: Fantasia (Luka and I; I made a redpoint ascent); Les Rivieres Pourpres (7b+, 545m) on Taoujdad (Luka and I, both onsight or flash); L'axe du Mal (7c, 500m) on Tadrarate (Luka and I, both redpoint); Canyon Apache (6c+, 355m) on Timrazine (Alenka and Tanja, Tanja on-sight); Au nom de la Reforms (6c, 340m) on Taoujdad (Alenka and Tanja, Tanja onsight); La Zebta (7b+, 260m) on the Paroi des Sources (Miha and Milena, Miha redpoint). Our trip to Taghia was excellent. We were

Luka Krajnc on (or off?) Fantasia pitch five (6c), Tagoujimt N'Tsoiant. *Andrej Grmovsek*

enraptured with its diversity and the hospitality of local people. And especially with the unbelievable amount of fine red walls, making it one of the best limestone regions we know.

ANDREJ GRMOVSEK, *Slovenia*

Timrazine Canyon, Capitan Tajin. Climbing almost every day from October 5 till the 17th, Abigail Pickett from France and Andrea Cattarossi, Daniele Geremia, Silvano Gosso, Marco Zaffiri, and I from Italy repeated beautiful routes and over three days created our own. This route is situated in Timrazine Canyon, known colloquially as Canyon Apache after the name of its most famous route, opened in 2003 by Arnaud Petit, Michel Piola, and Bênoit Robert (6c+,

Capitan Tajin, in Timrazine Canyon. *Francesco Fazzi*

Daniele Geremia equipping pitch four (7a+) of Capitan Tajin. Nasty loose block to his left was later cleaned. *Francesco Fazzi*

6b obl, 355m). Our new line lies 30 minutes walk from the village, on the true right wall (facing downstream) of the canyon. It is just beyond L'enfant du Sable (7a, 6c obl, 390m, Simone Sarti-Maurizio Oviglia, 2004, on-sight without using bolts) and the giant boulder that blocks the gorge. We climbed and equipped the 320m-high wall in eight pitches from the ground up, using 8mm bolts. The rock is really good, just a bit sandy in places, but the spacing between bolts is often long. While it is possible to rappel the route, it is better to descend on foot. We called it Capitan Tajin (7c+, 7a obl). The fifth pitch is the crux, though pitch six is 7b, and four and seven are 7a+ and 7a respectively. No pitch is easier than 6a+. Everybody who visits Taghia and stays in the *gites* (village guest houses) will understand the route name. The food is great, but not the variety: couscous or tajin, tajin or couscous. Nonetheless, we appreciate it—thanks Hamed!

FRANCESCO FAZZI, *Italy*.

MALI

Mata, northeast face, Akuna Matata. Claudio Mandrini, Paolo Stoppini, Alberto Zanada, and I left Italy on November 28 for Ouagadougou (Burkina Faso). From here we traveled almost entirely on dirt routes 380km to Daari, where we stayed at the campground run by Salvador Campillo and his wife, situated next to the Hand of Fatima. We climbed several established lines on the Hand, which provides a variety of routes. Then, after a couple of days scouting for a new rock wall, we discovered the northeast face of Mata, which was 40km from camp. It took us three days, December 4-6, to complete our route, which we named Akuna Mata-ta (320m, 7b). The route is bolted, but a good selection of cams and micro-Friends is essential. We were pleased with the rock throughout, and the quality of climbing. It's an elegant line with a high degree of exposure; we couldn't have asked for anything more.

ALBERTO ZUCCHETTI, *Italy*

NAMIBIA

Brandberg, Southern Crossing. Bushes, bird excrement, snake paranoia, exfoliating faces, incipient seams—all to get to one perfect crack climb. Throughout May, Peter Doucette, Kate Rutherford, and I explored Namibia. Chris Alstrin and Gabe Rogel joined us to document the trip. At the end, on our last possible climbing day, we completed a first ascent of Southern Crossing, a V 5.11+ (South Africa grade 26) on the Orabeskopf Face of Brandberg, Namibia's highest mountain. It took seven days of work to find the line, clean it, and do a one-day ascent.

Akuna Mata-ta on northeast face of Mata. *Alberto Zucchetti*

Namibia is not known for its climbing, which is why I wanted to visit. Better known as Africa's newest independent country, Namibia is the continent's largest source of uranium and diamonds and the locale of the Namib Desert, the Skeleton Coast, and tribal peoples. In the middle of the country lies Spitzkoppe, with over 80 established climbs. When I heard about it, I wondered where else in Namibia it might be possible to climb.

War, apartheid, and remoteness have combined to discourage exploration of many of Namibia's vertical landscapes. When I saw an out-of-focus photo of a 2,000' granite prow, with a mud Himba hut in the foreground, I knew I'd found my objective. The Himba are southern Africa's largest pastoral tribal group and have maintained their distinct cultural identity despite being on the borderline of battle, resources, and landscape. I wanted both things I saw in that photo: the culture and the climbing.

First we visited Spitzkoppe, an 1,800' granite dome with slab climbs reminiscent of Joshua Tree. We climbed there, then moved north, driving five long days on dirt roads to reach the Marienfluss Valley and the granite prow. It took only 15 minutes to realize that our 2,000' objective would be unwise. We were now 18 days into our expedition. We turned to the Himba instead and learned that a 200' 5.7 was just as valid as a 2,000' 5.12 when it comes to cultural connection.

We drove south. Plan C was a trip to the Brandberg and a granite face called the Orabeskopf: 1,500' of pure rock to a 7,200' summit. It is steep, riddled with cracks, and in the shade all day. The face had been climbed once, in 1974 by R. Blumgart and R. Lichman, who ascended the long, central chimney system. Since then, its remoteness has largely kept it off climbers' radar.

We started by trying to repeat the 1974 route but accidentally made a first ascent: Painted Giraffe (5.9, SA 18). We returned with six days' food, a triple set of cams and nuts, twelve bolts, seven hangers, a hand drill, and a single set of pins. We had one week before we were flying back across the Atlantic.

During our first day on the climb, Peter and I went all of 200', while Kate remained tent-bound after inhaling too much bird excrement the previous day, after a thwarted attempt on another line. It took two hours to navigate a 30'-high loose block that threatened to keep us from ever climbing a second pitch. And then there were the bushes. Peter and I quickly developed a routine of finding a stance with feet and one hand, using the other hand to attack foliage, sometimes with a nut tool. We had one goal those first two days: to make it to the brilliant orange and green corner above.

Climbers are generally seen as stewards of the land. But we had to clean these cracks heavily. We contemplated this every day. Would this be justified for any climb? I would say no. But this climb mattered, it was personal, and it was shaping into a phenomenal climb—a climb I

Orabeskopf face at Brandberg. From left to right: Dogbreath (5.5-5.8, Blumgart-Lichman, December 1974), Painted Giraffe (V 5.9, Burhardt-Doucette-Rutherford, May 2009), Southern Crossing (V 5.11+, Burhardt-Doucette-Rutherford, May-June 2009). Majka Burhardt

Majka Burhardt on pitch six of Herero Arch, Spitzkoppe, (5.12 A0, SA 26 A0). Gabe Rogel

knew would be repeated. This final element sealed our decision (and installed a corollary sense of responsibility to do an even better job cleaning). Peter and I fought those precious 70m for a total of eight hours in two days, progress directly proportional to one's tolerance for ingesting bird excrement and dirt. Each night we come back to camp by headlamp, on the way filling our water containers at a small hole, so that we carried up to 18 liters each trip.

I didn't expect to find great climbing in Namibia; I expected a brief stint of good climbing, followed by a long search for passable climbing. I'd gone to Africa before to merge climbing and culture, in Ethiopia and South Africa, and kept my climbing expectations low and my life-broadening hopes high. I'd told myself that utter climbing success might be impossible. I didn't say it out loud, thankfully, because if I had, we might not have found Orabeskopf. We might not have found a climb that was better than passable, maybe even great.

On June 1 we woke before dawn, placed our homemade grass brush in our backpack, filled our water bottles, and hiked for the last time across talus and grassy slopes filled with puffed adders, horned adders, and spitting cobras. We racked up and climbed 13 pitches to the top. I sunk my hands into freshly cleaned cracks, their grit pressing into my flesh. I brushed, blew, and kicked dirt off footholds—dirt we'd dropped there from our efforts in the crack above. We chimneyed, offwidthed, jammed, laybacked, and stemmed to the top of Southern Crossing, V 5.11+. It's climbing I would travel anywhere to do.

The ascent is chronicled in the documentary *Waypoint Namibia* by Alstrin Films. Get culture and insight into why Namibia might be the new model for African conservation at www.waypointnamibia.com. [Portions of this story were previously published in the 2010 Petzl catalogue: www.petzl.com.]

MAJKA BURHARDT, *AAC*

MALAWI

MULANJE MASSIF

Chambe, west face, Nkhalango Khoswe; lower Eastwood-Howell Route, first free ascent. Situated south of Tanzania and west of Mozambique, Malawi is a small country in southern Africa best known for its lake of the same name. A year ago Jeremy Roop and I had stumbled across a website describing a half-mile-long, 5,500' wall on the west face of Chambe, one of many peaks comprising the Mulanje Massif (9,850'). The wall was described as being broken after 2,000' by a large, broad jungle terrace, above which was an additional 3,500' wall. After reading the 1988 Frank Eastwood guidebook and firsthand accounts by two South African climbers, Alard Hufner and Mark Seuring, who had climbed on the west face in 1997, we decided it warranted further exploration. We found accounts of only two routes on the lower face and two on the upper face, three of which were pioneered by Eastwood in the late 1970s. We felt sure that we could find a new route to the top, preferably to the left of the Eastwood Route on the upper wall.

After arriving in Lilongwe, we began the hectic process of shuttling gear south through Blantyre to Likhubula, a town at the base of the Mulanje Massif. While in Blantyre, we chanced to meet Maggie O'Toole, Chairperson of the Malawi Mountain Club, who provided additional information about the Mulanje Massif. Five days after leaving the U.S. in late September, we arrived at a small Scottish mission (the CCAP House) in Likhubula, where we camped for a nominal fee. Heeding Maggie's recommendation, we hired a local guide for the first day of our approach to the lower west face of Chambe (called the Approach Slabs in the guidebook) and the start of the 1977 Eastwood-Howell Route. This turned out to be an excellent decision, as

The 5,500' west face of Chambe is split by the obvious jungle terrace. (1) West Face Direct-Approach Slabs (lower Eastwood-Howell Route, 2,000', UIAA V A1, Eastwood-Howell, August 1977). (2) West Face Direct, Main Wall (upper Eastwood-Howell Route, 3,500', UIAA VI A1, Eastwood-Howell, August 1977). (3) Nkhalango Khoswe (3,000+', IV 5.10, Forrester-Roop, October 2009). (4) Roshnik's Route (1,500', UIAA V, Bright-Strachan-Roshnik, September 1969). Not shown, left of (1), is Northwest Slab Route (2,000', UIAA V, Eastwood-Leisten, October 1976). *Jeremy Roop*

Joe Forrester climbing through a vegetated chimney high on Nkhalango Khoswe. *Jeremy Roop*

we had to transect private fields and weave our way intricately through increasingly thick jungle. In addition our guide Edwin taught us rudimentary Chichewa, the local language, which proved invaluable during our future unguided treks in the region.

On October 3 we awoke in the pre-dawn hours and walked four hours to the bottom of the lower west face, carrying a rope and light rack. Our goal was to climb the Eastwood-Howell Route, and then spend time perusing the upper west face for a potential new line. We soloed the first 1,000' quickly, the difficulties never more than 5.7. But the climbing was surreal. Large vellozia bushes and clumps of grass had recently been burned in a large wildfire, and we climbed upward among ash and charred trees, which lent a post-apocalyptical feel. The first major obstacle was an overhanging headwall created by a roof system crossing the lower face. According to the guidebook, the first ascensionists had attempted the obvious crack line but were forced to avoid it by drilling a bolt ladder. Approaching the crack, we found it entrenched with vegetation. Undeterred, Jeremy on-sighted the pitch, rating in 5.10d. The climbing was "fully jungle", with the crux an overhanging fist/offwidth to a "Tarzan vine" move. Above, the difficulty decreased, but the burned vegetation and ash increased, making climbing difficult. Despite these obstacles, we eventually reached the jungle terrace. We had completed the first known free ascent of the lower Eastwood-Howell route, at III 5.10d (2,000'.)

The terrace turned out to be bigger than it appeared from below and the jungle horrendous and devoid of trails or paths. Constantly fearful of cobras, mambas, and troops of unruly baboons, all of which we had been warned of, we clawed our way through knife-sharp grass and pricker bush. After three hours of "jungling," we arrived at the base of the upper Eastwood-Howell (we advise future parties to take one of the natural stream beds, instead of the pricker fields). To our disappointment the upper face of Chambe, left of the Eastwood-Howell, looked devoid of continuous natural features. While the granite featured

The new American route Nkhalango Khoswe seen from Chambe's lower west face-Approach Slabs. *Joe Forrester*

numerous edges, there were few crack lines, and the face was densely covered with grass. We felt this part of the wall would require siege tactics and substantial bolting, and not wanting to embark on such a mission, traversed the terrace south. We spotted a continuous crack system left of the 1969 Roshnik's Route, the only other known line on the upper west face. Stashing our gear at the base, we hiked off the terrace and back to Likhubula. After two days rest to heal jungle-induced wounds, we returned to the face and bivouacked at the base of our proposed route. Early on the 7th we started up the crack line, which from below had looked relatively clean. However, we found it to be a 3,000' nightmarishly vegetated slot, requiring every jungleering skill we had. We simul-climbed difficulties up to 5.8, and belayed four sections with difficulties up to 5.10. The majority of the climb was 5.5. The highlight was the 600' "Shelob's Lair," a huge, dark, bomb-bay chimney filled with spiders, scorpions, and other nasty critters. The climb became increasingly vegetated as we approached the summit, and we became adept at lassoing loosely adhered vellozia trees for protection. Six hours after starting, we reached the summit, leading or following each pitch free and onsight, leaving no fixed gear. We named the route Nkhalango Khoswe (Chichewa for Jungle Rats; 3,000+', IV 5.10.)

The Mulanje Massif is a magical place. The level of adventure was fantastic and the local people incredibly friendly, inviting us into their homes and making us feel part of the community. For further information talk with the Malawi Mountain Club, which can provide a wealth of information about access, conditions, and route activity. We thank the AAC and the Mountain Fellowship Grant for supporting this trip.

JOE FORRESTER, *AAC*

Norway

LYNGEN PENINSULA

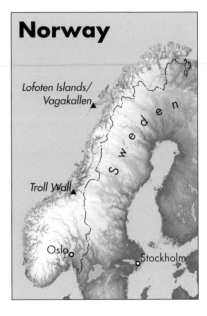

Stovelen, Northern Lights; various icefalls. April 2008: I'm eating dinner with Benoît Robert, who has just returned from a skiing and sailing trip to the Lyngen Alps. He shows me his pictures of Stovelen, a steep 850m face rising straight out of the sea and laced with thin lines. I'm immediately intrigued and must go there. There are so many first ascents to be made on that face, so the project is born. I log on to Google Earth. The region seems perfectly designed for the formation of ice climbs—cliffs topped by snow slopes.

The first obstacle is the cost. For a Frenchman, Norwegian prices are exorbitant. The price of renting a boat is equivalent to about six months' salary. But, despite the cost, eventually greatly reduced by our partners Millet and Petzl, there was no problem finding people who wanted to come along. I put together a team primarily of guides and aspirants, though I was the only person who knew all other members: Gérald Durant, Thierry Franc, Dorian Labeye, Benoît Robert, and Ludovic Seiffert. I also asked a friend, Bruno Peyronnet, a filmmaker. By making a film we hoped to finance the trip.

In early March we landed at Tromso after an exceptional winter season in France, where I'd climbed 50 days on ice. The captain of the boat, Ivar Bertelsen of Boreal Yachting, brought us to the base of Stovelen (N 69°43'32.04", E 20°16'54.07"). The face appeared drier than in the photos, and only one of the lines we'd envisaged seemed feasible. We climbed the couloir right of this coveted face to scope out the descent, which we would almost certainly have to do in the dark. The couloir was a delight to ski, as were the steep slopes directly beneath the summit of Stovelen.

At sunrise the following day, March 5, we headed for the face. The 25m approach from boat to shore was made in a Zodiac. We donned crampons and roped up on the beach. Above, ice and mixed sections were linked by snow slopes. These slopes concerned us, as it had been snowing recently, with much wind, making the stability of these slopes questionable. The first crux was a vertical dihedral plastered with snow. It ended with a snow mushroom, through which I had to tunnel. The route then climbed beautiful gullies, alternat-

Northern Lights on Stovelen rises straight from the sea. *Philippe Batoux*

ing mixed sections and snow slopes. The second crux was a chimney of unconsolidated snow, which we climbed with our backs on the rock and our crampons in the snow. It was the most runout section of the route, the only protection on the 60m pitch being a blue Camalot. But at least the belay was solid.

Eventually, we popped out into the exit couloir, directly beneath the summit. The couloir presented the easiest way to the top, but we were concerned about enormous overhanging cornices at the exit. We decided to branch left through mixed terrain threatened by avalanches and cornices. It was beginning to get dark. The last remaining obstacle was the summit cornice. I found a crack a few meters below it and placed a solid Alien. Now, well protected, I could commit to the final section. Fortunately, I found a small chimney that allowed me to climb easily without having to dig too much. We reached the top at nightfall. We named our route Northern Lights (V+/5+ M5+, 850m). Next day we climbed a sunny waterfall just above the sea, 500m of WI5/5+ and pure fun.

First pitch of Northern Lights, Stovelen. *Benoit Robert*

Most of the team had to head home to France for work, but Ludo and I stayed. We rented a car and headed out to explore the ice of the Lyngen Alps, making our approaches on ski. We had an amazing week, visiting a different location every day, never knowing whether the waterfalls we climbed had previously been ascended. It thrilled us to be ice climbing directly above the sea. The quality of ice was exceptional, often perfect plastic. Once, we climbed an entire pitch without swinging more than once to stick a pick. I have never seen such high-quality ice before; perhaps it is a result of being so close to the sea? For good quality ice to form, there needs to be a consistent temperature for

First crux section of Northern Lights, Stovelen. *Benoit Robert*

a long period, and it seems likely that the Gulf Stream helps by tempering variations in weather and temperature.

The most difficult line we climbed is located just above Massachusetts Institute of Technology Lynkspollen facility. It is a 350m waterfall with a final pitch of WI6—thin ice with a slightly overhanging section. The valley of Kafjordis is also appealing, with ice on both sides. Just above the south-side parking lot we met the only other climbers we saw during the entire trip: two Finns visiting for the weekend. We climbed a classic 300m waterfall of WI3/3+ and the beautiful wall just to its left, which gave 60m of 5+. We also went to the Ornersdal Gorge farther up valley, where we discovered many magnificent lines, including a 60m WI6, hidden at the end of a narrow corridor. A little farther into the gorge we climbed beautiful vertical walls, as wide as they were tall. We also climbed wonderful waterfalls above Furuflatten in the valley that leads to Jiehkkevarri. A one-hour approach reaches the classic climb of the valley, a wide, 100m flow of plastic ice. Just a few hundred meters to the left, we climbed another beautiful, slightly-steeper wall. During our stay in Lyngen we also crossed the sea with dolphins, made excellent ski descents, and were in awe of the aurora borealis. I have to come back; there are entire valleys filled with hundreds of waterfalls still waiting to be discovered.

In September, while descending the Matterhorn with a client, Gerald fell. Our trip and the film that we made (Stovelen et les garçons de Bruno Peyronnet ; www.realpiniste.com) are dedicated to his memory.

PHILIPPE BATOUX, *France (translated by Todd Miller).*

LOFOTEN

International Winter Meet. From March 8 to 15, 2009, the Norwegian Alpine Club (Norsk Tindeklub, NTK) invited nearly 40 climbers from all over the world to Lofoten, for a "come-as-you-are" climbing meet. The event was organized by Marius Morstad, and the philosophy was simple: put climbing and adventure in focus, without add-ons like sponsors, logos, DJ's, slideshows, and competitions—no public, no clinics, no organizers with yellow T-shirts. The ingredients of the meet were also simple: a wealth of mountains and a group of hungry climbers.

Most participants were very pleased with the meet. The climbing was adventurous, and everyone found his or her own personal challenges in the mountains. Wintertime in Lofoten is special. There are few route descriptions, no bolts, no directions. You have to rely on your own climbing and navigational skills, and are under constant threat of being overwhelmed by the scenery. Yet civilization is just around the corner. Many

Three new routes climbed on Andopshesten during meet (1) Den Norske Sor-Afrika Linja (WI5 M4, 700m, Thomas Mann-Sjur Nesheim). (2) Slovenian-Norwegian (Marko Prezelj-Trym Atle Saeland, not to summit). (3) American (Dave Turner, solo). Andy Cave and Dave Hesleden later started up Slovenian-Norwegian route and finished on American. *Dave Turner*

Haveren, with three new routes. (1) Forste Gang (V 4, Gina Bjornstro-Duncan Tunstall. (2) Shekina (AI7 M4, 500m, Bjorn Eivind Artun-Sjur Nesheim). (3) Arctic Mousaka (AI4, Dimitris Daskalakis-Mariza Daskalakis, excellent iced corner). *Bjorn Eivind Artun*

"As we drove south, the weather cleared and we spotted an isolated mountain with an inviting line splitting the face. Moderate mixed climbing led to a stout finish with detached ice and an overhanging chimney." Creatures of Love (5.10 M5, 400m, Ben Rosenberg-Hans Petter Watn) on Hoven. *Ben Rosenberg*

Rulten. (1) The Bullocks (M6+, 500m, Bjorn Eivind Artun-Marko Prezelj, beautiful thin ice and rime separated by easier sections). (2) Unnamed (Aymeric Clouet-Christophe Dumar est-Andreas Klastrom). (3) Original 2008 winter ascent (local Lofoten climbers). (4) Czech direct variant (M6, Martin Klonfar-Jiri Splichal). Not marked is Vestpillaren (AI5+ M6, Dimitris Daskalakis-Hans Petter Watn). Descent was via snow slopes right of 3. *Marten Blixt*

participants expressed their gratitude for been given the opportunity to climb under such conditions.

Routes described in this report are just a few climbed during the meet. Most of them are likely new, but it is amazing what old-timers achieved in the distant past.

Below is a selection of comments by participants, followed by one longer report:

"Climbing in the Lofoten Islands was a wonderful and breathtaking experience. The combination of mixed climbing on beautiful, steep mountains within a few meters of the arctic seashore was magical, and something we never believed existed."—DIMITRIS AND MARIZA DASKALAKIS, *Greece*

"Lofoten is an amazing winter climbing destination. The meet was totally informal, and it was up to each climber to make his day. This meant it was a meet for experienced climbers looking for adventure, and finding their own way. The conditions were great, and loads of new high-quality lines were climbed. Not a single bolt was drilled into the rock. The locals emphasized that placing bolts on Lofoten mountain routes was bad."—BJORN-EIVIND AARTUN, NORWAY

"It is difficult to describe my feelings about climbing in Lofoten, because it was so fantastic: great people, great climbing, and great landscape. Perhaps the best description of the week would be the single word from Bjorn, followed by silence, when I joined him on the summit of Rulten—MAGIC! Myself, often labeled a perfectionist, can just add 'Perfect!'"—MARKO PREZELJ, *Slovenia*

"I am prepared to stand up for Norway wilderness—it has given

me such pleasure and special memories. Norway has some of the biggest potential for adventure in the world, and it needs to be cherished."—ANDY CAVE, U.K.

"Information had been scant. All I was told was that 'you California boys will stand out.' As I am from Colorado, I was nervous."—BEN ROSENBERG, U.S.

"Rulten is the king of Lofoten mountains, with difficult access. Hospitable locals transported our small team of six climbers by boat. We landed beneath the mountain at sunrise. Visibility was poor, and as we were dependent on the boat ride back, we chose the easiest way up the north face—the original route. We made a hard four-pitch variant on the headwall—Scottish style mixed climbing on thin ice. A strong team of ice aces, Bjorn and Marko, were climbing close by, so we had great fun together. When we summited, the weather improved, offering lovely views of Lofoten's mountains and islands. 'What a magic day,' said Marco—the real truth. And there were more unforgettable days in the mountains."—JIRI SPLICHAL, Czech Republic

Describing Vagakallen and his new route, Glass Uhr: "A perfect wall. We were amazed at first sight—such a playground, yet with only one existing route. Unbelievable. We spent half a day on the wall, enjoying perfect ice and mixed climbing. Not too hard but pretty long. The descent from the top can be dangerous after heavy snowfall. The way back to civilization (Kalle), dubbed by locals 'the walk along the coast,' should be renamed 'the struggle for survival.' It proved an intense experience for a tired climber."—MARTIN KLONFAR, Czech Republic

Norwegian-Slovenian route (Marko Prezelj-Trym Atle Saeland) on Stauren. Not marked are British Route (Andy Cave-Dave Hesleden) and Norwegian Route (Anette Larsen-Trym Atle Saeland). *Marko Prezelj*

Trym Atle Saeland close to summit of Stauren. *Marko Prezelj*

(1) Norwegian-Slovenian route (Marko Prezelj-Trym Atle Saeland) on Stortinden. (2) Rosenberg and Watn line (WI4, 400m, Ben Rosenberg-Hans Petter Watn, good line on thick ice). *Marko Prezelj*

Vagakallen. (1) Mieux vaud tard que jamais (TD+ WI4 M6, 650m, Jonglez-Marceron-Marshal-Mouret-Plaze, 2004). (2) Glass Uhr (M5 80°, 650m, Klonfar-Splichal). *Jiri Splichal*

*And talking about his new route on Trollfestingen, Stop the Reactors, with Christophe Dumarest and Jiri Splichal: "A short, bold route. We were instructed by locals to 'walk up this valley, and when you see something hard, it's probably still unclimbed.' So we did. The route had three pitches. The first was hard M6/M7 with a poor belay on a few knifeblades. I led it with one fall. The third pitch was funny climbing on unstable snow crust. Christophe and I shared tools, both climbing with a special strategy: Nomic in left hand, Reactor in right. Hence the name of the route."—*MARTIN KLONFAR, *Czech Republic*

"*Lofoten was perfect. I don't think there could have been a better venue for this meet. One of the best aspects of these types of events is getting to know different climbers, from all over the globe, with whom you share a common bond but would otherwise not meet.*"—DAVE TURNER, *U.S.*

MARTEN BLIXT, *Norway*

Abrahams Tind, Nothing Compares to You. "Up here, there is more ice than in Europe and Canada combined." Bold words from Marius Morstad, who invited two alpinists from every UIAA country for an international gathering in Lofoten. "We promise fresh fish daily." OK, I'm convinced.

I land in Narvik with Patrick Rothlin and meet the French and Czech teams. In a car loaded beyond capacity, Andreas Klarstrom, a young Norwegian ice climbing ace, races through the night, disregarding snow drifts and black-ice passages. He's in a bad mood. Two weeks previously foreign climbers completed one of the great lines in Norway—and placed a few bolts. This is taboo in Norway and remained the topic of conversation for the following week. The event organizers wanted to promote winter alpinism in Lofoten but maintain its adventurous character. The Norwegians are in agreement: on alpine terrain they want no bolts.

Abrahams Tind. Nothing Compares to You follows obvious thin ice line falling from just right of summit. *Urs Odermatt*

This doesn't present a problem for us; we only want to climb steep, compact waterfalls. And that's the problem on Lofoten. "Rock is rock, and ice is ice," says Marius, indicating that local climbers have a different understanding of ice-climbing from ours. Deeply influenced

Thin ice and mixed climbing on Nothing Compares to You.
Urs Odermatt

by Scottish mountaineers and their weather, ice-climbing here takes place on iced-up rock routes and snowed-over, moss-covered walls. *Torf* [turf] is what they call frozen grass tuffs, their eyes glowing when they speak of them. Frozen waterfalls are nowhere to be found. Keeping our expectations in check, we invest a day in discovering the potential of the region. Just half an hour's drive from our base at Kalle, we find a compact, perfectly formed, almost 400m-high rock pyramid. A hair-thin ice line runs directly down the wall, from summit to ca 50m from the ground, where it disappears into granite bedrock. Another line like this does not exist, perhaps could not exist. Without hesitation we decide to attempt it the following day.

As mountain guides we are used to getting up early, but don't necessarily want to during vacation. Despite the Russian team creating a ruckus at 6 a.m., no one else gets out of bed before 7 a.m. Carrying heavy sacks and wearing snowshoes, we attempt to shorten the approach by going directly across the frozen fjord. However, Patrick, who regards any turns on skis as a sign of cowardice, becomes the scaredy cat and panics at the thought of wet feet. So we slog around the entire waterway, arriving at the base of the route after almost 2½ hours. The line is clear: a vertical, moss-filled crack leading directly to an ice hose. It is every ice-climber's dream. Four hours later only 20m separates us from the start of this dream. That may sound good, but it means we had only climbed 30m. Then, with little danger of wet feet, Patrick showed his true colors. Fearlessly he scraped the small amount of ice from the crack, plugged in Friends, hammered wobbly pitons, and an hour later reached a point two meters above the stance." No way. We're either too wimpy or weak.

Next morning we cut the approach to 1½ hours and arrived at the foot of the wall pumped. This time we tried a crack system farther right. A perfect 10m-long hand crack helped us through the crux. Too bad that the only Friend that would fit was down on the beach. The suffering was long, but our words were short. Patrick made it. I was left with the pleasure of leading the remaining 40m of vertical moss-covered wall. Thank God it was time to rappel for dinner. Tomorrow is another day.

At our lodgings we swapped info with other teams. Again the topic of bolts arose. I've probably placed more bolts than some of these guys will clip during their entire lives, and I'm decidedly for bolts after having several bad experiences. Nonetheless we couldn't escape the fascination of working only with removable gear. We decided we would either climb our dream line clean or leave it for others.

Day three. It snowed during the night, and worse weather was forecast. It was time for one last try. Two steam engines raced to the base of the line. With snowshoes and crampons cached in the right places, and the trail broken, we regained our high point by 10:30 a.m., and were greeted by a cloud of spindrift.

The next seven hours were climbing heaven. Overhanging *torf* passages, ice-filled cracks—the climb exceeded all expectations. When the sun poked out from the clouds at noon, we took it as a bonus. In 400m we found no easy sections, nor a single ledge. The ice was continuously vertical, sometimes even overhanging. Five minutes before dusk we reached the summit. Even though it is visible from the road, Abrahams Tind had not previously been climbed. A local fisherman could hardly believe it was possible to reach its top, and we had a hard time believing it ourselves. Although the altitude would be insignificant in the Alps, a 900m summit can still be immensely fascinating. We called our route Nothing Compares to You (WI6 M6+, 420m).

While we ate breakfast two days later, the Czechs were in the process of repeating our route [Editor's note: The Czechs graded their ascent WI5 M6], while we were trying to decide whether to spend another day in Bacalao Cafe or tackle one of the short gullies above the street. Marius really didn't exaggerate. There is potential for millions of new routes along the coast of northern Norway.

URS ODERMATT, *Switzerland (translated by Martin Gutmann)*

Six ascents. Our trip had an adventurous spirit, partly because we are 19- and 20-year-old geology students with a lot of time and little money. And Norway is one of the last places in Europe where you can enjoy true adventure. For us, during our last year at high school, Lofoten was a dreamland. We traveled by bus to Oslo and hitchhiked for three days to Lofoten. We brought everything, including food and fishing rods, in really big bags. Cod was the mainstay of our menu. The only thing we had to buy in Norway was bread. We spent every night for six weeks in a tent or, when the weather

Goodbye High School on Pillaren. *Lukas Marecek*   Hungry Eyes on Maslitinden. *Lukas Marecek*

Sweet Home Moravia on Lille Vagakallen. *Lukas Marecek*

was bad, old, empty fishermen's huts. Our rules and goals were simple: first ascents in light, fast, clean alpine-style, without portaledges, bolts, or other non-adventure gear.

For us Moskenesoya is the most amazing of Lofoten's islands and still has great climbing potential. There were around 18 routes before our arrival; we added three, and other huge lines are still waiting. We don't understand why all Norwegians only climb around Hennings-vær, Kalle, and Svolvær.

We created our routes in harmony with Norwegian climbing ethics: no bolts. When seconding a pitch one of us was often heard to shout, "Hey, that was a fucking crazy run-out man!" The two new routes Goodbye High School (Norwegian 7-, 460m) on Pillaren, and Sound of Waves (6+, 450m) on Brandtuva are really bold and scary, with lots of unprotected slab climbing. Our most serious route was Ticket to Greenland (6+ A0, 550m) on Hel-vetestind, which has very steep, continuous climbing. Sweet Home Moravia (7- A2, 260m) on Lille Vagakallen is nice, with Chamonix-quality rock. We also put up Fish Restaurant (5+, 350m) on Djupfjord Buttress, and Hungry Eyes (6 A1, 420m) on Maslitinden.

We won't disclose more information on the routes; you should go try them yourselves. We climbed six new lines but more importantly had a great time, with much climbing and fishing in one of the most wonderful places on earth. We say to the Norwegian community, "Thanks for your enormous kindness. You helped us on many occasions."

LUKAS MARECEK AND JIŘÍ SVIHÁLEK, *Czech Republic*

Moskenesoya Island, Helvetestind, Thirst in the Clouds. During the summer Alexey Orudzhev, Alexander Shamakov, and Andrey Varvarkin from Russia made the first ascent of Thirst in the Clouds on the central section of the main face of Helvetestind, located in the southern part of the island. Their ascent completes a line attempted by Finn Jensen and Arild Meyer in 1984 or '85. The Norwegians bailed on their ninth pitch, a thin wet crack, after persisting August rain. Their high point matches the Russian's pitch 13. Arild returned the following year with Anne Fyhn but found the route too vegetated for a serious attempt. As far as they got Finn and Arild found the route neither difficult nor serious; the 14 bolts placed by the Russians must be questioned.

MARTEN BLIXT, ALPINKLATRING, *Norway*

Lillemola Island, Man Hands. Who wouldn't jump at the chance to establish a granite big-wall route on an uninhabited island, with crystal clear water in the inlet and a 100' approach to the base across a white sand beach? From June 25 to 28 Mike Brumbaugh, Andrew Burr, Brian Hep-

Ticket to Greenland
6+ A0, 550m

Ticket to Greenland on west face of Helvetestind (Hell's Wall). In 2009 Russian team also added a big wall route at F6a and A2+/A3 directly beneath the highest point in this photo. *Lukas Marecek*

Sound of Waves on Brandtuva. *Lukas Marecek*

pner, Ari Menitove, and I put up Man Hands (5.11+, 1,000') on an east-facing wall on Lillemola (Litlmolla), one of the smaller Lofoten Islands.

We flew to Kiruna, in northern Sweden, via Stockholm, and drove west to Lofoten. We'd seen a picture of the wall in a guidebook and thought it would be a fun adventure. When we asked for the island with the big wall, locals knew what we meant. Although a team had previously established an aid route, there were no recorded free climbs. We hired a jet boat from Svolvaer and with three days food and made base camp directly beneath our project. From camp to the base of the wall took less than five minutes, and we were climbing above the tent and white beach the whole time. Our island had one small cottage; some otherwise deserted islands have summer cottages that are used a weekend or two a year.

Man Hands was seven pitches long. Highlights were leaving beautiful dihedrals with finger and hand cracks, to face-climb over compact terrain toward the next crack system. If someone was to bring a drill and place a few bolts between non-connecting crack systems, this wall would provide many wonderful 1,000' routes that could then be climbed carrying only traditional gear. We rapped the route from nut and sling anchors. It was one of those once-in-a-lifetime experiences, which Andrew summed up with, "After major unearthing of the first pitch and heavy cleaning of pitches two and three, we completed the climb ground up in one push under the ever-lit sky of an Arctic summer. From the jet boat ride, to the man-eating mosquitoes, to the hermit crab fights on the beach, I loved every minute of it".

ROB PIZEM, *AAC*

Man Hands on Lillemola island. *Rob Pizem*

ROMSDAL

Trollveggen, French Route, first free ascent. In a remarkably fast two-day ascent, August 7-8, Sindre and Ole Johan Saether made the first free ascent of the French Route on Troll Wall. Since it was first sieged from July 22 to August 10, 1967, by Yves Boussard, Jérome Brunet, Patrick Cordier, Claude Deck, and Jean Frehel, there have been relatively few ascents of this direct line up the tallest part of the face left of the Rimmon Route. A topo from ca 2000 described the 1,200m route in ca 37 pitches up to Norwegian 6+ (5.10c) and A4. Sixteen of the pitches needed aid. The Norwegians made one attempt prior to their successful ascent and established a few variants while climbing the route at 8- or 5.12b. Sindre is considered to be ahead of his time in the context of Norwegian climbing. He prefers to climb hard in the mountains, with his father and close friends, but if he competed in national bouldering championships, he would certainly finish in the top three.

LINDSAY GRIFFIN, MOUNTAIN INFO, *from information supplied by Marten Blixt, Norway*

ROGALAND

Gloppedalen, south face, Civil Twilight. There are climbers, and there are *climbers*. The c*limber*, Johannes, who has honed his skills doing several serious solo climbs on Blamannen, is struggling midway to the great roof on the south face of Gloppedalen. Your humble narrator—the climber—who has lately spent too many hours on his laptop, is munching a chocolate bar 15m away. Johannes stops exhausted, biceps bulging from continuous maximal reaches, and digs out his first aid kit to get some power gel. It occurs to me that I'll have to bag this pitch as well, it being too steep to clean while jumaring.

South face of Gloppedalen, with Civil Twilight. *Marten Blixt*

I ended up in this miserable situation because of the wettest July in Rogaland in 25 years (this says something) and exceptional routefinding skills of my friend Johannes Karkkainen. The rain wrecked plans for multipitch free-climbing, so we drove between cliffs depicted in *Klatring I Rogaland*, looking for a dry valley. Eventually, in the parking lot of the mighty Gloppedalsura, Johannes dug out the ancient telescope that once belonged to his girlfriend's grandfather, and became obsessive about a potential aid route that would pierce the impressive, complex roof system of Gloppedalen south face.

Johannes negotiated the roof, while I hunched on the haulbag, shivering in soaked clothing. Following, I wasted a lot of energy trying to free a stuck Camalot but made it to the edge of the roof easier than expected. From there it was another 30 minutes of struggle with jumars stuck in a deep, narrow crack. We set up the portaledge and collapsed into a well-deserved but broken sleep. It was not the remaining part of the route that kept me awake but the thought of descending with a 40kg sack. The traditional descent involves scrambling down a notoriously slippery slope and finding a tree from which to rappel the last 100m. This, I quickly realized, was not an option, but luckily, after a phone call, a local contact came to our assistance. And before reaching the parking lot, we had to cross the god-forsaken boulder conundrum that probably still hoards the corpses of German soldiers from WWII. Weeks later, as I went climbing back home, I found my rock shoes full of lichen, a reminder that the last two pitches involved more bushwhacking and blueberry eating than climbing.

While the most memorable section was aiding across the big roof, it is at the start of the aid-climbing, where the line deviates from all-free route, Nr. 1, that the technical crux is found. Here a series of thin cracks requires precarious placements (A3) and a pendulum from dubious gear. Above, the next pitch (C1) could be free-climbed when dry.

We called our route Civil Twilight (A3, 11 pitches). It shares its first three pitches with Nr. 1; the last four are easy free-climbing. The rest are generally A2-A3. The route name refers to the time of day when the sun has set, but civil servants are still able to work. It kept appearing in the weather forecasts we checked several times each day, hoping that a dry summer might be on its way.

JUHA EVOKARI, *Finland*

Editor's note: there are 10 routes on the south face of Gloppedalan. After climbing the first three pitches of Nr. 1 (6+, 400m, Bjorgen-Price, 1995), Civil Twilight moves right to finish between Slipset (6+ A3, 425m, Basen-Bjorgen, 1993) and Reisen til Ixtalan (7, 425m, Diesen-Ormseth, 1993).

Kjerag, Russian Route. I've not been climbing in the mountains that long, and although I'd visited the Caucasus, Crimea, Tien Shan, and Khibiny peaks of the Kola Peninsula, I'd been fascinated by mountains outside the former Soviet Union. After training in summer 2008, we decided to visit Norway and enter the Russian Winter Championships by climbing a new route on the Troll Wall. However, the Troll Wall was well-known to Russian climbers, and the championships are oriented toward first ascents, so we consulted Andrei Varvarkin from St. Petersburg, who knows Scandinavian mountains well. He provided three alternatives, of which we chose Kjerag.

Kjerag is popular with local climbers, and there were at least 13 existing routes, with grades of Norwegian 6 and 7 free and A3+. According to the information we found, the left side of the central wall is taken by the 21-pitch Hoka Hey, first climbed in 1996 at Norwegian 7- A2+ and freed in 1999 at 7+ (5.11c/d). Toward the right is the 1995 route Skjoldet (A3, 18 pitches, climbed free at 8). We decided to create a direttissima between the two.

We started our journey on the night of February 20, with support from the Russian Mountaineering Federation and Sport Committee and friends who lent us equipment.

Galina Chibitok, Ivan Dozhdev, Vyacheslav Ivanov, Aleksey Lonchinsky, and I, with 10 huge bags in two cars, headed to the Finnish border. We spent a day on a ferry to Stockholm and the following night reached Oslo, where we stayed with friends, Marina and Feodor Iskhakov, who had been gathering information on Kjerag. We took a second ferry in the evening and finally reached Lysebotn, a small town that has become a Mecca for BASE jumpers and climbers. It's lively and well-populated in summer, but tourism stops in winter, and Lysebotn is transformed into a quiet village.

We reorganized our gear on Lysebotn's pier, separated from our goal by a short stretch of water, which we crossed in a canoe I'd brought. We set up base camp near the foot of the wall, and on our first day the weather was fine. However, the only other good day was during our descent. The rest of the time the weather astonished us by its diversity: rain at the base, cloud and wind higher, snow in all its various forms, and continuous humidity. It was the humidity that affected us most; despite only mild frost, we were always cold.

For the first 12 days on the wall we were continuously wet. Three of the team did all the leading, with a different leader each day, though sometimes changing during the day in bad weather. On the lower part of the wall we found several bolted rappel anchors. When we reached the crux, we discovered a bucket of canned food hanging from a bolt, the food dated 1999. We

Russian winter route on central wall of Kjerag. *Valery Shamalo*

took it with us. Then, in the overhanging section, we found two copperheads, the higher of which had a rappel loop. Above, the wall was featureless and had no sign of passage. We continued, risking still being there when our visas expired. We reached the top having climbed 95% of the route on aid. In summer it's my opinion that a strong leader could free climb 20-25%. Our route had an overall classification of Russian 6B.

VALERY SHAMALO, *Russia (translated by Ekaterina Vorotnikova)*

Editor's Note: The Russian route is a continuation of Aishan Rupp's attempt. He left much gear on the wall for a second try but was killed on the Matterhorn. The new line shares a pitch with Tsunami (Norwegian 6+ A4, Stein Ivar Gravdal-Trym Atle Saeland, 2003) at its steepest point, "and was not welcomed by local climbers, as it is rumored to be heavily bolted." According to Saeland there are ca 20 routes on Kjerag, and many climbers had eyed this new line but were waiting until they were competent to do it in good style. In 2008 Martin Jakobsson (Sweden) and Mikjel Thorsrud (Norway) made the first winter ascent of Skjoldet, leaving Lysebotn on January 9 and not returning till the 23rd.

Russia

CAUCASUS

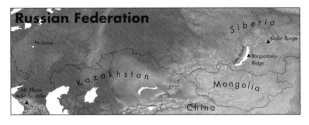

Mizhirgi (5,025m), north ridge, winter ascent. In early January 2009 Sasha Gukov, Sergey Kondrashkin, Alik Izotov, and Viktor Koval made the first winter ascent of the north ridge of Mizhirgi East Peak (4,927m). Mizhirgi is an eastern subsidiary summit of Dych-tau (5,204m), on the ridge toward Koshtun-tau (5,151m); its north face rises almost 2,000m above the Mizhirgi glacier basin. The route was first climbed in August 1952 by Vasiliy Pelevin's five-man team, at hard 5B, but is rarely repeated, due to poor rock and stonefall in the lower section. The 2009 team experienced much spindrift and bad weather, making five bivouacs before reaching the summit. On the third they spent most of the night keeping the tent from being crushed by snowfall; on the following morning the temperature was ca -30°C.

North ridge (NR) of Mizhirgi slants down left from East Peak. *Supplied by Anna Piunova*

From the East Peak, reached January 8, they traversed a sharp ridge to the West Peak and descended the south ridge (5A), continuing through the night to arrive on the Sella Glacier at 3 a.m. Next morning, while approaching the Jangi Kosh hut, Gukov was partially buried by an avalanche but managed to extract himself. Next day Kondrashkin was buried under half a meter of snow by another avalanche. His ski pole was visible, and teammates dug him out. They finally reached the Bezengi Glacier, to the west, and waded north down the moraine in a meter of fresh snow. This was one of the most impressive winter ascents in the CIS during 2009.

ANNA PIUNOVA, *www.mountain.ru*

On north ridge of Mizhirgi in winter. *Supplied by Anna Piunova*

Fisht (2,867m), west face. One of the most important first ascents in the Caucasus during 2009 was a direct route up the middle of the west face of Fisht, the most westerly snow-and-ice peak in the range. To enter the 27th Russian Championships for Alpinism in the First Ascent category, the team of Eugene Bolkovoy, Eugene Dmitrienko, Vasily Petyakshev, Dmitry Podlesny, and Alexander Spindonov (leader) chose winter and climbed the face, a 560m rock wall, from March 1 to 6. Because of poor weather, there were some days on which the team could climb no more than one pitch. They used fixed rope and a portaledge camp. They descended from the summit by the line of the ascent.

ANNA PIUNOVA, *www.mountain.ru*

SIBERIA

West face of Stolb, with Russian route and campsites marked. *Supplied by Anna Piunova*

Kodar Range, Stolb (2,850m), west pillar. Russians Bashkirtsev, Davydenko, Glazunov, Pedenko, and Veretenin, from the Siberian city of Irkutsk, made the first ascent of the pillar forming the left edge of the west face of Stolb, the southwest summit of Czar's Throne. The team climbed this 700m rock route in 14 60m pitches, from February 23 to 28. The overall grade was 6B. A large terrace splits the face at one-third height, and the team spent four nights here while working the route above. They made one more camp halfway up the headwall. They regained the foot of the face on March 1. Only the summit day was clear; on one day they were unable to move due to weather and wind. This route was one of seven nominations for the 2009 Russian Piolet d'Or.

The Kodar lies east-northeast of Siberian Lake Baikal. The highest summit rises to over 3,000m. In February 2003 a team from Krasnoyarsk established a new route on the 1,000m southwest face of Czar's Throne. Graded 6B, it was at that time probably the hardest on the mountain, though the poor quality of rock led to the amount of free-climbing being minimal.

ANNA PIUNOVA, *www.mountain.ru*

ALTAI

South Kurai, various ascents. In May Marc Bullock, Matthew Freear, Tim Moss, Nancy Pickup, Michael "Spike" Reid, and David Tett traveled to the South Kurai, becoming almost certainly the first non-Soviet mountaineers to visit this area of the Siberian Altai. The Kurai is a range of relatively low mountains north of the Taban Bogdo and northeast of Bielukha. Immediately south of the Kurai rise the more extensive North and South Chuisky.

After a long day's drive from Barnaul, followed by a two-day approach with horsemen, the team established base camp. Over the next eight days they placed two advanced camps and

Kurai panorama from Hammer and Sickle summit. (A) Peak 3,089m. (B) Peak 3,259m. (C) Peak 3,071m. (D) Peak 3,167m. *www.davidtett.com*

made five ascents. Their liaison officer, Igor Fediaev, from the Russian agency K2 Adventures, had visited the area but not ascended any mountains. He believed no one had climbed there, but the British found cairns and a hammer-and-sickle sign on a walk-up summit above base camp. On the four other summits climbed, Peak 3,071m (N 50°22.336', E 87° 45.829', PD, May 30), Peak 3,259m (N 50°21.925', E 87°45.842', PD, May 31), Peak 3,089m (N 50°22.414', E87°47.014', PD, June 2), and Peak 3,167m (N 50°23.938', E 87°45.045', F, largely walking, June 3), they discovered no sign of previous activity and feel these may have been first ascents. Climbs were on snow and rock, with no need for a belay.

At the end of the expedition Freear and Moss walked south into the fringes of the North Chuisky and on June 7 completed the locally well-known Teacher Horseshoe (F), which reaches an altitude of 3,179m at N 50°5.305', E 87°45.174'. Throughout the expedition the weather was perfect and surprisingly hot, meaning that snow conditions were generally poor, as indeed is the rock in this area.

LINDSAY GRIFFIN, *Mountain INFO, Tim Moss, U.K.*

Kyrgyzstan

PAMIR ALAI

KARAVSHIN

Asan (4,230m), northwest face, Timofeev Route, first free ascent. In August, as part of a Mammut Team Trip, I joined Austrian David Lama and Swiss Giovanni Quirici and Stephan Siegrist, and with photographer Rainer Eder, filmmaker Christoph Frutiger, and expedition organizer Robert Steiner (Germany) made a trip to the Karavshin.

After flying to Batkin and continuing by road, we trekked three days to reach base camp in the Kara-su, where we found other expeditions, mostly Russian and Ukrainian. We wanted to open a new free route on the 900m northwest face of Asan and spotted a potential line in the middle of the wall. However, after two pitches we retreated. As one of the Russians later explained, all possible routes on this wall have been climbed; away from existing lines the rock is shit. But the man gave us good advice on possibilities for free-climbing established routes, so we changed our objective to the Timofeev Route. [Editor's note: It was first climbed during the 1988 Soviet Championships, as primarily an aid climb, and given the hardest Russian grade of 6B. Later it became relatively popular and was downgraded to 6A. Some of the aid was eventually eliminated to give technical difficulties of F7a and A3 on sound rock.]

After two-three intro pitches, the next four pitches, on steep slabs, were hard, and had originally been climbed with Bathooks. Old Soviet 5mm bolts were in place. As there were no real cracks, we added new ones, side by side. With one exception there was no additional drilling on previously unbolted ground (bolts were added at belays and the route equipped for a rappel descent, but the standard of aid climbing will not have changed). This section proved to be the crux. Above, we continued up a fantastic series of cracks, fixing a total of 10 pitches before making our final attempt.

The northwest face of Asan showing the Timofeev route. *visualimpact.ch* | *Rainer Eder*

At base camp the alarm sounded at 1 a.m. We made the one-and-a-half-hour approach to the foot of the route, jumared 500m, and at 6 a.m., first light, we set off on the remaining pitches. Our idea was to redpoint every pitch, and this proved not to be so difficult, as the maximum grade was 7b, and the cracks and protection were supersolid. Lama, Quirici, Siegrist, and I reached the summit at 2 p.m.

We walked east to the Ak-su valley, where a large group of climbers from Geneva was based. Leading through on the Perestroika Crack, Giovanni and I on-sighted

Stefan Siegrist on pitch 4 (7b+) of the Timofeev Route. The rock wall behind and in shadow is a subsidiary buttress below Usan (4,378m). To its right, in the far distance, is Pik Piramidalny (5,509m), while below is the moraine-covered Kara-su Glacier. *visualimpact.ch* | *Rainer Eder*

every pitch. Stephan teamed with one of the Geneva climbers, Sébastien Pochon, as David had returned home, led the entire route, and on-sighted every pitch: the first one-day on-sight. We reached the summit in about eight hours, an effort that left me destroyed. There is still much potential in this region for aspiring free climbers, due to the climber-friendly granite - a climber's Eldorado as Saladin once described it.

NINA CAPREZ, *SWITZERLAND, with additional material from* ROBERT STEINER, *GERMANY*

Editor's note: The single crack splitting the west face of the Russian Tower is one of the world's classic big-wall free routes. Put up in 1991 by four Frenchmen at 7a and A2, with much of the climbing at around 6c, it can be climbed in anything from 18 to 24 pitches. Two years later it was climbed by Francois Pallandre, with only one pitch of aid, at 7a/7b. In 1995, in a single push of 28 hours, Greg Child and Lynn Hill freed it at 7b. The first on-sight was likely made in 2006 by Adam and Pawel Pustelnik, with Slawek Syndecki, though in a much longer time than the Swiss.

Pik 4,810m, east face. Previously unrecorded outside Korea, but an important event in the history of climbing in the Karavshin, was a new route, climbed free, on the giant east face of Pik 4,810m (Boston) above the Ak-su Valley. On July 17, 1994, Koreans Choi Byeong-gi and Shin Dong-seok started up the face seven or so meters to the right of the Sytnik route and climbed 25 pitches to the summit, at 5.10c. The two bivouacked at three-quarters height in the "Bomb Shelter" and reached the top the following afternoon. They report seeing gear on the Sytnik route but found none on their line. They rappeled the Verdernikov route to the north, bivouacked a second time, and continued their descent to base camp. It is thought that no other free ascent has been achieved on this face. The two climbers were part of a 12-man team, members of which were unsuccessful on other climbs apart from Lee Dong-yoon and Shin Sang-man, who repeated the Troschchinenko route on the north face of Rocky Ak-su (Ak-su North, 5,217m).

PETER JENSEN-CHOI, *Korea*

Pik 4810 from the east. (1) Southeast Ridge (unknown). (2) Pogorelov (1999). (3) Direttissima (1995). (4) Klenov (1993). (5) Sytnik (1989). (6) Korean (1994). (7) Vedernikov (1989). *John Arran*

Pik 4810 from the northeast. (1) Southeast Ridge (unknown). (2) Pogorelov (1999). (3) Direttissima (1995). (4) Klenov (1993). (5) Vedernikov (1989). (6) Sytnik (1986). *Shin Dong-seok, supplied by Peter Jensen-Choi*

Editor's note: There has been confusion regarding routes on Pik 4,810m, as on many other faces in the CIS that have seen former Soviet and foreign traffic. The Russians hold detailed information about their climbs but know little about ascents of others, such as Czechs, Germans, and Poles. And vice versa.

It wasn't until 1989 that routes were opened on the 1,100m east face. Toward the right side of the wall a mixed free and aid route was established by a team from Odessa Climbing Club led by M. Sytnik (Russian 6B, now considered 6A), while farther right Verdernikov's team climbed a shorter line on less-steep rock to gain the right-bounding rib, reaching it at around half-height and continuing to the summit (6A but low in the grade). Sytnik had already climbed the lesser-angled north face/ridge in 1986 at 5B, a route that has subsequently been used for descent. The Korean route also joins this rib and appears to follow similar if not identical ground to the Verdernikov in its upper section. Remarkably for the period, Sytnik did not enter his 1989 route, the first to breach the impressive east face, for the Soviet Championships.

The center of the face, dubbed "Africa" due to a large feature that resembles the outline of the continent, resisted all attempts until 1993, when it was climbed by a team led by Alexander Klenov (Borisov-Bruk-Devi-Donskih-Klenov). Klenov's route follows a logical but difficult line up the right side of Africa. There is only one decent ledge, a meter wide, at the top of the 13th pitch. Above, the route follows a crack system known as the "Eyebrow," with an exit right of the summit fall-line (going left seemed too dangerous, due to falling ice). This line gives more than 1,300m of climbing and was completed mostly free. It is 6B and considerably harder than the Sytnik, which Klenov's team repeated in 1994.

German climber Robert Steiner, who knows much of the history of the area and has climbed one of the big routes on the west face of 4,810m, is of the opinion that really talented rock climbers would be able to free-climb any of the routes on the peak.

From information provided by Anna Piunova (http://mountain.ru) and Robert Steiner

Pik Slesov (4,240m), northwest face, Odessa Route. I'm not sure why I first visited the Karavshin, but since my first visit in 1998 I have returned four times. The place stays the same, yet with every visit I find something new. This year we went early and summited on June 30. I saw nothing familiar. There was so much snow, even on steep faces, and it was so cold. But there were also positive aspects—long hours of daylight and snow on ledges for water. Our plan was simple: a new route on the northwest face of Pik Slesov (Russian Tower) between the Moroz Route and the Spanish Dihedral, and a repeat of Kritsuk's route on Pik 4,810. Long ago I visualized the line on Slesov while at home in Odessa. The final piece of the puzzle was to climb it.

The weather was bad from the beginning. Alexander Homenko, Taras Tsushko, and I approached the face in rain, which toward evening turned to snow. We spent the next day examining the wall. This proved a godsend, as we could see what falls from where, and then modify our original line. There was much ice in the upper section, and from noon onwards it began to fly, as on Cerro Torre. The saving grace was the steepness; the ice would pass well out from the face.

The next two days were sunny but cold. Our route led to the base of a chimney, which shocked us by its size and structure. It was formed by a giant detached flake leaning precariously against the wall. After two pitches it widened to 6-7m, so we had to traverse out right and climb 70m alongside.

Higher, the situation changed; there was a series of roofs with no cracks. Fortunately, 20m to the right we

Upper two-thirds of 900m northwest face of Pik Slesov, seen over lower walls of Central Pyramid. (1) Spanish Dihedral (6c A4, Gallego-Gomez-Seiquer, 1992). (2) Odessa Route. (3) Moroz Route (6A/6B). Huge corner close to right skyline is Klenov Route (6A/6B), and between this and Moroz are Semiletkin (6A/6B) and its variant Russian Shield (5.10 A4, Anker-Lowe, 1995). *Tony Whitehouse collection.*

spotted flakes. Reaching them required a 30m pendulum across a water runnel. The runnel is often bombarded by falling ice, but we were lucky as at that time there was no sun. In fact every day was poor, with rain and snow. Above the flakes, the route became fun. It was technically difficult, but the cracks were good and the rock solid. At the top of the 17th pitch we joined the Moroz Route and followed it to the summit. We named our new line Odessa Route and graded it Russian 6B.

After five days' rest we started up the Kritsuk on Pik 4,810. The most unpleasant part of this route is at the bottom, an overhanging broken corner. Above, it is better, and because there was snow everywhere we didn't have to haul water. We had three different route descriptions and, picking a line that averaged the three, never got seriously lost. However, one thing I couldn't understand: everyone talks about free-climbing, yet where did all the drilled holes for bathooks come from?

We reached the summit and descended in bad weather. We felt this route was easier but longer than our line on Slesov. With these two routes we won the 2009 Ukranian Championships. Incidentally, it was a great season on 4,810: two teams did Kritsuk, two did Sakharov, one climbed Voronov, and two completed the 5B Nazarov.

ALEXANDER LAVRINENKO, *Ukraine (translated by Marina Modlin)*

TIEN SHAN

WESTERN KOKSHAAL-TOO

Pik Vernyi (5,250m GPS), northwest face; Kyzyl Asker (5,842m), southeast face, attempt. I first visited the Kyzyl Asker region in August 2007. We set up base camp at 3,750m, in the valley leading to the Kyzyl Asker Glacier, but as we knew nothing about the area, we spent much

Vernyi from north-northwest. Belorussian-Russian ascent and portaledge camps marked. Left skyline is 2002 British route on north ridge. *Nikolai Banderet*

Southeast face of Kyzyl Asker after storm, showing Belorussian-Russian attempt. 1,500m pillar forming left edge of face was climbed in 2007 (*AAJ 2008*). Steep, narrow couloir left again has also seen several attempts. *Nikolai Banderet.*

time exploring. Nearly all the ascents we made from the West and East glaciers were straightforward.

In August 2009 I organized a second Belorussian-Russian expedition. Our aims were to climb the northwest face of Vernyi and to establish a new route on the southeast face of Kyzyl Asker, which had only the line climbed in 2007 by Mikhailov, Odintsov, and Ruchkin. We established base camp at the same spot as in 2007. After a short period of acclimatization, we attempted Vernyi as a team of five, as we thought this would be faster. Although the 700m wall is not huge, it is difficult, with an average angle of 82° and large smooth sections of granite. The lower and upper sections presented problems finding protection and belays. In the lower part cracks were full of ice, which restricted the use of cams, but was too thin and unstable to climb with ice tools. In the upper part a 100m vertical, wide chimney posed a problem, the side walls being very friable; this was probably the crux. These factors, with cold temperatures, meant that the amount of free-climbing was less than expected. Nonetheless, Dmitriy Golovchenko, Aleksander Malakhovskiy, Sergey Mikhailov, Sergey Nilov, and I reached the summit after three nights on the wall. We spent a fourth night on top because thick cloud prevented us seeing the descent. We graded the route 6B.

There is still much potential in this region for big rock routes, the main venues being Kyzyl Asker, Vernyi, and the Great Walls of China.

NIKOLAI BANDALET, *Republic of Belarus*
(translated by Ekaterina Vorotnikova)

Editor's Note. In recent years Vernyi has been referred to by a variety of names. It was first climbed in 1988 by Vladimir Turgaleva's four-man team, which climbed a rock rib to the right of the northwest face, finishing on the south ridge (5A). They named the summit Pik Vernyi (Faithful). The height attributed to the peak has been 4,850m, but the 2009 expedition recorded a much greater altitude by GPS. The second ascent was made in 2002 by Crampton and Fyffe who, unaware of a previous name, called it Pik Sabor (Cathedral). They climbed the north ridge (TD+, Scottish 6), which they felt to be 800m high. The following year it was repeated by five French, who thought it 500m high and M5. These French and other parties have attempted different lines on the northwest face. Other Russian teams reconnoitering the peak have dubbed it the Petit Dru of the Tien Shan.

Western Kokshaal-too, Komorova Glacier, various ascents; At Bashi Range, Acha Kaeyndi Valley, various ascents. In August Eddy Barnes (U.K.), Sari Nevala (Finland), Vanessa Wills (Australia), and I headed to Kyrgyzstan, intending to make first ascents in the Borkoldoy Range, an area that had primarily been explored by Pat Littlejohn's ISM expeditions. This was Eddy's first expedition, at the tender age of 20.

However, 20km from our intended destination we were waylaid by hunters on horse. They made it clear that we were unwelcome and should go elsewhere. We were constrained by transport, fuel, and information but took the view that we were meant to have an adventure. So we went to the nearest high point on the plateau, had a look-see, and drove off into the most interesting, but seemingly doable, part of the Western Kokshaal-too, in the far distance. This turned out to be the tri-tongued Komorova Glacier.

Most mountains in this area had already been bagged, but we summited five previously climbed

At Bashi. (A) Crow's Nest, (B) Dove Peak, and (C) Chook Mountain, with ascent routes. *Sally Brown*

Advanced base camp in upper Acha Kaeyndi Valley, At Bashi. (A) Ashes Peak (4,098m), (B) Shark Peak (4,249m), and (C) Crocodile Peak (4,352m). Marked between A and B is Wills-Brown Couloir. *Eddy Barnes*

summits, up to a height of 5,250m, and may have added a new one. These were three unnamed acclimatization peaks of 4,250m, 4,323m, and 4,416m, Pik Beggar (4,640m, PD+), Pik Jerry Garcia (5,250m, PD), and an unnamed peak that we have called Pik NikKaz (4,957m, PD+), a subsidiary summit to the north of Pik Jjin (ca 5,180m; the highest of the four teeth of Trezubets.) [*One was climbed by Russians in the 1980s and repeated by an ISM expedition, which also climbed two others from the east in 1999.*] We climbed this via the west face and north ridge. We attempted Pik Jerry Garcia via two routes, the southwest face and north ridge, aborting the

Looking south-southeast from summit of Icarus, At Bashi, toward virtually unknown peaks. Vanessa Wills in foreground. Eddy Barnes

north ridge at 5,100m. However, the views across the border from the southwest face were spectacular, particularly the Great Walls of China. There is huge potential for much harder routes, although descents could be entertaining.

On August 20 we drove west for eight hours to the At Bashi Range. As with the Western Kokshaal-too, we'd had no plans to climb here, so we had no maps and had conducted no research. In a hamlet on the south side of the river (opposite side from At Bashi Village), we found the start of an entertaining track leading south into the Acha Kaeyndi Valley. This valley lies about halfway along the At Bashi, a chain ca 80km long. After establishing a base camp at 2,790m and an advanced base at 3,513m, we summited 10 peaks in a northeast-facing cirque. The highest we dubbed Pik Icarus (4,537m). It is likely that four of the 10 were first ascents: Dove Peak (4,311m, PD+), Crow's Nest (4,155m, AD+ with several pitches of scantly protected British VS), Chook Mountain (4,063m, PD+), and Icarus (PD). The only good rock was on Crow's Nest.

The excellent, sustained Wills-Brown Couloir was the most technical ascent we achieved, involving 800m of ascent (including approach), with the final four pitches being on superb 70-80° water ice (NZ Grade 4/Alpine D). The route topped out at 4,242m on the ridge connecting Shark Peak (4,249m) and Crocodile Peak (4,352m).

The fluidity of visa regulations, the vagaries of Central Asian diplomatic relations, the dancing water fountains in the central square of Bishkek, the sweet, hydrating, red flesh of the ubiquitous watermelon, and the stark beauty and contrasts of the Kyrgyz mountain landscape, all contributed to make this expedition an unforgettable, not-to-be-missed roller coaster ride. Huge thanks go to the Winston Churchill Memorial Trust and the Mount Everest Foundation for their support.

SALLY BROWN, *U.K.*

Peak 4,863m, north ridge; unnamed Trezubet summit, north ridge; Pik 5,046m, south ridge; Pik ca 4,800m, Sarah's Daddy; Kyzyl Asker, north summit (ca 5,500m), Gladwin-Stewart Ridge. Buying supplies should not be the most dangerous part of an expedition. Bishkek's roads are such that pedestrians are often forced into suicidal bids to cross six lanes of moving traffic. At least in Kyrgyzstan getting to our base camp should not have been an issue, as

Pik 4,863m, with Bide-Hapuoja route on north ridge. *Carl Reilly*

(A) Pik Zuckerman (5,046m), (B) Pik 5,046m, with Reilly-Schofield route, and (C) Pik Vernyi (5,250m GPS) from Kyzyl Asker Glacier. *Carl Reilly.*

Pik ca 4,800m on Ochre Walls with (1) Sarah's Daddy (ED2 WI5, 500m), (2) Fire and Ice (ED1 Scottish VII, 600m), and (3) Beefcake (IV M6 WI4, 600m). Spanish route Ak-Saitan (A3+ 6a+ 80°, 600m) climbs granite buttress immediately left. *Tom Stewart.*

we were traveling in a six-wheel drive, 16-ton, ex-Soviet army truck. It beats donkeys and Alpacas, or so we thought.

We got off to a bad start with an eight-hour roadside delay caused by a puncture, flat spare, and ripped valve on a spare inner tube. I never understood what Sergy, the Russian driver, was aiming to achieve by hitting the tire with a mallet, but it seemed to do the trick. Things then went reasonably well for the next two days. We couldn't hear each other, so no one could offend anyone else, and the scenery was becoming more dramatic. On leaving the last remnants of a track, we crossed the plateau toward base camp. Things now went rapidly wrong. One second we were at normal height above the ground and were moving, the next we were a meter lower and not moving. The ground had turned to marsh, and the Soviet Beast had become intimately acquainted with it. It took 24 hours of furious digging, chocking, scraping, and lifting before the Beast awoke from its slumber and regained solid ground.

We never reached our intended base camp, settling instead for the more accessible Komorova Glacier. Here the six of us completed an array of new routes and explored large parts of the surrounding area.

On August 19 Tom Bide and Urpu Hapuoja climbed the north ridge of Pik 4,863m, on the divide between the eastern and central Komorova glaciers. They

Looking south up Kyzyl Asker Glacier. (A) Pik Vernyi (5,250m GPS). (B) Pik Panfilovski Division (5,290m). (C) Sculptura Chokursu, with Gladwin-Stewart Ridge marked. *Tom Stewart*

Dave Gladwin approaching steep ice smear of Sarah's Daddy. Ice line slanting up to right is Fire and Ice. *Tom Stewart*

ascended scree and snow to the crest, before continuing for five ropelengths to the summit (altimeter reading 4,920m, AD, Scottish 2/3). They rappeled a broad couloir on the west face.

On the 23rd we, Graeme and Carl, climbed unroped to the crest of the Trezubet Ridge between Piks Oleg and Jjin. After camping for the night on the eastern Komorova Glacier, we gained the crest via east-facing snow slopes. We then followed the crest south, crossing an initial summit, where we found footsteps [Pik Niknaz, 4,957m, climbed a week earlier by Sally Brown's expedition, see report below], and followed the ridge to a second, higher peak (Alpine D).

On the 28th Tom Reilly and I, Carl, climbed the west face and south ridge of unnamed Pik 5,046m near the south end of the Ochre Walls. [This peak lies south of Pik Zuckerman and is clearly seen between (B) Zuckerman and (C) Unmarked Soldier in *AAJ 1999*, p. 415.] After camping for the night on the Kyzyl Asker Glacier, we followed a heavily crevassed eastern fork to access a smaller glacier between the Ochre Walls and Pik Vernyi. We ascended this, finally climbing a snow slope, wide gully, and mixed ground (Scottish 3/4) onto the south ridge. The crest gave two short sections of steep granite cracks (Scottish 5/6 mixed), before we reached the summit. It was a fantastic, varied route of TD/TD+.

In the meantime the other two members of the expedition, Dave Gladwin and Tom Stewart, had also been climbing excellent routes. They started on the 17th, with what they believe was a similar line to Silent Bob (DeCapio-Isaac, 2001) on the west face of Pik Gronky (ca 5,080m). Their route involved 400m in an ice couloir, generally WI4 but with one hard ice/mixed pitch at WI5+/Scottish 6.

On the 18th the same pair climbed a new route, Sarah's Daddy (ED2 WI5, 500m), on the north-northeast face of the unnamed ca 4,800m summit between Piks Zuckerman and Carnovsky on the Ochre Walls. This route follows the initial big snow couloir of the 2001 DeCapio-Isaac route, Beefcake, and the 2004 Benson-Tresidder route, Fire and Ice, until they fork. It then climbs the ramps of Fire and Ice, but where Fire and Ice moves out right, it continues straight up steep ice to the ridge. The pair did not continue to the summit. This is the fifth route on the peak.

From the 24th to 26th Dave and Tom climbed the north ridge of Kyzyl Asker as far as the previously unclimbed north summit, which they estimate to be 5,500m. The amount of climbing was 2,000m, with a height gain of 1,400m. After a five-hour approach the previous day, they climbed 350m of 50° snow/ice, and then made a rightward traverse for 350m to reach open gullies leading up for 150m (55°) to a notch in the crest of the ridge. Here the main difficulties began, and they climbed at least 20 pitches to the summit. There were several bold leads, with technical difficulties up to UIAA VI, WI 3/4, and M6+/7. The overall grade was ED2/3, the crux being a very thin 10m-high crack in a granite wall—just wide enough to accept monopoints and picks.

After three 18-hour days they reached the north summit in a massive storm, which subsequently caused frostnip. On the fourth day they decided to rappel straight down the (unseen) 1,000m west face. Using Abalakovs, they made 15 rappels in a gully onto a hanging ice field, under the most intense bombardment of spindrift and falling ice either had witnessed. After traversing across the top of a serac barrier, they made a further 10 rappels down another thin, steep ice gully to reach the glacier, and regained the tent that day. They named the north summit Sculptura Chokursu (Sculptures' Peak).

CARL REILLY *and* GRAEME SCHOFIELD, *U.K.*

Pik Plaza (4,912m), northwest face, Z-K; Pik Granitsa (5,370m), north face, Nordic Walking. Inspired by impressive photographs of Pik Granitsa, provided by Paul Knott, who visited this area in 2005 (*AAJ 2006*), Michal Kasprowicz, Wojtek Ryczer, and I attempted peaks around the head of the Fersmana Glacier in the central section of the Western Kokshaal-too. We were aware that with limited time and finances our chances of success were modest, but we took the risk in order to have an adventure.

On August 20th we reached the snout of the Kotur Glacier, which was

Z-K on northwest face of Pik Plaza. First ascent of this peak was made by Slovenians from the far side. *Wojtek Ryczer*

as far east as our driver would take us, and set up base camp. On the 23rd we reached the foot of the divide between the Fersmana and Sarychat Glaciers, where Michal twisted his ankle so badly that he was unable to walk. We established a temporary camp, and Wojtek and I spent the next few days ferrying loads from base. On the 30th we moved camp onto the Fersmana Glacier, and the following day Wojtek and I climbed the northwest face of Pik Plaza to its vir-

North face of Granitsa. Solid black line is Nordic Walking, white dashed line is rappel descent. Peak was named in 2005, when attempted by west ridge (right skyline). Name means "border." Rounded summit to left lies in China and is unclimbed. *Michal Kasprowicz*

gin north summit. [Editor's note: In 2008 two Slovenians made the first ascent of this peak, which lies on the east side of the glacier opposite Byiely, by the southwest couloir and west ridge. See *AAJ 2009*. The peak has two distinct tops: the Slovenians reached the south top, which is separated from the north by a deep col] Our new route, which we named Z-K, is 600m high, with snow and ice at 60°, two pitches of 70° hard ice on the rightward diagonal traverse, and an 80° gully. We descended our line by rappel, mostly from Abalakovs.

In order to meet our return transport at Kotur base camp, we had to leave the Fersmana no later than September 5. We decided to attempt Pik Granitsa immediately, planning the line by studying a photo on our camera's display. On September 2 we woke at 3 a.m. to heavy snowfall. However, by 6 a.m. the weather seemed perfect, so we hurried to the base of the climb and began the route at 11 a.m. As we had time for just one attempt, we opted for a line much farther right, which we felt offered greater chance of success. We climbed until dark, overcoming the two hardest pitches (AI5/5+), then after a memorably cold and windy bivouac without sleeping bags, continued up moderate ground (AI4 and M4, with a short section of M5) to reach the corniced ridge, which we followed to the summit. That second day snowfall was heavy, so we stayed on top just 15 minutes. We downclimbed the ridge and then rappeled directly to the glacier using Abalakovs. We regained the tent just before midnight on the 3rd and returned to Kotur base camp with Michal over the next two days.

This was the first ascent of Granitsa and we named our route Nordic Walking, as this activity seemed to be our main occupation during the expedition. The north face is 800m high, but our route was far longer due to its convoluted line. The Fersmana still offers ample opportunity for worthwhile first ascents. We thank the Polish Mountaineering Association (PZA) for financial support, and all the good people who helped with information on the area.

RAFAL "WALDORF" ZAJAK, *PZA*

Sarychat Glacier, various ascents. On August 11 and 12 Martin Jones, Edward Lemon, Jacob Wrathall, and I, from King's College London Alumni Mountaineering Club, achieved first ascents of five peaks on the western side of the Sarychat Glacier.

We arrived in the range July 26 but, due to circumstances, had to ferry equipment for nine days to reach our base camp at 3,520m on the west side the Sarychat valley, near the confluence of the Aytali and Sarychat rivers. Although this helped enormously with acclimatization, once we had explored the glacier, we were left with little time for climbing.

Looking west across Sarychat Glacier into Arwyn cwm. (A) Fers III. (B) Hilaire. (C) Sylvie. (D) Katherine. (E) Thornes. (F) Lyell. *Gareth Mottram*

Gareth Mottram and Edward Lemon moving along ridge toward Sylvia and Hilarie. Unclimbed Fers III is fine pyramid to right. *Jacob Wrathall*

Gareth Mottram approaching Sarychat-Fersmana divide. Big peak far left is Kosmos (5,940m), and peak above and right of climber's head is Krylia Sovetov (5,480m), first climbed in 1998. *Jacob Wrathall*

Our initial approach to the glacier above stayed on the west side of the river and traversed extremely difficult moraine, similar to that described by the Slovenian FreeApproved expedition on the neighboring Fersmana Glacier to the west (*AAJ 2009*). It took four hours to cross the moraine. The glacier was then found to be heavily crevassed, and the traverse to planned targets on the eastern side of the glacier proved slow and difficult. Our first attempt to reach these peaks was abandoned due to the difficulty of approach and bad weather. However, on the descent we discovered a relatively easy gully on the east side of the moraine, which was much faster but necessitated wading the thigh-deep river to regain base camp.

We used this faster approach on our second trip up-valley but then moved into a cwm, which we named Arwyn, to the west of the glacier. The Sarychat falls into the eastern sector of the range, where the rock is not the featured granite characteristic of the west, but disappointing shale.

On the 11th, from a camp in the cwm, we climbed as two independent pairs the aptly named Slush and Rubble (Scottish 2 or soft 3) to the crest of a ridge and from there traversed to two previously unclimbed summits. We named these after former King's College lecturers: Pik Lyell (4,864m GPS) for 19th-century geologist Charles Lyell and Pik Thornes (5,014m GPS; 4,989m on the 2005 American Alpine Club Map) for John Thornes, a recently deceased geographer and pioneer in the field of erosion modeling.

Next day Martin and Jacob climbed a mixed route up a chimney in a rock buttress on the north-facing wall of the cwm: Choss Bros. (Scottish 5). They then turned north and ascended Pik Katherine (4,840m GPS). Edward and I chose a line just to the left, staying on snow and ice for much of the way: Quartered Safe out Here (70°). Once on the crest we headed south along the ridge toward Fers III (5,210m), a superb unclimbed snow pyramid. We climbed two small peaks on the ridge—Sylvia (4,910m) and Hilarie (4,928m)—but lack of time and deteriorating weather prevented us continuing along the beautiful connecting snow ridge to Fers III.

GARETH MOTTRAM, *U.K.*

Editor's note: The only known mountaineers to have set foot previously on the Sarychat Glacier were Russians Danil Popov and friends. In 2003 they crossed a high pass from the head of the parallel Fersmana Glacier to the upper Sarychat, from where they made the second ascent of Krylia Sovetov, a high peak on the Chinese border.

KUILU RANGE

Kuilu, various ascents; Sun Kul Canyon, various ascents. This was the International School of Mountaineering's second trip to the Kuilu range, the first being in 2000, when we explored the Karator Glacier and its surrounding peaks. Our 2009 trip focused on the Bardytor valley immediately to the east, where records showed that only one peak had been climbed.

We set up base camp at the start of the valley and explored both branches of the glacier. We then split into two teams: Dean Clifford, Tomasz Dudek, Laura Plackett, and Stephen Taylor, with guide Adrian Nelhams; and Roger Elmer, Neil Lindsey, Brad Smith, John Vlasto, and Cindy Walters, with guides Vladimir Komissarov and me. We established two advanced base camps, Adrian's team at 4,020m on the eastern branch of the glacier and my team at 4,050m on the western branch.

Adrian's team was first to move up. Poor weather worsened to a heavy dump of snow. In spite of this they climbed to a shoulder at 4,500m on Pik 5,020m. Next day, in clearer but blustery conditions, they reached the summit, which they named Ak Sakal. It was a fine effort in difficult snow conditions. After a day's rest, they climbed a lower but more technical summit (Bakshi, 4,434m), before returning to base camp.

Meanwhile, my team climbed a small peak above advanced base in poor weather, after which a fine day gave us Pik Koopsyz (4,755m). *Koopsyz* means "safe" in Kyrgyz, and it was the only objective without serious avalanche danger. The plan was then to attempt an unclimbed 5,000er, but further heavy snowfall made conditions even more hazardous, so we decided to return to base camp and undertake the second part of the plan: Son Kul Canyon.

Son Kul was opened as a climbing area in 2008, when ISM teams climbed four routes from British HVS to E2, the longest being ca 10 pitches. This year we achieved bigger and better things, both ISM and the British team of Dave Barlow and Geoff Hornby. These ascents established Son Kul Canyon as the prime area for rock climbing in Kyrgyzstan.

Adrian's team climbed the north ridge (British HVS) of the 3,450m peak forming the east side of the canyon. This ridge links with a ridge he had climbed previously, making a route of more than 800m. Cindy, Brad, Neil, and I, followed by a second team of John and Roger, climbed the 600m ridge of Friendly Buttress (UIAA V-), a potential classic taking the easiest route from the canyon floor. The next objective for Adrian's team was the steeper, more compact buttress to the left of Friendly Buttress. This gave the fantastic Manaschi Rib (British HVS), a 14-pitch route, which Adrian declared was the best rock climb he had ever done. John, Neil, and I now turned to the untouched east-facing side of the canyon, wading the river to climb the huge spur running up to the highest point. Though not sustained, Eastern Spine gave some interesting British 5a pitches and serious climbing on a loose headwall.

Vladimir had been exploring another canyon to the west of Son Kul, and this gave John and me our final route, the impressive groove of Striker (E2 5c), while Adrian rounded off the trip by climbing a small pinnacle in the canyon, on immaculate limestone, at E1. We left more impressed than ever with Son Kul Canyon and eager, as always, for our next trip to Kyrgyzstan.

PAT LITTLEJOHN, *ALPINE CLUB*

TENGRI TAG

Pik Pobeda (7,439m), north face to west ridge. At the end of August, Russians Vitaly Gorelik and Gleb Sokolov made the first ascent of the north face of the formation known as the Camel on the west ridge of Pik Pobeda. The objective dangers on the lower section of the 2,400m mixed buttress on Pobeda, climbed alpine-style in seven and a half days, were high, and the pair had spent several years trying for the right conditions before setting foot on the route. Steep sections of technical ice and mixed climbing were made more difficult by poor weather on the upper part of the wall. On reaching the west ridge, close to two snow humps, the pair continued to a high point of 6,950m. They did not go to the main summit but descended the standard Medzmariashvilli route (5B) over the top of Pobeda West (Pik Pavel Pshavel, 6,918m) and down its north ridge to Dikiy Pass. This ascent was nominated for a 2010 Piolets d'Or. Sokolov, who was nearly 56 at the time of the ascent, has written a full account that appears earlier in the *Journal*.

KAZAKHSTAN

ZHUNGAR ALATAU

Kyoabl–Kapacau and Tblwkah valleys, various ascents. Landing at Almaty on August 2, Liam Hughes, Paul Padman, John Temple, Stuart Worsfold, and I were met by Andrey Gundarev, our happily laid-back interpreter, and whisked to a monolithic hotel. It was a concrete throwback to Soviet times, and if you listened carefully, I'm sure you could hear the shouts of the party faithful echoing through the empty corridors. But it did the job. Next morning, after buying a few essentials, we set out on our 350km drive across the Kazakh steppe. After six hours on relatively good roads, passing through a military base and a military checkpoint, the six of us, with Uliya Polyakova, our beautiful base-camp manager and cook, reached the roadhead above Saryabel and contemplated the southern Zhungar Alatau, which rose in front of us for 3,000m. The Zhungar doesn't do foothills: it changes from football-pitch-flat, desiccated steppe to 4,000m alpine peaks in less than 2km. The contrast is extraordinary.

We were enthusiastic about climbing peaks on which no one had set foot. The Zhungar was particularly attractive, as there were no records (or knowledge) of mountaineering activity in the southern sector. We had old military maps but practically no other information. It was a great feeling. Three heavy carries and six river crossings later, we established our first camp just above the confluence of two rivers, the Kyoabl–Kapacau and Tblwkah. We had arrived. The next day three groups set out in different directions, trying to find the best way to penetrate farther into the range. After dubious navigation and adventurous river crossings by some

Ak Tau, showing line of first ascent. *Jamie Goodhart*

Julie Tau, showing the two routes ascended. *Jamie Goodhart*

and opportune discoveries by others, particularly the "Padman Traverse," we returned to camp. None of the routes we discovered was suitable for carrying heaving loads, so we renamed our camp base camp, though it was 1,000 vertical meters and 8km from the planned site.

With four days food, we followed the Padman Traverse into the Kyoabl–Kapacau Valley, avoiding four river crossings. For much of the way we moved at snail's pace, slowed by loose, steep shale, chest-deep scratchy juniper, and torrential rain. We made barely a kilometer an hour. Higher the going got easier and we eventually set up camp on a large green plateau at 3,156m, surprised to find two derelict huts resembling garden sheds. Over the next three days we summited six peaks, one of the most lovely being Julie Tau. On reaching the summit ridge, we were greeted with a stupendous panorama of the steppe and 278km away, poking above the curvature of the earth, was the mighty spike of Khan Tengri (6,995m); it was stunning. The weather during our stay in this most beautiful of valleys was largely good, and all the ascents we made were around PD in standard.

After a rest and celebratory cake at base camp, we took five days food and headed up the Tblwkah, where we had originally intended to establish base camp. After two days we set up camp on grass at 3,000m, among a herd of feisty horses. The weather was mixed for a few days, but we managed some climbing, notably Ak Tau, the whitest peak in the valley, and Jasmine Tau, a stunning triangle at its head. The return to base included a night around a campfire

Unclimbed rock walls above Tblwkah-Kaupakmbl confluence. *Jamie Goodhart*

Jasmine Tau. Padman and Worsfold climbed behind right skyline ridge, following a gully to ca 20m from summit, where they saw a survey cross. *Jamie Goodhart*

below a spectacular rock face near the Tblwkah-Kaupakmbl confluence. There was much speculation on the fantastic potential of the area for alpinism, rock climbing and particularly ski touring. The snow is rumored to be consistent throughout winter, though the cold will be severe. In summer, we recommend that future parties set a higher base camp, using hired horses, which can certainly reach at least 3,100m.

We spent 17 days in the region and climbed 16 peaks, which we mostly named ourselves (potential first ascents marked with *): Pk. 2,664m, (N 44°30.263', E 80°07.010', Goodhart-Hughes, August 4); Kapacau (2,528m, N 44°30.446', E 80°06.188', Goodhart-Hughes, August 4); First Hurrah* (3,939m, N 44°34.968', E 80° 07.081', Goodhart-Hughes-Padman-Worsfold, August 6); Julie Tau* (3,996m, N 44°34.144', E 80°07.444', Goodhart-Hughes-Padman-Worsfold-Temple, August 7); Mt. Caroline* (3,905m, N 44°34.777' E 80°05.437', Goodhart-Hughes, August 8); The Cairn* (3,910m, N 44°34.736', E 80°05.228', Goodhart-Hughes, August 8); Tash Tau* (3,877m, N 44°34.736', E 80°05.228', Goodhart-Hughes, August 8); Christaline Peaks* (3,956m N 44°3507', E 80°0544.9'; 3,896m, N 44°3456.4', E 80°0542.1'; 3,847m, N 44°3456.5', E 80°0551.4', Padman-Worsfold, August 8); Pk. 3,638m (ca N 44°30', E 80°10', Gundarev-Polyakova, August 9); The Cross (3,877m, N 44°34.193', E 80°12.374', Goodhart-Hughes, August 12); Ak Tau* (4,162m, N 44°32.126', E 80°14.513', Goodhart-Hughes, August 13); Jasmine Tau (4,042m, N 44°3416', E 80°1440.3' Padman-Worsfold, August 13); Fern Tau* (3,623m, west of Ak Tau, Temple, August 13); Pk. 3,821m (N 44°32.126', E 80°14.513', Goodhart-Hughes, August 17); Bnanmoctb (3,865m, north-northwest of Pk. 3,821m, Gundarev-Polyakova, August 18), and Tut Tau* (4,080m, northeast of Julie Tau, Padman-Worsfold, August 18).

It was clear that some of the peaks had been climbed (some even sported survey cairns), but nine gave no indication of previous ascent (rocky summits without cairns). I am working on the premise that one-third of our ascents were new, though it will be almost impossible to verify this.

Military border permits and base camp logistics were provided by Kan Tengri (www.kantengri.kz). Thanks to the Mount Everest Foundation for financial assistance.

JAMIE GOODHART, *Alpine Club*

TAJIKISTAN

PAMIR

Muzkol Range, Zartosh (6,128m). In August, Jock Jeffrey, Graham Rowbotham, Simon Woods, and I arrived in the Muzkol Range, We wished to make the first ascent of Zartosh, a peak that had been attempted in the late 1990s and 2000 by commercial expeditions organized by EWP, a UK outfit. They had made three attempts via the northwest face from the col below neighboring White Pyramid and a fourth, in 1999, by the spectacular north face, which ended in tragedy.

Viewed from north: (A) Zartosh, (B) White Pyramid, and (C) Leopard's Tooth. *Adam Thomas*

A four-day drive from Dushanbe brought us to base camp at 3,870m. From there we spent the next week establishing a camp on the glacier at 5,100m. The weather had been stable, although notorious Pamir winds picked up each afternoon and made base camp dusty and unpleasant. This changed on the night of August 16, and it snowed lightly every night for the next week.

After carrying tents a little higher to the foot of Zartosh's

Jock Jeffery on east ridge of White Pyramid with northwest face of Zartosh behind. Route up Zartosh gained foreground col from left, then climbed obvious snow gully and steep mixed ground to gain summit ridge. Highest point is behind. *Graham Rowbotham*

800m north face, Simon and I made an attempt on the 22nd. We reached a height of ca 5,650m on the face, before retreating due to unconsolidated snow on technical terrain.

On the same day Jock and Graham set off to climb White Pyramid (6,060m), first summited in 1998 by an EWP expedition (*AAJ 1999*). Deep snow on the slopes leading to the Zartosh-White Pyramid col hampered progress. After crossing a seemingly safe area of snow at the top of the slope, Graham suddenly felt a tug on the rope and, looking around, saw no sign of Jock, only the rope leading into a hole. A few moments later snow-caked sunglasses flew out of the hole, and then Jock hauled himself out. However, Jock is a tough, determined bugger, and after a chocolate fix kicked in, only a little encouragement was required to get him up the final 100m ridge to the summit.

I was keen for another try at Zartosh, and although Graham was not overenthusiastic

Looking across north face of Zartosh from approach slopes to col between Zartosh and White Pyramid. *Graham Rowbotham.*

about slogging back up to the col, the summit of White Pyramid had proved a good vantage point for studying the northwest face of Zartosh, and he had seen a reasonable line.

At 5 a.m. on the 24th we set off for the col. Although the previous tracks had filled with spindrift, Graham was delighted to find the going much easier than it had been. Above the col the terrain became more challenging. Graham led a gully of loose powder and, above the first rocks, a section of precarious climbing on loose snow over ice. A snow/ice gully led to a steep and technical rock step. A groove that Graham had spotted from White Pyramid proved the key to overcoming this section, and also provided the route's crux. The summit ridge was a perfect knife-edge of snow, with huge cornices over the north face and broken rock and snow to the south. We reached the summit cornice in time for a late lunch. Descent was by the same route, rappelling from Abalakovs and downclimbing.

On the return trip to Dushanbe, we took a more southerly route along the Wakhan Corridor, which provided magnificent views of peaks in the Hindu Kush. We thank the Mount Everest Foundation for its generous support.

ADAM THOMAS, *Alpine Club*

Southwestern Pamir, Pik Tb GU (6,142m), northwest flank and north ridge; Pik Engels (6,510m), northeast face and north ridge, attempt. Peter Poljanic and I arrived in Dushanbe on July 30, with the aim of climbing Pik Karl Marx (6,723m) and/or Pik Engels from the Shaboy Glacier. For

Looking south up Naspar Valley. From left to right, Piks Tb GU, Chiurlionisa (5,794m), Danelaytisa (5,837m), and Engels. (A) East ridge (6A+, A. Kustovskiy, 1964). (B) Upper section of Chunovkin Route (6A, Chunovkin, 1971). (C) Upper section of north-northwest ridge (6A, P. Budanov, 1964). (D) Line followed by Jost and Poljanic. *Matic Jost*

Pik Tb Gu, with route followed by Slovenians. Bivouac sites marked.
Matic Jost

transport we used Ergash Fayzul-lobekov (tourdepamir@yahoo.com). At the roadhead at Javshan-goz local people had little interest in helping us with horses or donkeys, so we persuaded the driver to continue into the lower Naspar Valley, immediately east of the Shaboy. We made our base camp near a shepherds' encampment and found them extremely hospitable. They offered us meals, and donkeys for our trek up-valley.

We placed an advanced base close to the northeast face of Engels and went for an acclimatization climb on the strangely named Tb GU. From August 7 to 10 we climbed and descended the northwest flank and north ridge from the Naspar Glacier. Climbing was mostly on snow and ice up to 60°, but there was a 10m rock step of UIAA V+ on the north ridge. Just above our second bivouac we found old pitons.

We then climbed a line on the far right side of the northeast face of Engels, to gain the north-northwest ridge at 5,572m (GPS). We climbed through the night for eight hours, mostly on ice but with one steep section of rock (UIAA V A0), just before reaching the crest. We rested on the crest that day and bivouacked at the same spot that night. The following morning, though, we didn't feel strong enough to continue, so we descended.

On the way back to Dushanbe we stopped at Kalai Husein (Husein's Forest), where we hoped to climb new rock routes. However, we found the walls to be formed of very bad rock and did only one climb. We named it Flying Circus (V+, 200m), a serious route with awful rock, particularly on the crux first pitch.

In the past most expeditions to the southwestern Pamir came from parts of the old Soviet Union. They were well-organized teams that climbed in Russian style and established impressively hard and sometimes dangerous routes. The main potential now lies in repeating routes free, in alpine-style, but there is also space for new routes of all grades. Despite the fact that roads lead close to these mountains, climbers rarely visit the Karl Marx-Engels area, and there is almost no trekking activity. Local people are friendly, and the region offers spectacular, unspoiled scenery, with no crowds and great faces to climb.

MATIC JOST, *Slovenia*

Afghanistan

PAMIR

Tegerman Su Valley and eastern sector Aq Su Valley (Little Pamir), exploration. The far eastern part of the Wakhan Corridor has never seen many foreign visitors. During the Afghan climbing boom of the 1960s and 70s it was too remote and access too difficult to draw major attention, with high virgin peaks available two hours' drive from Ishkashim. Now, when most peaks in the High Hindu Kush have been climbed, it's worth re-examining this eastern region. Apart from being home to Kirghiz nomads, the area also hosts three interesting ranges: Lupsuq Hindu Kush, Pamir-i-Wakhan, and Kohe Aq Su. These mountains have remained almost untouched by alpinists, and more than 400 peaks above 5,000m await first ascents. Climbing one and gathering more information for future expeditions was my goal.

At the beginning of July I arrived in Afghanistan from Uzbekistan. After reaching Mazar-e-Sharif, I continued east through Kunduz and Faizabad. This wasn't the safest or quickest option, as the road around Kunduz was supposedly receiving attention from the rebels (the accepted route to the Wakhan these days is through Tajikistan, but in Warsaw there is no Tajik embassy, only Uzbek, so it was easier to obtain a visa.) After arriving in Ishkashim (the "gateway" to the Corridor), I bought food and arranged a permit and transportation. Ishkashim is the last place where you can buy provisions. Permits may be arranged prior to arrival, e.g. through Mountain Unity, to reduce time spent in the town. Otherwise permits can take up to three days. A jeep is required to get to Sarhad-e-Broghil, some way up the Corridor. The journey takes one or two days, depending on the water level, and costs $400-600 per day.

Qalandar Zom (5,909m) seen from Kashch Goz to the north. This peak lies on the Afghan-Pakistan border northwest of 4,630m Khora Bhurt Pass in the Lupsuq Hindu Kush. *Bartek Tofel www.tofel.eu*

Seen from Kashch Goz to the northwest, the outer peaks of Pamir-i-Wakhan rise to ca 5,000m. *Bartek Tofel www.tofel.eu*

Qara Jilga I (6,094m) in Pamir-i Wakhan seen from the north-northwest. This summit lies northwest of the border peak Sakar Sar. *Bartek Tofel www.tofel.eu*

Looking approximately north to ca 800m rock faces near Uween-e-Sar (4,887m), close to the Tajik border. *Bartek Tofel www.tofel.eu*

After reaching Sarhad-e-Broghil, I arranged for a donkey to carry my gear and set off in the direction of the Aq Su Valley or Little Pamir and the westernmost Kirghiz summer encampment of Kashch Goz. The journey took six days and crossed three passes, the highest of them being Uween-e-Sar (4,887m). Near this pass, in the Kohe Wakhan range, there are many rock faces up to 800m high, with peaks up to ca 5,700m. I reached the Kirghiz camp on July 27. It is possible to reach Kashch Goz faster, along the "low" or "river" route. It takes two or three days, but may be impossible when the water level is high (or locals view it as such).

At Kashch Goz I switched to horses. In the Wakhan, when you rent an animal, it comes with a person who takes care of its needs. That person serves as a guide (but not a mountain guide) and some-times as a cook. The hire prices of animals are much the same every-where, and in 2009 were $10 a day for a donkey, $16-20 for a horse, yak, or camel.

From Kashch Goz I contin-ued east along Lake Chaqmaqtin and the Kohe Aq Su range. The valley floor lies at 4,000-4,200m, and surrounding peaks reach up to ca 5,800m. It took nine days to reach the easternmost part of the Wakhan Corridor and Afghani-stan—the Tegerman Su Valley. I stopped on the way to explore the Kohe Aq Su and had to change animals three times, but if in a great hurry, one can reach Teger-man Su from Kashch Goz in

An unclimbed rock wall near the Uween-e-Sar. *Bartek Tofel www. tofel.eu*

Looking southeast at the border peak of Sakar Sar (6,272m). The main peak on the left has been climbed twice from the far side—the southeast flank, from Pakistan—by Japanese in 1999 and 2004. *Bartek Tofel www.tofel.eu*

four days. There are no Kirghiz encampments beyond Sayutuk, from where it is one or two days to Tegerman Su, and the point where Afghan, Tajik, and Chinese borders meet. Here there are around two-dozen unclimbed peaks up to ca 5,500m, with the valley floor at ca 4,600m.

Tegerman Su is a sensitive area: Kirghiz report the possibility of robbery by neighboring Tajiks. Keeping alert or having an armed escort is advisable. I had two Kirghiz with me, both of whom carried old Russian-made rifles. We didn't encounter anyone, so it's hard for me to judge if there is any real threat. Security in other parts of Aq Su Valley is better, although the Kirghiz did tell me about Tajik bandits stealing their animals at night. If that's true, they should pose no threat to climbers in Kohe Aq Su, because the border is relatively distant. No Taliban, rebel, or warlike people exist in this area.

After spending two days at Tegerman Su and getting close to the Chinese border, we went back to the Aq Su Valley. I continued to Sarhad-e-Broghil by the "river route" and got back to Ishkashim on August 15.

BARTEK TOFEL, *Poland*

HINDU KUSH

Koh-i-Beefy (ca 5,400m). While working in Afghanistan with development projects, I was constantly impressed by the beauty of the Hindu Kush and excited about its climbing potential. "Being involved with projects that attempted to promote sustainable development for poor mountain communities, I was frustrated that insecurity in the region was stopping what could surely be a thriving mountain tourist industry, of great benefit to the local economy. "Economic development is desperately needed in a region where roughly 80 per cent of young men

Looking approximately south to Peak 5,454m at the western end of Kohe Aq Su. *Bartek Tofel www.tofel.eu*

Looking southeast toward Peak 5,711m at the western end of Kohe Aq Su. *Bartek Tofel www.tofel.eu*

leave their homes and families to pursue cash incomes overseas, often taking great risks to cross international boundaries illegally.

A trek in 2008 to the ruggedly beautiful Wakhan Corridor made me realize the huge potential offered by this one hidden corner of Afghanistan, as an "adventure holiday" destination for those who like to walk the slightly wilder side of life. The region has no history of violent conflict, and being Ishmaili there is zero tolerance for Taliban ideals. The Wakhan is easily accessible from Tajikistan, allowing travelers to avoid insecure "mainland" Afghanistan.

I was spurred into organizing a climbing expedition for summer 2009, to be part of a growing interest in this region and help promote the potential of the Wakhan to the wider world. Our team of two Kiwis and three Brits met in Dushanbe, Tajikistan, ready for the journey south to the Afghan border. An 18-hour 4x4 trip got us near the frontier, and the following day we crossed to Ishkashim, the border town and capital of Wakhan. Here we finalized simple formalities with the help of Mountain Unity staff, met our indispensable guide Gorg Ali, and did our shopping for the month-long trip. There would be no opportunities to buy food once we headed east into the Corridor.

Our objective, the Qala-i-Hurst, is one of many high-altitude valleys in the Hindu Kush dominated by jagged peaks. Climbers had only visited this valley twice before, and all significant peaks remained unclimbed. Qala-i-Hurst is situated toward the eastern end of the Wakhan and can be reached in one day's drive from Ishkashim—but bank on two as the road is seriously rough and claims many tires. As few foreigners ever visit Wakhan, local people greet you with a mixture of excitement and curiosity. "We took a Polaroid camera, which was definitely appreciated by local families.

On September 15 Chris Philipson and I climbed the north ridge of Koh-i-Beefy (5,410m GPS, 5,379m Google Earth Digital Elevation, 5,288m on some sketch maps), named in memory of Jamie "Beefy" Fiddes. The day was clear and sunny, although a little chilly with autumn advancing. Our route follows a beautiful 600m line, which dominates the upper basin of the Qala-i-Hurst Glacier. It was mainly straightforward snow at AD+/D- but had three steep ice pitches of Scottish 4 (60-70°). The ridge also involved several easy rock towers of UIAA II. At around mid-height we left the crest, when snow conditions became too unstable, and moved onto the north face. "We encountered spectacular *penitentes* at various points, due to the arid, high-altitude environment. While the technical crux was the ice pitches, the psychological crux was definitely the summit tower, which involved loose, sugary snow on a relatively steep, exposed ridge, with no secure belay. We descended using snow bollards and Abakalovs for rappel anchors.

Stable weather, great rock and ice, countless unclimbed peaks, and the superb hospitality of local Wakhi make this a very special region in which to climb or trek. "This is one of the last unexplored mountaineering destinations that our shrinking world has to offer, and a true adventure. "We will be heading back in 2010 with the aim of climbing the stunning granite and ice-clad pyramid of Baba Tangi (6,513m).

A big thank you to our fantastic local guide Gorg Ali and David James at Mountain Unity, both of whom helped make this expedition a success. There is footage from our expedition at http://www.youtube.com/watch?v=m6iH-3YRCxM and more information, or help with organizing your own expedition to the Wakhan, at http://www.mountainunity.org/

JOEL FIDDES, *UK*

North ridge of Koh-i-Beefy. *Joel Fiddes Collection*

Upper Qala-i-Hurst Glacier. Koh-i-Beefy on left with north ridge facing camera. Other peaks are unclimbed. *Joel Fiddes*

Pakistan

Overview. The year 2009 was bleak for mountaineering in Pakistan, as the security situation adversely affected the inflow of tourists. Sixty-three teams applied to attempt various peaks, but 18 withdrew their applications, and two teams that had been granted permits did not turn up, leaving only 43 expeditions in the field.

It was a bad year on K2 and Broad Peak. As many as 55 climbers from six teams tried to climb K2, but none succeeded, and Italian Michael Fait lost his life. On Broad Peak 78 climbers from various teams tried their luck, but only one managed to reach the summit.

All three expeditions to Nanga Parbat were successful, putting 22 out of 41 climbers on top, including four Pakistani climbers. But again the "Killer Mountain" lived up to its nickname, as two climbers died after summiting on July 10.

All five expeditions on Gasherbrum I were successful, putting 18 out of 51 members on top. Four out of nine expeditions launched on Gasherbrum II were successful, putting 11 out of 98 climbers on the summit.

During 2009 the Pakistan Ministry of Tourism maintained a 50 percent reduction on royalty fees for peak permits. There is no royalty on peaks below 6,500m. The Alpine Club of Pakistan publishes a list of fees at www.alpineclub.org.pk/peak_royalties.php.

KARRAR HAIDRI, *Alpine Club of Pakistan*

HINDU KUSH

Raghshur (6,089m), attempt. Raghshur (Lagh Shar) is an unclimbed mountain east of the Istor-o-Nal group. Theodoros Christopoulos, Ioannis Kovanidis, and I established base camp beside the Raghshur Glacier (4,430m), north of the peak, in early August. On August 6, we crossed the bergschrund at 5,350m and climbed five pitches of 45°–60° ice and snow to reach a col in the west ridge at 5,530m. Here we found a rusty can from an Italian expedition that had attempted the peak in 1974.

The northwest face of unclimbed Raghshur (6,089m). Two expeditions, including one in 2009, reached the steep rocks on the west (right) ridge from the obvious saddle. *Theodoros Christopoulos*

After resting in base camp, we returned to the col on August 9. Over the next two days we explored possible routes past a prominent rock tower at 5,630m, the Italian team's high point. First we tried to traverse onto the south face, but there were no viable routes leading back to the ridge. Next we traversed left along the bottom of the tower to a couloir (60° max), but at the top was a huge cornice that we couldn't pass, so we gave up our attempt.

The only viable route on this side of Raghshur appears to be to traverse two or three more pitches across the northwest face and climb an exposed, mixed face (up to 70°), which would gain snow slopes and allow one to traverse back to the west ridge.

NIKOLAOS KROUPIS, *Hellenic Federation of Mountaineering and Climbing*

WESTERN HIMALAYA

NANGA PARBAT RANGE

Nanga Parbat, Austro-Canadian Northwest Buttress Route. After a year of research, we agreed on a plan to attempt a new route on the northwest buttress of Nanga Parbat (8,125m). Our group of close friends included Austrians Günther Unterberger, Hans Goger, and Sepp Bachmair, along with the two of us. We joined a big group of climbers from the OeAV (Austrian Alpine Club).

We arrived at Diamir Base Camp (4,250m) on June 17. After acclimatizing on Nanga Parbat's Kinshofer Route, the five of us prepared for our new line, which we hoped to climb in

The Diamir Face of Nanga Parbat. (1) The Austro-Canadian Northwest Buttress Route (2009). (2) Camp 4 on the Kinshofer Route (Kinshofer-Löw-Mannhardt, 1962). (3) Normal-route variation to Kinshofer Route. (4) Lower Kinshofer Route. *Guilhem Vellut*

pure alpine style, with no fixed ropes or porters. We took only two tents, three ice screws, two pitons, and 50m of 7mm static rope.

Leaving base camp on July 7, we walked up the Diamir Glacier and turned left up the Diama Glacier. We walked for two more hours along the base of the northwest wall and installed our first bivouac in a safe site at 5,300m, below the 900m couloir we planned to climb to reach easier slopes on the northwest buttress. This gully is between the French-Italian (Lafaille-Moro, 2003) and Czechoslovak (Belica-Just-Zatko-Zatko, 1978) routes, to the right, and the Diama Glacier route to the left (various attempts as high as 7,750m).

After crossing the bergschrund, we climbed 150m at 50° on the left side of the gully, followed by a 20m, 80° ice section. After about 700m of hard snow, we reached a 200m, 60°– 65° section of blue ice, covered by 10cm of snow. Here we used our rope for the first time. We placed our second bivouac at 6,300m, 100m past the exit of the couloir.

Continuing up the northwest buttress, we had to fight deep snow and strong wind. On the third day we climbed a 50° slope left of a gigantic serac to reach the col between two huge pinnacles at 6,600m. We continued to the right of the second pinnacle on easier but crevassed ground. A long snow slope led to our third bivouac (6,900m), on a flat but windy plateau.

We had hoped to continue up the northwest buttress to 7,400m and then traverse right to the Bazhin Basin. Late in the morning, we encountered steep rock, and after some hours of scrambling and routefinding, we realized our best chance to reach Nanga Parbat's summit was to traverse at 7,250m to Camp 4 on the Kinshofer Route. After this exposed traverse across deep 50° snow, we reached a rock ledge from which we could see Nanga Parbat's summit pyramid for the first time. We quickly descended to Camp 4 (7,100m) on the Kinshofer Route, having explored 2,300m of new ground. However, our celebration was brief.

At around 9 p.m. we received a call from our liaison officer in base camp, telling us that Go Mi-sun from Korea was requesting help. Go was climbing with six other Koreans and one of our Austrian companions, Wolfgang Kölblinger. This group had reached the summit in bad weather and was trying to descend to Camp 4.

Three Pakistani porters started up with warm drinks, oxygen, and a rope. We (Göschl and Rousseau) followed them at 3:30 a.m. Just before sunrise we came across the Korean team, which declined our offer of help and continued down to Camp 4. *[Editor's note: Go Mi-sun died in a fall lower on the mountain before reaching base camp.]* They had not seen Wolfgang since they'd reached the summit together at about 7 p.m.

Fearing the worst, we rushed toward the top. After discovering Wolfgang's backpack and ice axe at 8,064m, we reached the summit at 11:30 a.m. on July 11. From tracks in the snow, we inferred that Wolfgang had fallen to his death in the direction of the Mummery Rib. Goger and Bachmair, two of our partners on the new route, reached the summit later that day. We were the last to descend Nanga Parbat that year. A helicopter could find no trace of our friend.

GERFRIED GÖSCHL, *Austrian Alpine Club,* AND LOUIS ROUSSEAU, *Canada*

Corrected history of Laila Peak/Toshain II and Heran Peak; Schlagintweit Peak (5,971m), first ascent; Mamu Choti (ca 5,730m), possible first ascent; attempts on Toshain I and Peak 6,324m. This story begins with an old, awkward mistake. In 1997 some friends and I climbed a beautiful 6,132m peak in the Rupal Valley and claimed the first ascent (*AAJ* 1998), calling it Laila Peak. In April 2009 an e-mail from Roger D. Mellem revealed that he had climbed the same peak in 1974 with Willi Unsoeld and others (*AAJ* 1975, pp. 213-15). Although he had known this since 1998, he waited more than a decade to tell us because he didn't want to spoil our memories. What a nice gesture. We got the name Laila from locals. Unsoeld and friends called the peak Toshain II. Manfred Sturm, who did the second ascent in 1975, referred simply to Toshain. Since this is neither the first- nor second-highest peak in the group, perhaps Laila would be the best name.

(1) Heran Peak, 5,717m, with the north face line taken by Tanaka, et al, in 1990; Mark Twight soloed the northeast ridge (left skyline) in 1988. (2) Schlagintweit Peak, 5,971m, with the 2009 route on the west and northwest ridges. *Christian Walter*

Now that I had taken a fresh look at the old photos and maps, I was eager to visit the area again. We organized a team and traveled to the Rupal Valley in June. We camped on the right lateral moraine of the Toshain (Rupal) Glacier, at the so-called Mazeno Base Camp meadow (4,000m). For acclimatization, we attempted the 5,971m peak opposite base camp. Reinhold and Günther Messner had claimed the first ascent of that peak in 1970, climbing from the southeast, and called it Heran Peak. Locals call it Buldar Peak (Old Peak). Thomas Niederlein and I climbed the northwest ridge (PD) in three days. Since, to our knowledge, the

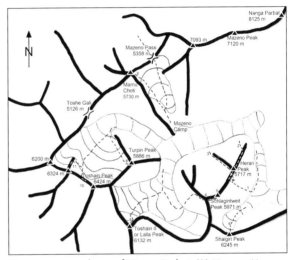

Known routes southwest of Nanga Parbat: (1) Messner-Messner, 1970; (2) Twight, 1988; (3) Tanaka, et al, 1990; (4) West ridge to Point 5,930m, Walter-Niederlein, 2009; (5) West ridge, Koschitzki, 2009; (6) Blanchard-Doyle-Robinson, 1988; (7) Jarrell-Mellem-Omberg-Unsoeld, 1974; (8) Rosenthal, et al, 1964; (9) Walter, et al, 2009; (10) attempt by Walter, et al, 2009; (11) attempt, Koschitzki-Walter, 2009. *Christian Walter*

peak was not virgin, we turned back where the northwest ridge meets the long, nearly horizontal summit ridge. But Robert Koschitzki followed our track the next day and continued to the mountain's highest point.

Back in Germany, Himalayan chronicler Wolfgang Heichel told us that neither the Messner brothers nor Sumio Tanaka and his Japanese team, who did the north pillar in 1990, had reached our summit. Nor had Mark Twight, who climbed northeast ridge in 1988. All of these climbs ended at the 5,717m east summit, or Heran Peak, 1.8km from the highest point. So it is likely that Koschitzki did the first ascent of the 5,971m peak on June 29, 2009. To unscramble the naming chaos, we suggest calling the higher summit Schlagintweit Peak, after the German scientist Adolph Schlagintweit, who visited the Rupal Valley in 1856.

Koschitzki, Niederlein, and I, plus Annette Longo, Norbert Trommler, and Gernot Frank, ascended another peak by a straightforward route (PD-) on July 1. It is the highest point between Mazeno Pass and the so-called Toshain Pass. We measured an altitude of 5,730m by GPS and called it Mamu Choti.

Next we attempted the virgin 6,424m Toshain main peak. It took us three days to find a route through the seracs of Toshain Glacier. From a camp at 5,700m, we reached the foresummit, 150m below the highest point, at midmorning on July 7. However, high avalanche danger prevented us from proceeding.

The next day Robert and I attempted neighboring Peak 6,324m, the second highest of the Toshain group. We climbed the north ridge to 6,100m, where Robert was caught in a slab avalanche. I was able to belay him, but we turned back.

CHRISTIAN WALTER, *Alpinclub Sachsen, Germany*

BATURA MUZTAGH

Karim Sar (6,180m), first ascent. On June 5 Paul Hersey and I arrived in Islamabad to discover security at an all-time high. We drove north up the Karakoram Highway against an endless tide of refugees fleeing a Taliban invasion of the Swat Valley. Three days after reaching the relative safety of Gilgit, we were ensconced at base camp beside the Shilinbar Glacier, under the 2,600m

Karim Sar (6,180m) from the southeast, above the Shilinbar Glacier. Pat Deavoll climbed a hidden gully with Paul Hersey (both unroped) to reach high camp at 5,100m. From there, Deavoll continued alone to the summit. The peak to the right is Aikache Chhok (6,595m). *Pat Deavoll*

south face of Karim Sar, a confusing mass of steep snow, hanging glaciers, and granite rock bands. It was a daunting sight.

As we acclimatized over the next week, the weather was snowy and unsettled. There was vastly more snow in the Karakoram than during the previous two years. At base camp Paul came down with an undiagnosed illness, recovered, and then decided he didn't want to go onto the mountain. I decided to try it alone and succumbed to angst-ridden, sleepless nights.

The morning of my departure, Paul announced he would come back up the glacier to advanced base camp (4,200m). I felt a flood of gratitude—even if Paul were thousands of feet below me, it would be a relief to know he was there. The next morning he agreed to belay me through a rock band a few hundred meters up the face. When we got beneath the short granite pitch, I decided to follow a gully system to the left. To my surprise, Paul decided to continue, though he had no overnight gear. I arrived on a small saddle at 5,100m at about 3 p.m., dug a tent platform, and watched Paul work his way up the slope. We both spent a sleepless night, Paul because he was lying in a large plastic pack liner, me because I was so damn nervous.

At 4 a.m. on June 25 I brewed up, handed my sleeping bag to Paul, and headed up a steep snow slope to the first obstacle: a small band of granite, covered in loose snow. I bridged up a gully for a few meters, had an "I can't do this" moment, and climbed back down. Taking a deep breath, I tried again and this time climbed 20m to the top.

Another steep snow slope led to a 100m cliff. Above and to the left were two ice cliffs, and between them a steep, narrow snow gully. I front-pointed 100m up the gully and found myself in a wide cwm rimmed by huge ice cliffs 300m above.

The cliffs seemed quiet, but I decided to climb onto a broad ice rib on the right of the cwm. I tried to hurry, but with snow almost to my knees progress was glacial. Conditions were better on the rib, however, and I sped up dramatically.

After climbing several hundred meters, passing sizeable crevasses, I came to a large rock band forming the base of the summit pyramid. From base camp it had looked as if this could be navigated on the left, but now I realized it would require a long traverse over steep ice with a 1,500m drop beneath. Far too scary! I accepted glumly that I'd have to drop 100m, traverse right under the rock band, and try to summit from the east side. The exposure was frightening, and with every step loose wet snow swished down alarmingly, gathering speed until it shot over the ice cliffs. After what seemed an eternity, I was able to start climbing toward the ridgeline. I was in the full sun and feeling tired.

At midday I hit the summit ridge above the east face. The only obstacle seemed to be a 60°–70° ice slope. "I can rappel that," I thought, and whizzed up the ice with renewed vigor. A five-minute wander along the final ridge put me on top. "Yippee! Now I can go down," was my reaction.

Two raps off V-threads got me nearly down the ice slope, and another three off rock bollards saw me back to the start of the traverse. The snow had deteriorated further, and by the time I reached the broad rib at the far end I was in tears. But progress down the rib was rapid, and I soon cheered up. Reversing the steep, narrow gully between the ice cliffs required concentration, followed by a nasty traverse back to the slope above camp. I spent 40 minutes cold-welding a stopper into a rotten crack for an anchor, and 30m lower repeated the procedure, to rappel the final rock band. Paul stuck his head out of the tent and waved.

I felt such an enormous sense of relief when Paul hugged me that I burst into tears for the second time. He had water and food ready. After 40 minutes he left to descend 1,000m to advanced base camp—another night in a plastic bag was beyond the call of duty! I fell sound asleep, and at dusk I woke, made another brew, and then passed out till 7 a.m. I descended the gully the next day, my legs like jelly.

PAT DEAVOLL, *New Zealand*

HISPAR MUZTAGH

Pumari Chhish East, attempt; Rasool Sar, first ascent; "Lunda Sar," first ascent of southwest face (no summit); Khani Basa Sar, first ascent. In the summer of 2009 Eamonn Walsh, Ian Welsted, and I traveled to Pakistan to play in bigger hills than the Canadian Rockies back home. With the support of a John Lauchlan Memorial Award, our primary objective was the unclimbed Pumari Chhish East (ca 6,900m).

The Canadian line on the southwest face of "Lunda Sar," a ca 6,300m peak west of Khani Basa Sar. The climbers' high point was the ridge, about 100m to 150m below the summit. *Raphael Slawinski*

On the summer solstice we arrived in base camp, at 4,500m, a wonderful grassy spot perched above the Yutmaru (Jutmaru) Glacier. While base camp had great bouldering, it also offered a front-row view of our objective, to remind us why we were there. The first order of business was to acclimatize, and on June 26 we summited a previously unclimbed 5,900m peak just to the northeast of camp, above the East Yutmaru Glacier, in an 11-hour round trip. We named the peak Rasool Sar in honor of our cook, guide, and friend Hajji Ghulam Rasool. While most of the "climbing" on Rasool Sar's southern flank consisted of slogging up a steep snow slope, there was an amusing bit of corniced ridge toward the top. After a few more acclimatization hikes, we declared ourselves ready for the main attraction.

Initially we had planned to attempt Pumari Chhish East via its south ridge, first tried in 2007 by Steve Su and Pete Takeda. But after we had wallowed in horrible snow on a few ridge climbs, the corniced south ridge lost some of its appeal. We turned our attention to the southeast face. On July 16 we bivied below the face at 4,800m. The following morning, starting well before dawn to take advantage of cooler temperatures, we made good progress up snow and ice fields, followed by a beautiful ice hose, to reach the base of a rock headwall at 5,700m. While Eamonn prepared a tent platform, Ian and I did one more pitch of reasonably difficult mixed climbing. Leaving a rope fixed, we descended to a waiting dinner. However, the effort of a big day, the altitude, and above all the heavy meal of freeze-dried chili and cheese had me throwing up all night. In the morning I could barely stand, and down we went.

On July 28 Ian and I (Eamonn having left to drink beer in Ireland) once again approached the southeast face. During the intervening 10 days the ice hose we'd climbed on the first attempt had melted out. While we sat deciding whether we should attempt the face, a large wet-snow avalanche swept the gully in question. That evening we were back in base camp.

The Canadian route on the southwest face of Khani Basa Sar (6,441m). A Korean expedition attempted the east face and upper south ridge in 2008. *Ian Welsted*

In between these two attempts (if they can be called that), the three of us climbed a route on a ca 6,300m peak directly north of the East Yutmaru Glacier and west of Khani Basa Sar. On July 20, starting from a bivy at 4,900m below the southwest face of the peak, we soloed 900m of serac-threatened snow and ice to reach a steep rock wall streaked with ice. We climbed this in eight sustained rope-lengths (WI4 M5), to reach the west ridge at 6,200m. The late hour, deteriorating weather, and snow that was waist-deep crud over rock slabs and hard ice combined to turn us around here. We rappelled through the night and arrived at our bivy site 22 hours after setting out. While we did not tag the summit, we were psyched to have climbed one of the best alpine mixed routes any of us had ever done. We propose a name for the still-unclimbed mountain: "Lunda Sar," which roughly translates as "Second-Hand Peak."

A few days before heading home, Ian and I made the first ascent of Khani Basa Sar (6,441m), a significant peak on the ridge separating the Yutmaru and Khani Basa glaciers. The peak had been attempted by several teams; during an acclimatization foray up its south ridge, we came across traces of a 2008 Korean expedition. Leaving our bivy at 4,800m at 3 a.m., we made for the southwest rib of the peak, which neatly separates two couloirs capped by giant seracs. After a few worrying moments when we thought we might have blundered into one of these gullies in the dark, we decided we were on route and continued up pleasant névé and rock scrambling.

Shortly after dawn we roped up at a short mixed wall and continued on 55° ice. The crux of the route was a narrow snow ridge leading to the summit plateau. One serac wall proved especially troublesome, but after I took a leader fall and landed on a pleasantly soft snow mushroom, we got up it. We summited around 6 p.m. and were rewarded with a panoramic view of the Karakoram. The descent was not entirely straightforward, especially reversing the snow ridge, but we persevered and stumbled back to our bivy exactly 24 hours after leaving it.

RAPHAEL SLAWINSKI, *Canada, AAC*

Tahu Rutum, attempt; Korea Youth Sar, possible first ascent. A seven-man Korean expedition led by Shim Kwon-sik attempted the west face of Tahu Rutum (6,651m) but gave up because of heavy snowfall, a porter strike, and other complications. Climbers Jeon Yong-hak and Hong Seung-gi, a high school student, made the possible first ascent of a nearby 6,000m peak with 1,400m of vertical relief above base camp; the two climbed alpine style, soloing up to 5,600m and then belaying to the top. They named the peak Korea Youth Sar.

Adapted from a report in Korean Alpine News

RAKAPOSHI RANGE

Spantik, new route on northwest face. Koreans Kim Hyung-il, Kim Pal-bong, and Min Jun-young completed a new route on the northwest face of Spantik (7,027m) in mid-July. The Korean route, which they graded VI WI4 M8, ascends steep snow to a difficult band of rock and mixed climbing near the top of the face, right of the famed Golden Pillar. The climbers spent five days on the face, from July 8 to 12, and needed another two days to climb to the summit via the gentle southwest ridge and descend to base camp.

This is believed to be the first alpine-style new route by Koreans on a peak taller than 7,000m; the climbers carried just two 100m ropes and left only two snow pickets on the mountain. A full report on their ascent may be found earlier in this *Journal.*

Japanese climbers Kazuaki Amano, Fumitaka Ichimura, and Yusuke Sato repeated the British route (Fowler-Saunders, 1987) on the Golden Pillar of Spantik, reaching the summit on July 12, one day before the Koreans. Both parties descended via the prominent snow and ice buttress far to the right of the pillar.

PANMAH MUZTAGH

Latok II, northwest ridge, first integral ascent and tragedy. In early August, Spanish climbers Álvaro Novellón and Óscar Pérez did the first complete ascent of the northwest ridge of Latok II (7,108m). This remarkable climb ended in tragedy, however, when a fall during the descent severely injured Pérez. With his partner unable to move, Novellón descended alone and called for help; an international rescue mobilized, but rescuers were unable to reach Pérez's position.

The pair first attempted the north ridge of Latok I, reaching only about 5,800m in very poor snow conditions. After switching

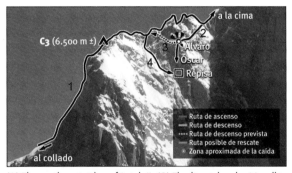

(1) The northwest ridge of Latok II. (2) The line taken by Novellón and Pérez during their descent from the summit in order to avoid the complex ridgecrest. After they fell, Novellón lowered Pérez to a ledge (box labeled "Repisa") and traversed to Camp 3 for supplies. The next day he returned to Pérez with their sleeping bags and food, and then traversed back to the ridge and descended alone over one and a half days. (3) The pair's planned traverse route back to Camp 3. (4) The line rescuers hoped to follow to reach Pérez. *Sebastian Alvaro, courtesy of* Desnivel

objectives to Latok II, on August 2 they began climbing on the northeast side of the ridge. They bivied that night on the 5,600m col between Latok II and Ogre II (Peak 6,950m). Climbing alpine-style directly up the ridge, they bivied again at 6,000m and 6,500m, where they left their tent and sleeping bags. Slow going forced an open bivy at 7,000m, before they reached the top on August 6.

Latok II from the northeast, showing the line of the first complete ascent of the northwest ridge, by Álvaro Novellón and Óscar Pérez. Previous attempts had approached the saddle on the right from the south, on the opposite side. In 1997 two Germans ascended the west face to reach the ridge at ca 6,600m and followed it to the summit. The black arrow points to the site of the accident that cost Pérez his life during the descent in 2009. *Sebastian Alvaro, courtesy of* Desnivel

The accident occurred as they descended toward their Camp 3. To avoid a complicated passage on the ridgecrest, they deviated onto the southwest face. While traversing unstable snow, Pérez fell and pulled them both off. The rope snagged on a ridge of snow and caught them, but Pérez could not move. After lowering his partner to a ledge, Novellón climbed to Camp 3 to recover their sleeping bags, food, and fuel; however, a storm forced him to spend the night there before returning to his partner. Unable to lower Pérez any farther, Novellón descended alone, using a cut rope to make dozens of 30m rappels down more than 1,600m of complicated terrain. This took a day and a half.

When Novellón reached base camp on August 8, he called his climbing club in Spain, El Pena Guara de Huesca, which began organizing a rescue. By August 14 a group of experienced climbers, including Spanish ace Jordi Corominas and American Fabrizio Zangrilli, plus a number of high-altitude porters, had set up a base camp on the Biafo Glacier, on the opposite side of the mountain from Novellón's camp. By the 15th the rescuers had fixed ropes to the col from the south, hoping to continue up the northwest ridge and reach Pérez. However, the weather turned bad on the 16th, making climbing and helicopter flights too dangerous. Given the length of time Pérez had been alone on the mountain, the rescue was called off.

Starting in the mid-1970s, several British teams had attempted the northwest ridge, approaching it from the south, and in 1987 a party led by Joe Brown reached a high point of about 6,800m. In 1997 Germans Franz Fendt and Christian Schlesener climbed the west face to 6,000m and then diagonaled left up a snow and ice couloir to reach the northwest ridge at 6,600m. From here, they continued to the summit, completing the third ascent of Latok II. However, no team had climbed the full ridge nor attempted the ridge from the north. Novellón said the northwest ridge was 2,400m high, with about 3,000m of climbing distance; the difficulties were VI 6a M6.

DOUGALD MACDONALD, *from information compiled by* Desnivel

Editor's note: An interview with Álvaro Novellón about this climb, the accident, and his difficult descent can be found at aaj.AmericanAlpineClub.org.

Latok IV, new route to just below northwest summit. Ondrej Mandula and I climbed a new route on the southwest side of Latok IV (6,456m) in July. We established advanced base camp four or five hours up the Baintha Lukpar Glacier from our base camp by the Biafo Glacier. The next day we crossed the heavily crevassed glacier under the southwest face of Latok IV and bivouacked without a tent on a small ridge at about 5,600m. We began climbing at 3 a.m. in the obvious gully system splitting the left side of the face. The first 200m was easy 50° snow, which we simul-climbed. We belayed as it got steeper (60°–70°) and icier. About 100m below the top, an overhanging chimney blocked the way. To bypass this we climbed rock on the right (crux), followed by a pitch with a 5m vertical ice chimney and then a nice mixed pitch to the summit

(1) Latok V (6,190m) and (2) Latok IV (6,456m), above the east arm of the Baintha Lukpar Glacier. (A) Czech Route (2009); (B) Japanese Route (Okano-Omiya, 1980). During the latter climb, Motomu Omiya made the first ascent of both the northwest (main) and southeast summits of Latok IV. The northwest peak has not been climbed again. *Martin Horak*

ridge, which we reached at 2 p.m. From here it appeared to be no more than 50m–100m of easy climbing to the top, but the weather was bad and we decided to rappel. We reached our bivy below the face at 9 p.m.

JIRI PLISKA, *Czech Republic*

Baintha Brakk (Ogre), attempt via southeast face and southeast ridge; HAR Pinnacle and Baintha Kabata, ascents. Julien Dusserre, Jérôme Para, and I established base camp at 4,600m on the Choktoi Glacier. On August 25, for acclimatization, we climbed a possible new route on the west face of HAR Pinnacle (5,490m), leaving base camp at 7 a.m. and returning at 9 p.m. Our route, Ruby Eternelle (400m, 6b), may share ground with the Ménard-Turgeon line of 2006. From August 29 to September 1 we climbed a 1,200m mixed line up the southeast arête of a ca 6,300m peak at the head of the Choktoi that we believed to be unclimbed. We had two days of bad weather during the four-day climb and found beautiful pitches of climbing up to 6a+ WI5 M4. After returning home, we

Baintha Brakk (the Ogre, 7,285m) from the east. (1) The French trio ascended the southeast face for two days to reach the east ridge. After traversing left for two days, they hoped to follow the upper southeast ridge to the top. But a storm forced them to descend the southeast ridge (2). *Colin Haley*

learned we had repeated the route climbed by Colin Haley and Maxime Turgeon in 2008 (in much better weather!); they called the peak Baintha Kabata.

After six days of poor weather, we began an attempt on Baintha Brakk (the Ogre, 7,285m), with a forecast for a week of good weather. We skied to the foot of the peak on September 8 and bivouacked there at just under 5,000m. After studying the conditions, we decided to avoid the serious objective dangers on the approach to the southeast ridge and instead started up the southeast face. Two days of climbing on steep mixed ground brought us to 6,250m on the east ridge, at the base of a steep rock headwall. From there, we traversed horizontally to the left toward the southeast ridge, following mixed terrain, with a pitch of exposed rock climbing. After a bivouac at 6,500m, we climbed snow and ice to the foot of the final tower at ca 6,800m. The weather was rapidly deteriorating, and in the morning it was impossible to climb. We descended the southeast ridge in high wind, making 20 rappels, and bivouacked a final time near the saddle between Ogre I and II. The next day we descended the icefall and returned to base camp.

AYMERIC CLOUET, *France*

Baltoro Muztagh

Trango Tower, Eternal Flame, first free ascent. In 1989 Kurt Albert, Wolfgang Güllich, Milan Sykora, and Christoph Stiegler climbed one of the most beautiful routes in the world: Eternal Flame on Trango Tower. They aided only four pitches, climbing approximately 80 percent of the route free, on compact, orange-colored rock with splitter cracks, with difficulties up to 5.12a. The fame of Güllich and Albert, and the pictures from their ascent, made the Eternal Flame one of the most desirable high-altitude rock climbs in the world.

In 2003 Denis Burdet, from Switzerland, free-climbed two of the four aid pitches, with difficulties up to 5.13a. A big step, but the 10th pitch with its bolt ladders still hadn't been freed, nor had the pendulum of the second pitch, with 4m of featureless granite. Another small piece was added to the mosaic in 2005, when Spanish climber Iker Pou discovered a variation to the right of the 10th-pitch bolt ladders and top-roped all the moves (up to 5.13b). Bad weather prevented him from redpointing the pitch.

Now it was our turn. On July 24 photographer Franz Hinterbrandner, Mario Walder, my brother Alexander, and I arrived at base camp beside the Trango Glacier. The weather had been bad until then, but we were lucky. After 10 days we established Camp 2 at the Sun Terrace, the huge shoulder at 5,500m, below the main headwall on the south face. Our curiosity dragged us onto the face above the same day. As we had been told, the granite of the second-pitch traverse was indeed featureless. But there was another possibility. From the beginning of the pendulum,

Trango Tower: Alexander Huber leads the first of two 5.12d pitches to bypass the 10th-pitch bolt ladder on Eternal Flame. Behind, Great Trango Tower. *Franz Hinterbrandner*

we climbed straight up using thin cracks for 30m and traversed left through nearly vertical but featured slabs toward the crack system of Eternal Flame. We named these two pitches Come on Baby and Light My Fire, with difficulties up to 5.12a.

Bad weather came in, and we rested in base camp. After three days, our meteorologist from Innsbruck, Karl Gabl, announced perfect weather for the upcoming week. At 3 a.m. on August 11 we set off, and six hours later we reached our Camp 2. After a short break we continued climbing. Alexander's and my goal was to free-climb as a team, swapping leads, without any falls by the leader or second. After repeating the new pitches to bypass the pendulum, we climbed another short crack pitch, Come Together, with which we rejoined the original route. We continued climbing for three more pitches, but then melt-water flowing down the rock stopped us.

The next day we climbed the ropes we had fixed the day before, then continued up an icy 5.11a to reach the 10th pitch. Here, Pou had top-roped a slab traverse, a hard boulder problem, and an ice-covered crack. It was a good idea, but his variation is only feasible in certain conditions. Four meters farther to the right, however, we discovered a trace of a crack, which, after 20m, led into the upper, drier part of the Pou variation. We named the first pitch of our variation Wish You Were Here and the second Burn for You, both 5.12d.

On day three the first three pitches above a great bivy ledge posed no big problems, with ideal jam cracks. Then came disenchantment: a slightly overhanging finger crack, only 15m high, but extremely thin. (Denis Burdet graded it 5.13a.) Only after an intense boulder session were we able to crack this hard nut. The following 5.12d double-cracks pitch finished us off. With some effort we both freed it, but we had to postpone the summit for another day.

After two 5.11 cracks the next morning, August 14, only easy ground remained below the 6,251m summit. Soon all four of us were there, surrounded by the giants of the Karakoram, overwhelmed by the great adventure we'd just experienced.

THOMAS HUBER, *Germany*

Uli Biaho Tower, attempt, first ascent of lower northeast wall. Basile Petiot, Benoit Monfort, and Mathieu Detrie, from France, and I, from Belgium, traveled to Pakistan in July, hoping to climb the direct northeast pillar of Uli Biaho Tower (6,109m), a virgin line of 2,100m. This is composed of two distinct parts. The first is a magnificent 1,000m big wall that ends at a hanging glacier. Above soars a mixed prow, also 1,000m. After studying the proposed line, we realized that the second part is very exposed to falling ice from the summit cornices. Given that the technical difficulties were likely to impose a slow pace, it was out of the question to risk such exposure.

We modified our objective: We would climb the lower pillar and then follow the hanging glacier to the left to reach the couloir that borders the east face; we would climb this for 600m to a col and finish with 500m of the upper south face. After a day of fixing the first 200m, we understood that the lower pillar would not be simple: The climbing was already 6B+ A3, and not one pitch gave way easily. We returned to base camp and prepared for our attempt.

After four days of bad weather, we started up the wall on July 25, heavily loaded. The climbing continued to be difficult, and we completed only four more pitches that day, much fewer than expected. Many of the cracks were dirty, and it was very steep. This wasn't Indian Creek! The aid climbing was in thin cracks, with micronuts, beaks, and knifeblades. We

The Belgian-French line on Uli Biaho Tower. The team completed the first ascent of the lower northeast face and continued to a saddle below the upper south face, but a storm prevented them from completing the route to the summit. They descended to the south (left) and climbed a small peak along the way, calling it Uli Biahette (ca 5,700m). *Jean-Baptiste Deraeck*

slept on a tiny, exposed ledge, as we did not bring portaledges or bolts. Already we were low on water, and the 600m above looked completely dry. We needed a little miracle. The next day we continued even slower, with yet another pitch of A3. We were completely dehydrated. But then the miracle took place: The ledge that would be our host for the night was supplied with a trickle of water. The next day was fantastic, and we arrived at the top of the wall after 22 pitches, eight with aid. Short on time, we did not walk up the easy ground to the actual summit of the pillar.

We left during the night to climb the ice couloir. It was very steep: sustained 55°, with numerous passages of 60° ice. The altitude, the weight of our packs, and fatigue from the previous days reduced us to a snail's pace. When we arrived at the 5,600m col that separates the east and south faces, we set up a comfortable bivouac on a ledge that overlooks the col. It began to snow. The following day it snowed all day. During a brief lull, we checked out the south face. The rock looked superb, but the first 250m would have sustained difficulties. We returned to our tent hoping for a lucky break. We had only two more days of food. We called for a forecast and learned that three to four more days of bad weather were predicted. We decided to go down. Near our descent route, we climbed a small consolation peak (5,700m) that we called Uli Biahette.

JEAN-BAPTISTE DERAECK, *Belgium*

Broad Peak, southwest face, new variation to 6,800m. Our group of 10, with Kiomars Babazadeh as leader and me as climbing leader, reached base camp for Broad Peak on June 30. Our goal was the first new route in the Himalaya by Iranians. On July 2 we began climbing the southwest face, following the same line attempted by two French climbers earlier in the season. It was a rather easy up to 5,200m, where we encountered an 80m step. A 50m ice and snow gully was followed by 30m of vertical and overhanging loose rock, which led to Camp 1 at 5,370m.

From there, rock and snow climbing led to 5,650m, followed by snow slopes to the ridgecrest at 6,220m. About 50m below the ridge we faced a major difficulty: a 75° ice slope covered by 40cm of snow that we had to shovel off to reach the ice. We reached the ridge on July 21, having fixed some 1,600m of rope. What we saw was not encouraging. Just past Camp 2, at 6,230m, was a 30m drop and then a knife-edge ridge leading to a gendarme.

(1) The normal route on Broad Peak's southwest face. (2) The Iranian variation, established in 2009. The Iranians fixed and later abandoned 1,600m of rope on the route, on which they placed two camps. They finished their climb at Camp 3 on the normal route, at ca 6,800m. A French pair had climbed alpine-style to 6,200m on the same variation earlier in the season. *Courtesy of Ramin Shojaei*

After a few days of rest at base camp in bad weather, we climbed back to the ridge on July 26 and climbed the gendarme, which was easier than expected. The next day we climbed a snow dome, the last 15m of which was 85° ice covered by snow, the crux of the whole route. Soon technical difficulties eased significantly, and after another 100m we reached a plateau that had been hidden from view.

The wide plateau was 1.5 km long. It led to a rock and snow spur, where, at 6,800m, we joined the normal route, just below Camp 3. *[Editor's note: The final part of this ascent, from the plateau to Camp 3, may have followed the route of the 1957 Austrian expedition that first climbed Broad Peak.]* Aidin Bozorgi and I slept at Camp 3, at 7,015m, on August 13, a windless and relatively warm night, but I could not go farther because of altitude sickness. We abandoned our summit attempt and left base camp on August 18.

RAMIN SHOJAEI, *Arash Mountaineers Club, Iran*

Editors note: French climbers Ludovic Giambiasi and Elisabeth Revol attempted this line May 30–June 1, 2009. Climbing alpine-style, they reached the ridge at ca 6,200m in two days. However, the narrow ridge beyond was loaded with early-season snow and appeared too dangerous, and the climbers retreated after their second bivouac. Also, it must be noted that, although the Iranian team cleaned its camps and garbage from the mountain, as well as garbage left by other expeditions on Broad Peak, unfortunately they also left 1,600m of fixed rope on their route.

Gasherbrum VI, northeast face, attempt. As far as we know, there have been only two or three attempts on Gasherbrum VI (7,004m), all via the south face, directly above Gasherbrum base camp. Paulo Roxo and I tried Gasherbrum VI alpine-style via the northeast face and east ridge, choosing the route that looked least prone to avalanches or cornice falls. We started climbing at 2 a.m. on July 12. The route began with slopes of 55°–60°, with reasonable snow and ice, and gradually became steeper. We stayed close to the rock to avoid possible avalanches and to try to find good protection. As a consequence, we found some mixed-climbing steps on

The northeast face of Gasherbrum VI showing the line of the Portuguese attempt. *Daniela Teixeira*

precarious rock. We mostly simul-climbed but sometimes belayed from pitons, ice screws, or snow stakes. Cams were mostly useless in the rotten rock.

We stopped about 60m below the east ridge. We were climbing 70° ice, and above us a narrow ice couloir led to vertical rotten rock. The only way to pass this was to climb vertical snow on either side. This loose powder must have blown over the ridge and plastered the face; protection was virtually impossible. We also could see that the east ridge had many large, overhanging cornices.

We started the descent around 12:30 p.m. The sun had hit the face, and it was hard to find good anchors in the wet snow and ice. We got to the bottom by rappelling from double Abalakovs and a few single-piton anchors, plus downclimbing.

This route is exposed to rockfall as soon as the sun shines on the face, and it is avalanche-prone in poor conditions (but less so than any other potential route we saw on Gasherbrum VI). It is advisable to climb as much as possible at night.

DANIELA TEIXEIRA, *Portugal*

CHARAKUSA VALLEY

Farol Far East (6,200m), first ascent, and other ascents. The Swiss team of Simon Riediker, Mirco Stalder, and I completed several routes in the Charakusa Valley, including the first ascent of a 6,200-meter peak. We arrived in the valley on July 19 and left August 15. In order to acclimatize, Mirco and I repeated a free-climbing route on a 5,400m rock tooth that we called "Dru Peak" after its resemblance to the Dru in Chamonix. The climb was six pitches (6a to 6c) on perfect rock. The next day Mirco and I tackled a beautiful crack system on a possibly unclimbed rock needle, south of Dru Peak, that we baptized Lady Finger. We placed two bolts on No More Immodium (180m, 7a).

Our next goal was the far eastern summit of the Farol group. This 6,200m peak had been tried several times without success. We hoped to reach the summit by the east ridge, which had been attempted by two Frenchmen in 2006. Simon had contracted pulmonary edema during the first night in base camp and was still recovering, so it was just Mirco and me again. We camped on the glacier at 5,000m and climbed to the saddle below the east ridge at 5,600m. However, that night brought 20cm of snow, and we returned to base camp. Two days later we returned to Camp 1, with 150m of extra rope, and the next day climbed to Camp 2 in the saddle and fixed three pitches above. The ridge had perfect rock and challenging mixed climbing. The more demanding passages forced us to change into rock-climbing shoes.

Early in the morning we jumared up the fixed ropes, moving agonizingly slowly. Above, four time-consuming mixed pitches brought us to a secondary peak. The main summit seemed miles away. A tough rocky ridge with huge cornices lay ahead; knowing that we had to return along this ridge the same day, we sped up as much as we could. A steep rock face below the foresummit provided some demanding crux pitches, but at 4:30 p.m. we finally made it to the main summit. (The difficulties had been up to 6c+ M6+.) We raised our home-sewn Swiss flag to commemorate our national holiday, August 1, and set off down the ridge. Around dusk, after 17 hours of climbing, we returned to our high camp, and the following day descended all the way to base camp.

In the meantime Simon had completely recovered and was eager for action. The three of us climbed Naisa Brakk via the north ridge. Next we completed a two-day approach to a camp at 5,800m, at the foot of the north ridge of Drifika (6,480m). The ridge provided demanding mixed climbing, bare ice, and powder snow, and our efforts were rewarded with a gorgeous panoramic view of the Karakoram.

Back at base camp we did a couple of rock climbs before we had to head home. First was the highest summit of the Iqbal Wall, which has a top shaped like a human head; we called it Gandel Peak (*gandel* means "head" in Balti). Four straightforward but beautiful pitches led to a seemingly blank 20m wall. But to our surprise we found small grips that allowed us to traverse to a perfect crack leading directly to the head (Human Touch, 300m, 7a).

(A) Farol East (6,350m), first ascent, solo, by Maxime Turgeon, September 2007. (B) Farol Far East (6,200m), first ascent by Simon Oswald and Mirco Stalder in July-August 2009. (C) The 5,600m saddle from which Oswald and Stalder attacked the east ridge. *Simon Oswald*

With the weather still great, we climbed a line on the left edge of the Iqbal Wall. Midway up the cliff, a band of quartz allowed us to switch cracks. In all it was a fantastic route, despite some occasional crumbly rock (The Last Move, 250m, 7b).

We returned via the Karakoram Highway, which, due to a shortage of diesel, was empty of traffic. Thanks to our liaison officer's far-reaching connections, we were able to fill our tanks and proceed toward home without impediment.

SIMON OSWALD, *Switzerland*

K7 West, southwest pillar, The Children of Hushe. The Karakoram 2009 Trentina Expedition—Michele Cagol, Fabio Leoni, Elio Orlandi, and I, all over 40—managed a new route up the southwest pillar of K7 West, reaching an altitude of ca 5,700m. The route was demanding, but our biggest difficulties came from the altitude. We set up base camp at 4,200m and moving up with loads, acclimatizing slowly, proved difficult.

We set off on July 31, ready to stay on the wall for an extended period. After a demanding first day, we established a bivy at 5,000m. After a light meal, we settled down for the night, but a few hours later I started to have trouble breathing. I remained awake all night, sitting up, and the next morning we descended to base camp, where I quickly started to feel better.

After a day's rest we were ready to start again, but that night Michele felt poorly. He had the same symptoms as I had, plus his limbs were swollen. We waited another day and set off yet again, burdened with a thousand uncertainties. This time we placed our tents at 5,200m. Here Elio started to feel the altitude, but thanks to Diamox he didn't have to descend—otherwise we would have risked running out of time. Despite everything, climbing determinedly, we completed our 1,100m rock route (7b A2) to the top of the wall on August 10. We called it the Children of Hushe to honor the village from which we departed and its remarkable young people.

By the time we descended, we were well-acclimatized, so Fabio and I used our final day to climb spectacular Naisa Brakk (ca 5,200m). We reached the summit on August 14, Pakistan's independence day, and from the top,

The Italian route on the southwest pillar of K7 West. In its upper half, the line lies immediately to the right of the 2007 Belgian-Polish route, Badal. *Rolando Larcher Collection*

1,000m above base camp, we listened to a party that the officers and cooks of various expeditions had organized; the national anthems of all the countries present—Pakistan, Italy, Switzerland, Germany, Australia, and New Zealand—were being played.

ROLANDO LARCHER, *Società Alpinisti Tridentini / Club Alpino Accademico Italiano*

Editor's note: Three lines have been climbed on the rock buttresses of the ca 6,200m subpeak southwest of K7 West (the "southwest pillar"): Badal (Favresse-Favresse-Pustelnik-Villanueva, 2007); Luna (Cesen-Sisernik-Hrastelj, 2008); and Children of Hushe (Cagol-Larcher-Leoni-Orlandi, 2009), each topping out at 5,500m to ca 5,800m. However, no team has continued to the summit of the 6,200m peak above the rock walls—an obvious prize.

Nafees Cap, Naughty Daddies. In August, the four-man team of Adrian Laing and Scott Standen from Australia and Bruce Dowrick and Jon Sedon from New Zealand free-climbed a variation to the route Ledgeway to Heaven (Favresse-Favresse-Pustelnik-Villanueva, 2007) on Nafees Cap, a prominent rock spire on the south side of K7. The team spent a total of nine nights on the southwest face, free-climbing about 20 pitches, up to 25 (5.12); they placed two protection bolts. Laing and Sedon reached a shoulder on the south ridge of the pinnacle and joined Ledgeway to Heaven, which they followed for two pitches before concluding it was too snowy to continue to the summit. They called the line Naughty Daddies (630m, 7b).

NANGMA VALLEY AND ENVIRONS

Denbor Brakk, south ridge to south tower. "Not even the American ambassador to Pakistan is getting past these gates. Closed means closed!" These are the words that welcomed us to the Kondus Valley of Pakistan…or just short of it. Months earlier Matt Hepp and I had applied for a "special permit" to explore unclimbed granite towers within this disputed territory of northern Pakistan. With the help of our local contact, Zafar Iqbal, and due to a humanitarian component of our expedition, we acquired clearances from all the necessary agencies. But even with official documents in hand and a local parliamentarian at our backs, a newly appointed brigade commander pulled the finely woven carpet out from under us.

During the week of our permit dispute, Zafar guided us to a number of mountain villages in need of basic services. Thanks to a Zack Martin Breaking Barriers Grant from the American Alpine Club, plus the help of the generous community in Ouray County, Colorado, we were able to teach villagers in Hushe and Kande how to quickly construct sturdy, heatable, post-earthquake and landslide shelters out of simple materials. The warm reception, helpful hands, and willingness to learn in these remote villages never ceased to surprise us.

With the Kondus Valley gates closed, and a limited amount of time, we decided to trek into the Nangma Valley. The snowy fall season had already closed in on peaks above 5,500m, so we lowered our sights to three 4,600m–4,800m peaks with promising lines.

The first and most striking route we attempted was on Green Tower (4,600m). Not knowing the tower's history, we chose a direct, aesthetic, and, unfortunately, north-facing line. We began our frost-nipped and short-lived journey at the top of a snow ramp. Not long into the Chia pet–choked cracks, we found a pin and some tat tucked into a hidden corner. Lacking the motivation for self-torture without pleasure or gain, we bailed. After returning to the U.S., we learned we had started up one of two known routes on the Green Tower: Inshallah Mi Primo (850m, 5.10b A3).

Feeling winter closing in, we scoped only sunny, south-facing options. The obvious south ridge of Denbor Brakk (4,800m) seemed an attainable objective. We began up a series of chimneys and wide cracks. A couple of pitches up, we encountered a lovely six-inch roof crack that rounded into a grass-packed fist crack. Many offwidths and ledges later, we blanked out against a prominent gendarme. Luckily, we were able to rap off the east shoulder of the peak into a high gully. Leaving our ropes fixed, we spent the night on the ground, recharging on pakora and dhal.

The next morning we ascended our ropes, flailed around the gendarme via another series of grass-choked wide cracks, and encountered about 50 feet of pleasantly garden-free hand jamming. The last pitches to the summit of the south tower were wide, hard, and especially exhausting at nearly 4,800m. Reaching the higher summit to the north would have involved a brutal amount of rappelling, traversing, climbing, more rappelling, and steep, dirty, wide cracks. So, late in the day, we rappelled off the east shoulder and headed beck to the comforts of camp.

We called the route Good From Zafar, But Zafar From Good (5.10 A1 G3—steep gardening), named after our friend Zafar Iqbal. I can't in good conscience recommend the route. It was good adventure, though.

After a couple of rest days, Matt and I started up a chimney system at the very tip of the apron below the south face of Zang Brakk (4,800m). At the top of the first pitch, a two-bolt belay greeted us. Since we only had a handful of days left in the valley, we decided to see where the route led. We continued up wide cracks (5.10 plus-ish) to a ledge below a 75m pitch of blank face climbing, with one bolt for protection. The pitch ended at a single-knifeblade belay. With darkness drawing near, we placed a bolt and rappelled 1,000 feet to the ground.

(1) Amin Brakk, 5,850m; (2) Nawaz Brakk, ca 5,700m; (3) Denbor Brakk, 4,800m; and (4) south tower of Denbor Brakk. Clint Estes and Matt Hepp climbed the south ridge (right skyline) to the south tower. *Clint Estes*

The next day we climbed as fast as we could to regain our high point. No signs of previous ascent were evident past the pin. Our route blanked out at the top of a nice hand crack. I made two attempts to link crack systems via hard face climbing, but fear set in, and I was unable to complete the moves. We then chose a less-appealing wide option to the right. After a couple of more pitches, a timely snowstorm blew in and gave us an excuse to retreat from our 1,300-foot high point. Nearly 1,000 feet of climbing remained. This route, I would recommend.

CLINT ESTES, *AAC*

Editor's note: On Zang Brakk, Estes and Hepp climbed the first 1,000' of Hasta La Vista David (Colnago-Davila-Lazzarini-Stucchi, 2004), before exploring variations on the upper wall.

Rustam Brakk (ca 5,450m) from the east. *Irena Mrak*

Bondid Valley, Rustam Brakk (5,450m), Ali Route. The Bondid Valley extends to the west of Kande village, opposite the well-known Nangma Valley. Mojca Svajger and I visited this valley in September, after an unsuccessful attempt on Rakaposhi. We set up base camp at 4,500m on the left side of the Muntin Glacier, where there is grass and running water. Our first goal was a mountain called Muntin (ca 6,500m), the dominant peak in the area. Conditions did not permit an attempt, though, so we chose a lower, neighboring mountain in a side valley northeast of Muntin.

On September 12 we climbed the east side of this peak (IV 80°/50°–70°, 400m), which we named Rustam Brakk after a porter from Kande. The climbing was great, and in the upper part we could see many unclimbed 5,500m–6,500m peaks in neighboring valleys.

Muntin appears to offer nice options for climbing, but one would have to be in the area earlier in the season, when the crevasses are still covered by snow. Rustam Brakk, on the other hand, can be climbed quite late in the season, and it appears that neighboring mountains could be climbable from May till September.

IRENA MRAK, *Slovenia*

The east side of Muntin (ca 6,500m). Rustam Brakk is located farther along the ridgeline to the right. *Irena Mrak*

India

Overview. In 2009 there were 64 Indian and 37 foreign expeditions in the Indian Himalaya, the total of 101 being the largest in recent years. Many Indian expeditions visited peaks that have been climbed many times (Satopanth, Chhamser Kangri), and many foreign groups were commercially organized trips to well-known mountains, such as Nun and Kun. Stok Kangri retained its status as the most-climbed 6,000m peak in the world, with the added tag of harboring one of the dirtiest, most foul-smelling base camps anywhere.

Both leading organizations in India had new Presidents. Ramkrishna Rao, former Director General of the Indo-Tibet Border Police (ITBP), was elected as President of the Indian Mountaineering Foundation, while a leading Indian mountaineer, Col. Ashok Abbey, took over the reins of the Himalayan Club.

Finally, the Indian Himalaya was severely affected by changes in the weather, and one can use the cliché that the only certainty about this year's weather was its uncertainty. The dry spells affected villagers' psyche too. The population of Langja, in Spiti, long suspected that the mountain rising above their village, with the romantic name Chau Chau Kang Nilda (Blue Moon in the Sky), affected their weather. This year they stopped three expeditions from proceeding to this peak, as they believed it would affect the crops: a curious effect of global warming.

HARISH KAPADIA, *Honorary Editor, The Himalayan Journal*

EAST KARAKORAM

Saser Muztagh, Plateau Peak (7,287m), attempt. The name "Plateau Peak" is something of a contradiction: the mountain is massive and wears a permanent ice cap. Despite several attempts, by 2009 the peak still remained unclimbed. Our five-member Indo-American team, consisting of Sudeep Barve, Rajesh Gadgil, Marling Geist, Bryce Green, and I, traveled to Leh on July 21. We trekked across the Lasermo La (5,400m) into the Nubra Valley and started our approach to the mountain from

The south face of Plateau Peak (7,287m) rises above the Sakang Lungpa Glacier. The summit is toward the right. *Divyesh Muni*

Pinchimic. The terrain was rough—long traverses on scree-covered rock slabs, loose mud, and exposed paths. It took 10 hours to gain the 1,000m height rise to Phonglas Camp at 4,400m. The next day, we established base camp (4,800m) at the snout of the Sakang Glacier [this point is marked as Yangbar on some maps and the glacier also referred to as the Sakang Lungpa].

We established ABC at 5,400m on the Sakang Glacier moraine by August 3. From the upper eastern basin we had to find a line up a wall of ca 1,000m to gain access to the east ridge of Plateau Peak. This line would exit at the base of Saser Kangri III, where we planned to place a camp. It would be a long traverse from there to Plateau Peak, but more direct access to the east ridge was subject to risk from seracs and avalanches. Our route followed a narrow gully to a height of 6,200m, from where a steep climb led to a leftward traverse below a rock band. This traverse was frightening due to extreme exposure and loose snow, the latter collapsing with every passage. On comple-

The line attempted by the Indo-American team on the far right side of the south face of Plateau Peak. The team almost reached the junction with the east ridge, which continues left off picture. The summit behind is Saser Kangri III (7,495m), first climbed in 1986 by the ITBP. *Divyesh Muni*

tion of the traverse, we climbed straight up a snow and ice slope that we called the Butterfly.

For seven days we persisted. As the sun touched the slopes and loosened rocks, the gully became a bowling alley. A few rocks found their mark. Our start time got earlier each day, to a point where we aimed to start by midnight. We reached a height of ca. 6,600m, after fixing 1,350m of rope. On August 15, Barve, Gadgil, Geist, and I visited the Sakang col (6,100m). This lay close by on the ridge between Saser III and 6,943m Sakang, and overlooks the North Shukpa Kungchang Glacier. Next day, the weather turned bad with strong winds and snowfall, which continued for the next eight days, making the route unsafe. In continuing bad weather the team returned to base camp on August 22.

Rajesh and I were keen to attempt a peak of 6,010m (as marked on the Survey of India Map: N 34°41.755, E 77°41.055) at the junction of the Sakang and its subsidiary glaciers. On the 24th the weather showed positive signs, so we shifted to Phonglas Camp at 4,400m. On the 25th, with Sherpas Mingma and Samgyal, we climbed steep scree slopes and traversed some nerve-racking rock slabs to establish a camp at 5,200m below the northwest face of the peak. Next day, despite cloudy skies, we decided to make an attempt, hoping the weather would hold. We climbed the north ridge, which held a few sections of steep ice, to the upper west ridge. All four reached the summit by 10:00 a.m. and were back in Phonglas Camp that evening. We named our mountain Tsumzong Kangri (Junction Peak). The expedition returned to Leh on the 28th.

DIVYESH MUNI, *Himalayan Club, India*

Saser Muztagh, Saser Kangri II (7,513m), attempt. Our Indo-American-British expedition included Indians Chewang Motup (co-leader), Dhan Singh, Konchok Tinles, and Tsering Sherpa; Americans Steve Swenson, Mark Wilford, and I (co-leader); and British climber Jim Lowther. Staff included Lakpa Boding, Pemba Norbu, Manbhadur Rai, Soop Singh, and Ang Tashi.

Our goal was the east summit of Saser Kangri II. The west summit was climbed in 1985 via the northwest ridge by an Indo-Japanese expedition (*AAJ 1986*), which felt the summits were of equal height. According to our maps and information, the east summit is higher and therefore should be referred to as Saser Kangri II Main. It is one of the highest unclimbed peaks in the world [the second highest by certain criteria].

Anglo-American attempt and high point on south face of Saser Kangri II. *Mark Richey*

On August 7 our expedition left the Nubra Valley, at 3,050m near the village of Tigur. We spent two days hiking up the Chameshan Lungpa Valley to the snout of the Sakang Lungpa Glacier. We established base camp in a side valley on August 11 at 5,180m, above and southeast of the Sakang Lungpa Glacier. To reach our intended objective, we needed to cross onto the South Shukpa Kunchang Glacier, the next valley east of base camp. On August 12 and 13 we made acclimatization and reconnaissance trips up the unnamed glacier behind base camp and established a camp at ca 6,000m on an unnamed pass above the South Shukpa Kunchang Glacier. On the 14th we dropped onto the South Shukpa Kunchang to explore the route to the foot of the south face of Saser Kangri II.

Due to bad weather we spent some days in the Nubra Valley, but on September 6 we climbed back to the

Day 2 on Saser Kangri II attempt. *Mark Richey*

pass in cold, windy conditions, with a forecast for a small window of good weather. Although this wasn't long enough to climb the mountain, we decided to use the opportunity to reconnoiter the route and assess snow conditions. On the 7th we made an advanced base below the south face, and the following day climbed 700m to ca 6,700m, before rappelling. There was no snow, just hard water ice, giving technical climbing on the lower slopes. As the rock is high-quality orange granite, there is no objective danger. We stayed on the far right side of the couloir to avoid debris falling from ice cliffs well to the left.

Bad weather kept us from the peak until the 19th. We reached a good bivouac at 6,700m relatively early in the day but stopped for the night, since there did not appear to be good sites higher until a ledge system at 7,000m. On the 20th we climbed steep ice in the main gully system before veering right into mixed terrain that would take us onto the major ledge system halfway up the face. We had a poor bivouac on small ledges chopped out of the ice and were not able to erect tents. Next day we progressed to the ledge system and established a better bivouac, spending nearly four hours chopping a ledge out of the ice. That night it snowed, and on the 22nd, due to cold and windy weather we decided to descend.

Climbing at this altitude late in August was very cold. We had nighttime temps of -13 to -17°C and highs during the day of -5 to -9°C. On the 25th we left base camp and reached the road in the Nubra Valley the same day.

MARK RICHEY, *AAC*

ZANSKAR

Zanskar, Lahaul, Ladakh, various ascents. In summer 2007 I made a number of ascents in the Indian Himalaya. I'd hoped to spend the winter of 2007–8 there, but lack of money and of motivation to remain in the mountains climbing alone drove me home. I returned the following summer to enjoy more ascents with friends and with clients while guiding. I believe most of the ascents described below are the first of the peak, though it seems

Gyaldop on Chu Kangri. *Sergi Ricart*

unlikely that two of the peaks were not climbed previously.

I began in Lahaul, where on June 22, 2007, I made the probable first ascent of a 5,400m summit I named Tara Parbat. It lies in the Milang Valley, directly opposite (west of) M8 in the Mulkila group, and southwest of Darcha on the Manali-Leh road. I climbed up and down the central ridge on the east face in a round trip of 10 hours from base camp at 4,300m. The route gained 800m of elevation, with rock, ice, and mixed difficulties. There were sections of UIAA IV and 65° snow/ice, and an 80°cornice. The top of the mountain was just 100m northwest of my exit onto the summit ridge. I named the route Samsara y Nirvana (D). The day previously I had attempted the peak immediately north, which I also believe to be virgin, but had to give up in a couloir at 5,000m when a crumbling rock wall blocked the way.

Le Ciudad Invisible, with bivouacs marked, on the First Aguja del Tzempuk. *Sergi Ricart*

Ahimsa on Dawa Mebar Kangri. *Sergi Ricart*

I moved on to Ladakh, and on July 12 Isidre Solé and I made a fine traverse of the Espolon de Shushot (3,600m), which lies one hour above the Leh-Shey road, just past Choglamsar (ca 10km from Leh). We took six hours in making the traverse from the south. The height gain is only 200m, but the length of the ridge is perhaps half a kilometer. There was much scrambling and eight roped pitches, up to UIAA V+ A1, and the granite was wonderful. The descent on the far side was short and easy, and it seems likely that this summit had been previously visited.

Isidre and I then climbed in the Stok Kangri region, where, among other peaks, we climbed Parcha Kangri (5,880m) by the northwest face and northeast ridge. It took four hours, on July 17. The 400m route was AD (55°), and we descended the north face directly, with two rappels. We assume this summit had been reached before, due to its proximity to Stok Kangri.

We moved north from Leh into the Nubra Valley and trekked up the Sakang Nala to the Saser Kangri Glacier, where we established a base camp. We made advanced base at 5,300m in the Dzomoriong Nala to the east. From there, on July 28, I climbed Lingmey Ri (5,700m), at the start of the ridge that separates the two branches of Dzomoriong Glacier. I climbed the west face solo on generally good rock, with strenuous sections in cracks. The climbing was mostly UIAA IV and V. I named the route Foc al Faro (D+ UIAA V+, 250m).

On the 29th and 30th Isidre and I climbed Dawa Mebar Kangri (6,250m, N 34°45', W 77°48') at the head of the Dzomoriong Glacier. It took three-and-a-half hours to reach the foot of the southwest face, five hours to climb it via a route we named Ahimsa (D-, 70°, 400m), and 13 hours to descend and return to base camp.

In September 2007 I soloed Tantak O la Vida Simple (PD+ 55°, 300m), the north face and east ridge of Sultanlango (5,793m), southwest of the Tongde La in Zanskar. I descended the east ridge (PD). This took place during a week's self-supported, ca 100km, solo traverse from Tongde to Reru, which required carrying a huge sack.

In 2008 I was back in Lahul. A peak I have named Chu Kangri (5,700m) stands on the opposite side of the Shingu Nala from Ramjak (6,290m), south of the Shingu La. Albert Ortega and I made base camp at Chumik Nakpo (4,630m) and walked three-and-a-half hours up the Khakurkur Nala to the east to reach an advanced base at 5,025m, below the north side Chu Kangri. On July 13 Albert and I climbed the north face and east ridge (PD+ 50°, 650m). It took four-and-a-half hours for the ascent and two hours to descend. We named the route Gyaldop.

Escher Revisited on Namay Skayrak Kangri. *Sergi Ricart*

During August 2008 I was in Zanskar. On the 16th, on our second attempt, Lluc Pellisa and I climbed Shawa Kangri (5,600m), which lies in the valley that runs south from Tungri on the Padam road, immediately west of Haftal Valley and Sani Gompa. We climbed snow/ice slopes, up to 65°, on the northwest face to reach a col at the base of the northeast face—a sound granite wall. We climbed this in five pitches, up to UIAA V+. We descended the route by rappel, naming it Rolling Stones (D+).

Namay Skayrak Kangri (5,700m) lies south of the Malung Tokpo Valley, connecting Ating to the Umasi La. Laia Acero, Lluc, and I established base camp at 4,000m in the valley, two hours walk past Dzongkul Gompa. We then headed south into the Gaora Lungpa, making an advanced base at 4,700m. From there, on August 30, we climbed Namay Skayrak Kangri by the northeast face and north ridge. It was a classic ice slope, 16 pitches from berg-

Rolling Stones on Shawa Kangri. *Sergi Ricart*

Samsara y Nirvana on Tara Parbat. *Sergi Ricart*

schrund to crest. We named the route Escher Revisited (D 60°, a step of UIAA II just before summit, 700m). We descended the north ridge for a considerable distance, before rappelling to the bottom of the face.

Finally, from September 2 to 4, we three climbed the First Aguja del Tzempuk (4,700m). This lies northeast of Namay Skayrak Kangri, directly opposite our base camp. We climbed the 600m northwest face with two bivouacs (22 hours effective climbing time), completing 19 pitches on good granite up to 6b A1. The climbing, in a series of cracks and corners, was excellent. We called the route Le Ciudad Invisible (TD/TD+). We descended the northeast flank easily in two hours to base camp.

SERGI RICART, *Spain*

Haftal Kangri (6,178m), northwest face. On August 4 Simon Deniel, Pauline Parmier, Elsa Pommarel, and I made a probable first ascent of a peak referred to by locals as Haftal Kangri. This peak is located above the east side of the Haftal Valley, which rises southwest toward the Kishtwar Himalaya a little east of Sani Gompa, shortly before reaching Padam on the road from Pensi La. It is invisible from Padam, and we weren't able to find any information about our proposed route from the west. People from Sani told us that one expedition had tried to reach the mountain before but had problems with horse transport and were unable to establish base camp. We trekked up the right side of the valley and placed base camp at 3,796m (GPS). How-

Haftal Kangri with ascent and traverse, seen from close to advanced base. (C1) Camp 1. (W) waterfall. (S) summit. (R) rappel on descent. Two high rock towers on left are below 6,000m and unclimbed. *Jonathan Crison*

ever, the only way we could cross the river to the east was to retrace our steps 300m and make a Tyrolean traverse. For this we placed two bolts in a large rock beside the river.

Once on the other side of the river, we ascended a side valley and made an advanced base at 4,329m. From there we scrambled up a stony couloir, crossed to the right above a waterfall and made Camp 1 at 5,131m, below the northwest face of our peak. The route above climbed snow slopes right of a rock rib (45-55°), then crossed it to similar slopes on the left, finally joining the rib to reach the summit ridge. Snow and mixed slopes led to the top. We named the route Yackattack (1,000m, D+ F3 WI3+ 55°). We then descended the north ridge, rappeled to snow slopes that we climbed down to a small col, and headed west down a couloir until we could traverse back to Camp 1. Around our base camp were many fine-looking but relatively compact rock walls. We were told that many years ago a Japanese alpinist climbed a big wall route somewhere close by.

JONATHAN CRISON, *France*

Reru Valley, exploration. In August four senior Japanese mountaineers, Kiyoaki Miyagawa (68), Mitsuhiko Okabe (68), Akira Taniguchi (71), and I, (69), explored the Reru Valley. Well-known Indian mountaineering authorities, Satyabrata Dam and Harish Kapadia, did not know of any previous climbing in this valley, so we traveled to Padam and made the short trek to the area to identify virgin peaks for future expeditions.

On the 16th we camped at Bardan Gompa School and saw an attractive rock peak of 6,071m, west of the entrance to the Reru Nala. Realizing that there are many mountains in the vicinity, we named them numerically, starting with Reru 1 (6,071m, R1) and continuing counterclockwise to R36 (5,825m) at the western end of the group. The accompanying map identifies these peaks. Next day by 1 p.m. we reached the village of Reru at the entrance to the valley, a beautiful campsite but noisy with trekkers. Our guide Tsewang and our horseman talked with the headman in Reru, who told them that the village had controlled Reru Valley for many years, that only villagers used it, and that no climber or trekker had ever entered it. To be granted access, Tsewang agreed to pay 100 rupees per tent per day. The headman

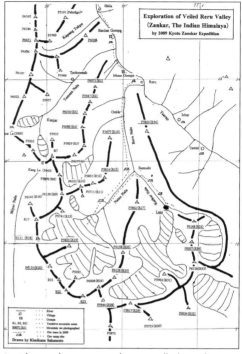

British expedition operated in a small glacier basin to northeast of that drawn east of R35. One or two peaks marked on watershed with Miyar Valley may have been climbed. *Kimikazu Sakamoto*

told us that the left branch of the valley has an easy trail from Sumudo, but the right branch has a rocky step that would be difficult for horses. He also told us the local names of peaks visible from the village: Skanglaya (R1) and Usuchan (R36).

On the 18th we walked south to Sumudo, where the valley forks, noting that R26 and 27 are fine rock peaks. The weather was poor next day, and we were tired, so we didn't move, but on the 20th we trekked to a camp in the right branch—the Nateo Nala. By climbing onto the glacier we were able to make a good photographic record of the mountains around its head, noting a fine snow pyramid (R20, 6,110m) and the highest summit in this sector, R18 (6,111m), to its north. These peaks lie on the watershed with the Miyar Nala. [Several identified peaks on Nateo-Miyar divide may have been climbed from the west by British and Japanese in the early 1980s or more recently by Italians.] The following two days we visited the left branch or Katkar Nala, making our second camp below the lake, from where we noted the attractive R35 (6,148m). On the 23rd we left the valley, wondering whether strong young climbers will come to attempt such difficult peaks as R3 (6,036m) and R4 (6,080m). We photographed 21 peaks believed to be virgin, but may have made mistakes in identifying some peaks in this complex massif. We encourage climbers to visit the area and contact us with corrections to the map.

KIMIKAZU SAKAMOTO, *Japan*

Katkar Valley, Skilma Kangri (5,979m), north face and west ridge; Mt. Jules (5,800m), south face. In late summer Al Boardman, Jane Cooper, Elliot Forge, and I set out to explore the remote Katkar Valley, hoping to reach its head. To reach our lakeside base camp took 12 days and included flights, acclimatization in Leh, car to Padum and then Reru, and two days approach on foot. We bought supplies in Leh and Padum and had them transported by horses. We had a cook, an assistant, and on-call backup in Padum and U.K. From the lake we reconnoitered a hanging valley to the southeast. This was the site of our originally proposed base camp, but we realized that horses would find the steep, rocky approach too difficult. Apparently, yaks would have coped. We then climbed to 5,000m, to discover that the surrounding peaks would require one or two camps above an advanced base. Unfortunately, we had only one spare tent and not enough time.

Looking south up main Katkar Glacier. (A) R33 (6,128m). (B) R29 (5,817m). (C) R28 (5,944m). *Jason Bailey*

North face and west ridge of Skilma Kangri. *Jason Bailey*

We ruled out having an advanced base on the southern glacier because of falling rock and ice threatening the approach. Eventually, we settled on another hanging valley farther east, which terminated northeast of the lake and rose southeast to three unclimbed peaks. We established an advanced base at 5,200m and the following day began breaking trail through deep snow. We barely covered one kilometer in two-and-a-half hours. At this point, day 18 of our expedition, morale dropped to a low. Concerns were expressed about time. I realized how difficult it is to find a new mountain, let alone the route. After another day of photography and route-planning, we tackled the middle of the three peaks.

At 2:30 a.m. we set off, retracing our previous tracks. It took only one hour to cover the first kilometer but a further four hours for the next one-and-a-half, through deep powder a skier would envy us for. At the bottom of our intended route a fine avalanche drifted past, missing us but obliterating our path. Had it been 10 minutes before, we would have been in the bergshrund. We had planned to ascend via the right-hand shoulder but found only brittle granite. The shallow gully we'd hoped for didn't appear, so we resigned ourselves to the 400m north face.

We dealt with a mixture of steep ice, deep powder, and compacted snow, sharing the lead and topping out after four hours, calves on fire and the tedium of counting paces finally over. We climbed up the west ridge over compact snow and brittle granite to reach the top at 1 p.m. on September 19. We graded the route D+.

We had to downclimb the face, as there seemed no other way off the mountain. This proved the most unnerving aspect of the day, and we were thoroughly exhausted by the time

Looking southwest from summit of Mt. Jules. (A) Peak 5,860m. (B) Skilma Kangri 5,979m. (C) Unnamed. (D) Peak 35 (6,148m). Only Skilma Kangri is known to have been climbed. *Jason Bailey*

we arrived at advanced base, 14 hours after leaving. We named this peak Skilma Kangri, which means "central snowy mountain."

Al and Elliott descended to base camp, and Jane came up to advanced base. On the 21st Jane and I scrambled up south-facing snow slopes (F) to summit a peak north of Skilma Kangri, which we named Mt. Jules (5,800m). Views were stunning, more so with the knowledge that no other team had climbed in this area.

JASON BAILEY, *U.K.*

LAHAUL

Peak 6,184m; Trident Peak. We arrived in Delhi during mid-September and after three days' coach travel reached the village of Darcha on the well-used Manali-Leh military road. Three short days of trekking along the Jankar Nala, northwest of Darcha, got us to base camp (4,300m) in a dry, dusty valley west of the river. Our aim was to attempt peaks a little east of the well-known mountain in this area, Gangstang (6,162m), but our primary objective was Peak 6,184m, a summit previously tried by Japanese in 1999

The south face of Saravsati, showing the line of the first ascent. *David Bingham*

and 2003, and again in 2008 by an expedition organized by the guide Martin Moran, who also organized our trip. The 2008 expedition attempted the south-southeast ridge, reaching a height of 5,850m, but was stopped by unusually high snowfall.

Toward the end of September we explored the glacier leading to Peak 6,184m and with the help of high-altitude porters established an advanced base at 5,000m. From here it was four hours' walk on easy glacier terrain to the bottom of the south face at 5,585m.

Trident Peak (ca 5,700m) is the low summit on the right. It was climbed by the northeast ridge, the curving snow crest facing the camera, and back left along the almost-horizontal summit ridge. The fine pyramid behind and to the left is Gangstang (6,162m). *David Bingham*

On the 30th three members descended from advanced base, while the remaining six attempted a summit close to the southwest ridge of Peak 6,184m. It was unnamed on the map, but because of the three rocky tops we dubbed it Trident Peak. Unconsolidated snow led to the crest of the elegant northeast ridge. Benjaman Fry, guides Jonathan Preston and Robin Thomas, and I made it to the main summit, ca 5,700m. We found a cairn at the summit, probably constructed by one of the Japanese expeditions. We rated the climb PD+. We descended to base camp for a rest before attempting our main goal.

David Bingham on the summit of Sarasvati (6,184m). The elegant pyramid behind is Gangstang. *David Bingham Collection.*

On October 2 six of us left for Peak 6,184m, staying the first night in advanced base and the second at high camp below the south face. For the first time during the trip we noticed a build up of high cloud, and during the night it snowed. By 9:30 a.m. on the 4th the skies were clearing and a cold wind blowing, so Jonathan

Looking northeast from Gangstang to Saravsati. The glaciated south face, the route of the first ascent, is bounded by the long southwest and southeast ridges, the latter attempted in 2008 to 5,850m. *Martin Moran*

Preston and Robin Thomas set off to fix rope in the initial couloir. After 150m of easy ground, they reached a narrow, steeper section and fixed 100m up terrain of Scottish II. They returned to camp, where it snowed for most of that evening.

By 1:00 a.m. on the 5th the weather improved, and by 2:30 a.m. we were away, climbing in three ropes of two. Ben Gibbison and Emma Read left another long rope at the fixed section, enabling 100m rappels on the descent, but they retreated from this point. We continued, climbing seven 55m pitches (50° maximum) to reach a level section on the summit ridge. We circumvented a final prominent rock tower by an elegant snow ridge on the northeast flank, and Preston and Fry reached the summit at 7:42 a.m. They spent 45 minutes recording a GPS altitude of 6,165m. Thomas and I arrived just after they left.

With the help of two HAPs, we cleared all equipment and were down at base camp on the 6th. We felt the grade of the climb to be about AD+ and have proposed the name Saravsati for the peak.

In the meantime Marc Booysen, Steve Foster, Stuart Irving, and our liaison officer explored up-glacier toward the Jankar Billing Range. Here they found peaks of ca 5,500–5,600m, all likely unclimbed.

DAVID BINGHAM *U.K.*

Lower Karcha Parvat (6,060m). A three-member Japanese team, led by Tsuneo Suzuki, established base camp in the Karcha Nala at 4,420m. They made Camp 1 at 4,700m and Camp 2 at 5,200m, from where Ritsuyu Matsubara and three high-altitude porters climbed the northwest face, reaching the summit on July 18. They propose that this previously unnamed peak be named Lower Karcha Parvat. It is not clear where this summit is situated in relation to the higher and popular Karcha Parvat (6,271m), north of the Karcha Nala.

HARISH KAPADIA, *Honorary Editor, The Himalayan Journal*

WESTERN GARHWAL

GANGOTRI

Bhagirathi IV (6,193m), III (6,454m), and II (6,512m). During autumn, Slovenians Rok Blagus, Luka Lindic, and Marko Prezelj blitzed the Bhagirathi Group, making three significant first ascents. The trio was reasonably lucky with the weather; during a month in the area, only the first week was poor. When conditions improved, they set off for their first objective, Bhagirathi IV, a small summit, with no recorded ascent, on the ridge between two grander neighbors, Bhagirathi II and III.

The west side of Bhagirathi IV is characterized by an elegant rock pillar leading to summit shale bands, this shale forming an infamous obstacle on most Bhagirathi peaks. The pillar had been attempted several times in the past, notably by Slovenians. To the left, a broad, moderately angled snow couloir leads up the south-southwest face of Bhagirathi II, to a shelf that can be traversed right to the ridge just north of Bhagirathi IV. Gaining this shelf has sometimes been threatened by seracs, but in mid-September the Slovenians accessed it without much difficulty, via a steep, right-leaning ice/mixed ramp through the rock wall below. From here they reached the north ridge and continued to the summit of Bhagirathi IV. The 1,000m route was graded D+ and downclimbed, with four rappels.

South-southwest face of Bhagirathi II, with 2009 Slovenian route and bivouac sites marked. Route shares ground with Rolling Stones on initial snow slopes and gully and for several pitches above first bivouac site, before moving right to finish on southwest ridge (left skyline). *Marko Prezelj*

A week later the three squeezed a 1,300m hard new mixed route onto the southwest face of Bhagirathi III, between the original route on this face, now a classic of the Gangotri—1982 Scottish Pillar (TD+, 1,300m, 44 pitches, Barton-Fyffe)—and the 1993 Czech Express on the central pillar (TD+, 1,300m, Michalec-Slachta). The Slovenian route more or less shares three pitches with the Scottish route in the upper section but is independent of the Czech. The three climbed their line with one bivouac, overcoming difficulties of 6b, M5, and WI5 (and making two diagonal rappels), giving the route an overall grade of ED. After reaching the summit, they descended the original 1933 Kirkus-Warren route on the southeast ridge and then walked out north down the Vasuki Glacier.

After a well-deserved rest, the trio completed a hat trick of new lines by climbing the 1,300m south-southwest face of Bhagirathi II. The face had been climbed once before, at the end of September 1989 by Slovenians Andreja Hrastnik and Franci Knez. This pair worked a little on the route, before climbing it with one bivouac at ED+. This 1989 team climbed 26 pitches up to UIAA VIII+ to the crest of the southwest ridge (crux near the top) but descended without going to the summit. They named their 800m route Rolling Stones.

In 1984 Italians Vincenzo Ravaschietto and Andrea Sarchi, having equipped the first 300m with Egidio Bonapace, climbed the southwest ridge in four days. The central section was UIAA VI+ A2, the rest IV and 55° snow/ice; the route gave more than 1,800m of climbing to the summit.

Blagus, Lindic, and Prezelj started in the same gully system as Hrastnik and Knez. However, the latter soon moved right to a steep rock pillar, while the former continued directly to a huge corner system that gave hard ice and mixed climbing. At the top they bivouacked and continued the next day with several pure rock pitches of the 1989 line, before moving right and climbing more hard rock to the southwest ridge. A few rock pitches along the crest brought them to their second bivouac, and the next day, October 1, they climbed mixed ground on the right flank to reach the upper crest, which they followed to the summit. Once again they traversed the mountain, descending via the classic 1938 Austrian Route on the east face to the Vasuki Glacier. The ascent had pitches of 6b+, M8, and WI 6+, and an overall grade of ED+/ABO. Marko Prezelj's photo feature appears earlier in the *Journal*.

Meru South (6,660m, left) and Meru Central showing line and high point of Slovenian attempt on the Shark's Fin. *Andrej Grmovsek*

Meru Central (6,310m), northeast pillar (Shark's Fin), attempt. At the end of August, Marko Lukic, Silvo Karo, and I traveled to Gangotri, hoping to climb the infamous and still virgin Shark's Fin on Meru Central. This line has already repulsed more than 20 expeditions, many of them strong teams. However, in 2008 Anker, Chin, and Ozturk reached a point just 150m below the summit, spending 20 days on the wall climbing in capsule style (*AAJ 2009*).

Assisted by beta from Anker's team, we planned to climb fast, light, and in alpine style. After reaching base camp at Tapovan, we used unsettled weather to prepare advance base, acclimatize on the lower slopes of Shivling, and study the face. Our second phase of acclimatization was stopped by heavy snowfalls lasting almost one week. There was more than 1.5m of fresh snow at higher elevations, and our tent at advanced base was destroyed. The weather then became stable and very cold. Despite the face being plastered in snow and ice, and our having acclimatized only to 5,600m, we decided to make an attempt. The weather forecast was good, deep snow on Shivling made our acclimatization program dangerous, and time was running out.

The approach to the face took two laborious days; we waded through deep, soft snow, excavating our advanced base camp tent and equipment, and crossing the dangerous Meru Glacier. On September 17 at 1 a.m. we started to climb. Our plan was to make the ascent in four days, spending the first night in a tent, and then hoping to find small ledges on the steep upper wall that would accommodate sitting bivouacs. On the lower snow slopes we found channels of reasonably hard snow and climbed quite fast.

After eight tiring hours we completed the initial 700m snow slope and started to climb rock on the diagonal ramp. The granite was covered with snow in many places, making climbing and route-finding harder than expected (up to M8). The two climbers following had to jumar with gear for all three, and our two tiny 9.1mm Joker ropes got worn super-fast on sharp granite edges. We got increasingly tired and finished the rock ramp just before nightfall. We expected to find a good place to set the tent but instead spent one hour cutting a small ledge out of snow and ice on which to sit. We were so tired and unmotivated that we didn't melt snow for drinks or cook soup. The night was cold and uncomfortable, and Silvo's feet got dangerously cold; he sustained minor frostbite.

Marko Lukic on mixed pitches below headwall. *Andrej Grmovsek*

Morning brought sunshine and an easy decision—to go down. We were tired, many things had not gone according to plan, and the hardest part lay above. Our tactic was wrong: we were climbing too fast, we were too heavy, we had unsuitable equipment, we were not acclimatized, and there wasn't enough motivation. With hard and complex climbs like Meru Shark's Fin, these "beginner's" mistakes count.

ANDREJ GRMOVSEK, *Slovenia*

CENTRAL GARHWAL

Mukut Parvat (7,242m). Lionel Albrieux's eight-member French team approached this high mountain from Ghastoli, establishing base camp at 4,800m on the Pachhimi (West) Kamet Glacier. After putting an advanced base at 5,300m, they climbed alpine-style up the south ridge. One member left for home early due to altitude problems, but Albrieux, Sébastien Bohin, Damine Cabane, Sébastien Giacobi, Didier Jourdain, Emmanuel Pellissier, and Marion Poitevin reached the summit on October 2 from a camp at 6,500m.

Mukut Parvat was first climbed in 1951 by Earle Riddiford's New Zealand expedition, via the northwest ridge from the Dakhhini Chamrao Glacier. They had previously reconnoitered the West Kamet Glacier but found it too challenging. Edmund Hillary was a member of this team, and although he did not summit, his involvement was one of the reasons he was selected to join the next Everest expedition. The peak had a second ascent in 1992, by an expedition of the Indo-Tibet Border Police.

HARISH KAPADIA, *Honorary Editor, The Himalayan Journal*

KUMAON

Changuch (6322m), first ascent. On June 9, an Indo-British team made the first recorded ascent of Changuch, an elegant sharp-edged peak that was one of the last major virgin summits in the region. Changuch lies northwest of Nanda Kot on the divide between the Lawan and Pindar valleys, directly opposite the southeast face of Nanda Devi East. Three previous attempts from the Pindari side had failed, and in 2007 an ice avalanche in the Pindari icefall killed two Sherpas. The northern approach from the Lawan Valley is much easier, and our first ascent team found a line up snowy ramps and couloirs at 45–55° to gain the northwest ridge at a 5,850m col. From here the final ridge rises in several steps, mixed ground giving way to exposed snow/ice slopes of 55–60°. The summit team of Paul Guest, Rob Jarvis, Luder Sain (Liaison Officer), Leon Winchester, and I left the col camp at 12:30 a.m. and summitted at 9 a.m. We descended

The north face of Changuch (6,322m) rises above the Lawan Glacier. The first ascensionists climbed from advanced base at (5,150m) to Camp 2 on the col at 5,850m, and from there up the northwest ridge to the summit. *Martin Moran*

The northwest ridge of Changuch (6,322m) seen from the slopes below Longstaff's Col. *Martin Moran*

by the same route. We graded the climb Alpine D.

We had earlier acclimatized by making an ascent of Nanda Lampak (5,782m) via the south ridge at AD (60°). The expedition then turned to its primary target, Nanda Devi East via the south ridge from Longstaff's Col (5,910m). However, lacking resources and manpower for a prolonged attempt, we abandoned our attempt at 6,100m and switched our attention to Changuch. Indian Mountaineering Foundation rules allow a switch of objective in return for an additional 50% peak royalty. In the case of Changuch this was only $450. As the expedition Liaison Officer was also one of the summit climbers, we faced no bureaucratic hurdles in making the change.

A few days later we crossed Traill's Pass (5,312m), between the Lawan and Pindar valleys. This famous glacier crossing was first made in 1830 in an attempt to forge a trade route direct from Almora to Tibet. The 2009 crossing was only the 6th known repeat and the first for 15 years. Glacial recession has rendered the crossing progressively more difficult, and we avoided the Pindari Glacier icefall altogether in favor of a mixed route down the west side of the valley (overall grade AD with snow/ice to 60°).

MARTIN MORAN, *Alpine Club*

Editors Note: The first expedition to make a serious inspection of Changuch took place in 1987, when Geoff Hornby's joint Indo-British team, approaching via the Pindari Glacier to the south, decided the southwest face was impractical and turned instead to Laspa Dhura (5,913m), making its first ascent. In 1997 a Northern Ireland team led by Gary Murray climbed part way up a neighboring peak in order to reconnoiter a line on the same southwest face. Snowfall made an attempt on their main objective impossible. Another 10 years would elapse before the next attempt. In 2007 an Indian expedition, jointly organized by the Navy and the Indian Mountaineering Foundation, was led by the accomplished Satya Dam. The expe-

Paul Guest and Luder Sain climb into the sun on Changuch's northwest ridge. *Martin Moran*

dition was one of several sponsored by the IMF to promote technical climbing by nationals in the Indian Himalaya. These climbers made far more progress than the previous two attempts, climbing the left side of the southwest face towards Traill's Pass, then more directly through the Pindari Icefall to gain the crest of the northwest ridge. Members reached a height of 5,600m on the ridge but retreated when a bad storm moved in. Next day an avalanche, caused by serac fall, hit Camp 1 at ca. 5,000m, killing two Sherpas and leaving a third critically injured. The surviving occupants of this camp were subsequently airlifted to safety in a daring helicopter rescue and the expedition abandoned.

SIKKIM

Kellas Peak (6,680m), attempt from south; Peak 6,252m. In autumn Graham Hoyland, Mark Lambert, Anindya Mukherjee, George Rodway, Dukpa Tsering Sherpa, Phurba Sherpa, Thendup Sherpa, and I were fortunate to gain permission to enter northwest Sikkim and make an attempt on Kellas Peak. Since western mountaineers had not ventured into the region for more than 75 years, the team relied heavily upon the work of Indian pundits and British luminaries such as Douglas Freshfield, Frank Smythe, and Alexander Kellas to help them reach their objective. From Gangtok the team headed north by 4x4 vehicle through the district capital of Lachen, before eventually reaching the roadhead at Tanggu. Here, with the help of local yak owners and the Indo-Tibet Border Police, we hired animals, crossed the Lungnak La, and made base camp near the temporary settlement of Rasum. We then established four further camps along the Goma Chu before we made an attempt on our target.

Kellas Peak is situated on the frontier ridge between Lhonak Peak (6,710m) to the north and Jongsang Peak (7,462m) to the south. Frank Smythe and members of the 1930 International-al Himalaya Expedition named the mountain in honor of the Scottish explorer and scientist Alexander Kellas. From 1907 to 1920 Kellas made six visits to the region, completing a number of first ascents that included Pauhunri (7,125m) and Chomoyummo (6,829m). As a member of the 1921 Everest Reconnaissance Expedition, Kellas took ill during the approach march and died near Kampa Dzong. At that time there was no one with more high-altitude experience. This, together with an academic background in biochemistry and a considerable knowledge of human physiology, led him to predict in 1920 that Everest could be climbed without supplemental oxygen: "Mt. Everest could be ascended by a man of excellent physical and mental constitution in first rate training, without adventitious aids, if the physical difficulties of the mountain are not too great." Kellas was ahead of his time; it would take more than 50 years for Reinhold Messner and Peter Habeler to prove him right.

At first we were confused as to which was our mountain, mistaking it for the higher

Looking west from Chombu in northeast Sikkim toward Tibetan border. (A) Part of Jongsang. (B) Peak 6,252m. (C) Kellas Col. (D) Kellas Peak. (E) Lhonak La. (F) Lhonak Peak. (G) Chorten Nyima (6,972m). *Lindsay Griffin*

Lhonak Peak. We tried to reach the upper slopes by climbing toward the Lhonak La. Eric Shipton and Lawrence Wager had descended these slopes in 1933, after a possible ascent of Lhonak Peak. However, the dangers posed by numerous avalanches and hidden crevasses forced us to cross the South Lhonak Glacier and ascend the northern slopes of Jongsang, in order to make an attempt from the south. Further

Lhonak Peak from southeast. *Jeremy Windsor*

crevasses and loose rock led us to abandon the attempt and turn our attention to Kellas Col (6,343m) and unclimbed Peak 6,252m.

We reached both on November 2. From a search of Alpine Club archives, it appears that Kellas Col had been reached twice before, during attempts on nearby Jongsang. The first was made by Kellas and his native companions in 1909, the second 21 years later by Smythe and members of the International Himalaya Expedition. In *The Kangchenjunga Adventure* Smythe described the ascent to Kellas Col as "hard work" and made light of the dangers: "We climbed roped, for there were several concealed crevasses, two or three of which were only discovered by trial and error."

Our journey through northwest Sikkim also provided a fine opportunity to study further

Chorten Nyima (6,927m), on Sikkim-Tibet border northeast of Kellas Peak, seen from east. *Jeremy Windsor*

opportunities in this area. Many can be located on the *Sikkim Himalaya* map published in 2006 by the Swiss Foundation for Alpine Research. We spotted a number of attractive unclimbed peaks in the Lungnak, Muguthang, and Lhonak valleys. Provided access to these areas remains possible, the northwest corner of Sikkim should attract mountaineers for years to come.

A biography of Alexander Kellas, by Ian Mitchell and George Rodway, will be published in 2010 by Luath Press (Edinburgh).

JEREMY WINDSOR, *Alpine Club*

Tinchenkang (6,010m), ascent and tragedy. A team of five from the Mumbai Chakram Hikers Club attempted Tinchenkang in October. On the 19th the leader, Mangesh Deshpande, and Sadasivan Sekar, with Sherpas Ang Dorje and Mingma, reached the summit at 1:30 p.m. After descending 100m, the party fell 50m. Deshpande and Sekar were fatally injured, while the Sherpas were severely injured. Rescue operations were launched with the help of local government, high-altitude Sherpas, and military authorities. The remoteness of this area and poor weather made the rescue operation difficult, but eventually both Sherpas were evacuated by Indian Air Force helicopters and taken to a hospital, where they survived.

HARISH KAPADIA, *Honorary Editor, The Himalayan Journal*

Nepal

NALAKANKAR

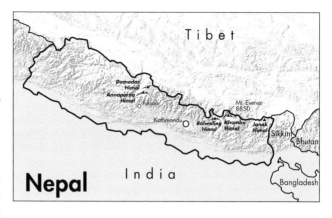

Kanti Himal, Kaptang (5,965m), north face; Kojichuwa Chuli (6,439m), attempt. The prolific mountain explorer Tamotsu Ohnishi and four companions visited the Kanti Himal in June. Their aim was the first ascent of three peaks: Kaptang, Kojichuwa Chuli, and Danphe Sail (6,103m)—peaks first opened in 2002 or 2003 and, apart from Kojichuwa Chuli, previously unattempted. They flew to Nepalgunj and then to Jumla, arriving on May 20. From here they trekked north to Rara Lake and then to the hamlet of Mugu, continuing up the Mugu Valley to establish base camp on June 2 at 4,300m. On the 8th they made an advanced camp at 5,492m, south of Kaptang, which lies on the frontier ridge southeast of the Namla La. On the 9th Gomba Sherpa, Toshitsugi Irizawa, and Ohnishi climbed to the summit. They left advanced camp at 6 a.m., reached the top at 2 p.m., and were back at their tents by 4 p.m. The three crossed to the Tibetan side and climbed the north face, fixing 400m of rope and overcoming a 70° section. Koji Mizutani, Hisashi Suzuki, and Kazuo Tauji repeated the climb the following day.

The expedition now retraced its steps down-valley to the south and moved east-north-east up the Kojichuwa Khola above Mugu. On the 16th they established base camp at 4,600m, and on the 21st Gomba, Irizawa, Suzuki, and Tauji climbed toward the ca 5,500m Kojichuwa La, on the frontier ridge northwest of Kojichuwa Chuli, with the goal of ascending its northwest ridge. Four hours above base they reached 5,565m, where they decided they were too tired to continue. They abandoned plans for climbing Danphe Sail, and returned toward Jumla. However, Tauji contracted a stomach illness, they requested a helicopter, and the team flew out on the 21st from Ringmo to Nepalgunj.

LINDSAY GRIFFIN, *Mountain INFO*, ELIZABETH HAWLEY, *AAC Honorary Member, Nepal, AND Richard Salisbury, The Himalayan Database.*

Kanti Himal, Kojichuwa Chuli (6,439m), attempt. In October 2008 José Maria Alvarez, Antonio Fernandez, and Josue Roibal, all from the Spanish island of Mallorca, flew via Nepalgunj to Talcha (2,748m, three hours walk from Rara Lake), and trekked via Mugu to the Kojichuwa Valley (possibly also referred to as Gokichuwa). Their goal was to reconnoiter a route on Kojichuwa Chuli for an ascent the following spring. Alvarez, Fernandez, and Da Dorche Sherpa climbed to the Kojichuwa La (5,550m) and moved a short distance up the frontier ridge to 5,625m, from where they could see that to continue to the summit of Kojichuwa Chuli would be hard. After noting that the Tibetan flanks looked relatively gentle, they returned to base camp and climbed a small (ca 5,400m) peak above the valley before returning home. One outstanding peak noticed during this exploration was the unnamed 6,310m summit on the fron-

Unnamed, unclimbed 6,047m peak on southeast side of Kojichuwa Valley. *Josue Roibal*

tier ridge immediately south of Kojichuwa Chuli, which they dubbed Mugu Chuli.

Both Kojichuwa Chuli and Mugu Chuli were "on the list" when Fernandez and Roibal returned in April 2009 with Santiago Amengui, Rodrigo Rodriguez, Luis Miguel Lopez, and Pedro Navarro. The team again helicoptered to Talcha, and then trekked along the Mugu Khola and up the Kojichuwa Valley, to establish base camp at 4,750m west of Mugu Chuli. They first examined the impressive west face of Mugu but found it too threatened by serac fall and avalanches. Lopez Narravo and Dawa Sherpa then moved up to the Kojichuwa La but found it a dangerous affair due to loose and falling rock. As their ascent was to be a siege and they deemed fixing this section impracticable, the team gave up further climbing and investigated the Koji Valley immediately to the southeast.

LINDSAY GRIFFIN, *Mountain INFO*, JOSUE ROIBAL, *Spain*, ELIZABETH HAWLEY, *AAC Honorary Member, Nepal*, AND RICHARD SALISBURY, *The Himalayan Database*.

Kanti Himal, Kojichuwa Valley, exploration. The second team visiting the Kojichuwa Valley, arriving as the Spanish were leaving, was the four-man British group of Nick Colton, Ed Douglas, Julian Freeman-Attwood, and Rob Greaves. In 2007 Colton and Freeman-Attwood had been part of a team that explored the neighboring Koji Valley and climbed two peaks on the frontier ridge west-southwest of Rongla South (*AAJ 2008*). In April '09 they established base camp lower in the valley than the Mallorcans and explored the area, climbing six small peaks of 4,900m–5,400m. The first two were on the south-

Looking northeast into upper Kojichuwa Valley. (A) Kojichuwa Chuli (6,439m), (B) unnamed ca 6,300m spire, (C) Mugu Chuli (6,310m), (D) Churau (Kanti Himal, 6,419m) and (E) unnamed 6,047m peak. *Nick Colton*

Unclimbed Churau or Kanti Himal (6,419m) from west-southwest. This peak lies on Tibet border northwest of main Koji Valley. *Julian Freeman-Attwood*

east side of the lower main valley more or less opposite base camp, while the remaining four, including the smallest, lay farther up on the opposite side of the valley, and to the southwest of the Spanish base camp. One was a prominent rock peak climbed from the back, and the rest were on a ridge running northwest from this peak. It is possible the Mallorcans also climbed one of these. Some involved snow slopes; others were rough scrambles over snow-covered scree and broken rock. The team noted an excellent ice/mixed line on the west face of Mugu Chuli.

LINDSAY GRIFFIN, *Mountain INFO,* *from information provided by* NICK COLTON AND JULIAN FREEMAN-ATTWOOD

KANJIROBA HIMAL

Kanjiroba Sanctuary exploration. You might recall our adventure in the fall of 2008, when we searched for the simplest route from Jagdula Khola through chaotic gorges to reach Kanjiroba base camp. Following the paths of Tichy and Tyssen, we climbed Dudh Kundali (*AAJ 2009*). But above all we inaugurated the Honeymoon Trail, and the idea of a new high route was born. In the spring of 2009 I returned with my girlfriend Sonia to the wild massif of Kanjiroba. We approached from the south, via the tiny airport at Jumla. On the agenda was an ascent of Bijora Hiunchuli (6,386m), a beautiful unclimbed peak on the ridge north of Dudh Kundali. We also wanted to scope out a new route through a col to the Kanjiroba Sanctuary. Foul weather buried our summit dreams under tons of snow. We only had enough time to take a look at the heart of the massif, confirming the possibility of the new high-level route. All that remains

Unclimbed Bijora Hiunchuli from northwest. *Paulo Grobel*

Looking into the Kanjiroba Sanctuary. But which peaks are these? *Paulo Grobel*

to be done is to complete it via a traverse across the mountains from the village of Huricot in the south to the village of Talphi. This is a wonderful area far from tourist economy, with attractive unclimbed peaks and much opportunity for exploratory travel. We'll be back in 2010.

PAULO GROBEL, *France (translated by Todd Miller)*

Kanta Gaton (5,910m). A French family expedition made the first known ascent of this small peak in the southeast corner of the Kanjiroba Himal, on the ridge immediately southwest of 6,005m Norbu Kang (climbed from the north in 2003 and 2008). The team flew to Juphal in early August. From here they trekked via Ringmo to a base camp at 4,885m, next to Chalugai Lake. On August 15 they established a high camp at 5,300m and the next day overcame several steep steps through seracs and an icefall on the glacier, before they set foot on the moderately angled southeast ridge. Two members turned back, but Abel Minelli, Eienne Minelli, Jean-René Minelli, Sarah Minelli, and Pemba Jangbu Sherpa reached the summit after four hours of climbing. They found no trace of previous traffic and are confident their ascent is the first of the route, if not the mountain.

LINDSAY GRIFFIN, *Mountain INFO,* ELIZABETH HAWLEY, *AAC Honorary Member, Nepal, and* RICHARD SALISBURY, *The Himalayan Database.*

MUKUT HIMAL

Anige Chuli (6,025m); Typhoon Peak (6,066m). In West Mustang, on the border with Tibet, lies Araniko Chuli (6,034m). The name is not Tibetan, so who christened this peak and why? This is a bizarre story of alpinism in which mysterious characters cross paths over the centuries. It begins with Araniko, also known as Arniko or Anige Jing. Born in 1245, he was one of the greatest Nepalese artists. Araniko was also a resident in the court of the Mongol emperor Khubilai Khan. We also have Ekai Kawaguchi, a Japanese Buddhist monk and scholar, who traveled through Mustang on his way to Tibet in 1899. Kawaguchi dreamed of studying the sacred texts of Buddhism within Tibet, although the country was off-limits to foreigners at the turn of the 20th Century [*Kawaguchi became the first foreigner to enter Tibet, reaching Lhasa from Nepal. On route he stayed in Mustang for nearly a year studying Tibetan language and a local sect of Tibetan Buddhism. He eventually reached Tibet in the summer of 1990 via Jomsom, Sangda, Chharka, and a high pass in Dolpo*].

Panch Himal from Typhoon Peak. Anige Chuli is far right summit and was ascended by snow slope on the right (in shadow). *Paulo Grobel*

Typhoon Peak from Anige Chuli. High camp was by the two lakes; mountain ascended by obvious snow tongue. *Paulo Grobel*

A century later, in 2002, the Japanese mountaineer and explorer Tamotsu "Typhoon" Ohnishi, set off for the interior of Mustang to follow in the footsteps of Kawaguchi. His aim was to explore the region and climb Araniko Chuli (6,034m), which he did by the rocky southwest ridge [*On this expedition Ohnishi followed Kawaguchi as far as Sangda, then headed north over several high passes. He returned in 2003 for more exploration of the area with a different group, some of whom made the second ascent of the peak*]. Then there is Kenneth Bauer, an American anthropologist, whose work highlighting the changes taking place in Dolpo sheds a different light on the Oscar-nominated cult film *Caravan,* by Eric Valli. Bauer made me want to see what it was really like in Chharka, a small West Mustang village "at the end of the world."

In the fall of 2009 I set off to continue my explorations of the "Lost Valley" of Nepal. After our 2008 trek from Mustang to Phu—the "incredible journey" (*AAJ 2009*, p. 324)— Dolpo to Mustang represented the impossible journey, because of the complexity of securing permits to get through these two regions. However, thanks to the permit we eventually obtained to climb Araniko Chuli, we were able to link Chharka to Dolpo to Lo Manthang to Mustang, by a new, captivating route. Just the descent into Lo itself is worth the journey.

We made our long trek in a roundtrip from Jomsom, which we gained by air. After reaching Chharko, we trekked northeast toward our mountains but gave up thoughts of trying to climb Araniko Chuli from the south; it is simply a horrible pile of scree. Instead, Frank Bonhomme, Jocelyn Chavy, Denis Flaven, Gyalzen Sherpa, and I climbed Peak 6,025m, a few kilometers along the ridge running south from Araniko. We ascended easy snow slopes on the north-northwest face and named the peak Anige Chuli. Bonhomme, Gyalzen, and I also climbed Peak 6,060m, east of Araniko, naming it Typhoon Peak as a tribute to Ohnishi. It is still not clear whether one of Ohnishi's two expeditions climbed Anige Chuli, but we found a cairn on the summit. Later a Spanish team led by Jesus Calleja visited the area, decided not to attempt Araniko, but instead climbed Anige Chuli, which they named Pico Cuatro for a TV company that provided sponsorship. At the time they were seemingly unaware of our ascent. We continued our trek northeast, crossing the Kekyap La before descending to Lo Manthang and following the well-traveled route south through Mustang to Jomsom.

My website provides information on a potential route up Araniko by its northeast side (www.paulogrobel.com/05_expes/Fiches_PDF/araniko_2009/araniko_2.htm).

There will be an aesthetic approach, with a large glacier and a new "Very Lost Valley."

PAULO GROBEL, *France (translated by Todd Miller)*

DAMODAR HIMAL

Pokharkan (6,372m), north face, Cassis Arête. We planned to climb the northeast ridge on Pokharkan, but the arrival of a violent wind, with gusts of 80-100 km/hour at 6,000m, forced us to find a route that was more sheltered. Nevertheless, heavy snow, the cold (-15°C or lower), and strong winds rendered climbing conditions very difficult and only Hugues de Varax, with the young Nepalese Bishal Rai, Chhotemba, Kishor Gurung, Pasang Sherpa, and Renzi, made the summit, which they reached on September 20 from

North face of Pokharkan with Cassis Arête. From top of marked line the route descends left to upper glacier and climbs to far ridge, then back right to main summit, which is more or less visible in right background. Original 2002 route lies farther right. *Paulo Grobel*

Camp 3 on upper glacier, north face of Pokharkan. Marked is talus descent from Cassis Arête. Impressive Lugula (6,899m; officially unclimbed) in background. *Paulo Grobel.*

our Camp 3 at 5,800m. The Cassis Arête of Pokharkan is technically reasonable, with no objective dangers. It is a snow route of PD-, with just a short descent through talus to reach the upper glacier. We attained our primary goal: to establish an easy, aesthetic route that could become a classic on a 6,000m peak near the village of Phu.

Our second goal was to figure out an approach to Amotsang (6,393m), an unclimbed summit in the Damodar massif west of Pokharkan. The base camp at 4,850m that we used to climb Pokharkan is the ideal point of departure for this new route, which would begin by traversing to the Amotsang Pass at 5,600m. The most difficult task remains: climbing to this beautiful, mysterious summit.

PAULO GROBEL, *France (translated by Todd Miller)*

Editor's Note: Pokharkan was first climbed at the end of October 2002 by Koichi Kato and Pa Nima Sherpa via the north ridge. It was climbed again two weeks later via the south face to the east summit (6,250m, first ascent), and then the east ridge to the main summit by Kaji Sherpa, Martin Scott, and Dave Wynne-Jones. The Cassis Arête is similar to the original route in the lower section but continues left to reach the northeast ridge just left of the east summit, before continuing over it and on to the main summit.

Amotsang (6,393m) and Pokharkan (6,372m), attempts. Chris Warner and I planned to attempt Amotsang during August and September. In 2003 a French expedition led by Paulo Grobel reconnoitered the south and west sides, finding no feasible route. Moving to the north flank, they decided the best approach would be directly from the east, but made no attempt on the mountain. Using maps and Google Earth, I felt an approach was possible via a col to the north of Pokharkan, dropping from the col west into a valley east of Amotsang, before climbing into a glacial cirque north of the peak. However we

Unclimbed Peak 6,085m, immediately south of Amotsang, seen from north face of Pokharkan. In between lies unexplored valley of upper Loha Khola. *Damien Gildea*

only got to see the second part of this route once, for an hour, due to terrible visibility, and that was late in the trip. It is certainly feasible for a small team, but porters would help.

We eventually attempted a new line on the north face of Pokharkan, from a high camp on the north col (ca 5,400m), but only reached 5,900m. I stopped due to poor visibility and minor avalanche danger; there was a lot of light rain, very cloudy up high, and hard to see where to go. Some past reports have indicated August and September to be fine for this area, due to the rain shadow formed by the Annapurnas and Chulus. This was not so in our case.

April and May might be too early, with snow blocking approaches, and October is often very windy up high, as in Mustang. Late May through June or late September is probably best.

DAMIEN GILDEA, *Australia*

ANNAPURNA HIMAL

Annapurna South (7,219m), East Pillar. In a roundtrip of 40 hours from base camp and back, Jozef "Dodo" Kopold made an audacious first ascent, solo, of the central pillar on the east face of Annapurna South. His route, completed in early April, tops out more or less at the ca 7,100m north summit, which was previously unvisited. From there he traversed the ridge southwest to the 7,219m main summit, returned to a low point on the crest where the 1964 Japanese Route—the original route on the mountain—emerges, and went straight down the southeast face through seracs, deep snow, and hidden crevasses. During the ascent he overcame difficulties of F5+ WI6 M5. His account appears earlier in the *Journal*.

There had been only two known previous attempts on this pillar. Sometime in the mid-1980s three Japanese got part way up the route on an unauthorized attempt, before disappearing. Locals later discovered their tent below the face, but not their bodies.

This event was unknown to a six-man British team before its arrival in the Annapurna Sanctuary in the spring of 1989. Members of this group reached just over half-height on the pillar but were dogged by poor weather, poor climbing conditions, and illness. However, they were surprised to find a Japanese bolt at 6,000m while dry tooling around a steep bulge on one of the central rock bands. The British team thought the upper section of the pillar looked extremely hard, with very steep fluted terrain capped by a difficult rock band.

Patal Hiunchuli (6,434m), north face, attempt and tragedy. The Choongbuk Alpine Federation Rescue Team, led by Park Yeon-soo, consisted of 10 members. They split into two groups and from August 27 to October 8 attempted the west-northwest ridge and north face of Hiunchuli in the Annapurna Sanctuary. Avalanches, rockfall, rotten crevasses, and bad weather forced them to abandon their attempts on the ridge.

Instead, they placed a camp on Tharpu Chuli (Tent Peak, 5,663m) directly opposite, used it for observing and photographing

Hiunchuli from the northeast. Pointed subsidiary summit on long east ridge (left skyline) is east summit (6,005m). 1995 Slovenian Route climbs triangular rock and ice wall below east summit, facing camera. Proposed Korean line followed broad depression to right, at first on vague rock and ice rib between two couloirs, then up right, and finally back left through serac barriers to summit. West-northwest ridge forms right skyline and leads toward Annapurna South. *Korean Alpine Federation*

the north face, and chose a detailed line of ascent. They hoped to reach the summit in four days.

On September 23 Min Jun-young, Park Jong-sung, and Park Soo-hwan left base camp and bivouacked as planned in a crevasse at 4,900m. The following morning they left for the face, while the remaining members established an observation site at 4,700m. At 10 a.m. the climbing party radioed that Park Soo-hwan was coming down, as he didn't feel he was in good enough shape for the climb. The remaining two continued and that night radioed that they had made a second bivouac at 5,350m. On the morning of the 25th the two men again radioed base camp to say they would be taking the right-hand couloir to reach the snowfield above and that both were in excellent condition. This was the last contact from the pair; bad weather engulfed the mountain, and sight of the climbers was lost. When nothing had been heard by 8 a.m. on the 26th, Kim Dong-hwa and Park Soo-hwan returned to the observation site, where they noted the weather was now even worse and avalanches were increasing. They returned to base camp at noon, and the team decided to contact friends in Korea for assistance. A helicopter arrived the following morning, and Park Soo-hwan accompanied the pilot on a search of the face and summit area. A second flight scoured the upper face and west-northwest ridge. Over the next three days Kim and Park, with Sherpa assistance, searched the base of the wall but found no trace of the missing climbers. On October 5 the expedition members agreed there was no possibility of the pair still being alive, and further searches, which had been financed by Cheongju City Hall and the climbing community in Korea, were abandoned.

Min Jun-young had made a possible first ascent of Jikji Peak (6,235m), Pakistan, in 2007 [*AAJ 2008*, p. 350] and a new route on the northwest face of Spantik (7,027m) in 2009 [see elsewhere in this *Journal*]. The latter, climbed in alpine style, constituted revolutionary progress in Korean alpinism. Min's loss has come as a great shock to the Korean climbing community.

KOREAN ALPINE FEDERATION INTERNATIONAL COMMITTEE (*translated by Peter Jensen-Choi*)

Editor's note: The only previously known attempts on this face were by Slovenians. In spring 1994 Tadej Golab and friends tried the northeast face, leading to the 6,005m east summit, but were forced down by poor weather and stonefall. They came back in the autumn but found the face too dry. In October 1995 Golab returned to the line with Tomaz Jeras and Dusan Polenik. The three climbed the initial 300m rocky section at UIAA VI/VI+ and A2, and continued on snow and ice, including a 50m pitch of 85° and a difficult serac barrier, to reach the east summit. Jeras remained there while the other two continued toward the main summit. However, they were thwarted by bad snow. Most of the 1,200m route (Terra Nostra, ED2) was climbed unroped, and they descended with only five rappels.

PERI HIMAL

Nemjung (7,140m), west-northwest face and upper west ridge. Himalayan veteran Osamu Tanabe led an eight-member Shinshu University Alpine Club expedition to Himlung Himal (7,126m) and Nemjung. On October 14 Shin Egawa, Nobusuka Oki, Tokihiro Takizawa, and Jaya Prakesh Rai reached the summit of Himlung via the standard route up the west ridge. They were followed next day by Hiroko and Yasuhiro Hanatani, and Michihiro Kadoya. Less than two weeks later Kadoya, Yasuhiro Hanatani, Oki, and

Japanese route on west-northwest face and upper west ridge of Nemjung. *Yasuhiro Hanatani*

Tanabe made a two-day approach from the north to the base of the west-northwest face of Nemjung, bivouacking at ca 6,000m. On October 29 they started up the 1,000m face, climbing 18 60m snow and ice pitches until nightfall, when they bivouacked at 6,840m. The following day they reached the upper west ridge, continued to the summit, and returned to their bivouac. On the 31st they rappeled the face and returned to base camp. Forty-eight-year-old Tanabe has climbed Everest, K2, and other 8,000m peaks. In 2006 he climbed the south face of Lhotse in winter but did not continue to the summit.

Climbing on west-northwest face. Col in shadow at foot of sharp, lower west ridge separates Nemjung from Gyaji Kang (7,074m). *Yasuhiro Hanatani.*

However, Nemjung was the first major Himalayan peak he has climbed alpine-style.

The only previous ascent of Nemjung was made in 1983 by Junji Kurotaki's Japanese expedition, via the east ridge, approaching from the southwest. Prior to 1992 there was confusion distinguishing Himlung and Nemjung, and most teams attempting what they believed to be Himlung were in fact trying Nemjung. The west ridge may have been tried during that period, but it was definitely attempted in 1994 by Peter Hudd's British expedition, which gained the ridge from the south, before retreating in bad weather from 6,370m. Subsequently several other expeditions attempted the ridge from both north and south sides without success, notably French teams in 2004 and '07, which reached higher than 6,500m.

DOUGALD MACDONALD, *Climbing.com*, HIROSHI HAGIWARA,
Rock and Snow, ELIZABETH HAWLEY, *AAC Honorary Member, Nepal*

MANASLU HIMAL

Samdo (6,335m), attempt. Babulal Lamu Tamang and Alexandre Ulcakar from France are the first known party to have attempted Samdo since the peak was brought onto the permitted list in 2003. The peak lies northeast of Manaslu on the Tibetan border, south of the Lajyung La. The pair reached the village of Samdo on the normal trek around the back of Manaslu, en route to the Larkya La, and established a high camp at 5,050m, hoping to climb the north ridge. However, from the outset the weather was terrible, with much snowfall, they made no further progress.

LINDSAY GRIFFIN, *Mountain INFO*, ELIZABETH HAWLEY, *AAC Honorary Member, Nepal*, AND
RICHARD SALISBURY, *The Himalayan Database*

Samdo (6,335m), north ridge; Panpoche I (6,620m), northeast ridge, attempt. Yoshitaka Kameoka, Kohei Kotani, Daisuke Nakatsuka, Seiya Nakatsukasa, Hiroki Yamamoto, and I as leader, all from the student section of the Japanese Alpine Club, hoped to climb the virgin peaks of Samdo and Panpoche I (Pang Phunch I or Kutang Himal). These are situated to the northeast of Sama village on the standard trekking route around Manaslu. Both peaks were brought onto the permitted list in 2003 [as was 6,504m Panpoche II, on the ridge southeast of the main summit]. We left Kathmandu on August 24 and established base camp on September 2 on a grassy terrace beside the Sonam Glacier, at 4,350m. On the 11th we made Camp 1 on the glacier at 4,600m and on the 14th Camp 2 at 5,600m, on the col at the foot of the north ridge of Samdo. This ridge forms the border with Tibet. On the 20th all six of us left Camp 2 at 4:15 a.m. and plowed through knee-deep snow on the crest of the ridge to reach the summit of Samdo at 10:20 a.m.

(S) Samdo and (P) Panpoche I from west. (BC) base camp hidden by foreground hill. (C1) and (C2) camps used for ascent of Samdo. (C3) site of top camp for attempt on Panpoche I. Route between Samdo and summit ridge of Panpoche not visible. *Yusuke Kuramoto*

The following day we moved our top camp farther up the north ridge, to 5,900m, and on the 28th made an attempt on Panpoche I. We again left camp at 4:15 a.m., climbed to the top of Samdo, but then continued southwest on a knife-edge ridge and descended 10m on the crest to reach the start of the main arête leading to Panpoche I. The next 200m were unstable rock and snow, and we could place neither rock pitons nor snow stakes. Realizing that if the ridge collapsed, we would not survive, we gave up at an altitude of 6,500m, 400m distant from the summit.

YUSUKE KURAMOTO, *Japanese Alpine Club*

On crumbling summit ridge of Panpoche I. Climbers turned back at this point. *Yusuke Kuramoto*

LANGTANG HIMAL

Langtang Lirung (7,227m), solo attempt and tragedy. No one knows what caused the death of Tomaz Humar on the south face of Langtang Lirung. On November 7 the 40-year-old Slovenian started up a wide couloir leading leftward and then diagonally up toward the south ridge. He bivouacked on the ridge at 6,100m. The forecast predicted strong winds. On the 9th he radioed to his base camp cook, "I'm here at 6,300m and not possible. I come down." Later that day he spoke again to his cook, who understood Humar to say that he had broken his leg and back. Before this second call he had talked with his girlfriend in Slovenia by satellite phone, saying, "I've had an accident. I'm dying." Finally, the next morning, he spoke once more to the cook and simply said, "This is my last call." He then either switched off the radio or the connection was lost. He was not heard from again.

The alarm was sounded but helicopter searches failed to locate Humar, as did a strong Sherpa team, who fixed ropes toward the point Humar had described as his location (first arriving on the south ridge at a point higher than Humar reported in his first radio message). Contacts in Slovenia mustered the services of the Air Zermatt Rescue, members of which arrived in Kathmandu on the 13th. The following day the Swiss flew with a Nepalese helicopter to Langtang, and co-pilot Robert Andenmatten located Humar at ca 5,600m on the southwest face, lower and much farther left than expected, in an area of steep rocky terrain. Zermatt guide Simon Anthamatten was lowered on a 25m static line and prepared Humar's body for evacuation. It was airlifted from the mountain and brought to base camp, literally frozen stiff.

Anthamatten thinks that Humar climbed an easy couloir on the left side of the southeast face, then moved onto the southwest face, continuing up below the crest of the south ridge. A camera in his pocket showed an extremely steep wide couloir, looking both up and down. Due to the frozen condition of his body, it was impossible to tell whether he had broken any bones, and the Nepalese doctors who perform autopsies said they were incapable of examining such a body. His clothing, camera, and other gadgets in his pockets were undamaged. His Slovenian doctor and good friend, Anda Perdan, who had come to Nepal with the Swiss, speculated that he had managed to descend several hundred meters to the point where he was found and then froze to death, though this seems less plausible given the nature of the terrain. Humar's body was cremated in Kathmandu and his ashes scattered over the Langtang Lirung base camp site.

ELIZABETH HAWLEY, *AAC Honorary Member, Nepal.* LINDSAY GRIFFIN, *Mountain INFO*

ROLWALING HIMAL

Gaurishankar (7,135m), southwest face, attempt. From December 23, 2008, to January 8, 2009, a six-member Korean expedition, led by Kang Sung-woo, attempted a new route on the southwest face of Gaurishankar. They planned to follow a line to the right of the 1984 American-Nepalese route (Wayne Culbreth–Ang Kami Sherpa), which itself is an upper-rightward variant to the original American-Nepalese route climbed in 1979 by John Roskelly and Dorje Sherpa. The Koreans accessed the bowl beneath the face by a gully between the Via Neithardt and the foot of the southwest ridge but gave up at 5,400m. They note that the Tseringma Glacier below the face has almost completely melted. Despite around 25 attempts, Gaurishankar has only been climbed three times, the last in January 1986—the only winter ascent—by Korean Choi Han-jo and Ang Kami Sherpa, repeating Ang Kami's own 1984 route.

PETER JENSEN-CHOI, *Corean Alpine Club*

Lunag Massif, nomenclature. A massif of high peaks, which forms the Nepal-Tibet border southwest of the Nangpa La, is generally unnamed on maps, although one of the northerly summits, 6,781m, is sometimes referred to as Jobo Rinjang (also Ribjang or Rabzang) and on the outdated HGM-MT map was marked with an altitude of 6,666m. In 2002 it was brought onto the permitted list of mountaineering peaks by the Nepalese government. Given that the nearest village and the glacier on the south side of the group are both named Lunag, it seems sensible to refer to the peaks as the Lunag Massif. In 2004 Stéphane Schaffter asked the Ministry to open this massif and agreed on the name Lunag Ri. In 2008 he received permission from the Ministry to attempt Peak 6,778m, the fine pyramid at the end of the 2km-long corniced snow and ice crest running east from Lunag's main summit and forming the cornerstone of the Lunag and Nangpa glaciers; the permit was issued with the name Jobo Rinjang and a height of 6,666m.

LINDSAY GRIFFIN, *Mountain INFO*

Jobo Rinjang (6,778m), south ridge, attempt; Jobo Rinjang West (ca 6,800m), southwest pillar, attempt; Mt. Antoine LeCoultre or Jobo LeCoultre (6,478m), northeast face and southeast ridge; Peak 5,777m. I reconnoitered the Lunag Massif in 2004 with the aim of documenting an ascent of a virgin summit by two of the greatest living mountaineers of the Sherpa and Balti communities, Apa Sherpa and Abdul "Little" Karim. The project was named *Un sommet pour la rencontre des Himalayas—Connecting talent in the Himalaya.* I planned the ascent of Jobo Rinjang for autumn 2009 and in October 2008 went to Nepal to prepare the route. I chose the south ridge, establishing base camp close to the foot. Then Vincent Colliard from France, Dawa Sherpa, Krishnar Bahadur Tamang, and I fixed 1,000m of rope to above 6,000m before retreating. There were sections of ice up to 80° and difficult mixed climbing. We left all rope in place for our 2009 attempt.

Mt. Antoine LeCoultre or Jobo LeCoultre. Northeast face to southeast ridge from Camp 1. *Stéphane Schaffter*

However, in spring 2009 Jobo Rinjang was climbed via the face to the left [see report and feature article in this *Journal*]. We returned in the autumn, and from October 6 to 15 Xavier Carrard, Jérôme Haeni, Dawa Sherpa, Krishnar Bahadur Tamang, and I attempted the southwest pillar, which falls from Point ca 6,800m on the ridge a little southeast of Lunag I. We refer to this point as Jobo Rinjang West (its east ridge leads to Jobo Rinjang). We abandoned our attempt at 6,100m because there was too much danger from stonefall for Sherpas and cameramen. Apa and Karim climbed with us to 5,800m. They were filmed by Carrard and photographed by Guillaume Vallot. I would like to return to finish this project.

From October 19 to 22 Carrard, Haeni, I, and, on the last day, Vallot—with some help in preparing the route from Dawa and Krishnar—made the first ascent of Peak 6,589m [Sch-

Moving left into central couloir at two-thirds height on northeast face of Jobo LeCoultre. *Stéphane Schaffter*

neider map, but 6,478m on HMG-Finn map]. This summit lies on the frontier ridge southwest of the Lunags, between them and Pangbuk Ri (6,625m). We fixed 900m of rope on the northeast face. From Camp 1 (5,200m) at the foot of the mountain, the first 200m were principally 45° snow slopes, leading to a short ice step of 70°, which gave access to the large central snow/ice field. Using the rocks on the right side we reached Vire de l'Orient, which would make a fine bivouac site.

A rising traverse of 150m on impressive ice flutes led into the central couloir. A section of 80° ice led to four steep pitches of mixed ground. After we returned to ice flutes for two pitches, three long mixed pitches led to a small notch on the frontier ridge, leading northwest to the summit. We continued over a series of cornices to the summit, the highest point being on top of a cornice entirely suspended over space. The elegance of the route matches its difficulty. The mountain is a climber's dream, and we proposed the name Mt. Antoine LeCoultre or Jobo LeCoultre to the Ministry.

On October 24 Apa, Carrard, Karim, Vallot, and I climbed Peak 5,777m just south of the Lunag Glacier. This will make a fine trekking peak.

STÉPHANE SCHAFFTER, *Switzerland*

Jobo Rinjang (6,778m), ascent and nomenclature. In April David Gottlieb and Joe Puryear made the first ascent of Jobo Rinjang, by the 1,700m south face. They were not aware the peak had been attempted [by Stéphane Schaffter's expedition; see above] until they arrived at the Ministry to collect their permit, nor did they see any fixed rope on the mountain; apart from a few cairns, there was little trace of anyone having been close to the peak. However, they also settled on Lunag as the most appropriate name for the group, and propose that the highest summit, which lies at the southern end of the chain, be named Lunag I (6,895m) and the summits farther north Lunag II (6,891m), III (6,795m), IV (6,781m, the old Jobo Ribjang), and V (6,550m). Peak 6,492m, west of Lunag I, they designate Little Lunag. Running east from Lunag I is a 2km corniced snow/ice crest, ending in the fine pyramid of Peak 6,778m, Jobo Rinjang. Puryear's account of his excellent alpine-style ascent appears earlier in the *Journal*.

Tengi Ragi Tau, south ridge, attempt. Oriol Baro and I arrived in Nepal on September 11 without firm plans, only pictures in the pocket. We acclimatized in the Khumbu, ascending the trekking peak Parchamo (6,279m). From here we saw an interesting wall; the south face of Tengi Ragi Tau (6,938m), which rises from the Tesi Laptsa pass (5,750m) on the well-known trekking route from Khumbu to Rolwaling. The weather was generally bad, so we made our base at a lodge in Thame (3,800m). Every time the sun came out, we had to climb nearly 2,000m to reach the foot of the face. We established a camp on the Khumbu side of the pass at 5,600m. To reach the start of the route, we crossed the pass and descended 100m on the west side, before traversing snow shelves into the base of a large couloir rising back right to the crest of the south ridge. During our first attempt, at the beginning of October, we left a rope fixed on a difficult rock pitch at 6,000m. Our final attempt took place from October 10 to 11, with a bivouac at 6,300m. We reached 6,600m on the south foresummit, after climbing 1,000m, with difficulties of ED V/M5 A1. Above, a snow ridge led to the main summit, but the weather was freezing,

South ridge of Tengi Ragi Tau seen from slopes of Parchamo. (1) Baro-Corominas attempt, 2009. (2) Approximate line of Japanese-Nepalese route (first recorded ascent of the mountain; Ezaki, Morishita, Onda, and Takahashi, with Dhanjit Tamang, Pasang Tamang, and Tul Bahadur Tamang over two days in December 2002). *Oriol Baro*

and my partner especially was suffering from cold feet, so we retreated. We made 20 rappels using 70m ropes and reached camp the same day.

JORDI COROMINAS, *Spain*

MALAHANGUR HIMAL – KHUMBU SECTION

Pasang Lhamu Chuli from southeast, showing (1) upper section of Slovenian Route and (2) Hook or Crook, with bivouacs marked. Lower section of (1) is hidden by Dzasampatze (D) in foreground. *Simon Anthamatten*

Pasang Lhamu Chuli (7,351m), southeast face, Hook or Crook. At 2:30 p.m. on October 29, Michael Lerjen, my brother Samuel, and I stood on the summit of Pasang Lhamu Chuli. We were not exactly full of joy. Pasang Lhamu Chuli hasn't got an easy way off down the backside. Like the Matterhorn, once you reach the summit, you are only halfway through. That evening we made it back to 6,900m and the following day regained base camp. It took 25 rappels from Abalakovs, stoppers, Camalots, a buried ice axe, and a buried segment of trekking pole.

After establishing base camp at 5,200m, we acclimatized with an ascent of Dzasampatze [the second known ascent

Simon Anthamatten on mixed terrain at 7,100m, southeast face of Pasang Lhamu Chuli. *Simon Anthamatten collection.*

Samuel Anthamatten leading on precarious ridge toward upper rock buttress on southeast face of Pasang Lhamu Chuli. *Simon Anthamatten*

of this 6,295m peak immediately south of Pasang Lhamu Chuli, the first having been made by Slovenians in 2004]. We began our new route on Pasang Lhamu Chuli on October 25, making a five-hour trek across the broken Somna Glacier to bivouac below the southeast face at 5,800m. The next day we were able to move fast: a little ice-climbing at first and then snow-trudging. In high spirits we camped on a snow mushroom at 6,500m, remaining tied in while we slept. The following day the climbing became more complex: snow mushrooms as big as trucks, between which lay steep ice walls. While climbing ice we were able to place good protection and to belay using ice screws, but on bottomless snow we could only move forward like voles, with no useful belay. Our nerves were on edge, as we often moved up one step only to fall back two. Regularly we asked ourselves what this had to do with climbing. We gained only 400m that day and squeezed our two-man tent into a gap in a mushroom at 6,900m. With three of us inside, the night was uncomfortable.

On the following morning our morale sank when we encountered a 150m rock wall at ca 7,000m. Steep slabs and vertical cracks taxed us, and, above, steep ice pitches sapped our remaining energy. Once over this, 300m of desperately tiring snow-trudging brought us to the summit. We made it thanks to team spirit and motivation, having to implement efficiently all the experience we'd gathered in the Alps, Patagonia, Canada, and Alaska. This was the first alpine-style ascent of Pasang Lhamu Chuli, and we named our route Hook or Crook (VI WI6 M5, 1,550m).

SIMON ANTHAMATTEN, *Switzerland*

Editor's Note: Formerly known as Nangpai Gosum I or Jasamba, Pasang Lhamu Chuli straddles the Nepal-Tibet border southwest of Cho Oyu. It was officially renamed by the Nepalese Government after the death in May 1993 of Pasang Lhamu, the Sherpani who became the first Nepalese woman to climb Everest but perished during the descent.

Cho Oyu (8,188m), southeast face. One of the most remarkable pre-monsoon ascents was the new route on the southeast face of Cho Oyu by Boris Dedeshko and Denis Urubko. The Kazakhs climbed the face to the left of the 1985 Polish Southeast Pillar, joining it at ca 8,000m. Climbing alpine-style, with Urubko leading, the two spent five days completing their 2,600m route, then crossing the summit plateau to give Urubko his 14th and last 8,000m peak. There was a difficult rock barrier low (6b A2/3) and a section of M6 high. The remainder was steep snow and ice. A full account of the Cho Oyu ascent appears earlier in the *Journal*. There are two other routes on the southeast face. In 1978 Austrians Alois Furtner and Edi Koblmuller, with only a trekking permit, made an ascent of the right side of the face, fixing some rope. In February 1985 a Polish team led by the great winter specialist, Andrzej Zawada, climbed the difficult central pillar, putting four climbers on the summit.

Tawoche (6,495m), Direct North Face. From November 26 to 29 Fumitaka Ichimura and I made the first ascent of Tawoche's north face. There was an obvious, logical line that was unclimbed, at an ideal altitude for an attempt in November.

On our first try, however, we failed because we took the wrong route. At 5,500m we traversed too far right, not realizing that we had strayed from our original plan. We spent the night on a tiny ledge and then tried and failed to climb through the rock band above. Three days later we started up the face at 5:30 a.m. At

Tawoche, showing Japanese Direct North Face. Bivouac sites are marked. Immediately left is northeast pillar climbed in 1995 by Mick Fowler and Pat Littlejohn. Left again is steep rock wall of east face, split by thin ice runnels and climbed in winter 1988 by Jeff Lowe and John Roskelly. *Genki Narumi*

midday we reached the spot where previously we had started the rightward traverse. This time we continued more directly, on moderate ice, until we reached the rock band. We now traversed right on steep ice, with few ice screw placements and poor rock gear. Our plan had been to reach the second icefield and be clear of the large, dangerous seracs above before making our first bivouac, at 5,600m. However, we only managed to reach the first icefield that night. During the bivouac we were hit by much spindrift and chunks of ice.

Our second day began with easy ice, but we continued on much steeper ice, with poor protection. The ice was too soft for screws and the rock often loose, or merely chunks of rock stuck in snow. Ichimura led a steep pitch in the dark, and at 9 p.m. we finally cut a site for our second bivouac (6,100m). It was just big enough that we could sit, and it was midnight before we finished our small meal.

On day three the terrain was mostly sugary snow, with some moderate ice climbing. Ichimura deluged me with spindrift; sometimes I was unable to open my eyes. We soon reached the summit ridge. Not far away was the main summit, but there was a massive gap before it, preventing us from reaching the true summit. On the descent we had to dig deep into the snow to find a layer hard enough to hold our weight. We made a rappel from a buried stuff bag filled with snow; it moved slightly as I descended. A second rappel from an Abalakov got us to a point where we could downclimb a short distance to a flat area above the east couloir. For the first time since starting the route we could take off our harnesses and lie down. The night was cold and windy. Next day we downclimbed and rappeled the east couloir, then walked back to Pheriche, where we arrived at 4 p.m. We climbed the route without tents, bivouac sacks, jumars, or aid, and carried food and fuel for just three days. The 1,500m Direct North Face was VI AI5 R.

GENKI NARUMI, *Japan*

Tibet restrictions, Everest bolting. Uncertainty about Tibet being open to climbers, indeed to any foreigners, led many to go to the Nepalese side of Everest, rather than wait in the hope of being granted permission to enter Tibet. Would-be Cho Oyu climbers and their expedition organizers switched to Manaslu or Baruntse. March 10 marked the 50th anniversary of the Tibetan uprising against Beijing authorities and shortly afterward the flight of the Dalai Lama across the Himalaya into India. In 2009 the important Buddhist holiday of Lhosar fell in late February, but the Tibetan community in Kathmandu did not hold their usual celebrations, instead mourning Tibetans who suffered during clashes last year.

By February 24 the few foreigners already in Tibet were told to leave, and tour organizers and other tourism operators were instructed not to accept bookings for March; visas valid for travel to Tibet were no longer being issued. By early March, as the *International Herald Tribune* reported, authorities had imposed an unofficial state of martial law on the Tibetan-inhabited highlands, with thousands of troops occupying areas they feared could erupt in riots on the scale of 2008. This was the largest deployment of military since the Sichuan earthquake the previous spring. A curfew was imposed on Lhasa.

The first reports of bolting on the normal Nepal route on Everest surfaced this season. The west face of Lhotse, the gateway to the South Col and final southeast ridge, was very dry during part of the climbing season (although during another period teams were paralyzed by a nearly week-long snowstorm), and some commercial expeditions had come prepared. The leader of a Swiss party brought a drill, which was used by a British assistant leader of a huge expedition and by the American leader of a smaller one. They placed about six bolts in the Yellow Band, at 7,700m on the Lhotse face. [More were added in spring 2010.]

The fitness of many people who sign up with expeditions seems open to question, considering high rates of dropouts and some fatalities. Take this spring's fatalities first: one died of chronic heart disease and one from intracerebral hemorrhage, both climbers surely not in a fit condition to tackle 8,000m summits. Another collapsed from exhaustion after summiting Everest. One disappeared, presumably fell, and five are known to have fallen for unrecorded reasons; some of these falls might have been caused by weariness.

ELIZABETH HAWLEY, *AAC Honorary Member, Nepal*

Everest (8,850m), southwest face, Park's Korean Route. At 3 p.m. on May 20, Jin Jan-chang, Kang Ki-seok, Shin Dong-min, and Park Young-seok stepped onto the summit of Everest, having completed a new route up the southwest face. This is the first new route climbed by Koreans on the mountain and their third attempt on this line, which lies left of the 1982 Soviet route.

The six-man Korean team, with eight Sherpas headed by Sirdar Sanggye Puri, left base camp on April 12 to establish Camp 1. On the 18th they established Camp 2 at 6,500m and on the 20th began climbing the left side of the southwest face. From here to Camp 3 (7,350m, dubbed Swallow's Nest) they climbed 28 pitches with an average angle of 50°. At one point their line shared common ground with Korean attempts of 2007 and '08. With less snow cover in 2009, crampons were not needed on 15 of the pitches. The average angle to Camp 4 (7,800m) was 60°. Sixty percent of the fixed rope used on this section had been left in place during the 2008 attempt. At the end of pitch 39 (ca 7,500m), the team collected 11 oxygen bottles deposited in 2007; four were useable.

Southwest face of Everest showing Park's Korean Route and camps (2 and 3 are hidden by foreground). The lower of the two C5s is camp used in 2008 attempt. *Park Young-seok Collection*

From Camp 4 the route made a rightward rising traverse across the face, partially in a couloir, to hit the west ridge at 8,350m, where the final camp would later be established. This section was the steepest part of the route, averaging 60° but with steps of 85°. Reaching the ridge involved crossing a huge rock band, which reportedly required 5.9 face-climbing at 8,100m. Sherpas, seeing this, dropped their loads and descended, leaving members to carry extra gear.

High on west ridge of Everest during summit day of Park's Korean Route. *Park Young-seok Collection*

At the end of April everyone descended to base camp for a rest; Lee Hyung-mo, who had a chest infection, decided not to return to the face. On May 8, making their first attempt on the summit, Dong-min and two Sherpas left Camp 4 and tried to establish Camp 5; Jan-chang, Ki-seok, and Young-seok left the same day from Camp 2 but were driven back by strong winds. On the next attempt all four Koreans reached 8,350m on May 19 and established Camp 5. This was at the same place as a Soviet camp, and the Koreans discovered old oxygen bottles.

On the 20th the four climbers divided 500m of rope between them and packed it in their sacks, which then weighed 20-30kg each. Carrying two or three oxygen bottles, 1½ liters of water, and three gel packets per person, the team climbed toward the summit, fixing a further 400m of rope. Above 8,600m (starting at a point more than 700m distant from the top), they made a new five-pitch variant to the upper west ridge. Fifteen hours after leaving Camp 5, all four reached the top and descended the Normal Route on the southeast ridge.

They named the new line Park's Korean Route. A total of 3,930m of rope was fixed. On new ground, between Camps 2 and 5, they climbed 68 pitches; from Camp 5 to the summit, 30 pitches.

In 1991 Park Young-seok attempted the southwest face by the 1975 British route. While he was leading at 7,000m, the Sherpa who was belaying him pulled the rope, causing Park to fall 150m. He had to drop out of the expedition, which later reached a high point of 8,350m. Park returned to attempt the new line, left of the 1982 Soviet Route, in the spring of 2007 and autumn of 2008. In 2007 his 10-man team, including two Sherpas, fixed rope to 8,000m. The day after he reached this high point, Lee Hyun-jo and Oh Hee-jun moved up to Camp 4 at 7,700m. While they were inside the tent, the first big avalanche to occur on the face during the expedition struck them, sweeping both climbers to their deaths. Lee and Oh were young and outstanding Korean mountaineers. In 2008 the Koreans placed Camp 5 at 8,200m, close to the west ridge, but were stopped from reaching the summit by severe winds.

CHRISTINE PAE, *Korean Alpine News*, WITH ADDITIONAL MATERIAL FROM ELIZABETH HAWLEY, *AAC Honorary Member, Nepal*

Melanphulan (6,573m), north face (not to summit). Marcin Michalek, Krzysztof Starek, and I arrived in the Khumbu hoping to climb the north face of Melanphulan, above the Nare Valley. During our first two weeks we acclimatized by trekking from base camp in the village of Pangboche (3,900m) to the foot of the face, where we established an advanced base at 5,100m, and then made two trips to Lobuje East. On the first we reached the so-called False Summit (ca 6,000m, PD). On the second Michalek and I continued on

North face of Melanphulan with line of Polish ascent to northeast ridge, 100m from summit. The only previously recorded ascent of the peak, in 2000 by Supy Bullard and Peter Carse, climbed west face on right direct to summit. *Wojtek Kozub*

the exposed east ridge to the rarely visited Main Summit (6,119m, D+). This ridge, between the two summits, took 4½ hours and was risky due to dangerous cornices. We then rested five days at base camp before climbing Melanphulan's north face in a round trip of five days from advanced base.

On October 30 we moved together up the first 300m of the face and cut a small tent platform on a narrow snow flute toward the right side of the wall. Our idea was to continue

Marcin Michalek and Wojtek Kozub on upper part of north face of Melanphulan. Highest peak on continuation ridge behind is 6,473m; below is upper Nare Glacier. *Krzysztof Starek*

Marcin Michalek on final section of East Ridge of Lobuje East. Nuptse, Lhotse and Makalu behind. *Wojtek Kozub*

from here non-stop. Next day our goal was to climb as far up the 300m crux section as possible. In Polish we refer to the crux as *Pralka*, which approximately translates to "nasty way." After three long pitches in the Pralka, we believed we could climb the rest of the route in a continuous push, which was just as well because there appeared to be no possible bivouac site on the hard and uniformly steep ice above. By late the following evening we reached the Pralka and climbed through it during the moonlit night. Next day we climbed many pitches of fluted ice toward the summit cone. We got dehydrated and began to develop frostbite. On most 55–60m pitches we were able to use three or four ice-screw runners, with main belays on ice screws and Abalakovs, placing the latter for our rappel descent and marking them with ribbon. However, because the ice was thin, there were some pitches where we could only place one or two screws, making the climbing psychologically demanding.

We reached the steep wall below the summit at dark. A pitch of 85°, followed by two easier ropelengths, led to the cornice. It was our fourth day on the face, we'd been climbing for 32 hours above camp, and it was 11 p.m. The leader could find no safe stance or belay, so he stopped just below the crest. We were 100m from the summit, but the intervening crest, festooned with highly delicate, often transparent cornices, seemed just too dangerous. We faced a dilemma: trying to reach the top would likely prove fatal, yet we were most unhappy about not continuing. *Ke garne*, as the Nepalis say (What to do?). We descended.

During the ascent the third man had constructed Abalakovs at each stance, so our descent was efficient, and we were back at camp in seven hours. We rested and then returned to advanced base the same day, November 3.

Prolonged sitting in harnesses while belaying, the low temperature, generally between -15 and -20°C, and wind at night meant that we all suffered frostbite in the toes. The height of the face is 1,400m and above our camp we climbed 18 55–60m pitches. We estimate the grade to be ED2/3 AI 4/5 85°. Our expedition was supported by grants from the Polish Alpine Association (www.pza.org.pl) and the Andrezj Zawada Award (www.fundacjakukuczki.pl).

WOJTEK KOZUB, *Polish Mountaineering Association (PZA)*

Mera Peak (6,470m), south ridge, In Memoriam. From October 29 to 31 I climbed a new route, solo, on the right side of Mera Peak's southwest face. I named it In Memoriam, as a tribute to Mal Duff and Ian "Tat" Tattersall; the only other route on this face is their 1986 Southwest Pillar. Ray Delaney was part of that expedition, and he accompanied me to the Sanu Valley, remaining at our 4,700m base camp while I completed the climb.

South ridge of Mera showing In Memoriam. (SR) Samivel Ridge, (B1) first bivouac, (R) rappels, (N) narrows and point of rockfall, (B2) second bivouac, and (RB) upper rock band. *Joe Simpson*

I started up a rock ridge at 5,150m. Easy climbing and scrambling on the crest led to a knife-edge snow ridge and then an area of broken rock ridge where I bivouacked at 5,900m. Another snow/ice crest led to a rock wall, 75m high. A huge serac barrier above looked extremely unstable and dangerous, so instead of climbing the rock wall, I traversed left across an ice slope to a point where I could make a series of diagonal rappels over vertical bands of shattered rock. From prior binocular examination I was hoping to reach an ice couloir, which ran up the left side of the serac barrier for 200m and regained the upper face. Since I only carried a single 50m rope, the rappels were committing. After pulling the rope on the first rappel, I was unable to climb back to my starting point. If the couloir was not where I expected, then with my small alpine rack I felt I might not be able to descend the ground below.

Fortunately, I reached the couloir (50-55°). As I climbed it, occasional overhanging rock walls provided some protection from the decomposing left side of the serac. Ironically, just as I was safely past the main danger, a football-sized rock from the summit headwall missed me by less than a meter. I bivouacked at 5 p.m. in a small crevasse at the top of the couloir where it joins the upper left edge of the serac at 6,250m. I'd intended to continue to the top, expecting to summit in the dark, but had been shaken by the rockfall and decided to take shelter. Next morning I climbed up left past crevasses marking the junction of the serac with the upper face. I reached an ice ridge and followed it toward the summit. A 50m rock band in the upper section gave UIAA III/IV and easy mixed climbing, and I reached the top at mid-day.

Descending the Normal Route, I plodded into Mera High Camp only to bump into a commercial group led by Tom Richardson. I've known Tom for 25 years, and he lives less than a kilometer from my house in Sheffield.

I found it difficult to grade the climb. Technically it wasn't hard but had a high seriousness factor. My best guess would be a Route Major (Mont Blanc) level of climb, with significantly greater commitment given the irreversible rappels and more time spent directly exposed to alarmingly unstable seracs. In years to come, if the seracs were to stabilize, a direct ascent of the rock wall and a route through the seracs would provide a more satisfying line, probably at D+. However, given the current risk of ice avalanche, I assess the 1,200m route at TD+/ED1.

JOE SIMPSON, *U.K.*

MAHALANGUR HIMAL – MAKALU SECTION

Pethangtse (6,739m), south face to southwest ridge. The summits of Everest and Makalu are 20km apart. Halfway between is Pethangtse, on the border of Nepal and Tibet. On October 30 Stephen Graham, Colin McLean, and I, with climbing Sherpas Dawa Gyalzen and Pema Tsering, were the first to reach the summit since the peak was officially opened for climbing in 2002. Our GPS read 6,770m on top. Ours may be the first ascent for 25 years. [Pethangtse was first climbed in May 1954 by Michael Ball, Norman Hardie, Brian Wilkins, and Urkien Sherpa from Edmund Hillary's Makalu reconnaissance expedition. After various ascents in the 1950s and 60s, a Spanish climber, Nil Bohigas, soloed the south face and descended the southwest

Looking west-northwest from summit of Pethangtse across Kangshung faces of Shartse II (7,457m), Shartse (Peak 38 or Shanti Shikar, 7,591m), Lhotse Shar (8,382m), Lhotse Middle (8,410m), Lhotse (8,516m), and Everest (8,850m). *David Graham*

Looking southeast along Tibet-Nepal border from Pethangtse, first toward Chago (6,893m), then Kangchungtse (Makalu II, 7,678m) and finally Makalu (8,485m). In far distant right is Tutse (6,758m) and to the right again Peak 4 (6,720m). *David Graham*

ridge in 1984. Since that time there are no known ascents, though it is possible that members from expeditions with Makalu permits also climbed it].

We made our base camp at Makalu upper base camp (5,300m). Above, it was exploratory for all of us, as our Sherpas had never been so far up the Barun Glacier. We followed the canyon of the Barun to a sprawling glaciated plateau, and after two days placed a high camp at 5,880m. The situation felt remote. From the start of our approach march in the foothills it

Pethangtse from south showing route of Canadian ascent. *David Graham*

had taken 17 days until we first caught sight of Pethangtse. From high camp we headed across the moderately crevassed upper Barun Glacier to the foot of Pethangtse's south face, at 6,000m. We climbed the face on 40–55° snow, avoiding obvious crevasses. A massive bergshrund 150m below the summit caused a pause for reflection before we worked left, mounted the rolling southwest ridge, and followed it to the top. The grade was AD-

The proximity of Chomolonzo, Makalu, Shartse, Lhotse Shar, the mountains of Tibet, and the Kangshung Face of Everest provided one of the world's great mountain vistas. It was Pethangtse's spectacular location, lost by the passage of time, which drew us to this utterly amazing place. For more information and photographs, including a summit panorama, visit www.pethangtse.wordpress.com

DAVID GRAHAM, *Canada*

Baruntse (7,219m), northeast face, attempt. If you're headed to Baruntse to seek a plumb line on a cleaved face, it'll be techy, heady, whatever you want. If you want off, it'll be scary. If you want in, it'll cost you about $6,000. If you want the top, be prepared for a few goes. That's what I think. When I met Elizabeth Hawley at the Nirvana Garden Hotel back in Kathmandu, she sat on my left, a man whose life I saved sat on my right, and Josh Butson was across from me. This was our first morning in the Nepalese capital after an exhilarating 10-day alpine-style attempt on a new line. We dis-

Baruntse from upper Barun Glacier to northeast. Main summit on left, north summit on right. Left skyline is normal route. Snowy east ridge in center descends to col, in front of which stands Peak 6,220m. To right, above glacier shelf, central rib of northeast face leads toward north summit. *Lindsay Griffin*

Camp at 6,400m on northeast face of Baruntse, with west face of Makalu in background and Peak 6,220m (which lies at foot of east ridge) in foreground behind tent. *Ben Clark*

cussed whether it had been a new line, but later research has shown that the central rib of Baruntse's northeast face, visible from the west side of Makalu, had not been previously attempted. The ridge above it and the ridge beside it had been climbed to the summit decades ago. We wanted to climb the rib, reach the summit, and ski down the lower-angled normal route, the Southeast Ridge. This would complete a first ascent, first ski descent, and fun traverse.

Butson, Jon Miller, and I spent 17 days approaching the mountain from an altitude of ca 500m and then committed to our project with little acclimatization but a hearty knowledge of Himalayan north faces. Our line, cutting through an hourglass-shaped face, was in places steep with chossy granite. We made three camps, the highest at 6,400m, where we spent three hours chopping a site out of the slope and then called it home for five nights, as we weathered a storm. Jon Miller fell ill, with a swelling of his brain impacting an anachroid cyst, leading to HACE-like symptoms. Going up was not possible, getting down was not probable, and this is where we did things one should not do in the mountains.

We had told our Sherpa cook staff that we would be back in eight days, but we didn't hit the moraine until day 10. We had self-rescued from 6,400m and were spent, though happy, with no scrapes or bruises. But we did have a time with the snow that accumulated in five days on the mountain. Avalanches were everywhere, steep slopes were settling. Somewhere in there is a spirit, even though we never reached the summit. I don't know how that gets recorded.

For more, visit http://skithehimalayas.com/blog/category/ski-the-himalayas-video-podcast

BEN CLARK, *AAC*

Editor's note: The three climbers established an advanced base at 5,335m and climbed to the col at the foot of the east ridge (climbed in 1980 on the second ascent of the mountain by Carlos Buhler and five Spanish alpinists). They camped here at 5,975m and then traversed across the glacier shelf to the right, below the northeast face, to camp again at 6,000m. On May 8th they climbed onto the snow rib in the center of this face, leading toward the 7,057m north summit. They followed it to 6,400m, where they were trapped by storm. A few days after their retreat to advanced base on the 15th, Butson and Clark attempted a different line farther left on the east face but abandoned it at ca 5,550m.

ELIZABETH HAWLEY, *AAC Honorary Member, Nepal,*
AND RICHARD SALISBURY, *The Himalayan Database.*

KANGCHENJUNGA HIMAL

Chang Himal, north face. In the autumn Nick Bullock and Andy Houseman made the first ascent of the 1,800m north face of Chang Himal (6,802m). The pair climbed the central spur in four days, finding the main difficulties on a series of rock bands, the second of which provided the crux at Scottish 7 mixed. The total amount of climbing was nearly 2,400m, often precarious and runout, with Peruvian-like steep, unconsolidated flutings in the upper section. The ascent was nominated for the 2010 Piolets d'Or; a full account by Houseman appears earlier in the *Journal*.

Brought onto the list of permitted peaks by the Nepalese Government in 2002, Chang Himal was referred to as Wedge Peak by the 1930 Kangchenjunga expedition. But it is also known as Ramtang Chang, perhaps the name that best identifies this summit. *Chang* means north, and Ramtang Chang rises north (actually northwest) of 6,601m Ramtang, a peak in the shadow of Kangchenjunga first climbed in 1930 by Frank Smythe. Bullock and Houseman's ascent of the north face was the first official ascent of the peak, though it had been summited previously. In the spring of 1974 a large Slovenian expedition climbed Kangbachen, the western subsidiary summit of Kangchenjunga. Taking time out from that ascent, Janez Gradisar, Bojan Pollak, and Michael Smola made an unauthorized climb of the long snowy southwest ridge of Chang Himal.

JANAK HIMAL

Dome Kang (7,264m), first ascent and correction of history. From 2002–2009 a group of Spanish mountaineers, which at different times included three doctors (Miriam Ferrer, Marian García, and Guillermo Mañana), a climber and cameraman (Dani Salas), a climber and biologist (Elena Goded), a climber and geographer (Pedro Nicolás), and four climbers (Miguel Bonet, Tente Lagunilla, Carlos Soria, and I), explored, climbed, despaired, and finally summited Dome Kang, a previously virgin peak on the Nepal-Tibet border north of Kangchenjunga. It took one reconnaissance trip (in 2002) and three full expeditions (in 2004, 2006, and 2009), before we reached the top.

Our quest was for the solitude of distant and relatively unknown mountains. Climbing new routes in alpine style is the most aesthetic approach, but we accepted that we didn't have that sort of ability above 7,000m, and therefore had to live with the classic, heavy-weight expedition, using fixed ropes, Sherpas, etc. We also recognize that without the help from the Sherpas and high-altitude porters, who assisted us during the three expeditions, each trip would have been a nightmare. We had 10 Sherpas throughout the three expeditions but the two that I would most like to mention are Muktu, the Sherpa leader of the first and second trips, and Chang Dawa, leader of the third.

On our first trip in 2002 we wanted to explore Janak (7,041 m), an unclimbed peak on the same plateau as Jongsang (7,462m) and Dome Kang. Officially, it is not possible to approach these peaks from Tibet and Sikkim due to border restrictions, so the only possibility to reach Janak, Jongsang, or Dome Kang is to climb the five-kilometer-long and one-kilometer-high barrier that defends the plateau on the Nepalese side. In 2002 we decided that Janak's south face would not be suitable for a heavy expedition: it was eventually climbed in 2006 by Stremfelj and Zalokar, as reported in *AAJ 2007*—a remarkable achievement.

The southeast face of Jongsang as seen from Camp 1 (6,200m). (A) Jongsang South Peak II. (B) Jongsang South Peak I (7,350m). (1) The 2009 Spanish line (snow, ice and mixed to UIAA IV+/V-, ca. 1,000m). (2) Touch of Silence (VI/4: c1,150m: Azman-Markovic, 2000). Dome Kang (7,264m) is some way behind and well to the right of South Peak I. *Salvador García-Atance*

Back in Kathmandu, in the library of our hotel, we found *The Kangchenjunga Adventure*, the book that covers the 1930 Dyhrenfurth expedition. Due to that accidental encounter, I began the research that convinced me Dome Kang was virgin. Jill Neate, in *High Asia* (1989), assigned the first ascent of Dome Kang (7,442m) to Dyhrenfurth in 1930 (see also the 2005 and 2007 *AAJ*). In the Kangchenjunga book, we read that Dyhrenfurth reached the summit of Jongsang after 1:00 p.m. Afterwards, he went to a subsidiary peak. Someone, somewhere, decided that this peak was Dome Kang.

This isn't the case. The name Dome Kang characterizes a big dome, and the only big dome on the plateau is a peak to the east of Jongsang, 200m lower, and two kilometers distant. Is it possible that a mountaineer, who at the time had just climbed the highest peak in history, reaching the summit in the afternoon, would descend 300m and then climb up another 100m to a summit two kilometers away? The reality was that Dyhrenfurth walked to the end of Jongsang's South Ridge, a point of altitude 7,442m, to have a look at the Jongsang Glacier below and his Corner Camp close to Pangpema. The big dome to the east was unclimbed. That conclusion was the basis of our three expeditions to Dome Kang. [Editor's note: this is also clear on the HMG-Finn map, where the 7,264m peak is labeled Domekhan. This peak was only brought onto the permitted list after the Spanish asked for a permit to climb.]

In 2004, we established base camp at Pangpema (5,000m), and then walked up the

Miguel Bonet, Dani Salas and Salvador García-Atance in the central couloir on the southeast face of Jongsang. *Salvador García-Atance Collection*

Jongsang Glacier to Jongsang La (6,100m). We had decided that Dome Kang lay close to the east ridge of the plateau, so the Jongsang La was the natural place to start the ascent. We set up Camp 1 at 6,100m on the east side of the glacier, and tried to climb the east ridge to the plateau. We got to 6,500m but had expended our strength on the glacier and had to go back. In 2006, we now knew the difficulties of the Jongsang Glacier, so we not only set up base camp at Dyhrenfurth's old Corner Camp (three hours closer to the mountain), but also prepared a complicated logistical system to carry equipment to Camp I (at the same place as on our first expedition). This time we reached 6,700m, but at that altitude the ridge was hazardous, possibly suitable for a strong team climbing in alpine style, but not for us. Back again.

Finally, in 2009 we mastered the logistics and set up base camp in the middle of the glacier, five hours above Pangpema and only eight hours from Camp 1. On this expedition we placed a new Camp 1 on the west side of the glacier at 6,200m. We also changed our route from the east ridge to the big couloir on the southeast face that was first climbed in 2001 by two young Slovenians [Editor's note: Urban Azman and Andrej Markovic made an alpine style ascent of the couloir, reaching the summit of 7,350m Jongsang South Peak I in a day. Azman and Markovic then traversed toward South Peak II and tried to descend its southeast spur in the dark. Not far into the descent a rappel anchor pulled and Markovic fell to his death.] In the first part we found difficult conditions (very icy, with sections of IV+/V- mixed), and we exited via snow ramps to the left, rather than following the couloir up right like the Slovenians. We fixed a total of 1,500m of rope and placed Camp 2 on the plateau at 7,200m. The day after, April 28, Carlos Soria and Tente Lagunilla, with Sherpas Chang Dawa, Karma Gyalzen, and Sonam, walked across the plateau for three hours to the summit of Dome Kang.

We learned by heart the beautiful meaning of the poem by Kavafis:
As you set out for Ithaka,
hope your road is a long one,
full of adventure, full of discovery.
Keep Ithaka always in your mind
Arriving there is what you are destined for
But don't hurry the journey at all
Better if it lasts for years
So you are old by the time you reach the island
Wealthy with all you have gained on the way
Not expecting Ithaka to make you rich

SALVADOR GARCÍA-ATANCE, *Spain*

China

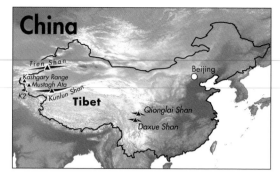

Kara Tagh, Shipton's Arch. From July 5 to August 15, on the first of my two Year of the Ox expeditions, I visited Xinjiang. Again I embarked on the ultimate challenges of a solo expedition, to get back to a relationship with myself that I can only find while going alone into the wilderness in search of world-class first ascents and moments of *now*. This was my fifth time in the area, and memories told me what to expect in the huge city of Urumqi, filled with Muslim Uygur and Chinese. Xinjiang Province has an entwined collection of signs written in both Arabic and Chinese characters: Chinese and Muslims coexisting.

But when I arrived, it was quite different from my previous trips. The streets were not packed with people. Markets of fresh vegetables, kebabs, and fried goodies, which once ruled alleyways, were nonexistent. Instead, Chinese military crowded every corner and street. Camouflaged trucks, several tanks, and even two bi-propeller helicopters were prominent on my way to the hotel. Young soldiers, emanating strict discipline, stood in battle-ready formation, all with machine guns, some with bazookas, and some with hand-combat weapons and large shields.

I had arrived on July 7, the day after a major terror and political battle between the local Uygur and Chinese, when over 600 people were brutally killed in the streets. The Chinese were embarrassed about their lack of control and shut down all communications. The situation changed my plans and military permits, and I canceled my initial goal to climb in an area of grand walls in the western Kokshaal-too, on the Kyrgyzstan border.

My liaison officer, who has helped me plan several expeditions in China, was concerned about my safety. He told me the previous day's terror now ruled the psyche and energy of every person in Urumqi, and likely all of Xinjiang. While in Urumqi, I left my hotel in hopes of finding food in the markets but ended up detained in a military jail and questioned for a day; they thought I was a reporter from *The New York Times*. A couple of days later I left with my Chinese friends for the 1,500km drive to the Kyrgyzstan border.

We passed through 14 military checkpoints; at three where I was questioned, it was not a polite situation. After several days we arrived at the roadhead, a spot I had visited before and just 20km from my potential base camp near dry glaciers. Then, at the last moment the military denied me permission. Devastation. The entire trip that had fueled my psyche for one of the most challenging solo adventures of my life, one for which I had worked for the past year to get the correct permits and paid more money than I will mention, was simply gone. When I politely tried to negotiate, the military officer got pissed off and took my papers. They told me there were terrorists hiding in the mountains, and I had to leave. My liaison officer drove me 1,500km back to Urumqi.

I'm addicted to optimism, so I had to devise a plan B. I knew of a mountain range that is home to Shipton's Arch. I took a 24-hour train from Urumqi to Kashgar, hired locals to drive me to the mountains, and proceeded to explore. There were steep, big walls up to 900m, made of mud and river stones. In the end I climbed three routes on Shipton's Arch and connecting formations. I repeated, rope solo, the west face of the Arch (5.10, 240m). There were in-situ anchors showing that it had previously been climbed. [The west arm of the Arch was climbed by Americans in 2000. They placed bolt anchors and climbed 180 vertical meters of generally loose conglomerate at 5.6 to reach the summit, for the first known ascent. *AAJ 2001*.] I then climbed the northeast face of a connecting summit, most likely a first ascent (5.10 A2, 270m). There were some strange rope-solo shenanigans with a cool chimney/tube. Finally, I climbed the north face of another connecting summit, which proved scary 5.10 A2 (270m) due to the need to overcome mud climbing on my own. These routes, on different walls, led to different summits. But the formations are connected at the base, and I refer to them all as part of Shipton's Arch.

Seen from north, Shipton's Arch in Kara Tagh, ca 40km northwest of Kashgar. *Mike Libecki*

It was a wonderful solo expedition. I plan to go back to the Chinese western Kokshaal-too as soon as permits become available. My chosen area has some of the most amazing untouched granite walls left on the planet, and I know of three formations that have faces at least 1,500m high, all waiting for a first attempt.

MIKE LIBECKI, *AAC*

TIEN SHAN

Xuelian massif, various ascents. Following exploration of the north side of the Xuelian massif in 2008 (*AAJ 2009*), Bruce Normand (Scotland) returned in August 2009 with Americans Jed Brown, Kyle Dempster, and Jared Vilhauer. Goals were the major satellite peaks of Xuelian Main (Xuelian Feng, 6,627m), all of which remained unclimbed. On August 3 Brown and Normand established an advanced base on the side glacier that runs below the northwest face of the Xuelian's west satellite (6,422m). On the 6th they made an acclimatization climb of a 4,000m summit directly north of the west satellite and the following day climbed the west ridge of Xuelian's north satellite (6,472m). A 600m snow couloir (50°) led to the crest, where the team pitched a tent at 5,300m. On the 8th they continued up largely rotten snow and then over the 6,150m forepeak to reach the summit. They noted that the continuation ridge to Xuelian Main would offer 300m of technical rock climbing, and sported considerable cornice formations.

6,150m forepeak below 6,472m north satellite of Xuelian. Brown-Normand route follows obvious large snow couloir to reach broader snow slopes of west ridge above narrower section. It then continues up these, along skyline ridge, and over forepeak to (hidden) north satellite. Visible top right is north ridge of Xuelian Feng. *Bruce Normand*

Looking west from Yanamax (6,332m) to main summits of Xuelian Massif. (A) east sub-summit (ca 6,400m). (B) main summit (6,627m). (C) north satellite (6,472m). (D) northeast sub-summit (6,231m). Approximately marked are lines followed by Brown and Normand on east ridge (1) and Dempster and Vilhauer on north face to east ridge (2). Distant peak at far left is Muzart (6,571m). *Bruce Normand*

On the 12th the pair reached the foot of a snow ramp leading to the crest of the east ridge of Xuelian's ca 6,400m east sub-summit. Next day they made a 1,700m push to the top, first climbing the ramp via a very thin ice pitch and a long section of unprotectable snow-covered rock to the crest and then strenuous wading through deep, rotten snow. Once on the ridge they were surprised to meet Dempster and Vilhauer, who had climbed a harder line up the north flank, involving much steep ice and difficult snow-covered rock in the last 500m. The pairs operated largely independently throughout the trip, but on this occasion they all combined forces for the last 800m.

Brown and Normand had planned a one-day round trip, but when the four were hit by bad weather during the descent, they crammed into a small bivouac tent brought by Dempster and Vilhauer. The storm produced the worst weather of the trip, and the tent saved the climbers from possible frostnip. The four climbers descended the Brown-Normand line on the 14th. The American-Scottish pair returned to base camp next day, but Dempster and Vilhauer remained on the upper Muzart Glacier for a further week, climbing a 1,600m ice route up the impressive northwest buttress of Yanamax, stopping on its 6,180m sub-peak (virtually a separate summit), which they named Yanamax II. The route, which took three days and had difficulties up to M4, they named Yanamaniacs.

In the meantime, on the 21st and 22nd, Brown and Normand tackled the west ridge of Xuelian's northeast sub-summit (6,231m). Bad snow conditions, together with knife-edge and rocky sections, made this particularly time-consuming, and that night they pitched camp below a hard rock section at 5,000m. Next day Brown led five tenuous snow-covered slab pitches, and by the time the pair reached 5,400m, it was obvious that the route would require

(A) Yanamax II (6,180m) and (B) northeast sub-summit of Xuelian (6,231m), seen from west-southwest. Marked are approximate lines of (1) Yanamaniacs and (2) west ridge attempt. *Bruce Normand*

Yanamax II (6,180m, left) and rounded summit of Yanamax (6,332m) from west-northwest. Marked is Yanamaniacs. *Bruce Normand*

considerably more time than was available. They retreated.

On the 24th Brown, Dempster, and Normand returned to the previously established advanced base below Xuelian's west satellite (6,422m), Vilhauer prudently opting out of further climbing after frostnipping a toe during the Yanamax II ascent. Over the next four-and-a-half days they climbed the fine 2,650m marble prow that separates the north-northwest and north-northeast faces. They descended the west ridge, then the southwest ridge, and finally rappeled onto the southwest face, regaining the west ridge at 5,200m, below its steepest section. Downclimbing the northern flank they reached advanced base that night. Kyle Dempster's account of this route, named *Great White Jade Heist* (5.7 WI5 M6 R), appears earlier in the *Journal.* The three climbers were recipients of one of the 2010 Piolets d'Or.

Lindsay Griffin, *Mountain INFO*

Altai

Keketuohai reconnaissance. Keketuohai or Koktokay lies in the southern Altai Range of China's Xinjiang Province, close to the border with Mongolia and 600km north-northeast of Urumqi. For three years I have attempted to travel to the area on the recommendation of non-climbing friends in China. In autumn I was finally successful and discovered a wealth of granite towers and walls that have yet to be visited by rockclimbers. I was told that there are 108 granite peaks here, and I estimate rock faces to reach a height of ca 300m, though I only saw part of the area. These walls are situated along the gorge of the Iyrtish River, and some reach the valley floor. Of all the valleys I have seen during world travels, Keketuohai compares closest to Yosemite, and locals assured me that no one has ever climbed there. Spring and autumn would be the best seasons: summer is just too hot, and in winter the temperatures regularly fall to -40°C and lower; it is one of the coldest places in China. While there is certainly no El Cap or Half Dome, the volume of rock is possibly greater than Yosemite, and there are also many good boulders in the valley bottom.

Divine Bell in Keketuohai National Geological Park. *Dennis Gray*

There are daily flights from Beijing to Urumqi and two scheduled flights a week from Moscow. From Urumqi an express bus, going toward Altai, will drop you off at Fuyun, where it is possible to catch a mini-bus from the Tourist Hotel for the remaining 70km to Keketuohai. Foreigners cannot hire vehicles in Xinjiang.

So why has no one climbed there? Keketuohai is a National Geological Site; visitors are taken part way into the valley on a battery-driven "golf buggy" along a newly constructed road.

The area is populated by Kazakhs, who are building the park infrastructure and visitor access. They are unlikely to allow rock climbing, unless sanctioned by higher authority in Beijing or Urumqi. This may be possible, as Chinese authorities are always interested in creating opportunities that will provide jobs and foreign currency. The Chinese Mountaineering Association is probably not aware of Keketuohai's climbing potential.

Granite scenery in Keketuohai. *Dennis Gray*

Currently, the situation in Xinjiang is fraught: no internet access and not possible to phone from abroad. Traveling is dangerous, due to ethnic tension between the Uighers and Han Chinese. There were large riots in July and many subsequent ethnic incidents. Al Qaeda has now declared a jihad on the Han Chinese. However, the local population, Kazakhs, have so far not involved themselves with this problem. Visiting Keketuohai would certainly necessitate one of the party having a basic grasp of Mandarin.

It may be that UIAA representatives could talk with CMA delegates about the possibilities of allowing rock climbing, or it might be that a group of climbers could arrive on spec, make friends with the Kazakhs, and hope that permission to climb was granted. But it's a long way to travel if the answer is no.

DENNIS GRAY, *Alpine Club*

KUN LUN

Qong Muztagh East (ca 6,976m). In September and October, Diana Borisova, Pavel Demesh-chik, Vasiliy Ivanov, Ivan Muyzhnek, Anna Pereverzeva, Sergey Zayko, and I visited the Western Kun Lun, near the northern border of Tibet. It was my fourth expedition to this remote region. The 2003 and 2005 expeditions (*AAJ 2006*) explored the western borders. The 2006 expedition focused on a detailed reconnaissance of the Ustjuntagh Range, which includes Qong Muztagh (*AAJ 2007*). During the 2006 expedition we found another peak with a height comparable to double-summited Qong Muztagh (6,962m). In 2000 the western summit of Qong Muztagh (6,937m SRTM) was climbed by Japanese (*AAJ 2001*). The eastern or main summit (6,962m) is still unclimbed.

Qong Muztagh lies a little east of the main range, which turns south at Peak 6,817m (SRTM). As a result, Qong Muztagh East, a separate mountain from Qong Muztagh and 700m south of Peak 6,817m, cannot be seen from the north. During our crossing of the Tibetan Pla-teau southeast of the range in 2006, the summits were hidden, and we failed to see this peak. SRTM data suggests that it is at least 6,946m. Since the difference between this and the heights of the two Qong Muztagh summits is slight, and in view of measurement error, the question as to which of the peaks is highest remained open. Possibly, the highest peak of the region was hidden from sight. This riddle was the focus of our expedition.

We wanted to go in 2007, but access to the region was restricted because of the massive rescue of a Russian rafting expedition. In 2008 the Beijing Olympics meant that Russian citizens encountered great difficulties getting Chinese visas. In 2009 there were riots in Xinjiang, and the atmosphere was tense when we arrived in Urumqi on September 12. However, we were able

View north-northeast from Pass of Chinese Friends. (A) Qong Muztagh (6,962m). (B) Peak 6,817m. (C) Qong Muztagh East, with route of ascent up southeast ridge. (D) Peak 6,878m. *Otto Chkhetiani*

Looking west from summit of Qong Muztagh East. (A) Peak 6,820m. (B) West top of Qong Muztagh (6,927m). (C) Qong Muztagh (6,962m). (D) Peak 6,670m. *Otto Chkhetiani*

Qong Muztagh and surrounding peaks, prepared in 2010 by Vadim Liapin. Part of Russian traverse, with campsites marked.

to drive across the Taklamakan Desert to Niya (Minfeng), and set off from there in two jeeps.

In 2006 we found that approaches to Qong Muztagh East from the north ran into deep, impassable canyons. The mountain can only be accessed from Tibet or through a ca 6,500m pass in the main range. It seemed that the simplest route of ascent would be either the southwest or southeast ridge.

We followed a mountain road that we discovered in 2006, via Yapal (4,632m) and over the Atyshdavan Pass (5,073m) to the Shor Koul Plain, spectacular but an extremely rough journey. Apparently used primarily by geologists and gold diggers, it follows an old trail from Tibet to Taklamakan oases. Roborovsky, Bogdanovich, and Deasy took this trail in 1890 and '98.

After scouting two valleys of the main range, we realized we'd have to cross the range much farther west than expected. To acclimatize we made a circular trek over six high passes between the Aksou, Koutaz-Dzhilga, and Keriya rivers, the highest pass being at 5,995m. We returned to the site of Baba Khatoun (4,784m) in the upper Keriya valley on September 24.

Our guess proved correct. Going west of Peak 6,150m (map height; 6,283m SRTM), we crossed the Nevidimka (Invisible) Pass, which we measured by GPS as 6,178m, and on the 29th, after traversing 20km-long ice fields, arrived at a barren, gently-sloping Tibetan plain southeast of the range. Next, we crossed the Pass of Chinese Friends (Kitayskikh Drouzey, 6,327m) and descended north to a region unapproachable from the north. From the pass we enjoyed an impressive view of Qong Muztagh and Qong Muztagh East, from which flowed a large crevassed glacier filling the valley. To the right stood Peak 6,878m, another high summit invisible from the north. It dominates the entire range on the Tibetan side and can be seen in a photo published in *AAJ 2007*, where it was incorrectly identified as Peak 6,470m. We dropped to moraines at 5,500m and then headed generally northeast toward our goal.

After passing though an icefall at 5,820m, we continued navigating numerous crevasses, leaving behind the spectacular and steep Peak 6,820m, which towers more than 1,000m above the glacier. At 6,000m we put on our lightweight, homemade snowshoes. Crossing a watershed ridge, we returned to Tibet and, below Qong Muztagh East, gained a 6,610m pass, where we found hard ice and some rocks, which we used to secure our tents. On the next day, October 5, we waited out a strong wind.

The 6th was our big day. There was no wind and the sky was clear. Crossing a 25-30° ice slope, we climbed onto the southeast ridge at 6,776m. It varied from three to seven meters wide, 30° maximum, so we moved together. However, just before the summit the crest narrowed and became corniced to the north. We belayed, the entire team finally climbing a short 40° pitch to the top. GPS readings ranged from 6,960 to 6,982m (an average of 6,976m, N 35.648990°, E 82.337070°). A barometric altimeter showed an elevation of 7,005m. The panorama was magnificent. Ahead was the double-summited Qong Muztagh. It was difficult to say whether it was higher, so an ascent of that peak is required to answer this question.

Next day we continued northeast and crossed Podnebesnyi (Celestial) Pass (6,541m). Then, after a long descent in snowshoes and crampons through a crevassed glacier with icefalls, we reached grass on October 8. From here we walked long days across the Koumboyan and Khokhlyk passes and the eastern tributary of the Keriya, to the Shor Koul Plain. While waiting for vehicles, we scouted several valleys in the Russian Range to the north. We met our jeeps on the 17th, by the north shore of Lake Shor Koul (4,503m, N 36.140170°, E 82.693630°). This was the end of our expedition, which traveled over 500 km through the Kun Lun, and we were back in Moscow on the 20th.

Unfortunately, there was a misunderstanding with Chinese authorities, who suspected us of being involved in illegal exploration. In our absence they searched our belongings and confiscated nearly all our photos, cameras, maps, and other items. We were told they would be returned in a week, but five months later we have received nothing. The GPS data and photos in this report are from one Garmin Vista HCx and a micro SD card, which by chance were missed.

OTTO CHKHETIANI, *Russia*

QINGHAI

QILIAN MOUNTAINS

Kangze'gyai (ca 5,800m), west face. Kangze'gyai (a.k.a.Tuanjiefeng), the highest peak in the Qilian Mountains, is located in Tianjun County within the Haixi Autonomous Prefecture of the Qinghai-Tibetan Plateau. From the town of Xining it took Li Yong, Yuan Wei, and I three days to reach base camp northeast of Hala Lake. We arrived on October 4. While Yuan remained to take care of camp, Li and I made the first ascent of Kangze'gyai's west face and south ridge in a three-day round trip.

We took neither tent nor fuel, carried only two sleeping bags, one liter of water,

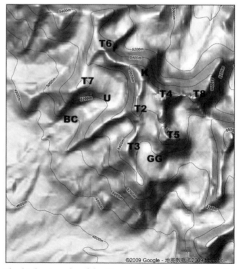

The highest peaks of the Kangze'gyai Group. Hala Lake is just off the map to the left. (BC) 2009 Chinese base camp. (U) Unnamed glacier. (GG) Ganalou Glacier.

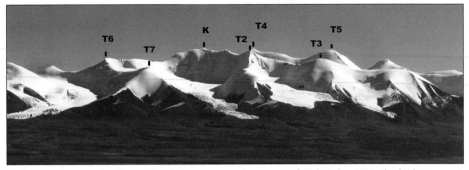

Looking northeast at the Kangze'gyai Group across the waters of Hala Lake. (K) is the highest summit Kangze'gyai (Tuanjiefeng): all others marked are unclimbed except T7. *Huang Zonghua*

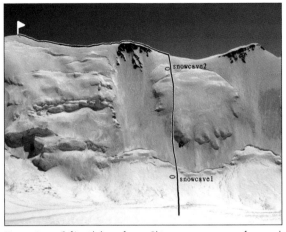

Kangze'gyai (left) with line of new Chinese route up west face and south ridge. Bivouac sites marked. Summit right of exit onto south ridge is unclimbed (T2 on map). *Huang Zonghua*

and a little food. We reached the bottom of the west face on the 5th, a day of fine weather, having climbed an unnamed, crevassed, and seracked glacier. This took longer than expected due to deep snow. By evening, as we approached the bergschrund, the weather was deteriorating, and we dug a snow hole at 5,343m for the night.

Next day the weather was terrible, with strong winds and snow. However, we continued our ascent, climbing directly toward the south ridge. A little below the crest, at 5,756m, we dug a second snow hole. The 7th was relatively clear with no snowfall, but the wind was still strong. At 2 p.m. we reached the summit, where we recorded a GPS height of 5,817m and coordinates N 38°30'22,68", E 97°43'01.98". We descended the unclimbed northwest ridge before cutting back south to the unnamed glacier, reaching base camp at 8 p.m. We named our route Darkness Wall (AI3+).

Kangze'gyai was first climbed in September 1958 by a large Chinese expedition, which approached from the southeast up the Ganalou Glacier. Leader Xu Jing and two others reached the summit on the 14th: Ten climbers followed on the 15th. In August 1999 a Sino-Japanese expedition repeated this route, believing it to be a first ascent. The 35-member expedition comprised seven Japanese and eight Chinese climbers, plus other camp personnel. The only other ascent in this compact range took place in 2008, when Chinese mountaineers Cao Yizhou, Lv Wei-bo, Pu Bai-lei and Zhen Han-bo ascended a peak above the north bank of the unnamed glacier west of Kangze'gyai.

HUANG ZONGHUA, *China*

SICHUAN PROVINCE

SHALULI SHAN

Yangmolong (6,066m), attempt. In 2007 Dick Isherwood, Peter Rowat, and I attempted Yang-molong (*AAJ 2008*). In September-October 2009 we returned with Derek Buckle to explore the northern approaches. We traveled up the Sanchu River valley and stayed at lower Sanglong Xi, before setting up base camp on the riverside east of Yangmolong, at an altitude of 4,000m. The local people identified the expedition as a suitable target for extortion, which became more serious following several thefts; binoculars, food, a stove, trekking poles, etc were stolen. The binoculars were eventually "ransomed." The police were summoned but tacitly admitted they were unlikely to obtain statements from the local community. For the duration of our time at base camp the support team slept virtually on top of remaining stores and was forced to hire "camp guards" from among the more law-abiding locals.

After several reconnaissance walks, we realized there was nothing for it but an arduous 1,000m ascent to an advanced base camp on glacial moraine below the east ridge of Yang-molong. A period of prolonged bad weather followed the establishment of this camp, dur-ing which we kicked our heels at base camp listening to rain hammering flysheets. When the weather finally cleared, we made several forays onto the flanks of the east ridge. However, we found no line that would offer a safe route to the crest. With time running out, Derek and I established a camp on a col at the head of the glacier cirque and prepared to tackle the shallow ridge and steep face above. However, more unstable weather rolled in, and after two days of abortive alpine starts we decamped to advanced base.

On the one remaining day available for climbing, Derek and I attempted the 5,700m sat-ellite peak to the north, but the upper part of the route proved too difficult in the deteriorating weather. The team evacuated the valley amid more tension and unpleasantness from the locals, including theft of money from the bus driver at the roadhead.

Something had changed significantly in this valley. In 2007 it had been populated by friendly, helpful people, but in 2009 we encountered only a few whom we recognized from

Yangmolong (6,066m, left) and Makara (a.k.a. Central Peak, 6,033m) from the north. Highest point of Yang-molong is just above left arm of seracs/hanging glacier left of center. Dangchezhangla (5,830m) is off picture to right. *Dave Wynne-Jones*

Broad summit ridge of Yangmolong (6,066m) from northeast.
Highest point is right of center. *Dave Wynne-Jones*

the earlier visit. Perhaps the 2008 disturbances, which resulted in a police house being burned down in a neighboring valley, had some influence. However, there seemed to be only two observable material changes: the illegal logging of virgin forest, which started in 2007, had been shut down by the government, although a new road and electricity pylons had been built to the village as compensation. And during 2007 there had not been a single monk or nun in evidence in the valley, while in 2009 there was a significant presence. No one on the team has any inclination to return. We wish to acknowledge the support given by the Mount Everest Foundation.

DAVE WYNNE-JONES, *Alpine Club*

Yangmolong (6,066m), south face attempt; Dangchezhengla (5,830m), south glacier to southeast face to northeast ridge. Our original plan was to approach Yangmolong from Sanglongxi (pronounced *song-lung-see,* a.k.a. Sanchu) Valley and climb from the east. We arrived in the valley on October 17 and spent the night in the lower village, which has a population of ca 300. The following morning the village secretary took us to a community meeting. The result of our 30-minute "talks": "You are not allowed to climb Yangmolong." Our stand-in liaison officer, Chen Li, with Zhang Jian, had a private meeting with village officials, which proved even worse. We were told to leave the valley that day or the villagers could not guarantee our safety. Climbing the mountain brings about ominous events such as bad weather, sickness, and natural disasters. Reasoning with superstitions is impossible.

Summit area of Dangchezhengla. Northeast ridge forms right skyline. (1) Ascent route taken by American-Chinese team. (2) Descent route. Top of high camp tent in lower right. *Jon Otto*

We had two options. One was to delay our climb, return to Chengdu, and work through official channels to negotiate access to Sanglongxi Valley, the other was to approach the mountain from Zhongba Valley to the south. We knew the south face of Yangmolong might not offer a feasible line to the summit, but returning to Chengdu would have wasted a lot of money and resources. Approaching from the south seemed worth the risk.

On the 19th we established base camp at 4,700m in the Zhongba Valley, by the northern shores of Lake Yangmogen (pronouced *jong-more-gen*). Here people were friendly, and we were easily able to hire horses. The head lama of a monastery told us that many of the surrounding peaks were sacred, but that nobody felt they should be banned to climbers. After a reconnaissance Tim Boelter, Kang Hua, Lao Wang, Su Rongqin, Yao Zhen, and I set up advanced base at 5,065m on a moraine directly below the south face.

A 600-700m wall of rock, snow,

Su Rongjin (left) and Jon Otto on summit of Dangchezhengla. Behind lie Makara and then Yangmolong. *Tim Boelter*

Tim Boelter on final section of Dangchezhengla northeast ridge. *Jon Otto*

and ice stood between us and the summit. A huge serac stretched across the entire face at mid-height, and the summit ridge had suspicious-looking cornices overhanging our route. On the morning of the 23rd, Tim, Kang Hua, Su Rongqin, and I started up the face. I tried not to notice that large parts had recently calved off and were lying in rubble at its base. I was in front, when a rock exploded 50m above. I quickly took cover but 20 minutes later saw a rock twice the size of a fist shoot down our route. The sun had hit the upper section of the south face, and the cliff 400m above us was coming apart. Disappointed, we descended, knowing that this route was unsafe.

Back on the glacier, we looked at another line, a thin couloir in the center of the face. Su Rongqin and I climbed the 45° cone flowing from the fissure, and I then led an almost vertical section of mixed rock and ice. This was followed by a long 30° snow couloir and a pitch of hollow WI3, running with water. It was getting late so we rappeled.

Next morning four of us jumared back up and continued climbing, but a chunk of ice hit Tim hard on the hand, and a few minutes later ice and rock flew past. The ice above was thin and melting fast. Further climbing was too risky. We retreated from 5,400m dejected, noticing that our first abandoned line was now a waterfall. We had done our best.

Next morning, the 25th, Tim, Su Rongqin, and I walked around to the central glacier leading to the col between Dangchezhengla and Makara (Yangmolong central peak, 6,033m).

It was full of crevasses, but they were obvious. We eventually reached a 100m wall of 70° ice, which we climbed to a flat spot at 5,554m, just below the Dangchezhengla-Makara col (5,565m). We camped there for the night.

Next morning we made a long traverse west below the northeast ridge, before climbing 70° snow and ice for 150-200m directly up the southeast face to reach the final section of ridge. We followed this to the summit, the steepest part at 80°. From the top we had a fabulous view of Yangmolong's upper ridge, which looked more challenging than we had imagined. We could also see Everest on the horizon and Namche Barwa to the west. We were the third team to summit this peak and Su Rongjin the first Chinese. We also believe we made a new variant. [In 2002 Japanese reached the Dangchezhengla-Makara col directly and then climbed the right side of the northeast ridge on very steep ice, 11 pitches from col to summit.] We made five 60m rappels directly down the southeast face, regained our traverse line, and followed it back to camp. Continuing down, we made it to base camp at midnight.

JON OTTO, *AAC*

Editor's note: A history of attempts and ascents in this small massif appears in AAJ *2008, p. 422. However, corrections are necessary. Makara is now reported to have been climbed from the south by Koreans in 2003, likely during an attempt to reach Yangmolong. It was attempted again in March 2007 by a Chinese team (which did not attempt Dangchezhengla, as stated), also likely as part of an attempt on Yangmolong. This attempt was not only unsuccessful but resulted in the death of one of China's most gifted climbers, Liu Xinan. There is now a memorial to him at Yangmogen Lake.*

DAXUE SHAN

MINYA KONKA RANGE

Peak ca 6,000m, southwest face, attempt; Jiazi (6,540m), west face, not to summit. In 2008, during an expedition to the Minya Konka Range (*AAJ 2009*, pp 350-352), Sébastien Moatti and I climbed a nameless summit of 5,200m in the Tshiburongi Valley north of Riuchi Gongga. While making this ascent, I noticed a towering granite wall rising from just beyond the base of the Tshiburongi Glacier. With its image burned into my mind, I returned in 2009 to tackle it with French guides Pierre Labbre, Rémi Sfilio, and Baptiste Rostaing-Puissant.

We established camp on October 3 at the foot of the Tshiburongi moraine. This would be our base for

1,600m west face of Jiazi. (1) Northwest ridge, attempted in 1981 by a British Army expedition that reached 6,100m. (2) West face couloir, climbed to summit ridge in 1982 by Americans Stutzman and Williams. A cornice collapse and dropped sack forced them to abandon the summit and descend east face. (3) 2009 French line, which reached a high point (H) on south ridge: (B) marks bivouac. (4) 2008 French attempt. High point was bivouac at 5,400m, reached after 600m of climbing. (5) South ridge followed by 1982 Americans to make first and only ascent of mountain. *Pascal Trividic*

Pierre Labbre approaching icefall in middle section of west face of Jiazi. *Rémi Sfilio*

Pierre Labbre on mixed terrain near top of west face of Jiazi. *Rémi Sfilio*

the next 22 days. We then required four days to ferry our technical equipment, including two portaledges, 200m of static line, and food, to the bottom of the face, a 900m vertical wall shaped like a cannon shell and topped by 150m of mixed terrain and ribs leading to a nameless summit of ca 6,000m. It took 3½ days to open the first 400m, where the rock varied from compact to crumbling flakes. During the third night a stone, falling from high above, hit my chest, the first in a series of misfortunes that would end our attempt. Next day a faulty rope maneuver, and the sack containing all our sup-

Ca 6,000m peak above north bank of Tshiburongi Glacier and line attempted by French. *Pascal Trividic*

plies fell to the foot of the wall. This conclusively forced our retreat.

To the high point we had climbed and equipped (one 8mm bolt and piton at each belay) eight pitches: the first three up a wide crack (6b and A2, 180m); a long traverse pitch on mixed ground (5 and M4, 80m), and four steep pitches (6b and A2, 200m).

While I was treated at Kangding's hospital (nothing broken, just a crushed muscle), Pierre and Rémi attempted the west face of Jiazi via a different line from the one we tried in 2008. It took 2½ days to reach the top of this 1,300m-long mixed face. The climb, which resembled the Colton-MacIntyre route on the Grandes Jorasses, followed a series of steep snow slopes, ice gullies, and mixed terrain (TD+, WI5+ and M4). They reached the south ridge and climbed to an altitude of 6,200m, before strong wind and poor snow conditions turned them back. They descended the south ridge to the col between Jiazi and Grosvenor, from where they rappeled the west face for 150m from Abalakovs to reach the glacier. They made two bivouacs; one at around two-thirds height on the face and a second on the col. This is the second route on the west face of Jiazi, yet neither has reached the summit.

PASCAL TRIVIDIC, *France*

Mt. Grosvenor (6,376m), northwest face direct, attempt. Three Korean climbers, Ahn Chi-young, Heo Young-cheol and Yun Young-Joon, from the Wand Alpine Club attempted the northwest face of Grosvenor from March 31 to April 21. They retreated from ca 5,600m in the central couloir that leads directly to the summit. This was the line attempted in spring 2003 by Andy Cave and Mick Fowler, who retreated from a point slightly higher than the Koreans when faced with a loose and protectionless slanting groove choked with powder snow. The mountain was climbed later in the year for its only ascent by Julie-Ann Clyma and Roger

Northwest face of Grosvenor with (1) 2009 Korean attempt, and (2) 2003 Clyma-Payne route to summit. *Wand AC Expedition, supplied by Peter Jensen-Choi*

Payne, who followed a much shorter line on the far right side of the face to gain the west ridge.

CHRISTINE PAE, *KOREA*, AND PETER JENSON-CHOI, *Corean Alpine Club and AAC.*

Peak 6,134m, Carte Blanche. Mikhail Mikhailov and I planned to be in Sichuan by mid-March. Our goal was the southeast face of Edgar (E Gongga, 6,618m), a large, steep, mixed granite wall. However, at the last minute the Chinese authorities canceled our permit because of the 50th anniversary celebrations in Tibet. Fortunately, a month later China reopened its doors, and it was not too late to continue with our project. We flew to Chengdu, traveled easily by road

to Moxi on the east side of the Minya Konka Range and walked for only three hours with horses up the Yangzigou Valley to an altitude of 3,150m. "Base camp is here," said the horsemen, and, pointing vaguely to the north as they set off for home, added, "and your mountain is somewhere there." We were also told that Koreans had climbed Edgar, when we thought it was still virgin.

We then had many days of mist and rain. We examined the gorge leading to the foot of the southeast face, but the wall itself remained invisible. We then decided to go for a four-day acclimatization trip up the valley. During this trip, through a brief clearing in the cloud, we saw a beautiful rock wall

Southwest face of Peak 6,134m above upper Yangzigou Valley. Right-hand line, with bivouac sites indicated, marks Carte Blanche. Left-hand line, descending from B6, shows descent. *Alexander Ruchkin*

A 360° panorama from top of southwest buttress of Peak 6,134m. (A) Summit ridge of 6,134m. (B) Grosvenor (6,376m). (C) Jiazi (6,540m). (D) Riuchi Gongga (Tshiburongi or Little Konka, 5,928m). (E) Nannemgoungou (Nan Men Guen) Valley. In far distance is snow-capped Lamo-She (6,070m). (F) Northwest face of Edgar (6,618m). (G) Peaks 6,130m. (H) Zhong Shan (Sun-Yat-Sen, 6,886m, second highest peak in Minya Konka Range). (I) Minya Konka (7,556m). (J) Daddomain (6,380m). (K) Peak 5,962m (unclimbed). (L) Dogonomba (5,960m, unclimbed). (M) Yangzigou Valley. *Alexander Ruchkin, stitched by Pedro Detjen*

Oil painting of view looking more or less north from summit of Minya Konka. (A) Grosvenor (6,376m, first ascent in 2003 via northwest face to gain southwest ridge—left skyline). (B) Peak 6,206m (unclimbed). (C) Peak 5,603m (N 30°36'15", E 101°54'03"). (D) Jiazi (6,540m; first ascent, in 1982, gained snowy south ridge, facing camera, via west face to left). (E) Peak 6,134m (climbed in 2009). (F) Lotus Flower Mountain (5,704m, N 30°16'07", E 101°57'48"). (G) Peak 6,130m (unclimbed). (H) Peak 6,130m (unclimbed). (I) Edgar (6,618m, climbed in 2001 by snowy west ridge falling toward Peak 6,130m). (J) Part of Lamo-She Massif. *A photo of this painting by Y Tanaka was supplied by Tamotsu Nakamura.*

on the south side of Peak 6,134m that cried out to be climbed. This virgin summit lies northwest of Edgar, close to 6,367m Grosvenor. We decided to waste no more time on a face we hadn't yet seen, on a mountain that may have been climbed, when there were so many virgin peaks. On May 4 we left base camp for the southwest buttress of 6,134m, assuming it was steep enough to shrug off fresh snow.

We camped at 4,200m and during three days of poor weather marked a route to the base of the wall. We started up the lesser-angled lower spur on the 8th and climbed it over three days in about 13 pitches. The rock, generally 70-75°, was often icy, but we climbed the spur free except for about five meters of aid. This led to the headwall, a rounded pillar dividing the south and west faces.

After climbing a couple of pitches on the headwall during the afternoon of the 10th, we completed the remaining nine up this steep buttress from the 11th to 13th. Despite the angle, which fluctuated between 85 and 95°, we climbed mostly free, using rock shoes, at difficulties up to 6b-6c. We climbed more than 90% of the route free, the rest requiring aid in short sections up to A2. We took no bolts and placed no skyhooks but used a full assortment of gear from copperheads to large cams. The rock was not perfect, and there were sections where we had to hold our breath as we made delicate moves around large detached flakes. We used a small tent for bivouacs, though on two nights there was barely room to sit down.

We reached the top of the buttress at 1:35 p.m. on the 13th, spent an hour there, and then followed the sharp and broken ridge to the northwest summit, from where we planned to descend. However, visibility was zero, so we pitched the tent for another night and the next day made 20 rappels down the snowy west face to the glacier. Bad visibility again hampered progress, and we had to spend another night out in the valley before reaching base camp on the 15th. After an absence of 12 days, we were greeted by our much-relieved cook and interpreter. We were very pleased with our 1,100m route (1,250m of climbing), mostly because we were able to climb largely free. We named it Carte Blanche.

ALEXANDER RUCHKIN, *Russia*

Mt. Edgar, tragedy. In late May Colorado residents Jonny Copp, Micah Dash, and Wade Johnson lost their lives in an avalanche below the southeast face of Mt. Edgar (E Gongga, 6,618m). The face was a much talked about objective, which has received wide publicity due to photos published by prolific Japanese explorer Tamotsu Nakamura. With Nick Rosen of Sender Films, who with Johnson hoped to document part of the expedition for a National Geographic TV series, the three established base camp below the mountain in May.

Rosen returned to Colorado, and on May 15 the remaining three left their liaison officer to establish an advanced base camp. They returned to base, having cached gear and food at a suitable site, reported to be five hours above when carrying a heavy load.

On the 20th Copp, Dash, and Johnson moved up toward advanced base. Dash and Copp would attempt the peak, while Johnson remained in camp. Nothing was heard from them after that date. When they failed to return to base camp and then missed their flight home, on June 3, Rosen alerted authorities.

On June 5 Guo Jie and Li Zong Li, of the Sichuan Mountaineering Association, discovered a body at 4,000m on the route between base camp and advanced base. Two days later Ci Luo and Li Fu Qing, of the Chinese Mountaineering Association in Beijing, discovered a second body 300m distant. The rescuers were able to identify the first body as Copp and the second as Johnson. There was no sign of Dash, though rescuers later found some of his gear in the vicinity.

In the meantime four experienced American mountaineers, Eric DeCaria, Nick Martino, Steve Su, and Pete Takeda, who were close friends of the three climbers, had been busy arranging flights and obtaining visas in order to assist with the search. On the 11th they helped the Chinese remove both bodies from avalanche debris in a wide couloir leading toward the face. The search for Dash's body was eventually called off; the area, frequently bombarded by rockfall and avalanche, was deemed too dangerous, and by this time chances of locating Dash or his remains seemed unlikely.

LINDSAY GRIFFIN, *Mountain INFO*

Nyambo Konka (6,114m), east face, attempt. During the last week of April and the first week of May, a four-person New Zealand-American team, comprising Lydia Bradey, Kenny Gasch, Penny Goddard, and I, attempted the east face of Nyambo Konka. This beautiful summit lies just south of Minya Konka. During more than a fortnight of humping loads and climbing, we established two camps in the Bawang River Valley due north of Bawang Lake, then a further camp in the east face cirque, and one more on the face itself. We climbed the east face and reached the summit (north) ridge, but it was heavily corniced and too dangerous to allow us to reach the top. Descending, we were caught in two substantial snowstorms, the first dropping a foot of snow, the second, two feet.

Two notes: (1) our Liaison Officer, Lenny/Chen Zheng Lin, purportedly of the Ganzi Tibetan Autonomous Prefecture Mountaineering Association, made our trip almost impossible, throwing up roadblocks at every opportunity. We advise climbers not to use him; (2) after our close calls with excessive snowfall, and the deaths of Jonny Copp, Micah Dash and Wade Johnson in avalanches just a couple miles away, it is clear that climbing in the Daxue Shan should be attempted only in very late fall or very early spring.

MARK JENKINS, *AAC*

The northwest face of Nyambo Konka (6,114m). The summit is behind and to the left. The New Zealand-American attempt reached the crest of the north ridge (left skyline) from the far (east) side, off picture to the left. *Pedro Detjen*

The unclimbed north ridge of Nyambo Konka from close to the New Zealand-American exit point from the east face. *Mark Jenkins*

SOUTH OF MINYA KONKA

Ren Zhong Feng (6,079m). On November 28 Martin Ploug and I, from Denmark, made the first ascent of Ren Zhong Feng, a little-known peak that was believed to be one of the few remaining unclimbed 6,000m summits in Sichuan Province.

We established base camp at 3,100m in the Gan Gou Valley northeast of the mountain, and a higher camp at 4,500m.

Lydia Bradey and large rucksack high on the east face of Nyambo Konka. *Mark Jenkins*

Northwest face of Ren Zhong Feng. Marked is upper section of Danish route, which climbs hidden east face to crest of north ridge. From point where route joins ridge, it is still 1,500m to summit. *Pedro Detje*

We decided to climb alpine-style up the right side of the east face to gain the north ridge. Our third member, Carsten Cooper-Jensen, opted out, feeling he would slow us. With no prior acclimatization we climbed to 5,200m the first day, in an open gully. We spent the next day resting, to improve acclimatization, and on the following day climbed to a second bivouac, at 5,500m. We spent our third day on the crest of the north ridge, at 5,675m. We had overcome most of the technical difficulties and most of the altitude, but still needed to reach the summit. However, the ridge above was 1½ km long, and often sharp. A storm and bulletproof ice made it a long, tiring climb; we reached the summit at 5:30 p.m. It took 18 hours to climb to the top and return to the bivouac site. Although the summit altitude is officially given as 6,079m, our altimeters and GPS recorded ca 5,800m.

Martin Ploug leads final ice wall on east face to gain crest of north ridge of Ren Zhong Feng. *Kristoffer Szilas*

Looking back along north ridge of Ren Zhong Feng. In background is Minya Konka (7,556m), and to the right: Long Shan (6,684m); Chu I (6,466m); Chu II (6,483m); Zhong Shan (6,886m), and Tai (6,410m). *Kristoffer Szilas*

Descending during the night, Martin slipped while trying to place an ice screw and fell 30m down the 1,000m west face. Luckily, I managed the classic maneuver of jumping down the east face and thus holding him on the rope. He was battered and bruised but, assisted by painkillers, made it back to our top bivouac. We rested on the 29th, before descending to base camp on the 30th. We graded the 1,300m route, which was free from objective danger, TD M4 WI4.

Logistics went smoothly. Tom Nakamura had been helpful in supplying us with information, and we used the company, Sichuan Earth Expeditions, that he had employed when visiting the area. Unfortunately, we paid the Sichuan Mountaineering Association for a virgin 6,000er and were unable to convince them that we were entitled to a refund, as the peak is likely 200m lower.

KRISTOFFER SZILAS, *Denmark*

Martin Ploug on north ridge of Ren Zhong Feng. *Kristoffer Szilas*

Editor's Note: No photographs existed of this peak until autumn 2008, when Japanese explorer Tom Nakamura traveled to the Daxue Shan to inspect an unnamed 6,079m peak south of Minya Konka (AAJ 2009). Nakamura took photographs from the south and northeast and suggested the name Ren Zhong Feng, as the summit lies in the valley north of Ren Zhong Lake. Nakamura's photographs were widely published, resulting in two groups applying for permission to climb Ren Zhong Feng last autumn.

Hungarians Peter Csizmadia, Veronika Mikolovits, Balazs Pechtol, and Katalin Tolnay approached from the northeast via the Gang Gou Valley, setting up base camp at 3,100m and, on October 17, an advanced base at 3,900m. It is thought they then made a reconnaissance up-valley, but they were never seen again. The Sichuan Mountaineering Association organized a rescue party (and later a military helicopter search), and noted that on the 22nd, the last day of contact as indicated by the Hungarians' website, a large avalanche from collapsing seracs swept the upper valley between 5,200m and 5,500m.

The Danes were unaware that Hungarians were already on the mountain until two weeks before leaving Denmark. One week before their departure, they heard that the Hungarians were overdue. After arriving at the Hungarian base camp, the three offered their assistance but didn't go as far as the assumed incident site, which they felt was extremely exposed to serac avalanche.

The Danes' barometric altimeters and GPS recorded a summit height some 200m lower than the generally accurate Chinese PLA maps. However, the German Pedro Detjen, who has visited the region and published Michael Brandtner's fine book on the Minya Konka Group and Tom Nakamura's on the Tibetan "Alps," has checked satellite data, which he considers reliable. (Much work on this has been done by Jonathan de Ferranti; see www.viewfinderpanoramas.org.) Original unprocessed SRTM-Data does not produce a spot height for the summit but records the nearest point as 5,876m. Better, newly processed ASTER-Data shows the summit to be at 5,966m.

Qonglai Shan

Siguniang National Park

Siguniang (6,250m), south face, The Free Spirits. From November 23 to 27 Zhou Peng and I climbed the central south face of Siguniang (a.k.a. Yaomei Feng), the main peak of Siguniang Shan (Four Girls Mountains). In December 2008 the Chinese Ultimate Expedition attempted this line using fixed rope and reached 5,600m. Zhou and I were on that expedition. In February 2009 we made another attempt, this time alpine style, reaching 5,950m. Here Zhou was trying to climb the upper part of the icefall right of the central couloir, when it collapsed.

For our third attempt we again climbed alpine style, starting from Rilong on November 23 with sacks weighing less than 15kg. Local porters carried our sacks as high as the traditional base camp at 4,800m. We camped that evening at 5,130m, a short distance below the bergschrund at the foot of the south face. The forecast predicted bad weather on the afternoon of the 26th, and we weren't taking chances. On 24th we crossed the bergschrund and climbed the snow-covered rock buttress that separates the main couloir from a black, steeper, subsidiary runnel to the left. We simul-climbed most of the way to a bivouac at 5,700m, only belaying three pitches, on more difficult rock sections.

On the 25th we began our summit push a little after 8 a.m., climbing over the right side of the rock step between 5,900 and 5,950m. Above, we climbed four mixed pitches of mainly rock, and then breached the cornice onto the windy southwest ridge. The time was 4 p.m. From here we followed the crest to the south summit, arriving at 6:10 p.m. (Siguniang has three summits on a horizontal summit ridge; the south is marked as the highest on the Chinese 1:50,000 military map, courtesy of climber Ma Yihua.)

We planned to descend the route the same day, but the entire face below was threatened by falling debris and too dangerous to rap in the dark. We spent the night in a snow cave dug beneath a cornice at 6,130m. Next day the rock and ice fall got worse, but we descended anyway, reaching our tent at 5,130m and moving it farther from the mountain after we found nearby several pieces of rock that weren't there when we set out. On 27th we slept until 10:30 a.m. and trekked down the glacier and back to Rilong.

The 1,000m route, the first all-Chinese new line on Siguniang, had difficulties of AI3+ and M4. We named it The Free Spirits, which is the name of our climbing partnership.

Yan Dongdong, *China*

Editor's Note: The Free Spirits marks arguably the first time in mountaineering history that a Chinese pair has made an alpine-style first ascent of a big technical route on home ground, and on a line that had been attempted previously several times.

South Face of Siguniang above Changping Valley. Marked is the Free Spirits, with first and second bivouacs. For other lines on the face see *AAJ 2007* p.423. *Yan Dongdong/Ma Demin Collection.*

This line, which is not a straightforward snow/ice gully but a complex mixed affair with steep rock steps, was rumored to have been attempted by Russians some years ago and was definitely attempted by Russians in early October 2009, when the St Petersburg team of Alexey Gorbatenkov and Svetlana Gutsalo climbed alpine style up the buttress slightly right of the couloir before being hit by a big snowstorm, with thunder and lightning, which forced a retreat from 5,800m. Before this, in autumn 2006, guide Philippe Batoux and a "young alpinists" group from the French Alpine Club planned an attempt but found the line dry, with an imposing rock barrier towards the top. Instead they slanted left from its base to reach the upper southwest ridge and the1992 Japanese Route but did not continue to the summit. The first known serious attempt took place in April 2007, when a Korean team pushed to 5,650m using fixed ropes. But their camp at 5,200m was taken out by avalanche, forcing a retreat.

Chinese Ultimate Expedition members, who attempted the line in dry conditions during December 2008, reaching 5,600m with fixed ropes, were Li Hongxue, Yan Dongdong, Liu Yunfeng, Wang Ting, and Zhou Peng. At about the same time Gu Jie, Luo Biao, and Sun Bin tried a line similar to the French attempt, reaching 5,750m, while Cai Yu, Ji Xing, Peng Xiaolong, Zhang Yusheng, Zhao Jianshan, and Zheng Chaohui attempted the Original 1981 Japanese Route up the southeast ridge, reaching 5,900m.

Siguniang (6,250m), northwest face, Bloody Sunset. Our expedition began as nine Russians from Irkutsk, Moscow, and St Petersburg. However, at base camp Evgeny Korol caught a cold that quickly developed into pulmonary edema, and we had to evacuate him rapidly. The St Petersburg team, Alexey Gorbatenkov and Svetlana Gutsalo, made an alpine-style attempt on a direct route up Siguniang's south face. They followed the buttress to the right of the line later climbed by Chinese, but were hit by a big snowstorm with thunder and lightning and retreated from ca 5,800m.

On October 5 the Irkutsk team of Evgeny Bashkirtsev and Denis Veretenin, with the team of Vladimir Molodozhen from St Petersburg and Valery Shamalo, Denis Sushko, and I from Moscow, started up the northwest buttress. The aim was to climb directly this steep rock pillar right of the 2002 Fowler-Ramsden route, the Inside Line (ca 1,100m, WI6). While our four-man team took the only obvious crack system that extends the height of the face, the guys from Irkutsk began 100m to the left. [Editor's note: They probably followed the line tried in 2005 by Chad Kellogg, Joe Puryear, and Stoney Richards, the only party to have previously attempted this 900m buttress. The buttress tops out a little below 6,000m, where it joins the right-slanting snow ramp of the Inside Line.]

Over two days both teams completed four pitches but were then hit by the storm that forced the pair on the south face to retreat. Avalanches pounded our portaledge, and we spent all night clearing snow to prevent damage to our shelter. In the morning we saw the Irkutsk pair retreating. They told us by radio that a heavy avalanche had scored a direct hit and broken their portaledge. Bashkirtsev was not belayed and did well to keep himself on the ledge. After that our team of four experienced snow every night, keeping us awake half the time.

This wall gets little sun, less with the frequent bad weather, and the temperature was always below 0°C. The temperature gradient itself was drastic; we felt every 100m of height gained. I've never experienced that before, and wonder if it is connected with Siguniang being 500m higher than neighboring summits.

The northwest face of Siguniang. The lower peak to the left is Siguniang North (5,700m). (1) The Inside Line. (2) Bloody Sunset. (3) Southwest ridge (1,900m, 5.11 A2 AI3+ M5, Johnson-Kellogg, 2008). For other lines and past attempts see p. 422, *AAJ 2007*). *Andrey Muryshev*

Starting the northwest buttress by the only obvious line running the height of the face. *Andrey Muryshev.*

boring summits. Near the top the cold was fierce (we had no thermometer but I suspect it could have been as low as -30°C). We all got frostbitten toes, though without serious consequence.

Free-climbing was impossible, and we typically made only one pitch a day. It was much slower than planned, but we were so keen to reach the summit that we sacrificed our return

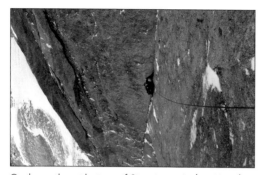
On the northwest buttress of Siguniang. *Andrey Muryshev*

flight tickets to do so. Had the weather been good, the route has enough features for long sections to be free-climbed. But we either had to aid the cracks with pins or clear them of ice so we could use cams. Near half-height we were forced to use skyhooks and the drill on a 100m compact section.

After 14 pitches, with time running out, we moved left to join the Fowler-Ramsden couloir. Life immediately got better; on the first full day in the couloir we climbed four pitches, and on the day after pushed for the summit. However, we had underestimated the amount of climbing remaining. It was delicate, thin ice over rock, and Denis spent three hours on one pitch, taking two falls, one of 15m. We fixed a rope and returned to the portaledge.

Next day, October 21, Denis felt too tired to continue, so only Valery and Vladimir went for the summit, reaching it at 5 p.m. Denis and I followed on the 22nd, then we all descended our route. It is the logical way down, as the buttress is solid and steep, the Fowler-Ramsden couloir is exposed to stonefall in the lower section, and we already had at least one bolt on each belay.

We named our route Bloody Sunset (1,150m, VI A4 90°). It has 14 pitches on rock, and then four steep ice and mixed pitches in the upper couloir to reach the snow/ice ramp, which although steep, proved to be comparatively straightforward. This route was the hardest big-wall effort of my life, and I was pleased when we were awarded first prize in the Russian Championships.

ANDREY MURYSHEV, *Russia*

Wuse Shan, Another Day. On February 10, 2010, Li Lan and I summited Wuse Shan ("Five Colors Mountain," 5,430m) via the south face. The North Face sponsored our climb. The peak had been attempted several times, but we believe our ascent was the first. We named the route Another Day (V 5.9+, 18 pitches). It's serious because of poor rock, especially in the lower limestone folds, and a constant threat of stonefall.

Located between Shuangqiao and Changping Valleys, Wuse got its name because of the many layers of different rock types visible on the peak, especially on the sunny south face. At the bottom there is limestone, above that is shale, and then granite to the summit. The limestone and shale are folded into a striped U, which can be seen from the road a few kilometers down Shuangqiao Valley (a popular ice-climbing area). Geologically, this face must be spectacular.

On February 8 we trekked from Shuangqiao Lodge to the foot of the talus slope beneath the face and set up camp at 4,800m. Leaving at 7:45 next morning, we scrambled up talus for an hour, only to find the limestone above impossible to protect or to climb. Handholds broke into powder in our fingers, so we struck out right, following the U shape for seven pitches of mostly easy 5th- and 4th-class climbing. However, protection was scarce and rockfall frequent. To the left a gap in the folds appeared and we climbed through it to reach more broken, featured shale. Two pitches brought us to a granite buttress. We traversed right along the base, and then scrambled

Striated south face of Wuse Shan. (1) Another Day. (2) Rappel descent. (B1) Bivouac on ascent and (B2) on descent. *Yan Dongdong*

Li Lan on west summit of Wuse Shan. In background is unclimbed Goromity (Riyue Baojing, Treasure Mirror or Left-hand Trumpet Shell, 5,609m). *Yan Dongdong*

up 4th-class rock for two more pitches before bivouacking.

On the 10th we began climbing at 8:15 a.m. The first half pitch was scrambling, but then it was continuous 5.7 until on our fifth pitch of the day, where we cut left onto a spur. The 6th pitch provided the crux of the climb, featuring an exposed traverse followed by 20m of vertical rock leading back to the crest of the spur. Above, a further half pitch led to one of twin summits; another summit to the east looked identical in height to the one we were on and less than a ropelength away. It was past 1:00 p.m., and the other summit looked hard to reach, so we didn't give it a try.

We started down our route at 2 p.m. The ropes stuck on the first rappel, and while Li Lan was prussiking to retrieve them, a piece of rock flew down and hit me close to the left eye, drawing blood. Because of the delay caused by this and the rope jam, we didn't get off the face before nightfall and didn't dare try continuing in the dark. The gas canister was still ¼ full, so we bivouacked about a pitch lower than the previous night, where there was snow to melt. (We had used up the bit of snow at the previous spot). The next day we rappelled seven more pitches to the talus. The ropes stuck again, on the penultimate rappel, and because the pitch mostly overhung and one rope end was out of reach, it was more than frustrating. Fortunately, we had dragged down just enough of the other rope that it was possible to sling a horn, tie the rope to the sling, and rap the last 15m on a single strand.

Li Lan is perhaps China's only true female alpinist—the only Chinese woman ready to lead a technical pitch on a high mountain. This was only our second climb together, and I got away with leading all the pitches. We might have simul-climbed some ground and made better time if we had known each other better. The previous month we had failed on a new route up the west side of Chibu (5,430m), a few kilometers north of Wuse. Maybe we'll try to finish it in September, when it should be warm enough to wear rock shoes.

Yan Dongdong, *China*

Tibet

CHANG TANG

Mayer Kangri and Jomo Ri massifs, reconnaissance, Mayer Kangri I East (6,053m). On September 23, 2008, Grzegorz Chwola and I flew from Kathmandu to Lhasa intending to reach the Mayer Kangri Massif on the Chang Tang plateau. As far as we could ascertain, these isolated mountains remained unexplored. Although the highest peak (6,266m, N 33°24', E 86°46') is called Mayer Kangri I on contemporary Western maps of Tibet and on Chinese road maps, it is referred to as Bonvalet Peak on Russian maps. Frenchman Gabriel Bonvalet was the first foreign traveler to see the mountain, during his journey through the Chang Tang and the central Arka Tagh in 1889-90, and the name Bonvalet Peak is also used on the map in Sven Hedin's book *Trans-Himalaya* (1909).

About 120km to the northwest lies the Zangser Kangri Group, whose highest summit (6,460m) was first climbed in 1990 by a Japanese-Tibetan expedition (*AAJ 1991*) and repeated in alpine style in 1997 by Frank Kauper and Stefan Simmerer during an unsupported south-north crossing of the Chang Tang (*AAJ 1998*). Three-hundred km to the east-northeast lies Purog Kangri, named the Dupleix Mountains by Bonvalet, who thought they were around 8,000m in elevation. The official altitude is 6,482 on the Chinese map (6,435m on the Russian): this is a different Purog Kangri to the one climbed by a Canadian-Danish-Swedish party in 2008 (*AAJ 2009*), which is part of the Zangser Kangri. Immediately southeast of Mayer Kangri, across the Kyarub Tsangpo, stands the Jomo Ri Massif. Four summits are over 6,000m, with the highest, Jomo I, indicated as 6,015m on the Russian map. The Kyarub Tsangpo was encountered by Jules Detreuil de Rhins and Ferdinand Grenard, who out of all the early explorers came closest to Mayer Kangri during their travels in 1893-94.

No Western traveler appears to have visited this region before the famous American biologist George Schaller. He made several journeys to the Chang Tang from 1987 to '94. The publicity he gave the region bore fruit, as in 1993 a 300,000 sq km Chang Tang reserve was created. Schaller includes reports of his journeys in his *Tibet's Hidden Wilderness: Wildlife and Nomads of the Chang Tang Reserve* (1997), In autumn 2008 Chinese Juntao Jiang made a cycle trip in the Jomo Ri region and posted photos in a Picasa Web album under the name of "Single Singer "(2008 Tibet).

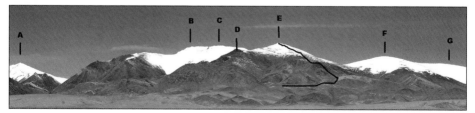

Highest peaks of Mayer Kangri Massif from the east. (A) Mayer Kangri IV (6,120m). (B) Mayer Kangri I (6,286m). (C) Peak 6,200m. (D) Peak ca 5,900m. (E) Mayer Kangri I East (6,065m). First ascent route marked. (F) Mayer Kangri II South (6,165m). (G) Mayer Kangri II North (6,120m). *Janusz Majer.*

Highest peaks of unclimbed Jomo Ri Massif. (A) Peak 5,600m. (B) Peak 5,800m. (C) Peak 5,480m. (D) Jomo Ri III (6,000m). (E) Jomo Ri II (6,010m). (F) Peak ca 5,900m. (G) Jomo Ri (6,015m). (H) Peak 5,800m). (KT) Kyarub Tsangpo. *Grzegorz Chwola*

Second highest sector of Jomo Ri Massif, seen from the northwest. Valley 2 on map separates this group of summits from highest peaks. (A) Peak 5,600m. (B) Peak 5,650m. (C) Jomo Ri IV (ca 6,002m). (D) Peak 5,950m. (E) Peak 5,700m. (F) Peak 5,600m. (G) Peak 5,720m. (H) Peak 5,500m. *Grzegorz Chwola*

On September 24, with two drivers, a guide, and a cook, we traveled in two Toyota Land Cruisers to Shigatse. From there we first had to reach the village of Nyima. Next day we headed north to the Kiku La (5,120m, N 30°14.941', E 89°18.340') in the Nyanchen Tanglha West but were stopped on the pass by Chinese police, who told us Shainzi District was closed to foreigners. We returned to Lhasa to try another route.

On the 27th we drove north on the Lhasa-Golmud highway to Nakchu and the next day turned west onto the prairie. Passing Baingoin and Serling Tso Lake, we reached Nyima, where we refueled the vehicles. Turning north, on October 1 we crossed a pass (4,900m, N 32°39.974', E 86°31.035'), got our first glimpse of Mayer Kangri, and descended to the last settlement, Rongma. We continued, crossing another pass, and after a night out took one of the Toyotas and went to look for a base camp. We found it close to the southeast flank of the range at 5,057m (N 33°24.776', E 86°48.760') and set up camp the same day. Nighttime temperatures here fell as low as -15°C. After reconnaissance to 5,700m on the hills south of Mayar Kangri, on October 5 we climbed to the east ridge of Mayar Kangri I. I stopped at 5,865m, but Grzegorz continued to the summit of Mayer Kangri I East (6,053m).

On the 6th we drove with nomads on motorbikes to the northern side of the massif, and the next day made a trip towards the Jomo Ri mountains to take more photographs. The day after, we left base camp and retraced our approach as far as Baingoin, where we took a different route back to Lhasa, via the well-known lake of Namtso and Largen La to the Golmud-Lhasa Road. We were back in Kathmandu on the 16th.

JANUSZ MAJER, *Poland*

NYANCHEN TANGLHA EAST

Nyanchen Tanglha East and Kangri Garpo ranges, exploration. Tsuyoshi Nagai, Tadao Shintani, and I returned from Tibet in November, after five weeks and 4,800km of travel. Accompanied by Zhang Jiyue of Sichuan Earth Expeditions, we had been exploring unknown peaks and glaciers in the Nyanchen Tanglha East and Kangri Garpo. The trip was not only satisfactory but enchanting, in spite of strict control of foreigners entering prohibited areas off the main road—the Sichuan-Tibet Highway—by the Public Security Bureau. Our Tibetan guide was most capable and helpful in negotiating with PSB officials. Blue sky welcomed us wherever we went, and I was fortunate enough to bring back plenty of photos of new peaks and glaciers, news, and stories. We explored three unfrequented valleys in Nyanchen Tanglha East and one in Kangri Garpo West. Two of them were unknown to foreigners since the early 20th century, and in one we were the first foreign visitors. Specifically, the areas we visited were Aigagong Glacier in the Niwu Qu of the upper Yi'gong Tsangpo; Lake Jambo Tso and Maraipo Glacier in Jingling

West face of Gutonchalagebo (5,511m), Botoi Tsang-po, north of Bomi. *Tamotsu Nakamura*

North face of Kang Ri Karpo (ca 5,800m), above headwaters of Dongchu Valley. *Tamotsu Nakamura*

East face of unnamed ca 5,800m peak, seen from Shiargung La, Jingling District. *Tamotsu Nakamura*

North face of unnamed 6,018m peak above left bank of Maraipo Glacier. *Tamotsu Nakamura*

District; Yuri North Glacier in the Botoi Tsangpo, north of Bomi; and Dongchu Tsangpo southwest of Songzong. The first three lie in the Nyanchen Tanglha, while the fourth, in the area with no previous foreign visit, is situated east of Namcha Barwa in the Kangri Garpo.

TAMOTSU NAKAMURA, *Japanese Alpine News*

A map of these travels and a greater selection of photographs appear on the Journal *website.*

KANGRI GARPO MOUNTAINS

Lopchin (Kangri Garpo II). In the autumn a joint expedition from the Alpine Club of Kobe University (ACKU) and the Mountaineering Association of China University of Geosciences (Wuhan, CUG) made the first ascent of Kangri Garpo II (KG II, 6,703m on old Soviet maps, 6,805m GPS). Lying a little northwest of Kangri Garpo I or Ruoni (Bairiga, 6,882m), KG II is the second highest summit in the Eastern Kangri Garpo mountains, and the only one of more than 30 6,000m peaks to have been climbed.

Lopchin (KG II, 6,805m, left) and KG III (6,726m) seen from Camp 1 on Ata Glacier at 4,890m. Moon is setting behind unclimbed KG III. Route on first ascent of Lopchin took left skyline. *Tatsuo Inoue*

East-northeast face of unclimbed Ruoni (6,882m), highest peak in Kangri Garpo, seen from 5,050m on Ata Glacier. *Tatsuo Inoue*

The expedition comprised two Tibetans and eight Chinese led by Dong Fan and seven Japanese led by me. Nine members were students. After a three-day, 920km drive from Lhasa to Lhagu and an additional one-day walk, we established base camp on October 18 in a moraine valley close to the snout of the north tongue of the Ata Glacier (4,320m, N 29°13.17', E 96°49.19'). Ten porters, who each ferried loads seven times, quickly established a deposit camp at 4,400m, below the first icefall.

It was obvious there had been little snowfall during the summer and early autumn, which was unusual. Trekkers and climbers who have visited the region in October and November report heavy snowfall and frequent avalanches. The Kobe University attempts on Ruoni in 2003 (*AAJ 2004*) and 2007 (*AAJ 2008*) were defeated by bad weather and excessive snow. These expeditions reported 40-50cm of fresh snow each night for periods of three or four

Eastern Kangri Garpo seen from 5,050m on Ata Glacier. On left is KG 27 (ca 5,850m), while fine pointed peak is KG 26 (ca 6,000m). Behind it and to right is Gheni (6,150m). *Tatsuo Inoue*

days. In contrast our expedition experienced a maximum of only 10cm on the glacier, which was quickly melted by strong sunshine. Although we had only two perfect days and over 20 snowy ones, no snow accumulated on the glacier. This had its good and bad points: glacier travel was relatively easy, but higher, where temperatures remained lower, deep snow on the ridges made for hard work and dangerous conditions.

Advanced base was sited on the 22nd at 4,660m, above the first icefall and crevasse maze. This site experienced wind-blown snow, as deep as 130cm, deposited from the south tongue of the Ata. In contrast, when we established Camp 1 (4,890m) on the 29th at the confluence of the three upper glacier forks, we placed the tents on bare ice. Above we fixed 600m of rope through the second icefall and placed Camp 2 at 5,680m.

On November 5 five members left Camp 2 at 3:30 a.m. under a full moon. Strong wind, deep snow, and difficult crevasses slowed progress, and three returned. Deqing Ouzhu and Ciren Danda, Tibetan students with the CUG, continued up the southeast ridge of KG II and reached its summit at at 1:18 p.m. in a mist. Above the col on the main divide between Ruoni and KG II (we refer to these two peaks and KG III as the Three Ata Sisters), the ridge was wide and gently angled to ca 6,300m. Above, it became steeper (average of 40°) and covered with deep, soft snow; not difficult but avalanche prone.

In the meantime, four Japanese had established Camp 3 on the col at 5,910m and prepared to climb next day. However, it remained windy and snowy, but on the 7th they had a lucky break, with a clear and relatively calm day. Koichiro Kondo and Masanori Yazaki left Camp 3 and reached the summit at 3:36 p.m., returning after dark at 8 p.m. Later, after consultation with the village leader of nearby Rhagu, we agreed to name KG II Lopchin (Lopchin Feng in Tibetan, Lou bu qin in Chinese), which means "male white hawk."

TATSUO "TIM" INOUE. *Japan*

HIMALAYA

ROLWALING HIMAL

Gaurishankar (7,135m), south summit, northeast face, attempt. After much negotiation with the CTMA, Kazuya Hiraide and I secured a permit to climb Gaurishankar in the autumn. Still we had a difficult time getting to the northeast side of this mountain. Our approach was up the Rongshar and Menlung valleys, but each time we tried to move forward, Chinese Police or Army would stop us for no good reason. We persevered with negotiations and were eventually allowed to continue. Many expeditions have failed to reach this side of the mountain, either because of political problems or climatic conditions.

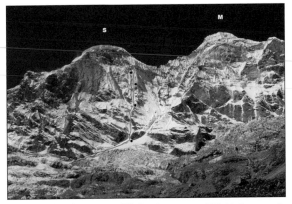

Gaurishankar from east. (S) South summit. (M) Main summit. Attempted route and bivouac sites marked. Ascents of south summit have finished up left skyline. Northeast rib leading to northeast ridge forms right skyline. Japanese planned to attempt east face to left of rib/ridge, directly below main summit. *Kei Taniguchi*

Talking about the weather, if you go too early, the east and northeast faces will be too dry, with much rockfall; if you are too late in the season, it may not be possible to get up the Rongshar Valley, due to snow.

On October 22 we arrived at base camp on Menlung meadow and then made several reconnaissance and acclimatization trips. We had planned to climb the east face to the main summit but found that, after the long period of prevailing good weather, the mountain had become quite dry, with little snow and ice. Seracs in the upper section were unstable. To the right the northeast rib rises to join the long northeast ridge at ca 6,200m. We first climbed the smaller, triangular northeast face, which lies between rib and ridge. Conditions were poor, so we changed our plan. We moved well left of the east face and attempted the northeast face of the 7,010m south summit. Leaving base camp on November 5, we found a way through the icefall to the bottom of the face. On the 7th we began climbing, following a line of couloirs with thin, rotten ice and sugary snow. After four days we had reached 6,850m, just below the summit ridge, but couldn't solve the problem of the crux rock band. With little food and fuel left, we retreated. During our descent on the 11th, the weather changed, and it began to snow.

Kazuya Hiraide tackles steep ice high on northeast face of Gaurishankar South. *Kei Taniguchi*

KEI TANIGUCHI, *Japan*

Editor's Note: in September 1997 Taeko and Yasushi Yamanoi climbed the north flank of the northeast ridge, reaching the crest and a high point of 6,300m, where it becomes steep, narrow, and mushroomed. They witnessed many serac falls and avalanches on this side of the mountain and recommended a visit later in the year. In early October 2005 Jess and John Roskelly appear to have tried this ridge from its base but gave up at only 5,450m because the rock was terribly loose and did not appear to improve. The south summit has had several ascents from Nepal since the first in 1979 by Pete Boardman, Pemba Lama, Tim Leach, and Guy Neithardt.

Malaysia

Tioman Island, Dragon's Horns, west face, Beckwith-Traver Route. On July 17 Mathew Traver and I traveled to the Malaysian Island of Tioman in the South China Sea. Our objective was the first ascent of the west face of Dragon's Horns (Bukit Nekek Semekut), a big wall rising from the canopy of the rainforest on the south coast of the island. The Horns (693m) are two grano-diorite towers and, according to legend, are the resting place of a mythical Chinese princess who decided to stop there while flying to her prince in Singapore. When seen from the west, the southeast arête shows a distinct nose, mouth, and forehead, presumably forming her face.

Getting to the closest village, Mukut, proved straightforward though time-consuming. Reliable buses run from Singapore and Kuala Lumpur to the port of Mersing, the main embarkation point for Tioman Island. A regular ferry service connects Mersing and Genting on Tioman, though the ferry operator saw fit to charge us an additional two passages for our five haul bags.

From Genting we hitched a ride on a fishing boat to the tiny village of Mukut, arriving on the 19th with our five bags and supplies for the wall. It took 10 days' trail-cutting through the undergrowth to reach the base of the west face and a further six days of ferrying loads to install ourselves at our jungle base camp, which became affectionately known as the "Trench" on account of its dank, muddy, and insect-infested nature.

South Dragon's Horn, Tioman Island. (1) Beckwith-Traver Route on the west face. (2) Approximate line of Waking Dream on the south face. *Matthew Traver*

The approach had been physically and mentally draining. The heat and humidity, coupled with the repetitive nature of load-carrying, had us both suffering from exhaustion. After a few days rest in Mukut, we headed back into the jungle to begin fixing.

We scrambled up 3rd- and 4th-class gullies to the base of the South Dragon's Horn and fixed two pitches to a large forested terrace. A good system of cracks led from the center of the terrace toward a conspicuous overhang dubbed the Great Roof. We fixed an additional two pitches from the terrace, before hauling our bags to the high point. We then pulled our ropes and went capsule-style.

Matthew Traver hooks a hollow flake toward the Great Roof. *Steve Beckwith*

We made a long hook traverse beneath the roof to reach a clean corner-crack. This led to a seam, which we climbed on aid to cross the roof. This section proved to be the most challenging and time-consuming of the route. The aid, primarily on hooks and marginal gear, took 12 hours to complete. The remainder of the route was a mixture of free climbing and moderate aid. Protection on the free pitches was poor and spaced, the climbing characterized by water-warn pockets and grooves, often friable. The majority of the aid pitches required multiple hooking and/or thin placements. Matt suffered an inflammation of the ankle when three days in, which not only restricted his mobility, but also coincided with a fever and an illness. Fortunately, as we were 400m up the route, it passed quickly.

Our planned exit was blocked by large blocks, perched precariously above the portaledge and belay. Not willing to risk dislodging them, we instead climbed through blocky overhangs to a curving crack that brought us to a steep and exposed wall. Three long pitches took us to the summit, which we reached on August 19.

From the time we launched capsule style, it took five days to reach the top. It took another day to rappel the route, regain the Trench, and shuttle out most of our load in a single push. We called our line the Beckwith-Traver Route (13 pitches, 5.10 A3). Throughout our time on the wall the weather was mostly dry, though often windless and a scorching 35°C.

From high on the face we could see deep into the untouched interior of the island. To the northwest lay Mumbar Peak, featuring a wall, estimated to be nearly 800m high, rising out of the forest to the summit plateau. Projecting from the top was a series of spires. Farther into the dense forest a number of smaller walls rose into needle-like spires. And the North Dragon's Horn remains unattempted.

Steve Beckwith *UK*

Editor's note: Prior to the arrival of the British pair, there was only one established route on the entire island, Waking Dream on the south face of South Dragon's Horn. This 10-pitch climb was put up in 1999 by Scotty Nelson and Nick Tomlin at 5.9 and A2; it was repeated in 2002 by Malaysians Rosmann and Sharin, supported by Abudullah Danial, Akmal Noor, and Al Haleq. These five created an important, mostly free, variant above half-height; the climb attracted so much national attention that the ascent made front-page news in the Malaysian Star. In 2004 Americans Hank Jones and Dave Sharratt visited the island and made the third ascent. After working the route, they eventually climbed it free in a single push at 5.13a.

The never-attempted 3,300m west face of Namcha Barwa (7,782m) in the Great Bend of the Brahmaputra River, Tibet. Photo taken from Se Ti La (4,500m). *Tamotsu Nakamura*

AMERICAN ALPINE CLUB GRANTS

The American Alpine Club provides resources for climbers and explorers to attempt new challenges, conduct scientific research, and conserve mountain environments. The AAC awards more than $40,000 annually, although the size and number of awards vary from year to year. For more information on all the

Hunting for a bivy on Xuelian West. *Jed Brown*

grant programs, please visit www.AmericanAlpineClub. org. The information below about 2009 grant recipients and their objectives was accurate at the time of the grant; in some cases, they may have decided to attempt other objectives. Expeditions labeled with an asterisk (*) are reported in this *Journal*.

LYMAN SPITZER CUTTING-EDGE AWARDS

Kyle Dempster, Salt Lake City, Utah
*Northern Tien Shan, China**
$2,500

Pat Goodman, Banner Elk, North Carolina
Peak 5,592m, China
$1,500

Toby Grohne, Jackson, Wyoming
Northwest face of Siguniang, China
$1,500

Joe Puryear, Leavenworth, Washington
*Lunag Ri, Nepal**
$2,000

Pete Takeda, Boulder, Colorado
Pumari Chhish East, Pakistan
$2,500

Dave Turner, Sacramento, California
*Sam Ford Fjord, Baffin Island**
$2,000

MCNEILL-NOTT AWARDS

Nate Farr, Camas, Washington
*Caraz II, Cordillera Blanca, Peru**
$1,500

Caroline George, Salt Lake City, Utah
Pharilapche, Nepal
$1,000

Brianna Hartzell, Bellevue, Washington
*Desire Mountain, British Columbia**
$1,500

Tyler Jones, Sun Valley, Idaho
"Forgotten Wall," Denali, Alaska
$1,500

Zack Smith, Boulder, Colorado
*Kichatna Spire, Alaska**
$1,500

MOUNTAIN FELLOWSHIPS (FALL 2008)

Dustin English, Anchorage, Alaska
Pika Glacier, Alaska
$1,000

Josh Hoeschen, Anchorage, Alaska
Pika Glacier, Alaska
$1,000

Aaron Jones, Richmond, Kentucky
Howser Towers, British Columbia
$300

Walter Mackey, Boulder, Colorado
Torres del Paine, Chile
$1,000

Althea Rogers, Bozeman, Montana
Torres del Paine, Chile
$500

Todd Tumolo, Anchorage, Alaska
Pika Glacier, Alaska
$1,000

MOUNTAIN FELLOWSHIPS (SPRING 2009)

Mason Earle, Concord, Massachusetts
Cerro Catedral, Chile
$600

Joe Forrester, Castle Rock, Colorado
Chambe Peak, Malawi*
$600

Brianna Hartzell, Bellevue, Washington
Desire Mountain, British Columbia*
$850

Blake Herrington, Vancouver, Washington
North Taku Tower, Alaska*
$850

Jeremy Roop, Lambertville, New Jersey
Chambe Peak, Malawi*
$600

Nathan Smith, Salt Lake City, Utah
Jebel Shams, Oman
$400

Sevve Stember, Bemidji, Minnesota
Wild Cat Point, California
$500

ZACK MARTIN BREAKING BARRIERS GRANT

Matt Hepp, Ouray, Colorado
Demonstration earthquake shelters and granite towers in Pakistan*
$1,500

SCOTT FISCHER CONSERVATION GRANT

Cullen Kirk, Grand Canyon, Arizona
Patagonia Sustainable Trails Project
$450

NIKWAX ALPINE BELLWETHER GRANT

Ann Piersall, Whitefish, Montana
Socio-ecological dimensions of glacial retreat in the Tien Shan, Kyrgyzstan
$2,000

Tracie Seimon, Nyack, New York
World's highest amphibian populations' response to climate change, Peruvian Andes
$1,000

RESEARCH GRANTS

Sean Collett, American Fork, Utah
Reproduction of quaking aspen in mountainous landscapes of the western U.S.
$600

Paul Firth, Boston, Massachusetts
Effects of extreme altitude on the mental cognition of climbers
$500

Kevin Ford, Seattle, Washington
High-elevation alpine meadows' response to climate change
$2,000

Caitlyn Florentine, Bozeman, Montana
Paleoclimate records in relic ice layers within rock glaciers
$850

Nathan Furman, Salt Lake City, Utah
Risk-taking decisions of backcountry skiers in avalanche terrain
$1,000

Jon Kedrowski, San Marcos, Texas
Crowding and climber-induced hazards in Denali National Park
$1,000

Dave Ohlson, Seattle, Washington
Precise location of Vittorio Sella photographic positions near K2 to determine glacial changes in the past 100 years
$1,000

Ann Piersall, Whitefish, Montana
Socio-economic impact of glacial retreat on village water supplies in the Tien Shan
$1,000

Christopher Serenari, Raleigh, North Carolina
Interviewing local mountain guides in the Garhwal Himalaya, India, to assist their communications with western tourists
$1,800

BOOK REVIEWS

EDITED BY DAVID STEVENSON

K2: Life and Death on the World's Most Dangerous Mountain. ED VIESTURS, WITH DAVID ROBERTS. BROADWAY BOOKS, 2009. 342 PAGES. COLOR AND BLACK & WHITE PHOTOS. HARDCOVER $26.00.

K2: Lies and Treachery. ROBERT MARSHALL. CARREG LIMITED, 2009. 232 PAGES. BLACK & WHITE PHOTOS. HARDCOVER £20.00 (IN UK; U.S. PRICE VARIES, $26.00 OR HIGHER).

These two books, though different in approach, enrich the K2 literature. Ed Viesturs, one of the world's most accomplished high-altitude climbers, teams with David Roberts to focus on the "six most dramatic seasons in the mountain's history." These include the classic pioneering efforts in 1938, 1939, 1953 and 1954, and the disastrous 1986 and 2008 seasons, when a total of 24 climbers lost their lives. Viesturs' aim is not merely to tell the stories of those campaigns, but to "glean their lessons." This fine book, in Viesturs' evocative phrase, is a "hymn of praise" to K2, the most difficult and dangerous of the 8,000 meter peaks. It will absorb readers from start to finish.

The springboard for Viesturs was his own 1992 climb of K2. On his summit day, he made what he calls the greatest mistake of his climbing life. Instead of retreating in the face of deteriorating weather, he kept going. This was not the result of a decision, but the opposite, his "perverse inability to make a decision." He, Scott Fischer, and Charley Mace eventually summited in sunshine, but their descent into a maelstrom of clouds became a desperate epic, complicated not only by the storm and avalanche conditions that nearly engulfed them, but their moral obligation to assist the pulmonary edema-stricken Gary Ball down the mountain. Viesturs came away from that K2 experience a changed person, making a vow that he rigidly followed for 13 more years, in completing his quest of the remaining 8,000-meter peaks: *Your instincts are telling you something. Trust them and listen to them.*

Most readers will be familiar with the two American attempts on K2 in the late 1930s and the most storied of them all—the 1953 "Brotherhood of the Rope" saga—but Viesturs and Roberts add to our knowledge with their combined perspective. What makes this book so compelling, though, is how ably Viesturs uses his own K2 experience to assess, measure, and reflect on what his predecessors went through. We gain renewed appreciation of those magnificent efforts. His inclusion of entries from Dee Molenaar's expedition diary illuminates prior accounts of the 1953 expedition and shows his true grit. Clearly homesick, Molenaar felt the pull of his family, but refused to succumb to the "crumping" that lets the hardship and danger of expedition life drain a climber of ambition.

This book also provides a needed corrective to Putnam and Kauffman's *K2: The 1939 Trag-*

edy on the subject of Fritz Wiessner's leadership of that ill-fated expedition. The fact that Wiessner led from the front is consistent with other pioneering Himalayan expeditions, such as Maurice Herzog on Annapurna. In Viesturs' view, Wiessner not only made the right decision to turn back at 27,500 feet when his Sherpa companion, Pasang Dawa Lama, refused to go higher, but the morally responsible one. For this he rightly admires Wiessner more than if he had reached the summit. Finally, Viesturs powerfully describes the role of Sherpas on K2, both in 1939, when three of them did not return from a heroic effort to save the life of the stranded Dudley Wolfe, and in 2008, when Pemba Gyalje and his compatriots acted similarly to rescue climbers after tons of debris fell from the huge ice cliff above the Bottleneck, obliterating the fixed ropes. Two of the Sherpas died in the process. Their acts of heroism deserve to be as hallowed in K2's history as the 1953 expedition's valiant attempt to bring Art Gilkey down the Abruzzi Ridge.

Robert Marshall's *K2: Lies and Treachery* is concerned with a single K2 expedition, the Italian ascent in 1954, when Achille Compagnoni and Lino Lacedelli became the first persons to stand on the summit. What happened high on K2 the last two days of July stirred up a bitter controversy lasting over five decades. At the center of the storm was Walter Bonatti, in Ed Viestur's estimation "one of the most phenomenally gifted climbers of all time." The trouble started with a selfless act of Bonatti and his Hunza companion, Mahdi, that made success possible. They carried up two 42-pound loads of bottled oxygen 2,300 feet to where it had been agreed the two summit climbers would place their highest camp. But when Compagnoni and Lacedelli moved the campsite just far enough away to prevent Bonatti from reaching it, he and Mahdi were forced to endure an open bivouac at 26,568 feet before descending the next morning. Both men survived the bitterly cold night, Bonatti remarkably unscathed but Mahdi with severely frostbitten extremities.

Then the lies started, with Compagnoni's dubious claim that he and Lacedelli had run out of oxygen 650 feet below the summit because Bonatti had used the precious gas during his bivouac, intending to go to the summit himself. In leader Ardito Desio's official account, the summit pair are described as yelling to Bonatti to "leave the masks" with the oxygen bottles, falsely asserting that this vital equipment was in Bonatti's possession, when in fact Compagnoni and Lacedelli had them. They also falsely claimed an earlier start time to fit the bogus oxygenless finish to the climb. Bonatti became the sacrificial victim of what amounted to a cover-up to assuage the consternation of Pakistani authorities about the permanent injuries Mahdi suffered. With astonishing dedication, Bonatti spent the next 50 years clearing his name and establishing the facts, finally officially accepted in 2007 by the CAI (Club Alpino Italiano).

This long battle was mostly fought alone, but Bonatti was fortunate that Marshall, an Australian surgeon who had never climbed a mountain, took up his cause. Marshall became so proficient in Italian that he was able to produce a better English translation of Bonatti's two prior autobiographical volumes and combine them, in 2001, as *The Mountains of My Life*, adding an important new section on Bonatti's writings in response to the attack on his character. It was Marshall's careful analysis of photos of Compagnoni and Lacedelli on the summit that buttressed Bonatti's contention that the pair had lied not only about their oxygen running out below the summit but also their placement of the highest camp and the start time for the summit. In this book, Marshall brings the story up to date with an exhaustive, comprehensive account, including the remarkable denouement.

After maintaining silence for all those years, Lacedelli startlingly revealed his own version in 2004 (published in English as *K2: The Price of Conquest*, 2006). Although he still claimed that the oxygen had run out below the summit, he conceded this had happened at a point above which "the climb was less steep," much higher than where he and Compagnoni had always claimed. This is a significant admission, because the final slope becomes less steep only after the low-angle summit ridge is attained, a few easy steps from the top. Aside from the oxygen issue, Lacedelli—unlike Compagnoni, who went to his grave in 2009 still proclaiming his innocence (Lacedelli also died last year)—confirmed Bonatti's account in all respects. As inexcusably late as it came, no longer was it one person's word against another. If this sounds like an arcane debate, it is not. It is much more, something that goes to the very core of mountaineering. Walter Bonatti should—and will—be remembered as much for his unyielding commitment to historic truth as his unparalleled genius as a climber.

JIM WICKWIRE

Beyond the Mountain. STEVE HOUSE. FOREWORD BY REINHOLD MESSNER. PATAGONIA BOOKS: 2009. HARDCOVER. 285 PAGES. $29.95.

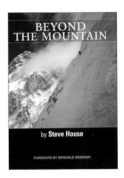

Beyond the Mountain is Steve House's self-described tale of "Commitment on Steroids," with selected insights into one of alpinism's most accomplished characters. Why am I compelled to be such a smart ass and think of the book as "Beyond the Image"? Am I envious for shortchanging my own commitment to alpinism, or am I just too far out of The Show to discern fact from fiction? So who is House House *beyond the image*? Is he our pop-culture icon, a self-created hero? Is the book any good? Does it answer any serious questions? Does it redefine alpinism, move the bar, or change one's view of climbing? What questions has House's career presented that *Beyond the Mountain* might answer?

This book gives us a few powerful insights, the first of which is House's assessment of his success in understanding and then articulating the age-old question of *Why*. In the book's introduction House admits he failed to answer "why" and for the most part I agree. That said, he *is* successful in bringing the reader close to the experience of being in that moment of total awareness that high-stakes living on the sharp end affords. His narratives of soloing Beauty is Rare Thing on Denali and Hajji Brakk in the Karakoram are where we see the characteristic that is embedded in House's DNA and defines great climbers, namely depth and intensity of focus. In these passages House brings the reader face to face with the ultimate free-soloist question—up or down?—when success, failure, and death are all that remain. While most shrink from the question, throughout the book House strives to re-enter this transcendent state of being, but then struggles for meaning when the edge grows dull from accomplishment.

What House wrote in *Alpinist* magazine a few years ago about his experience with Bruce Miller on Nanga Parbat in 2004 left me (and others) wondering if House had lost his moral compass. To apparently blame your partner for personal failure and not honor the commitment of the partnership was appalling. House explores this imbalance in *Beyond the Mountain* and comes clean with an explication of his state of mind. Ironically, when I heard about Miller saving House a second time after his 25-meter fall this March on Mt. Temple, I wondered how many times Miller would be called upon before he got credit. Fortunately, House had already resolved the earlier transgression in writing this book. Nonetheless, I would like to learn more about House's journey between those disparate states of mind: from blaming to honoring the man who most contributed to success on Nanga Parbat.

House has executed what others envisioned. For example, whose idea was the single-push ascent of the Czech Direct on Denali? While the book does not provide explicit insight, I believe the answer reveals a great deal about the Mark Twight–Scott Backes–House relationship. (Note: on their non-stop 60-hour third ascent of the 9,000-foot Czech Direct, this team cut about nine days off the first ascentionists' time and four off the second ascentionists' time.) Whoever of the three first believed it possible brilliantly envisioned success without the benefit of bivy ledges, or indeed, bivying at all.

One difference between Twight's writing and House's (in this book) is that while Twight challenged his own ideas, House expresses disappointment but little self-doubt. At times it seems that we are reading a re-telling of House's journal, which makes me wonder how the story would have unfolded if he had honored the journal by using its original voice.

Is House simply hooked on the dopamine rush these intense climbs afford? The high that a climber achieves by living through such high-stakes experiences has an addictive quality that makes them incredibly desirable yet ever more difficult to re-create. This possibility becomes evident in House's retelling of his and Rolo Garibotti's one-day accent of Mt. Foraker's Infinite Spur. When that beautiful route went so easily, and they failed to be pushed, House and Garibotti left with both the experience and their relationship somehow diminished.

Is the book any good? I think so. Mostly because it is witness to the intense effort and commitment Steve House has brought to the project of building himself into a climber capable of succeeding on the toughest routes in the world. The Acknowledgments section alone makes the book worth purchasing. There we see the man, the authentic emotion, House's character, and the value he places on those most influential to his development as a world-class athlete, alpinist, and man searching for acceptance and meaning.

Whether *Beyond the Mountain* will change others' view of alpinism depends on the era in which one enters the sport. As a teenager I found Messner's *The Seventh Grade* among a pile of library books and was immediately transformed. Desmaison's *Total Alpinism* still makes my palms sweat. Will *Beyond the Mountain* have a similar effect on another young aspirant? Given my late middle-age stage in life, I don't think I can know the answer, but I hope it does.

While he may have failed to answer "why," *Beyond the Mountain* offers a glimpse of an answer through *knowing by doing*. That precept, *knowing by doing*, is rare enough, and we can only hope House will share more in his future work.

CHARLIE SASSARA

To Be Brave, My Life, Volume 1. ROYAL ROBBINS. PINK MOMENT PRESS, 2009. 221 PAGES. PAPERBACK. $19.95.

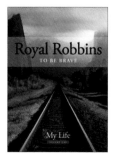

Royal Robbins was the outstanding climber of the Golden Age of Yosemite climbing. More important, he was the most influential. He was probably the first American-born climber to climb 5.9 on this continent. His uncompromising vision of how to approach the great walls, from Half Dome to El Capitan's Nose and later the North American Wall, echo through the decades and speak to climbers to this day.

Less well known is that it was Robbins who triggered the clean-climbing revolution in this country. After a trip to the U.K., Robbins returned home imbued with the ethos of using natural features and chocks to protect rock climbs. Chouinard and Frost immediately understood the implications, applied their design and production genius to improving the chocks available from the U.K., and commissioned Doug Robinson's seminal essay, "The Whole Art of Natural Protection," in the Chouinard Equipment catalog. This was followed by John Stannard, on the East Coast, publishing his brilliant newsletter, "The Eastern Trade." The revolution swept on, but it was Robbins who triggered it.

Thus an autobiography by Robbins is a must read for anyone interested in the modern history of American climbing. It helps that it is so well done and consistently engaging.

As a device, Robbins recounts his 1963 solo of Warren Harding's amazing route on the Leaning Tower in Yosemite. His clear descriptions of the technical aspects of the climb are accessible to the non-climber, but are gripping enough to satisfy the most experienced among us. Alone on the wall for days, Robbins looks back on his hardscrabble youth, growing up in post-WWII Los Angeles. Always supported by his long-suffering mother but without a steady father figure, he recounts his youthful adventures, and misadventures, with an uncompromising eye and an amazing memory for detail. His discovery of climbing and his calling gives us a window for understanding his resolute character.

This is the first of a seven-volume undertaking. I look forward to the rest with great anticipation.

JIM MCCARTHY

Early Days In the Range of Light: Encounters With Legendary Mountaineers. DANIEL ARNOLD. COUNTERPOINT, 2009. 432 PAGES. HARDCOVER. $29.95.

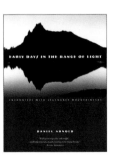

When it comes to mountaineering literature, California's Sierra Nevada is perhaps the most storied of North American ranges. Not that other mountains lack narratives, but the Sierra seems to have attracted more than its share of gifted chroniclers, among them Clarence King, John Muir, and Francis Farquhar. Now add to this illustrious company the name of Daniel Arnold.

An accomplished climber as well as scholar, Arnold immersed himself for ten years in the history of Sierra mountaineering, reading all the classic texts, from William Brewer's *Up and Down California in 1860-64* to Norman Clyde's essays, as well as the old climbing accounts published in the *Sierra Club Bulletin*. From this veritable massif of alpine material, Arnold identified "the most adventurous climbs made by the most headstrong climbers," then spent four summers re-doing the routes himself, following in the paths of "the climbing ancestors."

Not only did he follow the exact routes of these predecessors, he did it on their terms, leaving at home modern climbing gear and opting instead for vintage equipment. Or no equipment at all. When John Muir made the first ascent of Mt. Ritter in October 1872, he walked 25 miles across rugged high country to reach the peak. Afterward, he walked back the way he came. He wore light clothes and carried only a tin cup, a notebook, and a bundle of bread. Arnold, in retracing Muir's route, did the same, right down to the bundle of bread. At one point he reflects upon his efforts to meet the old-time mountaineers on their own ground, confessing, "In all honesty, my possessions were disconcertingly light—each easy step forward reminded me that I carried nothing to defend myself against the darkness and the cold."

The book presents 15 narrative accounts, "the most difficult and notable routes along with the stories of the men who climbed them." In each case Arnold deftly weaves his own story in with that of his subject. At times the writing is so seamless, the reader is almost charmed into believing that Arnold has dissolved the barrier of years and has joined the climbing ancestors on their historic climbs, "shamelessly eavesdropping on their hundred-year-old conversations." But more importantly, he treats each climber he writes about with a profound sympathy, which has the effect of shifting the reader's attention away from the technicalities of mountaineering to the complications of the human heart. Instead of rehashing the all-too-familiar myth of the hero-mountaineer, Arnold leads the reader toward those inexpressible privacies that abound in the souls of those who would climb mountains.

The most poignant character in this regard is the legendary Norman Clyde. Before he gave his heart to the Sierra, Clyde was married to a woman named Winnie Bolster, who died tragically young from tuberculosis only a few years after they married—"before he had the chance to do much more than feel the potential of their future, but apparently she remained with him all his life." Her spirit, it would seem, was his constant companion, unseen by the others who occasionally climbed with him, yet attending him to the end of his long days. A sad and moving story of love lost, to be sure, but Arnold also sees in Norman Clyde a cautionary tale for any creative spirit. When he wasn't out and about in the mountains, Clyde was holed up in his cabin, grinding away at his writing, struggling to get into words exactly how the Sierra made him feel. It was a lifelong labor, and he never really found the audience for his work that he hoped for. When he died in 1972 at the age of 87, he left behind reams of unpublished manuscripts. As Arnold sums it up, "To me, the strongest warning against Clyde's path is the simple fact that Clyde himself, who seems to have been better equipped than anyone to handle solitude and the unrelenting pressure of raw beauty, struggled so hard to find his place in the borderland between the mountains and civilization—and only surrendered to the peaks after exhausting the possibilities in between."

One comes away from this book with the uncanny sense that rare is the high Sierra peak that is not haunted. As Arnold so eloquently expresses it, "The mountains have a way of propagating human echoes."

JOHN P. O'GRADY

The Stonemasters: California Rock Climbers In the Seventies.
DEAN FIDELMAN, JOHN LONG, AND OTHERS. T. ADLER BOOKS/
STONEMASTER PRESS, 2009. MANY PHOTOGRAPHS. 196 PAGES.
HARDCOVER. $60.00.

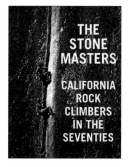

"We made this book square, like a block of granite," said Dean Fidelman, the photographer. That's how much he and John Long, the writer, wanted it to reflect the experience of being a Stonemaster. It's exciting how well their big volume succeeds, by diving deep into the legend to locate the sparks that set a few high school kids so on fire they ignited a generation. The story is vivid, thanks to the penetrating writing of their chief spokesman, John Long.

How did it all start? Long "organized a high school rock-climbing club for the sole purpose of enlisting a partner who had access to a car." The club quickly sank under the weight of teen drunkenness when "a foreign exchange student from Hyderabad [India]—who'd shown such promise on The Blob earlier that day—was found wandering the desert in her panties." But Long had already hooked up with Rick Accomazzo and "a powder-blue Ford Pinto we drove into the tundra over the next few years." Step on the gas and wipe that tear away.

Fidelman's iconic shots are everywhere, opening with John Bachar hanging oh-so-casually off the lip of The Molar for a dedication page. Yet they don't dominate. Instead, their classiness is deliberately upstaged by snapshots that start out reflecting self-conscious poses from reading too much Herman Buhl, but soon dissolve into the warmth and plain goofiness of hanging out in Josh with your buds.

Likewise, Long is too good to just go big with his own language. The book sweeps together writings from many others who were there as the tribe swelled and became the statement, the identity, of a generation. Right away we get multiple views of climbing Valhalla, their initial entrance exam, from Accomazzo and Mike Graham. Plus rare writing from John Bachar, as he steps it up to the first solo of Butterballs, and sweet Tobin Sorenson going alpine.

The Stonemaster legend has loomed, creating a hunger for this book. It wouldn't have taken much to satisfy the hunger, but we get filled right up by a rich choir of voices, set off by candid moments on Kodachrome.

It's the start of an era of red two-inch swamis, worn like a pirate's sash over painter's pants, long hair, an insouciant stance. They might have been tempted to tighten that circle as more aspirants clamored. Instead, the Stonemasters did a remarkable thing. They threw open the gates and became a generation that wouldn't quit until it had run itself out on enduring icons like Astroman, the Nose-in-a-Day, and the Bachar-Yerian.

"Dime edges," we often say, when in truth most of them were larger coin. Long wryly acknowledges "centavo" size as they build early skill bouldering on Mt. Rubidoux before tackling the "holdless" slabs of Suicide Rock, where the drill stances were "round as a wine grape and smoother, too."

The Stonemasters were the last great trad climbers, pulling the rope after a fall and trying from the ground or the last no-hands stance to send it straight through.

Steve Roper's slim volume, *Camp 4,* gestated 30 years before committing to history the Golden Age of Valley climbing. He got it so right, reflecting by turns the serious and farcical, all with painstaking accuracy. A hard act to follow. All the more interesting then that we waited out the same delay in documenting this next great era, one that couldn't really be contained by the walls of The Gulch. Hardly a tombstone, this volume cracks open with the invitation to make your own mischief and keep it real.

I keep returning to Long's piece that opens the book, "A Short History of the Stonemasters." Like a solo on the sax, it has evolved over the years since it was first published with subtle twists and big surprises. By the time I encountered them in the Valley, the Stonemasters were already a movement at flood stage and had recruited the best of the Bay Area boys, like Dale Bard and Werner Braun, Ron Kauk and John "Yabo" Yablonski, not to mention sweeping in their King-of-the-Valley predecessor, Jim Bridwell.

The brilliance in this volume calls out its dark side, which surfaced with a couple of bodies shattered by long falls, the early death of Tobin Sorenson, and a sick obsessiveness oozing out of Yabo that even the strong medicine of climbing itself could not hold in check forever. Lynn Hill digs into the story of sparring with Yabo as no 18-year-old girl should have to, yet so many do. Emotional blackmail forces her hand, and in the heat of the moment they end up practically soloing a line that is lost forever. But its acid-etched tale could be the strongest piece in a very strong book.

The Stonemasters scatters a lot of gripping writing among grainy snapshots and epic landscapes. It also innovatively uses a lot of short snippets culled fresh from tossed-off posts on SuperTopo.

Okay, so I'm kind of smitten by the Stonemaster legend. It is truly a thrill to trace their roots, exposed as never before in this excellent book.

DOUG ROBINSON

The Last Of His Kind; The Life and Adventures of Bradford Washburn, America's Boldest Mountaineer. DAVID ROBERTS. WILLIAM MORROW, 2009. 352 PAGES. HARDCOVER. $25.99.

I never understood Bradford Washburn.

Or rather, I never understood his place in the climbing pantheon. I always thought of Washburn as a remarkable photographer who happened to climb a dozen (or so) prominent peaks; a genius mapmaker who happened to climb a dozen (or so) prominent peaks; a great writer, a careful naturalist, a serious scientist, a devout museum guy—who happened to climb a dozen (or so) prominent peaks. Even a wingnut who battled other wingnuts about the activities of the ultimate wingnut, Dr. Frederick Cook.

As biographer Roberts makes clear, Washburn certainly was a climber. He was, in fact, just a big kid who carried on doing everything we all do as youngsters (exploring, climbing, taking pictures, and writing about our experiences) for much of his adult life.

Today we're used to 12-year-olds training in gyms and becoming 5.12 climbers by their early teens. That's not how it used to be, especially in the climbing-naive 1920s and '30s. For precocity, though, Washburn's life was a surprising exception.

His writing career started as an eight-year old, in 1918, when he was living with his family in New York. He penned a piece about fishing on the docks along the Hudson and East rivers that was published in *The Churchman* in 1919. An interest in geography was in full tilt by the time he was in fifth grade, and by 14, if not earlier, he was drawing maps and plotting routes around New Hampshire's Squam Lake, where his family had a cabin. He also had a thirst for knowledge about the natural world, and as a young student wrote school papers on subjects as esoteric as ferns.

He was introduced to climbing at age 11, finding that the higher he went, the less hay fever bothered him. He shortly thereafter climbed Mt. Washington, and in the summer of 1926 he spent a month climbing difficult technical routes in the Alps, as well a few of the highest peaks, with a guide. Roberts observes: "In one month, at sixteen, Brad had amassed an alpine experience that could be matched by no more than a score of American climbers of any age."

By the time he was 17, after a second season in the Alps, he had written his first book—*Among the Alps with Brad Washburn* (published by Putnam). By the time he was a Harvard freshman, he had a professional lecture agent. In Washburn's teens, Charles Lindbergh's Atlantic flight stirred an interest in aviation (Washburn learned to fly at 24). In his early 20s, he was courted by *National Geographic* and other publications.

The die had been cast.

Exploring, climbing, writing, flying, and an insatiable curiosity about unknown places were to make this life remarkable in many ways. And while he originally looked to the Himalayas, by the time he was partway through his undergraduate education, Washburn had figured out the final, crucial element to his career, a vast area where he could do all of the above with the style of a born Olympian: Alaska and northwestern Canada.

The deeds he performed there, we know well: Mt. Crillon in 1934, Lucania in 1937, mts. Marcus Baker and Sanford in 1938, Mt. Bertha in 1940, Mt. Hayes in 1941, Mt. Deception in 1944, Mt. Silverthrone in 1945, McGonagall Mountain in 1947, Denali's West Buttress and Kahiltna Dome in 1951, and Mt. Dickey in 1955, to name the most prominent. Roberts tells the stories of these climbs—and his subsequent years as a father, mapmaker, Everest height-adjuster, and museum director—richly, in detail, and expertly placed within their historical context.

But *The Last of His Kind* has its uncomfortable moments for even sporadic readers of mountain literature. Roberts spends considerable time covering climbing history that has been repeated dozens of times (the history of the 8,000-meter peaks, for example). The ascent of Lucania gets its own chapter. There are lengthy descriptions of other climbers' careers (e.g., Terris Moore) that, though related to Washburn's trajectory, seem superfluous. At times I felt like I was rereading James Ramsey Ullman's *High Conquest*.

While Roberts does a terrific job of assembling Washburn's personal story, what's covered at times seems unbalanced (Brad's broken engagement to an Eleanor Kelsie covered most of eight pages). The epilogue hints as to why.

Roberts knew Washburn, and he is not just his biographer, but was a friend, student, and, as he calls himself, protégé of the great man. As a mountaineering publisher friend recently pointed out, "It must have been incredibly difficult for David to write that book. Even if Washburn wasn't there, he must have felt Brad looking over his shoulder."

This sense is the source of the epilogue's awkwardness. It describes the Washburn–Roberts relationship and is part memoir, part celebration, and part justification as to why Roberts was the man to write this book (even though several other Washburn biographies exist). Thirty-one pages long, it leaves the reader with the impression that Roberts feels he's the heir apparent to Washburn, which, though plausible enough, gives the reader pause after 300 pages of expert, if occasionally bumpy, storytelling.

Quibbles aside, *The Last of His Kind* is a great read and offers the details necessary to fully understand Washburn—who he was, how he was raised, what motivated him, how he achieved so much in so many fields, and how he sat at this great intersection of the things he loved as a boy. And how he put them to use to ultimately join the pantheon.

CAMERON M. BURNS

Pickets And Dead Men: Seasons on Rainier. Bree Loewen. Mountaineers Books, 2009. 189 pages. Paperback. $16.95.

After Bree Loewen graduated from college with a degree in philosophy at age 17, she spent four years as a climbing bum and ambulance jockey. We meet her at age 21, when she was rescued from a training climb of Mt. Rainier in a "highly televised extravaganza less than a month before [being] hired to rescue others." *Pickets and Dead Men* is her first-person account of the three seasons she spent as a climbing ranger on the highest mountain in Washington State.

The book is arranged in rough chronological order, detailing her experiences as a female ranger in a male-dominated industry. Her adventures are numerous and eclectic, and the bulk of the book is comprised of her stories. She describes participating in dangerous, high-profile rescues, cleaning the outhouses at Camp Muir in her "out-on-the-town" jacket, routefinding in some of the world's most extreme mountain weather, determining which breakfast burrito is most satisfying after a 24-hour shift, and accidentally climbing solo in whiteout conditions. Several themes become clear, including Loewen's struggle to gain the respect of her male coworkers, her constant internal self-doubt, and a continual pondering of that never-ending question: Why am I here? She touches on both the macabre (excavating bodies from crevasses) and the whimsical (she hopes her last mortal thought will be about white chocolate macadamia cookies). Her engaging prose is often underscored with a reverence for the mountain on which she lived, worked, and played.

Loewen's candor, utter lack of pretension, and matter-of-fact honesty make *Pickets and Dead Men* funny, poignant, and entertaining. But while her wry bluntness and self-deprecation in presenting her own quirky perspective endear her to readers immediately, there's also a danger to her casual prose: she uses the same unfiltered language to describe multiple real-life situations, co-workers, and climbers, but with a less-than-humorous undertone. Of her fellow climbing rangers, for example, she says "the intolerance, egomania, and 'lone wolf' attitude... led to many awkward situations involving offensive language, uniform requirements, substance and beverage regulations, and sometimes a lack of human decency." Names have been changed, but strong personalities and delicate situations are sometimes portrayed as more one-dimensional than we know them to be in real life.

Her trademark honesty does not waver in the Afterword, when Loewen offers her conclusion: "Neither of my twin philosophies, that shared hardship increases camaraderie nor the doctrine 'that which doesn't kill you makes you stronger,' worked out for me. The mountain irrevocably broke me in many ways, but it also kept me focused on what I wanted in my life: good friends to grow old with.... If this experience had been the sum of my life, then this book would have outlined a tragedy. Fortunately, it was only a summer job I had for three years in my early twenties."

Readers—especially those well-versed in the challenges that come with choosing climbing as a lifestyle, rather than a hobby—may have mixed feelings about the ultimate conclusion of *Pickets and Dead Men.* But the real value of the text isn't in the message; rather, it's in the playfulness of the stories, and in the simple bravery it took for Loewen to tell her truth. Spending her summers on Mt. Rainier as a climbing ranger might not have ultimately been right for her, but luckily for us, that summer job left Loewen with some wonderful tales to tell.

Charlotte Austin

Hooker & Brown. JERRY AULD. BRINDLE & GLASS, 2009. 240
PAGES. PAPERBACK. $19.95 (CANADIAN).

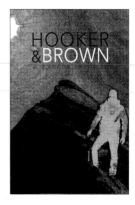

So few mountaineering novels exist that it feels wrong to make gen-
eralizations from such a small sampling. Nonetheless, *Hooker &
Brown* is more ambitious than most. This is a serious literary novel
that tells the story of its first-person narrator, known to us as Rumi,
the Ruminant, not after the "Sufi poet of love," but because as he
begins his season of working trail crew he appears to his co-workers
as a deer in the headlights. The book is organized by the seasons and
Rumi climbs in all four, the climbs being part of the structure that
supports his quest for self-understanding.

The novel takes its title from the mythical peaks, Hooker and
Brown, "observed" by David Douglas during his early 19th-century exploration of the Rockies as
the highest peaks on the continent. By 1902 the search was given up, but Rumi, enamored of the
history of exploration and of the idea of blank spaces on the map, seems to want to will the peaks
into being. Early on, Rumi's glimpse of a peak hidden in the clouds arouses his curiosity and
desire and leads him on the path to the legendary peaks, as well as the actual rock and ice of Mt.
Assiniboine. As he proceeds throughout the year, this is just one of many quests he undertakes;
he also climbs more, works the trail crew, deliberates whether to return to graduate studies in
geology in the city or surrender to the mountain life. He also pursues, but not very aggressively,
the Interpreter, a young woman who longs for a small mountain lake, as Rumi longs for Hooker
and Brown.

Rumi's fascination with early 19th-century explorers is passed along to readers through journal excerpts of David Thompson, David Douglas, Arthur Coleman, and Norman Collie. Rumi also
tells stories of these to the Interpreter, who likes her history in story form. No small part of this
book's charm comes from its respect for this history and Rumi's deeply felt connection to it: "I want
to follow Norman Collies' path. Collie followed Arthur Coleman, who followed old Indian maps.
Coleman found the pass but no mountains fitting the descriptions of Hooker and Brown." And
from an earlier observation: "Coleman and I are connecting…. [He] wandered out into the wilderness—an impulse that strikes me as boyish and uncomplicated. That's the life I want."

Rumi's travels (and Auld's—doubtless this is writing of the kind that blurs the fiction/
nonfiction boundary) create a wonderfully, deeply felt sense of the Canadian Rockies. Many of
the places he describes I know from experience and from reading, and I found myself cross-
referencing one of my favorite guidebooks, Sean Dougherty's *Selected Alpine Climbs in the
Canadian Rockies.* Auld's story, as a story of place, so lovingly and accurately evokes those
mountains that I found myself wanting to follow Rumi as he follows the explorers.

The book opens and closes with descriptions of climbs, and there are more in between.
There is never a doubt that Auld knows exactly of what he speaks, but better yet is that he gives
it to us fresh: it's familiar, but we never saw it in quite this way. For the author of a book so filled
with history and topography (in other words, it's *discursive*), Auld has a very light touch—
Rumi's story and his voice carry us through. The book will appeal particularly to those of us
who have struggled to find balance between the siren call of the mountains and the traditional
adult worlds of schooling and careers; in other words, to all of us.

DAVID STEVENSON

In Memoriam

EDITED BY CAMERON M. BURNS

STIMSON BULLITT 1919–2009

Stim Bullitt, by his own admission, was born with a silver spoon in his mouth, and he spent the rest of his life trying to live it down. Being delivered to school in his mother's Rolls Royce, he would lie on the floor and beg the chauffeur to drop him off a block away so that his classmates would not see him arrive in this ostentatious manner. While a student at Yale, he joined the varsity boxing team, "so that I could compete with the poor black boys from Harlem, man-to-man." When taking the train home to Seattle, he declined his mother's preferred accommodations, a Pullman car. Instead, he would "ride the rails" in cold, dirty cattle cars with hobos, whom he respected ("They were not bums, they were hobos!").

Stimson Bullitt. *Cliff Leight*

It is small wonder that his love of nature, combined with his spirit of independence, resulted in enthusiasm for climbing. Stim's exposure to the outdoors of the Pacific Northwest started with family outings and the Boy Scouts. Later he took his own children on hiking trips, but it wasn't until he turned 50 that he discovered the joy of actual mountaineering. Still later came the thrill of climbing hard rock, which eventually made him a legend.

He was in his sixties when he climbed Denali—on his third attempt. He teamed with Fred Beckey for first ascents of peaks in the Coast Range of British Columbia. When he couldn't find climbing partners, he would not hesitate to solo routes—routes normally done by roped teams. It was just the expedient thing to do. He found his true passion in climbing hard rock, savoring multi-pitch routes on Liberty Bell, Slesse, Squamish Chief, and Mt. Sir Donald, to mention but a few. One indoor climbing competition included a "Masters" division for anyone older than 50. I was 54 and was proud to get third place. Stim got first place, at 74.

When his stamina for carrying heavy loads started to wane, he focused on sport climbs. Always pushing himself to the limit, he sought routes that were aesthetically attractive. One such route, Illusion Dweller, is rated 5.10b. At the age of 83 he led this classic. Patagonia ran a full-page photo showing Stim struggling up the final move. "Alex, this is one of the happiest days of my life," he declared with a boyish grin when he finished the climb. This accomplishment inspired climbers all over the world. "This gives me hope that I may still climb when I'm 83," I often heard young climbers say when they realized I was there to belay Stim.

Stim was a lawyer until his mid-seventies. For a time he was president of King Broadcasting Corporation, a communications conglomerate his mother founded. Nevertheless, this president of the largest television station in the region disdained watching television. He was a prolific reader and writer. One of his proudest moments came when he heard that his name was on President Nixon's "enemies list," an honor earned for his vocal opposition to the Vietnam War. He made most of his many millions through the real estate development company he founded—rebuilding inner city areas of Seattle and expanding ski resorts in the Cascades.

He strongly believed in helping rectify social and racial injustices and contributed most of his considerable wealth to such causes, often as an anonymous donor. He co-founded the Bullitt Foundation, which is still addressing the conservation needs of America's wilderness and mountain areas. True to his principles, he made sure that he was broke (or nearly so) when he died, sitting in his house in view of the mountains he loved.

ALEX BERTULIS

RICCARDO CASSIN 1909–2009

In 2009 the (British) Alpine Club accorded its honorary member-ship to Riccardo Cassin, one of the legends of Italian mountain-eering. Cassin had celebrated his 100th birthday just three and a half months before. Though he could not travel to Chamonix to receive the certificate, he was still in good health. Four months later, however, he died at his home at Piani Resinelli, facing the spectacular crags of his Grigna.

Riccardo Cassin in 1987.

Cassin was born in Friuli, an eastern region in northern Italy, which then was one of the poorest in the country. His father had emigrated to the United States, hoping to have his family rejoin him, but was killed in an accident at work. Little Riccardo, bound to help his mother and younger sister, moved to Lecco (in northernmost Italy just below the Swiss border) with an uncle and worked as an apprentice at a blacksmith's shop. Cassin loved to recount his amazement arriving at Lecco—a wonderland to him, with a beautiful lake and astonishing hills a few minutes from anywhere in town. He worked hard at the smith's shop, yet he had time in summer daily to swim, run, and scram-ble uphill, all without spending a cent. He loved sports and was fit for many. He ran on foot because he had no bike and he borrowed one to win bicycle races. Those were the years when the Italian Government, created free gyms for working people, where Cassin practiced boxing. He was very good at it, but his coach told him that he had to choose between boxing and rock climbing. He opted for rock.

For climbers, Lecco was, and is, a paradise, with steep walls rising all around the town and, higher, the Grigna unfolding a countless number of even steeper towers and spires. The Grigna has been the first playground for generations of climbers. An extraordinary woman alpinist, Mary Varale, also came to the Grigna. She was from the Mediterranean Liguria region and was rich enough to climb all over the Alps. At Piani Resinelli, the departing point for ascents of the south face of the Grigna, she met Cassin. They climbed together, appreciated each other's ability, and Mary returned with Emilio Comici, a famous climber from Trieste who knew the sophisticated techniques being practiced by Austrians. He taught those tech-niques and skills to Riccardo and his friends, transforming them from rough amateurs into formidable alpinists.

The deeds and achievements of Riccardo Cassin are well known and recorded in numer-ous anthologies and histories of mountaineering. What made Cassin and his partners so dif-ferent from almost all other climbers in the 1930s was their talent on both rock and ice. What distinguished Cassin from his partners, though they were as skilled and tough as he, was his strength of character and his determination. He was a born leader, and he prided himself on accomplishing his ascents during his first push. So it was in 1935 at Torre Trieste and on the north face of the Cima Ovest di Lavaredo in the Dolomites, in 1937 on the northeast face of the Piz Badile, and in 1938 on the Walker Spur of the Grandes Jorasses. Those are only the most famous of his long list of first ascents.

After World War II, during which he led a squad of partisans, Cassin resumed climbing and fully displayed his talent as a leader. This also caused him grief, when after a reconnaissance up the Baltoro Glacier with Ardito Desio in 1953, Desio was named leader of the Italian expedition to K2 the following year and excluded Cassin from the team. It was clear that Desio, a dictatorial boss, could not bear another leader in his group.

Cassin's revenge was the Gasherbrum IV expedition in 1958. Under his leadership, the summit of the extremely difficult 7,925-meter mountain was reached by Walter Bonatti (another victim of Desio's authoritarian intolerance—see the K2 book review earlier in this *AAJ*) and Carlo Mauri. But Cassin's masterpiece was what is now called the Cassin Ridge on the south face of Mt. McKinley, where in 1961, he led his entire team of Ragni di Lecco (Lecco Spiders) to the summit and down. Other expeditions followed: to the Caucasus (1966), Jirishanca in the Andes (1969), and Lhotse in the Himalaya (1975). In 1987, to celebrate the 50th anniversary of his first ascent on the northeast face of Piz Badile, he climbed it at the age of 78. After the ascent Fulvio Mariani, a filmmaker and friend of his, complained about not having been informed.

"We could have filmed you," Mariani said.

"Why not?" said Cassin. "Let's do it again."

So he climbed the Badile once more. But he scolded journalists who wrote that he had repeated his own route twice. "The second ascent was not valid," he said, "because there was not the descent: a helicopter came to the top to fetch me!"

That was Riccardo Cassin.

MIRELLA TENDERINI

JONATHAN COPP 1974–2009

Of all my friends who *live* their lives, I never thought that he would die. And even if he did, I thought he would surely rise like a Phoenix and keep on living.

We last climbed together in the summer of 2008—life gets busy, I guess—and not much had changed with our usual late-start junk-show reminiscences of airport and travel fiascos. By mid-morning we stood in the Chasm Lake Cirque.

"What should we climb?"

"Maybe something up there?" came Jonny's characteristic reply. "We'll figure it out."

Jonny Copp on the summit of Fitz Roy in 2005. *Self portrait*

Strong as hell. Good at everything. Wild eyes that burned with life. A mystic who embraced the unknown and unknowable. The best hugs. Huge, toothy grin. Without a doubt the partner you wanted if—and when—the shit hit the fan. He'd just laugh. The greatest laugh. He had an unrelenting optimism.

"Nah, I think it'll work out!" seemed the most common phrase when we climbed.

Some partners offer an unspoken gift that, just by being with them, somehow makes you better than you thought you could be. And then, sometime, before you really know it, you begin believing in yourself.

As we racked up I saw what looked like a dowel hanging from his harness.

"Dude, what in *the hell* is that?"

"It's a flute!" he said, and kicked steps up the snow toward the wall.

Oh, well, of course.

I tried my best to mock the hippie flute, but I got quiet when the crux randomly came on my lead. "This is too hard for me," I thought. But I knew he'd tell me to try, and I knew he'd be right. Toward the top of the pitch, as notes drifted upward from the belay and without even realizing it, I danced.

Now he's gone. Some things are too big, too powerful and there is no Santa Claus. Later we console ourselves with talk of inspiration and memories, and how the ones we lost wouldn't want us to be sad. We whisper wistful "if onlys," but it remains undeniable that risks are part of the equation, as are all the experiences that make us who we are—that the close calls and willingness to *go* come with the love and laughter and joy and inspiration, and you cannot go back and remove one component from an integral whole. It *was* him. All of it.

Higher, he saw a chossy corner: "Let's head up that!"

We'd find another way to return to our packs—it'd all work out. Now I struggle to believe that everything will all work out, but I guess it has to, somehow.

The summer of his death I returned to the cirque. While kicking steps up the sun-cupped snow, as firey alpenglow bathed the rock, I stopped. I looked everywhere, studying the air and the wind and the rock, and though Jonny didn't rise from the ashes, I still heard the sounds of his flute.

△

Jonathan Copp was born on March 26, 1974, in Singapore. His parents, John and Phyllis, loaded him into their camper van when he was one year old, and they took a 28,000-mile road trip from Bangkok to Amsterdam. Jonny was held by holy men in India, monks in Nepal, and nomadic horsemen in Afghanistan. From the start his world became one of adventure, love, and life. He climbed around the world, establishing standard-setting alpine climbs practically everywhere. A world-class climber and photographer, and a brilliant writer, he created the now international and growing Adventure Film Festival, touched everyone he met, and left too soon when an avalanche in the pre-dawn hours of May 20, 2009 took him, Micah Dash, and Wade Johnson below the unclimbed east face of Mt. Edgar, in China. The Jonny Copp foundation has been established in his memory (www.jonnycoppfoundation.org). He will never be forgotten.

KELLY CORDES

MICAH DASH 1977–2009

In late spring 2009, Micah Dash, a 32-year old professional climber, died in a massive avalanche while climbing the east face of Mt. Edgar (6,618m), on the Gongga Shan massif, located in western Sichuan Province, China. The above is cold fact, like an alpine colossus in entropy, like a corpse buried in rock and snow. It reveals little of the vitality and beauty of the man recently departed. But mountains are indifferent, unconcerned with your safety or CV, and they extend safe passage with one hand and obliteration with the other. The paradox of feeling intensely alive when so close to ruin emerges from this polarity of life and death. Micah led a resolute life, focused on being the best climber his body and mind

Micah Dash in 2008. *Dean Fidelman*

could produce. In his last blog he wrote of his exercise regimen, stating, "...this kind of training won't necessarily make you a better climber, you need to climb to do that, but what it will do is make you hard to kill in the alpine."

You remember your brushes with fate; this is important since those close calls impart wisdom—until they're so close that only those left behind learn the lesson. Micah got the chop. He'd say it about me. It's not so much gallows humor, the universal relief valve, as it is the simple truth, a cruel truth that confirms the loss of a cherished person. I remember Micah always being thankful for what he created in the last decade of his life, especially the last few years when he finally earned what was to him the most intoxicating commodity: recognition. He was making a good living being a badass dude, recounting tales to inspired audiences, and he lived in larger shoes than he wore. But who's perfect? He was petty, insecure, loud, and cheap, yet he had a heart of gold. His way out was to go up, from being whacked out desperately on hard drugs to gaining independence, from dropout to University of Colorado grad, from Free Rider to Nameless Tower.

Micah signed off his blog posts with the word "Always," and the irony stings and embarrasses me as I think, "Hmm, not really." But there is an undying embodiment of the word. I ponder the law of conservation of energy that states that energy cannot be created or destroyed, that it remains the same in a closed system—say, our climbing community. I wonder about the cumulative power of Micah's prolific crunching of baby carrots, cabbage salad, and his abs; about his manic attempts at success on his current project, be it a redpoint of a single-pitch finger flayer or an alpine style first ascent in a distant range; about the mounting wattage of his obsessive, nervous twitching, never ceasing mind, and globe trotting spirit. If energy is only transformed from one state to another, then all the potential he possessed at the time of impact was unleashed and broadcast into the living world to be tuned in and absorbed by us.

Micah, my brother, you were absolutely killing it in your final months and I revel in the knowledge that you were experiencing the deepest love, boldest climbs, and most profound career success. We miss you deeply: the honesty of your self doubt, the ecstatic triumph of your victories, your incessant hunting and gathering of calories, the rising staccato of your laughter, how with a nose like a trumpet you brought us to tears with your hilarious tunes of self-deprecation and satire. The empathy you felt when someone got smacked down informed us that you'd been sharply struck yourself and felt the ache. And especially your rise from a runty outsider from the Mojave Desert to the center of a band of loyal, loving rock monkeys who cherished you entirely, your every vulnerable shortcoming and noble strength. Your whole being equaled so much more than simply the sum of your parts. We long to hear your shrill astonishment again, "Oh my god, I did it, I fucking sent it," or your rigid dismissals, "That's not cool, that's just not cool at all dude." And of course we will never forget your life's tag line, the acknowledgement of insatiability in every aspect of your life: "Are you going to eat that?"

We will Micah. We will consume and assimilate the remainder of your existence, not mere crumbs but a massive heartfelt serving of humanity, of rising up, of working hard, of carrying on to the last dying breath. And even though you may have been killed doing what you loved, at least you don't have to do anymore of the things you hated. Know that I will live strongly and follow your example of being more fearful of not living than of dying, for the latter is a certainty and the former is a call to action. Carpe Micah.

TIMMY O'NEILL

CHARLES SNEAD HOUSTON 1913–2009

The wise old guru and mentor for so many of us died peacefully in his Vermont home on September 27. He was 96, the last of the Harvard Mountaineering Club Five, with Terris Moore, H. Adams Carter, Bradford Washburn, and Robert Bates.

Charlie was scarcely 40 when he swore off mountaineering, but he packed a lot of it into the preceding two decades. During his Harvard undergrad years, first ascents of mounts Crillon and Foraker were among the crown jewels. While a supposedly serious medical student at Columbia, he conceived what was to be the first ascent of Nanda Devi in 1936, the highest mountain climbed until the French ascent of Annapurna 14 years later. He managed to

Charles Houston. Anne-Marie W. Littenberg

enlist three seasoned Brits, Bill Tillman, Noel Odell, and Graham Brown, to join his young team. Two years later Charlie and Bob Bates put together an AAC-sponsored reconnaissance of K2. They might have reconnaissanced themselves to the top had they not run out of matches.

After Nepal opened its doors to Westerners, in 1950 Charlie and his father Oscar, Andy Bakewell, Betsy Cowles, and Bill Tillman pioneered a new approach to Everest. Charlie and Tillman became the first Westerners to view its infamous Icefall.

Fifteen years after their first K2 trip, Charlie and Bob Bates were back in the Baltoro with a team of young hard men. The 1953 K2 expedition is, like Shackleton's voyage of the Endurance, one of those magnificent failures that provoke us all to reexamine our definition of success. The team was high on the mountain positioned for a summit attempt when the weather packed in, and Art Gilkey developed what Charlie diagnosed as thrombophlebitis. For him and his teammates, there was no choice but to try to lower Art down the mountain even though they figured the odds of succeeding were about zilch and that their own chances of getting down alive would be much diminished. That assumption was validated when one of the team fell, pulling off a sequence of four others in entangling ropes. It was only Pete Schoening's ice-ax belay of Gilkey's makeshift litter that kept all seven from hurtling thousands of feet to their deaths. Charlie, in his later years, came to call this iconic camaraderie of that team the "Brotherhood of the Rope," used as the title of both a film he put together in his 90s about the two K2 expeditions and of his biography by Bernadette McDonald.

Even before K2 in 1953, Charlie's affair with thin air was morphing into its next incarnation, that of high-altitude research. Though Charlie had no formal training, here too he dreamed big and with the same remarkable ability to make dreams happen. In 1946, while a flight surgeon in the Navy, he convinced his superiors to allow himto place Navy "volunteers" in an altitude chamber for 40 days, gradually acclimatizing them to higher and higher altitudes. The payoff was to demonstrate the value of acclimatization to fighter pilots flying unpressurized aircraft, but Charlie's personal mission in Operation Everest was to demonstrate that an acclimatized person could survive at the summit of Everest, which had yet to be climbed.

After K2, Bob Craig and, Walter Paepcke, brought Charlie to Aspen. Here, another pivotal event occurred when he rescued an ailing backcountry skier and discerned his breathing problem was something new. The result was a seminal report in the *New England Journal of Medicine* in 1960 on the entity we now call HAPE or high-altitude pulmonary edema. Then came the Logan years, 1967 to 1982, summers at 17,000 feet pursuing field research on human performance at altitude, including the discovery of high-altitude retinal hemorrhages. In 1985 Charlie pulled off his magnum opus, Operation Everest II. Volunteers gradually ascended to the equivalent of the summit of Everest in a hypobaric chamber. This effort yielded some three-dozen publications from an all-star cast of investigators. Two other major bits of his research legacy were the initiation of the International Hypoxia Symposium in 1979, a biennial gathering of scientists from many disciplines and many places, and the publication the following year of *Going High*, the story of how humans fare in thin air; the 5th edition, *Going Higher*, was completed in 2005, when Charlie was 92 and blind.

In 1962 Charlie, his wife Dorcas, and their three children left Aspen for India, where Charlie directed the Peace Corps. As the 1963 American Mount Everest Expedition was returning home through New Delhi, our paths connected for the first time, though Charlie had entered my teenage life many years before from within the pages of James Ramsey Ullman's mountaineering history *High Conquest*. I shared with Charlie our adventure on Everest's West Ridge. His clear pleasure with our accomplishment was seasoned with a wistful wondering about whether it could have been done without supplemental oxygen. That encounter was my first exposure to his philosophy that mountains should be approached simply and with humility. Over the more than half century that we subsequently shared, I came to realize that this was more than a philosophy of mountaineering; it was a philosophy of life.

Charlie Houston was an explorer, scientist, caring doc, mentor, and a totally committed and at times stubbornly principled spokesman for making this world a better place. This self-effacing, sometimes courageously blunt and downright exasperating curmudgeon was his own harshest critic. Charlie is too marvelous and complex a character to capture in these few words, but to me two of his most precious gifts were his sorcerer's ability to turn fantasy to reality and his total commitment to those he cherished.

THOMAS HORNBEIN

CHARLES SNEAD HOUSTON 1913–2009

I have always felt there was a kind of classical Grecian quality about Charlie's life. This was perhaps best expressed by Charlie's and my boss, the great Walter Paepcke, founder of the Container Corporation of America and the Aspen Institute, who once said to me, "I think Charlie Houston is driven by the pursuit of virtue." I don't know whether this pursuit was inspired by his impressive father, Oscar, or by "Angel Bunny," his equally impressive mother. I do know that the keeper of the flame of virtue was his Minerva-like wife, Dorcas. Virtue in the Greek sense demanded also the pursuit of excellence and certainly Charlie exemplified that in whatever he undertook. I also believe the absence of virtue in so much of contemporary life fueled his curmudgeonliness. He was happiest in the perfections of nature, of dogs, of children, and good science. He was an uncommon man and a great and demanding friend.

ROBERT CRAIG

TOMAŽ HUMAR 1969–2009

Tomaž Humar. *Tomaž Gregorič*

Tomaž Humar's first climbing experiments took place in the basement of the family home, where he leapt from beam to beam above his father's tools. He soon ventured out to the nearby Kamnik crags, clad in his first harness: a discarded Fiat seatbelt. He joined the local mountain club in 1987, but politics intervened and Humar went to war. As a Yugoslavian soldier stationed in Kosovo, he was shocked at the treatment of ethnic Albanians. When his conscription ended, he asked to return home. Instead he was detained, brainwashed, and mistreated before being abandoned, filthy, hungry, and thirsty, at a Kosovo train station. Humar's wartime experiences of torture and degradation affected him deeply.

When he returned home, he coped with post-traumatic stress syndrome by fleeing to the mountains. He became increasingly bold, soloing routes that many in his club referred to as "sick." The club was part of the highly regulated Slovenian Mountaineering Association. Novices had to adhere to a strict training program, and the most promising climbers, chosen by a small but powerful committee, were groomed for expeditions. The system produced a generation of high-performance Himalayan climbers. Humar was seen as a rising star.

At 25 he went on his first Himalayan expedition, to Ganesh V in Nepal. He performed well and was invited to Annapurna in 1995 by Tony Škarja, the most powerful man in Slovenian climbing. But when Škarja ordered Humar down off the mountain, Humar ignored him and went to the summit alone. The decision fatally undermined his relationship with the Slovenian climbing establishment, but it didn't stop him from climbing. In 1996 he and Vanja Furlan summitted the Northwest Face of Ama Dablam, a climb that was heralded as futuristic and that won them the prestigious Piolet d'Or. Less than six months later, Humar was back in Nepal and soloed 6,808-meter Bobaye. The following year he returned for the West Face of Nuptse, a climb that many regard as his finest. Climbing with Janez Jeglič, they reached the summit on October 31st. When Humar arrived, shortly after Jeglič, all he could see were footprints in the snow and the radio that Jeglič had been carrying. Jeglič had simply disappeared.

After an epic descent, Humar was praised for this climb, but some blamed him for the death of Jeglič, who had been a favorite of many. Emotionally and physically crushed, he conclued that "the wrong man came back from Nuptse." The psychological scars from Nuptse went deep, and from then on Humar climbed mostly alone. His next big effort was the steep, dangerous south face of Dhaulagiri, in 1999. The world's response to the climb was intensified by the enormous traffic on his website, which he had set up to monitor the climb.

A few months later he sustained multiple compound fractures when he fell while building his house. After a series of botched surgeries and a couple of brushes with death, it appeared that he would never walk again. But he did return to the mountains: Shishapangma in 2002, the south face of Aconcagua in 2003, Jannu in 2004, and Cholatse in 2005.

Later in 2005 he attempted a new route on the Rupal Face of Nanga Parbat. He had climbed to around 6,300 meters when a brief window of good weather closed in. He dug into the slope and hunkered down, waiting for a change in weather and reduced avalanche activity. That change didn't materialize and finally, after days on the face, he called for a rescue. The dangerous rescue had a happy ending for Humar, his family, the brave Pakistani pilots, and his team. But he was vilified by climbing journalists and his peers. In Slovenia the reaction was different. For 10 days people had been glued to their television sets and, when he was plucked from his icy coffin on the Rupal Face, he became a national hero. Many Slovenians urged him to run for President. He probably could have won.

After the Nanga Parbat rescue in 2005, many climbers dismissed Humar as a has-been who had disgraced himself and the climbing community. But he retrenched, alone, in his spiritual center—the forest—and in the Kamnik Alps, and he continued to climb.

Among his post-rescue climbs was a solo of the east summit of Annapurna in October 2007. His last expedition, again climbing solo, was in November 2009, to Langtang Lirung in Nepal. He suffered multiple injuries part way up and managed one last call on his satellite phone, indicating his weak condition. A rescue team from Air Zermatt found his body on November 14th. Later that month several thousand people gathered in a meadow near his home in the Kamnik Alps to bid their farewell. [A detailed account of the Langtang Lirung tragedy appears in the Nepal reports earlier in this *Journal*.]

His climbing career mirrored his personal life: explosive, futuristic, visionary, and controversial. His vision was defined by the one constant in his life, the mountains that defined his soul, made him feel alive, and gave him joy. It was through alpinism that Tomaž felt those rare moments of grace: "I carry out a climb for my soul."

Tomaž Humar is survived by his ex-wife Sergeja and their two children, Tomi and Ursa.

BERNADETTE MCDONALD

CRAIG LUEBBEN 1960–2009

News of Craig Luebben's death while preparing for an AMGA guide's exam in the North Cascades on August 9 was a devastating blow to his vast network of friends and the climbing community. But his legacy and dedication to education and climbing live on through his publications, photographs, and countless personal relationships.

I first met Craig, as many did, sitting around a campfire in the desert, in 1998. I had perceived him as being an offwidth master, best known for his onsight of Lucille (5.13a) in Vedauwoo, Wyoming. As I prodded into his career over many nights at the campfire, I found he had logged more than 2,000 days bouldering at Horsetooth Reservoir, developed hundreds of routes across the country and world, sent the nation's gnarliest wide cracks, made

Craig and Guilia Luebben. *Luebben Collection*

a free-solo link-up of two classic Colorado ice climbs, the Ames Ice Hose and Bridalveil Falls, and bagged several big mountains—all before I started climbing, in 1995.

An Iowa native, Craig was adopted as an infant and moved to Colorado at seven when his father Bob took a job with the Denver Post. One day a local church group took Craig and a rowdy bunch of young teens to hike a fourteener. After that he was hooked on the outdoors and never looked back. Despite his newfound climbing lifestyle, he always venerated his parents for having accepted him into their family, a trait he would emulate throughout his life with his limitless love and generosity.

Craig was also analytical and creative. In college he recognized that offwidths lacked adequate protection. In 1984, he designed an expandable tube chock to protect wide cracks. Although the Big Bro was a small first step, improving climbing safety became a pursuit that Craig would continue for the rest of his life through gear testing, clinics, articles, and an excellent series of how-to books.

Craig's life was also dedicated to teaching. His vast technical knowledge base was a tremendous asset for climbing camps with Lynn Hill and Arno Ilgner, guide-instructor courses offered by the American Mountain Guides Association, and introductory classes at a local community college. Even outside of classes, Craig sought to educate and instill a sense of passion in everyone he met. He loved to see people succeed, regardless of ability level. Craig also worked hard to develop positive relationships between the climbing community and land managers. As good friend Tom Kelley notes, he founded the Horsetooth Hang and an assortment of stewardship events that brought the community together and were fundamental building blocks for later grassroots activism.

Craig loved international travel. He didn't speak a second language and didn't care. His wife, Silvia, whom me met in 1995 and married in 1997, was one of his best travel companions, and he shared countless adventures with her. In recent years Craig focused less on exotic destinations and more on a curly haired girl with a mischievous grin: his daughter, Giulia, born in 2003. On her first birthday, he carried her to the top of Colorado's Mt. Bierstadt (14,060 feet). By the time she was five, she was skiing black diamonds at Arapaho Basin, had summited the Third Flatiron, and was wiggling up offwidths. Craig would proudly relate her latest achievements to anyone who'd listen.

Craig is survived by Silvia, six-year-old Giulia, parents, sister, brother, and close friends around the world. Perhaps in time, the pain of his absence will ease—perhaps not. Either way, the depth of his experience and influence will continue to enrich us. As consolation I reflect on wise words he would tell Giulia, "Be kind, be strong, be happy, and try hard."

Please consider making a donation to the Craig Luebben Memorial Fund (nococlimbing. org/get-involved/), to help his daughter Giulia attend college. To submit a fond memory of Craig for Giulia to read later, visit nococlimbing.org/craig/.

CAMERON CROSS

CLIFTON H.W. MALONEY 1938–2009

Clifton H.W. Maloney, 71, an investment banker and a long-time member of the New York Section, perished at a high camp on Cho Oyu on September 25 after reaching the summit the day before. He thus became the oldest American to summit an 8,000-meter peak and probably the oldest person to have reached the summit of Cho Oyu. His last words before falling asleep, never to awake, were "I'm the happiest man in the world. I've just climbed a beautiful mountain." Dozens of his friends, who had been following his progress via daily Internet reports from his guide Marty Schmidt and who were about to celebrate his triumphant return home, were plunged into shock and disbelief. Clif was more than an exceptionally fit and able climber, with all the Seven

Summits except Everest under his belt, but a force of nature, always good humored, sincere, loyal, and seemingly indestructible. With his 96-year-old mother still very active, he also had the genetic components. A few weeks before, both of us were attending Bob Street's 70th birthday party in Colorado Springs. Not content just to take in a great party for his old climbing partner, Clif took the occasion to climb Pikes Peak with a 50-pound pack. I tagged along with my five-pound rucksack, but he matched me step for step. This was not surprising, for Clif, a 20-times-plus marathoner, was consistently at or near the top of his age group in the New York City marathon and as fit a contemporary as I've known.

Clifton Maloney in 2008. *Maloney Family*

His memorial service in New York was jammed with friends, from not only the climbing community but also from the world of business and government, including Bill Clinton. It was a marvelous service, but perhaps the most authentic remembrance was a memorial hike and reception a few weeks later in the Hudson Highlands, where Clif would assiduously train. Present were 30 or so of Clif's AAC buddies, along with his wife, Congresswoman Carolyn Maloney and their two daughters. At the reception afterwards, at the Galligan home, we felt he was still with us, enjoying his usual glass of Heineken's after a good workout and talking about getting ready for his next climb.

In her touching remembrance of her friend Clif's passing, Susan Schwartz raised some of the existential questions that a sudden, unexplained death of an ostensibly fit climber inevitably raises: "Some of us climb, I believe, as a way to bring order and control to our personal universe. But climbing has a way of yanking hard on our chain to remind us that there is a limit to how much we can control. At some point, no matter how stubborn, talented or hard working we are, we step out of our world of personal control and into one of cosmic caprice, whether it be Everest, Cho Oyu or cancer."

PHILIP ERARD

ROBERT MODEL JR. 1973–2009

I have still not quite come to terms with the truth that Bobby Model is dead. I knew Bobby for almost 20 years, traveled five continents with him, and tied in with him for hundreds of climbs. Bobby saved my life on a couple of occasions and will forever rest in my mind as one of the finest men I've known.

Bobby was born in May, 1973. The son of Anne Young and Robert Model, he grew up on a ranch outside Cody, Wyoming. An athletic and outdoor-driven youth, he hunted, hiked, and adventured in the mountains near his home. In high school he discovered ski racing, which became his passion until climbing took over in his early years of college. While attending classes in Laramie, Bobby was also a student at the "University of Vedauwoo," becoming a well-rounded, bold climber.

Bobby Model. *Steve Bechtel*

Already an accomplished ice and rock climber, at age 22 he joined fellow Wyoming climbers for an ascent of Trango Tower via the Cowboy Direct (VII 5.13a). A budding photographer, Bobby's images from that trip were published in a story on the climb in *National Geographic's* April 1996 issue. Over the next half-dozen years, he climbed and photographed routes on big walls, 8,000-meter peaks, seaside sport climbs, and boulders across the globe. At the same time Bobby contributed to his "local" climbing areas. From long ice climbs in the South Fork near Cody to sport routes in Tensleep, to hard cracks throughout Wyoming, he was a climber who gave something back to the sport.

Gradually Bobby's photographic interests changed. Although he remained a dedicated climber and adventurer, his passion became capturing the peoples of the world on film. In 2003 he relocated to Nairobi, Kenya. From there he made frequent trips to countries of Africa and the Middle East, working on assignment for *National Geographic Adventure* and as a contributor to other publications. Bobby's photography has received international recognition, including being exhibited at the Banff Centre for Mountain Culture. In 2006 he was selected as an Emerging Explorer by the National Geographic Society Missions Program. For the past several years he worked documenting the lives of the Balti of northern Pakistan. On climbing in the area he said, "Expeditions are one thing, but I couldn't do that for the rest of my life. It feels strange to enter a cultural environment—carrying tons of equipment, bags of money, and bright synthetic clothing—and then disappear without really getting to appreciate the people you meet along the way. I have this idealistic streak in me. I always hope I will get the shot that makes people understand what it's like for people who live lives completely different from their own."

Bobby's climbing partners were lucky. He was a solid partner, had a wonderful sense of humor, and could be counted on to get great snapshots of every climbing day. Where many photographers rely on their subjects to help rig ropes for shots, Bobby often would lead a pitch first and then give his subjects beta as he shot from above.

Bobby's memorial service, held in his hometown of Cody, drew over 500 people. Some knew him as a climber, some as a photographer, some as a friend from school, and some as a kid from a local ranch. Held in the Cody Auditorium, decorated with his photos, the service featured reflections of friends, talks by his sisters and parents, and a breathtaking slide and video show of his life created by his closest friend, Peter Mallamo.

Bobby is survived by his mother Anne Young and stepfather Jim Nielson, father Bob Model and stepmother Mona Model, sisters Faith and Austine Model, and an extraordinary collection of friends and extended family from around the world whose outpouring of love, humor, grace, and prayers was an enormous support for Bobby and his family.

STEVE BECHTEL

SEAN PATRICK 1951–2009

Sean Patrick, founder of the HERA Women's Cancer Foundation, died of complications related to ovarian cancer on January 20 at Aspen Valley Hospital in Colorado. Patrick was loved by many, and her passion for saving the lives of other women affected by ovarian cancer, and for living life to the fullest, will resound through HERA's outreach for years to come.

Patrick founded HERA (Health, Empowerment, Research, Awareness) and the first annual Climb4Life event in 2002, while she recovered from her seventh ovarian cancer surgery. The Climb4Life

Sean Patrick

series, which raises money for ovarian cancer research and awareness initiatives, takes place in Washington, D.C., Salt Lake City, and Boulder, Colorado, annually. Prior to the first Climb4Life, a friend of Patrick's said, "The day you get climbers to go to an event about ovaries is the day pigs fly."

Climbers, however, attended in overwhelming numbers. HERA has funded 20 research projects aimed at increasing awareness of, and finding better detection methods for, ovarian cancer. To Patrick the challenge of climbing paralleled her fight against ovarian cancer, and she used that comparison as a catalyst for change.

"When you're out there on a ledge and there's a storm rolling in, you can't just cut the line," she would say. "You have to keep on going, and fighting." She also said "Ovarian cancer is where breast cancer was 25 years ago. When we started talking about breast cancer, we started saving women's lives. Our job is to start…talking about ovarian cancer."

Born on April 5, 1951, in Peekskill, New York, Patrick graduated from Skidmore College in Saratoga, New York, in 1973, with a fine arts degree. After graduating, she took an art fellowship in Florence, Italy, and in the following years worked in New York, Oklahoma, and Colorado. In 1988 she founded the Impact Group, a strategic marketing and design firm in Carbondale, Colorado. She continued her work with the Impact Group until she was diagnosed with cancer in 1997. She had no family history of the disease.

Patrick was a climber, skier, scuba diver, and cyclist. By the time she was 46, she was climbing 5.12. With an ear for language, Patrick loved to immerse herself in the culture of a new place. She spoke fluent French and Italian.

After her diagnosis, Patrick eventually underwent nine surgeries and was a part of numerous clinical trials. Her fight with cancer for more than 11 years inspired many; in 2004 she was featured on a television special with Jane Pauley. "Cancer does not mean life is over," said Patrick. "You can survive and thrive, do new things, and learn new skills." Patrick will be remembered for her uplifting spirit and unflinching persistence. "Life happens, and the only thing you have control of is your attitude," she said. "You can deal with it with a bad attitude or a good one … and life is just more fun with a good attitude."

To continue her legacy, please make donations to the HERA Foundation, www.herafoundation.org.

WHITNEY BOLAND *[A version of this tribute originally appeared in* Rock and Ice *magazine.]*

NECROLOGY

William E. Briggs	Mark D. Givens	Craig Luebben
Stimson Bullitt	Peter M. Hart	Clifton H. Maloney
Riccardo Cassin	Kathryn Hess	Sean Patrick
Jonathan Copp	Charles Snead Houston, M.D.	Keith Spencer
Paula Craig	Thomaz Humar	Robert J. Swanson
Micah Dash	Wade Johnson	

CLUB ACTIVITIES

EDITED BY FREDERICK O. JOHNSON

ALASKA SECTION. The Alaska Section has been moving forward with a program to replace the aging Snowbird Hut in the Talkeetna Mountains near Hatcher Pass. Built over 30 years ago, the hut sits on a wood foundation that has become unstable due to its age and the settling of the moraine it rests on. The north side of the dome-shaped structure has been damaged by heavy snow loads over the years. Rim Architects of Anchorage developed the new hut design, preserving the style of the small wilderness hut, yet offering a much more efficient and usable space. The new structure will have an 18' x 18' floor plan and will comfortably sleep six people. It will be located slightly above the old hut and will command a better view of the glacier and surrounding summits. Logistics for constructing the new hut will require airlifting materials into the glacier. Construction of the hut is planned for 2010 by a volunteer crew under the supervision of Harry Hunt and former AAC treasurer Charlie Sassara. The Bear Tooth Theater Pub hosted a successful fundraiser for the hut, with a showing of the video *Flakes*, featuring Anchorage telemark champion, Paige Brady, to a sellout crowd.

The monthly public slideshows were a great success, bringing Club members and the public together at the BP Green Energy Center in Anchorage. Among the presentations were: Harry Hunt's ascents of Shaken Not Stirred on the Moose's Tooth and other climbs; Ryan Hokanson's report on climbing with Sam Johnson in the Arrigetch Peaks of Alaska; Dave Hart's review of his three most recent expeditions in the Wrangell/St. Elias and Kluane National Parks; and Kelsey Gray's epic road trip with friends driving 18,000 miles across North America and climbing over 180 routes in 25 states, 3 Canadian Provinces and Mexico.

The Alaska Section was a sponsor of Anchorage's 1st Annual Alaska Ice Climbing Festival held from March 6–8 at Hunter Creek. The event included clinics, a competition, food, beverages, slideshows, live music, and an awards ceremony. Prizes and awards were donated by Black Diamond, Petzl, Mountain Hardwear, Alaska Mountaineering & Hiking, Ice Holdz, and others.

HARRY HUNT, *Chair*

SIERRA NEVADA SECTION. Dave Riggs, Section Chair since 2006, transitioned to the AAC Board of Directors and deserves many thanks for his fine leadership these past years.

The Section again hosted its popular annual "Climb-munity" gatherings, with the first being the January ice-climbing weekend in Cold Stream Canyon near Truckee. The Sierra summer climbing season started in June with the Donner Summit Climb-munity, which was followed by the Tuolumne Meadows Climb-munity in August. Both these events afforded our members not only great rock climbing, but also great camaraderie with group camping, barbecues, parties and raffles.

In September Royal and Liz Robbins and Tom Frost hosted their final Pinecrest Climb-In. This popular gathering of members and friends enjoyed cragging at Gianelli Edges and a wonderful party at the Robbins' cabin. The Section intends to carry on this fine tradition with Royal, Liz, and Tom as our guests.

Throughout the year the Section reached out to the climbing community and promoted the AAC. In April Section members represented the AAC at the Rockpile Rendezvous at Pinnacles National Monument. This event celebrated the 70-year history of climbing at the Pinnacles and recognized the conservation and stewardship ethics that climbers have practiced there during that time. Also, the Section continued to sponsor the year-round climbers' coffee held every Sunday morning in Yosemite with the climbing rangers, where members interact with other climbers and spread the good word about the AAC. Further, AAC Yosemite Committee Chair Linda McMillan continued to lead the Saturday evening slideshow series in Yosemite as part of the climbers' interpretive program, which generates further goodwill and exposure for the AAC.

As for conservation activities, in September our members represented the AAC at the Yosemite Facelift clean-up week organized by the Yosemite Climbers Association. In conjunction with the Access Fund, the Section underwrote commemorative Facelift bandanas that were given away to all the Facelift volunteers. In October the Section coordinated with the Friends Of The Inyo and the Access Fund to organize the Fall High Ball in Bishop to raise funds for a solution to the human waste management issue that exists in the nearby bouldering areas. The weekend included a volunteer trail restoration/clean-up workday and a slideshow by Section member Doug Robinson. The event raised almost $5,000.

The year ended with our Holiday Dinner, highlighted by AAC Treasurer/Board Member Jack Tackle, who presented his outstanding slideshow on "Alaska Alpine Style," which attracted a record turnout. At the dinner special recognition was given to those members who have provided valuable leadership and support to the Section and to the entire AAC over the years.

TOM BURCH, *Chair*

FRONT RANGE SECTION. As a result of the AAC Sections Committee's work, the Central Rockies Section was divided into smaller, more locally focused sections. One of them is the Front Range Section, composed of the eastern half of Colorado and the southeastern corner of Wyoming. During this reorganization the previous Central Rockies Chair, Majka Burhardt, decided it was a good time to focus on other ventures, and I took on the role of Chair for the Front Range Section.

Due to the reorganization the Section's primary event in 2009 was the Ninth Annual Lumpy Trails Day, managed by longtime volunteer and previous Section Chair, Greg Sievers. In partnership with the Macgregor Ranch, the Access Fund, the AAC, and Rocky Mountain National Park, 45 volunteers showed up for a day of trail work on the Sundance trail in the Black Canyon Falls area at the west end of Lumpy Ridge. We were happy to have a beautiful fall day to work. After fantastic breakfast support from several Estes Park establishments, the NPS trail crew quickly organized their teams to tackle the severely eroded trail leading to the rock face. In all, 51 wood water bars and 87 rock steps were constructed. We wrapped up the seven-hour day with great raffle prizes from local and regional sponsors. It was a pleasant surprise to see each and every attendee receive gifts. Everyone involved was very pleased with the noticeable progress from the day.

CHRIS PRUCHNIC, *Chair*

NEW ENGLAND SECTION. The New England Section held its 13th annual Formal Dinner in March, once again at the elegant Henderson House in Weston, MA. New Hampshire legend Steve Arsenault was our guest speaker, whose topic was "From Cathedral Ledge to the Wind River Range." Bill Atkinson stepped down as Chair after 14 years of dedicated service. Nancy Savickas stepped in as Chair, and Rick Merritt is now Vice-Chair.

June saw our annual BBQ, sharing the spotlight with past Club President Mark Richey, who celebrated his 25th wedding anniversary with wife Teresa Richey. Titoune Meunier hosted the event in North Conway. Prior to the party Bill Atkinson and Rick Merritt climbed with Nancy at Square Ledge, where a good time was had by all.

Despite the deluge a large crowd turned out for October's BBQ, hosted by Henry and Jill Barber at their home at Cathedral Ledge in North Conway. Rick Merritt once again acted as grill master, spending the better part of the evening under a tarp manning the grill.

In November Chad Hussey hosted an open day of climbing at Ragged Mountain, where Nancy along with Yuki Fujita and Judy Bayliss got the grand tour of the awesome Connecticut stone. Also, in early November Bill Atkinson and Nancy went to the Gunks to support the Gunks Climber Coalition in a fundraiser. Prior to the evening's festivities John Reppy lead Bill, now 84, and Nancy (no age deliberately given) up the first pitch of Andrew despite the frigid temps. Walt Hampton along with his wife Ann and son Luke made an assault on Denali. They were turned back due to bad weather but will be at it again this spring with another attempt on American's tallest summit. Best of luck to them. Finally, Big Kudos to Yuki Fujita, who climbed the Walker Spur on the Grande Jorasses with his climbing partner, Paul Cleary, from Manchester, England.

NANCY SAVICKAS, *Chair*

NEW YORK SECTION. The beginning of any new decade brings with it a moment of reflection and analysis. During the 2000's the New York Section Alpine Club Community almost doubled in size. Perhaps more important than membership growth, however, was a heightened spirit of community and brotherhood, manifested in consistently sold out events and a high degree of volunteerism. We reached several milestones: Our Adirondack winter outing, where good conditions seem to be the norm, is a year short of its 20th anniversary, while the June Ausable Club weekend, which began around 1980, is now close to celebrating its 30th anniversary. Meanwhile, an active program of slideshows, films, and other indoor events continues as in the past.

Of note, our Annual Black Tie Dinner in November is now known throughout the climbing world, gathers members from the far reaches of the country, consistently sells out, and makes a meaningful contribution to the Club's financial well being. Since its start 30 years ago, the Dinner has raised over $250,000 for the Library and *Journal*. It is also a family reunion, with old faces celebrating their friendships and newcomers being welcomed to the Brotherhood of the Rope, to Charlie Houston would say.

Some of the highlights of 2009 were the launch of Olaf Soot's new book, Alpine Americas, with page after page of the most beautiful and inspired photographs of peaks from Barrow to Cape Horn. Also, Fritz Selby published a fine memoir of his postings and adventures in Nepal in the 1960's in his "Postcards from Kathmandu." As the first Section to have its own Web site, we took a major step forward with the creation of a Section blog, where members are invited to post trip reports, photos and videos. Our thanks go to Vic Benes for years of dedicated editorship and to Conor Moran for revamping the site and creating http://nysaac. blogspot.com.

At the Dinner our two Mikes, Michael Lederer and Mike Barker, returned the Section flag from a winter exploratory mountaineering expedition to the English Mountains of Labrador. The main event, however, was our special guest speaker, Stephen Venables, who, in his droll, witty and Oxonian accent, took the audience back to the 1988 Kangshung Face Everest Expedition with a small, lightweight team; to Sarmiento with John Roskelley; and to South Georgia with Reinhold Messner and Conrad Anker.

Just a month before, however, the Section suffered a tragic loss. Clif Maloney, after summiting Cho Oyu and thus becoming, at age 71, the oldest American to climb an 8,000-meter peak, perished on the descent. Present at the Dinner and accepting our tribute were Clif's widow Carolyn and their two daughters. Two weeks later about 30 of Clif's close friends and family gathered for a memorial hike in the Hudson Highlands where he had spent so many hours training. Later that day we gathered for a sumptuous reception at the Galligan home in Garrison to reminisce and tell stories about our dear friend and brother.

PHILIP ERARD, *Chair*

SOUTHERN APPALACHIAN SECTION. In early 2009 the AAC Sections Committee announced a significant restructuring of the Club's Southeast Section to divide it into two smaller, more locally focused sections. The Deep South Section would cover Georgia, Florida, Alabama, and Mississippi. The Southern Appalachian Section was established to serve North Carolina, South Carolina, and Tennessee. I accepted the role of Chair and was assisted in launching the new section by AAC Ambassadors Max Poppel in Chattanooga and Chad Steiner in Memphis.

The Section's primary objective in 2009 was to establish itself as relevant to our membership as well as to the broader climbing community across the southern Appalachian mountains. Our membership has more than doubled over the past three years, and our numbers continue to grow. What makes these numbers important is the leverage that growth provides the Section in planning local events. Greater critical mass of membership has provided a much broader range of ways the Club can serve the climbing community locally.

One fine example of leveraging membership growth was the AAC Wilderness First Aid class, delivered in the Raleigh/Durham area. Over the weekend of July 18–19 the Section offered its members a unique opportunity to acquire Wilderness First Aid certification through a class designed for climbers, taught by a climber. The class was attended by 12 of our members. Instructor and AAC member Danny McCracken developed the class to Red Cross WFA certification standards with significant customization to focus on climbing-accident first response. Additional AAC-sponsored WFA classes are planned for 2010.

Another example of a new event in a growing area of the Section was the AAC Last Days of Fall cue, held on November 14 in Memphis. AAC Ambassador Chad Steiner and his wife Jeana hosted a get-together for members and their guests featuring burgers, beer, and climbing films. On a more traditional note, the 5th Annual Eastern North Carolina AAC Barbecue was held on November 14 in Wake Forest, NC. Thirty members and their guests gathered at the home of Brigitte Weston and Keith Nangle to socialize with old climbing partners, meet new ones, and discuss over food and drink how the local AAC community could help one another achieve our climbing goals. The featured speaker was local member Chip Popoviciu, who presented his slides from his 2008 ascent of Mt. Everest.

I would like to thank all of the AAC staff for their support for our Section in our inaugural year. In 2010 the Southern Appalachian Section will focus on recruitment of additional AAC Ambassadors, an increased focus on alpine conservation issues in the Appalachian Range, and the continuing effort to build a strong AAC community across our region.

DAVID THOENEN. *Chair*

DEEP SOUTH SECTION. The Deep South Section had an active inaugural year, with our members taking a stance in the climbing and conservation communities throughout the southeast. Our Section covers Georgia, Alabama, Florida, Mississippi, and Louisiana, and includes groups like the Atlanta Climbing Club and the activist climbing organization, the Southeastern Climbers Coalition. The first event the AAC hosted was an evening with Ken Kamler, M.D. Ken is the author of two books, *Doctor on Everest* and *Surviving the Extremes*. He was the only doctor on Mt. Everest during the 1996 catastrophe. The event was co-sponsored by High Country Outfitters in Buckhead, Atlanta and the Explorers Club. We had a great turnout, with beer and barbecue and silent auction items from High Country, the AAC, and Patagonia.

Ours is a diverse and dedicated group. One of our star members, Frank Nederhand, was featured in the AAC E-News regarding his global warming research/climbing project in the Cordillera Blanca. I also made it to Peru and attempted a new route on Yannapaccha (5,460m). Other members in the Section went to the Himalaya. Members get together almost every weekend for climbing excursions, while numerous trail clean-up days tend to have great turnouts. We sponsored a few smaller events in the region through our ambassador, Jay Love. We're looking forward to expanding into Alabama and Florida in 2010

CHADWICK HAGAN, *Chair*

David Gottlieb on the 1,700-meter south face of Jobo Rinjang in the Lunag Massif, Nepal. *Joe Puryear*

INDEX

COMPILED BY RALPH FERRARA AND EVE TALLMAN

Mountains are listed by their official names. Ranges and geographic locations are also indexed. Unnamed peaks (eg. Peak 2,340) are listed under P. Abbreviations are used for some states and countries and for the following: Article: art.; Cordillera: C.; Mountains: Mts.; National Park: Nat'l Park; Obituary: obit. Most personnel are listed for major articles. Expedition leaders and persons supplying information in Climbs and Expeditions are also cited here. Indexed photographs are listed in bold type. Reviewed books are listed alphabetically under Book Reviews.

A

Åartun, Bjorn-Eivind 113, 221
Abbe, Mt., Massif (Fairweather Rg., AK) 131-2
Abrahams Tind (Norway) 223-5
Acha Kaeyndi Valley (Kyrgyzstan) 239-40
Ackerman, Jorge 180, 189-90
Aconcagua (Andes, Argentina) 178-80, **179**
Acopan Tepui (Venezuela) 166-8, **167**
Afghanistan 253-7
Africa 207-17
Agparssuit (Greenland) **151**
Ak Tau (Kazakhstan) 247-9, **248**
Akuliarusinguaq Peninsula (Greenland) 151-3
Alaska (US) arts. 58-63, 64-9; 110-35
Alaska Rg. (AK) arts. 58-63, 64-9; 112-25
Alberta, Mt. (Canadian Rockies, CAN) 143
Albrieux, Lionel 294
Alexey Turchin, P. (Antarctica) 199-200
Almaraz, Guillermo 177
Altai (Russia/China) 232-3, 329-30
Alvarez, José Maria 299-300
Amin Brakk 277-9, **278**
Amotsang (Damodar Himal, Nepal) 304-5
Amqah Tower (Oman) 203-5
Anderson, Jerry 99
Andes (Argentina/Chile) 176-83
Andopshesten (Norway) **220**-3
Anemaqen II (Qinghai, China) art. 78-86
Anglada, Oriol 148
Anige Chuli (Mukut Himal, Nepal) **302**-3
Annapurna Dakshin see Annapurna South
Annapurna Himal (Nepal) art. 48-51; 305-6
Annapurna South "Annapurna Dakshin, Modi P." (Nepal) art. 48-51, **50**; 305
Antarctic Peninsula 193-8
Antarctica 193-200
Anthamatten, Samuel 114-5, 312-3
Anthamatten, Simon 114-5, 309, 312-3
Antoine LeCoultre, Mt. "Jobo LeCoultre" (Rolwaling Himal, Nepal) **310**-11
Aq Su Valley "Little Pamir" (Afghanistan) 253-5
Arenales, Cajon de (Argentina) 182-3
Argentina 176-80, 182-3, 187-90
Asan (Karavshin, Kyrgyzstan) **234**-5

Asgard, Mt. (Baffin Island, CAN) **145**-8, **147**
Ashes P. (Acha Kaeyndi Valley, Kyrgyzstan) **239**
Ashley, Mt. (South Georgia, Antarctica) **198**-9
Aslaksen, Jeremy 101
Assassin Spire (Cascade Rg. WA) 91
At Bashi Rg. (Kyrgyzstan) 239-40
Auer, Hansjörg 190
Austin, Charlotte 371
Austria, P. (C. Real, Bolivia) 174-**5**

B

Babazadeh, Kiomars 272-3
Baffin Island (CAN) 144-8
Bailey, Jason 288-9
Baintha Brakk "Ogre" (Panmah Muztagh, Pakistan) **269**
Balchen, Mt. (Hayes Rg., AK) **112**-3
Baltoro Muztagh (Pakistan) 270-4
Bandalet, Nikolai 237-8
Baraiazarra, Jabi 176
Baranow, Richard 127-8
Baro, Oriol 311-2
Barrill (Alaska Rg. AK) 120-1
Baruntse (Mahalangur Himal, Nepal) **321**-2
Batoux, Philippe 218-20
Batura Muztagh (Pakistan) 262-4
Bechtel, Steve 107-8, 383-4
Beckey, Fred 124-5, 135
Beckwith, Steve 357-8
Beitzel P. (Antarctica) 193
Beluga Spire (Baffin Island, CAN) **144**-5
Benowitz, Jeff apple 116
Bertha, Mt. (Fairweather Rg., AK) 131-**2**
Bertulis, Alex 373-4
Bhagirathi II (Garhwal, India) art. 25-33; 291-2
Bhagirathi III (Garhwal, India) art. 25-33; 291-2
Bhagirathi IV (Garhwal, India) art. 25-33, **27**; 291-2
Bijora Hiunchuli (Kanjiroba Himal, Nepal) **301**-2
Billy Budd, P. (South Georgia, Antarctica) 198
Bingham, Dave 289-91
Bird, Bryan 104
Birnbacker, Eduard 153-4
Bizot, Henry 177-8
Black Canyon of the Gunnison (CO) 108-9
Blagus, Rok art. 25-33; 291-2
Blixt, Marten 220-3, 226

Blow Me Down (Newfoundland, CAN) 148
Bogda Feng (Xinjiang, China) *art.* **84**
Boland, Whitney 384-5
Bolivia 173-5
Bolkovoy, Eugene 232
Bondid Valley (Pakistan) 279
Bonilla, Mikel 172
Book Reviews 362-72
　　To Be Brave, My Life, Volume 1 by Royal Robbins
　　　365-6
　　Beyond the Mountain by Steve House 364-5
　　Early Days in the Range of Light, Encounters with
　　　Legendary mountaineers by Daniel Arnold 366-7
　　Hooker & Brown by Jerry Auld
　　K2: Life and Death on the World's Most Dangerous
　　　Mountain by Ed Viesturs with David Roberts 362-4
　　K2: Lies and Treachery by Robert Marshall 362-4
　　The Last Of His Kind; The Life and Adventures of
　　　Bradford Washburn, America's Boldest
　　　Mountaineer by David Roberts 369-70
　　Pickets And Dead Men: Seasons on Rainier by Bree
　　　Loewen 371
　　The Stonemasters: California Rock Climbers In the
　　　Seventies by Dean Fieldman and John Long 367-9
Bougie, Ryan 116
Bracey, Jon 119-20
Brandberg (Namibia) 213-5, **214**
Brandtuva (Norway) 226-**7**
Brayshaw, Drew 138-9
Brazil 169
Broad P. (Baffin Island, CAN) 144-**5**
Broad P. (Pakistan) 258, 272-**3**
Broken Tooth (Alaska Rg. AK) 122
Brooks Rg. (AK) 110-11
Brown, Jed *art.* 34-41; 327-9
Brown, Nate 101-4
Brown, Sally 239-40
Brujo, Torres del (Chile) 181-2
Bugaboos (CAN) 142-3
Buhler, Carlos 171
Bullitt, Stimson *obit.* 373-4
Bullock, Marc 232-3
Bullock, Nick *art.* 42-7; 323
Burdick, Dave 135
Burhardt, Majka 213-5
Burkett Needle (Coast Rg., AK) *art.* **58**-63; **134**-5
Burkett, Mt. (Coast Rg., AK) *art.* **58**-63
Burns, Cameron M. 369-70, 373-85
Bute, Mt. (Coast Rg. CAN) **141**-2
Byeong-gi, Choi 235

C

California (US) 95-100
Campanini, P. (Andes, Argentina) 180
Canada 136-49
Canadian Rockies (CAN) 143-4
Cape Farewell (Greenland) 162-3
Caprez, Nina 234-**5**
Carrascal, Sergio Ramírez 170, 172-3
Cascade Rg. (WA) 90-5

Cassin, Riccardo *obit.* 374-5
Caucasus (Russia) 231-3
Cave, Andy 221-2
Cenotaph (Ren Land, Greenland) **155**-6
Chago (Mahalangur Himal, Nepal) **320**
Chaleur Bay (Newfoundland, CAN) 148
Challenger, Middle (Cascade Rg. WA) 91
Chalten Massif (Patagonia, Argentina) 187-90
Chambe (Mulanje Massif, Malawi) 215-7, **216**
Chang Himal "Wedge P. or Ramtang Chang" Nepal
　　art. 42-7; 323
Chang Tang (Tibet) 351-2
Changuch (Kumaon, India) 294-6, **295**
Chañi Chico (Argentina) **176**
Charakusa Valley (Pakistan) 274-7
Chau Chau Kang Nilda (Spiti, India) 280
Chile 181-7, 190-92
China *arts.* 34-41; *Origins of Mountaineering* 78-86;
　　326-50
Chinese Mountaineering Assoc. *art.* 78-86
Chi-young, Ahn 340
Chkhetiani, Otto 331-3
Cho Oyo (Mahalangur Himal, Nepal) *art.* 16-24, **23**;
　　314
Chorten Nyima (Sikkim, India) 296-8, **297**-8
Chouinard, Yvon 186-7
Chu Kangri (Lahaul, India) **283**-6
Chugach Mts. (AK) 127-8
Churau (Nepal) **300**-1
Church, Mt. (Alaska Rg. AK) 117-9, **118**
Clark, Ben 321-2
Clouet, Aymeric 269
Coast Rg. (AK/CAN) *art.* 58-63; 132-5, 138-42
Cochamó (Patagonia, Chile) 184-5
Cohete, El (Arenales, Argentina) 182-3
Colchuck Balanced Rock (Cascade Rg. WA) 94-**5**
Colombia 165-6
Colorado (US) 108-9
Colton, Nick 300-1
Combatant, Mt. (Coast Rg. CAN) **140**-1
Condor, Cerro (Patagonia, Chile) **183**-4
Confluence P. (Zion) *see* Sub P.
Copp, Jonny 36, 120, 342; *obit.* 375-6
Coquenzi (C. Apolobamba, Bolivia) 173-**4**
Cordes, Kelly 35-6, 375-6
Cordillera Apolobamba (Bolivia) 173-4
Cordillera Blanca (Peru) 170-1
Cordillera Central (Peru) 172
Cordillera Huayhuash (Peru) 172
Cordillera Real (Bolivia) 174-5
Cordillera Yauyos (Peru) 172-3
Cordón de la Jaula (Andes, Argentina) 180
Corominas, Jordi 267, 311-2
Cortial, Mathieu 193-8
Craig, Robert 379-80
Crison, Jonathan 286
Crocodile P. (Acha Kaeyndi Valley, Kyrgyzstan) **239**
Cross, Cameron 381-2
Crosson, Mt. (Alaska Rg. AK) 116
Cuerno, Cerro (Andes, Argentina) 180

D

Dalton Dome (Coast Rg. CAN) 138
Damodar Himal (Nepal) 303-5
Dangchezhengla (Shaluli Shan, China) **336**-8
Dash, Micah 120, 342; *obit.*377-8
Daskalakis, Mariza 221
Daudet, Lionel 193-8
Davis- Robbins, Crystal 182-3, 185
Dawa Mebar Kangri (India) 283-6, **284**
Daxue Shan (China) 338-46
De Gregori, Esteban 188
Deavoll, Pat 262-4
Dedeshko, Boris *art.* 16-24; 314
Della Bordella, Matteo 148, 161-2
Dempster, Kyle *art.* 34-41; 327-9
Denali Nat'l Park (AK) 113-22
Denali, Mt. (Alaska Rg. AK) 113
Denbor Brakk (Nangma Valley, Pakistan) 277-9, **278**
Deraeck, Jean-Baptiste 271-2
Desire, Mt. (Coast Rg. CAN) 139-**40**
Disappearing Dome (Sierra Nevada, CA) **99**
Dome Kang (Janak Himal, Nepal) 323-5
Dome P. (Cascade Rg. WA) **91-2**
Donahue, Topher 109
Donaldson, Marcus 171
Dongdong, Yan *art.* 78-86, 346, 349-50
Douglas P. (Antarctica) 193
Dragon's Horns (Malaysia) **357**-8
Duck Walk Wall (Greenland) 158-60, **159**

E

E Gongga (China) *see* Edgar, Mt
East Fork Valley (Wind River Mts. WY) **106**
Eastern Barnard Glacier (St. Elias Rg., AK) **129**-30
Edgar, Dave 115
Edgar, Mt. "E Gongga" (Minya Konka Rg., China) 340-2
Ellsworth Mts. (Antarctica) 193
Engels, P. (Pamir, Tajikistan) **251**-2
English Mts. (CAN) 149
Erard, Philip 382-3
Estes, Clint 277-9
Everest, Mt. (Nepal/Tibet) 315-7, **316**
Evokari, Juha 228-30
Eye Tooth (Alaska Rg. AK) 120-1

F

Fainberg, Fernando 181
Fairweather Rg. (AK) 131-2
Falaise de Machkour (Morocco) 207-9, **208**
False Cape Renard (Antarctica) 193-8
Fan, Doug 354-5
Far Out P.(Chugach Mts., AK) 127-**8**
Farol East (Pakistan) **275**
Farol Far East (Pakistan) 274-6, **275**
Favresse, Nicolas 146-8
Favresse, Olivier 146-8
Fazzi, Francesco 211-12
Fede, Pico El (Andes, Argentina) 180
Fickweiler, Martin 155-6
Fiddes, Joel 255-7

Fiddler, Claude 98
Fillot, Jean Francois 172-3
Fiorenza, Luciano 188-90
Firestone, Asa 184-5
First Aguja del Tzempuk (India) 283-6, **284**
Fisher Towers (UT) 101
Fisht (Caucasus, Russia) 232
Fitz Roy, Cerro (Patagonia) 188-90, **189**
Five Colors Mtn. (China) *see* Wuse Shan
Foraker, Mt. (Alaska Rg. AK) 113, 116
Formidable, Mt. (Cascade Rg. WA) 90
Forrester, Joe 215-7
Foster, Mt. (Antarctica) **193**-8
Fox Jaw Cirque (Greenland) 161-2, **160**
Franco-Argentina, P. (Andes, Argentina) 177-8
Frechou, Eliseu 168-9
Freeman-Atwood, Julian 300-1
Freile, Cerro (Andes, Chile) **181**
French, Joe 101, 103
Fritz, Sarah 113
Frost, Ryan 102
Fryatt, Mt. (Canadian Rockies, CAN) 143-4

G

Galligan, Gerry 174-5
Gangotri (India) 291-4
Gantzhorn, Ralf 191-2
García-Atance, Salvador 323-5
Gargitter, Helmut 165
Garhwal Himalaya (India) *art.* 25-33; 291-4
Garibotti, Rolando 187-8
Garlick, Sarah 148
Garrett, James 106
Gasherbrum I (Pakistan) 258
Gasherbrum II (Pakistan) 258
Gasherbrum VI (Pakistan) 273-**4**
Gatt, Erich 188
Gaurishankar (Rolwaling Himal, Tibet) 355-**6**
Geisler, Chris 139
Gemelos, Los (Patagonia, Chile) 190-**1**
Gietl, Simon 188
Gildea, Damien 193-8, 304-5
Givens, Mark 104-5
Gliozzi P. (Antarctica) 193
Gloppedalen (Norway) **228**-9
Glowacz, Stefan 169
Gomez, Milena 188
González, Curro 125-7
González, Pablo 180
Good Neighbor P. (St. Elias Rg., AK) 130-1
Goodhart, Jamie 247-9
Gorelik, Vitaly *art.* 70-7; 247
Goromity (Siguniang Nat'l Park, China) **350**
Göschl, Gerfried 259-61
Gottlieb, David *art.* 52-7; 311
Graham, David 320-1
Granitsa, P. (Kokshaal-Too, Kyrgyzstan) 243-**4**
Gray, Dennis 329-30
Green Tower (Nangma Valley, Pakistan) 277-9
Greenland 150-63

Griffin, Lindsay 161-2, 228, 232-3, 299-302, 307-10, 327-9, 342
Grmovsek, Andrej 210-11, 293-4
Grobel, Paulo 301-4
Grosvenor, Mt. (Alaska Rg. AK) 119-120
Grosvenor, Mt. (Minya Konka Rg., China) **340, 341**
Gruhn, Steve 127-8
Guillaumet (Patagonia) 188
Gukov, Sasha 231
Gutonchalagebo (Tibet) **353**
Guyana 168-9

H

Haas, Jason 101
Haeussler, Peter 122
Haftal Kangri (Zanskar , India) **286**
Hagiwara, Hiroshi 306-7
Haidri, Karrar 258
Haley, Colin 114, 138-9, 269
Hamilton, David 193
Harden, David 98
Hart, Dave 127
Hasson, Max *art.* 58-63; 135
Haveren (Norway) 220-3, **221**
Hawley, Elizabeth 299-302, 306-9, 315-7, 321-2
Hayes Rg. (AK) 112-3
Helling Rüdiger 209-10
Helling, Josh 205-6
Helvetestind (Norway) 226, **227**
Heran P. (Nanga Parbat Rg., Pakistan) **260**, 261-2
Herrington, Blake 92-4, 132-4
Hicks, Kurt 90
Himalaya (Tibet) 355-6
Hindu Kush (Afghanistan/Pakistan) 255-7, 258-9
Hispar Muztagh (Pakistan) 264-6
Höbenreich, Christoph 199-200
Hoinkes P. (Antarctica) 193
Hokanson, Ryan 128-9
Holden, Seth 122-4
Holeczi, Steve 143-4
Holsten, Jens *art.* 58-63; 135
Hornbein, Thomas 378-9
Houseman, Andy *art.* 42-7; 323
Houston, Charles Snead *obit.* 378-80
Huancasayani Valley (Bolivia) 173-4
Huantsan (C. Blanca, Peru) **171**
Huasteca Nat'l Park (Mexico) 148
Huber, Thomas 270-1
Huck, Daron 125
Huey Spire, East 136-7
Huey Spire, Middle 136-**7**
Humar, Tomaž *obit.* 308-9
Hunter, Mt. (Alaska Rg. AK) 114-**5**
Huntington, Mt. (Alaska Rg. AK) *art.* 64-9; 113-4, 117-8
Hyung-il, Kim *art.* 87-9
Hyung-il, Kim 266

I

Ibañez, P. (Andes, Argentina) 176
Ice Pyramid (Revelation Mts., AK) 122-4, **123**

Illimani (C. Real, Bolivia) 175
India *art.* 25-33; 280-98
Inoue, Tatsuo "Tim" 354-5
International Winter Meet (Norway) 220-3

J

Jabal Asala (Oman) **202**-3
Jabal Dhawi (Oman) **201**-2
Jabal Kawr (Oman) **203**-5
Jabal Misht (Oman) 203-5, **204**
Jabal Nakhus (Oman) 201-5, **204**
Janak Himal (Nepal) 323-5
Jan-chang, Jin 315-7
Jasamba (Nepal) *see* Pasang Lhamu Chuli
Jasmine Tau (Kazakhstan) 247-9, **249**
Jbel Tadline (Morocco) **207**-9
Jebel Tadrarate (Morocco) **209**-10
Jeffrey, Daniel 91
Jenkins, Mark 105-6, 342-3
Jensen-Choi, Peter 235, 340, 309
Jianshanzi (Sichuan, China) *art.* 84
Jiazi (Minya Konka Rg., China) **338**-9, **341**
Jimmy Boy, P. (Neacola Mts., AK) 125-7, **126**
Jobo LeCoultre (Nepal) *see* Antoine LeCoultre, Mt
Jobo Rinjang "Ribjang or Rabzang" (Rowaling Himal, Nepal) *art.* **52**-7, **54**; 309-12
Jobo Rinjang West (Rolwaling Himal, Nepal) 310-11
Johns Hopkins Glacier (Fairweather Rg., AK) 131-2
Johnson, Jeff 186-7
Johnson, Samuel 112-3, 127
Jomo Ri Massif (Chang Tang, Tibet) 351-**2**
Jones, Crag 198-9
Jongsang (Janak Himal, Nepal) 323-5, **324**
Jonsson, Krister 158-60
Jost, Matic 251-2
Jules, Mt. (Zanskar , India) 288-9
Julie Tau (Kazakhstan) 247-9, **248**
Jun-young, Min *art.* 87-9, 266

K

K2 (Pakistan) 258
K7 West (Charakusa Valley, Pakistan) **276**-7
Kang Ri Karpo (Tibet) **353**
Kangchenjunga Himal (Nepal) *art.* 42-7; 323
Kangri Garpo II (Tibet) *see* Lopchin
Kangri Garpo Rg. (Tibet) 353-5
Kangze'gyai "Tuanjiefeng" (Qilian Mts., China) *map* 333-**4**
Kanjiroba Himal (Nepal) 301-2
Kanjiroba Sanctuary (Nepal) **301**-2
Kanta Gaton (Kanjiroba Himal, Nepal) 302
Kanti Himal (Nepal) 299-301
Kapadia, Harish 280, 291, 294, 298
Kaptang (Nepal) 299
Kara Tagh (Xinjiang, China) 326-7
Karakoram (India/Pakistan) *art.* 87-9; 280-3
Karavshin (Pamir Alai, Kyrgyzstan) 234-7
Karim Sar (Batura Muztagh, Pakistan) **262**-4
Karo, Silvo 293-5
Kathar Valley (Zanskar , India) **288**-9

Kaufmann, Joel 188
Kay, Bruce 141-2
Kazakhstan 247-9
Keketuohai "Koktokay" (Altai, China) 329-30
Kellas P. (Sikkim, India) 296-8, **297**
Kellogg, Chad 178-80
Kelly, Damien 138
Ken Minaret (Sierra Nevada, CA) 98
Khani BasaSar (Hispar Muztagh, Pakistan) 264-6, **265**
Kigluaik Mts. (AK) 111-2
Kinesava, Mt. (Zion Nat'l Park, UT) **101**
Kjerag (Norway) 229-**30**
Klick, Matt 110-11
Klonfar, Martin 222
Kluane Nat'l Park (CAN) 136
Knott, Paul 131-2, 201-5
Kodar Rg. (Siberia, Russia) 231
Kohe Aq Su (Afghanistan) 253-5
Koh-i-Beefy (Hindu Kush, Afghanistan) 255-**7**
Kojichuwa Chuli (Nepal) 299-300
Kojichuwa Valley (Nepal) **300**-1
Kokshaal-Too (Kyrgyzstan) 237-46
Koktokay (China) *see* Keketuohai
Komorova Glacier (Kyrgyzstan) 239-40
Kopold, Jozef "Dodo" *art.* 48-51; 305
Korea Youth Sar (Pakistan) 266
Korean Alpine Federation International Committee
     305-6
Kozub, Wojtek 317-9
Kristine, Cerro (Patagonia, Chile) **186**-7
Kroupis, Nikolaos 258-9
Kruczyk, Marcin 173-4
Kruk, Jason 143
Kuilu Rg. (Kyrgyzstan) 246-7
Kumaon (India) 294-6
Kun Lun (China) 331-3
Kurai, South (Altai, Russia) 232-**3**
Kuramoto, Yusuke 307-8
Kwon-sik, Shim 266
Kyoabl-Kapacau Valley (Kazakhstan) 247-9
Kyrgyzstan *art.* 70-7; 234-47
Kyzyl Asker (Kokshaal-Too, Kyrgyzstan) 237-**8**, 240-3

L

La M (Neacola Mts., AK) **125**-7
Labrador (CAN) 148-9
Ladakh (India) 283-6
Lagh Shar (Pakistan) *see* Raghshur
Laguna Grande de la Sierra (Colombia) **166**
Lahaul (India) 283-6, 289-91
Laila P. "Toshain II" (Pakistan) 261-2
Laing, Adrian 277
Lama, David 187
Langley, Mt. (Sierra Nevada, CA) **100**
Langtang Himal (Nepal) 308-9
Langtang Lirung (Langtang Himal, Nepal) 308-9
Larcher, Rolando 276-7
Lars Christensen P. (Antarctica) 193-8
Larson, Rolf 91
Latok II (Panmah Muztagh, Pakistan) 266-8, **267**

Latok IV (Panmah Muztagh, Pakistan) **268**-9
Latok V (Panmah Muztagh, Pakistan) **268**
Lavigne, Joshua 140-1
Lavrinenko, Alexander 236-7
Layton, Mike 91-2
Lederer, Michael 149
Lee, Zack 102-4
LeMay, Joe 99-100
Leoni, Fabio 276-7
Lhonak P. (Sikkim, India) 296-8, **297**
Libecki, Mike 205-6, 326-7
Lille Vagakallen (Norway) 225-**6**
Lillefjord (Greenland) 153-4
Lillemola Island (Norway) 226-7
Lindic, Luka *art.* 25-33; 291-2
Linek, Vlado 167-8
Lingmey Ri (India) 283-6
Littlejohn, Pat 246-7
Liverpool Land (Greenland) 153-4
Lofoten (Norway) 220-7
Logan Mts. (CAN) 136-7
Lopchin "Kangri Garpo II" (Tibet) **354**-5
Lopez, Camilo 166
Lower Karcha Parvat (Lahaul, India) 291
Luang Massif (Rolwaling Himal, Nepal) *art.* **52**-7; 309-12
Luebben, Craig *obit.* 381-2
Lugula (Damodar Himal, Nepal) **304**
Lunda Sar (Hispar Muztagh, Pakistan) **264**-6
Lupsuq Hindu Kush (Afghanistan) 253-5
Lyngen Peninsula (Norway) 218-20

M

MacDonald, Dougald 266-8, 306-7
Madinabeitia, Adolfo 166-7
Maggioni, Michele 150-1
Mahalangur Himal (Nepal) *art.* 16-24; 312-22
Majer, Janusz 351-2
Majestic, Mt. (Zion Nat'l Park, UT) **102**
Malawi 215-7
Malaysia 357-8
Mali 212-13
Maloney, Clifton H. W. *obit.* 382-3
Mamu Choti (Nanga Parbat Rg., Pakistan) 261-2
Manaslu Himal (Nepal) 307-8
Marecek, Lukas 225-6
Mashanig Towers (Yemen) 205-6
Maslitinden (Norway) **225**-6
Massih, Erik 162-3
Mata (Mali) 212-**13**
Matthiesen, Stewart 94-5
Maturano, Anibal 177-8
Mayer Kangri Massif (Chang Tang, Tibet) **351**-2
Mayer Kangri I East (Chang Tang, Tibet) **351**-2
McCarthy, Jim 365-6
McDonald, Bernadette 380-1
McDonnell P. (Ren Land, Greenland) 155-**6**
Mckinley, Mt. (AK) *see*Denali
McKinnon, Guy 131-2
McRae, Ian 111-2
Mealy Mts. Nat'l Park (CAN) 149

Melanphulan (Mahalangur Himal, Nepal) 317-9
Mendenhall Towers (Coast Rg., AK) 132-4, **133**
Mera P. (Mahalangur Himal, Nepal) 319-320
Mercedes Sosa, P. (Patagonia) 188
Merrick, Dan 97-8
Meru Central (Gangotri, India) **293**-4
Mexico 148
Middle Cathedral Rock (Yosemite, CA) 95-6
Mills, J. 143-4
Minelli, Abel 302
Minya Konka Rg. (China) 338-43
Missing Toof (Alaska Rg. AK) 120-1
Mitoma, Iku 116
Mizhirgi Caucasus, Russia) **231**
Mocha Spire (Alaska Rg. AK) **122**
Model, Robert Jr. *obit.* 383-4
Modi P *see* Annapurna South
Moose's Tooth (Alaska Rg. AK) 113
Moran, Martin 294-5
Moreno, Mario 91
Moretta, Gabriel 180
Morocco 207-12
Morro Von Ronsen (Andes, Argentina) **176**
Morstad, Marius 220-3
Moskenesoya Island (Norway) 226
Mosquito Pass Wall (Kigluaik Mts., AK) 112
Mottram, Gareth 244-6
Motup, Chewang 282-3
Mrak, Irena 279
Mugu Chuli (Nepal) 299-**300**
Mukut Himal (Nepal) 302-3
Mukut Parvat (Central Garhwal, India) 294
Mulanje Massif (Malawi) 215-7
Muni, Divyesh 280-1
Muryshev, Andrey 347-9
Muzkol Rg. (Pamir, Tajikistan) 250-1

N

Nafees Cap (Charakusa Valley, Pakistan) 277
Nakamura, Tamotsu 346, 353-4
Nalakankar (Nepal) 299-301
Nalumasortoq (Greenland) 162-**3**
Namay Skayrak Kangri (India) 283-6, **285**
Namibia 213-5
Nanga Parbat (Pakistan) 258, **259**-61
Nanga Parbat Rg. (Pakistan) 259-62
Nangma Valley (Pakistan) 277-9
Nangpai Gosum I (Nepal) *see* Pasang Lhamu Chuli
Narumi, Genki 115-6, 314-5
Nawaz Brakk 277-9, **278**
Neacola Mts. (AK) 125-7
Negra, Aguja (Andes, Argentina) 176
Nemjung (Peri Himal, Nepal) **306**-7
Nepal *arts.* 16-24, 42-7, 48-51, 52-7; 299-325
Nesakwatch Spire, South (CAN) 139
Newfoundland (CAN) 148-9
Nicholson, Ian 190-1
Nielsen, Nils 113
Nkhalango Khoswe (Malawi) 215-7
Normand,Bruce *art.* 34-41; 327-9

North America 90-149, 164
North Fork Glacier (Neacola Mts., AK) 125-7
Northumberland Island (Greenland) 151-3
Norway 218-30
Novellón, Álvaro 266-8
Nuevo León (Mexico) 148
Nyambo Konka (Minya Konka Rg., China) 342-**3**
Nyanchen Tanglha East (Tibet) 353-4

O

Odermatt, Urs 223-5
Odin, Mt. (Baffin Island, CAN) 146-8, **147**
Ogden, Jared 109
O'Grady, John P. 366-7
Ogre (Pakistan) *see* Baintha Brakk
Ohnisha, Tamotsu 299
Oman 201-5
O'Neill, Timmy 377-8
Orlandi, Elio 276-7
Orudzhev, Alexey 226
Orvin Fjella (Antarctica) 199-200
Oswald, Simon 274-6
Otto, Jon 83, 336-8
Ozturk, Renan 120-1, 142

P

P. 1,636m (Ren Land, Greenland) **157**-7
P. 11,300' (Alaska Rg. AK) **117**-9
P. 38 (Nepal) *see* Shartse
P. 4,800m (Kokshaal-Too, Kyrgyzstan) 240-3, **241**
P. 4,810m (Karavshin, Kyrgyzstan) **235-6**
P. 4,863m (Kokshaal-Too, Kyrgyzstan) 240-3
P. 5,046m (Kokshaal-Too, Kyrgyzstan) 240-3, **241**
P. 5,454m (Hindu Kush, Afghanistan) **256**
P. 5,711m (Hindu Kush, Afghanistan) **256**
P. 5,777m (Rolwaling Himal, Nepal) 310-11
P. 5,800m (Tibet) **353**
P. 6,000m (Minya Konka Rg., China) 338-**9**
P. 6,018m (Tibet) **353**
P. 6,047m (Nepal) 299-**300**
P. 6,085m (Damodar Himal, Nepal) **304**
P. 6,134m (Minya Konka Rg., China) 340-2, **341**
P. 6,150m (Xuelian Massif, China) 327-9, **328**
P. 6,252m (Sikkim, India) 296-8, **297**
P. 6,324m (Nanga Parbat Rg., Pakistan) 261-2
P. 7,240' (Coast Rg., AK) *art.* 62
P. 7,260' (Fairweather Rg., AK) **131**-2
P. 710m (Liverpool Land, Greenland) **153**-4
P. 715m (Liverpool Land, Greenland) 153-**4**
P. 8,599' (Fairweather Rg., AK) **131**-2
P. 9,365' (St. Elias Rg., AK) **128**-9
Padilha, Edemilson 169
Pae, Christine 315-7, 340
Paine, Central Tower (Patagonia, Chile) 190
Paine, North Tower (Patagonia, Chile) 190
Paine, Torres del (Patagonia, Chile) 190-1
Pakistan *art.* 87-9; 258-79
Pal bong, Kim *art.* 87-9, 266
Palma, Fabio 161-2
Palmada, David 101

Pamir (Afghanistan/Tajikistan/Kyrgyzstan) 234-7, 251-5
Pamir-i-Wakhan (Afghanistan) 253-5
Panfilovski Division, P. (Kokshaal-Too, Kyrgyzstan) **242-2**
Panmah Muztagh (Pakistan) 266-9
Panpoche I (Manaslu Himal, Nepal) 307-**8**
Papert, Ines 136-7
Parcha Kangri (India) 283-6
Parry, Mt. (Antarctica) 193-8, **194**
Pasang Lhamu Chuli "Nangpai Gosum I or Jasamba" (Nepal) **312**-13
Pass Out P. (Chugach Mts., AK) 127-**8**
Patagonia (Chile/Argentina) 183-91
Patal Hiunchuli (Annapurna Himal, Nepal) **305**-6
Patrick, Sean *obit.* 384-5
Pedferri, Simone 161-2
Pellin, Matteo 198
Peri Himal (Nepal) 306-7
Perkins, Matt 91
Peru 170-5
Pethangtse (Mahalangur Himal, Nepal) 320-**1**
Picket Rg. (Cascade Rg. WA) 90
Pike, Gavin 117-9
Pillaren (Norway) **225**-6
Pinto, Beto 170, 172
Pipsqueak P. (Coast Rg., AK) 135
Pissis (Andes, Argentina) 177
Piunova, Anna 231-2, 236
Pizem, Rob 226-7
Plateau P. (Karakoram, India) **280-1**
Plaza, P. (Kokshaal-Too, Kyrgyzstan) **243**-4
Pliska, Jiri 268-9
Pobeda (Kyrgyzstan) *art.* 70-7, **71**; 247
Poincenot, Aguja (Patagonia) 188
Pokharkan (Damodar Himal, Nepal) **303**-5, **304**
Polaco, P. (Andes, Argentina) 177-**8**
Porto, Thiago C. 184
Pou, Eneko 176
Pou, Iker 176
Presidente Perón, Cerro (Andes, Argentina) 177
Prezelj, Marko *art.* 25-33; 221, 291-2
Pucaraju (C. Blanca, Peru) **171**
Pumari Chhish (Hispar Muztagh, Pakistan) 264-6
Puryear, Joe *art.* 52-7; 311
Puscanturpa (C. Huayhuash, Peru) 172
Pyramid P. (Cascade Rg. WA) 91

Q

Qalandar Zom (Lupsuq Hindu Kush, Afghanistan) **253**-5
Qara Jilga I (Pamir-i-Wakhan, Afghanistan) 253-5, **254**
Qilian Mts. (Qinghai, China) 333-4
Qinghai (China) 333-4
Qinghai Mountaineering Assoc. *art.* 78-86
Qong Muztagh East (Kun Lun, China) **331**-3; *map* 332
Qonglai Shan (China) 346-50
Queen Maud Land (Antarctica) 199-200

R

Raghshur "Lagh Shar" (Pakistan) **258**-9
Rakaposhi Rg. (Pakistan) *art.* 87-9; 266
Ramada Rg. (Andes, Argentina) 177-8

Ramtang Chang (Nepal) *see* Chang Himal
Ranrapalca, Nevado (C. Blanca, Peru) **170**
Rasool Sar (Hispar Muztagh, Pakistan) 264-6
Rauch, Robert 175
Ravier, Christian 207-9
Ravtanna (Greenland) 158-60, **159**
Reilly, Carl 240-3
Ren Land (Greenland) 155-8
Ren Zhong Feng (China) 343-6, **344-5**
Reru Valley (Zanskar , India) 287
Revelation Mts. (AK) 122-5
Ricart, Sergi 283-6
Richey, Mark 282-3
Richiger, Aaron 181-2
Ricklin, Nate 100
Rik, P. (Neacola Mts., AK) 125-7
Ritacuba Blanco (Columbia) **165**
Ritter, Mt. (Sierra Nevada, CA) 98
Robie Reid, Mt. (CAN) **139**
Robinson, Doug 367-9
Rogaland (Norway) 228-30
Roibal, Josue 299-300
Rolwaling Himal (Nepal/Tibet) *art.* 52-7; 309-12, 355-6
Romsdal (Norway) 228
Roop, Jeremy 108
Rooster Comb (AK) *art.* 64-9; 117-8
Roraima, Monte (Guyana) 168-**9**
Rosa, P. (Andes, Argentina) 180
Rosenberg, Ben 106-7, 222
Rousseau, Louis 259-61
Rowe, Jay 122
Ruby P. (Sierra Nevada, CA) 99-**100**
Ruchkin, Alexander 340-2
Ruddy, Dana 143
Rulten (Norway) 220-3, **221**
Rurec, Nevado (C. Blanca, Peru) 171
Russia 231-3
Rustam Brakk (Pakistan) **279**
Rutford, Mt. (Antarctica) 193

S

Sabor, P "Vernyi, P." (Kokshaal-Too, Kyrgyzstan) 237-9, **238, 241-2**
Saether, Sindre 228
Sakamoto, Kimikazu 287
Sakar Sar (Afghanistan) 253-**5**
Salazar, Eloy 170
Salisbury, Richard 299-302, 307, 321-2
Sambataro, Joe 201-2
Samdo (Manaslu Himal, Nepal) 307-**8**
San Esteban, P. (Andes, Argentina) 180
Sarmiento, Monte (Tierra del Fuego, Chile) 191-**2**
Sarvasati (Lahaul, India) **289**-91
Sarychat Glacier (Kyrgyzstan) 244-6, **245**
Saser Kangri II (Karakoram, India) **282**-3
Saser Muztagh (Karakoram, India) 280-2
Sassara, Charlie 364-5
Savoia (Antarctica) 193-8, **194**
Scanu, Marcelo 176-8, 180
Schaefer, Mikey 95-6, 168

Schaffter, Stéphane 309-11
Schlagintweit P. (Pakistan) 261-2
Schmitt, Hans-Martin 176
Schofield, Graeme 240-3
Schweizer, Paul 130-1
Schweizerland (Greenland) 158-62
Scottish Wall (Denali Nat'l Park, AK) *art.* 64-9, **66**; 117-8
Sculptura Chokursa (Kokshaal-Too, Kyrgyzstan)
    240-3, **242**
Sentinel (Zion Nat'l Park, UT) **102**-3
Shaluli Shan (Sichuan Province, China) 335-8
Shamalo, Valery 229-30
Shanti Shikar (Nepal) *see* Shartse
Shark P. (Acha Kaeyndi Valley, Kyrgyzstan) **239**
Shark's Fin (Gangotri, India) **293**-4
Shartse "P. 38 or Shanti Shikar" (Nepal) **320**
Shartse II (Mahalangur Himal, Nepal) **320**
Shawa Kangri (Zanskar , India) 283-6, **285**
Shepton, Bob 151-3
Shlosar, Zach 124-5
Shojaei, Ramin 272-3
Siberia (Russia) 232-3
Sichuan Province (China) 335-8
Siegrist, Stephan 234-5
Sierra Nevada (CA) 97-100
Signorelli, Luca 198
Siguniang (Qonglai Shan, China) 346-9, **347-8**
Siguniang Nat'l Park (China) 346-50
Sikkim (India) 296-8
Silly Wizard P. (Coast Rg., AK) *art.* 58-63, **61**
Simmons (Antarctica) 193
Simpson, Joe 319-20
Skilma Kangri (Zanskar , India) **288-9**
Slawinski, Raphael 143-4, 264-6
Slesov, P. (Karavshin, Kyrgyzstan) 236-**7**
Slesse, Mt. (CAN) 138
Sloan P. (Cascade Rg. WA) 92
Smith, Jay *art.* 64-9; 117-8
Smith, Zack 120-1
Smoot, Brian 102
Snowcap Mtn. (Revelation Mts., AK) **124**-5
Snowpatch Spire (Bugaboos, CAN) **142**-3
Socotra Island (Yemen) **205**-6
Sokolov, Gleb *art.* 70-7; 247
Sortehul Fjord (Greenland) 151-3
South America 165-92
South Georgia (Antarctica) 198-9
Southgate, Dominic 156-7
Spantik (Rakaposhi Rg., Pakistan) *art.* 87-9; 266
Spicer, Dominic 193
Splichal, Jiri 222
Squire Creek Wall (Cascade Rg. WA) 91-**3**
St. Elias Rg. (AK/CAN) 128-31, 136
Stairway Glacier (St. Elias Rg., CAN) 136
Stanhope, Will 138-9, 143
Statham, Mt. (Antarctica) 193-8, **196**
Stauren (Norway) 220-3, **222**
Steidle, Christian 183-4
Steiner, Robert 234-6

Stevenson, David 362-72
Stikine Ice Cap (AK) *art.* 58-63
Stolb (Kodar Rg., Russia) **232**
Stortinden (Norway) 220-3, **222**
Stovelen (Norway) **218**-20
Streaked Wall (Zion Nat'l Park, UT) **103**
Stuart, Mt. (Cascade Rg. WA) 93-**4**
Sub P. "Confluence P." (Zion Nat'l Park, UT) **104**
Sugar Tooth (Alaska Rg. AK) 120-1
Sukakpak Mtn. (Brooks Rg., AK) **110**-11
Sultanlango (Zanskar, India) 283-6
Suluun (Kigluaik Mts., AK) **111**
Sun Kul Canyon (Kuilu Rg., Kyrgyzstan) 246-7
Sung-woo, Kang 309
Suzanne, Mt. (Coast Rg., AK) *art.* 58-63, **62**
Svihálek, Jiri 225-6
Swenson, Steve 282-3
Szilas, Kristoffer 343-5
Szybinski, Boryslaw 166

T

Tackle, Jack *art.* 64-9; 117-8
Taghia (Morocco) 207-12
Tagoujimt N'Tsouiant (Morocco) 210-**11**
Tahu Rutum (Hispar Muztagh, Pakistan) 266
Tajikistan 250-2
Tamang , Babulal Lamu 307
Tanabe, Osamu 306-7
Tangle Ridge (Canadian Rockies, CAN) **143**-4
Taniguchi, Kei 116, 355-6
Tara Parbat (Lahaul, India) 283-6, **285**
Tasermiut Fjord (Greenland) 162-3
Tatewari, (Mexico) **148**
Tawoche (Mahalangur Himal, Nepal) **314**-5
Tb GU, P. (Pamir, Tajikistan) **251-2**
Tblwkah Valley (Kazakhstan) 247-9
Tegerman Su Valley (Afghanistan) 253-5
Teixeira, Daniela 273-4
Temple P. (Wind River Mts. WY) 107-8
Tenderini, Mirella 374-5
Tengi Ragi Tau (Rolwaling Himal, Nepal) 311-**2**
Tengri Tag (Kyrgyzstan) *art.* 70-7; 247
Teton Rg. (WY) 104-5
Thomas, Adam 250-1
Thomas, Chris 113-4
Thunder Mtn. (AK) *art.* 64-9, **68**; 117-8
Tibet 351-6; *restrictions* 315
Tibet Mountaineering Guide School *art.* 78-86
Ticlla, Nevado (C. Yauyos, Peru) 172-**3**
Tien Shan (China) *art.* 34-41; 327-9
Tien Shan (Kyrgyzstan) 237-46
Tierra del Fuego (Chile) 191-2
Timrazine Canyon (Morocco) 211-12
Tinchenkang (Sikkim, India) 298
Tioman Island (Malaysia) 357-8
Tirokwa, Mt. (Baffin Island, CAN) **146**-8
Tito Carrasco, Aguja (Patagonia) 188
Tofel, Bartek 253-4
Toilsome P. (Chugach Mts., AK) 127
Tomaszewski, Marcin 166

Tompkins, Doug 186-7
Torre, Cerro (Patagonia) 187-8
Toshain I (Nanga Parbat Rg., Pakistan) 261-2
Toshain II (Pakistan) *see* Laila P.
Tower 4 (Coast Rg., AK) 132-4, **133**
Trango Tower (Baltoro Muztagh, Pakistan) 270-1
Trata Trata (C. Apolobamba, Bolivia) 173-**4**
Trident Peak (Lahaul, India) 289-91, **290**
Trividic, Pascal 202-3, 338-9
Trollveggen (Norway) 228
Tuanjiefeng (China) *see* Kangze'gyai
Tupalik (Schweizerland, Greenland) **158**-60
Turner, Dave 144-5
Twenty-Hour Tower (Wind River Mts. WY) **105**-6
Twin needles (Cascade Rg. WA) 90
Typhoon P. (Mukut Himal, Nepal) **302**-3

U

Uli Biaho (Baltoro Muztagh, Pakistan) 271-**2**
Ulysses, Aguja (Neacola Mts., AK) 125-7, **126**
United States 90-109
Upper Tittman Glacier (St. Elias Rg., AK) 129-30
Urubko, Denis *art.* 16-24; 314
Urus Central (C. Blanca, Peru) **170**
Utah (US) 101-4
Uttaranchal (India) 294-6
Uumannaaq Fjord (Greenland) 150-1

V

Vagakallen (Norway) 220-**3**
Van Biene, Matt 139-40
Venezuela 166-8
Vernyi, P. (Kyrgyzstan) *see* Sabor P.
Vicuñita, Nevado (C. Central, Peru) **172**
Vilhauer, Jared *art.* 34-41; 327-9
Villanueva, Sean 146-8
Vinson Massif (Antarctica) 193
Vinson, Mt. (Antarctica) 193
Volcán Salín (Andes, Argentina) 176

W

Wallace, Wayne 90-2
Walsh, Eamonn 143-4
Walsh, Jon 143, 145-6
Walt, Mt. (Sierra Nevada, CA) 98
Walter, Christian 261-2
Wandel P. (Antarctica) 193-8, **195**
Washington (US) 90-5
Watchtower (Wind River Mts. WY) 106-**7**
Watchtower (Sierra Nevada, CA) **97**-8
Wedge P. (AK) **116**
Wedge P. (Nepal) *see* Chang Himal
Weeding, Mark 136
Whiskey Pillar (Greenland) 158-**60**
Whitelaw, David 92-3
Wickwire, Jim 362-4
Wilson, Mt. (Canadian Rockies, CAN) 143-4
Wind River Mts. (WY) 105-8
Windsor, Jeremy 296-8
Wojciech, Chaladaj 173-4

Woldendorp, Gemma 162
Worrisome P. (Chugach Mts., AK) 127
Wuse Shan "Five Colors Mtn." (China) 349-**50**
Wynne-Jones, Dave 335-6
Wyoming (US) 104-8

X

Xinjiang (China) *art.* 34-41; 326-7
Xuebaoding (Sichuan, China) *art.* 78-86, **83**
Xuelian Feng (Xinjiang , China) *art.* 34-41; 327-9
Xuelian Massif (Tien Shan, China) *art.* 34-41; 327-9, **328**

Y

Yanamax II (Tien Shan, China) *art.* 34-41; 327-**9**
Yangmolong (Shaluli Shan, China) **335**-8, **336**
Yates, Simon 130-1
Yemen 205-6
Yeon-soo, Park 305-6
Yosemite Valley (US) 95-6
Yukla, Mt. (Chugach Mts., AK) 127
Yuzhu, Mt. (Kunlun Mts., China) *art.* 78-86, **80**

Z

Zajak, Rafal "Waldorf" 243-4
Zalaqueni (Yunnan, China) *art.* 84
Zang Brakk (Nangma Valley, Pakistan) 277-9
Zanskar (India) 283-9
Zartosh (Muzkol Rg., Tajikistan) **250-1**
Zerua P. (Antarctica) 193-8, **195**
Zhungar Alatau (Kazakhstan) 247-9
Zion Nat'l Park (UT) 101-4
Zonghua, Huang 333-4
Zucchetti, Alberto 212-13
Zuckerman, P. (Kokshaal-Too, Kyrgyzstan) **241**

INTERNATIONAL GRADE COMPARISON CHART

To download the complete "American Alpine Journal International Grade Comparison Chart," including alpine and ice grades, go to: aaj.americanalpineclub.org

This chart is designed to be used with the *American Alpine Journal* to help decipher the difficulty ratings given to climbs.

Seriousness Rating:

These often modify the technical grades when protection is difficult.

R: Poor protection with potential for a long fall and some injury.

X: A fall would likely result in serious injury or death.

YDS	UIAA	FR	AUS	SAX	CIS	SCA	BRA	UK	UK
5.2	II	1	10	II	III	3			D
5.3	III	2	11	III	III+	3+			
5.4	IV- / IV	3	12		IV-	4			VD
5.5	IV+		13		IV	4+			S
5.6	V-	4	14		IV+	5-		4a	HS
5.7	V / V+		15	VIIa		5		4b	VS
5.8	VI-	5a	16	VIIb	V-	5+	4 / 4+	4c	HVS
5.9	VI	5b	17	VIIc		6-	5 / 5+	5a	E1
5.10a	VI+	5c	18	VIIIa	V	6	6a	5b	
5.10b		6a							E2
5.10c	VII-	6a+	19	VIIIb		6+	6b		
5.10d	VII	6b	20	VIIIc	V+	7-	6c		E3
5.11a	VII+	6b+		IXa			7a	5c	
5.11b		6c	21	IXb		7	7b		
5.11c	VIII-	6c+	22	IXc	VI-	7+			E4
5.11d	VIII	7a	23				7c	6a	
5.12a	VIII+	7a+	24			8-	8a		E5
5.12b		7b	25	Xa	VI	8	8b		
5.12c	IX-	7b+	26	Xb		8+	8c		
5.12d	IX	7c	27				9a	6b	E6
5.13a	IX+	7c+	28	Xc		9-	9b		
5.13b		8a	29				9c		
5.13c	X-	8a+	30	XIa		9	10a	6c	E7
5.13d	X	8b	31		VI+		10b		
5.14a	X+	8b+	32	XIb			10c	7a	E8
5.14b	XI-	8c	33						
5.14c	XI	8c+		XIc		9+		7b	E9
5.14d		9a							

YDS=Yosemite Decimal System; UIAA=Union Internationale des Associations D'Alpinisme; Fr=France/Sport; Aus=Australia; Sax=Saxony; CIS=Commonwealth of Independent States/Russia; Sca=Scandinavia; Bra=Brazil.